OXFORD EC LAW LIBRARY

General Editor: F. G. Jacobs
Advocate General, The Court of Justice
of the European Communities

EU ANTI-DISCRIMINATION LAW

OXFORD EC LAW LIBRARY

The aim of this series is to publish important and original studies of the various branches of EC Law. Each work provides a clear, concise, and original critical exposition of the law in its social, economic, and political context, at a level which will interest the advanced student, the practitioner, the academic, and government and Community officials.

Other Titles in the Library

EU Anti-Discrimination Law

EVELYN ELLIS

OXFORD
UNIVERSITY PRESS

OXFORD

UNIVERSITY PRESS

Great Clarendon Street, Oxford OX2 6DP

Oxford University Press is a department of the University of Oxford.
It furthers the University's objective of excellence in research, scholarship,
and education by publishing worldwide in

Oxford New York

Auckland Cape Town Dar es Salaam Hong Kong Karachi
Kuala Lumpur Madrid Melbourne Mexico City Nairobi
New Delhi Shanghai Taipei Toronto

With offices in

Argentina Austria Brazil Chile Czech Republic France Greece
Guatemala Hungary Italy Japan Poland Portugal Singapore
South Korea Switzerland Thailand Turkey Ukraine Vietnam

Oxford is a registered trade mark of Oxford University Press
in the UK and in certain other countries

Published in the United States
by Oxford University Press Inc., New York

© E. Ellis, 2005

British Library Cataloguing in Publication Data

Data available

Library of Congress Cataloging-in-Publication Data

Ellis, Evelyn, 1948-
    EU anti-discrimination law / Evelyn Ellis.
        p. cm.
    Includes index.
    ISBN 0-19-926683-2
    1. Discrimination—Law and legislation—European Union countries. I. Title;
European Union anti-discrimination law. II. Title.
    KJE5142.E445 2005
    342.2408'7—dc22

                                                        2005002269

Typeset by Newgen Imaging Systems (P) Ltd., Chennai, India
Printed in Great Britain
on acid-free paper by
Biddles Ltd., King's Lynn

ISBN 0-19-926683-2   EAN 978-0-19-926683-8

1 3 5 7 9 10 8 6 4 2

For Brian, Jeremy, Stephen and Laurie

General Editor's Foreword

The earlier editions of this work provided a leading text on EC sex equality law. Equal treatment for men and women is a subject which raises many fundamental issues of principle; it is also a subject of great practical importance; and it is an area where EC law has had a profound impact on the law of the Member States.

In this edition, the book is transformed into *EU Anti-Discrimination Law*, and covers a far wider field. That transformation reflects a new stage in the development of the European Union itself. The law on sex equality developed from a principle set out in a relatively obscure provision of the original EEC Treaty, Article 119, which called for equal pay for men and women for work of equal value. The inclusion of that principle in the Treaty was not then seen as a matter of fundamental rights, but rather had an economic rationale. The remarkable body of case law of the Court of Justice, and implementing legislation, which put flesh on the bones of that principle, were the subject of previous editions and remain an outstanding feature of this book.

The scene has been transformed, however, by the Treaty of Amsterdam, which amended the EC Treaty by introducing new and wide-ranging provisions on fundamental rights, and which also introduced a wholly new, and far broader, anti-discrimination provision, now Article 13 of the EC Treaty.

Article 13 is placed, significantly, in Part One of the Treaty, which sets out the basic principles on which the Community is deemed to be founded. It enables the Community to enact legislation, and to take other necessary measures, against many different forms of discrimination; as formulated, it empowers the Community to 'take appropriate action to combat discrimination based on sex, racial or ethnic origin, religion or belief, disability, age or sexual orientation'.

On the basis of that Article, two major pieces of legislation—the Race Directive and the Framework Directive—have been enacted, outlawing discrimination on all of the above grounds other than sex, while that new legislation has itself generated important changes to the existing legislation on sex equality. The provisions of these Directives are required to be transposed into the legislation of the twenty-five Member States of the European Union; many of them will be directly enforceable, and they will prevail over any conflicting provisions of national law.

It is therefore clearly desirable that this book should cover the new forms of discrimination now prohibited by European and national law. But this new edition is all the more welcome because it seems likely that the learning which underlies sex equality law will be particularly valuable in resolving many of the fundamental issues which will arise in the new fields. The author's previous work thus makes her exceptionally well placed to throw light on these issues. In the absence of any authoritative judicial interpretation of the new legislation, its very broad and general provisions are illuminated by careful analysis, inspired by the author's established expertise on the scope and application of the principle of equal treatment, and on the questions to which they are likely to give rise in the national courts and the Court of Justice.

Francis G. Jacobs
December 2004

Preface

There has, since the publication of the second edition of *EC Sex Equality Law* in 1998, been an extraordinary amount of activity in the field to which this book is devoted. Those six years have witnessed the entry into operation of the Amsterdam Treaty and a consequentially enhanced emphasis on the protection of fundamental human rights within the context of EU law; the Treaty of Nice has been agreed and has also entered into force; no fewer than ten new Member States have acceded to the EU, and a draft Constitution has been signed. Above all, of critical importance to the scope and content of EU anti-discrimination law has been the enactment of two new directives in 2000: the Race Directive, outlawing discrimination on the ground of racial or ethnic origin, and the Framework Directive, outlawing discrimination on the grounds of religion or belief, disability, age, and sexual orientation. These new instruments have in turn precipitated changes to the legislation governing sex discrimination, in particular the amendment in important respects of the Equal Treatment Directive.

All these developments have necessitated a wholesale re-structuring of this book and the inclusion of much new material. Considerable space is of course now devoted to the new directives themselves, their scope and detailed provisions, together with the numerous exceptions to their terms. A new section has been introduced discussing the concepts of non-discrimination and equality, and alerting the reader to the varying, and sometimes inconsistent, philosophical objectives which can be the goals of these familiar-sounding terms. The book also examines the ways in which these various objectives are reflected in the current body of EU law. There is a new chapter dealing with concepts common to all the areas in which discrimination is now forbidden, for example, direct and indirect discrimination, causation, harassment, and mainstreaming. The likely meanings to be attached to the recently-added grounds of religion or belief, disability, age, and sexual orientation are analysed. In addition, a special focus is afforded in this new edition to both the current and the potential significance of general principles, especially those deriving from the European Convention on Human Rights and those expressed in the EU's Charter of Fundamental Rights.

Important cases have also been decided since 1998 by the European Court of Justice across the whole gamut of sex discrimination law, including many decisions on equal pay, equal treatment, pregnancy discrimination, defences, and social security. Of particular note are decisions dealing with the boundary between State and occupational pensions, the permitted scope of comparison in equal pay claims, and the highly vexed issue of positive action. Because of the similarity between many of the rules on sex discrimination and those in the new areas in which discrimination is proscribed in EU law, such decisions are likely to have a broader impact than merely in relation to gender discrimination. Some significant rulings have also been made by the Court on the basic principles of EU law. These clearly affect the practical enforcement and operation of all the anti-discrimination rules. Of particular note have been the analyses provided by the Court of the inability of directives to take horizontal direct effect, its clarification of the scope of the *Francovich* principle, and its decisions on the principle of procedural autonomy in the field of equal pay in the UK.

Because of the recent origin of the Race Directive and the Framework Directive, the European Court of Justice had not by the time of writing yet rendered any judgments on them. The new instruments also leave considerable discretion in the hands of the Court. A feature of this work is therefore that quite a large part of it is speculative in nature. However, it is hoped that this speculation may at least provide a starting point for those faced with the inevitable task, likely to be faced in the near future, of deciding issues pursuant to the new law.

As with previous editions, the author has tried not to stray into discussion of domestic law, except where its content is vital to understanding an issue of EU law. However, given the untested nature of the EU rules on race, religion, disability, age, and sexual orientation, some mention has been made of relevant provisions of UK law, in order in particular to shed light on the possible interpretation to be given to specific provisions of the new directives.

The author would like to express her huge thanks: to Advocate General Francis Jacobs for his continued advice and support throughout the preparation of this edition; to her colleague Professor Tony Arnull for being prepared to engage in numerous nit-picking discussions of the minutiae of EU law; to the staff of the Birmingham University Harding Law Library for their patient help in retrieving information; and to her husband Brian, who has had to endure what must have seemed endless hours of rumination on the subject of anti-discrimination law. For the opinions expressed in this book, as well as for any errors, the author is of course solely responsible.

Evelyn Ellis
Ombersley, Worcestershire
November 2004

Contents

Table of Cases

European Court of Human Rights

European Court of Justice

Alphabetical

European Court of Justice

Chronological

Court of First Instance

Alphabetical

Chronological

Opinions

Other Jurisdictions

France

Germany

Greece

United Kingdom

United States of America

Table of Legislation

European Union

Decisions

Directives

Recommendations

Regulations

Treaties

Denmark

Ireland

United Kingdom

Statutory Instruments

United States of America

Table of Treaties and Conventions

Abbreviations

CFI	Court of First Instance
CLJ	*Cambridge Law Journal*
CMLR	*Common Market Law Reports*
CMLRev	*Common Market Law Review*
CYELS	*Cambridge Yearbook of European Legal Studies*
ECHR	European Convention on Human Rights
ECJ	European Court of Justice
ECR	*European Court Reports*
ECSC	European Coal and Steel Community
EHRLR	*European Human Rights Law Review*
EHRR	*European Human Rights Reports*
ELJ	*European Law Journal*
ELRev	*European Law Review*
EOC	Equal Opportunities Commission
EOR	*Equal Opportunities Review*
EPL	*European Public Law*
EU	European Union
Euratom	European Atomic Energy Community
ICR	*Industrial Cases Reports*
IGC	Intergovernmental Conference
ILJ	*Industrial Law Journal*
IRLR	*Industrial Relations Law Reports*
JCMS	*Journal of Common Market Studies*
JSWFL	*Journal of Social Welfare and Family Law*
LIEI	*Legal Issues of European Integration*
LQR	*Law Quarterly Review*
MLR	*Modern Law Review*
NLJ	*New Law Journal*
nyr	not yet reported

OJ	Official Journal of the European Communities
OJLS	*Oxford Journal of Legal Studies*
PL	*Public Law*
TEC	Treaty establishing the European Community
TEU	Treaty on European Union
YEL	*Yearbook of European Law*

1

Introduction

The importance of anti-discrimination law

Earlier editions of this book were entirely concerned with the law on sex equality, an area in which, from the beginning of its existence, the European Economic Community[1] possessed rules forbidding discrimination. The right to equality of opportunity irrespective of sex is fundamental to a civilized society since, without it, the individual's talents cannot be exploited to the full, human dignity is compromised, and the person concerned cannot make the most of what life has to offer: inequality on the ground of sex is simply unfair. The community at large suffers too since valuable resources go untapped and potential gifts remain unrealized. The law and the apparatus by which it is administered, of course, play a vital part in sustaining the notion of equality as between the sexes; the law cannot do the whole job, since peoples' attitudes and cultural and other influences will always overlay it, but it can prove highly instrumental in shaping behaviour and expectations.[2]

As will be seen later in this chapter, economic and political forces combined to produce the first European Community anti-discrimination legislation in the fields of sex and nationality. It was not until the dawn of the third millennium that similar laws came into existence to forbid discrimination on the grounds of race, religion, disability, age, and sexual orientation. In addition, it will be seen that other expressions of the equality principle have begun to creep into EU law. It is undeniable that this later generation of anti-discrimination law is every bit as significant as its predecessors in human, moral, political, and economic terms. The aspirations which lie behind it are justice and an improved quality of life for literally millions of people within the European Union.[3] The present volume therefore

---

[1] A brief account of the development of the three original European Communities, and their subsequent metamorphosis into the European Union, is given below.

[2] See further Byre, 'Applying Community Standards on Equality', in Buckley and Anderson (eds), *Women, Equality and Europe* (Macmillan, London, 1988); Mancini and O'Leary, 'The New Frontiers of Sex Equality Law in the European Union' (1999) 24 ELRev 331; and Osborne and Shuttleworth (eds), *Fair Employment in Northern Ireland: a generation on* (Blackstaff Press and the Equality Commission for Northern Ireland, Belfast, 2004). For an expression of the view that EU law is not committed to the principle of real sex equality, see Fenwick and Hervey, 'Sex Equality in the Single Market: New Directions for the European Court of Justice' (1995) 32 CMLRev 443. Similarly, see Fredman, 'European Community Discrimination Law: A Critique' (1992) 21 ILJ 119, where powerful arguments are marshalled to demonstrate that EU law fails to address the underlying structural obstacles to progress for women.   [3] Henceforth EU.

attempts to examine the scope and coverage of EU law on all the grounds (bar one) upon which it currently forbids discrimination and seeks to promote equality between people; the law forbidding discrimination on the ground of nationality is not covered in depth (though occasional reference is made to it where the context requires) for reasons of space and also because its rationale is very different from that of the other grounds, rooted as it is in the importance of the free movement of persons to the achievement of a single economic market; in addition, its scope is somewhat different from that of the other categories of discrimination and, furthermore, the whole area of nationality discrimination is being subsumed today into the wider notion of citizenship of the Union.[4]

Non-discrimination and equality

Despite the length of time which it took the EU to outlaw discrimination on this portfolio of grounds, it is not actually difficult for most people today to embrace the broad notion that at least some types of discrimination are unacceptable and should be forbidden by law. Of course, the word 'discriminate' is capable of two distinct connotations, the first of which expresses the usually laudable activity of making those kinds of choices which everyday life presents to human beings; thus, we speak, for example, of being 'discriminating' consumers of food or art, meaning that we make informed and critical judgements about these matters. This is not, however, the sense which legal systems attach to the word 'discriminate'; the law is concerned with discrimination only when it is in some generally recognized way unacceptable. As Feldman has explained, discrimination becomes 'morally unacceptable' when it takes the form of treating a person less favourably than others on account of a consideration which is 'morally irrelevant'.[5] The critical question which then has to be decided by the legal system is when a consideration is to be considered morally irrelevant. If taken to extremes, this principle could effectively stultify decision-making by requiring the positive justification of every matter taken into consideration by the decision-maker. Legal systems frequently, therefore, attempt to classify or to enumerate those matters which are morally irrelevant in specified contexts. Thus, there is some consensus today that many matters which fall outside the control of an individual, such as sex, race, and disability, are generally speaking morally irrelevant bases on which to disfavour people in fields such as the workplace and education. Control is not, however, the invariable key to deciding this matter. Age, for example, although outside control, may often be considered to be morally relevant to the doing of a job: a five-year-old may not be the best person to pilot a jumbo jet! Even more doubt surrounds those issues over

---

[4] See in particular Case C-85/96 *Martínez Sala* [1998] ECR I-2691 and Case C-184/99 *Grzelczyk v Centre Public d'Aide Sociale* [2001] ECR I-6193. See also Spaventa, 'From *Gebhard to Carpenter*: Towards a (Non-) Economic European Constitution' (2004) 41 CMLRev 743.

[5] Feldman, *Civil Liberties and Human Rights in England and Wales*, 2nd edn (Oxford University Press, Oxford, 2002), 135–9.

which, arguably, people have some control, such as their choice of religion or (more controversially) sexual orientation.

A legal system which outlaws discrimination has also to be acutely aware of the many different ways in which discrimination manifests itself. The law cannot restrict its prohibition to conscious or deliberate acts founded on prejudice, since these are certainly not the only ways in which disadvantage grounded upon discrimination arises. Much discrimination results from the traditional, unquestioning ways in which society is ordered and the ways in which it functions in practice. For example, the ineffectual and haphazard pursuit by the London Metropolitan Police Service of the murderers of the black teenager Stephen Lawrence constituted institutional discrimination, irrespective of the wrongdoing of individual officers. In very important words, which should serve as a reminder to all legislators in this area, Sir William Macpherson's Inquiry into the matter defined the concept of 'institutional racism' as:

The collective failure of an organisation to provide an appropriate and professional service to people because of their colour, culture, or ethnic origin. It can be seen or detected in processes, attitudes and behaviour which amount to discrimination through unwitting prejudice, ignorance, thoughtlessness and racist stereotyping which disadvantage minority ethnic people.

It persists because of the failure of the organisation openly and adequately to recognise and address its existence and causes by policy, example and leadership. Without recognition and action to eliminate such racism it can prevail as part of the ethos or culture of the organisation. It is a corrosive disease.[6]

In addition to difficulties surrounding the identification and definition of discrimination, it has become clear from the practical operation of systems of anti-discrimination law that it is not enough to focus simply on the negative concept of non-discrimination. If the moral basis on which the law forbids discrimination is that there is a fundamental human right to be treated in the same way as other human beings,[7] the aim must logically be to produce substantive equality. This is a much more positive and value-laden concept than non-discrimination, although courts not infrequently conflate the two ideas.[8] In particular, it involves taking an active attitude to dismantling the obstacles which stand in the way of equality (however 'equality' is to be defined).[9] Thus, for example, it is not sufficient for the achievement of equality simply to require the same conditions for all people, whether male or female, black or white; this is because in practice some sections of

[6] *The Stephen Lawrence Inquiry*, Cm 4262-I (HMSO, London, 1999), para 6.34.
[7] In addition to this goal of neutrality as between different groups of people, Fredman has argued that the non-discrimination principle also furthers individualism and personal autonomy: see Fredman, 'Equality: A New Generation?' (2001) 30 ILJ 145.
[8] For example, in Case T-45/00 *Speybrouck v Parliament* [1992] ECR II-33, the Court of First Instance stated that 'the principle of equal treatment for men and women in matters of employment and, at the same time, the principle of the prohibition of any direct or indirect discrimination on grounds of sex form part of the fundamental rights the observance of which the Court of Justice and the Court of First Instance must ensure' (at 46).
[9] For a compelling critique of Europe's existing race discrimination laws from this perspective, see Hepple, 'Race and Law in Fortress Europe' (2004) 67 MLR 1.

the community have been historically so disadvantaged as to be unable to compete in the race in the first place. Although most people would probably agree at a relatively rarefied plane of abstraction that equality is a proper goal, there is scope for a great deal of debate over the lengths to which it is proper to go in order to provide such a level playing-field.[10] In addition, there is the even more difficult problem of deciding to what extent equality embraces respect for minority practices and requires the recognition of diversity, as distinct from identity of treatment.[11]

There are many different ways in which the concept of equality can be expressed and in which it can be attempted to be realized in practical terms.[12] It has been described by one commentator as 'one of that genre of words . . . which have both a vague conceptual meaning and a rich emotive meaning—with the conceptual meaning being subject to constant redefinition'.[13] The same author draws attention to three main (though not exclusive) expressions of the principle of equality, namely 'formal' equality (consistency of treatment), equality of opportunity, and equality of results.

In addition, although many different models of equality can be articulated and described, legal systems often adopt their own individualized views of these various models. Current EU law, as will be seen throughout this book,[14] espouses differing approaches to the concept,[15] and is indeed subject to competing influences in this regard.[16] There are, in short, no absolutes in this area in practice, although absolute positions can be defined in theory.

The picture can perhaps best be viewed in terms of a continuum. At one end lies what is often called 'formal' equality; this is the minimal, Aristotelian postulate that like cases should be treated alike and that different cases should be treated differently, unless there is an objective reason not to do so. Thus, for example, two people with identical qualifications and experience should be paid the same wage,

[10] For a seminal, though now in part historical, analysis of the causes of inequality and the panoply of responses to it which are open to society, see McCrudden, 'Institutional Discrimination' (1982) 2 OJLS 303.

[11] See Barmes with Ashtiany, 'The Diversity Approach to Achieving Equality: Potential and Pitfalls' (2003) 32 ILJ 274. The proposed Constitution, discussed below, rather engagingly adopts a 'motto' for the EU, which is to be 'United in diversity': see its Art I-8.

[12] See McCrudden, 'Equality and Non-Discrimination', in Feldman (ed), English Public Law (Oxford University Press, Oxford, 2004), ch 11; Barnard, 'The Principle of Equality in The Community Context: P, Grant, Kalanke and Marschall: Four Uneasy Bedfellows?' (1998) 57 CLJ 352; Fredman, 'A Critical Review of the Concept of Equality in UK Anti-Discrimination Legislation', Working Paper No 3 (Cambridge Centre for Public Law and the Judge Institute of Management Studies, 1999); and Fredman, 'The Future of Equality in Britain', Working Paper Series No 5 (EOC, 2002).

[13] Barrett, 'Re-examing the Concept and Principle of Equality in EC Law' (2003) 22 YEL 117, at 120.

[14] But see ch 3 in particular.

[15] See Fenwick, 'From Formal to Substantive Equality: the Place of Affirmative Action in European Union Sex Equality Law' (1998) 4 EPL 507; Barnard and Hepple, 'Substantive Equality' (2000) 59 CLJ 562; Bell and Waddington, 'Reflecting on Inequalities in European Equality Law' (2003) 28 ELRev 349.

[16] See Flynn, 'Equality Between Men and Women in the Court of Justice' (1998) 18 YEL 259, and McCrudden, 'International and European Norms Regarding National Legal Remedies for Racial Inequality' in Fredman (ed), Discrimination and Human Rights (Oxford University Press, Oxford, 2001).

irrespective of any dissimilarities which they may possess. This is also frequently referred to as the 'merit' principle: individuals ought to be rewarded according to their merit and not according to stereotypical assumptions made about them on account of the group to which they belong. However, such a principle is of course deceptively simple, for how is it to be judged, for example, that the qualifications and experience of two individuals are identical?[17] And to precisely which situations and decisions is the principle to be applied?[18] In addition, this analysis does nothing to improve the condition of an under-class, since it is satisfied where two individuals are treated equally badly, as well as where they are treated equally beneficially. If one of the prime rationales of equality law is the improvement of the lot of human beings, this simply will not do.

These sorts of difficulties lead some legal systems to focus on factual scenarios which can be shown empirically to produce specially severe or marked injustice and hardship ('suspect classifications' in American terminology), and then to enact quite specific laws which attempt to remedy the situation. For example, it is often perceived that, as a result of stereotyping, women and people from ethnic minorities are treated unequally in the workplace by comparison with men and the prevailing ethnic majority. A frequent legislative response is therefore to enact legislation making it unlawful to discriminate on the grounds of sex and ethnic origin in the context of employment.

A more fluid version of this principle is also encountered. This acknowledges specific instances of discrimination in practice but then tries to generalize and to cater for similar, but not yet classified, examples of discrimination. Such a model typically covers a broad range of situations in which discrimination is rendered unlawful and contains an *eiusdem generis* provision allowing the prohibition to develop organically to deal with fresh situations as they manifest themselves. McCrudden characterizes this model as prevalent in relation to the 'protection of particularly prized "public goods", including human rights'. He goes on to explain that the focus here is on the distribution of the public goods, rather than on the characteristics of the recipient, except for the purpose of justifying different treatment.[19]

These models, however, share a common shortcoming which is often analysed in terms of symmetry. In the example taken here, the rules apply identically to men

[17] See further McCrudden, 'Merit Principles' (1998) 18 OJLS 543.
[18] This sort of problem manifested itself in Joined Cases C-122 & 125/99P *D and Sweden v Council* [2001] ECR I-4319, which concerned the alleged entitlement of a Community employee, who had a registered same-sex partnership under Swedish law, to identical treatment to that accorded to a married employee. The ECJ found that the then existing laws of the Member States showed great diversity in approach to same-sex partnerships and that they did not generally assimilate them to marriage; it held that the employee's situation was therefore not comparable with that of a married employee. On same-sex partnerships, see further Wintemute and Andenas (eds), *Legal Recognition of Same-Sex Partnerships: A Study of National, European and International Law* (Hart, Oxford, 2001). In the UK, a Civil Partnership Bill was introduced in the House of Lords and brought to the House of Commons on 5 July 2004; this proposed legislation would grant legal recognition to same-sex partnerships and place civil partners in the same position as married people as regards discrimination on the ground of their status. At the time of writing, it had not been enacted. [19] McCrudden, op cit, n 12, at para 11.05.

and women, and to people from all ethnic backgrounds; indeed, this is at the heart of their philosophy since they are usually predicated on a principle of fundamental human rights and the dignity which should be accorded to all human beings. However, the underlying injustice which they actually seek to counter applies predominantly to women and to people from ethnic minorities. In seeking to treat everyone alike, the law in effect forces a male, ethnic majority paradigm on all. This, it is argued, may appear to produce equality but it is in reality only a formal, super-ficial kind of equality which reinforces the pre-existing hegemony.[20] In addition, as Fredman has pointed out, these types of model also ignore the fact that cumulative disadvantage makes it difficult for members of the disadvantaged group ever to attain the threshold of equal qualification or merit with the dominant group.[21] Further-more, these models usually rely heavily upon individual action, normally through litigation, to vindicate the rights protected. They do not provide either the support or the subsequent legal protection offered by a collectivist or group-based remedy. In addition, they may never actually achieve legal redress, since there may never emerge a particular 'wrong-doer' whose actions can be challenged; many manifesta-tions of disadvantage result from an agglomeration of factors and circumstances for which no one person or body may be legally responsible.

Some systems and some bodies of law therefore approach equality from a differ-ent angle.[22] Rather than attempting to be blind to differences, they actually focus on differences, especially those which produce disadvantage in practice, and in doing so they clearly come into headlong conflict with the basic non-discrimination principle. They characteristically aim for equality of results, but the extent to which they inter-vene into the activities of people and organizations varies considerably. In some, there is little more than an obligation to be aware of differences and to endeavour to offer equal participation to all. Others expressly require public authorities actively to promote equality of opportunity.[23] And some are openly re-distributive, for ex-ample allocating jobs and other opportunities on the specific basis of membership of an under-privileged group.[24] Such models are clearly, though to varying extents, in tension with the liberal, non-collectivist view of equality which sees it as an individual human right.[25]

---

[20] MacKinnon, *Feminism Unmodified: Discourses on Life and Law* (Harvard University Press, Cambridge, Mass/London, 1987); Fredman, 'European Community Discrimination Law: A Critique' (1992) 21 ILJ 119; Lacey, 'From Individual to Group' in Hepple and Szyszczak (eds), *Discrimination: The Limits of Law* (Mansell, London, 1992).

[21] Fredman 'The Future of Equality in Britain', op cit, n 12. See also Fredman, *Women and the Law* (Clarendon Press, Oxford, 1997).

[22] See further O'Cinneide, 'Extending Positive Duties Across the Equality Grounds' (2003) 120 EOR 12.

[23] Notable examples of this approach in the UK include the Northern Ireland Act 1998, s 75, and the Race Relations (Amendment) Act 2000, s 2.

[24] The clearest example of this approach in the UK is to be found in the Police (Northern Ireland) Act 2000; pursuant to the so-called 'Patten' reforms to the Northern Ireland police service, a 50:50 split between Catholics and Protestants was, on a temporary basis, required for recruits to that force.

[25] For a thought-provoking attempt to resolve this tension, see Collins, 'Discrimination, Equality and Social Inclusion' (2003) 66 MLR 16; the author asserts that 'deviations from equal treatment are

It must be emphasized that these models are often much less distinct from one another in practice than these descriptions might suggest. Legal systems frequently blur the distinctions concerned, in particular by combining the principle of non-discrimination with a requirement to promote equality of opportunity and to celebrate diversity and pluralism.[26] Such blurring is sometimes also a consequence of the fact that a court may be required to enforce law from several different sources simultaneously. In addition, it should be acknowledged that different times and political climates require different and increasingly sophisticated responses, and that this is an area where one must therefore expect a constantly shifting legislative, as well as judicial,[27] response to society's demands. The title of the present work reflects the fact that the substance of most of the existing EU law in this area refers primarily to the principle of non-discrimination; however, it is not to be taken to preclude discussion of the concept of equality, which is (as will be seen) also often referred to both in the legislation and in judicial decisions.[28]

The dynamism inherent in EU law

EU law has proved an ideal vehicle for upholding the principle of sex equality, in part at least because of the EU's undoubted potential for growth. That growth has taken place, and continues to occur, in a number of different ways. With the expansion of the Union's concerns to cover other grounds of discrimination, it would appear well-nigh inevitable that what has been true in the past for sex equality will also hold good for other fields of equality law.

When the European Coal and Steel Community (ECSC) Treaty was concluded in 1951, and the Treaties establishing the European Economic Community (EEC) and European Atomic Energy Community (Euratom) were concluded in 1957, their chief instigators intended their immediate end to be economic welfare but their long-term goal to be political integration amongst the States of Europe.[29] The architects of the three European Communities had personally witnessed the destructive forces of nationalism; many had seen their countries overwhelmed and

---

required in order to achieve the distributive aim of social inclusion. This aim requires preference or priority to members of a particular group, if the group can be classified as socially excluded. The preferential measures required are those that will contribute to the reduction of social exclusion' (at 40).

[26] See Schiek, 'A New Framework on Equal Treatment of Persons in EC Law?' (2002) 8 ELJ 290.

[27] See, eg, Lord Lester's account of attitudes to discrimination expressed in the past by UK courts and judges in 'Equality and United Kingdom Law: Past, Present and Future' [2001] Public Law 77. See also the analysis of the EU case law on sex discrimination by Pager in 'Strictness v Discretion: The European Court of Justice's Variable Vision of Gender Equality' (2003) 51 American Journal of Comparative Law 553; the author there argues that the EU's judiciary adapts the level of scrutiny which it applies according to the nature of the provision under review.

[28] For discussion of the way in which the draft EU Constitution (examined further below) reflects notions of formal and substantive equality, negative and positive duties, and diversity, see Bell, 'Equality and the European Union Constitution' (2004) 33 ILJ 242.

[29] See in particular Ionescu, *The New Politics of European Integration* (Macmillan, London, 1972) and Kitzinger, *The Politics and Economics of European Integration* (Greenwood Press, Westport, Conn, 1963).

occupied during the Second World War. They were increasingly aware of the rise of the then 'Super Powers' and of the threat of Communism in the East. The Schuman Declaration of 9 May 1950, which preceded the formation of the ECSC, made very clear its author's ultimate political aspirations. Robert Schuman, the French Minister for Foreign Affairs, proposed that the whole of the French and German coal and steel production industries be placed under a common 'high authority', within the framework of an organization open to participation by the other countries of Europe. He went on to explain:

> The pooling of coal and steel production will immediately provide for the setting up of common bases for economic development as a first step in the federation of Europe, and will change the destinies of those regions which have long been devoted to the manufacture of munitions of war, of which they have been the most constant victims. The solidarity in production thus established will make it plain that any war between France and Germany becomes, not merely unthinkable, but materially impossible.

His overall plan was to build a united Europe 'through concrete achievements, which first create a *de facto* solidarity'. The Coal and Steel Community was to be just a first step in an ever-tightening web of economic, and thus political, integration. It was believed that the integration of the coal and steel industries would create common spheres of interest as between the French and the (then West) Germans, which would encourage greater political friendship between those nations; further common economic and social issues would then begin to present themselves and a political framework would have to be established to deal with them. Gradually, the process would gather momentum. This scheme for 'rolling interdependence' between the States of Europe is now, and was from the start, clearly echoed in the founding Treaties. It was taken a stage further when the Member States pledged themselves in the Single European Act of 1986 to make greatly increased use of majority voting in the Council, thereby relinquishing a significant portion of their national sovereignty in favour of the Community. Furthermore, despite the antagonism of many, in particular the British Government, to the use of the word 'federal' in the Treaty on European Union of 1993,[30] it is clear that that Treaty nevertheless continued the progress towards tightening the web; its Preamble proclaims the Member States:

> Resolved to mark a new stage in the process of European integration undertaken with the establishment of the European Communities,
> ... [And] Resolved to continue the process of creating an ever closer union among the peoples of Europe...

It also transformed the nature of the enterprise so as to create the 'European Union'. Founded upon the European Community which was still governed by its own Treaty,[31] the EU was also to direct its attention (albeit in a looser and less supranational fashion) to the wider issues of a Common Foreign and Security

---

[30] Henceforth referred to in the present work as the TEU. This Treaty is also known colloquially as the Maastricht Treaty.   [31] Henceforth normally referred to in the present work as the TEC.

Policy and Justice and Home Affairs; the way was also paved for economic and monetary union.[32] The Amsterdam Treaty of 1997, concluded after the holding of an Intergovernmental Conference (IGC) mandated by the TEU,[33] made numerous technical changes intended to reinforce the economic, social, political, and other links between the Member States.[34] The Member States, however, made clear their unease with the existing constitutional arrangements surrounding the EU in a Declaration on the Future of the Union which was issued in Nice in 2000, and they therefore decided to convene a new IGC, intended to agree the necessary Treaty amendments. A further Declaration made at Laeken in the following year established a Convention under the chairmanship of ex-President Giscard d'Estaing of France, charged with providing a discussion document for the IGC. This Convention produced a draft Constitution for the Union in 2003, an amended text of which was signed by the Heads of State or Government of all the Member States (but subject to ratification by all of them in accordance with their respective constitutional requirements) on 29 October 2004;[35] it is to enter into force on 1 November 2006, provided that it is duly ratified by that date.[36] The Constitution is an amalgam of legal provisions, both articulating the most fundamental of principles on which the Union is based and also containing a mass of detailed rules, substantive and institutional; it consolidates much existing law and also amends and rationalizes other areas. If and when it enters into force, it will repeal all the preceding Treaties. The third recital to its Preamble proclaims that 'the peoples of Europe are determined to transcend their former divisions and, united ever more closely, to forge a common destiny'.[37] Thus, it is evident that, although public relish for formal federalization has perceptibly waned over recent years, the process of European integration is set to continue, probably bringing in its wake yet further legislation supporting closer economic and political ties which are well-nigh certain to touch on the spheres of equality and non-discrimination.

The process of European integration has not, however, been restricted to the deepening of ties between the States of Europe. It has also been significant because it has hugely broadened the geographical scope of the enterprise. The Treaties,

---

[32] The original title 'European Economic Community' was abbreviated to the 'European Community' by the TEU. The EU was hereafter the pediment (essentially a single institutional framework) over-arching three so-called 'pillars': these pillars are constituted at the time of writing by (i) the Economic Community and Euratom, (ii) the Common Foreign and Security Policy, and (iii) Police and Judicial Cooperation in Criminal Matters.   [33] See TEU, Art N(2).

[34] Art 12 and the Annex to the Treaty of Amsterdam renumbered the articles of both the TEU and the TEC. The discussion which follows adopts the new numbering.

[35] The draft Constitution collapses the pillar structure and, in Art I-1, simply establishes 'the European Union'. It is for this reason that, although equality law is formally at the moment governed only by the EC pillar, the decision has been made to refer in the present work to 'EU' equality law, except where the context demands otherwise. In any event, the term 'EU law' is increasingly used in practice now, notwithstanding the technicalities of the matter.

[36] Art IV-447 of the Constitution. If not ratified by this date, it is to enter into force on the first day of the second month following the deposit of the instrument of ratification by the last ratifying State.

[37] See also Recital 1 of the Preamble to Part II of the Constitution.

of course, provide for the accession of new Member States[38] and, although only six States joined in the wake of the original Schuman Declaration,[39] the EU today consists of 25 Member States and spans most of Western and Central Europe.[40]

A third way in which the development of modern Europe has provided important support for the principle of equality is through its enhanced emphasis in recent times on the protection of human rights.[41] The Treaty of Amsterdam amended the TEU so as to articulate this emphasis. Article 6 of the TEU now provides:

1. The Union is founded on the principles of liberty, democracy, respect for human rights and fundamental freedoms, and the rule of law, principles which are common to the Member States.

2. The Union shall respect fundamental human rights, as guaranteed by the European Convention for the Protection of Human Rights and Fundamental Freedoms signed in Rome on 4 November 1950 and as they result from the constitutional traditions common to the Member States, as general principles of Community law.

Moreover, a procedure was introduced by Article 7 of the TEU for dealing with a 'clear risk of a serious breach by a Member State of the principles mentioned in Article 6(1)'; in the event of such a breach being established, certain of the defaulting Member State's Treaty rights, including the right to vote in the Council, may be suspended. The Cologne European Council of June 1999 proclaimed the protection of fundamental rights as an 'indispensable prerequisite' to the EU's legitimacy, and a decision was taken to promulgate a Charter of Fundamental Rights. This Charter was formally proclaimed by the European Parliament, the Council, and the Commission in Nice in December 2000[42] and contains a number of provisions protecting people from discrimination and guaranteeing equality. Although the Charter was not originally intended to have legal force, it now occupies Part II of the draft Constitution and will in effect become the Union's Bill of Rights if and when the Constitution is adopted.[43]

The Constitution itself clearly emphasizes the importance of human rights protection to the Union. The opening recital of its Preamble states that the signatories:

Drawing inspiration from the cultural, religious and humanist inheritance of Europe, have developed the universal values of the inviolable and inalienable rights of the human person, freedom, democracy, equality and the rule of law.

---

[38] See now TFU, Art 49.

[39] France, West Germany, Italy, Belgium, The Netherlands, and Luxembourg.

[40] The UK, Ireland, and Denmark became members of the Communities from 1 January 1973; Greece acceded as of 1 January 1981, Spain and Portugal as of 1 January 1986, and Austria, Finland and Sweden as of 1 January 1995. The latest accessions took place on 1 May 2004 and brought into membership of the Union Hungary, Poland, the Czech Republic, Slovakia, Slovenia, Malta, Cyprus, Estonia, Latvia, and Lithuania.

[41] For a highly sceptical view of the approach of the EU to human rights, see Williams, *EU Human Rights Policies: A Study in Irony* (Oxford University Press, Oxford, 2004).

[42] OJ [2000] C364/01.

[43] Its provisions on non-discrimination and equality are discussed more fully in ch 7.

Article I-2 also provides that the Union is 'founded on the values of respect for human dignity, freedom, democracy, equality, the rule of law and respect for human rights, including the rights of persons belonging to minorities'.

These aspects of the development of the EU are vital to an understanding of its equality laws. The Treaties and their present provisions are in no sense intended to be an end in themselves but rather a staging-post in an ultimate design. The social provisions, especially those protecting fundamental human rights, are growing and developing as the linkage between the Member States becomes closer. Furthermore, the Union's geographical extension brings its jurisdiction to bear over a vastly expanded population. What this means in practical terms is that a continuously developing body of equality law now reaches a very large, and ever-expanding, group of people. An element of dynamism is contained within this formula which is almost always lacking in any wholly domestic context.

Sources of EU anti-discrimination law

Crucial to the concept of federation is the existence of a distinct legal system, belonging exclusively to the federation itself. This means that a federation must be able both to create its own laws and to enforce them effectively through its own system of courts or tribunals. The drafters of the European Community Treaties, eager as they were to create the germ from which a federation would grow, were aware of these needs and therefore provided for a system of Community law, together with appropriate law-making powers, enforceable through the medium of the European Court of Justice (ECJ)[44] and the local courts. Essentially, they made provision for both primary and secondary tiers of Community law. Interestingly, the existing Treaties stop short of the use of the actual word 'legislation' in describing the legal system which they create, presumably for the political and psychological reasons that this might have proved unacceptable to national parliaments at the time of their accession to the European Communities.[45]

The Constitution contains a number of provisions which, if the instrument is ratified, will have a direct and important impact in the field of non-discrimination and equality law. In particular, it proclaims in Article I-2 that the Union's values 'are common to the Member States in a society in which pluralism, non-discrimination, tolerance, justice, solidarity and equality between men and women prevail'.

Article I-3 includes amongst the Union's objectives the combating of 'social exclusion and discrimination' and pledges to 'promote social justice and protection, equality between men and women, solidarity between generations and protection of the rights of the child'. Article I-45, entitled 'The principle of democratic

---

[44] The ECJ's sister court, the Court of First Instance (hereafter the CFI), was created in 1988 and began work on 31 October 1989. If the Constitution becomes effective, the CFI will be re-named 'the General Court': see Art I-29.

[45] However, such qualms were not experienced by the drafters of the Constitution and, as will be discussed below, that document does refer to 'legislative acts' of the Union.

equality', provides: 'In all its activities, the Union shall observe the principle of the
equality of its citizens, who shall receive equal attention from its institutions,
bodies, offices and agencies'.[46]

(i)   The EC Treaty (TEC)

The main primary source of Community law at present is the founding Treaties,
together with the amendments which have been made to them over the years.
Of the three founding Treaties, the only one to make specific reference to equality
is the Treaty establishing the European Community, the TEC, and it is with that
Treaty, as subsequently amended, that this book is therefore mainly concerned.[47]

The TEC contains a number of provisions which are relevant in this field. Such
provisions are of two types, namely, those which themselves convey substantive
rights and those which confer enabling authority on the institutions of the EU to
make secondary legislation.

Taking first the substantive provisions, the importance to the Union of outlawing sex discrimination is indicated by the enumeration in Article 2 of the TEC
of the promotion of 'equality between men and women' in the list of 'tasks' of the
European Community. Furthermore, Article 3(2) provides that, in engaging in all
its activities, 'the Community shall aim to eliminate inequalities, and to promote
equality, between men and women'. Article 141[48] enunciates the principle of
equal pay for equal work irrespective of sex. As the Treaty was originally drafted,
this was the only explicit mention anywhere in it of the principle of sex equality,[49]
and so it provided the inspirational springboard for the subsequent developments in
this area. As it is currently drafted, the Article also protects the wider principles of
equality of opportunity and equal treatment in the world of work.

The second type of Treaty provision relevant in the present context is that
which provides the legal authorization for further, secondary legislation. The
Treaty makes clear the need for specific authorization for particular measures of
secondary legislation in Article 249, which enables the European Parliament, the
Council, and the Commission[50] to make secondary legislation 'in order to carry

---

[46] Art III-257(3) also pledges the Union to 'endeavour to ensure a high level of security through
measures to prevent and combat crime, racism and xenophobia'.

[47] Henceforth, unless otherwise stated, all Treaty references in the present work will therefore be to
the TEC.

[48] Under the pre-Amsterdam numbering, the substance of what today are the first two paragraphs of
Art 141 were contained in Art 119. Many of the older cases cited in the text therefore refer to Art 119.
For the sake of verbal simplicity, discussion in the text of the present work will just refer to Art 141,
unless the context demands otherwise. If and when the Constitution enters into effect, Art 141 will be
metamorphosed once again, this time into Art III-214.

[49] A number of references to sex equality were added by the Amsterdam Treaty, as will be discussed.

[50] For general discussion of the powers and functions of the main institutions of the Communities,
in particular the European Parliament, the Council, Commission, and ECJ, see *Wyatt and Dashwood's
European Community Law*, 4th edn (Sweet & Maxwell, London, 2000); and Weatherill and Beaumont,
EU Law, 3rd edn (Penguin, London, 1999).

out their task', but only 'in accordance with the provisions of this Treaty'. In other words, the institutions may create fresh secondary legislation only where a particular provision of the Treaty authorizes this. They possess no inherent or implied law-making capacity.

Article 141 itself conferred no secondary law-making power until its amendment by the Amsterdam Treaty. A new para (3) was, however, inserted by that Treaty, providing:

The Council, acting in accordance with the procedure referred to in Article 251,[51] and after consulting the Economic and Social Committee,[52] shall adopt measures to ensure the application of the principle of equal opportunities and equal treatment of men and women in matters of employment and occupation, including the principle of equal pay for equal work or work of equal value.[53]

The breadth of this enabling provision is noteworthy; it permits measures in general and is not limited to any one form of legislative instrument.[54] It is expressed to extend to measures ensuring equality of opportunity and is not restricted to those simply outlawing discrimination.[55] Furthermore, it encompasses not merely pay equality but also other aspects of equal treatment. The important issue of how far it will be permitted to extend to equal treatment outside the traditional world of paid work will depend on the policy adopted by the ECJ in relation to the interpretation of the word 'occupation'.

The Amsterdam Treaty also created what is now Article 13(1):[56]

Without prejudice to the other provisions of this Treaty and within the limits of the powers conferred by it upon the Community,[57] the Council, acting unanimously on a proposal from the Commission and after consulting the European Parliament,[58] may take appropriate action to combat discrimination based on sex, racial or ethnic origin, religion or belief, disability, age or sexual orientation.[59]

[51] Art 251 gives a power of 'co-decision' to the Council and the European Parliament; this involves a complicated process of exchange and negotiation between the two institutions.

[52] This Committee consists of 'representatives of the various economic and social components of organised civil society, and in particular representatives of producers, farmers, carriers, workers, dealers, craftsmen, professional occupations, consumers and the general interest': Art 257.

[53] The substance of this provision will be contained in Art III-214(3) of the proposed Constitution, if and when that instrument enters into force.

[54] See discussion below of the different legislative instruments available in EU law.

[55] See discussion above.

[56] As to the genesis of Art 13, see Flynn, 'The Implications of Article 13 EC—After Amsterdam, Will Some Forms of Discrimination be More Equal Than Others?' (1999) 36 CMLRev 1127.

[57] Note the subtly different opening words of Art 12 on nationality discrimination: 'Within the *scope of application of this Treaty* and without prejudice to any *special* conditions contained therein' (emphasis added). It remains to be seen whether any significance will be ascribed by the ECJ to these verbal differences.

[58] The marginal role assigned by Art 13 to the European Parliament is ironic, given that this area touches the very heart of social policy. The difference between the Parliament's role under Art 13 and that under Art 141(3) has led to differences in the texts of the instruments adopted pursuant to these respective provisions.

[59] Considerable disagreement between the Member States preceded the adoption of this Article. Whilst most agreed on the need to include sex, race, and religion, there was much less commitment to the other grounds. The UK, under Conservative administrations, was opposed to any EU instrument on discrimination; this attitude changed only with the election of a Labour Government in 1997, whose

It is noteworthy that this Article is to be found in Part One of the TEC, headed 'Principles'; this will enable the ECJ, if it is so inclined, to emphasize the constitutional importance of the instruments adopted pursuant to Article 13. The opening phrase of the Article indicates that it is not to be used where other, more specific enabling authority exists, and Article 141(3) will thus usually be the appropriate provision for legislation dealing exclusively with sex discrimination; however, Article 13 could be used for the enactment of a composite measure which addressed discrimination based on sex as well as the other prohibited classifications. Like Article 141(3), Article 13 authorizes all types of legislative or other instrument,[60] but it should be noted that its ambit is restricted to the prohibition of discrimination and that it does not extend to measures to promote equality of opportunity on the wider scale.

Before the creation by the Amsterdam Treaty of enabling provisions dealing expressly with sex equality, more general enabling provisions had to be utilized for the enactment of secondary legislation in this area. The most obvious candidates were Articles 94 and 308. Article 94 permits the Council, acting unanimously on a Commission proposal and after consulting the European Parliament and the Economic and Social Committee, to make directives[61] 'for the approximation of such laws, regulations or administrative provisions of the Member States as directly affect the establishment or functioning of the common market'. This is often called 'harmonization' legislation. Article 308 is generally a little wider in its scope and provides:

If action by the Community should prove necessary to attain, in the course of the operation of the common market, one of the objectives of the Community and this Treaty has not provided the necessary powers, the Council shall, acting unanimously on a proposal from the Commission and after consulting the European Parliament, take the appropriate measures.

Some further bases for harmonization legislation were provided by the Single European Act of 1986, in particular what was then Article 118a. This was used to mandate Council directives for improving the health and safety of workers.[62] The Amsterdam Treaty generalized the provision[63] and today its successor,

support made possible the unanimous agreement necessary for the adoption of the new Article. The Irish Presidency of the Council in the second half of 1996 is widely credited for the eventual text of Art 13. (Ireland's enthusiasm for such legislation was also manifested shortly afterwards by the adoption of its own wide-ranging national Employment Equality Act 1998.)

[60] See Waddington, 'Testing the Limits of the EC Treaty Article on Non-discrimination' (1999) 28 ILJ 133. If and when the Constitution comes into operation, Art 13(1) will be slightly modified: Art III-124 of the proposed Constitution provides authority for anti-discrimination legislation on the same grounds as Art 13, but it will require the Council to act unanimously 'after obtaining the consent of the European Parliament'. Note: this does not involve the full co-decision procedure and, although increasing the Parliament's powers in this area from its present powers, somewhat limits its input to the debate over new measures.   [61] For the definition and characteristics of a directive, see below.
[62] In this form it provided the authorization for the Pregnancy Directive (Directive 92/85, OJ [1992] L348/1), discussed in ch 5.
[63] It absorbed into the body of the TEC the provisions which had formerly been contained in the Agreement on Social Policy, discussed below.

Article 137,[64] provides that the Community will support and complement the activities of the Member States in a number of fields including:

(a) improvement in particular of the working environment to protect workers' health and safety;
(b) working conditions;
(c) social security and social protection of workers;
...
(h) the integration of persons excluded from the labour market . . . ;
(i) equality between men and women with regard to labour market opportunities and treatment at work.

To these ends, the Council is authorized to adopt directives setting 'minimum requirements for gradual implementation, having regard to the conditions and technical rules obtaining in each of the Member States'.[65] Such directives must not, however, impose administrative, financial, and legal constraints in a way which would hold back the creation and development of small and medium-sized undertakings.[66] The Council is also permitted to adopt measures

designed to encourage co-operation between Member States through initiatives aimed at improving knowledge, developing exchanges of information and best practices, promoting innovative approaches and evaluating experiences, excluding any harmonisation of the laws and regulations of the Member States.[67]

Such action is to be in accordance with Article 251, after the Council has consulted the Economic and Social Committee and the Committee of the Regions.[68] Exceptionally, however, in order to take action *inter alia* in the fields of social security and social protection, the Council has to act unanimously on a proposal from the Commission, after consulting the European Parliament, the Economic and Social Committee, and the Committee of the Regions.[69]

Until its repeal by the Amsterdam Treaty, the Protocol on Social Policy annexed at Maastricht to the TEC provided a vehicle for a special kind of secondary legislation.[70] The Protocol contained an Agreement on Social Policy, acquiesced in by all the Member States apart from the UK, which refused whilst under Conservative administration to be involved in any further extension of the powers of the Community in the field of social policy.[71] Legislative action[72]

[64] If and when the proposed Constitution enters into force, this will become Art III-210.
[65] Art 137(2)(b).   [66] Ibid.   [67] Art 137(2)(a).   [68] Established by Art 263.
[69] Art 137(2).
[70] Art 311 provides that Protocols annexed to the TEC are to form 'an integral part thereof'.

[71] It was suggested by some writers that the UK's social policy opt-out could be contrary to a 'higher principle' of Community law (ie, superior in legal force to the written rules of the Treaty), such as that of the uniform application of EC law or the principle of legal certainty, and that it was therefore invalid. See Hartley, 'The European Court, Judicial Objectivity and the Constitution of the European Union' (1996) 112 LQR 95; Whiteford, 'Social Policy After Maastricht' (1993) 18 ELRev 202; and Curtin, 'The Constitutional Structure of the European Union: a Europe of Bits and Pieces' (1993) 30 CMLRev 17.

[72] Art 2(2) permitted the Council to adopt directives in accordance with the procedure referred to in Art 252, after consulting the Economic and Social Committee. Art 2(3) permitted unspecified action to be taken by the Council unanimously on a proposal of the Commission, after consulting the European Parliament and the Economic and Social Committee, in areas which included social security and the protection of workers. Art 4 envisaged Community level collective agreements which could, in certain

pursuant to the Agreement took place according to the usual EC institutional procedures, but without the participation of the UK in the relevant Council meetings since such legislation did not bind the UK.[73] It could supplement but could not detract from the pre-existing *acquis communautaire*.[74]

Several instruments were concluded under the aegis of the Protocol and Agreement, the first being the Directive on Works Councils.[75] This was followed by a European-level collective agreement on Parental Leave signed on 14 December 1995. The agreement was subsequently enacted in the form of a directive in June 1996.[76] A directive on parental leave had been proposed as long ago as 1984, but was consistently opposed by the UK Government on financial grounds. The proposal was resurrected after the Social Policy Agreement came into force. Another measure which had remained stalled for a long time because of the intransigence of the UK Government of the day was a proposed directive on the burden of proof in sex discrimination cases and on the definition of indirect discrimination; the social partners decided that they did not wish to negotiate an agreement on this matter, but progress was made towards the enactment of legislation when unanimous political agreement[77] was reached on a common position at a Council meeting in the Summer of 1997.[78] In addition, an agreement between the social partners was reached in June 1997 on discrimination against part-time workers, subsequently transposed into a directive in the Summer of 1997.[79] A framework agreement on fixed-term work was concluded on the same basis and later transposed into a directive.[80] After its election in May 1997, the new Labour Government of the

circumstances, be implemented by a Council decision on a proposal from the Commission. See further Fitzpatrick, 'Community Social Law After Maastricht' (1992) 21 ILJ 199 and Watson, 'Social Policy After Maastricht' (1993) 30 CMLRev 481.

[73] Thus the Agreement created for the first time the potential for a 'two speed Europe'. For the view that the Protocol created a real danger of 'social dumping', in other words, 'investment by companies in the United Kingdom where labour costs are lower than in other Member States, which will result in workers in those other Member States being forced to accept lower standards in order to avoid unemployment', see Watson, op cit, n 72.

[74] See the opening recital to the Protocol. Curtin, op cit, n71, questioned the legal status of such 'legislation', pointing out that the wording adopted by the Protocol authorized the participating States to adopt acts 'among themselves' and arguing that the products of such agreements could not constitute EC law with the qualities set out in Art 249. The Commission, however, asserted that 'the Community nature of measures taken under the Agreement is beyond doubt, which means that the Court of Justice will be empowered to rule on the legality of directives adopted by the Eleven and to interpret them' (Communication concerning the application of the agreement on social policy presented by the Commission to the Council and to the European Parliament COM(93) 600 final). To the same effect, see also Bercusson, 'The Dynamic of European Labour Law After Maastricht' (1994) 23 ILJ 1.

[75] Directive 94/45, OJ [1994] L254/64, as to which see also Burrows and Mair, *European Social Law* (Wiley, Chichester, 1996), ch 14. At a lecture in the University of Birmingham in 1995, Prof Giorgio Gaja pointed out that the adoption of the usual EC system for the numbering of such directives was deceptive because it implied that they were ordinary instruments of EC law; furthermore, he asserted that this confused the legislative system.

[76] Directive 96/34, OJ [1996] L145/4, discussed in ch 5.   [77] Including that of the UK.

[78] COM (96) 340 final. The provisions of the eventual directive are discussed in ch 3.

[79] Directive 97/81, OJ [1998] L14/9, discussed in ch 5.

[80] Directive 1999/70, OJ [1999] L175/43, also discussed in ch 5.

UK announced its intention to commit itself to all the instruments hitherto agreed by the other Member States under the Social Policy Agreement.[81]

(ii)   Secondary legislation

Secondary EC law is currently of three types: regulations, directives, and decisions. Article 249 defines the basic attributes of each. Regulations are stated to have 'general application', which means that they create binding legal obligations for every person within the Union. This is not to say that they necessarily in fact impinge on the legal situation of each and every legal person within the Community, since they are frequently of a highly specialized nature and regulate only specific activities or industries. They do, however, create general law and thus have the potential actually to affect the legal position of any legal person within the Community. Their nearest equivalent in domestic legal terms is Parliamentary legislation. Article 249 goes on to provide that regulations are binding in their entirety and 'directly applicable in all Member States'. The meaning of this latter phrase is not at once self-evident, but it is clear from comparison with what Article 249 goes on to say about the effects of directives that it is intended to indicate that regulations have automatic legal force and require no implementing measures to be taken by the legislative or other authorities in the Member States. The ECJ has also confirmed this interpretation.[82] It follows that regulations are the appropriate instrument for achieving uniformity or identity of legal provision throughout the Community.[83]

Directives, unlike regulations, are expressed by Article 249 to be addressed to States rather than being of 'general application'. A directive is binding 'as to the result to be achieved' on each Member State to which it is addressed, but it leaves to the national authorities 'the choice of form and methods'. Directives thus do not take effect within the legal systems of the Member States as they stand. Rather, they require the Member States to legislate to achieve a particular end-product. They require translation into national law and always contain a time-limit by which such translation must have been carried out. They are chiefly of use when mutually compatible, or harmonized, laws are needed amongst all the Member States, as distinct from where identical provisions are required.[84]

---

[81]   The existing instruments were re-enacted with the agreement of the UK under Art 94; as Usher observes in *EC Institutions and Legislation* (Longmans, London, 1998), this suggests that the matters covered by the Agreement on Social Policy fell within the mainstream of Community law all along.

[82]   In Case 93/71 *Leonesio v Italian Ministry of Agriculture and Fisheries* [1972] ECR 287, the ECJ said (at 293): 'Therefore, because of its nature and its purpose within the system of sources of Community law it has direct effect and is, as such, capable of creating individual rights which national courts must protect. Since they are pecuniary rights against the State these rights arise when the conditions set out in the regulation are complied with and it is not possible at a national level to render the exercise of them subject to implementing provisions other than those which might be required by the regulation itself.'

[83]   Pursuant to Art I-33 of the proposed Constitution, regulations are to become known as 'European laws'.

[84]   Also pursuant to Art I-33 of the proposed Constitution, directives are re-named 'European framework laws'.

In practice, all the secondary legislation to date in the fields covered by the present work has taken the form of directives, so that their nature and effects are particularly significant in the present context. The directives thus far enacted have been clustered around three broad themes, namely, sex equality, non-discrimination on the ground of race, and non-discrimination on the remaining grounds set out in Article 13. The major instruments concerned are: the Equal Pay Directive[85] and Equal Treatment Directive,[86] which supplement Article 141 of the Treaty and proscribe sex discrimination;[87] the Race Directive,[88] which implements the principle of equal treatment irrespective of racial or ethnic origin; and the so-called 'Framework' Directive,[89] the purpose of which is to combat discrimination on the grounds of religion or belief, disability, age, or sexual orientation.

A decision, according to Article 249, is addressed to a particular legal person or group of such persons. Such persons can include individual people, corporations, and States. The decision is 'binding in its entirety upon those to whom it is addressed'. It does not therefore appear capable of creating any kind of generalized legal obligations.[90]

All three instruments of secondary legislation are required to state the reasons on which they are based and must refer to any proposals or opinions which the Treaty required to be obtained.[91] Because of the breadth of their legal consequences, all regulations and most directives are today required to be published in the Official Journal of the European Union.[92]

The relevant enabling article in the TEC has to be examined in order to discover what type of secondary law is permitted in any given instance.

(iii) Decisions of the ECJ and CFI

As will become evident in the rest of this book, judicial decisions have played, and continue to play, an extremely important role in shaping EU law in the area of equality and non-discrimination. Many vital concepts, words, and phrases have either been left undefined in the relevant legislation, or have been defined only

---

[85] Directive 75/117, OJ [1975] L45/19.   [86] Directive 76/207, OJ [1976] L39/40.

[87] But note that there are a number of other directives which also support the principle of sex equality and are discussed elsewhere in the present work.   [88] Directive 2000/43, OJ [2000] L180/22.

[89] Directive 2000/78, OJ [2000] L303/16. Like the Race Directive, the Framework Directive was adopted pursuant to Art 13. For the argument that Art 13 was a less appropriate Treaty base than Art 137 for the Framework instrument, and the suggestion that reasons of pragmatism and political expediency influenced the choice, see Bell and Whittle, 'Between Social Policy and Union Citizenship: the Framework Directive on Equal Treatment in Employment' (2002) 27 ELRev 677.

[90] See Greaves, 'The Nature and Binding Effect of Decisions Under Article 189 EC' (1996) 21 ELRev 3.   [91] Art 253.

[92] Art 254 provides that regulations, directives, and decisions adopted in accordance with the procedure referred to in Art 251, together with regulations of the Council and the Commission and directives of those institutions which are addressed to all Member States, must be published in the Official Journal. They enter into force on the date specified in them or, in default of such specification, on the twentieth day following that of their publication. Other directives and decisions must merely be notified to those to whom they are addressed and take effect on such notification.

broadly; their articulation and effect are therefore in the hands of the ECJ. Although the Court does not adopt a formal system of precedent, and remains free to change its mind in subsequent decisions, in practice it establishes core areas of jurisprudence which act as sources of law. This is recognized in the proposed Constitution, which provides in Article IV-438(4) that the case law of the ECJ and CFI on the interpretation of the Treaties which preceded the Constitution, as well as of the secondary legislation enacted pursuant to them, is to remain 'the source of interpretation of Union law and in particular of the comparable provisions of the Constitution'.

The exclusive jurisdiction enjoyed by the ECJ over the preliminary rulings procedure[93] has meant that in practice the ECJ's jurisprudence has so far been vastly more influential in this area than that of the CFI, since preliminary rulings have provided the vehicle for most anti-discrimination litigation.

(iv) Instruments for the protection of fundamental human rights

A number of internationally agreed instruments seek to protect fundamental human rights and they exert at least an indirect influence on the content of EU law. Their relevance in the specific field of equality and anti-discrimination law will be discussed further in chapter 7. Of prime importance in this respect is the European Convention on Human Rights.[94] It has already been seen that the TEU expressly enjoins the Union to respect the principles of the ECHR, and this is a formal acknowledgement that the Convention operates as a secondary source of EU law.[95] Also of importance in this context are the European Social Charter of 1961, revised in 1996, and the Community Social Charter of 1989, both referred to in the Preamble to the TEU.[96]

Potentially of even greater significance is the Charter of Fundamental Rights, planned to become Part II of the proposed Constitution of the Union. It too is discussed in further detail in chapter 7.

(v) Other indirect sources

Since the European judicature has a wide measure of discretion in interpreting and applying anti-discrimination and equality law, it is inevitably thrown back on a number of other sources when deciding what policy consideration should guide it.

---

[93] This is a procedure which enables national courts to seek the help of the ECJ in interpreting and applying EU law. It is discussed more fully in ch 2. The Treaty of Nice, which came into operation on 1 February 2003, made it possible for the CFI in the future also to be given jurisdiction to make preliminary rulings in specified areas. [94] ETS No 5, 1950. Hereafter the ECHR.
[95] For recent examples of the influence of the ECHR on EU law, see Case C-60/00 *Carpenter v Secretary of State for the Home Department* [2002] ECR I-6279 and Case C-224/01 *Köbler v Austria* [2003] ECR I-10239, discussed in ch 2. [96] See Recital 4.

Amongst such sources should be listed, no doubt *inter alia*, the constitutional provisions of the Member States, international instruments, and non-binding instruments of EU law (so-called 'soft' law). The part they play is discussed more fully in chapters 2 and 7.

The grounds on which EU law forbids discrimination

The picture which emerges from a consideration of the numerous sources of EU equality and non-discrimination law is a complex one. There are a number of instruments to which a court must have regard in deciding an issue within this area, and the European judicature, in seeking to resolve ambiguities and unclear matters, must have recourse to many different instruments. Nevertheless, in the current state of the law, there is only a limited list of grounds on which EU law actually contains an outright prohibition on discrimination. These are nationality, sex, part-time and temporary employment, racial or ethnic origin, religion or belief, disability, age, and sexual orientation.

(i) Nationality

A number of provisions of EU law forbid discrimination against persons on the ground of their possessing the nationality of one of the Member States. The most important are Article 12 of the TEC, prohibiting such discrimination in general terms and authorizing the Council to adopt rules designed for this purpose, and Articles 39–55, providing for the free movement of workers, the right of establishment, and the freedom to provide services within the Community. A substantial body of secondary law has also been enacted to support these rights. However, for reasons already set out, discrimination on the ground of nationality is not dealt with extensively in the present work.

(ii) Sex

That the improvement of the quality of life for the peoples of the Communities is an ideal underlying the EU is clear from the Preamble to the TEC[97] and from the aspirations of the founders of the Communities discussed above. However, at the time the original TEC was being drafted, there were two radically opposed conceptions of the relationship between social policy and the establishment and functioning of the proposed Common Market. The French view was that the harmonization of the 'social costs' of production was necessary in order to make

[97] See in particular Recital 3: 'Affirming as the essential objective of their efforts the constant improvements of the living and working conditions of their peoples.'

sure that businesses competed on a fair and equal basis once the barriers to the free movement of persons and capital were removed. At the time of the negotiations, there were important differences in the scope and content of the social legislation in force in the States concerned. France, in particular, had on her statute book a number of rules which protected workers and were consequently expensive for employers. For example, legislation of 1957 mandated equal pay for men and women. Workers in France also had longer paid holidays than workers in the other States, normally a minimum of twenty-four days. They were, in addition, entitled to overtime pay after fewer hours of work at basic rates than elsewhere. All this meant that the French feared that the indirect costs of production of goods in France would make French goods uncompetitive in the proposed Common Market and would damage French industry. They therefore sought to persuade the other negotiating States that social costs should be equalized throughout the Community. Germany, however, took a very different line, arguing that the harmonization of indirect or social costs would inevitably follow from the setting up of a Common Market. The Germans were also strongly committed to a minimum level of government interference in the area of wages and prices.

A compromise was ultimately reached and the two differing viewpoints were both reflected in the Treaty's social policy provisions.[98] In particular, the French delegation succeeded in persuading the others to accept two specific provisions, which would protect French industry from the kind of 'social dumping' of which it was afraid. These are what are today Article 141, on equal pay for men and women,[99] and Article 142, which provides that the Member States will 'endeavour to maintain the existing equivalence between paid holiday schemes'.

Despite this somewhat unedifying origin, there emerged a principle which both the Union and the ECJ were to regard as of fundamental importance, namely, the equal treatment of men and women. Social policy generally came to play an increasingly prominent role in practice because it provided a useful mechanism by which to emphasize the human face of the Community, against a background of criticism that it was exclusively economic, capitalist, and uncaring. Social policy legislation was also made more necessary as a result of economic recession and mass unemployment. So, by 1972, the communiqué issued by the Paris Summit Meeting stated that the Heads of State or Government attached 'as much importance to vigorous action in the social field as to the achievement of monetary

[98] That the debate between the two positions is not yet over has been shown in more recent times by the altercations between those who would seek to de-regulate employment and their opponents who advocate harmonized social policy legislation as the only route to real future progress in Europe. A more recent example of the practical issues involved can be seen in the decision of Hoover, a US company, to close its factory in Dijon and transfer production to Scotland, where the burden of social protection provisions was perceived to be less than that in France: see Editorial Comment, 'Are European Values Being Hoovered Away?' (1993) 30 CMLRev 445.

[99] See Forman, 'The Equal Pay Principle under Community Law' (1982) 1 LIEI 17. Note that despite its legislative history, the equal pay article makes no suggestion (and neither has the subsequent case law of the ECJ) that it protects only women and not men.

and economic union'. A 'Social Action Programme' followed in 1973,[100] which was approved by the Council in January 1974.[101] The Social Action Programme had three main aims: the attainment of full and better employment; the improvement of living and working conditions; and the increased involvement of management and labour in the economic and social decisions of the Community, and of workers in the life of undertakings. Among other things its objectives included the bringing about of a 'situation in which equality between men and women obtains in the labour market throughout the Community, through the improvement of economic and psychological conditions, and of the social and educational infrastructure'.

Gradually, equality of opportunity as between the sexes took its place at the forefront of EU social policy.[102] In addition to the enactment of a series of directives on the subject, five 'Action Programmes' have been mounted covering the periods 1982–5, 1986–90, 1991–5, 1996–2000, and 2001–2005.[103] These have sought to enforce the equality legislation on a practical level in numerous ways, a matter of the utmost importance if the kinds of structural disadvantages faced by women which have been discussed earlier in this chapter are to be dismantled.[104] An 'Advisory Committee on Equal Opportunities for Women and Men' was established in 1982 to help the Commission to formulate and implement policy on the advancement of women's employment and equal opportunities, and to arrange for the exchange of information between interested bodies in this field.[105] In addition, the Amsterdam Treaty gave a strong new emphasis to equality of opportunity irrespective of sex.

Quite why sex equality has been accorded this sort of priority by the Community is open to speculation. On an economic level, it is clearly important to prevent competitive distortions in a now quite highly integrated market. On the political level, perhaps it has been selected because it provides a relatively innocuous, even high-sounding, platform by means of which the Community can demonstrate its commitment to social progress. Barnard has also suggested that the promotion of the concept of equality by the ECJ has served, in times of uncertainty

[100] 24 October 1973, COM (73) 1600.   [101] OJ [1974] C13/1.
[102] For an account of the processes at work to achieve this end, see Harlow, 'A Community of Interests? Making the Most of European Law' (1992) 55 MLR 331.
[103] See Action Programme 1982–5, OJ [1982] C186/3; Equal Opportunities for Women Medium-term Community Programme 1986–90, Bull EC Supplement 3/86 and Bull EC 6–1986, point 2.1.116; Third Medium-term Community Action Programme COM (90) 449 final; Fourth Equality Action Programme 1996–2000, OJ [1995] L335/37; Council Decision of 20 December 2000 establishing a Programme relating to the Community framework strategy on gender equality (2001–2005), Decision 2001/51, OJ [2001] L17/22.
[104] However, the Report from the Commission to the Council, the European Parliament, the European Economic and Social Committee, and the Committee of the Regions on Equality Between Women and Men (19 February 2004, COM (2004) 115 final) exposes some dispiriting statistics, in particular that the average gender pay gap in the EU remains at 16% and has hardly changed in recent years; similarly, sex segregation in the labour market has also remained more or less constant, at around 25% for occupational segregation and 18% for sectoral segregation.
[105] Commission Decision 82/43/EEC of 9 December 1981, OJ [1982] L20.

about the future of the EU, to legitimize the Union and to strengthen political integration.[106]

The part played by the European Parliament in the process will provide an interesting study for the historians of future generations. The Parliament, which has a higher proportion of women members than have the national parliaments,[107] has since 1984 possessed an influential Standing Committee on Women's Rights and has on several occasions provided the impetus for Community action in this field.[108] To some extent, it may be that to accede to demands made by the Parliament in the sphere of equal rights between the sexes has provided the Community's executive with a useful way out of heeding its advice in other fields.[109]

The ECJ has also made clear the importance which it attaches to the principle of sex equality. In its seminal decision in *Defrenne v Sabena*,[110] it held:

The question of the direct effect[111] of Article 119 must be considered in the light of the nature of the principle of equal pay, the aim of this provision and its place in the scheme of the Treaty. Article 119 pursues a double aim. First, in the light of the different stages of the development of social legislation in the various Member States, the aim of Article 119 is to avoid a situation in which undertakings established in states which have actually implemented the principle of equal pay suffer a competitive disadvantage in intra-Community competition as compared with undertakings established in states which have not yet eliminated discrimination against women workers as regards pay. Secondly, this provision forms part of the social objectives of the Community, which is not merely an economic union, but is at the same time intended, by common action, to ensure social progress and seek the constant improvement of the living and working conditions of their peoples, as is emphasized by the Preamble to the Treaty. This aim is accentuated by the insertion of Article 119 into the body of a Chapter devoted to social policy whose preliminary provision, Article 117, marks 'the need to promote improved working conditions and an improved standard of living for workers, so as to make possible their harmonization while the improvement is being maintained.' This double aim, which is at once economic and social, shows that the principle of equal pay forms part of the foundations of the Community. Furthermore, this explains why the Treaty has provided for the complete implementation of this principle by the end of the first stage of the transitional period.[112]

---

[106] Barnard, op cit, n 12.

[107] See Valance, 'Do Women Make a Difference? The Impact of Women MEPS on Community Equality Policy' in Buckley and Anderson (eds), *Women, Equality and Europe*, (Macmillan, London, 1988) and CREW Reports (1990), Vol 10, No 5, 11. After the 1994 elections, women represented 25.7% of the membership of the European Parliament. By 1996, this percentage had increased to 27.6. This is to be compared with the average percentage of women in the national parliaments of the Member States, which stood at 15 in 1996, notwithstanding the accessions of Sweden and Finland which both have an exceptionally high number of women in parliament: see *Equal Opportunities for Women and Men in the European Union: Annual Report 1996* (Commission, Luxembourg, 1997). The percentage of women MEPS rose to 30% in both the 2000 and the 2004 elections.

[108] See, eg, its Resolution of 11 February 1981 on the Situation of Women in the EC (Bull EC 2-1981, point 2.3.7), which prompted the production of the first 'Action Programme'.

[109] See O'Donovan and Szyszczak, Equality and Sex Discrimination Law (Blackwell, Oxford, 1988), in particular ch 7.

[110] Case 43/75 [1976] ECR 455, the so-called Second Defrenne case, noted in [1976] Journal of Business Law 296. See also Wyatt, 'Article 119 EEC: Direct Applicability' (1975–6) 1 ELRev 418, and Crisham, 'Annotation on Case 43/75' (1977) 14 CMLRev 108.

[111] The meaning of 'direct effect' is discussed in ch 2.

[112] [1976] ECR 455, at 471–2. For discussion of the similar rationales for EU race discrimination law, see McInerney, 'Bases for Action against Race Discrimination in EU Law' (2002) 27 ELRev 72.

This passage explains two vital elements of the ECJ's reasoning in relation to the principle of equal pay for men and women. First, it sees equal pay as part, but only part, of the social objectives of the Community. This has enabled it in later cases to develop an allied general principle of equality as between the sexes. It has also undoubtedly contributed to the Court's purposive reading of the secondary legislation on sex discrimination. France's 'foot-in-the-door' negotiating stance when the original TEC was being drafted therefore paid off in a way which could hardly have been anticipated in 1957. Secondly, because Article 141 is an important element in the development of Community social policy, it is not to be read narrowly or restrictively;[113] its meaning and effects must be understood in the light of its purposes, and this can lead to very much more extensive constructions of its terms, and those of the implementing directives, than would normally be expected.

It might be thought that the definition of 'sex' was a straightforward biological matter and that the only question marks which would be encountered in enforcing the principle of sex equality would concern its scope, rather than the ground itself. However, the ECJ has made it clear that the principle of non-discrimination on the ground of sex extends in two important ways beyond the obvious case of a comparable man and woman receiving different treatment. In arriving at these decisions, it has concentrated on 'gender' as well as 'sex', in other words, the social, psychological, and cultural constructs which accompany a person's membership of one or other sex, in addition to the biological difference of sex.

First, the principle of sex discrimination has been interpreted by the ECJ as providing automatic protection against discrimination based upon pregnancy.[114] In *Dekker v Stichting Vormingscentrum Voor Jonge Volwassen Plus*,[115] the Court held that the Equal Treatment Directive forbade an employer to refuse to employ a pregnant woman, who was otherwise suitable for the job which she had been offered. The fact of her pregnancy was the most important reason for her non-employment and, since this is a condition which can apply only to members of the female sex, this meant that the employer's action necessarily constituted direct discrimination on the ground of sex.[116] In *Handels-OG Kontorfunktionaerernes Forbund i Danmark v Dansk Arbejdsgiverforening (acting for Aldi Marked K/S)*,[117] the Court added that this principle holds good throughout the relevant period of maternity leave.[118] It is clear from *Dekker*, and also from the ECJ's subsequent decision in *Webb v EMO (Air Cargo) Ltd*,[119] that there is no need to resort to comparison with the treatment

---

[113] See, eg, the comment of Darmon AG in Joined Cases C-399, 409 and 425/92, C-34, 50 and 78/93 *Stadt Lengerich v Helmig* [1994] ECR I-5727, at 5731. See also Case C-1/95 *Gerster v Freistaat Bayern* [1997] ECR I-5253, in which the ECJ held that Art 141 applies to employment relationships in the public service.   [114] This matter is discussed in further detail in ch 5.
[115] Case 177/88 [1990] ECR I-3941, noted by Asscher-Vonk in (1991) 20 ILJ 152.
[116] The meaning of 'direct' discrimination is discussed in ch 3.
[117] Case 179/88 [1990] ECR I-3979; both *Dekker* and *Aldi* are noted by Nielsen in (1992) 29 CMLRev 160. See also More, 'Reflections on Pregnancy Discrimination under EC Law' [1992] JSWFL 48.   [118] See also discussion in ch 5 of the Pregnancy Directive.
[119] Case C-32/93 [1994] ECR I-3567.

afforded, or which would be afforded, to a member of the opposite sex where the detrimental treatment complained of can be shown to be referable to pregnancy; thus, it is incorrect to draw comparisons between the treatment received by a pregnant woman and that which would, for example, be received by a male comparator suffering from some temporary medical ailment.[120] Treatment based upon pregnancy is *ipso facto* treatment based on sex.

Secondly, the principle of sex equality has been held to apply to discrimination based upon gender reassignment. In *P v S and Cornwall County Council*,[121] the ECJ held that the Equal Treatment Directive prohibited the dismissal of an employee[122] where the true reason for the dismissal had been found by the referring court to be the employee's proposal to undergo gender reassignment.[123] The Court explained that the Directive:

. . . is simply the expression, in the relevant field, of the principle of equality, which is one of the fundamental principles of Community law. Moreover, . . . the right not to be discriminated against on grounds of sex is one of the fundamental human rights whose observance the Court has a duty to ensure . . .

Accordingly, the scope of the Directive cannot be confined simply to discrimination based on the fact that a person is of one or other sex. In view of its purpose and the nature of the rights which it seeks to safeguard, the scope of the Directive is also such as to apply to discrimination arising, as in this case, from the gender reassignment of the person concerned.

Such discrimination is based, essentially if not exclusively, on the sex of the person concerned. Where a person is dismissed on the ground that he or she intends to undergo, or has undergone, gender reassignment, he or she is treated unfavourably by comparison with persons of the sex to which he or she was deemed to belong before undergoing gender reassignment.

To tolerate such discrimination would be tantamount, as regards such a person, to a failure to respect the dignity and freedom to which he or she is entitled, and which the Court has a duty to safeguard.[124]

---

[120] But for discussion of the extent to which the ECJ has compromised this principle in its subsequent decisions, see ch 5.

[121] Case C-13/94 [1996] ECR I-2143. See Campbell and Lardy, 'Discrimination Against Transsexuals in Employment' (1996) 21 ELR 412, and Flynn's comments in (1997) 34 CMLRev 367.

[122] In *Goodwin and I v UK* (2002) EHRR 447, the European Court of Human Rights held that the UK's failure to accord legal recognition (specifically, through an amended birth certificate) to the reassigned gender of a post-operative transgender person violated the right to private life pursuant to Art 8 of the ECHR; furthermore, the State's refusal to recognize that reassigned gender for the purpose of marriage violated the right to marry under Art 12. The UK responded by enacting the Gender Recognition Act 2004, which permits an amended birth certificate to be issued to a transsexual person who registers pursuant to the Act. Since, as discussed above, the ECHR operates as a secondary source of EU law, *Goodwin* is likely to induce the ECJ to take an increasingly broad view of the protection granted by EU law to transsexuals.

[123] This conclusion was of particular significance in the UK where the Sex Discrimination Act 1975 had not been interpreted hitherto as extending to this situation on the basis that the treatment received by the applicant would have been no different whether the gender reassignment had been male to female or *vice versa*. See *White v British Sugar Corporation* [1977] IRLR 121. However, subsequently in *Chessington World of Adventures Ltd v Reed* [1997] IRLR 556, the Employment Appeal Tribunal held that the Sex Discrimination Act could be construed so as to cover unfavourable treatment on the ground of a declared intention to undergo gender reassignment. The Act was subsequently formally amended so as to preclude discrimination against transsexuals by the Sex Discrimination (Gender Reassignment) Regulations 1999, SI 1999 No 1102.

[124] [1996] ECR I-2143, at 2165. Tridimas has commented: 'The case provides a prime example of the way the Court views the principle of equality as a general principle of Community law transcending

Tesauro AG added:

I regard as obsolete the idea that the law should take into consideration, and protect, a woman who has suffered discrimination in comparison with a man, or *vice versa*, but denies that protection to those who are also *discriminated against*, again by reason of sex, merely because they fall outside the traditional man/ woman classification.[125]

The spirit of this decision was followed in *KB v National Health Service Pensions Agency*.[126] A female nurse employed by the National Health Service complained that the restriction of survivors' benefits in her pension scheme to widows and widowers infringed her right to equal pay pursuant to Article 141.[127] She was living in a stable relationship with R, a female-to-male transsexual, and UK law did not at the relevant time permit marriages other than between two people of the opposite biological sex; neither did it recognize the possibility of a legal change of sex.[128] The ECJ held that a decision to restrict benefits to married couples, excluding all unmarried couples, did not *per se* amount to sex discrimination since it applied to both sexes. However, the situation in question did involve an 'inequality of treatment' which, although it did not directly undermine the enjoyment of a right protected by Community law, affected one of the conditions for the grant of that right; in other words, the inequality did not relate to the award of the widower's pension but to a necessary precondition for the grant of such a pension, namely, the capacity to marry. The Court noted that the UK law prohibiting marriage between transsexuals and preventing the alteration of birth certificates had recently been held by the European Court of Human Rights to constitute a breach of Articles 8 and 12 of the ECHR.[129] This led it to conclude:

Legislation, such as that at issue in the main proceedings, which, in breach of the ECHR, prevents a couple such as KB and R from fulfilling the marriage requirement which must be met for one of them to be able to benefit from part of the pay of the other must be regarded as being, in principle, incompatible with the requirements of Article 141.[130]

However, the Court went on to hold that it is for the Member States to determine the conditions under which they give legal recognition to gender reassignments; it

the provisions of Community legislation. In effect, the Court applied a general principle of unwritten human rights law, according to which discrimination on arbitrary criteria is prohibited, rather than the provisions of the Equal Treatment Directive, a literal interpretation of which does not support the Court's finding' (Tridimas, *The General Principles of EC Law* (Oxford University Press, Oxford, 1999), at 70). For further discussion of the general principle of equality, see ch 7 of the present work.

[125] Ibid, at 2153. See Barnard, '*P v S*: Kite Flying or a New Constitutional Approach?' in Dashwood and O'Leary (eds), *The Principle of Equal Treatment in EC Law* (Sweet & Maxwell, London, 1997). In *Chief Constable of West Yorkshire Police v A (No 2)* [2004] 2 WLR 1209, the House of Lords held that it followed from *P v S and Cornwall County Council* that, for the purpose of identifying unlawful discrimination, a transsexual person must be regarded as having the sexual identity of the gender to which he or she has been reassigned.   [126] Case C-117/01 [2004] 1 CMLR 28.

[127] The applicability of Art 141 to pension schemes, and in particular to survivors' benefits, is discussed in ch 4.   [128] But see now the Gender Recognition Act 2004.

[129] *Goodwin v UK* (2002) 35 EHRR 447, as to which see ch 7.

[130] [2004] 1 CMLR 28, at [34].

was therefore for the national court in *KB* to determine whether KB could rely on Article 141 in order to gain recognition of her right to nominate R as the beneficiary of her survivor's pension.

The broad interpretation of the concept of 'sex' for the purposes of the Directive given by the ECJ in *P v S and Cornwall County Council*, combined with the Court's references to the fundamental right to equality and to dignity and freedom, lent force to the view that the Directive might also extend to discrimination on the ground of homosexuality.[131] Thus, for example, in *R v Secretary of State for Defence, ex parte Perkins*,[132] Lightman J commented in the High Court:

> After the decision in the *Cornwall* case, it is scarcely possible to limit the application of the Directive to gender discrimination, as was held in the *Smith* case,[133] and there must be a real prospect that the European Court will take the further courageous step to extend protection to those of homosexual orientation, if a courageous step is necessary to do so. I doubt, however, whether any courage is necessary, for all that may be required is working out and applying in a constructive manner the implications of the Advocate General's Opinion and the judgment in the *Cornwall* case.[134]

Furthermore, in *Grant v South-West Trains Ltd*,[135] which concerned travel concessions granted by an employer in respect of the common law opposite-sex spouse of an employee but refused to a lesbian employee who was living with a female partner, Elmer AG submitted that discrimination on the ground of sexual orientation was indeed forbidden by EU law. Although the *Cornwall* case technically concerned the Equal Treatment Directive, he argued that it had equal significance for Article 141, 'which sets out the basic principle prohibiting discrimination based on sex'. In order to give full effect to that principle, he reasoned that Article 141 must be construed so as to preclude forms of discrimination against employees based on gender, and he continued:

> The provision must, in order to be effective, be understood as prohibiting discrimination against employees not solely on the basis of the employee's own gender but also on the basis of the gender of the employee's child, parent or other dependent. The provision must therefore also be regarded as precluding an employer from, for instance, denying a household allowance to an employee for sons under 18 living at home when such an allowance in otherwise equivalent circumstances was given for daughters living at home.[136]

---

[131] Support could also be derived for the application of the Equal Treatment Directive to discrimination on account of homosexuality from the fact that Art 2(1) (even after its amendment) refers to discrimination on 'grounds' (plural) 'of sex'. In *R v Ministry of Defence, ex parte Smith* [1996] IRLR 100 (noted by Skidmore in 'Homosexuals Have Human Rights Too' (1996) 25 ILJ 63) and *Smith v Gardner Merchant Ltd* [1996] ICR 790, UK courts held that UK sex equality legislation did not protect homosexuals against discrimination on grounds of sexual orientation. For further discussion, see Wintermute, 'Recognising New Kinds of Direct Sex Discrimination: Transsexualism, Sexual Orientation and Dress Codes' (1997) 60 MLR 334, and Waaldijk and Clapham (eds), *Homosexuality: A European Community Issue* (Martinus Nijhoff, Dordrecht, 1993).

[132] [1997] IRLR 297. The *Perkins* case challenged the Ministry of Defence's policy of dismissing all members of the armed services who had a homosexual orientation. The request for a preliminary ruling in this case was, however, withdrawn after the ECJ's decision in Case C-249/96 *Grant v South-West Trains Ltd* [1998] ECR I-621, discussed below.   [133] Op cit, n 131.

[134] [1997] IRLR 297, at 303.   [135] Op cit, n 132.   [136] Ibid, at 627.

His conclusion was that:

[A] provision in an employer's pay regulations under which the employee is granted travel concessions for a cohabitee of the opposite sex to the employee but refused such concessions for a cohabitee of the same sex as the employee constitutes discrimination on the basis of gender which falls within the scope of [the Treaty] Article . . . [137]

Despite these robust assertions, in its decision in *Grant* the ECJ nonetheless ultimately rejected the view that the equal treatment principle contained in Article 141 extended to discrimination on the ground of homosexuality.[138] It did however note expressly that the Treaty of Amsterdam had inserted what is now Article 13 into the TEC, and that this would enable future legislative action to outlaw discrimination on the ground of sexual orientation. As seen above, such action was taken shortly after *Grant* in the form of the Framework Directive.

The Equal Treatment Directive also refers, in Article 2(1), to discrimination in relation to marital or family status. The ECJ has never ruled specifically on the meaning of the phrase 'marital status'. However, it would appear to embrace any type of marital status, so that it seems to protect alike those who are married, those who have never been married, and those who were once married but whose marriage has ended because of death, divorce, or nullity.[139] The meaning of discrimination on the basis of 'family status' is less obvious, but it is perhaps designed to cover discrimination on the basis of a person's position within a family, for example, as a parent, a child, or a grandparent. It remains unclear whether discrimination on the grounds of marital and family status are prohibited *per se*, or whether they are prohibited only where they also constitute some form of sex discrimination, whether direct or indirect. The latter construction is probably the more likely—the main object of the Directive is to prohibit sex discrimination— and the phrase 'by reference in particular to marital or family status' suggests that these are merely examples of situations in which sex discrimination can occur.

(iii)   Part-time and temporary employment

Two other grounds on which discrimination is today prohibited by EU law have also developed out of the law on sex discrimination. As will be seen in chapter 3, the concept of indirect discrimination enables the ECJ to treat as unlawful practices which, though apparently neutral, have a disadvantageous effect upon a protected class of persons. Thus, since the vast majority of part-time workers throughout the

---

[137] Op cit, n 132 at 629–30.

[138] For criticism of this decision, see Terrett, 'A Bridge too Far? Non-Discrimination and Homosexuality in European Community Law' (1998) 4 EPL 487; Bamforth, 'Sexual Orientation Discrimination after *Grant v South-West Trains*' (2000) 63 MLR 694; and the comment of McInnes in (1999) 36 CMLRev 1043. See also Joined Cases C-122 & 129/99P *D and Sweden v Council* [2001] ECR I-4319.

[139] Cf the British Sex Discrimination Act 1975, s 3, which forbids discrimination on the basis of marital status only as far as married persons are concerned. The Civil Partnership Bill, if enacted, will extend protection against discrimination to same-sex couples who have registered a civil partnership.

EU are female, practices which produce a negative impact for part-time workers have consistently been treated by the ECJ as contrary to the principle of sex equality. The same is true for practices which produce an adverse impact for workers employed on fixed-term contracts of employment. Today, however, it is not always necessary to resort to the concept of indirect discrimination in these situations since, as will be discussed in chapter 5, discrimination on the grounds of both part-time and temporary working is independently rendered unlawful by the Directive on Part-Time Work[140] and the Directive on Fixed Term Work.[141] This independent regulation has the consequence that male part-time and temporary workers also have legal protection against discrimination.

(iv)   Racial or ethnic origin

The Race Directive prohibits discrimination on the grounds of 'racial or ethnic origin'.[142] Its background was mounting international concern at the prevalence of racism, in particular because of the resurgence of Far Right activities and racist violence in parts of Europe.[143] 1997 was proclaimed the European Year against Racism,[144] and the same year witnessed the creation of the European Monitoring Centre on Racism and Xenophobia.[145] The European Council meeting in Tampere in October 1999 invited the Commission to come forward as soon as possible with proposals to implement Article 13 in the field of race, an invitation which was accepted with alacrity.[146] The Commission was particularly concerned about discrimination in parts of Central and Eastern Europe, especially as regards the Roma and persons with learning disabilities; it was therefore keen to send out a signal about the importance of respect for fundamental rights to the countries of Central and Eastern Europe which were at that time seeking accession to the EU. In addition, it wished to ensure that the new Article 13 legislation formed part of the *acquis communautaire* to which those countries would be required to accede.[147] There is, nevertheless, undoubtedly also an economic basis for the Race Directive[148] (as indeed for its sister instrument, the Framework Directive).[149] Fredman has argued that discrimination helped to establish the Common Market by creating a pool of cheap labour, and it was only with the acceptance of a 'convergence

---

[140] Directive 97/81, OJ [1998] L14/9.   [141] Directive 99/70, OJ [1999] L175/43.

[142] Op cit, n 88. See, in particular, Arts 1 and 2 of this Directive.

[143] See Gearty, 'The Internal and External "Other" in the Union Legal Order: Racism, Religious Intolerance and Xenophobia in Europe' in Alston (ed), with Bustelo and Heenan, *The EU and Human Rights* (Oxford University Press, Oxford, 1999). See also Brown, 'The Race Directive: Towards Equality for *All* the Peoples of Europe' (2002) 21 YEL 195.   [144] OJ [1999] C237/1.

[145] See Regulation 1035/97, OJ [1997] L151/1.

[146] See also the account of the remarkable haste with which the Race Directive was ultimately adopted, given by the Select Committee on the European Union in 'The EU Framework Directive on Discrimination', HL Session 2000–01, 4th Report, HL Paper 13, para 7.

[147] See Select Committee on the European Union, 'EU Proposals to Combat Discrimination', HL Session 1999–2000, 9th Report, HL Paper 68, para 36.   [148] See, eg, Recital 9 of its Preamble.

[149] See Recital 11 of the Preamble to the Framework Directive.

between economic goals, and goals of justice and fairness that a generalised power to legislate in the discrimination field was enacted'.[150]

It is to be noted that the Directive contains no definition of the elusive expression 'racial or ethnic origin',[151] although a few textual clues about its intended meaning can be garnered from the lengthy Preamble. In particular, Recital 6 provides:

The European Union rejects theories which attempt to determine the existence of separate human races. The use of the term 'racial origin' in this Directive does not imply an acceptance of such theories.

Thus, the Directive appears to be predicated on the basis that the human race itself, although a single generic entity, consists of different racial groups. The concept of racism is on several occasions[152] linked in the Preamble with 'xenophobia', defined in the *Shorter Oxford English Dictionary* as a 'morbid dread or dislike of foreigners'; this might perhaps indicate that the Directive is primarily targeted at discrimination against racial groups (whatever they may be) whose origin is outside the EU.

The notion of ethnicity is arguably even more elusive than that of race. However, it may perhaps be hazarded that more cases will turn on the meaning of ethnic origins than of racial origins because, whilst 'racial' suggests physiological but generally unprovable distinctions between people, 'ethnic' primarily connotes sociological or cultural distinctions (albeit sometimes transient ones) with which the judiciary is likely to feel more comfortable. Thus, for example, the *Shorter Oxford English Dictionary* definition suggests that 'ethnic' indicates the distinctive characteristics of different racial groups or peoples. Recital 8 of the Preamble refers to 'ethnic minorities', suggesting perhaps that it is minorities within a State's population who are uppermost in the mind of the legislature. Recital 10 refers to a Commission Communication on 'racism, xenophobia and anti-Semitism', the only hint given by the instrument that religion or religious heritage may play a part in defining ethnicity.

Recital 14 highlights the very important practical point that women from racial minorities frequently encounter discrimination on the grounds both of their race and of their sex:

In implementing the principle of equal treatment irrespective of racial or ethnic origin, the Community should, in accordance with Article 3(2) of the EC Treaty, aim to eliminate inequalities, and to promote equality between men and women, especially since women are often the victims of multiple discrimination.

A further deduction to be made from this statement would seem to be that the relevant substantive provisions of EU law on racial and sexual equality should, as far as possible, be interpreted and applied consistently with one another.

---

[150] Fredman, 'Equality: A New Generation?' (2001) 30 ILJ 145, at 149.

[151] Attempts to provide a scientific explanation for the attribution of race are, mercifully, generally discarded today. Thus, as Fredman has observed, race today is really 'a social construct, reflecting ideological attempts to legitimate domination, and heavily based on social and historical context... Racism is...not about objective characteristics, but about relationships of domination and subordination...'(Fredman, 'Combating Racism with Human Rights: The Right to Equality' in Fredman (ed), *Discrimination and Human Rights: The Case of Racism* (Oxford University Press, Oxford, 2001).

[152] Recitals 7, 10, and 11.

On a more negative note, Recital 13 explains that the Directive applies to the nationals of third countries but 'does not cover differences of treatment based on nationality and is without prejudice to provisions governing the entry and residence of third-country nationals and their access to employment and to occupation'.[153] It is immediately evident that this limitation will lead to some idiosyncratic distinctions; thus, for example, a white Zimbabwean whose antecedents were of European origin might be unable to complain of unlawful discrimination occurring in a Member State of the EU in circumstances where a black compatriot, of African descent, could do so. It is noteworthy that the primary British legislation outlawing race discrimination refers to 'colour, race, nationality or ethnic or national origins'.[154] 'Colour' has not been included in the Directive, though it seems probable that it will play an indirect role in establishing ethnicity; this is in many ways a strange omission, since much racial discrimination is in reality grounded upon the visible element of the colour of the victim's skin.[155]

It is therefore clear that much discretion has been left in the hands of the ECJ as regards the definition of 'racial or ethnic origin'. As will be seen in chapter 2, the ECJ's position is crucial, since any definition it formulates will create binding law in all the Member States. Even if it opts to delegate a measure of discretion over the meaning of 'racial or ethnic' in different national contexts to the courts of the Member States, the outer limits of any such discretion will be patrolled by the ECJ. Although experience in the field of sex discrimination suggests that confidence can be placed in the ECJ to articulate sensible and workable principles in this area, the disadvantage of the present arrangements is that the law will remain uncertain until such time as it does so. This is undesirable for applicants and respondents alike.

British case law on racial discrimination is probably the most advanced of all the Member States of the EU. It is therefore likely to provide at least guidance to the ECJ in formulating its definition of 'racial or ethnic origin'. In practice, most of the litigation has concerned the meaning of 'ethnic', perhaps because the inclusion of 'colour' in the Race Relations Act definition has made it less necessary to concentrate on the meaning of 'race'. The leading decision is that of the House of Lords in *Mandla v Dowell Lee*.[156] A Sikh boy had been refused admission into a school because he refused to cut off his hair and remove his turban. Since Sikhs cannot be identified by reference to colour, race, nationality, or national origin, it was necessary to prove that they formed an ethnic group if they were to be protected by the Act. Lord Fraser set out two essential, and five other relevant, characteristics of an ethnic group; in practice, his test is routinely applied today by British courts and tribunals hearing discrimination cases. The *essential*

---

[153] This exception is discussed in more detail in ch 6.
[154] Race Relations Act 1976, s 3(1). Cf the new legislation introduced to implement the Race Directive; the Race Relations Act 1976 (Amendment) Regulations 2003, SI 2003 No 1626, refer only to racial, ethnic, or national origin.
[155] See discussion by Brennan in 'The Race Directive: Recycling Racial Inequality' (2002–3) 5 CYELS 311.   [156] [1983] AC 548.

characteristics are:

- a long shared history, of which the group is conscious as distinguishing it from other groups, and the memory of which keeps it alive;
- a cultural tradition of its own, including family and social customs and manners, often but not necessarily associated with religious observance.

The *relevant* characteristics are:

- either a common sense of geographical origin, or descent from a small number of common ancestors;
- a common language, not necessarily peculiar to a group;[157]
- a common literature peculiar to the group;
- a common religion different from that of neighbouring groups or from the general community surrounding it;
- being a minority, or being an oppressed or dominant group within a larger community.

Lord Fraser added that a group which included enough of these characteristics would be capable of including converts, such as people who marry into it. The House of Lords concluded that Sikhs did constitute an ethnic group. They were originally a religious community but are now no longer purely religious in character. However, they are a distinctive and self-conscious community, with a history going back to the fifteenth century. They have a written language, which a small proportion of Sikhs can read but which can be read by a much higher proportion of Sikhs than Hindus, and they were at one time politically supreme in the Punjab.

Applying Lord Fraser's test, Rastafarians were held not to constitute an ethnic group in *Crown Suppliers v Dawkins*,[158] since sixty years does not amount to a long shared or group history. Similarly, Muslims are not regarded by British courts as forming an ethnic group since they include people of many different nationalities and colours, who speak many different languages.[159] On the other hand, in *CRE v Dutton*,[160] members of the 'traveller' community (formerly known as 'gypsies') were found to be an ethnic group because they do have a long shared history and a common geographical origin (coming from Northern India via Persia in medieval times); they also have some customs of their own, especially as regards cooking, washing, dressing, and furnishings. They have a language or dialect of their own and, although without a common religion or literature, they have a repertoire of folk tales and music passed down the generations.[161]

---

[157] A common language, on its own, is insufficient to establish a racial group under British law: *Gwynedd County Council v Jones* [1986] ICR 833.   [158] [1993] ICR 517.

[159] This assumption underlies the decision of the Employment Appeal Tribunal in *J H Walker Ltd v Hussain* [1996] IRLR 11. Cf the discussion below on discrimination on the ground of religion or belief.

[160] [1989] QB 783.

[161] In *Seide v Gillette Industries* Ltd [1980] IRLR 427, the Employment Appeal Tribunal held that Jewish people could be said to share a common ethnicity.

(v) Religion or belief

The grounds of religion or belief, disability, age, and sexual orientation are all contained in the Framework Directive. As was the case with the Race Directive, the Commission made it clear at the time of proposing the instrument that an important part of its motivation was that this anti-discrimination legislation should form part of the *acquis communautaire* before the accession of the new Member States. The grouping of the four, seemingly somewhat disparate, grounds together was also part of the Commission's strategy; it believed that the Member States were more enthusiastic about some of the grounds than about others, and it wanted to exploit the political momentum to ensure that it achieved legislation on all the bases mandated by Article 13.[162] Nevertheless, this approach involves the risk of false consistency, in other words, that the attempt to shoe-horn four different grounds into a single legislative instrument will produce a model which is not wholly appropriate to one or more of them.

As in the case of racial or ethnic origin contrary to the Race Directive, the Framework Directive makes no attempt to define 'religion or belief', so that similar problems of uncertainty occur here, as indeed also in relation to disability, age, and sexual orientation. In using the bare but alternative expression 'religion or belief', the Directive presumably means to encapsulate both religious beliefs (however 'religion' is to be defined) and other philosophical beliefs on major issues such as life, death, and morality akin to, but not amounting to, religion; thus, a belief in a divine being or deity would appear to be unnecessary. So, for example, it seems likely that the intention is to cover Buddhism. What remains to be clarified by the ECJ is whether other typical facets of religious practice, such as some form of communal or individual worship, will be required; if they are, this might rule out belief systems such as humanism, pacifism, atheism, and vegetarianism. In addition, the Court will have to draw the difficult line between religion or belief on the one hand and political opinion on the other, a problem of heightened importance in a world in which religious fundamentalism often marches hand in hand with political ideology.

Further guidance will be available from the ECHR, Article 9 of which provides:

Everyone has the right to freedom of thought, conscience and religion; this right includes freedom to change his religion or belief and freedom, either alone or in community with others and in public or private, to manifest his religion or belief, in worship, teaching, practice and observance.

As already noted, the law flowing from the ECHR operates as a source of EU law and, therefore, the meaning attached by the European Court of Human Rights to the concept of religion is relevant to its interpretation by the ECJ. It is thus relevant to note that, although it has not decided many cases directly on the point, the European Court of Human Rights has taken an essentially broad view of Article 9,

---

[162] See Select Committee on the European Union, op cit, n 147, para 40.

not confining it to the major world religions[163] but extending it also to fringe religions[164] and to non–religious beliefs, including atheism and agnosticism.[165] Before its demise,[166] the European Commission on Human Rights also recognized as 'religions' some movements which might be referred to popularly as 'cults'.[167]

UK law did not, before the enactment of the Framework Directive, define religion or belief for the purpose of anti-discrimination law; this was because no statute applying to mainland Britain prohibited religious discrimination *per se*[168] and, although the Fair Employment and Treatment (Northern Ireland) Order 1998[169] prohibits discrimination on the ground of 'religious belief or political opinion',[170] in the practical context of Northern Ireland it is clear that the Catholic and Protestant religions are those which were uppermost in the mind of the legislature.[171] The only former purpose for which UK law had to define religion was for the law of charities, since one of the permitted objects of a charity is the advancement of religion.[172] The UK courts, understandably, have never sought to arbitrate between different religions, nor to decide on the veracity of their respective claims.[173] However, for charitable status, a religion requires that its adherents believe in a god[174] and, furthermore, that they engage in some form of worship.[175]

In the UK, the prohibition on religious discrimination is implemented by the Employment Equality (Religion or Belief) Regulations 2003.[176] These define 'religion or belief' as 'any religion, religious belief, or similar philosophical belief'.[177] The Department of Trade and Industry Explanatory Notes which preceded the

---

[163] Although of course the major world religions are included. See, eg, *Cha'are Shalom Ve Tsedek v France*, App No 00027417/95, Reports of Judgments and Decisions 2000-VII, which implicitly regards Orthodox Judaism as covered by Art 9.

[164] For example, the Jehovah's Witnesses: *Hoffmann v Austria* (1994) 17 EHRR 293 and *Thlimmenos v Greece* (2001) 31 EHRR 411; and the Pentecostal Church: *Larissis v Greece* (1999) 27 EHRR 329.

[165] *Kokkinakis v Greece* (1994) 17 EHRR 397.

[166] Protocol 11 to the ECHR, which came into force on 1 November 1998, replaced the Commission and the old Court with a new full-time Court of Human Rights.

[167] For example, Druidism (*Chappell v UK* (1987) 53 DR 241), Scientology (*X and Church of Scientology v Sweden* (1979) 16 DR 68), the Divine Light Zentrum (*Omkarananda and the Divine Light Zentrum v Switzerland* (1981) 25 DR 105), Pacificism (*Arrowsmith v UK* (1978) 19 DR 5), Veganism (*H v UK* (1993) 16 EHRR CD 44), and the Krisna consciousness movement (*Iskcon v UK* (1994) 76A DR 90).

[168] However, as noted in the preceding section, religion plays a part in determining ethnicity within the provisions of the Race Relations Act 1976.   [169] SI 1998 No 3162 (NI 21).

[170] For the purposes of the Order, references to a person's religious belief or political opinion include references to '(a) his supposed religious belief or political opinion; and (b) the absence or supposed absence of any, or any particular, religious belief or political opinion': reg 2(3).

[171] See, eg, reg 4 of the Fair Employment and Treatment (Northern Ireland) Order 1998.

[172] See generally Picarda, *The Law and Practice Relating to Charities*, 2nd edn (Butterworths, London, Dublin, and Edinburgh, 1995).   [173] *Neville Estates Ltd v Madden* [1962] Ch 832.

[174] *Bowman v Secular Society* [1917] AC 406.

[175] See the Decision of the Charity Commissioners of 17 November 1999 to the effect that the Church of Scientology did not attract charitable status since, although members of the Church believed in a god, they did not engage in veneration of their god. See also *R v Registrar General, ex parte Segerdal* [1970] 2 QB 697.   [176] SI 2003 No 1660.

[177] Ibid, reg 2.

enactment of the Regulations add that the courts and tribunals will probably wish to consider factors such as whether the potential 'religion or belief' involves collective worship, a clear belief system, and a profound belief affecting a person's way of life or view of the world. The ACAS Guide counsels employers to be aware that the Regulations 'extend beyond the more well known religions and faiths to include beliefs such as Paganism and Hinduism . . . and those without religious or similar beliefs'.[178]

(vi)   Disability

As with the other grounds specified in the Framework Directive, no definition is provided of the term 'disability'; the suggestion of the House of Lords Select Committee on the EU that some non-exhaustive examples might be given was not taken up.[179] The result is especially unsatisfactory in relation to such an extremely vague and open-ended term as disability.

Once again, some guidance might be obtained from the UK's domestic legislation, in this case the Disability Discrimination Act 1995. Section 1(1) defines disability for the purposes of the Act as 'a physical or mental impairment which has a substantial and long-term adverse effect on [the] . . . ability to carry out normal day-to-day activities'. Schedule 1 supplements this provision by defining such things as the types of mental illness covered, the meaning of 'long-term', the relevance of medical treatment, and the correct approach to progressive conditions; in doing so, it well illustrates the difficulties inherent in this area and thus the current lacuna in EU law. However, the UK's domestic legislation, focusing as it does on impairment, adopts a highly 'medical' view of disability; there is a competing and wider model of disability which sees it as a social construct, in other words, a result of the person's disadvantaged position in society. As one writer has put it, '[w]hilst the medical model sees disability as a functional impairment, the social model sees disability as a particular relationship between the impaired individual and society';[180] she goes on to argue that EU law takes an increasingly social view and that the UK's domestic law may therefore fall short of its demands.[181]

(vii)   Age

Age is similarly left undefined by the Framework Directive. The only conclusion which can be drawn from this, in the absence of explanatory case law from the

---

[178] ACAS, *A guide for employers and employees: Religion or belief and the workplace*, 2004, www.acas. org.uk.

[179] See Select Committee on the European Union, op cit, n 147, para 69.

[180] Wells, 'The Impact of the Framework Employment Directive on UK Disability Discrimination Law' (2003) 32 ILJ 253.

[181] See also Whittle, 'The Framework Directive for Equal Treatment in Employment and Occupation: an Analysis from a Disability Rights Perspective' (2002) 27 ELRev 303.

ECJ, is that the Directive is intended to protect all age groups and not merely older people,[182] despite the demographic trend towards an increasingly elderly population in Europe.[183] However, as will be seen in chapter 6, the Directive contains a widely drafted exception where age discrimination can be justified by reference to a legitimate aim; this might well exonerate national legislation restricting the application of the principle in specific instances to older people.[184]

(viii)   Sexual orientation

In common with the other prohibited categories, 'sexual orientation' remains to be defined by the ECJ. Its most obvious intended application is to homosexuals; this conclusion is reinforced by the ECJ's reluctance to interpret 'sex' for the purposes of Article 141 so as to include discrimination against homosexuals,[185] and the clear hints in its jurisprudence that this is a matter for legislative, not judicial, decision-making. However, the prohibition in the Directive also extends to discrimination against heterosexual, and bisexual people.[186] It is to be hoped that sexual orientation for this purpose includes those who merely incline towards homosexual, heterosexual or bisexual attraction without actively indulging in such sexual activity, since otherwise the practical application of the provision will be severely undermined; similarly, it will enhance the effectiveness of the Directive if the proscription is held to extend to discrimination on the ground of a person's behaviour (for example, his or her manner of dressing), as well as on the ground of his or her underlying sexual preference.[187]

It is not yet clear whether the Court will be prepared to apply the legislation, in addition, to those with minority sexual preferences such as, for example, sado-masochism. This is not the view taken by UK law, which limits 'sexual orientation' to:

[A]n orientation towards—

(a) persons of the same sex,

(b) persons of the opposite sex, or

(c) persons of the same sex and of the opposite sex.[188]

---

[182] But it is to be noted that Recital 6 of the Preamble to the Framework Directive refers expressly to the integration of 'elderly' people, and Recital 8 speaks of supporting 'older workers'.

[183] Cf the American law on age discrimination; the Age Discrimination in Employment Act 1977 protects only workers who are aged 40 and over.

[184] For support for such an argument, see Rubenstein, 'US court upholds older worker preferences' (2004) 129 EOR 18.   [185] See discussion above.

[186] There is, however, a body of opinion which questions whether sexual identity can be separated into rigid categories; see Oliver, 'Sexual Orientation Discrimination: Perceptions, Definitions and Genuine Occupational Requirements' (2004) 33 ILJ 1, and the literature cited therein.

[187] See further discussion in ch 3.

[188] The Employment Equality (Sexual Orientation) Regulations 2003 (SI 2003 No 1661), reg 2(1).

2

Essential characteristics of EU law

The nature and effects of EU Law

Because of the power,[1] and indeed sometimes the duty,[2] of national courts of the Member States of the EU to seek preliminary rulings from the ECJ[3] in cases pending before them, it has been for the ECJ on numerous occasions to define the nature and effects of EU law. The ECJ's jurisdiction in the preliminary rulings procedure extends to explaining the meaning and effects of particular pieces of EU law, but the Court does not have the power to apply its rulings to the facts of the given case; that remains the role of the referring national court. In defining the characteristics of EU law, the ECJ has clearly been strongly influenced by the federalist ideal underlying the conception of the Communities. It has been able to distil certain specific and vital qualities of EU law, which differentiate it clearly both from the national laws of the Member States and also from traditional international law.[4] In practice, as events have turned out, there has probably been no other field of substantive law in which these principles developed by the ECJ have proved to be more important than sex discrimination. There is every reason to suppose that such principles will come to have similar significance in relation to the new fields of equality law too.

[1] The main power to seek a preliminary ruling is given by Art 234 (formerly Art 177). Art 234(2) confers discretion on national courts and tribunals to request a preliminary ruling where a question of EC law has to be decided before that court or tribunal can arrive at a judgment. Exceptionally, however, lower courts have no discretion to seek preliminary rulings in relation to questions arising under Title IV of the Treaty on 'Visa, Asylum, Immigration and other policies related to the free movement of persons'. (It should be noted that, pursuant to Protocols annexed to the TEU and TEC, Title IV does not apply to the UK, Ireland, or Denmark, unless they decide to opt in.) The ECJ does not, however, have jurisdiction to give preliminary rulings on Council measures connected with the removal of controls on the movement of persons across internal borders 'relating to the maintenance of law and order and the safeguarding of internal security': Art 68(2). TEU Art 35 gives additional jurisdiction to the ECJ to give preliminary rulings on matters governed by Title VI of that Treaty ('Police and Judicial Cooperation in Criminal Matters'), provided that the national State concerned has accepted the Court's jurisdiction in this respect. For further discussion of the preliminary rulings procedure, see Arnull, Dashwood, Ross, and Wyatt, *Wyatt & Dashwood's European Union Law*, 4th edn (Sweet & Maxwell, London, 2000), ch 11.
[2] In the case of courts and tribunals against whose decisions there is no judicial remedy under national law; see Art 234(3) and Art 68(1).
[3] Art 225 provides that this jurisdiction remains exclusive to the ECJ, notwithstanding the creation of the CFI. However, Art 225(3) permits the Statute of the Court of Justice to confer jurisdiction on the CFI to give preliminary rulings in specific areas.
[4] Cf Hartley, 'The Constitutional Foundations of the European Union' (2001) 117 LQR 225.

The case in which the ECJ first began to express the particular characteristics of EU law was *Van Gend en Loos v Nederlandse Tariefcommissie*.[5] This case concerned the legal effect within The Netherlands of the prohibition, contained in what is today Article 25[6] of the TEC, on any increase in customs duties in trade between Member States of the Community. The ECJ made a now-famous statement of principle:

> The objective of the EEC Treaty which is to establish a Common Market, the functioning of which is of direct concern to interested parties in the Community implies that this Treaty is more than an agreement creating only mutual obligations between the contracting parties. This view is confirmed by the Preamble to the Treaty which refers not only to governments but to peoples. It is also confirmed more specifically by the establishment of institutions endowed with sovereign rights, the exercise of which affects Member States and also their citizens. Furthermore, it must be noted that the nationals of the States brought together in the Community are called upon to cooperate in the functioning of this Community, through the intermediary of the European Parliament and the Economic and Social Committee. In addition the task assigned to the Court of Justice under Article 177, the object of which is to secure uniform interpretation of the Treaty by the national courts and tribunals, confirms that the States have acknowledged that Community law has an authority which can be invoked by their nationals before those courts and tribunals. The conclusion to be drawn from this is that the Community constitutes a new legal order in international law for the benefit of which the States have limited their sovereign rights, albeit within limited fields, and the subjects of which comprise not only the Member States but also their nationals. Independently of the legislation of Member States, community law therefore not only imposes obligations on individuals but is also intended to confer upon them rights which become part of their legal heritage. These rights arise not only where they are expressly granted by the Treaty, but also by reason of obligations which the Treaty imposes in a clearly defined way upon individuals as well as upon the Member States and upon the institutions of the community . . . Article 12 must be interpreted as producing direct effects and creating individual rights which national courts must protect.[7]

It follows from these remarks of the ECJ that EU law possesses two special characteristics in particular: it is 'supreme' over conflicting national law in the Member States, in other words, prevails over such law;[8] and it is, on occasion at least, enforceable by individuals bringing proceedings in the courts of the Member States.[9] In later litigation, the ECJ has taken the opportunity to develop and refine these vital principles.[10]

---

[5] Case 26/62 [1963] ECR 1.   [6] Formerly Art 12.

[7] [1963] ECR 1, at 12–13. See also Case 28/67 *Molkerei-Zentrale Westfalen/Lippe GmbH v Hauptzollamt Paderborn* [1968] ECR 143, at 152–3.

[8] The primacy of the law of the Union over that of the Member States is formally asserted by Art I-6 of the Constitution, which, as seen in ch 1, was not in force at the time of writing.

[9] Reference should be made to more general works on EU law for a full discussion of these concepts, in particular Weatherill and Beaumont, *EC Law*, 3rd edn (Penguin, London, 1999), chs 11 and 12; Kapteyn and Verloren Van Themaat, *Introduction to the Law of the European Communities*, 3rd edn (Kluwer Law International, London, 1998), ch II; and Arnull et al, op cit, n 1, ch 4. The discussion which follows in the present text is confined, so far as possible, to those aspects of the concepts which have special significance in the context of anti-discrimination and equality law.

[10] See further Van Gerven, 'Bridging the Gap Between Community and National Laws: Towards a Principle of Homogeneity in the Field of Legal Remedies?' (1995) 32 CMLRev 679.

The supremacy of EU law

In *Van Gend en Loos*, the supremacy of EU law was an implication to be made from the ECJ's statements: an individual legal person was held entitled to have Article 25 of the Treaty enforced in preference to the conflicting domestic law of The Netherlands. Having surmounted this tricky political hurdle—in effect, telling a Member State that its own law was to be ignored—the ECJ gathered courage and became bolder in its formulation of the concept of supremacy of EU law.

Costa v ENEL[11] was a strong case in which to test the doctrine of supremacy of EU law because the potential conflict arose in the situation where the impugned domestic law post-dated the contrary EU law, in other words, the situation where, in a purely domestic context, a court would normally hold that the later law in time prevailed. The ECJ held:

> The Italian Government submits that the request of the *giudice conciliatore* is 'absolutely inadmissible', inasmuch as a national court which is obliged to apply a national law cannot avail itself of Article 177. By contrast with ordinary international treaties, the EEC Treaty has created its own legal system which, on the entry into force of the treaty, became an integral part of the legal systems of the Member States and which their courts are bound to apply. By creating a Community of unlimited duration, having its own institutions, its own personality and its own legal capacity and capacity of representation on the international plane, and, more particularly, real powers stemming from a limitation of sovereignty or a transfer of powers from the States to the Community, the Member States have limited their sovereign rights, and, albeit within limited fields, have thus created a body of law which binds both their nationals and themselves. The integration into the laws of each Member State of provisions which derive from the Community, and more generally the terms and the spirit of the Treaty, make it impossible for the Member State, as a corollary, to accord precedence to a unilateral and subsequent measure over a legal system accepted by them on a basis of reciprocity... The transfer by the States from their domestic legal system to the Community legal system of the rights and obligations arising under the Treaty carries with it a permanent limitation of their sovereign rights against which a subsequent unilateral act incompatible with the concept of the Community cannot prevail. Consequently, Article 177 is to be applied regardless of any domestic law, whenever questions relating to the interpretation of the Treaty arise.[12]

In subsequent cases, the ECJ has extended its formulation of supremacy so as to encompass not merely the law created directly by the Treaty but also secondary legislation made by the institutions.[13] So, for example, a provision contained in

[11] Case 6/64 [1964] ECR 585.

[12] Ibid, at 593–4. The principle of supremacy means that EU law prevails over both incompatible national legislation and administrative decisions, whether the latter are general abstract rules or specific individual decisions: see Case C-224/97 *Ciola v Land Vorarlberg* [1999] ECR I-2517.

[13] See, eg, Case 43/71 *Politi Sas v Minister of Finance* [1971] ECR 1039; and Case 38/77 *Enka BV v Inspecteur der Invoerrechten en Accijnzen* [1977] ECR 2203, discussed below. But note the exception contained in Art 307: the provisions of the TEC have no effect on rights and obligations resulting from treaties concluded before the entry into force of the TEC between a Member State and a third country. This provision was relied upon in Case C-158/91 *Levy* [1993] ECR I-4287 to justify a ban on night work by women in France which had earlier been held by the ECJ in Case C-345/89 *Stoeckel* [1991] ECR I-4047 (discussed in ch 5) to contravene the Equal Treatment Directive; the ban was pursuant to a pre-existing commitment to an ILO Convention, which France had not at the relevant time denounced. *Levy* was followed in Case C-13/93 *Office National de l'Emploi v Minne* [1994] ECR I-371.

a regulation must prevail over conflicting national law. However, the doctrine of supremacy does not mean simply that any conflict between EU and national law must be resolved in favour of EU law. Supremacy provides a guarantee that the minimum standards set by EU law must be achieved in all the Member States. Thus, the principle of supremacy does not prevent a Member State from exceeding the protection conferred by EU law.[14]

In *Amministrazione delle Finanze dello Stato v Simmenthal*,[15] the ECJ explained that the concept of supremacy of EU law entails the automatic inapplicability of conflicting national law and that it also precludes the valid adoption of new national legislation which would conflict with EU law. This led the Commission to argue in *Ministero delle Finanze v IN.CO.GE.'90 Srl*[16] that a national provision which is incompatible with EU law is 'non-existent'. However, the ECJ rejected this view, holding that such an incompatible national law is merely inapplicable.

In support of its conclusions that EU law is supreme over conflicting national law, the ECJ has put forward several reasons. The one most frequently referred to is the essentially federalist notion of a limitation of sovereignty on the part of the Member States when they acceded to the Communities. The Member States are taken to have transferred a portion of their legislative powers to the new organization, and in the areas where that transfer has taken place the States are consequently now incapable of making their own national legislation.[17] Another, similar line of argument which is discernible in *Costa v ENEL* is that it follows from the whole nature and spirit of EU law that it must be of a kind different from, and higher than, national law. The whole set-up of the Union is such that its laws must be intended to be supreme; Member States undertake to carry out certain actions and to suffer particular restrictions only provided that all the other Member States are placed in exactly the same position.[18] Of course, if the Member States possessed general powers to contradict EU law by means of their own national legislation, then all Member States would not be placed in the same position. The notion of reciprocity is central to the Union, and reciprocity would not exist without the doctrine of supremacy of EU law.

A related rationale which the Court has also sometimes relied on is the principle of *effet utile*.[19] This refers to the fact that the effectiveness of the Treaty would be

[14] See Case C-50/96 *Deutsche Telekom v Schröder* [2000] ECR I-743, Joined Cases C-270 & 271/97 *Deutsche Post v Sievers and Shrage* [2000] ECR I-929, and Joined Cases C-234 & 235/96 *Deutsche Telekom AG v Vick and Conze* [2000] ECR I-799; see also the comment on these cases by Besselink in (2001) 38 CMLRev 437.   [15] Case 106/77 [1978] ECR 629.
[16] Joined Cases C-10 to 22/97 [1998] ECR I-6307.
[17] This reasoning is evident in the early cases of *Van Gend en Loos* and *Costa v ENEL* and, in more recent times, in Case 63/83 *R v Kent Kirk* [1984] ECR 2689. See also Usher, *European Community Law and National Law: The Irreversible Transfer?* (George Allen & Unwin, London, 1981).
[18] This reasoning has become somewhat compromised in recent years, with the recognition by the Maastricht, Amsterdam, and Nice Treaties of the concept of 'flexibility', namely, the principle that certain Member States may opt out of specific aspects of EU law and that integration may proceed at different rates for different groups of Member States.
[19] See Case 14/68 *Walt Wilhelm v Bundeskartellamt* [1969] ECR 1.

undermined if Member States could contradict its provisions. If, by national legislation, the Member States were able to contradict EU law, there would be absolutely no means of ensuring that EU law functioned uniformly and therefore effectively throughout the EU.[20]

It is important that the national courts of the Member States also accept the principle of supremacy of EU law; if, as the ECJ holds, the Union so much resembles a developed federation as to confer legal rights directly on individual legal persons, then it follows as a matter of practicality that those rights must be enforceable in national courts. If the national courts were, at this stage, unprepared to enforce EU law in preference to conflicting national law, much of the value of direct enforcement would be lost. The courts of the original six Member States took a little while to accept what must to them have seemed the very radical notion of supremacy of EU law;[21] however, in the main today it appears that in all the Member States of the Community the idea of supremacy of EU law has gained general acceptance,[22] albeit that the logical route which judges have followed to lead them to this conclusion has not always been the ECJ's theory of the limitation of national legislative sovereignty.

In the UK, the supremacy of EU law has faced a particular difficulty: that of the rival doctrine of the supremacy of the UK Parliament. If, as British judges have traditionally held, the UK Parliament can always do whatever it pleases, how could it ever be constrained by the limitation that it is not to contradict EU law? In particular, if EU law is rendered effective in the UK by an Act of Parliament, as constitutional theory dictates, what is to prevent the repeal of the implement-ing Act by a later piece of UK legislation which contradicts EU law? Is not the latest Act of Parliament the indication that the judges must unerringly follow if democracy is not to be undermined?

---

[20] The ECJ has also, on occasion, given other ancillary reasons for holding that EU law is supreme. In particular, it pointed out in *Costa v ENEL* that wherever the Treaty does allow the Member States a unilateral right to legislate, it does so in special provisions. However, these provisions are clearly by way of exception, and they would, of course, be quite unnecessary if the Member States anyway had power to pass conflicting national legislation. See [1964] ECR 585, esp at 593–4.

[21] Difficulties were encountered in particular in Italy, France, and West Germany. See, eg, the decision of the Italian Constitutional Court in *Costa v ENEL* [1964] 3 CMLR 425, that of the French Conseil d'Etat in *Cohn-Bendit v Ministre de l'Intérieure* [1980] 1 CMLR 543, and that of the Federal German Constitutional Court in *Internationale Handelsgesellschaft GmbH v Einfuhr-und Vorratsstelle fur Getreide und Futtermittel* [1974] 2 CMLR 540.

[22] See in particular *Frontini v Minister of Finance* [1974] 2 CMLR 372; *SpA Granital v Amministrazione delle Finanze*, Decision No 170 of 8 June 1984, (1984) 21 CMLRev 756; *Re the Application of Wunsche Handelgesellschaft* [1987] 3 CMLR 225; *Administration des Douanes v Société Jacques Vabre* [1975] 2 CMLR 336; and *Nicolo* [1990] 1 CMLR 173. Cf *Brunner v European Union Treaty* [1994] CMLR 57. See also Steiner, 'The Application of European Community Law in National Courts—Problems, Pitfalls and Precepts' (1980) 96 LQR 126; Pettricione, 'Supremacy of Community Law over National Law' (1986) 11 ELRev 320; Gaja, 'New Developments in a Continuing Story: The Relationship between EEC Law and Italian Law' (1990) 27 CMLRev 83; and Hoffmeister, 'German Bundesverfassungsgerichrt: Alcan Decision of 17 February 2000; Constitutional Review of EC Regulation on Bananas, Decision of 7 June 2000' (2001) 38 CMLRev 791.

This problem has, in practice, been neatly side-stepped by the European Communities Act 1972, and in particular by the artful wording of s 2(4) thereof.[23] This provides that 'any enactment passed or to be passed, other than one contained in this Part of this Act, shall be construed and have effect subject to the foregoing provisions of this section'. The 'foregoing' s 2(1) has already provided that all Community rights are to be available in law in the UK. The ECJ has explained, as has already been seen, for example, in *Van Gend en Loos*, that the right to have EU law treated as supreme is a Community right which can be claimed by a litigant. Thus, the effect of s 2(4) is that, at least until such time as the European Communities Act is repealed, all Acts of the UK Parliament must 'be construed and have effect' subject to the principle that EU law is always supreme over them in the event of conflict.[24] The device relied upon by the European Communities Act is therefore the delegation to the EU institutions of those law-making functions which fall within the purview of the Treaty; the legal system has not gone to the full lengths which the ECJ says EU law demands and there has, in reality, been no out-and-out transfer of law-making powers from the UK Parliament to the EU institutions.[25]

In practice, UK judges have tried wherever possible to utilize what might be called the first limb of s 2(4) of the European Communities Act and to hold that the relevant domestic legislation is susceptible of a variety of meanings, but that, in the light of s 2(4), they will adopt the construction which most clearly accords with the demands of EU law. The first statement and application of this approach in the House of Lords came in *Garland v British Rail*.[26] Confronted here with an apparent conflict between s 6(4) of the Sex Discrimination Act 1975, which at the time of the litigation permitted sex discrimination in relation to retirement, and Article 141 of the Treaty requiring equal pay for men and women, their Lordships chose to construe the UK statute in such a way as to make it accord with Article 141. Lord Diplock, delivering the only speech made, said:

[E]ven if the obligation to observe the provisions of [the] Article . . . were an obligation assumed by the UK under an ordinary international treaty or convention and there were no questions of the treaty

---

[23] Cf Wade, 'Sovereignty—Revolution or Evolution?' (1996) 112 LQR 568. For criticism of Wade's view that a constitutional revolution has occurred through the fettering of Parliament's legislative powers by s 2(4), see Allan, 'Parliamentary Sovereignty: Law, Politics and Revolution' (1997) 113 LQR 443.   [24] See *Thoburn v Sunderland City Council* [2002] 3 WLR 247.
[25] See Jaconelli, 'Constitutional Review and s 2(4) of the European Communities Act 1972' (1979) 28 ICLQ 65; Ellis, 'Supremacy of Parliament and European Law' (1980) 96 LQR 511; Eekelaar, 'The Death of Parliamentary Sovereignty—A Comment' (1997) 113 LQR 185; and Craig, 'Sovereignty of the United Kingdom Parliament after *Factortame*' (1991) 11 YBEL 221.
[26] [1982] 2 WLR 918. See also *Pickstone v Freemans plc* [1988] 2 All ER 803, and *Litster v Forth Dry Dock and Engineering Co Ltd* [1989] ICR 341, in the latter of which Lord Oliver commented at 354: 'The approach to the construction of primary and subordinate legislation enacted to give effect to the UK's obligations under the EEC Treaty . . . is not in doubt. If the legislation can reasonably be construed so as to conform with those obligations—obligations which are to be ascertained not only from the wording of the relevant Directive but from the interpretation placed upon it by the ECJ at Luxembourg—such a purposive construction will be applied even though, perhaps, it may involve some departure from the strict and literal application of the words which the legislature has elected to use.'

obligation being directly applicable as part of the law to be applied by the courts in this country without need for any further enactment, it is a principle of construction of UK statutes, now too well established to call for citation of authority, that the words of a statute passed after the Treaty has been signed and dealing with the subject matter of the international obligation of the UK, are to be construed, if they are reasonably capable of bearing such a meaning, as intended to carry out the obligation and not to be inconsistent with it. *A fortiori* is this the case where the Treaty obligation arises under one of the Community treaties to which section 2 of the European Communities Act 1972 applies.[27]

Where, however, the 'construction' approach is impossible, the UK courts have also been prepared to rely on the other limb of s 2(4) of the European Communities Act, and to hold that UK law which conflicts with EU law does not take effect.[28] This was most dramatically demonstrated in *Macarthys Ltd v Smith*.[29] This case concerned a demand for equal pay by a woman who had been employed on the same work as a man but in succession to him. In the Court of Appeal, Lord Denning MR had been prepared to adopt the 'construction' approach, and this led him to the conclusion that the British Equal Pay Act of 1970 was ambiguous as to whether or not it covered situations of successive, as distinct from contemporaneous, employment of a man and a woman doing the same job; Article 141 of the Treaty, on the other hand, he felt, clearly governed situations of successive employment. On this basis, he would have been prepared to construe the Equal Pay Act so as to cover successive employment. The other members of the Court of Appeal disagreed with this approach, however, holding that the Equal Pay Act was unambiguous and was clearly confined to situations of contemporaneous employment. The case was then referred to the ECJ for a preliminary ruling as to the meaning and scope of Article 141, and the ECJ held that Article 141 did indeed govern successive employment cases. A head-on conflict was thus produced between Article 141 of the Treaty and the later-enacted[30] Equal Pay Act. In these circumstances it was conceivable that the judges might hold that the latest expression of Parliament's will should prevail and that they should therefore enforce the national legislation. On the contrary, however, the Court of Appeal was unanimous in upholding the applicability of Article 141 in this situation.[31] It expressly approved of the doctrine of supremacy of EU law[32] and explained that it was made effective by the European Communities Act 1972, at least until such

---

[27] [1982] 2 WLR 918, at 934–5. Cf *Duke v GEC Reliance Ltd* [1988] 2 WLR 359, and *Finnegan v Clowney Youth Training Ltd* [1990] 2 WLR 1305.

[28] An alternative view is that there are not two limbs of s 2(4) at all because the word 'and' in the subsection is truly conjunctive. If this were the correct analysis of the subsection, the supremacy of EU law would be denied where domestic law could not be construed so as to accord with it, which, as is discussed in the text, is not in practice found to be the case.

[29] [1979] 3 CMLR 44. See also Guy and Leigh, 'Article 119 EEC: Discrimination on Grounds of Sex' (1979) 4 ELRev 415.

[30] The Equal Pay Act 1970 was amended and then brought into operation by the Sex Discrimination Act 1975.

[31] [1980] IRLR 209. On the same principle, see also *Pickstone v Freemans plc* [1987] 3 WLR 811 and [1988] 2 All ER 803; *Parsons v East Surrey Health Authority* [1986] ICR 837; and *R v Secretary of State for Education, ex parte Schaffter* [1987] IRLR 53.

[32] See also *Chief Constable of the West Yorkshire Police (No 2) v A* [2004] 2 WLR 1209.

time as that Act was repealed and the Treaty repudiated by the UK.[33] The same principle was reiterated *obiter* by the House of Lords in *R v Secretary of State for Transport, ex parte Factortame Ltd*.[34] The issue there was a potential conflict between Part II of the Merchant Shipping Act 1988, governing the registration of British fishing vessels, and EU law. Lord Bridge commented:

> By virtue of section 2 subsection 4 of the 1972 Act, Part II of the Act of 1988 is to be construed and take effect subject to directly enforceable Community rights, and those rights are, by section 2 subsection 1 of the Act of 1972, to be 'recognized and available in law, and ... enforced, allowed and followed accordingly ...' This has precisely the same effect as if a section were incorporated in Part II of the Act of 1988 which in terms enacted that the provisions with respect to registration of British fishing vessels were to be without prejudice to the directly enforceable Community rights of nationals of any Member State of the EEC. Thus, it is common ground that, in so far as the applicants succeed before the ECJ in obtaining a ruling in support of the Community rights which they claim, those rights will *prevail* over the restrictions imposed on registration of British fishing vessels by Part II of the Act of 1988 ... [35]

A practical application of the principle of supremacy in the field of discrimination occurred in *Bossa v Nordstress Ltd*.[36] The applicant had been rejected for a job offered in the UK on the ground of his Italian nationality. His claim for unlawful race discrimination was met with the argument that s 8 of the British Race Relations Act 1976 excepted from its operation jobs performed wholly or mainly outside Great Britain, which appeared to be the situation in which the applicant found himself. The Employment Appeal Tribunal simply held that s 8 must be disapplied because it conflicted with Article 39 of the Treaty, which prohibits discrimination based on nationality between workers of the Member States. In the words of Morrison J:

> It is possible to give effect to the supremacy of European law by simply disapplying, in this case, section 8. That means that the industrial tribunal will consider the complaint in the normal way

---

[33] See Ellis, op cit, n 25, and Allan, 'Parliamentary Sovereignty: Lord Denning's Dexterous Revolution' (1983) 3 OJLS 22.   [34] [1989] 2 WLR 997, discussed in greater detail below.
[35] Ibid, at 1011, emphasis added. See also his remarks when the case returned to the House of Lords after a preliminary ruling by the ECJ: [1990] 3 WLR 818, esp at 857–8. In the Court of Appeal, Lord Donaldson MR elaborated on the way in which conflicts between UK and EU law commonly arise, saying: ' ... underlying the whole of this problem is the unusual (to a British lawyer) nature of Community law, which is long on principle and short on specifics ... the result is often that the British courts are faced with an undoubted right or duty under British law and a *claim* that an inconsistent right or duty exists under Community law. If the British court can ascertain the nature and extent of this competing right or duty, there is little difficulty in resolving any inconsistency on the basis that Community law is paramount. That is the *acte clair* situation, but it is a comparative rarity. Much more commonly the British court cannot ascertain the nature and extent of the competing right or duty and it is to meet this problem that the right to seek a ruling by the European Court is provided under Article 177 of the Treaty of Rome. But it would be a mistake to think of that court merely as having a greater expertise in Community law than a British court, although this is undoubtedly true. Whatever the formal position, its true function in appropriate cases is actually to make new law by the applications of principle to specific factual situations. A challenge to national law based upon Community law may, when properly analysed, amount to a submission not that the national law is inconsistent with Community law as it then exists, but that upon a reference being made to the European Court, that court will give a ruling creating new and inconsistent rights and duties arising out of settled principles albeit with retroactive effect. In other words, national law is effective at present, but its life-span is predictably short' (1989) 139 NLJ Pt 1, 540, at 540–1.
[36] [1998] IRLR 284. See also *Davies v Neath Port Talbot County Borough Council* [1999] IRLR 769.

and, if appropriate, make such orders with regard to remedy as lies within their competence under the Act.[37]

Direct enforcement of EU law by individuals

(i)   Origins of the principle

The other twin pillar of EU constitutional law which was first described by the ECJ in *Van Gend en Loos*,[38] is the right of individual legal persons to have certain of its provisions enforced in the national courts of the Member States.[39] Such a notion is essentially federalist in its basis. Classical international law is concerned primarily with regulating the relations of States *inter se*, rather than with creating rights directly for their subjects. EU law, however, as the legal system for an embryo-federation, is concerned at the levels of both States and individuals, because a major part of its *raison d'être* is the improvement of the position and quality of life of individuals.

Apart from this somewhat philanthropic rationale, the ECJ is, however, aware of another good reason for giving individuals rights directly under EU law. Many aspects of EU law require implementing action on the part of the Member States, or at least require the Member States to refrain from taking any action which would inhibit their operation. If the Member States act in breach of these duties, Articles 226 and 227 provide for their prosecution before the ECJ by the Commission and other Member States. Such proceedings are, however, cumbersome and consuming of the Commission's time. In practice, it would be quite impossible for all such breaches to be dealt with through these channels. If individuals, therefore, can enforce their rights directly in their national courts, the procedure is short-circuited. The national court in effect rules that the Member State's action is in breach of EU law, and will often grant the individual a specific remedy in respect of it. So, for example, as in *Van Gend en Loos* itself, a demand for an increased customs duty made by a Member State in breach of Article 25 of the Treaty cannot be enforced in a national court and an individual charged is not liable to pay the sum involved.[40] As the ECJ expressed the principle in *Van Gend en Loos*, 'the vigilance of individuals interested in protecting their rights creates an effective

---

[37] [1998] IRLR 284, at 287.   [38] Op cit, n 5.

[39] See generally Pescatore, 'The Doctrine of "Direct Effect": An Infant Disease of Community Law' (1983) 8 ELRev 155, and Dashwood, 'The Principle of Direct Effect in European Community Law' (1977) 16 JCMS 229. For a powerful critique of the doctrine of direct effect, see Sebba, 'The Doctrine of "Direct Effect": A Malignant Disease of Community Law' [1995] LIEI 35.

[40] An example from the field of sex discrimination law is provided by Case C-317/93 *Nolte v Landesversicherungsanstalt Hannover* [1995] ECR I-4625, discussed in ch 8. The Commission was considering whether to proceed against Germany under Art 226 in respect of the exclusion of certain categories of workers from its social security system when Ms Nolte, a victim of such exclusion, brought an action seeking the direct enforcement of the equal treatment principle. Had her action been successful, the national legislation would have proved ineffective in the face of the contradictory EU law.

control additional to that entrusted by [what are today Articles 226 and 227] to the diligence of the Commission and the Member States'.[41]

A provision of EU law which, like Article 25 of the Treaty, is capable of being enforced directly by individuals is referred to in various ways. The ECJ sometimes uses the phrase 'directly applicable' in this context, and at other times uses the expression 'directly effective'. International lawyers also sometimes use a third term, 'self-executing'. Several terms to describe the same concept are at the best of times confusing. In this particular context, however, confusion is even more readily created because the TEC itself, as has already been seen, also refers to 'directly applicable' provisions: Article 249 provides that regulations are 'directly applicable in all Member States'. By 'directly applicable' here, it appears to mean 'automatically the law in the Member States'.[42] Whilst this matter is obviously related to the question of whether an individual can enforce the particular provision in a national court, it is not logically identical. Since the Treaty is the most authoritative source available here, the present writer therefore prefers to reserve the expression 'directly applicable' to describe the automatic legal force attributed to regulations by Article 249. The phrase 'direct effect' will be taken to refer to those provisions which are capable of enforcement by individuals.[43]

In the early years of its operation, the ECJ dealt with a number of cases in which the major issue was the possible direct effect of a provision of the Treaty. It gradually articulated the characteristics required of such a provision to render it 'legally complete' and thus directly effective. That there are four such characteristics was originally made clear in *Van Gend en Loos*, and was later explained further through the case law of the ECJ. The provision in question must be clear[44] (since judges in a great variety of national courts will have to apply it, and should be able to do so without an unacceptable element of variation), unconditional, non-discretionary,[45] and final, in the sense of not requiring any legislative intervention

---

[41] [1963] ECR 1, at 13. See also Lecourt, *L'Europe des juges* (Bruylant, Brussels, 1976). Another procedure available in the UK where it is alleged that national legislation infringes the Community's anti-discrimination legislation, is an action for judicial review at the suit of the relevant statutory commission: *R v Secretary of State for Employment, ex parte EOC* [1994] 2 WLR 409, also discussed in chs 4 and 5. See also Moore, 'Sex Discrimination and Judicial Review' (1994) 19 ELRev 425; Deakin, 'Part-Time Employment, Qualifying Thresholds and Economic Justification' (1994) 23 ILJ 151; Gordon, 'Judicial Review and Equal Opportunities' [1994] PL 217; and Morris, 'Rights and Remedies: Part-Time Workers and the EOC' (1995) 17 JSWFL 1.   [42] See discussion in ch 1.

[43] See also Winter, 'Direct Application and Direct Effect: Two Distinct and Different Concepts in Community Law' (1972) 9 CMLRev 425. Cf Steiner, 'Direct Applicability in EEC Law—A Chameleon Concept' (1982) 98 LQR 229.

[44] Case 18/71 *Eunomia di Porro v Italian Ministry of Education* [1971] ECR 811. See also the remarks of Warner AG in Case 131/79 *R v Secretary of State for Home Affairs, ex parte Santillo* [1980] ECR 1585, at 1604.

[45] The precise nature of this element has evolved over the years. See in particular Case 28/67 *Molkerei-Zentrale Westfalen/Lippe GmbH v Hauptzollamt Paderborn* [1968] ECR 143, at 152–3; Case 27/67 *Fink-Frucht GmbH v Hauptzollamt Munchen* [1968] ECR 223; Case 57/65 *Lutticke v Hauptzollamt Sarrelouis* [1966] ECR 205; Case 13/68 *Salgoil SpA v Italian Ministry of Foreign Trade* [1968] ECR 453; Case 41/74 *Van Duyn v Home Office* [1974] ECR 1337; Case C-271/91 *Marshall v Southampton and South-West Hants Area Health Authority (No 2)* [1993] ECR I-4367 (discussed in detail in ch 5); Joined Cases C-6 & 9/90 *Francovich and Bonifaci v Italy* [1991] ECR I-5357 (discussed below); and Case C-91/92 *Faccini Dori v Recreb Srl* [1994] ECR I-3325 (also discussed below).

by either the Member States or the Community institutions to make it effective. Thus, Article 13(1) of the TEC[46] is undoubtedly incapable of taking direct effect, since all it does is permit future action (forbidding discrimination) by the Community institutions. However, the fact that a particular Treaty provision is expressly addressed to the Member States does not mean that it necessarily confers any element of discretion on them, and is therefore not enough on its own to preclude direct effect;[47] this principle enabled the ECJ to hold that Article 141(1) (on equal pay for men and women) takes direct effect.[48]

(ii)   Direct enforcement of secondary EU legislation

Having established the conditions under which Treaty provisions are enforceable directly by individuals, the ECJ then turned to the question of whether, and if so when, the secondary legislation of the EU might also be held to be directly effective. The problems in this area were very much simpler to resolve in the case of regulations than in the cases of directives and decisions. Since regulations are, by Article 249, 'directly applicable', and thus automatically the law in all the Member States without the need for any implementation on the parts of national legislatures, there can be no objection in principle to regulations being, on occasion at least, directly enforceable at the suit of individuals. There is a clear parallel with national parliamentary legislation, some of which is aimed at regulating the position of individual legal persons and so is enforceable by them in the courts, and other aspects of which are not. It thus seemed likely that the ECJ would hold regulations to be capable of producing direct effects, provided that they fulfilled the same four requirements as were applied to Treaty provisions. In practice, because of their very nature as immediately operative legislation, regulations are less likely than Treaty provisions to be too vague or general for direct effect, and so the Court has devoted little or no detailed attention to this aspect of their enforcement by individuals. It has, however, held on a number of occasions that regulations are 'capable of creating individuals rights which the national court must uphold'.[49]

In the cases of directives and decisions, however, the problems were acute. Not being 'directly applicable' under the terms of Article 249, these instruments clearly require legislation by the national authorities of the Member States before they can penetrate into the national legal orders. The intentions of the drafters of the Treaty, it is clear from Article 249, were to make directives and decisions binding legal instruments, but the spheres of obligation which they create were undoubtedly

---

[46] Discussed in ch 1.

[47] See, eg, Case 28/67 *Molkerei-Zentrale Westfalen/Lippe GmbH v Hauptzollamt Paderborn* [1968] ECR 143.

[48] Case 43/75 *Defrenne v Sabena* [1976] ECR 455, discussed in ch 4; the case actually concerned the predecessor to Art 141(1), namely Art 119.

[49] Case 93/71 *Leonesio v Italian Ministry of Agriculture and Forestry* [1972] ECR 287, at 293. See also Case 43/71 *Politi Sas v Minister of Finance* [1971] ECR 1039, esp at 1048–9, and Case 41/74 *Van Duyn v Home Office* [1974] ECR 1337, esp at 1347.

intended to be limited. If directives and decisions are not therefore the law in the Member States until implemented, how could it ever be said that such instruments, taken on their own and in isolation from national implementing legislation, create rights which individuals may enforce in their national courts? It will be recalled that this issue is of special significance in the field of anti-discrimination law, where enabling authority for secondary legislation has until recently been sparse and where all of the secondary legislation takes the form of directives.

Notwithstanding the basic logical obstacle, there is an obvious reason of policy for seeking to hold directives and decisions capable of direct effect. Member States are notoriously slow in legislating to give effect to their EU obligations. The remedy of imposing a penalty on them for non-compliance with a decision of the ECJ became available only when it was introduced by the TEU.[50] Thus, at least until relatively recently, the main inducements on States in practice to comply with rulings of the ECJ were the political embarrassment and corresponding diminution in their negotiating power vis-à-vis their partners which would result if they disobeyed them, together with the fear that other Member States might retaliate. This being so, it is understandable that the Court should have been eager to extend the notion of direct effect to directives and decisions: by doing so, it was enabled to rule that that which ought to have been done had in effect been done, even where a Member State was in default and had not in fact passed the required legislation. The argument discussed earlier in the context of the direct effect of Treaty provisions, that the vigilance of individuals provides an important additional means of ensuring that the Member States carry out their EU obligations, is a particularly compelling one where directives and decisions are concerned.

The ECJ, in the early 1970s, seems to have been carried away by the utility of the notion of direct effect as applied to directives and decisions. This led it to pronounce such instruments capable of direct effect without giving sufficient attention to the underlying difficulties of principle. The process began with *Grad v Finanzampt Traunstein*,[51] where it held that a combination of a decision, a Treaty provision, and two directives was directly effective; and *SACE v Italian Ministry of Finance*,[52] in which it held a Treaty provision together with a directive to be directly effective. In neither case was there detailed discussion by the Court of the critical question as to how an instrument which was not the law in the Member States could be enforced in the courts of those Member States. For example, in *Grad* the Court held:

However, although it is true that by virtue of [what is today Article 249], regulations are directly applicable and therefore by virtue of their nature capable of producing direct effects, it does not follow from this that other categories of legal measures mentioned in that Article can never produce similar effects. In particular, the provision according to which decisions are binding in their entirety on those to whom they are addressed enables the question to be put whether the obligation created by the decision can only be invoked by the Community institutions against the addressee or whether such a right may

---

[50] See Art 228.   [51] Case 9/70 [1970] ECR 825.   [52] Case 33/70 [1970] ECR 1213.

possibly be exercised by all those who have an interest in the fulfilment of this obligation. It would be incompatible with the binding effect attributed to decisions by [what is today Article 249] to exclude in principle the possibility that persons affected may invoke the obligation imposed by a decision. Particularly in cases where, for example, the Community authorities by means of a decision have imposed an obligation on a Member State or all the Member States to act in a certain way, the effectiveness (*l'effet utile*) of such a measure would be weakened if the nationals of that state could not invoke it in the courts and the national courts could not take it into consideration as part of Community law. Although the effects of a decision may not be identical with those of a provision contained in a regulation, this difference does not exclude the possibility that the end result, namely the right of the individual to invoke the measure in the courts, may be the same as that of a directly applicable provision of a regulation.

Article 177, whereby the national courts are empowered to refer to the Court all questions regarding the validity and interpretation of all acts of the institutions without distinction, also implies that individuals may invoke such acts before the national courts. Therefore, in each particular case, one must examine whether the nature, background and wording of the provision in question are capable of producing direct effects in the legal relationships between the addressee of the act and third parties.[53]

Such a statement amounts to little more in reality than a vindication of the principle that directives and decisions *ought* to be capable of direct effect. However, these cases marked the beginning of a series of decisions in which the ECJ upheld the direct effect in particular of the provisions of certain directives. Perhaps the most important case in the series was *Van Duyn v Home Office*,[54] in which the Court upheld the direct effect of Article 3 of Directive 64/221[55] on the exceptions to the principle of the free movement of workers. The UK Government argued that, since Article 249 distinguishes between the effects of regulations, directives, and decisions, it was to be presumed that the Council, in issuing a directive here rather than a regulation, must have intended that the directive should have an effect other than that of a regulation, and accordingly that the former should not be 'directly applicable'.[56] The ECJ nevertheless repeated its remarks in *Grad* almost verbatim, and held that the necessity for direct effect in this situation justified the Court in reaching its conclusion.[57]

A significant development as regards the doctrine of direct effect of directives occurred in 1977 in the *Verbond* case.[58] The ECJ was asked about the possible

[53] [1970] ECR 825, at 837.   [54] Case 41/74 [1974] ECR 1337.
[55] OJ Sp Ed, 1963–4, 117.
[56] This argument was somewhat undermined by the fact that the relevant enabling article in the Treaty, today Art 46(2), only permits action here by directive and not by regulation.
[57] Mayras AG tried to be a little more analytical than the Court itself. He pointed out that the Court had said in the *SACE* case (op cit, n 52, at 1223) that a directive is directly effective 'whenever by its nature the provision establishing (the) obligations is directly applicable'. Mayras AG concluded that 'when faced with a directive, it is therefore necessary to examine in each case whether the wording, nature and the general scheme of the provisions in question are capable of producing direct effects between the Member States to which the directive is addressed and their subjects' ([1974] ECR 1337, at 1355). For decisions as to the direct effect of provisions of Directive 64/221, see Case 67/74 *Bonsignore v City of Cologne* [1975] ECR 297; Case 48/75 *State v Royer* [1976] ECR 497; Case 30/77 *R v Bouchereau* (1977) 2 CMLR 800; and Case 36/75 *Roland Rutili v Minister of the Interior* [1975] ECR 1219. See also Easson, 'The "Direct Effect" of EEC Directives' (1979) 28 ICLQ 319, and Green, 'Directives, Equity and the Protection of Individual Rights' (1984) 9 ELRev 295.
[58] Case 51/76 *Verbond v Inspecteur der Invoerrechten en Accijnzen* [1977] ECR 113.

direct effect of a provision of a directive harmonizing turnover taxes. The Court upheld the direct effect of the provision, notwithstanding that the directive had been made under the authority of Article 94 of the Treaty. Although the express reasoning of the Court in this case adds nothing to that of its predecessors, the substance of the decision does. In the earlier cases, the enabling article of the Treaty on which the directive was based had itself always been directly effective; the direct effect of the directive could thus be seen as, in a sense, merely an extension of the Treaty. There can be no question, however, of Article 94 being directly effective: it is exclusively an enabling provision, and certainly does not produce any 'final' or complete legal right for individuals. The directive itself therefore, in such a situation, is the source of the whole of the individual's rights. This is, of course, vital in the field of discrimination, where the existing secondary legislation (apart from the amendments to the Equal Treatment Directive which are authorized by Article 141(3)[59]) is based on general and non-directly effective enabling provisions. This fact alone does not present a barrier to the enforcement by an individual of such a directive.

A further important principle which seemed to have been implicitly assumed hitherto was articulated in the *Enka* case.[60] The ECJ held here that the provisions of a directly effective directive must take precedence over any national measures which prove to be incompatible with its terms. In particular, an individual can rely on a directive before a national court in order to ask that court to check whether, in the exercise of any discretion left to it by the directive, the Member State has kept within the permissible bounds of that discretion. The directive therefore can act either as a 'sword', giving the individual legal rights where national law does not do so, or as a 'shield', protecting that individual from having national law enforced against him or her where it conflicts with the terms of the directive. Again, this principle is of great potential significance in the field of anti-discrimination law, where the Member States have a corpus of national laws on the subject, which may on occasion conflict with the EU directives.

Given the policy-driven way in which the ECJ's doctrine of direct effect of directives developed, it hardly seems surprising—at least in retrospect—that serious criticism came to be levelled at it. The clearest and most persuasive criticism came from the French Conseil d'Etat in *Cohn-Bendit v Ministre de l'Intérieure*.[61] Cohn-Bendit, a West German citizen and a leader of the Paris student revolts in 1968, had been deported from France in that same year. In 1975, the Minister of the Interior refused Cohn-Bendit's request to cancel the deportation order, without giving any reasons. Cohn-Bendit argued that this action breached Article 6 of Directive 64/221, which required a 'worker' such as himself to be given an explanation for a refusal to allow him to enter another Member State on the ground of

---

[59] Directive 2002/73, OJ [2002] L269/15.
[60] Case 38/77 *Enka BV v Inspecteur der Invoerrechten en Accijnzen* [1977] ECR 2203.
[61] [1980] 1 CMLR 543.

public policy.[62] He claimed the right to enforce Article 6 of the Directive[63] before the Conseil d'Etat.[64] The Commissaire du Gouvernement lucidly summed up the logical arguments against the direct effect of directives. The validity of the ECJ's case law in this area did not, he considered, 'spring forcefully to the eye'.[65] In particular, he pointed out that the ECJ had never explained how an unimplemented directive could have an internal legal effect in the Member States. As to the argument so often referred to by the ECJ that the direct effect of directives greatly helps the enforcement of EU law, he commented:

[According to the third paragraph of Article 249] a directive should limit itself to formulating an obligation as to the aim to be achieved while leaving to the Member States the task of laying down the form and the means which will allow it to be achieved. And one cannot refrain from thinking that it is not only the effectiveness of the directive that has to be promoted; the effectiveness of the third paragraph of Article [249] deserves as much and even more to be protected by reason of the primacy of primary Community law over secondary Community law.[66]

He also made the point that to permit directives to take direct effect is to blur the Treaty-made distinction between regulations and directives and this makes nonsense of the Treaty's stipulation in many instances that the institutions may act by directive, but not by regulation. The Commissaire's preferred solution would have been to refer the case to the ECJ and ask it to reconsider its jurisprudence on the direct effect of directives. Notwithstanding this advice, the Conseil d'Etat nevertheless declined to seek a preliminary ruling and, after pointing out that Directive 64/221 is based on what is today Article 46(2) of the Treaty, which authorizes the issue of directives only and not of regulations, it held:

It follows clearly from Article [249] . . . that while . . . directives bind the Member States 'as to the result to be achieved' and while, to attain the aims set out in them, the national authorities are required to adapt the statute law and subordinate legislation and administrative practice of the Member States to the directives which are addressed to them, those authorities alone retain the power to decide on the form to be given to the implementation of the directives and to fix themselves, under the control of the national courts, the means appropriate to cause them to produce effect in national law. Thus, whatever the detail that they contain for the eyes of the member States, directives may not be invoked by the nationals of such states in support of an action brought against an individual administrative act. It follows that M Cohn-Bendit could not effectively maintain . . . that [the deportation] decision infringed the provisions of the directive . . . [67]

The gauntlet was thus thrown down to the ECJ to go back to first principles and surmount the logical hurdle which it had hitherto avoided. This it finally did in *Pubblico Ministero v Ratti*,[68] where it held that a 'Member State which has not

---

[62] Art 6 provides: 'The person concerned shall be informed of the grounds of public policy, public security, or public health upon which the decision taken in his case is based, unless this is contrary to the interests of the security of the State involved.'

[63] Following the ECJ's decision on the direct effect of this provision in Case 36/75 *Rutili*, op cit, n 57.

[64] The Conseil d'Etat is the highest court in the hierarchy of French administrative courts.

[65] [1980] 1 CMLR 543, at 550.   [66] Ibid, at 554.

[67] Ibid, at 562–3. See Simon and Dowrick, 'Effect of EEC Directives in France: The Views of the Conseil d'Etat' (1979) 95 LQR 376.   [68] Case 148/78 [1979] ECR 1629.

adopted the implementing measures required by the directive in the prescribed periods may not rely, as against individuals, on its own failure to perform the obligations which the directive entails'.[69] Reischl AG explained the mechanism, which is essentially a procedural one, rather more fully:

It is certainly inappropriate to speak of the direct applicability of a directive. That term is used in Article [249] of the Treaty only for regulations, that is to say, for directly applicable Community legislation, which may also create legal relations between individuals. However, it is clear from the Treaty and has also been emphasized again and again in the case law that a clear distinction must be drawn between regulations and directives, the latter creating obligations only for the Member States. So under no circumstances can one say . . . that directives may also have the contents and effects of a regulation; at most directives may produce similar effects . . . The essence of such effects is that in certain cases, which however constitute the exception to the rule, Member States which do not comply with their obligations under the directive are unable to rely on provisions of the internal legal order which are illegal from the point of view of Community law, so that individuals become entitled to rely on the directive as against the defaulting state and acquire rights thereunder which the national courts must protect. So in such cases one should more properly speak—and that has always happened in the case law—only of the direct effect of directives.[70]

This method of explaining how an unimplemented directive may take direct effect in internal law expressly requires the Member State to be in the wrong; this will not be the case until the time stipulated in the directive for compliance with its terms has run out. It follows that there is an additional requirement to be satisfied before a directive can take direct effect. In the words again of Reischl AG:

[A]s far as directives are concerned, direct effect is hardly an automatic consequence, but merely a reflex effect: it occurs when a Member State does not comply with its obligations and consists in the fact that the state is deprived of the possibility of relying as against individuals and undertakings on its failure to comply with Community law. Accordingly the fact that a directive becomes binding on its notification is not sufficient to produce that legal consequence, rather is it the expiry of the period laid down in the directive for the adaptation of national law which is material.[71]

As to the other requirements for direct effect of a directive, he said:

The decisive test is whether it may be said from the nature, general scheme and wording of a directive that it imposes clear, complete and precise obligations on the Member States, does not lay down any

---

[69] Case 148/78 [1979] ECR 1629, at 1642.
[70] Ibid, at 1650. These remarks were foreshadowed by Warner AG in Case 38/77 *Enka BV*, op cit, n 60, at 222b, when he said: 'Article [249] of the Treaty, although it leaves to each Member State the choice of the "form and methods" whereby it is to give effect to a directive, does not allow it the choice of not giving effect to the directive at all, or of giving effect to it only in part. On the contrary, Article [249] says in terms that a directive "shall be binding, as to the result to be achieved, upon each Member State to which it is addressed." A Member State that fails fully to give effect to a directive is in breach of the Treaty, so that to allow it (through its executive or administrative authorities) to rely upon that fact as against a private person in proceedings in its own courts would be to allow it to plead its own wrong.' See also Warner, 'The Relationship between European Community Law and the National Laws of Member States' (1977) 93 LQR 349.   [71] [1979] ECR 1629, at 1653.

conditions other than precisely defined ones and does not leave the Member States any margin of discretion in the performance of the obligations.[72]

The utility of the concept of direct effect is not, however, confined to cases in which a directive has not been implemented correctly; it may also come to the aid of an individual where a Member State has enacted proper implementing legislation. This emerged from *Marks & Spencer plc v Commissioners of Customs & Excise*,[73] where the ECJ explained that:

[T]he adoption of national measures correctly implementing a directive does not exhaust the effects of the directive. Member States remain bound actually to ensure full application of the directive even after the adoption of those measures. Individuals are therefore entitled to rely before national courts, against the State, on the provisions of a directive which appear, so far as their subject-matter is concerned, to be unconditional and sufficiently precise whenever the full application of the directive is not in fact secured, that is to say, not only where the directive has not been implemented or has been implemented incorrectly, but also where the national measures correctly implementing the directive are not being applied in such a way as to achieve the result sought by it.

... [I]t would be inconsistent with the Community legal order for individuals to be able to rely on a directive where it has been implemented incorrectly but not to be able to do so where the national authorities apply the national measures implementing the directive in a manner incompatible with it.[74]

(iii)   Directives and horizontal effect

At least one highly significant consequence follows from the ECJ's chosen method of explaining how a directive may take direct effect: it does not provide any mechanism for the enforcement of a provision contained in a directive by an individual *against another individual*. The capacity of EU law to be enforced against an individual—in other words, the creation of obligations as well as rights for individuals by EU law—is usually termed 'horizontal direct effect'.[75] It has long been clear that a Treaty provision may create obligations not just for Member States but also for individuals.[76] It was sometimes argued that there was little real

---

[72] Ibid, at 1650. In its later decision in Case 8/81 *Becker v Finanzampt Munster-Innenstadt* [1982] ECR 53, the ECJ confirmed this approach, saying (at 71): '[W]herever the provisions of a directive appear, as far as their subject matter is concerned, to be unconditional and sufficiently precise, those provisions may, in the absence of implementing measures adopted within the prescribed period, be relied upon as against any national provision which is incompatible with the directive or in so far as the provisions define rights which individuals are able to assert against the state'. Cf the remarks of Warner AG in Case 131/79 *R v Secretary of State for Home Affairs, ex parte Santillo* [1980] ECR 1585, at 1609. See also Usher, 'Direct Effect of Directives: Dotting the i's . . .', (1980) 5 ELRev 470.

[73] Case C-62/00 [2002] ECR I-6325, commented upon by Ruffert in (2003) 40 CMLRev 729.

[74] Ibid, at 6358–9. For an interesting discussion of the role of the doctrine of direct effect in today's EU legal order, see Prechal, 'Does Direct Effect Still Matter?' (2000) 37 CMLRev 1047.

[75] The term 'vertical direct effect' refers to the situation where EU law is enforced against the State or one of its organs.

[76] See, eg, Case 36/74 *Walrave and Koch v Association Union Cycliste Internationale* [1974] ECR 1405, and Case C-281/98 *Angonese v Cassa di Risparmio di Bolzano SpA* [2000] ECR I-4139.

difference between a Treaty provision addressed to the Member States, such as Article 141 which was held to create obligations for individuals in *Defrenne v Sabena*,[77] and a directive. Furthermore, it was pointed out that anomalies would arise in practice if directives could not be enforced against individuals, whilst Treaty provisions could.[78] However, the estoppel-type reasoning adopted in the *Ratti* case is inapposite where a directive is sought to be enforced against an individual: the individual is not at fault in consequence of the non-implementation of the directive by the Member State, and thus there can be no question of the individual relying on his or her own wrongdoing before the court.[79] The ECJ perhaps believed that it had made this matter clear in the *Ratti* case and in its later jurisprudence on the direct effect of directives.[80] However, its history of policy-led decisions in this area created a slim possibility that it would find a way around this difficulty and that it would eventually rule in favour of the horizontal direct effect of directives.[81]

That this was not to be was demonstrated by *Marshall v Southampton and South-West Hants Area Health Authority*,[82] where the ECJ held: '[A] directive may not of itself impose obligations on an individual and . . . a provision of a directive may not be relied upon as against such a person . . . '[83] This conclusion was reiterated by the full Court in *Faccini Dori v Recreb Srl*,[84] a stronger case in this respect than *Marshall*[85] since the application of the principle here actually resulted in the plaintiff losing her action. Whilst waiting on Milan station, Ms Faccini Dori had entered into a contract with a private commercial undertaking to take an English language correspondence course. She later sought to cancel this contract, and relied for her right to do so on Directive 85/577 concerning the protection of the consumer in

[77] Case 43/75 [1976] ECR 455, discussed in detail in chs 3 and 4.

[78] Szyszczak has also argued that the legal definition of Citizenship of the Union embraces the imposition of duties on individuals, since Art 17(2) of the Treaty provides: 'Citizens of the Union shall enjoy the rights conferred by this Treaty and shall be subject to the duties imposed thereby': see 'Future Directions in European Union Social Policy Law' (1995) 24 ILJ 19.

[79] In addition, before the amendment of what is now Art 254 (as to which see ch 1) by the TEU, directives were not required to be published in the Official Journal, and it was argued that grave injustice would result if an individual could be placed under an obligation by an instrument whose terms he or she had no means of discovering.

[80] See, eg, its remarks in Case 8/81 *Becker*, op cit, n 72, quoted above.

[81] For discussion, see Arnull et al, op cit, n 1, at 98–102; Arnull, 'Sanctioning Discrimination' (1984) 9 ELRev 267; Green, 'Directives, Equity and the Protection of Individual Rights', (1984) 9 ELRev 295; Easson, 'Can Directives Impose Obligations on Individuals?' (1979) 4 ELRev 67; id, 'The Direct Effect of EEC Directives' (1979) 28 ICLQ 319; and Wyatt, 'The Direct Effect of Community Social Law—Not Forgetting Directives' (1983) 8 ELRev 241.

[82] Case 152/84 [1986] ECR 723, discussed in detail in ch 5. See Foster, 'Equal Treatment and Retirement Ages' (1986) 11 ELRev 222, and Arnull, 'The Direct Effect of Directives: Grasping the Nettle' (1986) 35 ICLQ 939.   [83] [1986] ECR 723, at 749.

[84] Case C-91/92 [1994] ECR I-3325, noted by Bernard in 'The Direct Effect of Directives: Retreating from *Marshall (No 1)*?' (1995) 24 ILJ 97, and by Robinson in (1995) 32 CMLRev 629. See also Case 14/86 *Pretore di Salo v Persons Unknown* [1987] ECR III-2545, Case C-168/95 *Arcaro* [1996] ECR I-4705, and Case C-192/94 *El Corte Inglés SA v Rivero* [1996] ECR I-1281.

[85] In *Marshall*, the defendants were found to be an organ of the State and the directive could therefore be enforced vertically.

respect of contracts negotiated away from business premises.[86] At the material time, Italy had not taken any steps to implement this directive, even though the time for doing so had expired. Notwithstanding that the relevant provisions of the directive were held to take direct effect, the Court ruled that they could not be relied upon against a private person.[87]

Despite the apparent force of the Court's determination not to accord directives horizontal direct effect, there have nevertheless been subsequent decisions which have cast renewed doubt on the scope of the doctrine by creating a kind of 'incidental' horizontal effect for directives in certain circumstances. A significant characteristic shared by these cases is the involvement in them of two private parties, in addition to the State.[88] Foremost amongst these decisions is *CIA Security v Signalson*.[89] CIA marketed an alarm system in Belgium, which had not received type approval under the relevant Belgian legislation. In a commercial dispute with a rival organization, in which it was also argued that CIA was criminally liable, CIA argued that the national legislation enacted during the 1990s was invalid because it had not been communicated to the Commission as required by Directive 83/189.[90] An important issue for the Court was whether CIA could rely on the directly effective notification requirement in its dispute with another individual; if it were allowed to do so, this would be seriously detrimental to that other individual's case. Elmer AG distinguished this situation from that in *Faccini Dori* because, in his view, it was the intention of the present directive only to impose obligations on the Member States; it did not seek to impose obligations on individuals. He submitted that it was clear that if the State had tried to bring criminal proceedings against CIA for non-compliance with the national legislation, it would have been precluded from so doing by the direct effect of the directive. He continued:

The fact that the question in this case has been raised in the context of a private action, however, in my view can make no difference whatsoever. It is the State which lays down rules on penalties, prohibitions on marketing etc, and it is the courts who must impose such sanctions regardless of who, under the national rules on procedure, might have brought the case.[91]

---

[86] OJ [1985] L372/31.

[87] The denial by the ECJ of horizontal direct effect to directives has been the subject of considerable criticism. See in particular the submissions of Van Gerven AG in Case C-271/91 *Marshall v Southampton and South-West Hants Area Health Authority (No 2)* [1993] ECR I-4367, those of Jacobs AG in Case C-316/93 *Vaneetveld v SA Le Foyer* [1994] ECR I-763, at 770–6, and those of Lenz AG in Case C-91/92 *Faccini Dori v Recreb Srl* [1994] ECR I-3325. See also Tridimas, 'Horizontal Effect of Directives: a Missed Opportunity?' (1994) 19 ELRev 621; Coppel, 'Rights, Duties and the End of *Marshall*' (1994) 57 MLR 859; Mastroianni, 'On the Distinction Between Vertical and Horizontal Direct Effects of Community Directives: What Role for the Principle of Equality?' (1999) 5 EPL 417; and Colgan, 'Triangular Situations: The Coup de Grâce for the Denial of Horizontal Direct Effect of Community Directives' (2000) 8 EPL 545.

[88] Sometimes called 'triangular' or 'multi-angular relationships': see Prechal, *Directives in European Community Law* (Oxford University Press, Oxford, 1995), esp 65–9.

[89] Case C-194/94 [1996] ECR I-2201. See Coppel, 'Horizontal Effect of Directives' (1997) 26 ILJ 69.

[90] OJ [1983] L109/8.

[91] [1996] ECR I-2201, at 2226. See also the view of Lord Hoffmann, delivering the judgment of the House of Lords in *R v Secretary of State for Employment, ex parte Seymour-Smith* [1997] 1 WLR 473, at 478.

The full Court, without referring to *Faccini Dori*, agreed that individuals could rely on the notification requirement contained in the directive, with the result that the national court must decline to apply a national technical regulation which had not been notified in accordance with the directive.[92]

Bernáldez[93] concerned civil liability in respect of a road accident caused by a drunk driver. The driver had been held liable, and his insurers absolved from liability, under Spanish legislation. However, the Public Prosecutor appealed against this decision, seeking joint liability for the insurers on the basis of the requirements of two directives. Without making any mention of *Faccini Dori* and basing its reasoning entirely on the policy underlying the directives, namely, the harmonization of insurance and the protection of victims of accidents throughout the Community, the Court held that the directives precluded national legislation from relieving insurers of the obligation to compensate the victims of drunk drivers, although national legislation might provide that in such cases the insurer had a right of recovery against the insured. The net effect of this ruling was thus that, irrespective of the provisions of national law, the directives placed an obligation on a body which was not part of the State (an insurance company), and this obligation could be invoked by another private party (the victim).

In the same vein was *Panagis Pafitis v Trapeza Kentrikis Ellados AE*,[94] concerning an inconsistency between a company law directive[95] and a provision of Greek law which permitted an increase in a company's capital without the consent of the general meeting of its shareholders. Again without making any reference to *Faccini Dori*, the Court held that this national law was precluded by the directive, thereby implying that the directive created rights enforceable against the temporary administrator of the company concerned. Tesauro AG, however, regarded the situation as one of vertical effect, saying that the administrator's appointment and duties were subject to legislative ratification.[96]

Several explanations have been advanced for these, apparently aberrant, decisions.[97] Stuyck maintains[98] that everything depends on the nature of the proceedings

---

[92] See the Court's similar ruling in Case C-443/98 *Unilever Italia SpA v Central Food SpA* [2000] ECR I-7535, but note the powerful dissent of Jacobs AG and the strong criticism of the Court's ruling by Weatherill in 'Breach of Directives and Breach of Contract' (2001) 26 ELRev 177. See also Case C-77/97 *Unilever GmbH v Smithline Beecham GmbH* [1999] ECR I-431. In Case C-226/97 *Lemmens* [2000] ECR I-3711, the Court limited the scope of its ruling in *CIA Security* by stating that failure to notify technical regulations rendered such regulations inapplicable only inasmuch as they hindered the use or the marketing of a product which did not comply with them.

[93] Case C-129/94 [1996] ECR I-1829.

[94] Case C-441/93 [1996] ECR I-1347. See also Case C-215/97 *Bellone v Yokohama* [1998] ECR I-2191.   [95] Directive 77/91, OJ [1977] L26/1.

[96] [1996] ECR I-1347, at 1358. For the view that Case C-180/95 *Draehmpaehl v Urania Immobilenservice ohG* [1997] ECR I-2195, discussed in ch 5, also constitutes an exception to the principle that directives do not take horizontal effect, see Ward's comments on the case in (1998) 23 ELRev 65. Cf Dougan, 'The Disguised "Vertical" Direct Effect of Directives?' (2000) 59 CLJ 586, and id, 'The Equal Treatment Directive: Retaliation, Remedies and Direct Effect' (1999) 24 ELRev 664.

[97] Lackhoff and Nyssens argue that the crux of the matter is to find a balance between ensuring the *effet utile* of Community law and protecting the rule of law as set out in the Treaty: see 'Direct Effect of Directives in Triangular Situations' (1998) 25 ELRev 397. See also Dougan, 'The "Disguised" Vertical Direct Effect of Directives?', op cit, n 96.   [98] (1996) 33 CMLRev 1261.

pending in the national court; where proceedings are brought by an individual
with the aim of enforcing a right against State interference, he concludes that the
ECJ allows a directive to confer obligations on individuals. Slot,[99] in commenting
on *CIA Security*, has pointed out that the parties in that case did not base their
claims directly on the directive, and their situation could therefore be distinguished
from that of the plaintiffs in *Marshall* and *Faccini Dori*. He reasons that private parties
can *indirectly* invoke a directive in order to prevent the application of contradictory
national legislation, concluding that '[j]ust as the public authorities cannot enforce
national legislation that is contrary to provisions of directives . . . , so individuals
cannot achieve such a result'.[100]

It is submitted that these latter views have much to commend them, and that
further supporting and explanatory *dicta* are to be found in the ECJ's decisions. It is
important to note the Court's formulation that a directive may not 'of itself' impose
obligations on an individual.[101] This appears to imply that obligations may nevertheless result for the individual as a more circuitous consequence of a directive.
Elucidation may be found in the Court's case law on the supremacy of Community
law, which emphasizes, as has been seen above, the limitation of national sovereignty and legislative power which the ECJ considers to flow from adherence to
the TEC.[102] At the very least, this means that national legislation which contradicts
EU law in the shape of the Treaty or a regulation is inapplicable; some might go
further and argue that it is invalid or *ultra vires*. The effect of this reasoning in the
sphere of directives was examined by Mancini AG in *Teuling v Bedrijfsvereniging voor
de Chemische Industrie*:[103]

The Commission takes up and develops a view which has received authoritative support in academic
circles according to which even where the directive does not contain an express standstill clause, its
notification generates a 'blocking effect' inasmuch as it prohibits Member States from adopting measures
contrary to its provisions . . . [T]he particular objective of the directive [here] . . . is to harmonize the laws
of the Member States by removing existing legislative and administrative differences. Clearly, therefore,
the very fact of its adoption places an obligation on the Member States to refrain from introducing new
measures which may increase those differences.

It may be suggested that such a proposition conflicts with . . . *Ratti* . . . In paragraph 44 of the decision
in that case the Court held that until the expiry of the period prescribed for the implementation of the

[99] (1996) 33 CMLRev 1035.   [100] Ibid, at 1049–50.
[101] Case 152/84 *Marshall*, op cit, n 82, at 749. See also Case C-192/94 *El Corte Inglés*, op cit, n 84, at
1303, and Joined Cases C-74 & 129/95 *Criminal Proceedings Against X* [1996] ECR I-6609, where the ECJ
said that it had consistently held 'that a directive may not of itself create obligations for an individual and
that a provision of a directive may not therefore, as such, be relied upon against such a person' (at 6636). In
Case C-443/98 *Unilever Italia SpA v Central Food SpA*, op cit, n 92, the Court stated (at 7584–5): 'Whilst
it is true . . . that a directive cannot of itself impose obligations on an individual and cannot therefore be
relied on as such against an individual (see Case C-91/92 *Faccini Dori* [1994] ECR I-3325, paragraph 20),
that case-law does not apply where non-compliance with Article 8 or Article 9 of Directive 83/189,
which constitutes a substantial procedural defect, renders a technical regulation adopted in breach of
either of those articles inapplicable.' See also Case T-172/98 and T-175-177/98 *Salamander AG v
European Parliament and Council* [2000] ECR II-2487, Case C-456/98 *Centrosteel Srl v Adipol GmbH*
[2000] ECR I-6007, and Case C-185/97 *Coote v Granada Hospitality Ltd* [1998] ECR I-5199.
[102] See also Lenz, Sif Tynes, and Young, 'Horizontal What? Back to Basics' (2000) 25 ELRev 509.
[103] Case 30/85 [1987] ECR 2497, also discussed in ch 8.

directive 'the Member States remain free in that field'. As with all freedoms, however, that freedom too is subject to limits, and primarily to limits dictated by common sense. Thus there is no doubt that it entails the power to retain in force rules or practices which do not comply with the directive. However, as I have just stated, it is equally certain that such freedom does not include the power to aggravate the defect which the directive is intended to remedy. Indeed it may be that measures adopted during the prescribed period must of necessity be measures intended to transpose the Community provisions. Such measures must at least not conflict with the requirements laid down in those provisions.

That is not, however, sufficient. Further support for the solution which I propose is to be found in the Treaty. The second paragraph of Article 5 [now Article 10] requires Member States to abstain from adopting measures liable to 'jeopardize the attainment of the objectives' of the Treaty. The failure to fulfil that general obligation, the lack of co-operation and solidarity which form the substance of that obligation, is in fact the first ground on which the Commission should rely as against Member States which it charges under Article 169 [now Article 226] of the EEC Treaty with having disregarded the 'blocking effect', and thus the prohibition of the adoption of retrograde measures, which follows the notification of the directive. Moreover, the Court has often referred to the second paragraph of Article 5 and clarified the limits of Member States' powers in connection with Community measures which are not directives, but which, like them, generate rights and obligations at the end of a prescribed period . . . [104]

This position was confirmed by the decision of the ECJ in *Inter-Environnement Wallonie ASBL v Region Wallonne*,[105] where it held that, during the period permitted for implementation of a directive, the Member States must refrain from taking any measures liable seriously to compromise the result prescribed by the instrument; it added that a national court which is called upon to assess the 'legality' of a national measure enacted during the implementation period must determine whether the measure passes this test.[106] These remarks effectively equate the contravention by a Member State of a directive with its contravention of a Treaty provision or regulation. In other words, they suggest that a lightly modified version of the doctrine of supremacy applies to directives: whilst the implementation period

---

[104] Case 30/85 [1987] ECR 2497, at 2513–14. See also Case C-262/88 *Barber v Guardian Royal Exchange Assurance Group* [1990] ECR I-1889, at 1937 in which Van Gerven AG submitted that a directive has, 'as from the time of its adoption and *a fortiori* as from the expiry of the period prescribed for its transposition into national law, become part of Community law and as such takes precedence over *all* provisions of national law' (quoted more extensively below). See also the submissions of Darmon AG in Case C-229/89 *Commission v Belgium* [1991] ECR I-2216, and of Saggio AG in Case C-187/98 *Commission v Greece* [1999] ECR I-7713. For a limited exception to the 'blocking effect' principle, see Case C-420/92 *Bramhill v Chief Adjudication Officer* [1994] ECR I 3191, discussed in ch 8.

[105] Case C-129/96 [1997] ECR I-7411, discussed by Kaczorowska in 'A New "Right" Available to Individuals under Community Law' (1999) 5 EPL 79.

[106] In his submissions in *Inter-Environnement Wallonie*, Jacobs AG did not, however, subscribe to such a wide general proposition: 'I do not rule out the possibility that a Member State might in some circumstances . . . be considered to be in breach of its duty of faithful co-operation under Article [10] of the Treaty (although possibly not its duty to implement under Article [249]) if it were to enact without justification, after the adoption of a directive, measures which were wholly contrary to the spirit and tenor of a directive, especially one which conferred rights on individuals. That might particularly be so where the measures, although repealed before the final date for implementation, continued to produce practical effects after that date . . . However, such cases would be exceptional . . . I do not think it would be appropriate to interpret Articles [10] and [249] as entailing a general blocking effect' ([1997] ECR I-7411, at 7422).

for a directive is running, although contradictory domestic law remains applicable, no new contradictory domestic legislation may be enacted and, once the implementation period has elapsed, existing contradictory domestic legislation becomes inapplicable.[107] Powerful support for this analysis is to be found in the Opinion of Saggio AG in *Quintero*,[108] where he submitted:

I believe that a correct application of the principle of the primacy of Community law over national law and the need to guarantee uniform application of the Community provisions imply that non-transposed directives may, once the period prescribed for their transposition into national law has expired, have the effect of precluding application of the conflicting national rule, even if, for want of precision or because they have no effect in horizontal relations, they do not confer upon individuals rights that can be relied on before the courts. The duty to co-operate ... which is incumbent on every national body within the framework of its own powers, requires courts and administrative authorities to 'set aside', as it were, the incompatible national law ...

[T]he Court has ... recently examined other consequences resulting from the fact that directives rank higher, in the hierarchy of sources, than rules of domestic law. And this—it should be emphasised—has also been the case with disputes involving private persons only, a correct distinction being made here, albeit implicitly, between the direct effect of a provision of Community law, understood in the strict sense as the right to rely upon that provision as against another person in judicial proceedings, and its capacity to serve as a parameter of legality for a provision which ranks lower in the hierarchy of sources.[109]

This means that a distinction is rightly to be made between those cases where a directive is the only relevant legal provision and those cases where there is contradictory national law. Where a directive stands alone, *Faccini Dori* makes it clear that a claim cannot succeed where the defendant is a private party; the directive does not 'substitute' a new EU legal obligation. However, where there is contradictory national law, once the period allowed for implementing the directive has passed, the directive renders that national law unenforceable; this is sometimes described as the 'exclusionary' effect of a directive, and it may produce the indirect consequence that a legal obligation flowing from the directive is thereby placed on a private party, as occurred, for example, in *CIA Security, Bernáldez*, and *Pafitis*.[110]

---

[107] See also Case 21/78 *Delkvist v Public Prosecutor* [1978] ECR 2327, where the ECJ held: 'Article 2(2) of the directive provides that pending co-ordination at a later date, each Member State shall determine the provisions relating to good repute which must be satisfied by the applicant. That provision leaves the Member States a wide margin of discretion as to the requirements relating to good repute imposed on applicants ... A provision of national law whereby an applicant who has a criminal conviction may be regarded as not being of good repute ... cannot be regarded as exceeding the margin of discretion left to a Member State. Therefore the answer to Questions 3 and 4(a) should be that a statutory provision such as Article 78 of the Danish Penal Code is to be regarded as a provision *validly* enacted by the state within the limits of the directive' (at 2339, emphasis added). See also Prechal, op cit, n 88, esp 25–6, and the literature further cited therein.

[108] Case C-240-244/98 *Océano Grupo Editorial SA v Quintero* [2000] ECR I-4941.

[109] Ibid, at 4955–7. The ECJ decided the case on a different basis, as to which see Stuyck's comment in (2001) 38 CMLRev 719. See also Case C-287/98 *Luxemburg v Linster* [2000] ECR I-6917, especially the submissions of Léger AG.

[110] See also the discussion in Craig and de Búrca, *EU Law: Text, Cases, and Materials*, 3rd edn (Oxford University Press, Oxford, 2003), at 220–7.

If this reasoning is correct, it means that, even disregarding the other principles developed by the ECJ to mitigate the lack of horizontal direct effect of directives (discussed below), the scope of the rule that directives cannot take horizontal effect is narrower than was initially appreciated. Once again, because of the important role played by directives in anti-discrimination law, this is especially significant in the present context.

(iv) Meaning of the 'State'

The case law limiting the direct enforceability of directives against defendants who are private parties has focused attention on the meaning to be attached to the term 'State'. In *Marshall v Southampton and South-West Hants Area Health Authority*,[111] the ECJ indicated the broad stance which it was to take on this matter, saying:

[W]here a person involved in legal proceedings is able to rely on a directive as against the state he may do so regardless of the capacity in which the latter is acting, whether employer or public authority. In either case it is necessary to prevent the state from taking advantage of its own failure to comply with Community law.[112]

Slynn AG explained:

What constitutes 'the state' in a particular national legal system must be a matter for the national court to decide. However (even if contrary to the trend of decisions in cases involving sovereign immunity where the exercise of *imperium* is distinguished from commercial and similar activities), as a matter of Community law, where the question of an individual relying upon the provisions of a directive as against the state arises, I consider that the 'state' must be taken broadly, as including all the organs of the state. In matters of employment . . . this means all the employees of such organs and not just the central civil service. I would, thus, reject the argument put to the court that a distinction should be drawn between the state as employer and the state in some other capacity. For present purposes the state is to be treated as indivisible, whichever of its activities is envisaged. It was argued that, where the state is acting as an employer, it should be treated in the same way as a private employer, and that it would be unfair to draw a distinction. I reject that argument. The state can legislate but a private employer cannot. It is precisely because the state can legislate that it can remedy its failure to implement the directive concerned. This consideration puts it at the outset in a fundamentally different position from a private employer, and justifies its being treated differently as regards the right of a person to rely upon the provisions of a directive.[113]

In its decision in *Johnston v Chief Constable of the RUC*,[111] the ECJ gave a generous interpretation of the 'State' for the purpose of determining who derives obligations from directives. It held that the Chief Constable of the Royal Ulster Constabulary was part of the apparatus of the 'State', despite the UK Government's

---

[111] Case 152/84, op cit, n 82, discussed in detail in ch 5.

[112] Ibid, at 749. See also the submissions of Jacobs AG in Case C-2/94 *Denkavit Internationaal BV v Kamer* [1996] ECR I-2827, where he said: 'the principle according to which an unimplemented directive can impose obligations only on the state is a principle which has to be understood broadly, if it is not to have arbitrary consequences' (at 2840).   [113] [1986] ECR 723, at 735.

[114] Case 222/84 [1986] ECR 1651.

argument that he was constitutionally independent of the executive. The ECJ ruled:

> [I]ndividuals may rely on the directive as against an organ of the state whether it acts *qua* employer or *qua* public authority. As regards an authority like the Chief Constable, it must be observed that . . . the Chief Constable is an official responsible for the direction of the police service. Whatever its relations may be with other organs of the state, such a public authority, charged by the state with the maintenance of public order and safety, does not act as a private individual. It may not take advantage of the failure of the state, of which it is an emanation, to comply with Community law.[115]

The trend continued in *Foster v British Gas plc.*[116] Six female employees of the British Gas Corporation were dismissed in 1985 and 1986 when they reached British Gas's compulsory retirement age of 60 for women. They complained of unlawful sex discrimination, since male employees would not have been required to retire until they reached the age of 65. They could not rely on UK domestic law since, at the date in question, it did not extend to this situation. They argued, therefore, that EU law governed their case. At the relevant time, British Gas had not yet been privatized.[117] The industrial tribunal dismissed their applications on the ground that Article 5 of the Equal Treatment Directive,[118] which otherwise appeared to govern this situation, could be relied on only as against bodies which were 'organs of the State', and that British Gas was not such an 'organ of the State'. The Employment Appeal Tribunal dismissed the applicants' appeal, as did the Court of Appeal,[119] which held that the Directive gave rise to legal rights for employees of the State itself and of any organ or emanation of the State, an emanation of the State meaning an independent public authority 'charged by the state with the performance of any of the classic duties of the state, such as the defence of the realm or the maintenance of law and order within the realm'.[120] As a matter of English law the Court of Appeal found that British Gas, a nationalized industry, did not fall within this definition since its powers were not within the province of government. The House of Lords sought a preliminary ruling from the ECJ, asking whether the Directive was enforceable against British Gas. The ECJ delved into the facts in unusual detail for a preliminary ruling and pointed out that, by virtue of the Gas Act 1972, which governed British Gas at the relevant time, British Gas was a statutory corporation responsible for developing and maintaining a system of gas supply in Great Britain, over which it possessed a monopoly. The members of the British Gas Corporation were appointed by the Secretary of State, who also had the power to give the British Gas Corporation directions of a general character in relation to matters affecting the national interest and instructions concerning management. The British Gas Corporation was obliged to submit to the Secretary of State periodic reports (which were laid before Parliament) on the exercise of its functions, its management, and its programmes,

---

[115] Ibid, at 1691.   [116] Case 188/89 [1990] ECR I-3313.
[117] This occurred in August 1986.   [118] Discussed further in ch 5.
[119] [1988] 2 CMLR 697.   [120] Ibid, at 701, *per* Lord Donaldson MR.

and it had the right to submit proposed legislation to Parliament. It was required to run a balanced budget over two successive financial years and the Secretary of State could order it to pay certain funds to the Department of State, or to allocate funds to specified purposes. This emphasis on the factual background lent force to the ECJ's ultimate conclusion on the principle of EU law at stake and left no doubt at the end of the day as to how the relevant EU principle was to be applied to the facts of the case. It pointed out that it had:

[H]eld in a series of cases that unconditional and sufficiently precise provisions of a Directive could be relied on against organizations or bodies which were subject to the authority or control of the state or had special powers beyond those which result from the normal rules applicable to relations between individuals. The Court has accordingly held that provisions of a Directive could be relied on against tax authorities (the judgments of 19 January 1982 in Case 8/81 *Becker*... and of 22 February 1990 in Case C-221/88 *ECSC v Aciaierie e Ferriere Busseni (in liquidation)* [1990] ECR, local or regional authorities (judgment of 22 June 1989 in Case 103/88 *Fratelli Costanzo v Commune di Milano* [1989] ECR), constitutionally independent authorities responsible for the maintenance of public order and safety (judgment of 15 May 1986 in Case 222/84 *Johnston v Chief Constable of the RUC* [1986] 3 WLR 1038), and public authorities providing public health services (judgment of 26 February 1986 in Case 152/84 *Marshall*...).[121]

From all this, the Court concluded that:

[A] body, whatever its legal form, which has been made responsible, pursuant to a measure adopted by the state, for providing a public service under the control of the state and has for that purpose special powers beyond those which result from the normal rules applicable in relations between individuals is included[122] in any event among the bodies against which the provisions of a Directive capable of having direct effect may be relied upon.[123]

The EU concept of the 'State', for the purposes of the doctrine of horizontal direct effect, is thus characterized by the presence of four factors, namely:

- the body in question must have been given its powers by the State;
- it must have been made responsible for providing a public service;
- its powers must be exercisable under the control of the State; and
- its powers must be special ones, distinguishable from those possessed by individuals.[124]

---

[121] [1990] ECR I-3313, at 3348. See also Case C-31/87 *Beentjes BV v Holland* [1988] ECR 4635.
[122] In *NUT v Governing Body of St Mary's School* [1997] ICR 334, Schiemann LJ pointed out that it is clear from the use in this passage of the words 'is included' that this was not intended to be an exclusive formula.
[123] [1990] ECR I-3313, at 3348–9. Cf the Court's statement earlier in its judgment, and quoted above in the text, that 'unconditional and sufficiently precise provisions of a Directive [can] be relied on against organizations or bodies... subject to the authority or control of the state *or* [which have] special powers beyond those which result from the normal rules applicable to relations between individuals' (at 3348, emphasis added).
[124] These criteria were specifically applied by the CFI in Case T-172/98 and T-175-177/98 *Salamander AG*, op cit, n 101.

It is clear therefore that the 'State' in this context has the potential to cover a wide range of organizations and bodies, including, for example, educational establishments such as schools[125] and universities, local government,[126] the central civil service, and nationalized industries.[127] The editors of the *Equal Opportunities Review* made the point in the aftermath of the *Foster* decision that, even after its privatization, British Gas still seemed to fall within the ECJ's definition of an organ of the State since it continued to have responsibility for providing a public service for which it had special powers, and it was under the control of the State at least to some extent since it was a creature of statute.[128] It is perhaps not an exaggeration to comment that this issue remains a minefield, despite the efforts of the ECJ in *Foster* to articulate its concept of the State. Its formulation requires further elaboration, in particular as regards the meaning of 'public service', 'control of the State', and 'special powers'. The matter of course is of critical importance in an anti-discrimination case where, if an equality directive has not been properly implemented by a Member State, the success or failure of the claim may depend on whether the employer is or is not to be regarded as an organ of the State.[129]

The policy of the ECJ in this area has clearly been to try to compensate for the fact that directives may not be enforced, on their own, against anybody except for an organ of the State, by giving the State as generous as possible a definition. However, this has in turn led to a certain dilution of the logic behind the doctrine of direct effect. As has been seen, the mechanism permitting the enforcement of a directive against the State is the estoppel principle, whereby the State is denied the chance to assert that it has not legislated in circumstances in which it should have legislated. The further that the concept of 'organ of the State' moves from the central, legislation-controlling limbs of government, the more fictitious becomes this

[125] In *NUT v Governing Body of St Mary's School*, op cit, n 122, the Court of Appeal held that once a voluntary aided school had decided to enter the State system and had been granted voluntary aided status, its governing body was to be regarded as an emanation of the State. The Court of Appeal considered that it was incorrect to treat the *Foster* criteria in the same way as a statutory definition, and that the main underlying issue was whether the State would benefit from its own wrongdoing in not implementing the relevant directive if the governors were not treated as an emanation of the State. On the facts of this case, if the governors had not been treated as part of the State, the State would have directly benefited financially from its failure properly to transpose the directive. This led the Court of Appeal to its conclusion despite the fact that not all of the *Foster* criteria were satisfied, namely: (1) the governors had been made responsible pursuant to a statutory instrument; (2) they provided a public service, ie the provision of education; (3) that service was under the control of the State because of the statutory powers and duties possessed by the Secretary of State and local education authorities; but (4) the governors did not have special powers beyond those applying between individuals because their one distinctive power, that of being able to spend public money, was not the sort of power which the ECJ had had in mind in *Foster*.

[126] Case 103/88 *Fratelli Costanzo v Commune di Milano* [1989] ECR 1839. In *NUT v Governing Body of St Mary's School*, op cit, n 122, Schiemann LJ confirmed that, in his judgment, local authorities were certainly emanations of the State.   [127] Cf *Doughty v Rolls-Royce plc* [1992] ICR 538.

[128] See (1990) 33 EOR 40.

[129] For discussion of the approach of the UK courts in sex discrimination cases to the public/private employer dichotomy, see Arnull, 'The Incoming Tide: Responding to *Marshall*' (1987) PL 383. See also Curtin, 'The Province of Government: Delimiting the Direct Effect of Directives in the Common Law Context' (1990) 15 ELRev 195.

estoppel mechanism.[130] Nevertheless, in purely pragmatic terms, it is undeniable that any such development is in the interests of potential anti-discrimination claimants.

(v) Mitigating the lack of horizontal enforceability of directives

The ECJ has developed two extremely significant lines of jurisprudence, the ostensible policy of which is to mitigate the failure of directives to take horizontal direct effect. The first is the so-called doctrine of 'indirect effect'. This is the principle that, even where the defendant to an action is not part of the State, so that the directive itself cannot be enforced directly against that person, the terms of the directive may nevertheless be of assistance to the claimant. This is because the wording of the directive must be taken into account by the national court when it is interpreting any national law dealing with the same subject-matter; if the national court finds an ambiguity in that national law, then that must be resolved so as to make the national law conform to the directive wherever possible. As the ECJ explained in *Von Colson and Kamann v Land Nordrhein Westfalen*:[131]

The Member States' obligation arising from a directive to achieve the result envisaged by the directive and their duty under Article [10] of the Treaty to take all appropriate measures, whether general or particular, to ensure the fulfilment of that obligation, is binding on all the authorities of Member States including, for matters within their jurisdiction, the courts. It follows that, in applying the national law and in particular the provisions of a national law specifically introduced in order to implement Directive 76/207, national courts are required to interpret their national law in the light of the wording and the purpose of the directive in order to achieve the result referred to in Article [249(3)].[132]

A claimant may thus indirectly benefit from the terms of a directive, in particular where national law has been enacted in order to implement it and that national law is susceptible of interpretation in accordance with it.[133] This principle applies

---

[130] See the comments of Van Gerven AG in this context in both *Foster* and Case C-262/88 *Barber v Guardian Royal Exchange Assurance Group* [1990] ECR I-1889. In the latter case, he said: 'individuals ...are...allowed to rely on [a Member State's] default vis-à-vis independent public authorities of the Member State which are not themselves responsible for failure of the latter to transpose a directive into national law. The *nemo auditor* principle has thus acquired a far-reaching ambit (not connected with personal default), with the result that the directive has to a degree been endowed with effect with regard to third parties, in particular to the detriment of the aforesaid public authorities' (at 1938).

[131] Case 14/83 [1984] ECR 1891.

[132] Ibid, at 1909. See also Case C-185/97 *Coote v Granada Hospitality Ltd* [1998] ECR I-5199. The ECJ there refers to the UK's Sex Discrimination Act 1975 as legislation which was specially introduced in order to comply with the Equal Treatment Directive. However, the Act was actually enacted in the year before the Equal Treatment Directive (although doubtless with the likelihood of imminent EU law uppermost in the mind of the UK's legislature).

[133] See also Case 262/84 *Beets-Proper v Van Lanschot Bankiers NV* [1986] ECR 773; Case 80/86 *Public Prosecutor v Kolpinghuis Nijmegen BV* [1987] ECR 3969; *Litster v Forth Dry Dock and Engineering Co Ltd* [1989] ICR 341; and Arnull, 'Some More Equal than Others?' (1986) 11 ELRev 229.

even where the time given to the States for compliance with the directive has not yet run out.[134]

Controversy, however, arose where national law dealing with the subject-matter of the directive pre-dated that directive, so that it could not properly be said to have been enacted in response to the directive. The wording adopted by the ECJ in the *Von Colson* case in the passage quoted above is broad enough to encompass this situation, since the Court refers to applying 'national law' generally so as to conform with a directive.[135] However, this aspect of the judgment was technically *obiter*, since the legislation in question in that case had in fact been adopted in response to the directive. In *Marshall v Southampton and South-West Hants Area Health Authority*, Slynn AG commented:

[W]here legislation is adopted to implement a directive, or consequent upon a Treaty obligation, national courts should seek so far as possible to construe the former in such a way as to comply with the latter. To construe a pre-existing statute . . . in order to comply with a subsequent directive, which the legislature or executive has not implemented, in breach of its obligation, when it has a discretion as to the form and method to be adopted, is, in my view, wholly different. I am not satisfied that it is a rule of Community law that national courts have a duty to do so—unless it is clear that the legislation was adopted specifically with a proposed directive in mind.[136]

Mischo AG agreed with these remarks in *Public Prosecutor v Kolpinghuis Nijmegen BV*,[137] and also addressed himself to the question whether EU law in fact even *permits* pre-existing national legislation to be interpreted in the light of a directive. He concluded:

There is no principle of Community law obliging a national court to be guided by the provisions of a directive which is applicable but which has not yet been implemented by the Member State in question in order to interpret a rule of national law which is insufficiently precise. The question whether it may do so in order to confirm the interpretation obtained from purely national elements of appraisal must be resolved on the basis of the national rules of interpretation. On the other hand, a court cannot rely on such a directive to alter, to the detriment of the individual, the interpretation obtained from national elements of appraisal.[138]

This reasoning was based on the inability of directives to produce obligations for individuals, whether directly or indirectly, and it is arguably incorrect. Since newly passed national legislation could create obligations for individuals, it is unclear why pre-existing national legislation should not be capable of being similarly construed. Van Gerven AG took a very different view of the matter in *Barber v Guardian Royal Exchange Assurance Group*,[139] where he said:

[A]n interpretation [of national law] in conformity with [a] directive may not be restricted to the interpretation of national legislation subsequent to the adoption of the directive concerned or national legislation specifically enacted for transposing the directive into national law . . . Frequently, national implementing legislation will be involved as in *Von Colson* but that need not be the case. It is difficult to

---

[134] Case 80/86, op cit, n 133.   [135] See also the Court's remarks, ibid.
[136] Case 152/84, op cit, n 82, at 733.   [137] Case 80/86, op cit, n 133.   [138] Ibid, at 3980.
[139] Case C-262/88, op cit, n 130.

justify a restriction of the requirement of interpretation in conformity with the directive to the implementing legislation itself (quite apart from the difficulty of determining whether or not a given national provision has been enacted for the purpose of transposing a directive into national law) since the directive has, as from the time of its adoption and *a fortiori* as from the expiry of the period prescribed for its transposition into national law, become part of Community law and as such takes precedence over *all* provisions of national law.[140]

The matter was resolved by the decision of a chamber of the ECJ in *Marleasing SA v La Comercial Internacional de Alimentacion SA*,[141] in which it was held that, in applying national law, whether prior to or subsequent to a relevant directive, a national court is obliged to interpret the national law so far as possible[142] in the light of the wording and purpose of the directive.[143] Such a conclusion is not lacking in logic to the extent that some have hitherto assumed: a Member State might deliberately draft national legislation in broad terms specifically in order that its meaning should be developed by later EU legislation. Alternatively, a Member State might leave an old Act on the statute book even after the passage of a directive because it believed that statute to be capable of being construed in accordance with the directive, and therefore to constitute compliance by the State with its EU obligations.[144] The ECJ added in *Wagner Miret v Fondo de Garantia Salarial*[145] that, when interpreting and applying national law, 'every national court must presume that the state had the intention of fulfilling entirely the obligations arising' from a directive.[146]

Exceptionally, however, the ECJ has held that a directive 'cannot, of itself and independently of a national law adopted by a Member State for its implementation, have the effect of determining or aggravating the liability in criminal law of persons who act in contravention of the provisions of that directive'.[147] In *Public Prosecutor v*

---

[140] Case C-262/88, op cit, n 130, at 1936–7. Differing views on this question were voiced by the House of Lords at this time. In *Garland v British Rail* [1982] 2 WLR 918, Lord Diplock (delivering the opinion of the House) envisaged the possibility of the meaning of the Sex Discrimination Act 1975 being influenced by the Equal Treatment Directive of 1976. However, in *Duke v GEC Reliance Ltd* [1988] 2 WLR 359, the House refused to take this course. See also *Finnegan v Clowney Youth Training Ltd* [1990] 2 WLR 1305, where the Northern Ireland Court of Appeal and the House of Lords refused to refer effectively the same issue to the ECJ.

[141] Case C-106/89 [1990] ECR I-4135, noted by Stuyck and Wytinck in (1991) 28 CMLRev 205, and by Maltby in '*Marleasing*: What is All the Fuss About?' (1993) 109 LQR 301.

[142] But note that much play has been made in the literature of the fact that the Court was inconsistent in its use of the phrase 'as far as possible'; contrast paras 8 and 13 of the judgment.

[143] *Marleasing* was expressly followed by the ECJ in Case C-456/98 *Centrosteel Srl v Adipol GmbH* [2000] ECR I-6007 and Case C-240-244/98 *Océano Grupo Editorial SA v Quintero* [2000] ECR I-4941. The principle was also accepted and applied by the House of Lords in *Webb v EMO (Air Cargo) Ltd* [1995] 4 All ER 577, commented on by Szyszczak in 'Pregnancy and Sex Discrimination' (1996) 21 ELRev 79, and id, 'Pregnancy Discrimination' (1996) 59 MLR 589, and by Deards in 'Indirect Effect After *Webb v EMO (Air Cargo) Ltd*: How Must National Law be Interpreted to Comply with a Directive?' (1996) 2 EPL 71. See also *Chessington World of Adventures v Reed* [1997] IRLR 556.

[144] See Ellis, 'EEC Law and the Interpretation of Statutes' (1988) 104 LQR 379; Arnull, 'The *Duke* Case: An Unreliable Precedent' [1988] PL 313; and id, 'When is Pregnancy Like an Artificial Hip?' (1992) 17 ELRev 265.   [145] Case C-334/92 [1993] ECR I-6911.

[146] Ibid, at 6932.

[147] Case 14/86 *Pretore di Salo v Persons Unknown* [1987] ECR III-2545, at 2570. See also Case C-168/95 *Arcaro* [1996] ECR I-4705. But note that this principle is confined to criminal liability and

Kolpinghuis Nijmegen BV,[148] the Court held that the 'obligation on the national court to refer to the content of the directive when interpreting the relevant rules of its national law is limited by the general principles of law which form part of Community law and in particular the principles of legal certainty and non-retroactivity'.[149] In *Criminal Proceedings Against X*,[150] it added:

More specifically, in a case such as that in the main proceedings, which concerns the extent of liability in criminal law arising under legislation adopted for the specific purpose of implementing a directive, the principle that a provision of the criminal law may not be applied extensively to the detriment of the defendant, which is the corollary of the principle of legality in relation to crime and punishment and more generally of the principle of legal certainty, precludes bringing criminal proceedings in respect of conduct not clearly defined as culpable by law. That principle, which is one of the general legal principles underlying the constitutional traditions common to the Member States, has also been enshrined in various international treaties . . . [151]

The principle of interpretation of domestic law so as, so far as possible, to make it coincide with the requirements of a directive has been extended by the ECJ to a recommendation. This is of particular significance in the light of the fact that, according to Article 249 of the Treaty, a recommendation has no binding legal force. In *Grimaldi v Fonds des Maladies Professionelles*,[152] the Court held that, even though the recommendation there in question produced no direct rights on which individuals could rely in their national courts, it did not follow that a recommendation had no legal effect whatsoever. It ruled that:

[N]ational courts are bound to take . . . [r]ecommendations into consideration in order to decide disputes submitted to them, in particular where they clarify the interpretation of national provisions adopted in order to implement them or where they are designed to supplement binding Community provisions.[153]

The expression 'soft law' has been used by some writers to describe those EU instruments which are not themselves binding but which act as aids to construction for national courts.[154] Wellens and Borchardt have defined soft law as rules which, although not formally binding, have as their aim and outcome an influence on the behaviour of the Community institutions, the Member States, and/or individuals and undertakings.[155]

The second major milestone in the ECJ's efforts to mitigate the lack of horizontal direct effect of directives was its decision in *Francovich and Bonifaci v Italy*.[156]

---

does not preclude the imposition of civil liability on an individual: Case C–456/98 *Centrosteel Srl v Adipol GmbH*, op cit, n 143.

[148] Case 80/86, op cit, n 133.   [149] Ibid, at 3986.

[150] Joined Cases C–74 & 129/95, op cit, n 101.   [151] Ibid, at 6637.

[152] Case 322/88 [1989] ECR 4407.   [153] Ibid, at 4421.

[154] See, eg, 'EEC Sexual Harassment Resolution' (1990) 32 EOR 28. See further Klabbers, 'Informal Instruments Before the European Court of Justice' (1994) 31 CMLRev 997.

[155] Wellens and Borchardt, 'Soft Law in the European Community' (1989) 14 ELRev 267.

[156] Cases C–6 and 9/90 [1991] ECR I–5357, noted by Bebr in (1992) 29 CMLRev 557, by Curtin in 'State Liability under Community Law: A New Remedy for Private Parties' (1992) 21 ILJ 74, by Szyszczak in (1992) 55 MLR 690, and by Parker in 'State Liability in Damages for Breach of

This proclaimed the liability in damages as a matter of Community law of a Member State where loss is caused to an individual by the State's non-implementation of a directive, provided that the directive prescribes the grant of rights to individuals, the content of those rights is identifiable on the basis of the provisions of the directive itself, and there is a causal link between the breach of the State's obligation and the loss suffered by the individual.[157] The directive in this instance was held not to take direct effect for want of precision,[158] but it would appear that the consequences for the individual claimants and the Member State would have been identical even had it done so, since the defendants to the action were not organs of the State and no action could therefore have succeeded on the basis of direct enforcement of the instrument.[159] The principle was formulated in terms of the liability of a Member State for loss resulting from breach of *any* of its Community obligations and was not restricted to the situation of non-implementation of a directive;[160] such a principle was held to be 'inherent in the system of the Treaty'.[161]

In *Francovich*, the Member State's non-implementation of the relevant directive was patently culpable since the period for implementation had expired many years before the action and the State had been successfully prosecuted before the ECJ by the Commission in respect of its inaction. The unanswered question posed was thus whether any, and if so what, lesser level of 'fault' on the part of the Member State would be sufficient to trigger such liability. The ECJ addressed this matter in *Brasserie du Pêcheur v Germany* and *R v Secretary of State for Transport, ex parte Factortame*.[162] In both cases, the Court had already held that the relevant Member State's actions breached the Treaty. The Court explained that the conditions under which a

Community Law' (1992) 108 LQR 181. See also Craig, '*Francovich*, Remedies and the Scope of Damages Liability' (1993) 109 LQR 595; Steiner, 'From Direct Effects to *Francovich*: Shifting Means of Enforcement of Community Law' (1993) 18 ELRev 3; Ross, 'Beyond *Francovich*' (1993) 56 MLR 55; and Tridimas, 'Member State Liability in Damages for Breach of Community Law: An Assessment of the Case Law' in Beatson and Tridimas (eds), *New Directions in European Public Law* (Hart Publishing, Oxford, 1998).

[157] As Tesauro AG commented in his submissions in Joined Cases C-46 & 48/93 *Brasserie du Pêcheur v Germany* and *R v Secretary of State for Transport, ex parte Factortame* [1996] ECR I-1029 (discussed further below), this principle has its origins, as has the doctrine of direct effect, in the ECJ's desire to ensure the effective implementation of Community law.

[158] Thus giving rise to speculation as to the precise meaning of the requirement set out by the Court in *Francovich* that the directive must envisage the grant of rights to individuals. See further Joined Cases C-178, 179, 188, 189, & 190/94 *Dillenkofer v Germany* [1996] ECR I-4845, discussed below.

[159] *Francovich* has now, however, entered the ranks of ground-breaking decisions whose own protagonists proved unable to take advantage of the new principle expressed: the directive in question was found not to include within its terms Mr Francovich's employer. See Case C-479/93 *Francovich v Italy* [1995] ECR I-3843.

[160] See also *Garden Cottage Foods Ltd v Milk Marketing Board* [1984] 1 AC 130; *Bourgoin v Ministry of Agriculture and Fisheries* [1985] 3 All ER 585 (esp the dissenting judgment of Oliver LJ); and *Kirklees Metropolitan Borough Council v Wickes Building Supplies Ltd* [1992] 3 WLR 170.

[161] [1991] ECR I-5357, at 5414.

[162] Joined Cases C-46 & 48/93, op cit, n 157, noted by Oliver in (1997) 34 CMLRev 635. See also Craig, 'Once More Into the Breach: The Community, the State and Damages Liability' (1997) 113 LQR 67.

Member State incurs liability for damage caused to individuals by a breach of Community law cannot, in the absence of particular justification, differ from those governing the liability of the Community in similar circumstances, since the legal position of the individual should not depend on who is the author of the breach. It went on to draw a distinction between cases where the Member State enjoys little or no discretion, such as where it is required to implement a directive, and those in which it has a wide discretion. Where there is a wide discretion, the parallel with Community liability for normative injustice requires that three conditions must be met in order for there to be State liability to an individual: the rule of law infringed must be intended to confer rights on individuals; the breach must be sufficiently serious; and there must be a direct causal link between the State's breach and the individual's damage.[163] As to the requirement that the breach be sufficiently serious, the decisive test is said to be whether the State has manifestly and gravely disregarded the limits on its discretion.[164] The Court went on to spell out that:

The factors which the competent court may take into consideration include the clarity and precision of the rule breached, the measure of discretion left by that rule to the national . . . authorities, whether the infringement and the damage caused was intentional or involuntary, whether any error of law was excusable or inexcusable, the fact that the position taken by a Community institution may have contributed towards the omission, and the adoption or retention of national measures or practices contrary to Community law.

On any view, a breach of Community law will clearly be sufficiently serious if it has persisted despite a judgment finding the infringement in question to be established, or a preliminary ruling or settled case-law of the Court on the matter from which it is clear that the conduct in question constituted an infringement.[165]

The Court added that such liability on the part of a Member State can be incurred through the actions of its legislature, and that it makes no difference of principle whether or not the Community provisions breached take direct effect. The amount of reparation payable[166] must be commensurate with the loss suffered by the individual;[167] it appears that, although the individual must mitigate the

---

[163] See also Case C-127/95 *Norbrook Laboratories v MAFF* [1998] ECR I-1531. For further discussion of causation in this context, see Anagnostaras, 'Not as Unproblematic as You Might Think: the Establishment of Causation in Governmental Liability Actions' (2002) 27 ELRev 663.

[164] See further Steiner, 'The Limits of State Liability for Breach of European Community Law' (1998) 4 EPL 69, and Van den Bergh and Schäfer, 'State Liability for Infringement of the EC Treaty: Economic Arguments in Support of a Rule of "Obvious Negligence"' (1998) 23 ELRev 552.

[165] [1996] ECR I-1029, at 1150. In *R v Secretary of State for Transport, ex parte Factortame Ltd (No 5)* [1999] 3 WLR 1062, the House of Lords subsequently held that the UK's conduct had been sufficiently serious to ground *Francovich* liability; for discussion of this decision, see Cygan, 'Defining a Sufficiently Serious Breach of Community Law: The House of Lords Casts its Net into the Waters' (2000) 25 ELRev 452.

[166] Note that Dougan has questioned whether the ECJ in its recent jurisprudence is departing from its original insistence that damages (as distinct from other remedies prescribed by national law) must be payable in successful *Francovich* claims: see 'The *Francovich* Right to Reparation: Reshaping the Contours of Community Remedial Competence' (2000) 6 EPL 103.

[167] Tesauro AG explained that the compensation awarded must be 'real and effective'; furthermore, it must be quantified so as to restore the situation to that which would have obtained had the

damage, damages are obtainable for loss of profit. Further, where exemplary damages would be obtainable in a similar claim under domestic law, they must be obtainable in a claim against the State for a breach of Community law.

Subsequent cases[168] have answered further questions about the respective liabilities of different constitutional organs of a State.[169] In *Konle v Austria*,[170] the ECJ was asked whether damage caused to an individual by national measures in a federal State must be paid by the State itself. The Court held that this was not necessary:

It is for each Member State to ensure that individuals obtain reparation for damage caused to them by non-compliance with Community law, whichever public authority is responsible for the breach and whichever public authority is in principle, under the law of the Member State concerned, responsible for making reparation. A Member State cannot, therefore, plead the distribution of powers and responsibilities between the bodies which exist in its national legal order in order to free itself from liability on that basis.

Subject to that reservation, Community law does not require Member States to make any change in the distribution of powers and responsibilities between the public bodies which exist on their territory. So long as the procedural arrangements in the domestic system enable the rights which individuals derive from the Community legal system to be effectively protected and it is not more difficult to assert those rights than the rights which they derive from the domestic legal system, the requirements of Community law are fulfilled.[171]

Haim II[172] concerned the refusal by a regional German Association of Dental Practitioners to enrol the applicant on grounds which were alleged to breach EU law. The ECJ repeated what it had said in *Konle* and added that, whether or not the Member State has a federal structure, where legislative or administrative tasks have been devolved to autonomous territorial bodies, or to other public law bodies which are legally distinct from the State, reparation to individuals in respect of national measures which breach Community law may be made by those bodies.

The most important of the group of cases concerning the liability of different constitutional parts of a State is *Köbler v Austria*,[173] in which it was established that the judiciary can engage *Francovich* liability.[174] An Austrian law provided for a

---

infringement had not taken place, at least in financial terms ([1996] ECR I-1029, at 1123). Such a test, of course, accords with the usual measure of tortious damages in English law.

[168] On these 'second generation' *Francovich* cases generally, see Tridimas, 'Liability for Breach of Community Law: Growing Up and Mellowing Down?' (2001) 38 CMLRev 301.

[169] See further Anagnostaras, 'The Allocation of Responsibility in State Liability Actions for Breach of Community Law: A Modern Gordian Knot' (2001) 26 ELRev 139.

[170] Case C-302/97 [1999] ECR I-3099, commented upon by Lengauer in (2000) 37 CMLRev 181.

[171] [1999] ECR I-3099, at 3140. See also Case C-118/00 *Larsy v Institut nationale d'assurances sociales pour travailleurs indépendants* [2001] ECR I-5063.

[172] Case C-424/97 *Haim v KVN* [2000] ECR I-5123.

[173] Case C-224/01 [2003] ECR I-10239.

[174] For a prescient discussion of State liability for judicial acts and its potential consequences, some years before the ECJ's decision in *Köbler*, see Anagnostaras, 'The Principle of State Liability for Judicial Breaches: The Impact of European Community Law' (2001) 7 EPL 281. The ECJ's decision in *Köbler* is commented upon by Wattel in (2004) 41 CMLRev 177; the author there makes the entertaining point that the logical deduction to be made from *Köbler* is that the Community itself should be liable in damages for manifestly erroneous decisions of the ECJ. See also Classen in (2004) 41 CMLRev 813, and Scott and Barber, 'State Liability under *Francovich* for decisions of national courts' (2004) 120 LQR 403.

special length-of-service increment to be included in the retirement pensions of professors who had worked in Austrian State universities for at least fifteen years. Mr Köbler was refused the increment on the ground that, although he had been a university professor in various Member States for more than fifteen years, he did not comply with the requirement that those universities be Austrian. He challenged this decision on the ground that it breached Article 39 on the free movement of workers, and the Austrian Supreme Administrative Court hearing the action sought a preliminary ruling from the ECJ. The ECJ queried whether the national court wished to maintain its request for a preliminary ruling in the light of the judgment in *Schöning-Koigebetopoulou v Freie und Hansestadt Hamburg*,[175] which had been delivered in the meantime. This recent case appeared to settle the issue in Mr Köbler's favour. The national court thereupon withdrew its request, but then, surprisingly, dismissed the application on the ground that the length-of-service increment constituted a loyalty bonus which objectively justified a derogation from the provisions on the free movement of workers; in so doing, it expressly contradicted its earlier finding (namely, that the payment did not constitute a reward for loyalty). Mr Köbler asserted that this judicial decision, made by a court from whose decisions there was no appeal under Austrian law, breached his Community rights and entitled him to *Francovich* damages. The court hearing this second application referred the matter to the ECJ. Léger AG gave a very full review of the existing case law and concluded that, in principle, the actions of a supreme court should be able to trigger *Francovich* liability, and that they might indeed do so on the facts of this case, since the administrative court's decision was 'inexcusable' (the actual decision on the facts being one for the national court). The ECJ agreed with the principle that the decision of a supreme court which breached Community law could engage State liability.[176] It repeated its familiar assertions that the principle of State liability for damage caused to individuals as a result of a breach of Community law is inherent in the Treaty and that it matters not which authority within the Member State is responsible for the breach. It went on to emphasize the essential role played by the judiciary in the protection of Community rights:

[A] court adjudicating at last instance is by definition the last judicial body before which individuals may assert the rights conferred on them by Community law. Since an infringement of those rights by a final decision of such a court cannot thereafter normally be corrected, individuals cannot be deprived of the possibility of rendering the state liable in order in that way to obtain legal protection of their rights.[177]

The conditions under which a final court can engage State liability are the same as those for any other organ of a State. As regards the seriousness of the breach, the Court explained:

[R]egard must be had to the specific nature of the judicial function and to the legitimate requirements of legal certainty... State liability for an infringement of Community law by a decision of a national

---

[175] Case C-15/96 [1998] ECR I-47.
[176] For analysis of the differences between the Advocate General's and the Court's approaches in this case, see Breuer, 'State Liability for Judicial Wrongs and Community Law: the Case of Gerhard Köbler v Austria' (2004) 29 ELRev 243.   [177] [2003] ECR I-10239, at 10306.

court adjudicating at last instance can be incurred only in the exceptional case where the court has manifestly infringed the applicable law.

In order to determine whether that condition is satisfied, the national court hearing a claim for reparation must take account of all the factors which characterise the situation put before it.

Those factors include, in particular, the degree of clarity and precision of the rule infringed, whether the infringement was intentional, whether the error of law was excusable or inexcusable, the position taken, where applicable, by a Community institution, and non-compliance by the court in question with its obligation to make a reference for a preliminary ruling under the third paragraph of Article 234.

In any event, an infringement of Community law will be sufficiently serious where the decision concerned was made in manifest breach of the case law of the Court of Justice in the matter . . . [178]

Although the determination of the question of whether liability has actually been established is normally a matter for the national court, the ECJ, according to its usual practice, was prepared in this case to supply guidance. It accepted that the *prima facie* indirect discrimination on the ground of nationality might be justifiable,[179] but denied that it was so justifiable on the argument adopted by the Austrian court; this was because the special increment involved in this case did not solely have the effect of rewarding the employee's loyalty to the employer,[180] and also because it led to a partitioning of the employment market for university professors in Austria and ran 'counter to the very principle of freedom of movement for workers'.[181] However, the ECJ accepted that the Austrian court had simply misunderstood the law on justification and, in particular, the judgment in *Schöning-Koigebetopoulou* (which had not answered the question of whether the loyalty argument could provide justification). The Austrian court, as a court of final instance, should indeed have referred this matter to the ECJ, and it breached Community law in not doing so.[182] Nevertheless, in these circumstances, the court's misconduct was not sufficiently 'manifest' for liability to be incurred.

R v HM Treasury, ex parte British Telecommunications plc[183] provided another illustration of a situation in which a Member State's breach of Community law was insufficiently grave to found a *Francovich* claim.[184] After reiterating that it is normally for the national courts to determine this matter, the ECJ held that in this instance it was in possession of all the necessary information to enable it to assess the gravity of the State's conduct itself. The allegation was that the UK had incorrectly implemented a directive and had caused consequential loss to BT. The Court held, however, that the relevant directive was imprecisely worded and reasonably

---

[178] [2003] ECR I-10239, at 10311–2.

[179] See ch 3 for discussion of the justification of indirect discrimination.

[180] This was because the increment rewarded professors who had worked for fifteen years in *any* State university in Austria, not just in the university which was their current employer.

[181] [2003] ECR I-10239, at 10320.

[182] For an interesting illustration of the obligations of final appellate courts pursuant to the principle of cooperation arising from Art 10, see Case C-453/00 *Kuhne & Heitz NV v Produktschap voor Pluimvee en Eieren*, judgment of 13 January 2004, nyr.

[183] Case C-392/93 [1996] ECR I-1631, noted by Oliver in (1997) 34 CMLRev 658.

[184] See also Cases C-283, 291, & 292/94 *Denkavit International v Bundesamt für Finanzen* [1996] ECR I-5063, and Case C-319/96 *Brinkmann Tabakfabriken GmbH v Skatteministeriet* [1998] ECR I-5255.

capable of bearing the meaning which the UK had in good faith given to it,[185] albeit that this interpretation later turned out to be erroneous. It was specifically noted that other Member States had shared the UK's interpretation of the directive, which was not manifestly contrary to its wording or objective, and that there was no case law of the Court to provide guidance as to its correct meaning.[186]

This decision is to be contrasted with those in *R v Ministry of Agriculture, Fisheries and Food, ex parte Hedley Lomas (Ireland) Ltd*[187] and *Dillenkofer v Germany*.[188] In the former, the UK had refused a licence for the export of live sheep for slaughter in a specified Spanish slaughterhouse because it suspected that the slaughterhouse in question was in breach of a directive on animal welfare. This was held to be a breach of what is now Article 29 on the free movement of goods and could not be justified by reference to Article 30, which allows exceptions 'for the protection of health and life of . . . animals', because one Member State is not permitted to adopt unilateral measures designed to obviate a breach of EU law by another Member State. In relation to the issue of whether this conduct was sufficiently serious to provide the basis for a claim in damages against the UK, the Court held:

[W]here, at the time when it committed the infringement, the Member State in question was not called upon to make any legislative choices and had only considerably reduced, or even no, discretion, the mere infringement of Community law may be sufficient to establish the existence of a sufficiently serious breach. In that respect, in this particular case, the UK was not even in a position to produce any proof of non-compliance with the directive by the slaughterhouse . . .[189]

In *Dillenkofer*, the main issue was the liability of Germany to would-be holidaymakers who had lost money when certain tour operators became insolvent; had Germany implemented a 1990 directive on package travel by the date stipulated, national law would have been in place guaranteeing the reimbursement of the plaintiffs. Germany argued that, since in its view the period provided for transposition of the directive was inadequate, it was not liable because its breach of Community law had not been manifest and grave; late transposition in itself, Germany maintained, was not enough to render a State liable in damages. The ECJ rejected these submissions, explaining that there was no inconsistency as between its decisions in *Francovich* and the later cases:

[T]he condition that there should be a sufficiently serious breach, although not expressly mentioned in *Francovich*, was nevertheless evident from the circumstances of that case. When the Court held that the conditions under which state liability gives rise to a right to reparation depended on the nature of

[185] The concept of good faith as applied to a State and its legislative machinery might be said to be somewhat elusive.
[186] In similar vein, see also Joined Cases C-283, 291, & 292/94 *Denkavit International v Bundesamt für Finanzen* [1996] ECR I-5063, and Case C-319/96 *Brinkmann Tabakfabriken GmbH v Skatteministeriet* [1998] ECR I-5255.
[187] Case C-5/94 [1996] ECR I-2553, noted by Oliver in (1997) 34 CMLRev 666. For further discussion of the *Brasserie, Factortame, BT*, and *Hedley Lomas* cases, see Emiliou, 'State Liability Under Community Law: Shedding More Light on the *Francovich* Principle' (1996) 21 ELRev 399.
[188] Joined Cases C-178, 179, 188, 189, & 190/94 [1996] ECR I-4845, noted by Oliver, op cit, n 187, at 675.   [189] [1996] ECR I-2553, at 2613–4.

the breach of Community law causing the damage, that meant that those conditions are to be applied according to each type of situation. On the one hand, a breach of Community law is sufficiently serious if a Community institution or a Member State, in the exercise of its rule-making powers, manifestly and gravely disregards the limits on those powers ... On the other hand, if, at the time when it committed the infringement, the Member State in question was not called upon to make any legislative choices and had only considerably reduced, or even no, discretion, the mere infringement of Community law may be sufficient to establish the existence of a sufficiently serious breach ...

So where, as in *Francovich*, a Member State fails, in breach of the third paragraph of Article [249] of the Treaty, to take any of the measures necessary to achieve the result prescribed by a directive within the period it lays down, that Member State manifestly and gravely disregards the limits on its discretion.[190]

Consequently, such a breach gives rise to a right to reparation on the part of individuals if the result prescribed by the directive entails the grant of rights to them, the content of those rights is identifiable on the basis of the provisions of the directive and a causal link exists between the breach of the state's obligation and the loss and damage suffered by the injured parties: no other conditions need be taken into consideration.[191]

The questions then arose of whether the directive entailed the grant of rights to individuals and, if so, whether the content of those rights was sufficiently identifiable. The Court held that the purpose of the directive was the protection of consumers[192] and that the fact that it might also have other objectives was irrelevant:

[I]t must be concluded that the result prescribed by ... the directive entails the grant to package travellers of rights guaranteeing the refund of money that they have paid over and their repatriation in the event of the organizer's insolvency.[193]

These rights were fully defined in the directive, as were the consumers it was intended to protect. It made no difference that the directive left the Member State considerable latitude as to how to achieve its results. The content of the rights conferred was therefore sufficiently identifiable.[194]

---

[190] Cf the ECJ's later qualification of this principle in Case C-319/96 *Brinkmann Tabakfabriken GmbH v Skatteministeriet* [1998] ECR I-5255.

[191] [1996] ECR I-4845, at 4879–80. See Hervey, '*Francovich* Liability Simplified' (1997) 26 ILJ 74.

[192] If such a general aim is sufficient for this purpose, it being clear from *Francovich* that the instrument need not be precise enough to take direct effect, it is difficult to imagine a provision which would *not* entail the grant of rights to individuals. All legislation is surely enacted with the ultimate goal of benefiting human beings. But for a more limited view of this requirement, see Anagnostaras, 'State Liability and Alternative Courses of Action: How Independent Can an Autonomous Remedy Be?' (2002) 21 YEL 355.   [193] [1996] ECR I-4845, at 4883.

[194] *Dillenkofer* was followed in Case C-140/97 *Rechberger and Greindl v Austria* [1999] ECR I-3499, in which the ECJ held that the transposition of one article of the Package Travel Directive in a way which limited the protection it conferred to trips with a departure date four months or more after the period prescribed for transposing the directive constituted a sufficiently serious breach of Community law to ground a *Francovich* claim; this was notwithstanding the fact that the Member State concerned had properly implemented all the other provisions of the instrument. See also Tridimas, 'Member State Liability in Damages' [1996] CLJ 412. Considerable uncertainty remains in the UK as to the relevant procedure applicable to *Francovich* actions: are they, for example, subject to the three-month limitation period for public law claims, or should they be equated to private law claims and thus subject to a six-year limitation period? What is the appropriate forum for such an action? For further discussion of the enforcement in the UK of the principles analysed in this section, see Convery, 'State Liability in the United Kingdom after *Brasserie du Pêcheur*' (1997) 34 CMLRev 603, and Hervey and Rostant, 'After *Francovich*: State Liability and British Employment Law' (1996) 25 ILJ 259.

Considerable importance is to be attached to the Court's statement in the *Brasserie* and *Factortame* cases that the rights of the individual must not be permitted to depend on who is the author of the impugned breach of EU law. The statement caused renewed interest to arise in the question of whether one individual is to be held liable to another where he or she causes loss to that other by infringing a directly effective Treaty provision. The question had been asked, but not answered, in *Banks Ltd v British Coal Corporation*,[195] where Van Gerven AG submitted:

[T]he right to obtain reparation in respect of loss and damage sustained as a result of an undertaking's infringement of Community competition rules which have direct effect is based on the Community legal order itself. Consequently, as a result of its obligation to ensure that Community law is fully effective and to protect the rights thereby conferred on individuals, the national court is under an obligation to award damages for loss sustained by an undertaking as a result of the breach by another undertaking of a directly effective provision of Community competition law.[196]

In *Courage Ltd v Crehan*,[197] which concerned a breach of the EU's competition rules by a brewery and resulting commercial losses to one of its tenants, the ECJ held that a claim by one legal person against another was indeed possible:

[A]ny individual can rely on a breach of Article 85(1) of the Treaty[198] before a national court even where he is a party to a contract that is liable to restrict or distort competition within the meaning of that provision. As regards the possibility of seeking compensation for loss caused by a contract or by conduct liable to restrict or distort competition, it should be remembered from the outset that, in accordance with settled case-law, the national courts whose task it is to apply the provisions of Community law in areas within their jurisdiction must ensure that those rules take full effect and must protect the rights which they confer on individuals . . . The full effectiveness of Article 85 of the Treaty and, in particular, the practical effect of the prohibition laid down in Article 85(1) would be put at risk if it were not open to any individual to claim damages for loss caused to him by a contract or by conduct liable to restrict or distort competition. Indeed, the existence of such a right strengthens the working of the Community competition rules and discourages agreements or practices, which are frequently covert, which are liable to restrict or distort competition. From that point of view, actions for damages before the national courts can make a significant contribution to the maintenance of effective competition in the Community.[199]

Although this justification of its decision relies heavily on the importance of the effective enforcement of the competition rules specifically, it seems likely that the ECJ was giving its support to a general principle that one individual is liable to another for loss caused by the breach of a directly effective Treaty provision. This appears from its formulation earlier in the *Courage* judgment of the familiar 'new legal order' principle:

It should be borne in mind, first of all, that the Treaty has created its own legal order, which is integrated into the legal systems of the Member States and which their courts are bound to apply. Just as it imposes burdens on individuals, Community law is also intended to give rise to rights which become part of their

---

[195] Case C-128/92 [1994] ECR I-1209.
[196] Ibid, at 1251. See also Van Gerven, 'Bridging the Unbridgable: Community and National Tort Laws After *Francovich* and *Brasserie*' (1996) 45 ICLQ 507.
[197] Case C-453/99 [2001] ECR I-6297.   [198] Today Art 81(1).
[199] [2001] ECR I-6297, at 6323.

legal assets. Those rights arise not only where they are expressly granted by the Treaty but also by virtue of obligations which the Treaty imposes in a clearly defined manner *both on individuals* and on Member States and the Community institutions...[200]

(vi) The need to implement directives

In the light of all that has now been decided about the direct effect of directives, it might appear that the distinction between regulations and directives has been almost entirely eroded and that, in particular, the requirement of the legislative implementation of directives—at least where those directives take direct effect—has now been dispensed with. After all, if a directive is immediately enforceable by individuals in the national courts, why should the Member States go to the trouble of legislating to give it legal force? One reason for doubting the validity of this argument has already been discussed: a directive cannot of itself take horizontal direct effect so that, in the absence of national legislation, its provisions will not be fully effective and enforceable by everybody who falls within its purview. In order to render it fully enforceable against persons other than the State (where this is envisaged by the terms of the directive itself), national legislation will be required.[201]

Further reasoning supporting the continuing necessity to implement even directly effective directives was provided by the ECJ in *Commission v Belgium*.[202] It held that legal certainty and clarity require that national legislation be enacted, because individuals cannot know for sure (without legal proceedings) that the directive is directly effective and they may easily become confused, if similar national legislation remains in force, as to which law actually governs their situation. In addition, without national implementing legislation, it becomes impossible for the Commission to check whether directives are in fact being applied in a given Member State. It is therefore necessary for the Member State not only to legislate to implement all directives, but to legislate by means of provisions which are of the same type as those used by the Member State to regulate similar matters domestically. Thus, for example, if ministerial regulations are the normal method in the UK for regulating a particular matter, then a directive in the same area should also be implemented by ministerial regulations so as to avoid confusion to the ordinary person. The direct effect of directives the ECJ sees as providing only an essential safety net or 'minimum guarantee' where the Member State does not carry out its EU obligations. Furthermore, the Court added that domestic political difficulties, which render it difficult or impossible for a Member State's government to procure the necessary legislation to implement a directive, are not a

---

[200] [2001] ECR I-6297, at 6321, emphasis added.

[201] Query whether a judicial decision could ever suffice as the entire implementation mechanism for a directive; the ECJ left this question open in Joined Cases C-178, 179, 188, 189, & 190/94 *Dillenkofer v Germany* [1996] ECR I-4845. In Case C-382/92 *Commission v UK* [1994] ECR I-2435, however, the ECJ accepted that the scope of national laws (and thus their compatibility with EC law) must be assessed in the light of the interpretation given to them by national courts.

[202] Case 102/79 [1980] ECR 1473. See also Case C-354/98 *Commission v France* [1999] ECR I-4927.

sufficient excuse. The Member State remains in default until such time as the implementing measures are enacted.[203]

The protection of individuals and their legal rights was also stressed by the ECJ in *Commission v Denmark*,[204] where it was successfully alleged by the Commission that Denmark had not properly implemented the Equal Pay Directive:[205] the relevant domestic law provided only for equal pay for the 'same work' performed by men and women, whereas the directive requires equal pay also where the work performed by the two sexes is of 'equal value'. The ECJ held:

> In that respect the Danish law in question does not exhibit the clarity and precision necessary for the protection of the workers concerned. Even accepting the assertions of the Danish government that the principle of equal pay for men and women, in the broad sense required by the Directive, is implemented in collective agreements, it has not been shown that the same implementation of that principle is guaranteed for workers whose rights are not defined in such agreements. Since those workers are not unionized and work in small or medium-sized businesses, particular care must be taken to protect their rights under the directive. The principles of legal certainty and the protection of individuals thus require an unequivocal wording which would give the persons concerned a clear and precise understanding of their rights and obligations and would enable the courts to ensure that those rights and obligations are observed.[206]

It is thus absolutely clear now that, even where a directive takes direct effect, its provisions must nevertheless be carried into full legal force by appropriate implementing measures enacted by the Member States.

(vii)   The principle of procedural autonomy

A further issue in relation to direct effect, which is important in practice and has been discussed many times by the ECJ, is precisely what is meant when it is said that a provision is 'enforceable' by individuals. Are particular means of enforcement or particular remedies required, and what procedural rules apply to the enforcement? As will be seen in chapters 4 and 5, the Equal Pay Directive, the Equal Treatment Directive, the Race Directive, and the Framework Directive all make special provision for the enforcement of their own clauses. However, the ECJ has commented in other contexts on the consequences of direct effect in general terms. In *Rewe-Zentralfinanz, eG and Rewe-Zentral AG v Landwirtschaftskammer fur das Saarland*,[207] the ECJ was asked whether a time-bar prescribed by national limitation legislation could operate to preclude the recovery of sums paid contrary

---

[203] Similarly, the ECJ held in Case 48/75 *State v Royer* [1976] ECR 497, that '[t]he freedom left to the member States by Article [249] as to the choice of form and methods of implementation of directives does not affect their obligation to choose the most appropriate forms and methods to ensure the effectiveness of the directives' (at 519). In Case C-187/98 *Commission v Greece* [1999] ECR I-7713, the ECJ held that a constitutional guarantee of sex equality was not sufficient to satisfy the demands of the Social Security Directive (discussed in ch 8) where legislation which breached the Directive also remained on the statute book.   [204] Case 143/83 [1985] ECR 427, discussed further in ch 4.
[205] Directive 75/117, OJ [1975] L45/19, discussed in detail in ch 4.
[206] [1985] ECR 427, at 435.   [207] Case 33/76 [1976] 2 ECR 1989.

to a directly effective provision of EU law. In holding that such a situation did not contravene EU law, the ECJ commented:

Applying the principle of cooperation laid down in Article [10] of the Treaty, it is the national courts which are entrusted with ensuring the legal protection which citizens derive from the direct effect of the provisions of Community law. Accordingly, in the absence of Community rules on this subject, it is for the domestic legal system of each Member State to designate the courts having jurisdiction and to determine the procedural conditions governing actions at law intended to ensure the protection of the rights which citizens have from the direct effect of Community law, it being understood that such conditions cannot be less favourable than those relating to similar actions of a domestic nature. Where necessary, Articles [94 to 97] and [308] of the Treaty enable appropriate measures to be taken to remedy differences between the provisions laid down by law, regulation or administrative action in Member States if they are likely to distort or harm the functioning of the Common Market. In the absence of such measures of harmonization the right conferred by Community law must be exercised before the national courts in accordance with the conditions laid down by national rules. The position would be different only if the conditions and time-limits made it impossible in practice to exercise the rights which the national courts are obliged to protect. This is not the case where reasonable periods of limitation of actions are fixed. The laying down of such time-limits with regard to actions of a fiscal nature is an application of the fundamental principle of legal certainty . . . [208]

Warner AG added that this is really a matter of common sense:

Where Community law confines itself to forbidding this or that kind of act on the part of a Member State and to saying that private persons are entitled to rely on the prohibition in their national courts, without prescribing the remedies or procedures available to them for that purpose, there is really no alternative to the application of the remedies and procedures prescribed by national law. The plaintiffs submitted that to allow national law to apply in such circumstances was to allow it to override Community law. I do not think that that is a correct description of the situation. I see it as a situation in which Community law and national law operate in combination, the latter taking over where the former leaves off, and working out its consequences.[209]

Thus it is clear that no special rules or procedures are required for the enforcement of directly effective EU law in the courts of the Member States. The applicable principle is said to be that of the 'procedural autonomy' of the Member States.[210] This means that national remedies and procedures are satisfactory, so long as they are also applied to similar domestic areas of law (the principle of 'equivalence' or 'non-discrimination')[211] and so long as they do not frustrate the

---

[208] Case 33/76 [1976] 2 ECR 1989, at 1997 8. See also Case 45/76 *Comet BV v Produktschap voor Siergewassen* [1976] 2 ECR 2043; Case 6/60 *Humblet v Belgium* [1960] ECR 559; Case 28/67 *Molkerei-Zentrale Westfalen/Lippe GmbH v Hauptzollamt Paderborn* [1968] ECR 143; Case 13/68 *Salgoil SpA v Italian Ministry of Foreign Trade* [1968] ECR 453; Case 120/73 *Lorenz v Germany* [1973] 2 ECR 1471; Case 60/75 *Russo v AIMA* [1976] ECR 45; Case 35/74 *Mutualités Chrétiennes v Rzepa* [1974] ECR 1241; Case 26/74 *Roquette v Commission* [1976] ECR 677; and Case 61/79 *Amministrazione delle Finanze dello Stato v Denkavit Italiana Srl* [1980] ECR 1205.   [209] Ibid, at 2003.
[210] For more detailed consideration of this principle, see Craig and de Búrca, op cit, n 110, at 230–57.
[211] Clearly a considerable area of discretion surrounds the scope of the comparison implied here; see further Case 199/82 *San Giorgio* [1983] ECR 3595; Case 68/88 *Commission v Greece* [1989] ECR 2965; Case C-62/93 *BP Supergas* [1995] ECR I-1883; Case C-261/95 *Palmisani* [1997] ECR I-4025; and Case C-180/95 *Draehmpaehl v Urania Immobilienservice ohG* [1997] ECR I-2195.

enforcement of the EC law in question (the principle of 'effectiveness').[212] This last element has been expressed somewhat variously by the Court; so, for example, it has held that the national procedural constraints must not be such as to 'render virtually impossible',[213] 'excessively difficult',[214] or 'impossible in practice'[215] the enforcement of the EU right in question. In *Peterbroeck v Belgium*,[216] it refined this element further, saying:

... each case which raises the question whether a national procedural provision renders application of Community law impossible or excessively difficult must be analysed by reference to the role of that provision in the procedure, its progress and its special features, viewed as a whole, before the various national instances. In the light of that analysis the basic principles of the domestic judicial system, such as protection of the rights of the defence, the principle of legal certainty and the proper conduct of procedure, must, where appropriate, be taken into consideration.[217]

Heukels has commented that this new formulation of the principle of effectiveness entails a detailed examination of the national procedural rules in question by the ECJ, which 'may bring the Court into the heart of the national judicial systems, a domain traditionally reserved to the Member States'.[218]

The principles of effectiveness and non-discrimination have given rise to difficulties in the UK in the context of the equal pay legislation.[219] UK law used to contain a two-year limitation period in respect of arrears of pay in an equal pay claim. The question was asked whether this satisfied the principle of non-discrimination; in other words, whether it was as favourable as that applied in similar purely domestic claims. In *Levez v Jennings (Harlow Pools) Ltd*,[220] the ECJ held that, since the Equal Pay Act 1970 was passed to give effect to the EU principle of equal pay, it was not appropriate to compare the procedural rules for the two claims; the net must be cast wider in the search for a domestic action equivalent to an action for breach of Article 141; in particular, Léger AG submitted that the comparator should be sought amongst domestic actions for the recovery of salary arrears, especially through employment law. And in *Preston*,[221] the ECJ added that the national court must consider whether the respective actions are

[212] See also Steiner, 'How to Make the Action Suit the Case' (1987) 12 ELRev 102.
[213] Case 199/82 *San Giorgio*, op cit, n 211, at 3616.
[214] Joined Cases C-6 & 9/90 *Francovich and Bonifaci v Italy* op cit, n 156, at 5416.
[215] Case 33/76 *Rewe Zentralfinanze eG v Landwirtschaftskammer fur das Saarland* [1976] 2 ECR 1989, and Case C-128/93 *Fisscher v Voorhuis Hengelo BV* [1994] ECR I-4583, at 4599.
[216] Case C-312/93 [1995] ECR I-4599.
[217] Ibid, at 4621. See also Joined Cases C-430 & 431/93 *Van Schijndel v Stichting Pensioenfonds voor Fysiotherapeuten* [1995] ECR I-4705; Hoskins, 'Tilting the Balance: Supremacy and National Procedural Rules' (1996) 21 ELRev 365; Szyszczak and Delicostopoulos, 'Intrusions into National Procedural Autonomy: The French Paradigm' (1997) 22 ELRev 141; Prechal, 'Community Law in National Courts: the Lessons from *Van Schijndel*' (1998) 35 CMLRev 681; and Van Gerven, 'Of Rights, Remedies and Procedures' (2000) 37 CMLRev 501.   [218] Heukels, (1996) 33 CMLRev 337.
[219] See ch 4 for discussion of Case C-78/98 *Preston v Wolverhampton Healthcare NHS Trust* [1999] ECR I-3201, and Case C-246/96 *Magorrian and Cunningham v Eastern Health & Social Services Board* [1997] ECR I-7153.   [220] Case C-326/96 [1998] ECR I-7835.
[221] Case C-78/98, op cit, n 219.

similar 'as regards their purpose, cause of action and essential characteristics'.[222]
These considerations led the UK Government to conclude that the nearest similar
action to one for breach of the equal pay obligation was an action for breach of
contract. Since the limitation period in actions for breach of contract is six years in
England and Wales,[223] that same limitation period was extended to claims for
arrears of pay in equal pay claims in England and Wales.[224] It is to be noted,
however, that the UK's problems in this area may not yet be at an end; as will be
seen in chapter 4, the Race Directive and the Framework Directive also prohibit
discrimination in relation to pay. However, UK law appears to contain no limitation on the period for which arrears of pay in these claims can be made; there is
thus potential for a further allegation that the principle of equivalence is still being
breached in relation to sex discrimination claims.

   To the principle that normal limitation periods are generally permissible in
relation to the enforcement of EU rights there used to be one important exception.
The ECJ held in *Emmott v Minister for Social Welfare*[225] that where a directive had
not been correctly implemented in national law, time could not begin to run
against the State in any action based on the direct effect of that instrument.
It explained that:

So long as a directive has not been properly transposed into national law, individuals are unable to
ascertain the full extent of their rights. That state of uncertainty for individuals subsists even after the
Court has delivered a judgment finding that the Member State in question has not fulfilled its obligations
under the directive and even if the Court has held that a particular provision or provisions of the
directive are sufficiently precise and unconditional to be relied upon before a national court.

   Only the proper transposition of the directive will bring that state of uncertainty to an end and it is
only upon that transposition that the legal certainty which must exist if individuals are to be required to
assert their rights is created.

   It follows that, until such time as a directive has been properly transposed, a defaulting Member State
may not rely on an individual's delay in initiating proceedings against it in order to protect rights
conferred upon him by the provisions of the directive and that a period laid down by national law
within which proceedings must be initiated cannot begin to run before that time.[226]

The application and extent of this principle were never free from doubt.[227] Later
decisions of the ECJ therefore suggested an inclination to limit it. In particular,

---

[222] Case C-78/98, op cit, n 219, at 3263.   [223] Pursuant to the Limitation Act 1980, s 5.
[224] By the Equal Pay Act 1970 (Amendment) Regulations 2003, SI 2003 No 1656. The corresponding limitation period in Scotland is five years. In addition, the new Regulations respond to the
concern expressed by the ECJ in *Levez* that no national provision conferred discretion to depart from the
strict rule that proceedings must be begun within six months of the ending of the contract of
employment, even when the delay has resulted from an employer deceiving an employee into thinking
that there has been no sex discrimination: see reg 4.
[225] Case C-208/90 [1991] ECR I-4269, noted by Szyszczak in (1992) 29 CMLRev 604.
[226] Ibid, at 4299.
[227] For example, was the principle affected by the TEU requirement of the publication in the Official
Journal of most directives? What was the meaning of 'properly transposed'? Could it be said that, where
a Member State had adequately implemented one part of a directive but not another, the *Emmott*
principle applied with respect to the whole instrument? How could a provision in a directive

in *Steenhorst-Neerings*[228] and *Johnson (No 2)*,[229] the Court held that it was permissible for a Member State to limit claims to arrears of a social security benefit, even where entitlement to the benefit concerned depended on a directive which the State had not properly implemented. In addition, in *Denkavit Internationaal BV v Kamer*,[230] Jacobs AG submitted that *Emmott* depended heavily on its own facts:

[T]he judgment in *Emmott*, notwithstanding its more general language, must be read as establishing the principle that a Member State may not rely on a limitation period where a Member State is in default both in failing to implement a directive and in obstructing the exercise of a judicial remedy in reliance upon it, or perhaps where the delay in exercising the remedy—and hence the failure to meet the time-limit—is in some other way due to the conduct of the national authorities. A further factor in *Emmott* was that the applicant was in the particularly unprotected position of an individual dependent on social welfare. Seen in those terms the *Emmott* judgment may be regarded as an application of the well established principle that the exercise of Community rights must not be rendered 'excessively difficult'.[231]

The *Emmott* principle was eventually rejected by the ECJ in *Fantask A/S v Industriministeriet*.[232] The Court dealt with the point cursorily, saying merely that *Emmott* must be regarded as confined to its own circumstances.[233] However, Jacobs AG discussed the matter very fully, concluding:

[M]y main reservations about a broad view of the *Emmott* ruling are that it disregards the need, recognized by all legal systems, for a degree of legal certainty for the State, particularly where infringements are comparatively minor or inadvertent; it goes further than is necessary to give effective protection to directives; and it places rights under directives in an unduly privileged position by comparison with other Community rights. Moreover a broad view cannot be reconciled with the Court's subsequent case-law on time-limits.[234]

Subsequent case law of the ECJ has confirmed that it is resolved to confine the *Emmott* principle to its own facts, specifically to situations in which the relevant

simultaneously be precise enough to take direct effect but still be legally uncertain as far as concerned the individual?

[228] Case C-338/91 *Steenhorst-Neerings v Bestuur van de Bedrijfsvereniging voor Detailhandel, Ambachten en Huisvrouwen* [1993] ECR I-5475, noted by Sohrab in (1994) 31 CMLRev 875 and discussed in ch 8.

[229] Case C-410/92 *Johnson v Chief Adjudication Officer* [1994] ECR I-5483, noted by Docksey in (1995) 32 CMLRev 1447 and also discussed in ch 8.

[230] Case C-2/94 [1996] ECR I-2827.

[231] Ibid, at 2851. See also the submissions of Jacobs AG in Case C-62/93 *BP Supergas v Greece* [1995] ECR I-1883, and see Coppel, 'Time Up for *Emmott*?' (1996) 25 ILJ 153. For analysis of the efficacy of the principle of procedural autonomy in the field of sex equality law, see McCrudden, 'The Effectiveness of European Equality Law: National Mechanisms for Enforcing Gender Equality Law in the Light of European Requirements' (1993) 13 OJLS 320.

[232] Case C-188/95 [1997] ECR I-6783, commented upon critically by Notaro in (1998) 35 CMLRev 1385.

[233] Mastroianni has argued that the decision of the ECJ in *Fantask* is at odds with its insistence that unimplemented directives cannot impose obligations on individuals (as to which, see discussion above); the effect of the *Fantask* ruling, in Mastroianni's view, is that a duty is indeed cast on individuals, namely, the duty to be aware of the content of a directive in order to exercise in a timely fashion the rights it seeks to grant: see 'On the Distinction Between Vertical and Horizontal Direct Effects of Community Directives: What Role for the Principle of Equality?' (1999) 5 EPL 417.

[234] [1997] ECR I-6783, at 6811.

time-bar has the result of depriving the claimant of any opportunity whatever of relying on the Community right in question.[235]

(viii)   Balancing the claims of national law and EU law

Another major defect in the doctrine of direct effect was demonstrated before the British courts. It is the absence of any guaranteed interim or emergency remedy where the enforceability of EU law is arguable but not yet determined. *R v Secretary of State for Transport, ex parte Factortame Ltd*[236] involved a claim that Community rights were being defeated by British legislation. In an attempt to prevent over-fishing, the common fisheries policy had fixed quotas for national fishing fleets. In response, the Merchant Shipping Act of 1988 was passed in the UK, its aim being to define and restrict those vessels whose catch could be considered part of the UK quota. Under the Act, the Secretary of State was empowered to make regula-tions for a new register of British shipping vessels. The resulting Merchant Shipping (Registration of Shipping Vessels) Regulations of 1988 provided that vessels could be registered only if their owners, or their share-holders, were British citizens or domiciled in Britain. The applicants for judicial review of these regulations were the owners of a large number of vessels; most of them were Spanish, but their vessels had under the previous legislation been treated as British because their catch was landed in the UK. Unable to satisfy the nationality requirement of the new regulations, they faced enormous economic difficulties. They were ineligible to fish against the Spanish quota; to lay up their vessels pending the litigation would have been prohibitively expensive; and if they sold the vessels, the price would be disastrously low because the market would be glutted. In these dire circumstances, the applicants sought an interim remedy from the British courts, to protect their right to continue to fish against the British quota, until such time as the ECJ gave a preliminary ruling explaining their rights and the position generally under EU law; such a ruling had been sought already by the Divisional Court but was expected to take two years to obtain. The owners' argument was that EU law gave them an enforceable right to fish against the British quota, and that the newly enacted British legislation attempted unlawfully to defeat that right. Nevertheless, the House of Lords at first unanimously refused to grant them any interim relief. Although conscious of the unsatisfactory nature of this result, Lord Bridge, making the only speech in the House, clearly believed that the only practicable remedy was for the ECJ to expedite the procedures by which it gave its preliminary ruling. He held:

If the applicants fail to establish the rights they claim before the ECJ, the effect of the interim relief granted would be to have conferred upon them rights directly contrary to Parliament's sovereign will

---

[235] See Case C-90/94 *Haahr Petroleum v benra Havn* [1997] ECR I-4085; Joined Cases C-114 & 115/95 *Texaco and Olieselskabet Danmark* [1997] ECR I-4263; Case C-231/96 *Edis v Ministero delle Finanze* [1998] ECR I-4951; and Case C-260/96 *Ministero delle Finanze v Spac* [1998] ECR I-4997.

[236] Op cit, n 34.

and correspondingly to have deprived British fishing vessels, as defined by Parliament, of the enjoyment of a substantial proportion of the UK quota of stocks of fish protected by the common fisheries policy... [A]s a matter of English law, the court has no power to make an order which has these consequences.[237]

The House of Lords faced an additional problem in this case too, namely, that for it to grant emergency relief here would have meant ordering an interim injunction against the Crown. After reviewing the fairly extensive case law on this matter, in particular since the passage of the Supreme Court Act 1981, their Lordships held that this was impossible as a matter of British law. They thereupon sought a preliminary ruling from the ECJ, asking whether, in circumstances such as those occurring in *Factortame*, EU law either obliges a national court to grant interim protection to the Community rights claimed, or gives the national court a discretion to grant such interim protection; in the event that the national court merely enjoys a discretion here, the House of Lords also wished for guidance from the ECJ as to the criteria it should apply in exercising that discretion.

The ECJ's reply[238] was disappointingly evasive. It focused its attention on the rule of domestic law preventing the ordering of an interim injunction against the Crown. Reiterating the reasoning it had given in *Amministrazione delle Finanze dello Stato v Simmenthal SpA*,[239] it ruled that a national court which, in a case before it concerning EU law, considers that the sole obstacle which precludes it from granting interim relief is a rule of national law, must set aside that rule. This, of course, was not really what the House of Lords was waiting to hear, because the rule about interim injunctions against the Crown was not the sole obstacle it faced. The ECJ solved only the simpler and more mechanical part of the problems posed in *Factortame*. It unfortunately made no attempt whatever to deal with the much more difficult issue of the criteria which should guide a national court which is trying to decide whether to grant interim relief for the protection of disputed EU rights. The problem could be particularly acute in an anti-discrimination claim, where irreparable harm may well be done to a person's rights in the period intervening between the claim and any preliminary ruling needed to substantiate it.

The case thus returned to the House of Lords with nobody very much the wiser as to what should occur next, and with a very real danger of substantial variations in practice developing as between the different Member States. The House itself heard further evidence as to the predicament of the Spanish applicants and then granted them an interim injunction.[240] Its reasoning was given some three months later.[241] Lord Goff's was the leading speech in the House of Lords. He explained that the jurisdiction of the English courts to grant interim injunctions was contained in s 37 of the Supreme Court Act 1981, by virtue of which the court had power to grant an injunction in all cases in which it appeared to it to be just or convenient to do so; guidelines for the exercise of this jurisdiction were laid down

---

[237] Ibid, at 1014.   [238] Case C-213/89 [1990] ECR I-2433.
[239] Case 106/77 [1978] ECR 629.   [240] Order of 9 July 1990.   [241] [1990] 3 WLR 818.

by Lord Diplock in the House of Lords in *American Cyanamid Co v Ethicon Ltd*.[242]
As a result, in the words of Lord Goff:

It is now clear that it is enough if [a party seeking an interim injunction] can show that there is a serious
case to be tried. If he can establish that, then he has, so to speak, crossed the threshold; and the court can
then address itself to the question whether it is just or convenient to grant an injunction.[243]

The first issue, according to Lord Goff, is thus the adequacy of damages as a
remedy to either party. If damages are an adequate remedy for the claimant, this
will normally preclude the grant of an injunction. If damages would not provide
an adequate remedy for the claimant then the court has to consider whether, if an
injunction is granted against the defendant, there will be an adequate remedy in
damages to him or her under the claimant's undertaking in damages; if so, there
will be no reason on this ground to refuse to grant the interim injunction. The issue
assumes special significance in cases where the validity of legislation is at stake. For
example, it may not be thought right to impose an undertaking in damages against
the Crown. In addition, there is no general right in the UK to indemnity in respect
of damage suffered through invalid administrative action, so that no remedy in
damages would have been available to the applicant fishermen in this case for loss
suffered by them as a result of enforcement of the 1988 Act, should it eventually
turn out that that Act was in contravention of EU law. Conversely, a public
authority acting in the general public interest cannot normally be protected by a
remedy in damages because it will itself have suffered none. It follows, said Lord
Goff: '[T]hat, as a general rule, in cases of this kind involving the public interest,
the problem cannot be solved at the first stage, and it will be necessary for the court
to proceed to the second stage, concerned with the balance of convenience.'[244] In
relation to this second stage, in cases of this sort where one party is a public
authority performing duties to the public, particular stress has to be placed on the
importance of upholding the law. This means that if a public authority seeks to
enforce what is on its face the law of the land, and the person against whom such
action is taken challenges the validity of that law, 'matters of considerable weight
have to be put into the balance to outweigh the desirability of enforcing, in the
public interest, what is on its face the law . . .'.[245] Nevertheless, Lord Goff was
not prepared to go so far as to say that, in such cases, the party challenging the
validity of the law must show 'a strong *prima facie* case that the law is invalid'.
He concluded that:

[T]he court should not restrain a public authority by interim injunction from enforcing an apparently
authentic law unless it is satisfied, having regard to all the circumstances, that the challenge to the validity
of the law is, *prima facie*, so firmly based as to justify so exceptional a course being taken.[246]

Applying these principles to the facts of the case, two matters in particular
appeared to weigh with the House of Lords. The first was that recent case law of

---

[242] [1975] AC 396.   [243] [1990] 3 WLR 818, at 869.   [244] Ibid, at 870.   [245] Ibid.
[246] Ibid, at 871.

the ECJ[247] reinforced the likely strength in law of the applicants' case.[248] The second was the enormity and the immediacy of the damage they would suffer if the injunction was not granted and the legislation were subsequently to prove invalid. The House was therefore ultimately persuaded to exercise its discretion in favour of the grant of the injunction.

Further light has since been shed by the ECJ on the issue of the interim protection of alleged Community rights. In *Zuckerfabrik Süderdithmarschen AG v Hauptzollamt Itzehoe*,[249] the Court aligned the principles applicable to the suspension of national law which is alleged to conflict with Community rights with the suspension of national law implementing Community law which is alleged to be invalid. In *Kruger*,[250] it confirmed its earlier case law[251] on the criteria on the basis of which a national court may decide to suspend implementation of a domestic administrative decision because of its doubts as to the validity of the Community act which is its basis:

Interim relief can be ordered by a national court only if:

—that court entertains serious doubts as to the validity of the Community act and, if the validity of the contested act is not already in issue before the Court of Justice, itself refers the question to the Court;

—there is urgency, in that the interim relief is necessary to avoid serious and irreparable damage being caused to the party seeking the relief;

—the national court takes due account of the Community interest; and

—in its assessment of all those conditions, the national court respects any decisions of the Court of Justice or the Court of First Instance ruling on the lawfulness of the Community act or on an application for interim measures seeking similar interim relief at Community level.[252]

The Commission had argued that, in taking due account of the Community interest, a national court which is contemplating granting interim relief must give the Community institution whose act is being impugned an opportunity to express its views. To this the Court merely replied:

It is for the national court which has to assess the Community interest upon an application for interim relief to decide, in accordance with its own rules of procedure, which is the most appropriate way of obtaining all relevant information on the Community act in question.[253]

The constitutional scope of EU law

When the two qualities of supremacy and direct effect of EC law are considered together and in the light of the now highly sophisticated case law of the ECJ, it is

---

[247] In particular, Case 246/89R *Commission v UK* [1989] ECR 3125; Case C-3/87 *R v Minister of Agriculture and Fisheries, ex parte Agegate Ltd* [1989] ECR 4459; and Case C-216/87 *R v Minister of Agriculture and Fisheries, ex parte Jaderow Ltd* [1989] ECR 4509.

[248] As eventually demonstrated in Case C-221/89 *R v Secretary of State for Transport, ex parte Factortame Ltd (No 3)* [1991] ECR I-3905.   [249] Joined Cases C-143/88 & C-92/89 [1991] ECR I-415.

[250] Case C-334/95 *Kruger GmbH v Hauptzollamt Hamburg-Jonas* [1997] ECR I-4517.

[251] Joined Cases C-143/88 & C-92/89 *Zuckerfabrik Süderdithmarschen AG v Hauptzollamt Itzehoe* [1991] ECR I-415, and Case C-465/93 *Atlanta Fruchthandelsgesellschaft* [1995] ECR I-3761.

[252] [1997] ECR I-4517, at 4552–3.   [253] Ibid, at 4553.

obvious that they are of the utmost potential significance from the viewpoint of individuals claiming equality of opportunity. Together they make it possible for EU law to confer a 'constitutional' type of protection for the principles of non-discrimination and equality. There is a parallel here to be drawn with the attempts made some years ago in the USA to add an 'equal rights' amendment to the Federal Constitution, which would have protected citizens against unequal treatment by any of the States of the Union. Not only can the EU principle of equality be invoked by individuals in actions before their national courts, but it must prevail over any conflicting legislative provision in the Member States, even one contained in the country's constitution.

3

Key concepts in EU
anti-discrimination law

It was seen in chapter 1 that EU law contains specific prohibitions of discrimination on the grounds of nationality, sex, part-time and temporary working, racial or ethnic origin, religion or belief, disability, age, and sexual orientation. It was also seen that the concepts of non-discrimination and equality span a spectrum from the simple prescription of formal equality to the positive pursuit of equality of opportunity, fair participation, or even equality of results. EU law reflects a large part of this spectrum in its anti-discrimination provisions. Thus, the TEC expressly forbids 'discrimination' against specified groups of people;[1] however, it also refers to the broader principles of 'equal opportunities and equal treatment'[2] and offers as one of its aims 'ensuring full equality in practice between men and women in working life'.[3] Similarly, the secondary legislation seeks to put into effect in the Member States the 'principle of equal treatment'[4] and makes 'equality' one of its express goals.[5]

In practice, it is to the concept of 'discrimination' that the ECJ has given the most attention to date. Whilst the Treaty itself refers merely to 'discrimination', the secondary instruments of EU law[6] sub-divide the general concept into 'direct' and 'indirect' manifestations of discrimination. The Court's understanding of these expressions has evolved considerably over time. It has defined discrimination as: '[T]he application of different rules to comparable situations or the application of the same rule to different situations.'[7]

Without seeking to pre-empt the detailed discussion which follows about the meaning of direct and indirect discrimination, it needs to be explained broadly at the outset that direct discrimination occurs where, on one of the protected grounds,

---

[1] See, in particular, Arts 12, 13(1), 39(2), and 141(2).   [2] Art 141(3).   [3] Art 141(4).
[4] The Equal Treatment Directive, Art 1(1); the Race Directive, Art 1; and the Framework Directive, Art 1.
[5] The Equal Treatment Directive, in Art 1a, refers to 'the objective of equality between men and women'; the Race and Framework Directives refer rather more expansively to their objectives of 'ensuring full equality in practice' (respectively Arts 5 and 7).
[6] In particular, the Equal Treatment Directive, the Social Security Directive, the Burden of Proof Directive (Directive 97/80, OJ [1998] L14/6), the Race Directive, and the Framework Directive.
[7] Case C-279/93 *Finanzampt Koln-Altstadt v Schumacker* [1995] ECR I-225, at 259. For a practical example in the field of sex discrimination, see Case C-218/98 *Abdoulaye v Renault SA* [1999] ECR I-5723.

one person is treated less favourably than another person. The prohibition therefore seeks to protect the principle of formal equality. The rule against indirect
discrimination, on the other hand, represents an attempt to provide a greater degree
of substantive equality, in particular, equality of opportunity. Indirect discrimination is encountered where some requirement is demanded, some practice is
applied, or some other action is taken which produces an 'adverse impact' for a
protected class of persons. For example, in *Jenkins v Kingsgate (Clothing Productions)
Ltd*,[8] Warner AG, referring to earlier cases before the ECJ on the nationality
provisions, defined indirect discrimination as follows:

These cases . . . establish that a rule which, on the face of it, differentiates between people on the basis of a
criterion other than nationality nonetheless infringes a provision of Community law forbidding such
discrimination if its application leads in fact to the same result, unless the differentiation is justifiable on
'objective' grounds. I can see no reason for applying a different principle to sex discrimination.[9]

Because of its greater longevity, the law on sex discrimination and on nationality
has provided the back-drop for the ECJ's decisions to date on the concept of
discrimination. It seems indubitable, however, that the principles which it has
evolved will also (subject to legislative modification) embrace the fields occupied
by the Race Directive and the Framework Directive.

Direct discrimination

The ECJ's understanding of the concept of direct discrimination is largely to
be gleaned from the way in which it has contrasted it with indirect discrimination.
An early *excursus* into this distinction came with the Court's analysis of the ambit of
the equal pay principle, today contained in Article 141 of the Treaty. This requires
application of the principle of equal pay for male and female workers for equal
work, or for work of equal value. It thus *prima facie* requires simply the identical
treatment of men and women as regards pay; nothing whatsoever is to be permitted
to create a differential between the two groups. So formulated, the Article does not
appear to distinguish between sex-related distinctions and others. It simply forbids
all distinctions. However—and this is probably the only practicable line to take—
this is not how the ECJ came to apply the Article. Instead, it interpreted it as
meaning that there must be no discrimination between the sexes over pay where
they perform equal work or work of equal value, a conclusion reinforced by the
wording of the second paragraph of Article 141(2) and reflected in the national
legislation of the Member States. In other words, the Court held that there must

[8] Case 96/80 [1981] ECR 911. See also Crisham, 'The Equal Pay Principle: Some Recent
Decision of the ECJ' (1981) 18 CMLRev 601; Post, 'New Decisions of the European Court on
Sex Discrimination' (1981) 1 LIEI 77; and Plender, 'Equal Pay for Men and Women: Two Recent
Decisions of the European Court' (1982) 30 American Journal of Comparative Law 627.
[9] [1981] ECR 911, at 937. The concept of adverse impact discrimination was articulated by the
US Supreme Court in *Griggs v Duke Power Co* (1971) 401 US 425.

be no distinction made on the basis of sex within the scope of the Article.[10] This necessarily indicates that certain other distinctions over pay will be permitted, provided only that they are not in any way based on sex. It thus opens up the possibility of a causation-based defence to an equal pay claim.[11] It also led the Court to have to define discrimination. The real starting point came with its decision in *Defrenne v Sabena*,[12] where it held:

[A] distinction must be drawn within the whole area of application of Article 119 between, first, direct and overt discrimination which may be identified solely with the aid of the criteria based on equal work and equal pay referred to by the Article in question and, secondly, indirect and disguised discrimination which can only be identified by reference to more explicit implementing provisions of a Community or national character. It is impossible not to recognize that the complete implementation of the aim pursued by Article 119, by means of the elimination of all discrimination, direct or indirect, between men and women workers, not only as regards individual undertakings but also entire branches of industry and even of the economic system as a whole, may in certain cases involve the elaboration of criteria whose implementation necessitates the taking of appropriate measures at Community and national level.[13]

This early attempt to explain the difference between direct and indirect discrimination was confusing; direct discrimination is here linked with overt conduct, while indirect discrimination is linked with disguise. Yet, notionally at least, either sort of discrimination can be either overt or disguised; and, in practice, it is more often direct discrimination which is disguised by its perpetrator, whilst indirect discrimination is frequently quite overt. To take an example, an employer will rarely openly admit to preferring to appoint a man, even if this is in fact the reality of the position. Conversely, where an employer is guilty of indirect discrimination, say through the imposition of an unnecessary qualification for a particular job, the insistence on the qualification will often be quite overt. In addition, in relation to nationality at least, the Court had not hitherto refused to apply EU law directly just because the discrimination was covert.[14] Furthermore, the distinction that the ECJ appeared to be making did not correspond to the categories of direct and indirect discrimination generally recognized in national legal systems. In reality, the distinction which the Court seems to have been trying to make in *Defrenne* was simply between discrimination which can be identified without the need for further explanatory legislation and that which cannot. Van Themaat AG explained this in *Burton v British Railways Board*,[15] saying:

[T]he distinction drawn in the *Second Defrenne* judgment between overt and disguised discrimination which is important in determining whether or not Article 119 is directly applicable, does not coincide

[10] See also the remarks of Lord Lowry in *Hasley v Fair Employment Agency* [1989] IRLR 106, at 111.
[11] But it is important to notice that no other excuses or defences are articulated by Article 141 (except, possibly in relation to positive action, which is discussed in ch 6).
[12] Case 43/75 [1976] ECR 455, often referred to as the *Second Defrenne* case.   [13] Ibid, at 473.
[14] See the remarks of Warner AG in Case 69/80 *Worringham v Lloyds Bank Ltd* [1981] ECR 767, at 802–3.   [15] Case 19/81 [1982] ECR 555.

with a factual distinction between direct discrimination or discrimination in form, on the one hand, and indirect discrimination or discrimination in substance, on the other.[16]

Nevertheless, the Court repeated its original formula in *Macarthys Ltd v Smith*.[17] However, a year later, in *Worringham v Lloyds Bank Ltd*,[18] it changed its wording, and it dropped the expressions 'direct and overt' and 'indirect and disguised'. It could therefore be concluded that, henceforth, direct discrimination could be both overt and covert.

Today, the Equal Treatment Directive, the Race Directive, and the Framework Directive each contain statutory definitions of direct discrimination governing their respective fields of operation. Thus:

Direct discrimination: where one person is treated less favourably on grounds of sex than another is, has been or would be treated in a comparable situation.[19]

[D]irect discrimination shall be taken to occur where one person is treated less favourably than another is, has been or would be treated in a comparable situation on grounds of racial or ethnic origin.[20]

[D]irect discrimination shall be taken to occur where one person is treated less favourably than another is, has been or would be treated in a comparable situation, on any of the grounds referred to in Article 1.[21]

It is noteworthy that these definitions all embrace hypothetical comparisons, as well as comparisons with the treatment received by actual persons.[22] However, it should also be noted that this is the point at which the first schism is encountered between the different grounds of discrimination covered by EU law; this body of law is in general targeted at particular types of differentiation between human beings which have been legislatively deemed 'morally irrelevant' in the sense discussed in chapter 1. Thus, for example (subject to any specific defences permitted), racial or ethnic origin is treated by the law as irrelevant within the fields covered by

---

[16] Case 19/81 [1982] ECR 555, at 582. The direct enforceability of the non-discrimination principle is discussed further below.   [17] Case 129/79 [1980] ECR 1275.

[18] Op cit, n 14.

[19] Art 2(2) of the Equal Treatment Directive, as amended by Directive 2002/73, OJ [2002] L269/15. Recital 6 of the Preamble to this Directive states that this definition is intended to be consistent with the definition of direct discrimination for the purposes of the Race Directive and the Framework Directive. In Case C-79/99 *Schnorbus v Land Hessen* [2000] ECR I-10997, Jacobs AG explained further that discrimination on the ground of sex 'arises where members of one sex are treated more favourably than the other. The discrimination is direct where the difference in treatment is based on a criterion which is either explicitly that of sex or necessarily linked to a characteristic indissociable from sex' (at 11008). But note the unfortunate consequences of a less rigorously analytical application of such a concept in the submissions of Alber AG (not followed by the ECJ) in Case C-366/99 *Griesmar* [2001] ECR I-9383. Discrimination grounded on pregnancy is discussed in ch 5.

[20] Art 2(2)(a) of the Race Directive.

[21] Art 2(2)(a) of the Framework Directive. In the case of age, it is especially difficult to envisage how such a comparison is to occur; if someone aged (say) 60 alleges discrimination, with what other age is comparison to be made?

[22] In some domestic jurisdictions, the concept of direct discrimination also extends to hypothetical comparisons with how another person would be treated; see, eg, the UK's Sex Discrimination Act 1975, s 1(1)(a), and the Race Relations Act 1976, s 1(1)(a).

the Race Directive. However, one of the grounds contained in the Framework Directive is not defined in such general terms; disability is subjected to asymmetrical treatment. Article 1 of the instrument forbids discrimination 'on the ground... of... disability', with the result that it is only those who are disabled and not those who are able-bodied who are protected by the law. This formulation can be seen to reflect a different underlying philosophy for the disability provisions from the rest of the anti-discrimination legislation; they are more clearly directed to relieving the disadvantage experienced by the disabled section of society than to protecting a fundamental human right possessed by everybody.

Indirect discrimination

Perhaps not surprisingly in view of its more complex nature, the definition of indirect discrimination presented more problems for the ECJ than the definition of direct discrimination. Confusion resulted, in particular, from the existence during the evolution of the concept of different definitions of indirect discrimination in the various areas of anti-discrimination law.

It will be recalled that, broadly speaking, indirect discrimination occurs where an unjustified adverse impact is produced for a protected class of persons by an apparently class-neutral action. A serious problem arose over whether such adverse impact must actually have occurred, or whether it was sufficient for it merely to be anticipated. In the area of nationality discrimination, the ECJ was content, in *O'Flynn v Adjudication Officer*,[23] with proof of merely contingent harm:

[U]nless objectively justified and proportionate to its aim, a provision of national law must be regarded as indirectly discriminatory if it is intrinsically liable to affect migrant workers more than national workers and if there is a consequent risk that it will place the former at a particular disadvantage. It is not necessary in this respect to find that the provision in question does in practice affect a substantially higher proportion of migrant workers. It is sufficient that it is liable to have such an effect.[24]

However, this was not the line taken by its case law in relation to sex discrimination. In its first decision in this area, *Jenkins v Kingsgate (Clothing Productions) Ltd*,[25] the Court appeared to emphasize the importance of being able to prove actual adverse impact. A woman part-time employee complained that she received some 10% less pay per hour than a male colleague employed full-time on the same work. At the time of the proceedings, the part-time workers employed by the respondent were all female, with the exception of one male part-timer who had just retired and who had, exceptionally and for short periods, been allowed to go on working. This situation generally reflected the employment pattern of the UK, where the great majority of part-time workers, both at the date of the case and

---

[23] Case C-237/94 [1996] ECR I-2617.   [24] Ibid, at 2638–9.
[25] Case 96/80, op cit, n 8. See also Snaith, 'Sex Discrimination and the Part-Time Worker' (1981) 6 ELRev 196.

today, are women.[26] The Employment Appeal Tribunal wanted to know from the ECJ whether the Treaty forbade paying part-time workers less than full-time workers, when the category of part-timers is exclusively or predominantly composed of women. The ECJ ruled that:

[T]he purpose of Article 119 is to ensure the application of the principle of equal pay for men and women for the same work. The differences in pay prohibited by that provision are therefore exclusively those based on the difference of the sex of the workers. Consequently the fact that part-time work is paid at an hourly rate lower than pay for full-time work does not amount *per se* to discrimination prohibited by Article 119 provided that the hourly rates are applied to workers belonging to either category without distinction based on sex.[27]

However, the Court went on to add:

[I]f it is established that a considerably smaller percentage of women than of men perform the minimum number of weekly working hours required in order to be able to claim the full-time hourly rate of pay, the inequality in pay will be contrary to Article 119 of the Treaty where, regard being had to the difficulties encountered by women in arranging to work that minimum number of hours per week, the pay policy of the undertaking in question cannot be explained by factors other than discrimination based on sex. Where the hourly rate of pay differs according to whether the work is part-time or full-time it is for the national courts to decide in each individual case whether, regard being had to the facts of the case, its history and the employer's intention, a pay policy such as that which is at issue in the main proceedings although represented as a difference based on weekly working hours is or is not in reality discrimination based on the sex of the worker. The reply to the first three questions must therefore be that a difference in pay between full-time workers and part-time workers does not amount to discrimination prohibited by Article 119 of the Treaty unless it is in reality merely an indirect way of reducing the level of pay of part-time workers on the ground that that group of workers is composed exclusively or predominantly of women.[28]

As will be seen in later chapters of the present work, disadvantageous treatment of part-time workers compared to full-time workers has very often been treated as *prima facie* indirectly discriminatory by the ECJ, on the basis that many more women than men are obliged by their domestic responsibilities to opt for part-time work. However, this statement is deceptively simple; it can in

---

[26] See Robinson, 'Part-Time Employment in the European Community' (1979) 118 International Labour Review 299, and the evidence presented to the ECJ by the Commission in Case 171/88 *Rinner-Kühn v FWW Spezial Gebaudereinigung GmbH* [1989] IRLR 493. The 1995 New Earnings Survey showed that 80% of part-time workers in the UK at that date were female; in the EU as a whole at the same date over 80% of those working part time were women. see *Equal Opportunities for Women and Men in the European Union: Annual Report 1996* (Commission, Luxembourg, 1997). The figure for the whole EU was 81.4% in 2002: see *Advancing Women in the Workplace: statistical analysis* (EOC, Manchester, 2004). In all the Member States of the EU, a much larger proportion of women than men works part-time; in 2002, eg, 44% of the UK female workforce was part-time as against only 9.4% of the male workforce; in the EU as a whole, these figures were 33.5% and 6.6% respectively: European Foundation for the Improvement of Living and Working Conditions, www.eurofound.eu.int.

[27] [1981] ECR 911, at 925.

[28] Ibid, at 925–6. See also Case C-167/97 *R v Secretary of State for Employment, ex parte Seymour-Smith* [1999] ECR I-623. In Case C-333/97 *Lewen v Denda* [1999] ECR I-7243, the ECJ took judicial notice of the fact that women take parental leave far more often than men.

reality be difficult to determine when there actually is disadvantageous treatment for part-timers. For example, in *Elsner-Lakeberg v Land Nordrhein-Westfalen*,[29] a part-time teacher alleged indirect discrimination where, like her full-time colleagues, she was paid overtime only if she worked more than three extra hours per month. Was this facially equal treatment in fact disadvantageous to part-timers? Jacobs AG submitted that the critical issue was whether the overall pay of full-timers was higher than that of part-timers for the same number of hours worked. He relied for this principle on *Helmig*,[30] where overtime supplements were paid alike to full and part-timers who worked in excess of normal full-time hours; the Court there held that there was no discrimination because all employees received the same rate of overall pay. However, in *Elsner-Lakeberg*, Jacobs AG pointed out that where a part-timer, normally working 15 hours per week, worked an additional 2.5 hours, and thus clocked up 17.5 hours in the relevant week, he or she would not receive the same overall pay as that received by a full-timer for 17.5 hours worked. He therefore concluded that there was *prima facie* indirect discrimination on these facts. The Court reached the same conclusion, but on the significantly different basis that the burden to be discharged before qualifying for overtime was greater for part-timers than full-timers:

A full-time teacher must work an additional three hours over his regular monthly schedule of 98 hours, which is approximately 3% extra, in order to be paid for his additional hours, whilst a part-time teacher must work three hours more than his monthly 60 hours, which is 5% extra. Since the number of additional teaching hours giving entitlement to pay is not reduced for part-time teachers in a manner proportionate to their working hours, they receive different treatment compared with full-time teachers as regards pay for additional teaching hours.[31]

An unusual application of the principle that differential treatment of the part-time workforce is potentially indirectly discriminatory is to be seen in *Kachelmann v Bankhaus Hermann Lampe KG*.[32] German redundancy legislation required employers to have regard to 'social reasons' when selecting employees for redundancy; this was interpreted to mean that the employer must look at the individual circumstances of employees and decide to whom the loss of employment would cause the least harm. However, the legislation also provided that full-timers and part-timers could not be compared for this purpose. The ECJ ruled that this situation was potentially indirectly discriminatory, since the number of workers employed full-time in Germany (and probably throughout the Community) was significantly higher in all sectors than the number of part-time workers; thus, where jobs are being cut, part-time workers are in general at a greater disadvantage because they have a lesser chance of finding another comparable job.

[29] Case C-285/02, judgment of 27 May 2004, nyr.
[30] Joined Cases C-399, 409, & 425/92, C-34, 50, & 78/93 [1994] ECR I-5727, discussed further below.   [31] At para 17 of the judgment.
[32] Case C-322/98 [2000] ECR I-7505.

The definition of indirect discrimination was formalized for sex discrimination generally by Article 2(2) of the Burden of Proof Directive:[33]

For the purposes of the principle of equal treatment referred to in paragraph 1, indirect discrimination shall exist where an apparently neutral provision, criterion or practice disadvantages a substantially higher proportion of the members of one sex unless that provision, criterion or practice is appropriate and necessary and can be justified by objective factors unrelated to sex.

However, the matter became further confounded when the Race and Framework Directives were enacted, because each adopted a test for indirect discrimination based on contingent harm:

[I]ndirect discrimination shall be taken to occur where an apparently neutral provision, criterion or practice *would put* persons of a racial or ethnic origin at a particular disadvantage compared with other persons, unless that provision, criterion or practice is objectively justified by a legitimate aim and the means of achieving that aim are appropriate and necessary.[34]

There is much to be said in favour of such a contingent definition; in particular, although it may sometimes be fairly obvious as a matter of common sense that a practice produces an adverse impact for a particular group, it may prove very difficult in practice to produce statistical evidence to support such a claim.[35] This is especially true in relation to sensitive areas, such as discrimination on the ground of sexual orientation, where statistics are unlikely to be obtainable.[36] A contingent test of harm obviates the need for such evidence.[37] Moreover, where a law provides that a particular situation is prohibited, it is in principle not usually necessary to wait for actual harm to occur; most legal systems try to injunct such damage before it occurs. Arguments of this kind prevailed when the Race and Framework Directives were being negotiated, but it was also appreciated that it would be unacceptable to retain a different, and stricter, test for sex discrimination. Accordingly, the Equal Treatment Directive was amended in 2002,[38] so as to bring its definition of indirect discrimination in line with that operating for nationality, race, and the Framework Directive. Article 2(2) of the Equal Treatment therefore today defines indirect discrimination as occurring:

[W]here an apparently neutral provision, criterion or practice would put persons of one sex at a particular disadvantage compared with persons of the other sex, unless that provision, criterion or

---

[33] Directive 97/80, OJ [1998] L14/6.

[34] Art 2(2)(b) of the Race Directive, emphasis added. In identical vein, Art 2(2)(b) of the Framework Directive refers to provisions, criteria, or practices which 'would put' persons having a particular religion or belief, a particular disability, a particular age, or a particular sexual orientation at a disadvantage. The ECJ will have to clarify at the earliest possible opportunity how 'particular' is to be interpreted.

[35] Recital 15 of the Preambles to both the Race Directive and the Framework Directive states that rules of national law and practice may provide for indirect discrimination to be established by any means 'including' on the basis of statistical evidence.

[36] Some Member States, for example, Denmark and Sweden, are prohibited by their data protection laws from collecting statistical data relating to racial origin.

[37] For stringent criticism of the use of statistics, in particular in the context of preliminary rulings from the ECJ, see Barnard and Hepple, 'Indirect Discrimination: Interpreting *Seymour-Smith*' (1999) 58 CLJ 399.   [38] By Directive 2002/73, OJ [2002] L269/15.

practice is objectively justified by a legitimate aim, and the means of achieving that aim are appropriate and necessary.[39]

It is clearly crucial to the establishment of indirect discrimination that the complainant is able to identify a group of persons with whom to make a comparison so that it can be alleged that the comparators receive more advantageous treatment. The selection of the comparator group is an issue over which courts possess an important element of discretion, and the extent to which they take a sensitive approach to it bears directly upon the capacity of the concept of indirect discrimination to intervene to produce effective equality. A disappointing exercise of this judicial discretion can be seen in *Gruber v Silhouette International Schmied GmbH & Co KG*.[40] Ms Gruber terminated her contract of employment because she was unable to obtain childcare. The relevant Austrian legislation provided that, where an employment relationship had lasted for three years, the employee was entitled to a termination payment. However, this only applied to terminations instigated by the employee if the termination was for 'important reasons'. The important reasons listed did not mention childcare responsibilities; however, another legislative provision entitled workers who had worked for at least five years to half the usual termination payment where they left their job on childbirth. Ms Gruber alleged that this situation constituted indirect discrimination in breach of Article 141. It was clear that the termination payment was 'pay' for the purposes of that Article,[41] so the main issue was whether it was provided on sex discriminatory terms. Ms Gruber argued that the groups to be compared were workers who resigned from employment because of maternity and those who resigned for 'important reasons'. When this comparison was made, it was obvious that women were disadvantaged because the first group received only half the termination payment received by the second group. However, the employer responded that the comparator groups should be workers resigning for maternity and those resigning without 'important reasons'; if this basis was used, women were not disadvantaged since they at least received half the termination payment, whereas the comparator group received nothing. The ECJ therefore reasoned that the issue was whether maternity could be aligned with 'important reasons'. One might, in reliance on natural language and ordinary lifetime experiences, conclude that maternity must surely be regarded as an 'important reason'. However, unfortunately for Ms Gruber and others in her situation, the ECJ held that that was not so. This was because all the 'important reasons' listed in the legislation were related to working conditions in the undertaking or to the conduct of the employer, rendering continuing work impossible. These situations were 'in substance and origin' different from Ms Gruber's. It is noteworthy that Léger AG took a different view, saying that the comparator group should consist of those placed in

---

[39] Recital 6 of the Preamble to this Directive states that this definition is intended to be consistent with the definition of indirect discrimination for the purposes of the Race Directive and the Framework Directive. [40] Case C-249/97 [1999] ECR I-5295.
[41] See discussion in ch 4.

circumstances such that it would not be 'reasonable' to require them to continue in the employment relationship. The Court itself could without difficulty have arrived at a similar conclusion since it conceded that the 'important reasons' given in the national legislation were essentially matters which frustrated the contract of employment, as distinct from matters of personal preference, and in addition they were listed non-exhaustively. In failing to recognize this situation as indirectly discriminatory, it ignored the reality of the plight faced by what was acknowledged to be a much larger number of women than men.[42]

Curiously, in view of its previous insistence on actual adverse impact in sex discrimination claims, the ECJ has not demanded very precise proof of the degree of such adverse impact. As Léger AG observed in *Nolte v Landesversicherungsanstalt Hannover*:[43]

[I]n order to be presumed discriminatory, the measure must affect 'a far greater number of women than men' (*Rinner-Kühn*) or 'a considerably lower percentage of men than women' (*Nimz, Kowalska*) or 'far more women than men' (*De Weerd*).

Consequently, the proportion of women affected by the measure must be particularly marked. Thus, in the judgment in *Rinner-Kühn*, the Court inferred the existence of a discriminatory situation where the percentage of women was 89%.

In this instance, *per se* the figure of 60% . . . would therefore probably be quite insufficient to infer the existence of discrimination.[44]

Again, in *Gerster v Freistaat Bayern*,[45] national law provided that part-timers whose working hours exceeded two-thirds of normal working hours were deemed to have worked full-time for the purpose of calculating their length of service in relation to promotion. Part-timers whose working hours amounted to at least half of normal working hours were regarded as working two-thirds of normal working hours, but all working time was completely ignored in the case of those working less than half-time. Women accounted for 87% of part-timers in the relevant department. The Court effectively ignored the benefit which this system accorded to some part-timers and concluded:

It is common ground that the provision of national law at issue . . . treats part-time employees less favourably than full-time employees in so far as, since the former accrue length of service more slowly, they perforce gain promotion late . . .

[42] See the present author's comments in 'The Recent Jurisprudence of the Court of Justice in the Field of Sex Equality' (2000) 37 CMLRev 1403. See also Case C-220/02 *Österreichischer Gewerkschaftsbund v Wirtschaftskammer Österreich,* judgment of 8 June 2004, nyr, in which the ECJ apparently treated the non-recognition for the calculation of termination payments of time spent on parental leave as potentially indirectly discriminatory against women; however, it concluded that no indirect discrimination was proved because the comparator group chosen was those (mainly males) absent from work on military service whose situation was not in fact comparable. It is submitted that, if the rule impugned was the rule denying the recognition of time spent on parental leave, the correct comparator group would have been all workers otherwise eligible for termination payments whose employment was temporarily interrupted in order to discharge an important responsibility.
[43] Case C-317/93 [1995] ECR I-4625.
[44] Ibid, at 4640. See also the account of the statistical evidence which has satisfied the Court in other cases given by Cosmas AG in Case C-167/97 *R v Secretary of State for Employment, ex parte Seymour-Smith* op cit, n 28, at 658–9.   [45] Case C-1/95 [1997] ECR I-5253.

In a situation of that kind, it must be concluded that in practice provisions such as those at issue . . . result in discrimination against women employees as compared with men . . . .[46]

The matter of the degree of adversity arose expressly in *R v Secretary of State for Employment, ex parte Seymour-Smith*,[47] where the House of Lords referred to the ECJ the question of the 'legal test for establishing whether a measure adopted by a Member State has such a degree of disparate effect as between men and women as to amount to indirect discrimination'. Two employees had been dismissed before they had completed the period of two years' employment with the same employer, which was required under UK law before a complaint of unfair dismissal could be brought. They complained that the two-year rule constituted indirect discrimination on the ground of sex because fewer women than men were able to comply with it. The ECJ repeated its formulation that the statistics available must reveal that 'a considerably smaller percentage of women than men' could comply with the two-year rule.[48] It went on to say:

That could also be the case if the statistical evidence revealed a lesser but persistent and relatively constant disparity over a long period between men and women who satisfy the requirement of two years' employment. It would, however, be for the national court to determine the conclusions to be drawn from such statistics.

It is also for the national court to assess whether the statistics concerning the situation of the workforce are valid and can be taken into account, that is to say, whether they cover enough individuals, whether they illustrate purely fortuitous or short-term phenomena, and whether, in general, they appear to be significant . . . [49]

Despite the injunction on the ECJ applying the law it states to the facts of the case in giving a preliminary ruling, the Court was forthright in its view of the statistics presented in *Seymour-Smith* itself:

In this case, it appears from the order for reference that in 1985, the year in which the requirement of two years' employment was introduced, 77.4% of men and 68.9% of women fulfilled that condition.

Such statistics do not appear, on the face of it, to show that a considerably smaller percentage of women than men is able to fulfil the requirement imposed by the disputed rule.[50]

A further practical problem in relation to the proof of adverse impact also emerged in this litigation, namely, the appropriate moment at which to judge the impact of a rule. The Court explained that this can vary according to the circumstances of the claim:

[T]he requirements of Community law must be complied with at all relevant times, whether that is the time when the measure is adopted, when it is implemented or when it is applied to the case in point.

---

[46] Ibid, at 5284–5. Cf Joined Cases C-399, 409, & 425/92 and C-34, 50, & 78/93 *Stadt Lengerich v Helmig* [1994] ECR I-5727, discussed below. The Court did not explain why it accepted in *Gerster* that taking account of the shorter working time accrued by part-timers constituted indirect discrimination in relation to promotion but not (as in *Helmig*) in relation to pay.

[47] Case C-167/97, op cit, n 28. For highly critical comment on the quality of the ECJ's decision in this case, see Barnard and Hepple, op cit, n 37. See also the comment on the case by Moore in (2000) 37 CMLRev 157.   [48] See also Case C-50/96 *Deutsche Telekom AG v Schröder* [2000] ECR I-743.

[49] [1999] ECR I-623, at 683. See also Case C-226/98 *Jørgensen v Foreningen af Speciallaeger* [2000] ECR I-2447.   [50] [1999] ECR I-623, at 683–4.

However, the point in time at which the legality of a rule of the kind at issue in this case is to be assessed by the national court may depend on various circumstances, both legal and factual.

Thus, where the authority which adopted the act is alleged to have acted *ultra vires*, the legality of that act must, in principle, be assessed at the point in time at which it was adopted.

On the other hand, in circumstances involving the application to an individual situation of a national measure which was lawfully adopted, it may be appropriate to examine whether, at the time of its application, the measure is still in conformity with Community law.

With regard, in particular, to statistics, it may be appropriate to take into account not only the statistics available at the point in time at which the act was adopted, but also statistics compiled subsequently which are likely to provide an indication of its impact on men and women.[51]

Burden of proof

The question of how adverse impact is to be demonstrated is very closely related to the burden of proof which must be discharged in order for an anti-discrimination claim to succeed. A complainant in any discrimination claim normally faces considerable difficulties in proving the case. If the law places the entire burden of proof throughout the proceedings upon the complainant, then all the respondent needs to do in practice is to produce a colourable story which casts doubt on the complainant's version of events. Thus, for example, where a man has been chosen for a job in preference to a woman candidate who has slightly better qualifications than him on paper, the employer will escape liability for discrimination if the tribunal can be convinced that the man had a more appropriate personality for the particular job. This may be quite untrue, or at least an example of subconscious gender-stereotyping on the employer's part, yet it will save the case for the employer provided only that the tribunal does not conclude that the employer is lying. The real problem from the complainant's point of view is that it is extremely difficult, and sometimes quite impossible, to prove why she was not selected. This is a matter which is peculiarly within the employer's own knowledge, which is why the legal burden of proof should be reversed once a *prima facie* case has been made out and the employer should then be required to prove to the satisfaction of the tribunal the reason for the relevant decision.[52]

The ECJ has considered the issue of burden of proof on a number of occasions and, although the matter is complicated by differences between the adversarial and inquisitorial approaches to be found in the various Member States, the underlying difficulty which emerges is ascertaining the kind and weight of evidence from which a court or tribunal should infer discrimination. This question was addressed in the context of equal pay in *Handels-OG Kontorfunktionaerernes Forbund i Danmark*

---

[51] [1999] ECR I-623, at 679–80.

[52] But for distinguished opinion to the opposite effect, see the 17th Report (Session 1988–9) of the House of Lords Select Committee on the European Communities, 'Burden of Proof in Sex Discrimination Cases', July 1989, HL Paper 76, and especially the view of Anthony Lester QC expressed therein.

v Dansk Arbejdsgiverforening (acting for Danfoss),[53] which concerned a collective agreement between a staff union and an employers' association. The same basic minimum wage was paid to all workers in the same pay grade. Grading was determined by job classification. However, the collective agreement allowed the company to make additional payments to individuals within a grade on the basis of the individual's 'flexibility', vocational training, and seniority. The union argued that the pay system discriminated on the ground of sex because, within a pay grade, the average pay of women was less than that of men: specifically, it produced evidence of a statistical survey covering the pay of 157 Danfoss employees between 1982 and 1986, which showed a differential of 6.85% between the average pay of male and female workers within the relevant pay grades. The industrial arbitration tribunal sent a number of questions to the ECJ. The first issue raised was perceived by the ECJ to be in essence related to the burden of proof in equal pay claims:

[T]he issue between the parties . . . has its origin in the fact that the system of individual supplements applied to basic pay is implemented in such a way that a woman is unable to identify the reasons for a difference between her pay and that of a man doing the same work. Employees do not know what criteria in the matter of supplements are applied to them and how they are applied. They know only the amount of their supplemented pay without being able to determine the effect of the individual criteria. Those who are in a particular wage group are thus unable to compare the various components of their pay with those of the pay of their colleagues who are in the same wage group.

In those circumstances the questions put by the national court must be understood as asking whether . . . where an undertaking applies a system of pay which is totally lacking in transparency, it is for the employer to prove that his practice in the matter of wages is not discriminatory, if a female worker establishes, in relation to a relatively large number of employees, that the average pay for women is less than that for men.[54]

The answer given was that the burden of proof (and it would appear from the context that the Court meant the legal as distinct from merely the evidential burden of proof) was indeed so placed on the employer.[55] The Court's reasoning was that the employer might not shelter behind the grading scheme involved:

[I]n a situation where a system of individual pay supplements which is completely lacking in transparency is at issue, female employees can establish differences only so far as average pay is concerned. They would be deprived of any effective means of enforcing the principle of equal pay before the national courts if the effect of adducing such evidence was not to impose upon the employer the burden of proving that his practice in the matter of wages is not in fact discriminatory.

[53] Case 109/88 [1989] ECR 3199.   [54] Ibid, at 3225.

[55] The UK Government had intervened in the case and argued in favour of this solution to the effect that, in the UK in such a situation, the employer would already bear the burden of proof under the Equal Pay Act 1970. At first sight, this appears ironic, since the UK Government vetoed a draft directive on reversal of the burden of proof in sex discrimination claims in the late 1980s. However, that draft directive was seriously defective and would probably have increased rather than decreased confusion. In addition, the Government appeared to confine its submissions in *Danfoss* to the equal pay field, and would probably have opposed any extension of the principle to equal treatment generally.

Finally, it should be noted that under Article 6 of the Equal Pay Directive Member States must, in accordance with their national circumstances and their legal systems, take the measures necessary to ensure that the principle of equal pay principle is applied and that effective means are available to ensure that it is observed. The concern for effectiveness which thus underlies the Directive means that it must be interpreted as implying adjustments to national rules on the burden of proof in special cases where such adjustments are necessary for the effective implementation of the principle of equality.

To show that his practice in the matter of wages does not systematically work to the disadvantage of female employees the employer will have to indicate how he has applied the criteria concerning supplements and will thus be forced to make his system of pay transparent.[56]

Danfoss thus established the principle that, where a system of pay is non-transparent, the burden of proof is on the employer to show that that system is not sex discriminatory, where a woman can establish, by comparison with a 'relatively large' number of employees, that the average pay of women employees is 'lower' than that of male employees. This formula of course leaves uncertain how many employees must be involved (although clearly 157 was enough), for how long (here it was four years), and what percentage differential is sufficient to reverse the burden of proof (6.85% being established to be enough).

The Court proceeded to a more general statement of principle in *Enderby v Frenchay Health Authority*.[57] A speech therapist employed by the UK National Health Service complained that speech therapists, who were almost all female, were less well paid than clinical psychologists and pharmacists, who were pre-dominantly male, and who she claimed performed work of equal value. Both the Court and the Advocate General took a pragmatic approach as to how adverse impact might be demonstrated. The Court stated simply that the existence of a '*prima facie* case of discrimination' casts the burden of proving objective justification onto the employer,[58] and it added that such a *prima facie* case might be made out where 'significant statistics disclose an appreciable difference in pay between two jobs of equal value, one of which is carried out almost exclusively by women and the other predominantly by men'.[59] Lenz AG explained:

The basic legal position is that Article 119 . . . and the directives adopted for its implementation, as interpreted and applied by the Court of Justice, prohibit all forms of sex-related discrimination. Sex-related pay discrimination takes various forms, the categorization of which can pose a legal problem. In order to render them susceptible to legal categorization, the courts have adopted the categories of direct and indirect discrimination. The conceptual scheme applied should in no way be construed in the sense of any exclusiveness of possible forms of sex discrimination. A glance at the conceptual scheme applied in these proceedings under the laws of the UK bears this out. The reference there to intentional

---

[56] [1989] ECR 3199, at 3226. For the domestic sequel to *Danfoss*, see Precht, '*Danfoss* in the Danish Courts' (1992) 21 ILJ 323.

[57] Case C-127/92 [1993] ECR I-5535, noted by Fredman in 'Equal Pay and Justification' (1994) 23 ILJ 37, by Wynn in 'Equal Pay and Gender Segregation' (1994) 110 LQR 556, and by the present author in (1994) 31 CMLRev 387. See also Kentridge, 'Direct and Indirect Discrimination After *Enderby*' [1994] PL 198.

[58] See also Case C-381/99 *Brunnhofer v Bank der österreichischen Postsparkasse AG* [2001] ECR I-4961.

[59] [1993] ECR I-5535, at 5573.

or unintentional direct discrimination and to intentional or unintentional indirect discrimination shows that there are four possible ways of categorizing the same phenomenon for legal purposes.[60]

The purpose of a conceptual scheme is to comprehend methods by which women are placed at a disadvantage in their working lives and not to create additional obstacles to claims being made before the courts in respect of sex-related pay discrimination. For this reason, a formalistic approach should not be adopted when categorizing actual instances where women are placed at a disadvantage at work.[61]

Later, he added:

Attention should be directed less to the existence of a requirement or a hurdle by means of which women suffer a disadvantage, and more to the discriminatory result.[62]

It is, however, necessary to raise a *prima facie* case of indirect discrimination before the employer is required to justify a pay disparity.[63] *Stadt Lengerich v Helmig*[64] concerned a claim by women part-time workers that the denial to them of overtime pay when they exceeded their normal (part-time) working hours constituted indirect discrimination. Under the relevant collective agreements, all employees were entitled to overtime supplements, but only after they had worked a full-time week. The Court held that it must be asked, first of all, whether there was different treatment for part-time and full-time employees, and whether that difference affected considerably more women than men. Only if those questions were answered in the affirmative would a *prima facie* case arise which would require objective justification. The Court concluded:

There is unequal treatment wherever the overall pay of full-time employees is higher than that of part-time employees for the same number of hours worked on the basis of an employment relation. In the circumstances considered in these proceedings, part-time employees do receive the same overall pay as full-time employees for the same number of hours worked. A part-time employee whose contractual working hours are 18 receives, if he works 19 hours, the same overall pay as a full-time employee who works 19 hours. Part-time employees also receive the same overall pay as full-time employees if they work more than the normal working hours fixed by the collective agreements because on doing so they become entitled to overtime supplements. Consequently, the provisions at issue do not give rise to different treatment as between part-time and full-time employees and there is therefore no discrimination . . . [65]

Most of the cases so far litigated have involved alleged sex discrimination where work is paid at time rates. However, *Specialarbejderforbundet i Danmark v Dansk Industri, acting for Royal Copenhagen A/S*[66] raised questions relating to proof of discrimination in a piece-work system. The ECJ explained in *Royal Copenhagen*

---

[60] The relevance of intention in EU anti-discrimination law is discussed below.

[61] [1993] ECR I-5535, at 5557.   [62] Ibid, at 5560.

[63] For an example of a case in which this initial hurdle was not surmounted, see Case C-297/93 *Grau-Hupta v Stadtgemeinde Bremen* [1994] ECR I-5535.   [64] Op cit, n 46.

[65] Ibid, at 5754–5. For criticism of the excessive devotion paid by the ECJ in this case to the concepts of formal equality and the male norm, see Holmaat, 'Overtime Payments for Part-time Workers' (1995) 24 ILJ 387.

[66] Case C-400/93 [1995] ECR I-1275; see Bourn, 'The Devil is in the Detail' (1995) 20 ELRev 612, and Hervey, 'The Rise and Rise of Conservatism in Equal Pay' (1996) 18 JSWFL 107.

that the kind of group comparison which it uses in cases involving work paid at time rates cannot usually as a matter of logic be applied in piece-work systems:

> [I]n a piece-work pay scheme the principle of equal pay requires that the pay of two groups of workers, one consisting predominantly of men and the other predominantly of women, is to be calculated on the basis of the same unit of measurement. Where the unit of measurement is the same for two groups of workers carrying out the same work or is objectively capable of ensuring that the total individual pay of workers in the two groups is the same for work which, although different is considered to be of equal value, the principle of equal pay does not prohibit workers belonging to one or the other group from receiving different total pay if that is due to their different individual output.
>
> It follows that in a piece-work pay scheme the mere finding that there is a difference in the average pay of two groups of workers, calculated on the basis of the total individual pay of all the workers belonging to one or the other group, does not suffice to establish that there is discrimination with regard to pay.
>
> It is for the national court, which alone is competent to assess the facts, to decide whether the unit of measurement applicable to the work carried out by the two groups of workers is the same or, if the two groups carry out work which is different but considered to be of equal value, whether the unit of measurement is objectively capable of ensuring that their total pay is the same. It is also for that court to ascertain whether a pay differential relied on by a worker belonging to a group consisting predominantly of women as evidence of sex discrimination against that worker compared with a worker belonging to a group consisting predominantly of men is due to a difference between the units of measurement applicable to the two groups or to a difference in individual output.[67]

The principles relating to the burden of proof formulated by the ECJ in relation to equal pay came to be reflected in its case law on other aspects of sex discrimination.[68] In time, they were broadly consolidated for the purposes of sex discrimination claims into Article 4(1) of the Burden of Proof Directive:[69]

> Member States shall take such measures as are necessary, in accordance with their national judicial systems, to ensure that, when persons who consider themselves wronged because the principle of equal treatment has not been applied to them establish, before a court or other competent authority, facts from which it may be presumed that there has been direct or indirect discrimination, it shall be for the respondent to prove that there has been no breach of the principle of equal treatment.[70]

This Article does not prevent Member States from introducing rules of evidence which are more favourable to claimants;[71] it does not, however, apply to criminal proceedings[72] and need not be applied to inquisitorial proceedings.[73]

---

[67] [1995] ECR I-1275, at 1305–6.

[68] See in particular Lenz AG in Case C-127/92 *Enderby v Frenchay Health Authority* op cit, n 57, Van Gerven AG in Joined Cases C-63 & 64/91 *Jackson and Cresswell v Chief Adjudication Officer* [1992] ECR I-4737, and Darmon AG in Case C-189/91 *Kirsammer-Hack v Sidal* [1993] ECR I-6185. Cf McGlynn, 'Equality, Maternity and Questions of Pay' (1996) 21 ELRev 327.

[69] Directive 97/80, which was extended to the UK and amended by Directive 98/52, OJ [1998] L205/66.

[70] It is submitted that, in the light of this provision, Case 233/85 *Bonino v Commission* [1987] ECR 739 (in which the ECJ held that the principle of equal treatment did not require a respondent to provide reasons for decisions on promotion even though some of the candidates were women) and Case 111/86 *Delauche v Commission* [1987] ECR 5345, should no longer be considered good law.

[71] Directive 97/80, Art 4(2).   [72] Ibid, Art 3(2).

[73] Ibid, Art 4(3). The Commission has expressed the view that there is considerable confusion about the meaning of this provision and that it undermines legal certainty: see COM (2003) 657 final, at 16.

Identical rules are also today contained in the Race Directive[74] and the Framework Directive.[75]

Causation

A further vital aspect of the concept of discrimination was elucidated in the case law relating to sex discrimination. No intention or subjective motivation is required; it is enough simply that the adverse treatment received by the victim is grounded upon, or caused by, a prohibited classification. This was a logical conclusion for the ECJ to draw given that Article 141 was originally included in the Treaty in order to obviate inequalities in pay attributable to sex. It is in principle irrelevant to that objective to examine an employer's intention or motives where the effect of what has been done is in reality to the disadvantage of one sex. In the words of Lenz AG in *Enderby v Frenchay Health Authority*:[76]

[F]orms of direct sex discrimination are quite conceivable without sex being expressly mentioned in the contract of employment, pay scales or collective agreement as the criterion for the higher or lower pay. The conceptual scheme of that category makes it clear that discrimination does not even have to have been intentional.[77]

This view is also inherent in the ECJ's attitude to so-called 'gender-plus' discrimination. The expression 'gender-plus' was coined by the American courts in the context of sexual harassment. The problem is to know whether the law catches discrimination against a class or sub-class of women, so that the conduct has to be analysed as discrimination on the ground of sex-plus-something-else.[78] In common with their American counterparts, UK courts have come to accept that such conduct breaches the national anti-discrimination legislation: 'but for' the sex of the victim, the person would have been treated more favourably, and therefore the discrimination is 'on the ground of sex'; questions of intention and motivation are quite irrelevant to such a test.[79] In *Liefting v Directie van het Academisch Ziekenhuis bij de Universiteit van Amsterdam*,[80] where the gender-plus point was argued, the ECJ held that there was a breach of Article 141 where a system of making employer-contributions to certain types of pension scheme discriminated against women civil servants who were married to civil servants. There was no allegation that the system discriminated against women generally, or even against women civil

---

[74] Art 8 and Recital 21 of the Preamble to the Race Directive.
[75] Art 10 and Recital 31 of the Preamble to the Framework Directive; the latter adds: 'However, it is not for the respondent to prove that the plaintiff adheres to a particular religion or belief, has a particular disability, is of a particular age or has a particular sexual orientation.'   [76] Op cit, n 57.
[77] Ibid, at 5558.
[78] See, eg, *Barnes v Costle* (1977) 15 FEP Cases 345; *Hurley v Mustoe* [1981] IRLR 208; *Horsey v Dyfed District Council* [1982] IRLR 395; and *Hayes v Malleable Working Men's Club* [1985] ICR 703. Cf *Turley v Allders Department Stores Ltd* [1980] IRLR 4.
[79] See also the decision of the House of Lords in *James v Eastleigh Borough Council* [1990] 3 WLR 55. Cf Watt, 'Goodbye "but-for", hello "but-why?"' (1998) 27 ILJ 121.
[80] Case 23/83 [1984] ECR 3225.

servants generally, but only against that class whose husbands were also civil servants. The same analysis can be applied to *Worringham v Lloyds Bank Ltd*,[81] where the discrimination challenged was not against women employees generally but only against those aged under 25. In this later decision, the ECJ made a statement which is really only compatible with an objective test for direct discrimination, unrelated to any requirement of motivation or intention on the part of the employer. It said:

Article 119 of the Treaty applies directly to all forms of discrimination which may be identified solely with the aid of the criteria of equal work and equal pay referred to by the Article in question, without national or Community measures being required to define them with greater precision in order to permit of their application . . . This is the case where the requirement to pay contributions applies only to men and not to women and the contributions payable by men are paid by the employers in their name by means of an addition to the gross salary *the effect of which* is to give men higher pay within the meaning of the second paragraph of Article 119 than that received by women engaged in the same work or work of equal value.[82]

The ECJ in *Dekker v Stichting Vormingscentrum Voor Jonge Volwassen Plus*[83] also implicitly ruled out the need for intention in relation to direct discrimination, saying that

. . . if the employer's liability for infringement of the principle of equal treatment were made subject to proof of a fault attributable to him and also to there being no ground of exemption recognized by the applicable national law, the practical effect of those principles would be weakened considerably.[84]

As with direct discrimination, so also for indirect discrimination: no motive or intention is required on the part of the discriminator. The test for causation is an objective one. Although the ECJ appeared ambivalent about this matter in *Jenkins v Kingsgate (Clothing Productions) Ltd*,[85] in *Bilka-Kaufhaus GmbH v Weber Von Hartz*,[86] it held that Article 141 extended to unintentional indirect discrimination.[87]

---

[81] Case 69/80, op cit, n 14.

[82] Ibid, at 792, emphasis added. See also Case C-7/93 *Bestuur Van Het Algemeen Burgerlijk Pensioenfonds v Beune* [1994] ECR I-4471, at 4520.   [83] Case 177/88 [1990] ECR I-3941.

[84] Ibid, at 3976. Cf Watt, op cit, n 79; the author there argues that the ECJ abandoned its 'but for' approach in Case 179/88 *Handels-OG Kontorfunktionaereremes Forbund I Danmark v Dansk Arbejds-giverforening (acting for Aldi Marked K/S)* [1990] ECR I-3979; in *Aldi*, the ECJ refused to hold that there had been unlawful discrimination where a woman was dismissed for taking long periods of sick leave which were caused by an illness, which in turn was caused by an earlier pregnancy. (In ch 5, it is argued that this decision is explicable on the basis that the complainant did not receive adverse treatment, compared to that receivable by a male comparator, rather than on the basis of causation.) Watt also draws attention to recent decisions of some UK courts which suggest that they too are re-focusing on intention in determining causation in discrimination claims.

[85] Case 96/80, op cit, n 8.   [86] Case 170/84 [1986] ECR 1607.

[87] See also the opinion of Van Gerven AG in Joined Cases C-63 & 64/91 *Jackson and Cresswell v Chief Adjudication Officer* [1992] ECR I-4737, esp at 4770. In Case C-317/93 *Nolte v Landesver-sicherungsanstalt Hannover* [1995] ECR I-4625, Léger AG submitted: 'There is a presumption that indirect discrimination is present "once an apparently neutral measure in fact has a preponderant effect on workers of a given sex—without there being any need to establish the intention to discriminate"' (at 4632, quoting from Commission DGV 'Equal Treatment in Community Law' Social Europe, 3/91, p 79).

Ms Weber complained of indirect discrimination in that her ex-employer's pension scheme conferred rights on part-time workers only where they had been in full-time employment with the company for fifteen years out of a total of twenty years. Ms Weber, a part-time worker who could not satisfy this requirement, argued that it worked to the detriment of women workers, because they were more likely than their male colleagues to have to opt for part-time work because of their family and child-care commitments. The ECJ held:

Since, as was stated above, such a pension falls within the concept of pay for the purposes of the second paragraph of Article 119 . . . it follows that, hour for hour, the total remuneration paid by Bilka to full-time workers is higher than that paid to part-time workers.

If, therefore, it should be found that a much lower proportion of women than of men work full time, the exclusion of part-time workers from the occupational pension scheme would be contrary to Article 119 of the Treaty where, taking into account the difficulties encountered by women workers in working full time, that measure could not be explained by factors which exclude any discrimination on grounds of sex. However, if the undertaking is able to show its pay practice may be explained by objectively justified factors unrelated to any discrimination on grounds of sex, there is no breach of Article 119. The answer to the first question referred by the national court must therefore be that Article 119 of the EEC Treaty is infringed by a department store company which excludes part-time employees from its occupational pension scheme, where that exclusion affects a far greater number of women than men, unless the undertaking shows that the exclusion is based on objectively justified factors unrelated to any discrimination on grounds of sex.[88]

Since a lack of intention to discriminate cannot sensibly be regarded as an objectively justified factor unrelated to sex discrimination, it followed that the Court was saying here that even unintentional indirect discrimination is caught by Article 141.[89]

This principle was established even more clearly in *Rinner-Kühn v FWW Spezial-Gebaudereinigung GmbH*.[90] Ms Rinner-Kühn worked for ten hours a week. Her employers, strictly in accordance with the relevant German statutory provision, refused to pay her for a period of six days' absence owing to sickness. She complained to her local Labour Court, which referred to the ECJ the question:

Is a legislative provision excluding from the principle of continued payment of salary by the employer during illness those workers whose normal period of work does not exceed 10 hours a week or 45 hours a month compatible with Article 119 of the EEC Treaty and Council Directive 75/117/EEC of 10 February 1975 on the approximation of the laws of Member States relating to the application of the principle of equal pay for men and women—although the proportion of female workers suffering adverse effects from this exclusion is much higher than that of male workers?

[88] [1986] ECR 1607, at 1626–7. See also *Kowalska v Freie und Hansestadt Hamburg* Case 33/89 [1990] ECR I-2591.

[89] The objective nature of what is required for indirect discrimination was also emphasized by Léger AG in Case C-249/97 *Gruber v Silhouette International Schmied GmbH & Co KG*, op cit, n 40, when he submitted that the 'absolute nature of the protection conferred by [Article 141] on individuals who invoke it cannot be limited by considerations relating to the cause of the discriminatory situation' (at 5313).   [90] Case 171/88 [1989] ECR 2743.

The ECJ replied:

Under the German legislative provision in question only those employees whose contract of employment provides for a normal period of work of more than 10 hours a week or 45 hours a month are entitled to the continued payment of wages by their employer in the event of illness. Since such payment falls within the concept of 'pay' within the meaning of the second paragraph of Article 119, the German legislative provision in question accordingly allows employers to maintain a distinction relating to total pay between two categories of employees: those who perform the minimum number of weekly or monthly hours and those who, although performing the same type of work, do not work the minimum number of hours.

It is also clear from the order requesting a preliminary ruling that in percentage terms considerably less women than men work the minimum number of weekly or hourly hours required to entitle an employee to the continued payment of wages in the event of inability to work due to illness.

In such a situation, it must be concluded that a provision such as that in question results in discrimination against female workers in relation to male workers and must, in principle, be regarded as contrary to the aim of Article 119 of the Treaty. The position would be different only if the distinction between the two categories of employees were justified by objective factors unrelated to any discrimination on grounds of sex . . . [91]

It seems safe to assume that this same principle applies for the purposes of the Race and Framework Directives. In other words, whether the alleged discrimination is direct or indirect, all that is required to establish causation is that 'but for' the prohibited classification, the victim would not have sustained the disadvantage alleged. For this purpose, it is unnecessary to prove any particular motive or intention on the part of the respondent. An important rider, however, needs to be added in the context of the new grounds of discrimination in EU law. Whilst a person's sex is normally obvious, this is not the case in relation to some of the other prohibited classifications. As far as the victim is concerned, it is nevertheless irrelevant whether the treatment received is attributable to an actual state of affairs, or whether it is attributable merely to the discriminator's perceptions or assumptions; for example, it matters not to the victim whether, on the one hand, the reason for non-selection is that he or she is a Muslim, or, on the other hand, is because the discriminator thought this to be the case. It will therefore be important that the ECJ establishes the principle that causation is demonstrated both where the action is based on an actual ground and also where it is grounded on the discriminator's perception that that ground exists. [92]

---

[91] Ibid, at 2760–1. Shaw comments in 'The Burden of Proof and the Legality of Supplementary Payments in Equal Pay Cases' (1990) 15 ELRev 260, that the Court in *Rinner-Kühn* effectively grasped the legislative nettle and enacted the long-stalled proposal for a directive granting equality of treatment to part-time employees (OJ [1982] C62/7, and OJ [1983] C18/5); for discussion of the framework agreement on part-time work which was subsequently reached, see ch 5. It is noteworthy that no minimum number of hours of service per week was required by the ECJ in order to trigger the *Rinner-Kühn* principle.

[92] Express support for this principle in the context of sexual orientation discrimination was given by Richards J in *R (on the application of Amicus—MSF section) v Secretary of State for Trade and Industry* [2004] IRLR 430, especially at 442. See also Oliver, 'Sexual Orientation Discrimination: Perceptions, Definitions and Genuine Occupational Requirements' (2004) 33 ILJ 1.

In the case of sex discrimination, the ECJ has taken a firm line in relation to pregnancy and established the rule that discrimination is grounded on sex where it is attributable to an attribute (pregnancy) which can be demonstrated only by one sex.[93] To the extent that such a principle of causation can be extended to other grounds, it is likely to constitute a precedent. Thus, for example, even though colour is not specifically mentioned in the Race Directive, it seems probable that a requirement that a person be of a particular colour could similarly be inextricably connected to race.

However, some new difficulties in the field of causation are likely to be encountered by litigants who seek to rely on the Framework Directive. For example, in the field of disability, it is unclear from the wording of the instrument whether discrimination on the ground of disability covers not only adverse treatment which is based on the disability itself, but also extends to adverse treatment which is based on consequences which stem from that disability. It is to be hoped that the ECJ will construe disability to encompass its consequences, since otherwise the protection against discrimination will be seriously limited in this important area. Whilst there is certainly some discrimination simply on the grounds of particular disabilities (such as mental ill-health and epilepsy), it is undoubtedly the case that most discrimination results from the consequences of disability (such as restricted mobility).

In the case of all the prohibited classifications, the Directives merely forbid discrimination on the ground specified; they do not stipulate who must belong to the relevant class. Thus, as a matter of textual interpretation as well as principle, it seems probable that the instruments embrace discrimination not only on the ground of the victim's protected status, but also discrimination against a victim on account of someone else's protected status; in other words, they capture the situation where A treats B adversely because B refuses to discriminate against a protected class. An example would be where a shop-owner sacked an employee because that person refused to obey an instruction not to serve gay customers.

For religious discrimination, the question also arises as to whether the 'religion or belief' which lies at the heart of the alleged discrimination can be that of the discriminator. In part this will depend on how the ECJ opts to define 'religion or belief';[94] if it chooses to include absence of belief in its definition, this will widen the scope of the conduct prohibited, since it will then have the potential to cover adverse treatment meted out by somebody on the ground of his or her own religion or belief where that does not coincide with that of the victim. Thus, the usual case will no doubt involve A choosing, for example, not to employ B because of B's religion; however, the law would also embrace the situation where A, perhaps holding fundamentalist views, refuses to employ B because B has no particular religion, or does not share the beliefs of A. Even if the ECJ does not

---

[93] Case 177/88 *Dekker v Stichting Vormingscentrum Voor Jonge Volwassen Plus* [1990] ECR I-3941, discussed in ch 5.   [94] See discussion in ch 1.

adopt this view, it is still open to it to hold (admittedly bullishly) that A has discriminated against B in the situation posited because A's conduct is grounded upon 'religion or belief'.

In addition, it is not yet clear where the line is to be drawn between 'religion or belief' and the manifestation of religion or belief. For example, where an employer requires employees to wear a particular form of head-dress, is this direct discrimination against Sikhs whose religion demands the wearing of a turban; or is it instead indirect discrimination against them?[95]

In the field of sexual orientation discrimination, a similar issue arises. It will not be clear until the ECJ determines the matter whether the prohibition is restricted to orientation, or whether it also extends to behaviour which is associated with sexual orientation. If the former, the law would only forbid adverse treatment grounded upon a person's sexual orientation: 'I will not employ you because you are (or I believe you to be) homosexual'; if the latter, it would extend, much more widely, to adverse treatment grounded upon the manifestations of sexual orientation: 'I will not employ you because you dress and speak in a camp manner.'[96]

Very difficult questions are likely to arise where there is a collision between the different grounds of discrimination now covered by EU law. The most obvious example is where one employee holds religious views which proscribe homosexuality and expresses those views to the offence of a gay colleague. The gay employee may claim that this constitutes discrimination on the ground of homosexuality; but, equally, the religious employee may claim that disciplinary action taken by the employer infringes the right not to be discriminated against on the ground of religion or belief. The resolution of these sorts of difficulty is not a clear-cut matter but depends in part on the availability of the defences which are discussed in chapter 6.

Defences to a discrimination claim[97]

Since only discrimination based on the specified grounds is prohibited by EU law, it follows that differences between persons in otherwise comparable circumstances which are not based on such specified grounds are themselves lawful. Thus, for example, where the allegation is of direct discrimination contrary to

---

[95] This question is important because, as will be discussed below, indirect discrimination is subject to the defence of justification, whereas direct discrimination cannot usually be justified.

[96] In a decision on the interpretation of the UK's implementing legislation, Richards J held that 'sexual orientation and its manifestation in sexual behaviour are both inextricably connected with a person's private life and identity': R (on the application of Amicus—MSF section) v Secretary of State for Trade and Industry, op cit, n 92, at 436; he added that 'the protection against discrimination on grounds of sexual orientation relates as much to the manifestation of that orientation in the form of sexual behaviour as it does to sexuality as such' (at 446).

[97] On this subject generally, see Hervey, Justifications for Sex Discrimination in Employment (Butterworths, London, 1993).

Article 141, the way is open for the employer to plead that some factor other than sex is the cause of the pay discrepancy. As the ECJ explained in *Macarthys Ltd v Smith*:[98] '[I]t cannot be ruled out that a difference in pay between two workers occupying the same post but at different periods in time may be explained by the operation of factors which are unconnected with any discrimination on grounds of sex'.[99] The ECJ chose its words carefully here; this is in essence a matter of causation and not a matter of justification. Properly analysed, this is a situation where there is no discrimination, not one where proven discrimination can be excused.[100]

There is a logical, though not a verbal, parallel as regards causation in cases of indirect discrimination. Here, the respondent can defend the conduct if it can be shown that the discriminatory effect is explicable, in the words of the ECJ in *Bilka-Kaufhaus GmbH v Weber Von Hartz*,[101] by 'objectively justified factors which are unrelated to any discrimination': in other words, where the apparently objectionable effect is in fact not grounded in discrimination.[102] The Court went on in that case to explain that this principle is subject to a stringent test of proportionality:

It falls to the national court, which has sole jurisdiction to make findings of fact, to determine whether and to what extent the grounds put forward by an employer to explain the adoption of a pay practice which applies independently of a worker's sex, but in fact affects more women than men may be regarded as objectively justified [on] economic grounds. If the national court finds that the measures chosen by Bilka correspond to a real need on the part of the undertaking, are appropriate with a view to achieving the objectives pursued, and are necessary to that end, the fact that the measures affect a far greater number of women than men is not sufficient to show that they constitute an infringement of Article 119.[103]

This sets up a formidable hurdle for a respondent seeking to justify indirectly discriminatory conduct. The respondent must show to the satisfaction of the national court that there is a genuine need on behalf of the enterprise for the discriminatory factor,[104] that the means chosen are suitable for attaining the objective, and, most

[98] Case 129/79, op cit, n 17.
[99] Ibid, at 1289. See also the remarks of Capotorti AG in the same case, especially at 1295, and see Case C-381/99 *Brunnhofer v Bank der österreichischen Postsparkasse AG* [2001] ECR I-4961.
[100] See also Case 177/88 *Dekker v Stichting Vormingscentrum Voor Jonge Volwassen Plus*, op cit, n 93, where this point was specifically recognized by the ECJ, and Ellis, 'The Definition of Discrimination in European Community Sex Equality Law' (1994) 19 ELRev 563.
[101] Case 170/84 [1986] ECR 1607.
[102] This analysis was confirmed by the ECJ in Case C-381/99 *Brunnhofer*, op cit, n 99, and by Jacobs AG in Case C-79/99 *Schnorbus*, op cit, n 19.
[103] [1986] ECR 1607, at 1628. For further discussion of the role played by proportionality in the defence of discrimination, see Hervey, 'EC Law on Justifications for Sex Discrimination in Working Life' in Blanpain (ed), *Collective Bargaining, Discrimination, Social Security and European Integration*, (Kluwer, Deventer, 2003).
[104] In other words, the subjective beliefs of the respondent are not the essence of the matter. Unfortunately, the ECJ is not always scrupulously consistent in applying this requirement; see, eg, Case C-79/99 *Schnorbus*, op cit, n 19, which concerned a provision which expedited the entry into practical legal training of those who had completed military service. This provision was *prima facie*

strictly of all, that the means chosen are 'necessary' to attain the objective; it follows that, if reasonable alternative means are available to the respondent to attain the objective, the behaviour will breach the non-discrimination principle. There is a good reason for the law to take this approach, effectively reversing the burden of proof once adverse impact has been demonstrated in an indirect discrimination claim.[105] It will usually be very difficult, if not impossible, for the complainant to demonstrate that discrimination lies at the root of the adverse impact in these sorts of cases, and it therefore makes practical sense to place the burden of disproving discrimination on the shoulders of the respondent, who is in a much better position to explain what has occurred.[106]

An equivalent principle also applies where the alleged indirect discrimination stems from a legislative act of one of the Member States. Thus, in the words of the ECJ in *R v Secretary of State for Employment, ex parte Seymour-Smith*:[107]

[I]t is for the Member State, as the author of the allegedly discriminatory rule, to show that the said rule reflects a legitimate aim of its social policy, that that aim is unrelated to any discrimination . . . , and that it could reasonably consider that the means chosen were suitable for attaining that aim.[108]

When it comes to justifying alleged indirect discrimination contained in a Member's State's law, the respondent is not restricted to relying on the reasons put forward when the measure introducing the differential treatment was adopted.[109]

The role of justification in indirect discrimination was so well-established in EU law by the date of enactment of the Race Directive and the Framework Directive that the concept was expressly incorporated into those instruments. Thus, the definition of indirect discrimination contained in Article 2(2)(b) of the Race Directive[110] concludes with the words: 'unless that provision, criterion or practice is objectively justified by a legitimate aim and the means of achieving that aim are appropriate and necessary'. The Framework Directive contains identical wording.[111]

The application of the principle of justification in the substantive fields occupied today by EU anti-discrimination law will be discussed further in the later chapters of this work.

---

indirectly discriminatory, since only men were required to perform compulsory military service. Nevertheless, the Court held it to be justified in part because it was 'prompted solely by the desire' to counterbalance the delay caused to those concerned in embarking on their careers.

[105] See the opinion of Léger AG in Case C-317/93 *Nolte*, op cit, n 87, at 4641.

[106] Cf the decisions of the House of Lords in *Strathclyde Regional Council v Wallace* [1998] SC 72 and *Glasgow City Council v Marshall* [2000] 1 WLR 333, and the decision of the British Employment Appeal Tribunal in *Parliamentary Commissioner for Administration v Fernandez* [2004] IRLR 22.

[107] Case C-167/97, op cit, n 28.   [108] Ibid, at 686.

[109] Joined Cases C-4 & 5/02 *Schönheit v Stadt Frankfurt am Main*, judgment of 23 October 2003, nyr.

[110] See above.

[111] Art 2(2)(b)(i) of the Framework Directive. Additionally, indirect discrimination can be defended in cases of disability through the principle of 'reasonable accommodation': Art 2(2)(b)(ii); this is discussed further in ch 6.

Can direct discrimination be justified as a matter of EU law?

It has sometimes been suggested that it is not only indirect discrimination which may be justified, but that this concept may also be applied so as to legalize direct discrimination.[112] For example, in *Birds Eye Walls Ltd v Roberts*,[113] both the Commission and the defendant employers argued that alleged discrimination in relation to bridging pensions against female ex-employees aged between 60 and 65 who had retired early, could be justified. Van Gerven AG agreed that 'exceptionally' direct discrimination might be justified, apparently largely on the basis that it can be difficult to distinguish between direct and indirect discrimination.[114] He concluded:

> Since I consider that Birds Eye Walls can justify on objective grounds the policy with regard to pensions at issue here, I have come to the conclusion... that an employer is not in breach of Article 119... if, taking account of the difference between the pensionable age for men and that for women applied by the state and authorized for the time being, he operates an occupational scheme involving payment of a bridging pension using a method of calculation *designed to ensure* the same overall retirement pension (occupational pension and state pension combined) for male and female ex-employees.[115]

The Court avoided dealing with the issue in this case by holding that there was no discrimination at all on the facts. This appeared consistent with its earlier holding in *Dekker v Stichting Vormingscentrum Voor Jonge Volwassen Plus*[116] that the concept of justification has no place in the law relating to direct discrimination.[117] However, an indication that the Court might be able to be persuaded of the possibility of justifying direct discrimination was provided in *Smith v Avdel Systems Ltd*.[118] Van Gerven AG had again argued in favour of such a solution:

> Such a possibility... may be used only in exceptional situations, more specifically in order to take account of circumstances which are entirely unconnected with discrimination on grounds of sex and which meet an *acute* need concerning the very existence of the undertaking or the solvency of its occupational pension scheme.[119]

The Court itself held that Article 141 forbade raising the pension age for women members of the scheme from 60 to 65 in the period intervening between the

---

[112] See McCrudden, *Equality of Treatment Between Men and Women in Social Security* (Butterworths, London, 1994), esp at 215–7.   [113] Case C-132/92 [1993] ECR I-5579.

[114] See the Advocate General's submissions, ibid, at 5593. See also the somewhat ambiguous submissions of La Pergola AG in his Opinion in Case C-1/95 *Gerster v Freistaat Bayern* [1997] ECR I-5253, at 5363–4, and in Case C-243/95 *Hill and Stapleton v Revenue Commissioners* [1998] ECR I-3739, at 3748.

[115] [1993] ECR I-5579, at 5596; the supplied emphasis suggests that the Advocate General was in fact satisfied with subjective rather than objective justification. See also the same Advocate General's submissions in Case C-152/91 *Neath v Hugh Steeper Ltd* [1993] ECR I-6935.

[116] Op cit, n 93, also discussed in ch 5.

[117] See also Elmer AG in Case C-249/96 *Grant v South-West Trains Ltd* [1998] ECR I-621.

[118] Case C-408/92 [1994] ECR I-4435.   [119] Ibid, at 4448.

operative date of the *Barber* judgment[120] and the date on which the scheme rules were equalized for men and women. It went on to add:

Even assuming that it would, in this context, be possible to take account of objectively justifiable considerations relating to the needs of the undertaking or of the occupational scheme concerned, the administrators of the occupational scheme could not reasonably plead, as justification for raising the retirement age for women during this period, financial difficulties as significant as those of which the Court took account in the *Barber* judgment, since the space of time is relatively short and attributable in any event to the conduct of the scheme administrators themselves.[121]

Similarly, in relation to direct discrimination contrary to the Equal Treatment Directive, the Court has apparently countenanced the possibility of justification but without actually applying the principle.[122]

It is respectfully submitted that this is a misconceived and undesirable route for the ECJ to pursue.[123] It is misconceived because it is based upon a flawed analysis of the concept of discrimination.[124] Discrimination occurs where a person is treated adversely on a prohibited ground. The concept is a remedial one and, as Lenz AG pointed out in *Enderby v Frenchay Health Authority*,[125] it makes no sense to make technical distinctions between its direct and indirect manifestations. There are, therefore, broadly speaking, two elements of the tort of discrimination, whichever form it takes: adverse treatment (harm) and the grounding of that treatment in a prohibited classification (causation). It has already been seen that the ECJ recognized expressly in *Macarthys Ltd v Smith*[126] that where there is no causation there can be no discrimination. It has also been seen that objective justification reflects the element of causation where the discrimination is indirect: if the adverse consequences to one group can be shown to be attributable to an acceptable and discrimination–neutral factor, then there is no discrimination. The cause of the adverse impact is something other than discrimination. When one is dealing with direct discrimination, however, once adverse treatment and causation have been proved, this is the end of the matter; there can logically be no room for any further arguments about the roots of the adverse treatment. Justification is, therefore, not an applicable notion.[127]

---

[120] Discussed in ch 4.   [121] [1994] ECR I-4435, at 4468.

[122] See Case C-32/93 *Webb v EMO (Air Cargo) Ltd* [1994] ECR I-3567 and Case C-421/92 *Habermann-Beltermann* [1994] ECR I-1657. Cf Case C-109/00 *Tele Danmark A/S v Handels- og Kontorfunktionaerernes Forbund I Danmark (HK)* [2001] ECR I-6993 and Case C-320/01 *Busch v Klinikum Neustadt GmbH* [2003] ECR I-2041. All of these decisions are discussed in greater detail in ch 5.

[123] It is, however, important to note that the European Court of Human Rights has adopted a markedly different analysis of the concept of discrimination from the ECJ; for it, any *prima facie* discriminatory treatment (that is to say, the unequal treatment of comparable situations, or the equal treatment of different situations) can be excused by objective and reasonable justification: see the *Belgian Linguistics (No 2)* Case (1968) Series A, No 6, 1 EHRR 252, and further discussion in ch 7. It is submitted that this is a much weaker model for anti-discrimination law than that adopted by the ECJ, and that the EU approach is therefore to be preferred.

[124] This view was endorsed by Jacobs AG in Case 79/99 *Schnorbus*, op cit, n 19.

[125] Case C-127/92, op cit, n 57.   [126] Case 129/79, op cit, n 17.

[127] It is submitted that this is what was intended by Lenz AG in *Enderby*. Although he spoke of an employer 'justifying' differences of pay in cases of direct discrimination, he was dealing with proof that

The possibility of justifying direct discrimination is also undesirable[128] because it permits a raft of undefined excuses for discrimination which are not articulated in EU law.[129] This has the potential gravely to undermine the operation of the principle of equality and is, furthermore, contrary to the Court's usual rule that exceptions to fundamental principles are to be construed narrowly.[130]

It must, however, be conceded that there are today a few situations in which direct discrimination is expressly deemed capable of justification. In particular, in relation to discrimination on the ground of age, Article 6(1) of the Framework Directive provides:

Notwithstanding Article 2(2), Member States may provide that differences of treatment on grounds of age shall not constitute discrimination, if, within the context of national law, they are objectively and reasonably justified by a legitimate aim, including legitimate employment policy, labour market and vocational training objectives, and if the means of achieving that aim are appropriate and necessary.

This provision is considered further in chapter 5. In addition, the Directives on Part-Time Work[131] and Fixed-Term Employees,[132] also discussed in chapter 5, permit the justification of direct discrimination.[133]

Harassment and instructions to discriminate

There was a growing consciousness of the existence and prevalence of sexual harassment in both the USA and the EU during the closing decades of the twentieth century. The action taken by the EU in this field is discussed in chapter 5. The damaging potential of harassment in relation to all the groups protected from discrimination in EU law today is reflected in specific provisions outlawing both harassment and the giving of instructions to discriminate. Thus, both the Race

the pay difference was *caused* by sex discrimination; see the Advocate General's submissions: [1993] ECR I-5535, at 5558–9. For further support for this analysis, see Watson, 'Equality of Treatment: A Variable Concept?' (1995) 24 ILJ 33, Hepple, 'Equality and Discrimination' in Davies, Lyon-Caen, Sciarra, and Simitis (eds), *European Community Labour Law: Principles and Perspectives* (Clarendon Press, Oxford, 1996), Szyszczak, ' "The Status to be Accorded to Motherhood": Case C-32/93 *Webb v Emo Air Cargo (UK) Ltd*' (1995) 58 MLR 860, and Ellis, 'The Definition of Discrimination in European Community Sex Equality Law' (1994) 19 ELRev 563.

[128] See Hepple, Coussey, and Choudhury, *Equality: A New Framework* (Cambridge Centre for Public Law and the Judge Institute of Management Studies, 2000); the vast majority of people questioned pursuant to this inquiry did not consider that direct discrimination should be justifiable.

[129] See Hepple, 'Can Direct Discrimination Be Justified?' (1994) 55 EOR 48; Bowers and Moran, 'Justification in Direct Sex Discrimination Law: Breaking the Taboo' (2002) 31 ILJ 307; Gill and Monaghan, 'Justification in Direct Sex Discrimination Law: Taboo Upheld' (2003) 32 ILJ 115; and Bowers, Moran, and Honeyball, 'Justification in Direct Sex Discrimination: A Reply' (2003) 32 ILJ 185.

[130] Case 222/84 *Johnston v Chief Constable of the RUC* [1986] ECR 1651, also discussed in ch 6.

[131] Directive 97/81, OJ [1998] L14/9.   [132] Directive 99/70, OJ [1999] L175/43.

[133] Gill and Monaghan, op cit, n 129, argue that these directives are labour market, rather than human rights, measures; thus, justification reflects the balance which has to be struck between the interests of the workers concerned and their employers. 'Such differential treatment does not undermine the dignity of the worker' (at 119).

Directive and the Framework Directive include harassment and an instruction to discriminate within the concept of discrimination.[134] Article 2(3) of the Race Directive provides:

Harassment shall be deemed to be discrimination within the meaning of paragraph 1, when an unwanted conduct related to racial or ethnic origin takes place with the purpose or effect of violating the dignity of a person and of creating an intimidating, hostile, degrading, humiliating or offensive environment. In this context, the concept of harassment may be defined in accordance with the national laws and practice of the Member States.

Article 2(3) of the Framework Directive is cast in identical terms in relation to its field of operation. The amended Article 2(2) of the Equal Treatment Directive defines harassment similarly, and adds that 'sexual harassment' occurs 'where any form of unwanted verbal, non–verbal or physical conduct of a sexual nature occurs, with the purpose or effect of violating the dignity of a person, in particular when creating an intimidating, hostile, degrading, humiliating or offensive environment'. Article 2(3) states that such harassment and sexual harassment are to be 'deemed' to be discrimination on the grounds of sex; it adds that '[a] person's rejection of, or submission to, such conduct may not be used as a basis for a decision affecting that person'.[135] The difficulties caused both by the specificity of these texts and of the verbal disparities between them are examined in chapter 5.

The Race Directive, Framework Directive, and amended Equal Treatment Directive all prohibit the giving of instructions to discriminate, but none gives any definition of what is meant by this term.[136] In particular, the ECJ will have to decide whether 'instructions' have to be mandatory, or whether, alternatively, an expressed preference or encouragement would be included. The provision is presumably intended to catch such situations as where an employer tells a job agency not to send, for example, black or Muslim applicants for a post; however, it ought arguably also to extend to the situation where the (perhaps more wily) employer expresses a mere preference in this regard.

Positive action

Through its now quite sophisticated view of direct discrimination, EU law protects the principle of formal equality. However, as discussed in chapter 1, many factors inhibit the capacity of this principle alone to produce real equality (however that is

[134] It has been argued, however, that the restriction of the concept of harassment to cases which involve discrimination is too limiting, and that a broader Community measure outlawing bullying and mobbing is required: see Driessen–Reilly and Driessen, 'Don't Shoot the Messenger: A Look at Community Law Relating to Harassment in the Workplace' (2003) 28 ELRev 493.

[135] Recitals 8 and 9 of the Preamble to the amending Directive remind the Member States that harassment and sexual harassment take place not only in the workplace, but also in access to it and during vocational training.

[136] See Art 2(4) of the Race Directive, Art 2(4) of the Framework Directive, and Art 2(4) of the Equal Treatment Directive.

defined). Thus, legal systems often reach out beyond the pure principle of consistency of treatment to try to tackle the obstacles which stand in the path of real equality of opportunity. The chief means by which it is sometimes said that EU law attempts this difficult task is through the concept of indirect discrimination. As has been seen, the ECJ is quite rigorous in its definition of this concept, although later chapters will reveal that it is not invariably faithful to this approach in its application of the law. However, even if it were unfailingly rigorous, the concept of indirect discrimination in itself is essentially a non-dynamic, non-redistributive one. Although it seeks to take note of the hidden obstacles facing protected groups of people and to set them aside where they are irrelevant to the matter in hand, it does nothing to dismantle those obstacles or to change customarily stereotyped roles.[137] Thus, for example, in enthusiastically applying the concept of indirect discrimination to protect part-time workers, the Court recognizes the commitment of women (predominantly) to the care of their families and homes; however, this recognition arguably concretizes the position of women, giving implicit judicial blessing to the way in which domestic life is currently usually organized.[138] It does nothing to break down a work culture of long hours and family-unfriendly work conditions, yet these are the sorts of measures which are needed to give men and women truly equal opportunities in the workplace.

It is for this reason that the more positive measures referred to in chapter 1 are sometimes resorted to. Such measures run counter to the principle of formal equality and create a difficult tension which has to be resolved by the legal system. EU law contains several provisions permitting positive action, and these will be discussed in chapter 6. It will be seen that the legislative philosophy underlying these provisions has not yet been fully fleshed out by the ECJ. In particular, it is not clear whether they are restricted to operating in the shadow of the principle of formal equality, or whether, on the other hand, they are sometimes permitted to trump it.

Mainstreaming

It is also widely recognized that non-discrimination and equality law must be complemented by wider measures of social policy, designed to relieve historical and other types of structural disadvantage and to promote social inclusion. There can be no doubt that the EU today wields enormous power in this area, in particular through its Employment Strategy and the deployment of its Structural Funds. However, one especially noteworthy way in which the EU today gives

---

[137] See also Morris, 'On the Normative Foundations of Indirect Discrimination Law: Understanding the Competing Models of Discrimination Law as Aristotelian Forms of Justice' (1995) 15 OJLS 199.

[138] See also McGlynn and Farrelly, 'Equal Pay and the "Protection of Women Within Family Life"' (1999) 24 ELRev 202.

voice to the promotion of equality is through 'mainstreaming'. According to the Commission, mainstreaming in the context of sex equality

involves not restricting efforts to promote equality to implementation of specific measures to help women, but <u>mobilising</u> <u>all</u> <u>general</u> <u>policies</u> <u>and</u> <u>measures</u> specifically <u>for</u> <u>the</u> <u>purpose</u> <u>of</u> achieving <u>equality</u> by actively and openly taking into account at the planning stage their possible effects on the respective situations of men and women (<u>gender</u> <u>perspective</u>). This means systematically examining measures and policies and taking into account such possible effects when defining and implementing them: thus, development policies, the organisation of work, choices relating to transport or the fixing of school hours, etc may have significant differential impacts on the situation of women and men which must therefore be duly taken into consideration in order to further promote equality between women and men.[139]

Legislative underpinning for this type of activity in the field of sex equality is provided by the TEC itself, which lists the promotion of sex equality as one of the Community's 'tasks' in Article 2 and pledges, in Article 3(2), to 'aim to eliminate inequalities, and to promote equality between men and women' in the pursuit of all the Community's activities;[140] it has been argued that this legitimizes *inter alia* the promotion of sex equality in public procurement, so-called 'contract compliance'.[141] If and when the Constitution enters into force, it will reiterate this pledge[142] and will add that, in defining and implementing its policies and activities, the Union will 'aim to combat discrimination based on sex, racial or ethnic origin, religion or belief, disability, age or sexual orientation'.[143]

A similar duty in the field of sex equality is cast on the Member States by Article 1a of the Equal Treatment Directive:

Member States shall actively take into account the objective of equality between men and women when formulating and implementing laws, regulations, administrative provisions, policies and activities [in relation to the workplace and social security].

A Council Decision in December 2000 established a Programme relating to the Community framework strategy on gender equality, 2001–2005.[144] This provides in Article 2(1) that the Programme

is one of the instruments necessary for the implementation of the overall Community strategy on gender equality, which embraces all Community policies and action aimed at achieving gender equality, including gender mainstreaming policies and specific actions targeted at women.

The European Council in 2003 called on the Commission to report annually on gender equality and mainstreaming. The Commission's first response was a 'Report on equality between women and men, 2004',[145] in which it affirmed that

---

[139] Communication, 'Incorporating equal opportunities for women and men into all Community policies and activities', COM (1996) 67 final, at 2.

[140] It is noteworthy that Art 3(2) uses mandatory, not merely discretionary, language: '...the Community shall aim to eliminate inequalities...'

[141] See Tobler, 'Encore: "Women's Clauses" in Public Procurement under Community Law' (2000) 25 ELRev 618.   [142] In Art III-116.

[143] Art III-118.   [144] OJ [2001] L17/22.   [145] COM (2004) 115 final.

gender mainstreaming was underway both in the EU machinery of government and in the Member States, but that further action was necessary to compile data on gender equality, to develop indicators for the assessment of progress in this field, and to monitor progress.

The Commission is required to draw up a report to the European Parliament and the Council on the application of both the Race Directive and the Framework Directive. This report must, in accordance with the principle of gender main-streaming, provide an assessment of the impact of measures taken pursuant to the Directives on women and men.[146]

Even before the inclusion of Article 13 in the TEC, the Commission had committed itself to a policy of mainstreaming in relation to many of the other classes of people protected by the Article.[147] For example, its 1998 Action Plan against Racism pledged it to mainstream race when considering a number of important policy areas.[148] In November 2000, as a counterpart to the Race Directive and the Framework Directive, the Council established a Community action programme to combat discrimination during the period from 2001 until 2006.[149] This addresses all forms of discrimination prohibited under EU law, apart from sex discrimination, and aims to provide practical support and underpinning for the legislation. It seeks, for example, to foster the exchange of information, networking, and good practice, and it gives express emphasis to the mainstreaming of anti-discriminatory policies and practices.[150]

[146] Race Directive, Art 17(2); Framework Directive, Art 19(2).
[147] See further Bell, 'Equality and the European Union Constitution' (2004) 33 ILJ 242.
[148] COM (1998) 183.   [149] Decision 2000/750, OJ [2000] L303/23.
[150] See the Annex to the instrument, para 1(g).

4

Equal pay

Scope of the obligation

The principle that there must be no discrimination as regards pay applies in all the areas of substantive EU anti-discrimination law covered in the present work. Article 141 on equal pay for men and women devotes considerable attention to the scope of this principle, providing in particular:

1. Each Member State shall ensure that the principle of equal pay for male and female workers for equal work or work of equal value is applied.[1]

2. For the purpose of this Article, 'pay' means the ordinary basic or minimum wage or salary and any other consideration, whether in cash or in kind, which the worker receives directly or indirectly, in respect of his employment, from his employer.
   Equal pay without discrimination based on sex means:

   (a) that pay for the same work at piece rates shall be calculated on the basis of the same unit of measurement;
   (b) that pay for work at time rates shall be the same for the same job.[2]

It was not until the ECJ's decision in *Allonby v Accrington and Rossendale College*[3] that it ruled on the meaning of 'worker' for the purposes of Article 141. It pointed out that there is no single definition of 'worker' in Community law, and that the concept varies according to the area under consideration.[4] Because of the fundamental importance of the principle of sex equality in pay, 'worker' in this context must have a Community meaning and it must not be interpreted restrictively. A 'worker' for this purpose is:

A person who, for a certain period of time, performs services for and under the direction of another person in return for which he receives remuneration . . . [T]he authors of the Treaty did not intend that the term 'worker', within the meaning of Article 141(1) EC, should include independent providers of services who are not in a relationship of subordination with the person who receives the services.[5]

---

[1] Before its amendment by the Amsterdam Treaty, this provision read: 'Each Member State shall during the first stage ensure and subsequently maintain the application of the principle that men and women should receive equal pay for equal work.' If and when the proposed Constitution enters into force, Art 141(1) will become Art III-214(1); the only alteration in its wording is the reversal of 'male and female'.   [2] Art III-214(2) of the proposed Constitution.
[3] Case C-256/01, judgment of 13 January 2004, nyr.
[4] Case C-85/96 *Martinez Sala* [1998] ECR I-2691.   [5] Case C-256/01, at paras 67 and 68.

The Court added:

Provided that a person is a worker within the meaning of Article 141(1) EC, the nature of his legal relationship with the other party to the employment relationship is of no consequence in regard to the application of that article . . . The formal classification of a self-employed person under national law does not exclude the possibility that a person must be classified as a worker within the meaning of Article 141(1) EC if his independence is merely notional, thereby disguising an employment relationship within the meaning of that article.[6]

There would appear to be no reason to suppose that a different definition will be applied to persons who seek to invoke the equal pay provisions of the Race Directive and the Framework Directive.

The definition of 'pay' contained in Article 141 has provided the starting-point for a large body of case law, in which the ECJ has developed the meaning of the concept for the purposes of sex equality. It is likely that this case law will inform the meaning to be attached to pay for the purposes of the Race Directive and the Framework Directive, both of which expressly forbid discrimination over 'pay' in the fields which they occupy;[7] the discussion of the meaning of 'pay' which follows proceeds on this basis. Such a conclusion is fortified by Recital 13 of the Preamble to the Framework Directive, which suggests a correlation between the way in which Article 141 operates and the scope of the Framework Directive:

This Directive does not apply to social security and social protection schemes whose benefits are not treated as income[8] within the meaning given to that term for the purpose of applying Article 141 of the EC Treaty, nor to any kind of payment by the State aimed at providing access to employment or maintaining employment.

The tricky dividing line between 'pay' and social security benefits for the purpose of Article 141 is discussed below.

Article 141 is to be found under Title VIII of the TEC, 'Social Policy, Education, Vocational Training and Youth', which was substantially amended by the Amsterdam Treaty. The opening provision of this Title, Article 136, sets the agenda:

The Community and the Member States, having in mind fundamental social rights such as those set out in the European Social Charter signed at Turin on 18 October 1961 and in the 1989 Community Charter of the Fundamental Social Rights of Workers, shall have as their objectives the promotion of employment, improved living and working conditions, so as to make possible their harmonization while the improvement is being maintained, proper social protection, dialogue between management and labour, the development of human resources with a view to lasting high employment and the combating of exclusion . . .

---

[6] Case C-256/01, at paras 70 and 71. The Court added: 'In the case of teachers who are, vis-à-vis an intermediary undertaking, under an obligation to undertake an assignment at a college, it is necessary in particular to consider the extent of any limitation on their freedom to choose their timetable, and the place and content of their work. The fact that no obligation is imposed on them to accept an assignment is of no consequence in that context' (at para 72).

[7] Art 4(1)(c) of the Race Directive and Art 3(1)(c) of the Framework Directive.

[8] This is an infelicitous piece of drafting since Art 141 does not use the term 'income'.

Article 141 is thus an unusual type of Treaty provision. On the one hand, it represents a social ideal and an instrument with which at least indirectly to harmonize social policy. On the other hand, it states a complete legal obligation, a social and economic end in its own right. Its wording is based on that of Article 2(1) of International Labour Organization (ILO) Convention No 100, 1951,[9] which provides:

[E]ach Member State shall, by means appropriate to the methods in question for determining rates of remuneration, promote and, in so far as is consistent with such methods, ensure the application to all workers of the principle of equal remuneration for men and women workers for work of equal value.[10]

The meaning of 'pay' for the purposes of Article 141

The ECJ's now-famous statement in *Defrenne v Sabena*[11] about the purpose of the equal pay provision was quoted in chapter 1. It will be recalled the Court reasoned that the original Article 119 aimed both to eliminate competitive imbalances between the Member States and also to ensure social progress. It concluded that the principle of equal pay forms part of the foundations of the Community. This important statement of principle has conditioned the view the Court has taken of what is today Article 141, and has in general led it to attach a broad, purposive meaning to the word 'pay'. In particular, the ECJ has developed a large and influential body of case law on the relationship between Article 141 and occupational pensions, and for this reason, pensions and their legislative regulation in EU law are dealt with at an early stage in the present chapter.

Certain immediate conclusions can be drawn from the wording of Article 141(2) (set out in the previous section). For example, it is clear that the material form of the consideration is irrelevant for the purpose of Article 141; thus, all perks provided for employees by their employers are likely to constitute 'pay', so that Article 141 catches such things as company cars, and health and other insurance cover paid for by employers. It also follows that Article 141 must also cover compensatory payments made by an employer to an employee, such as the refund of expenses incurred in travelling or entertaining. In *Garland v British Rail*,[12] Article 141 was held to extend to concessionary rail fares provided for employees and ex-employees. Similarly, the notion of 'pay' is not confined to basic pay, but covers

---

[9] UNTS, Vol 165, 303.

[10] The Editor of the *Common Market Law Reports* pointed out in [1976] 2 CMLR, at 114, that the authentic English text of what was then Art 119 was translated from the original languages of the EEC Treaty and the translators did not, in doing so, pay any regard to the English authentic text of the ILO Convention. The major difference between Article 119 as it was originally phrased and the ILO Convention lay in the use of the phrases 'equal work' (Art 141) and 'work of equal value' (ILO Convention). However, the Amsterdam Treaty added 'work of equal value' to the EC text.

[11] Case 43/75 [1976] ECR 455.

[12] Case 12/81 [1982] ECR 359, noted by Bradley in (1982) 19 CMLRev 625.

overtime pay,[13] special bonus payments made by employers,[14] and termination payments.[15]

Article 141 refers specifically to consideration which the worker receives 'in respect of his employment'. This indicates that the payment must arise out of the worker's employment, but not that it is necessarily confined to payment for the work actually done.[16] One type of situation in which such a distinction may become relevant was highlighted in *Sabbatini v European Parliament*.[17] Two Community employees brought a staff action before the ECJ asking to have overturned the decisions of the Community institutions denying them 'expatriation allowances'. These allowances were paid to people having to live in a foreign country in order to work for the Community. One of the applicants' arguments was that the denial of these allowances amounted in the circumstances to a breach of Article 141. The issue therefore arose as to whether the allowances constituted 'pay'. The Commission argued that they were not 'pay' because they represented not payment for work done, but compensation for having to live away from home in order to work; they were therefore payable quite independently of the work done. The ECJ decided the case on a different basis,[18] but the Advocate General dealt with this issue. He submitted that account should be taken not just of wages *stricto sensu*, but also of all other payments made by reason of the links binding workers to their employers. Expatriation allowances fell within the notion of 'pay' because they were so closely linked with the employee's work.

Similarly, the Court has held that payments made by an employer to an employee who is absent from work can also constitute 'pay';[19] thus, maternity

[13] This was assumed by the ECJ in Joined Cases C-399, 409, & 425/92, C-34, 50, & 78/93 *Stadt Lengerich v Helmig* [1994] ECR I-5727; Darmon AG said that it was 'agreed that overtime supplements constitute pay for the purposes of the first paragraph of Art 119' (at 5731).

[14] See Case 58/81 *Commission v Luxembourg* [1982] ECR 2175, where the ECJ held a special 'head of household' allowance to be 'pay'. See also Case C-281/97 *Krüger v Kreiskrankenhaus Ebersberg* [1999] ECR I-5127, where an annual Christmas bonus was held to be 'pay'.

[15] Case C-249/97 *Gruber v Silhouette International Schmied GmbH & Co KG* [1999] ECR I-5295.

[16] In Case 19/81 *Burton v British Railways Board* [1982] ECR 555, Van Themaat AG said '[T]he decisive question is whether the benefits are received by the worker concerned from his employer owing to his employment. The French and Italian texts of Article 119 containing the words "en raison de l'emploi" and "in regione dell' impiego" also show that the test is not whether the payment is consideration for work performed. Only the English text of Article 119, which contains the words "in respect of his employment", might perhaps point to a more restrictive meaning. What is required for the purposes of the final words of the second paragraph of Article 119, and what incidentally I believe is also required by the English text logically construed, is rather an unseverable causal link between the payment and a worker's employment' (at 588–9). See also the remarks of Lamothe AG in Case 80/70 *Defrenne v Belgium* [1971] ECR 445. In Case C-342/93 *Gillespie v Northern Health and Social Services Board* [1996] ECR I-475, the ECJ stated: '... the concept of pay ... includes all consideration which workers receive directly or indirectly from their employers in respect of their employment. The legal nature of such consideration is not important for the purposes of the application of Article 119 provided that it is granted in respect of employment...' (at 498).   [17] Case 32/71 [1972] ECR 345.

[18] See ch 6.

[19] See, eg, Case C-360/90 *Arbeiterwohlfahrt der Stadt Berlin v Bötel* [1992] ECR I-3589; Case C-457/93 *Kuratorium für Dialyse und Nierentranslantation eV v Lewark* [1996] ECR I-243; and Case C-278/93 *Freers v Deutsche Bundespost* [1996] ECR I-1165. Cf the decision of the British Employment

benefit paid by an employer pursuant to legislation or to the woman's contract of employment is 'pay' because it is 'based on the employment relationship',[20] and therefore a woman is subjected to unlawful sex discrimination where she does not receive a pay rise awarded to her colleagues during the period of her maternity pay.[21] In *Lewen v Denda*,[22] the ECJ held that a Christmas bonus paid by an employer to all his employees constituted 'pay'; the reason for which the employer paid it was of 'little importance' provided that it was granted in connection with employment. Thus, even if paid voluntarily and as an incentive for future work, it fell within Article 141.[23]

The fact that the payment is notional only and never actually passes into the hands of the employee does not prevent it from falling within Article 141. This became evident in *Worringham v Lloyds Bank Ltd*,[24] where a bank had separate pension schemes for its male and female employees. The schemes were contributory for all male employees but only for those female employees who were over 25. In order to maintain pay parity with the other clearing banks, Lloyds added an extra 5%, corresponding to the cost of the contribution, to the salaries of all its contributing employees. This sum passed straight to the pension fund and was thus in effect merely a notional payment to the employee. However, if a man left Lloyds Bank before qualifying for a pension benefit, he received a refund of the contributions paid on his behalf, whereas if a woman under 25 left she received nothing. Two women under 25 complained that this treatment breached Article 141 and the ECJ held that it did. The 5% additions were included in an employee's gross salary and directly determined the calculation of other advantages linked to salary (such as redundancy payments, unemployment benefits, family allowances, and credit facilities). It did not matter that they were immediately deducted by the employer and paid into the pension fund.

Appeal Tribunal in *Manor Bakeries Ltd v Nazir* [1996] IRLR 604, which emphasized that the alleged pay must be received in respect of 'work'; this decision was later disapproved in *Davies v Neath Port Talbot County Borough Council* [1999] IRLR 769, but on the basis that the activity in issue there did in fact constitute 'work'.

[20] Case C-342/93 *Gillespie*, op cit, n 16, at 499, and Case C-218/98 *Abdoulaye v Renault SA* [1999] ECR I-5723; in the latter, the ECJ held that it made no difference that the payment was one-off, not indexed on salary, and paid to pregnant employees when they went on maternity leave. See McGlynn, 'Pregnancy, Parenthood and the Court of Justice in *Abdoulaye*' (2000) 25 ELRev 654, and id, 'Equality, Maternity, and Questions of Pay' (1996) 21 ELRev 327.

[21] Case C-342/93 *Gillespie*, op cit, n 16. See also Case C-147/02 *Alabaster v Woolwich plc and Secretary of State for Social Security*, judgment of 30 March 2004, nyr, but note the dissent of Léger AG from the principle that Art 141 applies to a woman on maternity leave, and see further discussion in ch 5.

[22] Case C-333/97 [1999] ECR I-7243.

[23] See also the submissions of Warner AG in Case 69/80 *Worringham v Lloyds Bank Ltd* [1981] ECR 767, at 805. And see Snaith, 'Article 119 EEC and Private Occupational Pension Schemes' (1981) 6 ELRev 193; Crisham, 'The Equal Pay Principle: Some Recent Decisions of the ECJ' (1981) 18 CMLRev 601; Post, 'New Decisions of the European Court on Sex Discrimination' (1981) 1 LIEI 77; Plender, 'Equal Pay for Men and Women: Two Recent Decisions of the European Court' (1982) 30 American Journal of Comparative Law 627; and Szyszczak, 'Occupational Pension Schemes and Article 119 EEC' (1981) 1 NLJ 527.   [24] Case 69/80 *Worringham*, op cit, n 23.

Similarly, in *Liefting v Directie van het Academisch Ziekenhuis bij Universiteit van Amsterdam*,[25] the ECJ held:

[A]lthough the portion which employers are liable to contribute to the financing of statutory social security schemes to which both employees and employers contribute does not constitute pay within the meaning of Article 119 of the Treaty, the same is not true of sums which are included in the calculation of the gross salary payable to the employee and which directly determine the calculation of other benefits linked to the salary such as redundancy payments, unemployment benefits, family allowances and credit facilities. This is also the case if the amounts in question are immediately deducted by the employer and paid to a pension fund on behalf of the employee.[26]

Can this principle be extended to compulsory deductions from salary demanded by an employer on a discriminatory basis, where the gross salary itself does not vary according to sex? In *Newstead v Department of Transport*,[27] a male civil servant, who described himself as 'a confirmed bachelor', complained of discrimination contrary to Article 141 in the requirement contained in the civil service pension scheme that all male employees contribute 1.5 % of their gross salary to a fund for widows' pensions. If the employee never married, his contribution was returned to him with interest when he left the civil service, or was paid to his estate if he died before then, but no such contribution was required of his female colleagues. He therefore contended that he was denied the immediate enjoyment of his full salary, unlike his female colleagues. The ECJ held that this situation did not breach Article 141, since gross pay was not affected and, unlike the situation in *Worringham* and *Liefting*, there was no consequential effect as regards other salary-related benefits. Critical to this ruling seems to have been the fact that the deduction was made for the purpose of providing a survivor's benefit in an occupational pension scheme which substituted for a part of the State scheme, a matter over which EU law appeared at the time of this case to permit sex discrimination.[28] It would seemingly have been otherwise had the purpose of the deduction been unrelated to an area where sex discrimination was permitted. So, for example, it would certainly appear to constitute a breach of Article 141 where an employer requires his male employees only to donate a percentage of their gross salaries to the local cats' home.

Although the ECJ has not yet determined this question, the Commission has committed itself to the view that the taxation of income from employment must also respect the principle of equality pursuant to Article 141. Thus, it argues that the Member States must ensure that their tax systems do not discriminate on the ground of sex.[29]

[25] Case 23/83 [1984] ECR 3225.   [26] Ibid, at 3239.

[27] Case 192/85 [1987] ECR 4753. See Arnull, 'Widows' Mite' (1988) 13 ELRev 135.

[28] The ECJ's decisions in Case C-262/88 *Barber v Guardian Royal Exchange Assurance Group* [1990] ECR I-1889 and succeeding pensions cases subsequently made it clear that sex discrimination was not permissible in such situations. See discussion below.   [29] See COM (2003) 657 final, at 5.

(i)   Are pensions 'pay' within Article 141?

It was seen above that Article 141 provides that, in order to be 'pay', the consideration must come, either directly or indirectly, from the employer. This requirement has presented a problem in relation to the practically very important issue of whether pension benefits fall within Article 141, a matter which has now been raised before the ECJ many times.[30] The issue has proved to be specially significant in the field of sex equality for a number of reasons, not least the different State pension ages traditionally stipulated in the Member States for men and women,[31] and the different working lives of the two sexes. However, it is also to be anticipated that the issue will prove to be highly relevant to discrimination on the newer grounds introduced into EU law, especially, it may be hazarded, discrimination on the grounds of disability, age, and sexual orientation.

Probably the first real hint from the ECJ itself that pensions might sometimes be within Article 141 came in *Burton v British Railways Board*.[32] The question here was whether the provision of early retirement pensions under a voluntary redundancy scheme contravened EU law because women became eligible at 55, but men only at 60. The Court held that

the question of interpretation which has been referred to the Court concerns not the benefit itself, but whether the conditions of *access* to the voluntary redundancy scheme are discriminatory. This is a matter covered by the provisions of Council Directive 76/207 . . . and not by those of Article 119.[33]

Later, it pointed out specifically that:

The option given to workers by the provisions at issue . . . enables a worker who leaves his employment at any time during the five years before he reaches normal pensionable age to receive certain allowances for a limited period. The allowances are calculated in the same manner regardless of the sex of the worker.[34]

Commenting on this case in the British Employment Appeal Tribunal, Browne-Wilkinson J said that he considered its implication to be that 'the quantum of benefit payable under a retirement scheme may be "pay" within the meaning of Article 119'.[35]

Razzouk and Beydoun v Commission[36] concerned sex discrimination contained in the Community's own Staff Regulations as regards the provision of survivors' benefits to the relatives of deceased employees. Slynn AG submitted that a retirement pension received by a Community employee, and also a survivor's pension

---

[30] The issue was originally ducked by the ECJ in Case 69/80 *Worringham*, op cit, n 23. For further discussion, see Curtin, 'Occupational Pension Schemes and Article 119: Beyond the Fringe?' (1987) 24 CMLRev 215.   [31] See further ch 8.

[32] Case 19/81 [1982] ECR 555, noted by Bradley in (1982) 19 CMLRev 625.

[33] Ibid, at 575, emphasis added.   [34] Ibid, at 576–7.

[35] *Barber v Guardian Royal Exchange Assurance Group* [1983] IRLR 240, at 243.

[36] Cases 75 & 117/82 [1984] ECR 1509.

received by such a person's widow or widower, was 'pay' and subject to a principle 'analogous' to Article 141. He explained that:

> In substance the official's entitlement to, for example, a retirement pension is part of the consideration (albeit deferred) which he receives in respect of his employment . . . The same can, in my view, be said of the survivor's pension even though it is not received directly by the official himself but is paid to his surviving spouse. It is still consideration received in respect of the official's employment for which in part he also makes general pension contributions.[37]

The Court itself preferred to base its conclusion in this case on the general principle of equal treatment of the sexes and said that:

> [I]n relations between the Community institutions on the one hand and their employees and those claiming under them on the other, the requirements arising from this principle are by no means limited to those flowing from Article 119 . . .[38]

The Court was much more forthcoming on the pensions issue in *Bilka-Kaufhaus GmbH v Weber Von Hartz*.[39] Bilka was part of a chain of department stores in Germany which employed several thousand people. Ms Weber Von Hartz, who had been employed by the company for a number of years, alleged that its occupational pension scheme discriminated against female employees because of the conditions it imposed for entry into the scheme. Darmon AG submitted that each pension scheme has to be examined individually in order to test whether it falls within the scope of Article 141, in particular in the light of the relevant national legislation. However, he considered that the pension provided by Bilka was within Article 141:

> [I]t is a voluntary scheme which complements and 'tops up' the statutory scheme, even if it was encouraged or organized by the authorities, and . . . it applies only in so far as it is incorporated in the employment relationship, after negotiations between the employer and the employees.[40]

The Court itself agreed, saying:

> [T]he occupational pension scheme at issue in the main proceedings, although adopted in accordance with the provisions laid down by German legislation for such schemes, is *based on an agreement between Bilka and the staff committee representing its employees* and has the effect of supplementing the social benefits paid under national legislation of general application *with benefits financed entirely by the employer. The contractual rather than the statutory nature of the scheme in question is confirmed by the fact that, as has been pointed out above, the scheme and rules governing it are regarded as an integral part of the contracts of employment between Bilka and its employees.* It must therefore be concluded that the scheme . . . does not constitute a social security scheme governed directly by statute and thus outside the scope of Article 119. Benefits paid to employees under the scheme therefore constitute consideration received by the worker from the employer in respect of his employment, as referred to in the second paragraph of Article 119.[41]

---

[37] Cases 75 & 117/82 [1984] ECR 1509, at 1540.   [38] Ibid, at 1530.

[39] Case 170/84 [1986] ECR 1607. See Arnull, 'Sex Discrimination in Occupational Pension Schemes' (1986) 11 ELRev 363.   [40] [1986] ECR 1607, at 1614.

[41] Ibid, at 1625–6, emphases added. It is noteworthy (particularly with the benefit of hindsight) that the Court did not follow the argument of the UK Government in this case to the effect that this was

It followed that there were in essence two requirements for payments under this type of supplementary pension scheme to fall within Article 141: the scheme must be funded in part at least by the employer, because otherwise payments would not represent consideration received from the employer within the wording of Article 141;[42] and the scheme must be contractual in origin rather than set up by statute.[43]

The second of these criteria represented an attempt by the ECJ to differentiate between social security payments and pay. Such a distinction appears to be implied by the social policy provisions of the TEC, since they make separate reference to the harmonization of social security systems. The first case to explore the dividing-line was *Defrenne v Belgium*.[44] Ms Defrenne had been an air hostess employed by Sabena Airlines. In common with her other female colleagues, the company required her to retire at the age of 40. She then found that she faced discrimination in relation to her pension arrangements. A Belgian Royal Decree established a pension scheme for 'all members of air crews with the exception of air hostesses'; this special scheme was far more lucrative than the general State pension and payable at the age of 55. Under the general State scheme, women could not claim their pensions until the age of 60. Ms Defrenne voiced two objections in particular: her years of service with Sabena before she reached the age of 40 were taken into consideration only under the less favourable general scheme; and she could not claim any pension at all until she was 60. The Belgian court before which she brought proceedings asked the ECJ whether a 'retirement pension granted under a social security scheme financed by workers' and employees' contributions, as well as by state grants', constituted 'pay' within the meaning of Article 141. The ECJ ruled that both general and special State pension schemes are excluded from the ambit of Article 141:

Although payments in the nature of social security benefits are therefore in principle not alien to the concept of pay, there cannot be brought within this concept, as defined in Article 119, social security

a problem of 'access' to benefits and therefore within the principle of Case 19/81 *Burton*, op cit, n 32. For further discussion of this issue, see ch 5.

[42] Thus, in Case C-226/98 *Jørgensen v Foreningen af Speciallaeger* [2000] ECR I-2447, the ECJ held that the price which a doctor receives for goodwill on selling her practice when she retires is not equivalent to a pension: 'The transfer of a practice is not necessarily linked to the age of the transferor and may occur at any time, whereas a pension is obtained only at a certain age and subject to a certain period of activity and payment of a specific amount of contributions. Furthermore, it is the person taking over the practice who pays the purchase price and not those who normally provide the doctor's remuneration . . .' (at 2483).

[43] Provided that the origin of the payment is not statutory, it has long been clear that it is not taken outside the scope of Art 141 simply because statute regulates certain aspects of the payment. Van Themaat AG commented in Case 19/81 *Burton*, op cit, n 32: 'I do not think that it is relevant, for the purpose of determining whether Article 119 applies, that the method of calculating the amount of the benefits partly depends on statutory provisions. As was rightly pointed out in the course of the proceedings, such a criterion would mean that statutory minimum wages which discriminated between the sexes would not fall under Article 119 either' (at 588).

[44] Case 80/70 [1971] ECR 445, the so-called *First Defrenne* case. See also the remarks of Mayras AG in Case 207/78 *Ministère Public v Even* [1979] ECR 2019, at 2038–9.

schemes or benefits, in particular retirement pensions, directly governed by legislation without any element of agreement within the undertaking or the occupational branch concerned, which are obligatorily applicable to general categories of workers. These schemes assure for the workers the benefits of a legal scheme, to the financing of which workers, employers and possibly the public authorities contribute in a measure determined less by the employment relationship between the employer and the worker than by considerations of social policy. Accordingly, the part due from the employers in the financing of such schemes does not constitute a direct or indirect payment to the worker. Moreover, the worker will normally receive the benefits legally prescribed not by reason of the employer's contribution but solely because the worker fulfils the legal conditions for the grant of benefits.[45]

A social security payment thus appeared to be one whose qualifying conditions were exclusively laid down by legislation and which was payable irrespective of whether the particular employer concerned had in fact contributed to its financing. In the words of Lamothe AG:

[T]here is no relationship at all between the employer's contribution and the pension and it is this absence of relationship which in this case as in that of the general scheme prevents the pension from being regarded as consideration which the employed person receives from his employer within the meaning of the provisions of Article 119.[46]

In more graphic terms, he explained that social security benefits are

[N]o more consideration received indirectly from the employer than are the road, water mains or sewer, the benefit of which the employed person has as a citizen and to finance which the taxes and duties paid by the employer have contributed.[47]

However, this analysis proved to be deceptively simple. In reality, there is considerable overlap between the notions of 'pension' and 'social security', in particular in the UK, where occupational pension schemes may be 'contracted-out' of the earnings-related element of the State pension scheme, provided that they satisfy certain statutory requirements. The occupational pension in such a situation thus substitutes, at least in part, for the State pension. Is such a contracted-out pension therefore removed from the scope of Article 141? This question was first put to the ECJ in *Worringham v Lloyds Bank Ltd*.[48] The ECJ itself managed to avoid answering it on this occasion. However, Warner AG did deal with it. He considered that benefits under the Lloyds Bank scheme would have fallen within Article 141 were it not for the 'contracting-out' element. It had been argued that the rights under such a contracted-out scheme were not received, even indirectly,

---

[45] [1971] ECR 445, at 451. The Court appears today to consider that the *origins* of a particular scheme are relevant in helping it to decide whether it falls within the definition of a social security scheme: in Case C-109/91 *Ten Oever v Stichting Bedrijfspensioenfonds voor het Glazenwassers- en Schoonmaakbedrijf* [1993] ECR I-4879, a scheme was differentiated from that in the *Defrenne* case where 'the rules . . . were not laid down directly by law but were the result of an agreement between both sides of the industry concerned', notwithstanding that 'at the request of such employers' and trade union organisations as were considered to be representative, . . . the scheme [was declared] compulsory for the whole of the industry concerned' (at 4943).   [46] [1971] ECR 445, at 461.
[47] Ibid, at 458.   [48] Case 69/80, op cit, n 23.

from the employer because others were concerned in their elaboration and financing. However, the Advocate General submitted:

In my view the circumstances that the terms of a scheme have to be discussed with and to be approved by others does not detract from the fact that, at the end of the day, its adoption is the act of the employer. Nor is the element of tax saving in my opinion relevant. Wages and salaries, which are undoubtedly 'pay', are also deductible in computing the employer's profits for tax purposes; and I hardly think that the circumstance that a member of the scheme is taxable on benefits he receives from it and not on contributions he makes to it can affect the issue. It was also pointed out that some of the benefits under the scheme were payable not to the member but to his dependants. The conferment of the right to those benefits on his dependants can, however, in my opinion, properly be regarded as an advantage to the member arising from his employment.[49]

But he went on to add:

To hold that Article 119 applied in relation to [these] schemes would mean holding that ever since that Article took effect (ie since the end of the first stage of the transitional period in the case of the original Member States and since 1 January 1973 in the case of the [UK]) a Member State operating such a system was under an obligation to ensure that a contracted-out scheme afforded equal rights for men and women whilst it was under no such obligation as regards its state scheme. That would, it seems to me, be an unbalanced result to reach, as well as one calculated to deter contracting-out. In my opinion, where a privately established pension scheme is designed, not as a supplement to the state social security scheme . . . but as a substitute for it or for part of it, it must be regarded as outside the scope of Article 119 and as falling to be dealt with under the broader headings in Article 118.[50]

The full ECJ itself ultimately reached a different conclusion on this matter in *Barber v Guardian Royal Exchange Assurance Group*.[51] The effect of its forthright ruling in the latter case was to bring contracted-out pensions squarely within the scope of Article 141. It held:

[T]he second question must be understood as seeking in substance to ascertain whether a retirement pension paid under a contracted-out private occupational scheme falls within the scope of Article 119 of the Treaty, in particular where that pension is awarded in connection with compulsory redundancy. It must be pointed out in that regard that [in the *First Defrenne* case] the Court stated that consideration in the nature of social security benefits is not in principle alien to the concept of pay. However, the Court

---

[49] Case 69/80, op cit, n 23, at 805.

[50] Ibid, at 806. Cf *Razzouk and Beydoun*, op cit, n 36, where Slynn AG commented: 'The judgment of the Court in Case 80/70 *Defrenne v Belgium* excluded from the scope of Article 119 "social security schemes or benefits, in particular retirement pensions, directly governed by legislation without any element of agreement within the undertaking or the occupational branch concerned, which are obligatorily applicable to general categories of workers". That description cannot, in my view, be applied to the benefits and pensions made available under pension schemes entered into by employers and employees outside a national system of social security. Nor does it in my view fit the benefits provided under the Staff Regulations. True, they are independent of and replace social security legis-lation for the officials concerned. On the other hand, although based on Community "legislation", ie a Council Regulation, the scheme in the Staff Regulations applies only to persons employed by the institutions and is therefore closer to a scheme applicable to employees rather than to citizens or workers generally. In substance the official's entitlement to, for example, a retirement pension is part of the consideration (albeit deferred) which he receives in respect of his employment . . .' (at 1540).

[51] Op cit, n 28. See Honeyball and Shaw, 'Sex, Law and the Retiring Man' (1991) 16 ELRev 47, and Fitzpatrick, 'Equality in Occupational Pensions—The New Frontiers After *Barber*' (1991) 54 MLR 271.

pointed out that this concept, as defined in Article 119, cannot encompass social security schemes or benefits, in particular retirement pensions, directly governed by legislation without any element of agreement within the undertaking or the occupational branch concerned, which are compulsorily applicable to general categories of workers. The Court noted that those schemes afford the workers the benefit of a statutory scheme, to the financing of which workers, employers and possibly the public authorities contribute in a measure determined less by the employment relationship than by considerations of social policy. In order to answer the second question therefore it is necessary to ascertain whether those considerations also apply to contracted-out private occupational schemes . . .

[I]t must be pointed out first of all that the schemes in question are the result either of an agreement between workers and employers or of a unilateral decision taken by the employer. They are wholly financed by the employer or by both the employer and the workers without any contribution being made by the public authorities in any circumstances. Accordingly, such schemes form part of the consideration offered to workers by the employer.

Secondly, such schemes are not compulsorily applicable to general categories of workers. On the contrary, they apply only to workers employed by certain undertakings, with the result that affiliation to those schemes derives of necessity from the employment relationship with a given employer. Furthermore, even if the schemes in question are established in conformity with national legislation and consequently satisfy the conditions laid down by it for recognition as contracted-out schemes, they are governed by their own rules.

Thirdly, it must be pointed out that, even if the contributions paid to those schemes and the benefits which they provide are in part a substitute for those of the general statutory scheme, that fact cannot preclude the application of Article 119. It is apparent from the documents before the Court that occupational schemes such as that referred to in this case may grant to their members benefits greater than those which would be paid by the statutory scheme, with the result that their economic function is similar to that of the supplementary schemes which exist in certain Member States, where affiliation and contribution to the statutory scheme is compulsory and no derogation is allowed. In its judgment [in the *Bilka-Kaufhaus* case] the Court held that the benefits awarded under a supplementary pension scheme fell within the concept of pay, within the meaning of Article 119.

It must therefore be concluded that, unlike the benefits awarded by national statutory social security schemes, a pension paid under a contracted-out scheme constitutes consideration paid by the employer to the worker in respect of his employment and consequently falls within the scope of Article 119 of the Treaty. That interpretation of Article 119 is not affected by the fact that the private occupational scheme in question has been set up in the form of a trust and is administered by trustees who are technically independent of the employer, since Article 119 also applies to consideration received indirectly from the employer.[52]

The consequence of *Barber* was that both supplementary and contracted-out occupational pension schemes were clearly subject to the principle of equality as between the sexes, and discrimination within their terms was therefore actionable via Article 141 itself.[53]

---

[52] [1990] ECR I-1889, at 1950–2. Part of the Commission's motivation for its arguments in the *Barber* case, and probably part of the Court's motivation in reaching its ultimate decision, was the aim of ensuring equality of treatment as between the Member States in this matter; in other words, if German employers operating *Bilka-Kaufhaus* supplementary pension schemes were to be bound by Art 141, then so ought British employers operating under the British system of contracted-out pensions.

[53] The enforceability of Art 141 is discussed below. The relationship between Art 141 and the Equal Treatment Directive is examined in ch 5.

The full Court subsequently analysed the relationship between State social security schemes and occupational pension schemes in the *Beune* case.[54] The main question referred to the ECJ was whether a statutory pension scheme for civil servants in The Netherlands fell within Article 141. The Court referred to Jacobs AG's exhaustive and lucid exposition of the factors which had been regarded as relevant in the earlier case law. It summed them up as follows:

[T]he statutory nature of a pension scheme, negotiation between employers and employees' representatives, the fact that the employees' benefits supplement social security benefits, the manner in which the pension scheme is financed, its applicability to general categories of employees and, finally, the relationship between the benefit and the employees' employment.[55]

However, it went on to point out that most of these criteria do not, at least taken alone, provide a conclusive answer to whether the payment is within Article 141. Thus, the fact that a scheme is directly governed by statute may provide an indication that it is a social security scheme, but both the *Barber* and *Second Defrenne* cases expressly included as within Article 141 discrimination which was statutory in origin. The Court stated that it has attached more importance to the criterion of whether the scheme is a result of a formal agreement. As to the supplementary nature of schemes, the Court pointed out that the *Barber* case itself demonstrates that this is not invariably required. In relation to funding arrangements, even though a pension is funded by employers' and employees' contributions and is managed independently in accordance with rules similar to those applicable to occupational pension funds, this does not in truth differentiate it from a social security scheme; the Court added that even the fact of a contribution to the scheme by the State is not necessarily decisive. The applicability of the scheme to a 'general category of employees', which *Defrenne I* indicates is typical of a social security scheme, is a difficult test to apply in practice. All this led that Court to conclude:

[T]he only possible decisive criterion is whether the pension is paid to the worker by reason of the employment relationship between him and his former employer, that is to say the criterion of employment based on the wording of Article 119 itself.

Admittedly, as the Court has recognised ever since *Defrenne I*, the employment criterion cannot be regarded as exclusive. Thus, as regards the inception and determination of pension rights, the pensions paid by statutory social security schemes may reflect, wholly or in part, pay in respect of work, but nevertheless fall outside the scope of Article 119.

On the other hand, considerations of social policy, of state organisation, or of ethics or even budgetary preoccupations which influenced, or may have influenced, the establishment by the national legislature of a scheme such as the scheme at issue cannot prevail if the pension concerns only a particular category of workers, if it is directly related to the period of service and if its amount is calculated by reference to the civil servant's last salary. The pension paid by the public employer is therefore entirely comparable to that paid by a private employer to his former employees.

---

[54] Case C-7/93 *Bestuur van Het Algemeen Burgerlijk Pensioenfonds v Beune* [1994] ECR I-4471. This was followed in Case C-147/95 *DEI v Evrenopoulos* [1997] ECR I-2057.

[55] [1994] ECR I-4471, at 4512.

It follows from all the foregoing considerations that a civil service pension scheme of the type at issue in the main proceedings, which essentially relates to the employment of the person concerned, forms part of the pay received by that person and comes within the scope of Article 119.[56]

It is submitted that this ruling was unacceptably vague both in not expressing clearly which indicia it regarded as critical to determining whether a payment is made by reason of an employment relationship and also in saying that the employment criterion is not exclusive. The Court has, however, subsequently gone some way towards remedying these deficiencies. In *Griesmar*,[57] it held that a pension scheme applicable to all French civil servants fell within the scope of the Treaty.[58] Following its reasoning in *Beune*, it pointed out specifically that civil servants constituted a particular category of workers and that the pension paid to them took account of the level, duration, and nature of their services. It was therefore paid by reason of the employment relationship. This conclusion was not ousted by the fact that, unlike The Netherlands scheme in *Beune*, the French scheme was not merely supplementary but also provided a basic pension; nor by the fact that The Netherlands scheme relied on contributions accumulated in a fund managed by a board, whereas the French benefits were paid directly out of the State budget.

Not long afterwards, in *Pirkko Niemi*,[59] the Court was faced with an even wider pension scheme, this time established under Finnish law, for all persons employed by the State. It reiterated its earlier formula:

[C]onsiderations of social policy, of State organisation, of ethics, or even the budgetary concerns which influenced or may have influenced the establishment by the national legislature of a scheme such as the one in question in the main proceedings cannot prevail if the pension concerns only a particular category of workers, if it is directly related to the period of service completed and if its amount is calculated by reference to the public servant's last salary. The pension paid by the public employer is in that case entirely comparable to that paid by a private employer to his former employees.[60]

Applying these three indicia, the ECJ concluded that the scheme in question did indeed fall within Article 141:

[P]ublic servants who benefit under a pension scheme such as that at issue in the main proceedings must be regarded as constituting a particular group of workers. They are distinguished from employees grouped within an undertaking or group of undertakings in a particular sector of the economy, or in a trade or inter-trade sector, only by reason of the specific features governing their employment relationship with the State, or with other public employers or bodies... Second,...a person is entitled... only if he is in a relationship with the State as a public servant or ordinary employee... [T]he

---

[56] [1994] ECR I-4471, at 4518. This decision was followed in Case C-50/99 *Podesta v CRICA* [2000] ECR I-4039. *Beune* rendered highly doubtful of the Employment Appeal Tribunal in *Griffin v London Pension Fund Authority* [1993] ICR 564, to the effect that pension payments made to local government workers throughout the country under the Local Government Superannuation Scheme are not pay.   [57] Case C-366/99 [2001] ECR I-9383.
[58] Alber AG reached the same conclusion, albeit reluctantly, on the basis of *Beune*. *Griesmar* was followed by the ECJ in Case C-206/00 *Mouflin v Recteur de l'académie de Reims* [2001] ECR I-10201.
[59] Case C-351/00 [2002] ECR I-7007.
[60] Ibid, at 7049. The ECJ repeated this formulation in Joined Cases C-4 & 5/02 *Schönheit v Stadt Frankfurt am Main*, judgment of 23 October 2003, nyr.

age-limit which gives rise to compulsory retirement, which in turn gives rise to entitlement to pension benefits, is in the present case directly related to the period of service completed . . . [T]he level of the pension paid . . . is determined by how long the person concerned has worked. Third, as regards the amount of the benefit, it must be noted that [the] pension benefits paid . . . are calculated on the basis of the pay received over a period limited to a few years directly preceding retirement. Such a basis of calculation essentially satisfies the criterion applied by the Court in *Beune* and *Griesmar*, according to which the amount of the pension is calculated on the basis of the official's last salary.[61]

(ii)   The principle of equality as applied to pensions[62]

The ECJ's decision in *Barber* left a number of issues unresolved.[63] First, there were problems as to the temporal scope of Article 141 in relation to pensions. It will be seen below that Article 141 generally takes direct effect and has been able to be relied upon since 8 April 1976.[64] However, in this specific context, the Court took a restrictive stance:

[T]he direct effect of Article 119 of the Treaty may not be relied upon in order to claim entitlement to a pension with effect from a date prior to that of this judgment, except in the case of workers or those claiming under them who have before that date initiated legal proceedings or raised an equivalent claim under the applicable national law.[65]

The date of the judgment was 17 May 1990. The Court gave unusually full reasons for reaching this conclusion, saying that it could:

[B]y way of exception, taking account of the serious difficulties which its judgment may create as regards events in the past, be moved to restrict the possibility for all persons concerned of relying on the interpretation which the Court, in proceedings on a reference to it for a preliminary ruling, gives to a provision . . .

   With regard to this case, it must be pointed out that Article 7(1) of [the Social Security Directive[66]] authorized the Member States to defer the compulsory implementation of the principle of equal treatment with regard to the determination of pensionable age for the purposes of granting old-age pensions and the possible consequences thereof for other benefits. That exception has been incorporated in Article 9(a) of [the Occupational Social Security Directive[67]] which may apply to contracted-out schemes such as the one at issue in this case.

   [61] Case C-351/00 [2002] ECR I-7007, at 7049–50.
   [62] For general discussion of this matter, see Whiteford, 'Lost in the Mists of Time: the ECJ and Occupational Pensions' (1995) 32 CMLRev 801; id, *Adapting to Change: Occupational Pension Schemes, Women and Migrant Workers* (Kluwer, The Hague, 1997); and Fredman, 'The Poverty of Equality: Pensions and the ECJ' (1996) 25 ILJ 91.
   [63] See Moore, ' "Justice Doesn't Mean a Free Lunch": The Application of the Principle of Equal Pay to Occupational Pension Schemes' (1995) 20 ELRev 159.
   [64] The date of the ECJ's decision in Case 43/75 *Defrenne v Sabena*, op cit, n 11.
   [65] Case C-262/88 *Barber*, op cit, n 28, at 1956. In Case C-147/95 *Evrenopoulos*, op cit, n 54, Jacobs AG submitted that 'the exception in favour of those who [have] already introduced a claim should not be narrowly construed. Rather, it is the temporal limitation introduced by the *Barber* judgment which, as a departure from the normal canons of interpretation, should be subject to strict construction' (at 2071).
   [66] Directive 79/7, OJ [1979] L6/24, discussed in ch 8.
   [67] Directive 86/378, OJ [1986] L225/40, subsequently amended in this respect and discussed further below.

In the light of those provisions, the Member States and the parties concerned were reasonably entitled to consider that Article 119 did not apply to pensions paid under contracted-out schemes and that derogations from the principle of equality between men and women were still permitted in that sphere.

In those circumstances, overriding considerations of legal certainty preclude legal situations which have exhausted all their effects in the past from being called in question where that might upset retroactively the financial balance of many contracted-out pension schemes. It is appropriate, however, to provide for an exception in favour of individuals who have taken action in good time in order to safeguard their rights. Finally, it must be pointed out that no restriction on the effects of the aforesaid interpretation can be permitted as regards the acquisition of entitlement to a pension as from the date of this judgment.[68]

It was far from clear how the Court's formulation of this prospective direct effect would actually work on the facts of particular cases involving occupational pension schemes. The Editors of the *Equal Opportunities Review*, for example, commented that the Court's statement was capable of being read in at least five different ways.[69] The financial implications were so serious for the pensions industry that the Member States took the unprecedented step of legislating directly on the matter. The TEU annexed the so-called 'Barber Protocol' to the TEC, providing:

For the purposes of Article 119 of this Treaty, benefits under occupational social security schemes shall not be considered as remuneration if and in so far as they are attributable to periods of employment prior to 17 May 1990, except in the case of workers or those claiming under them who have before that date initiated legal proceedings or introduced an equivalent claim under the applicable national law.

The ECJ subsequently ruled that this was what it had intended in *Barber*,[70] in *Ten Oever v Stichting Bedrijfspensioenfonds voor het Glazenwassers- en Schoonmaakbedrijf*,[71] it held:

The Court's ruling [in *Barber*] took account of the fact that it is a characteristic of this form of pay that there is a time lag between the accrual of entitlement to the pension, which occurs gradually throughout the employee's working life, and its actual payment, which is deferred until a particular age. The Court also took into consideration the way in which occupational pension funds are financed and thus of the accounting links existing in each individual case between the periodic contributions and the future amounts to be paid. Given the reasons explained in . . . the *Barber* judgment for limiting its effects in

[68] [1990] ECR I-1889, at 1955–6, emphasis added. The French text of the same passage omits the word 'all' in the emphasized section: 'Dans ces conditions, des considérations impérieuses de sécurité juridique s'opposent à ce que des situations juridique qui ont épuisé leurs effets dans le passé soient remises en cause alors que, dans un tel cas, l'équilibre financier de nombre de régimes de pensions conventionellement exclus risquerait d'être rétroactivement bouleversé.'
[69] In 'Occupational Pensions are Pay under EEC Law' (1990) 32 EOR 30. See also the analysis of Van Gerven AG in Joined Cases C-109, 110, 152, & 200/91 *Ten Oever v Stichting Bedrijfspensioenfonds voor het Glazenwassers- en Schoonmaakbedrijf, Moroni v Collo GmbH, Neath v Hugh Steeper Ltd*, and *Coloroll Pension Trustees Ltd v Russell* [1993] ECR I-4879.
[70] This was fortunate in the sense that a battle between the EU's legislature and its judiciary would have had disastrous consequences for the rule of law in the EU; on the other hand, it was unfortunate in that it meant that full equality in the area of pensions will not be achieved until about 2030.
[71] Case C-109/91, op cit, n 45. Van Gerven AG commented in his submissions that the Protocol had not been intended to alter the meaning to be placed on the Court's words in *Barber*, his view was that this is clear from the fifth indent of Art 2 of the TEU, which states that one of the Union's objectives is 'to maintain in full the "acquis communautaire" and build on it'.

time, it must be made clear that equality of treatment in the matter of occupational pensions may be claimed only in relation to benefits payable in respect of periods of employment subsequent to 17 May 1990, . . . subject to the exception in favour of workers or those claiming under them who have, before that date, initiated legal proceedings or raised an equivalent claim under the applicable national law.[72]

The consequence of this interpretation is that pension-providers must now calculate the proportions of each pension which are attributable to service before and after 17 May 1990, and make the necessary mathematical adjustments to ensure equality of treatment for the later period and not the earlier one. Where a particular pension benefit is not linked to length of service, such as a lump sum paid on the death of an employee during employment, then whether or not the principle of equality applies depends upon whether the triggering event occurred before or after 17 May 1990.[73]

The coincidentally named *Defreyn v Sabena SA*[74] raised the issue of what sorts of payments fall within the definition of 'benefits under occupational social security schemes' for the purpose of the Barber Protocol. The case concerned additional redundancy payments made pursuant to a collective agreement (on terms which were sex discriminatory); they were paid by the individual's last employer to workers receiving unemployment benefit. Ms Defreyn became redundant in 1987. The ECJ held that an occupational scheme such as the one in issue, 'which provides protection against the risk of unemployment by providing workers employed by an undertaking, in this case Sabena, with benefits intended to supplement the unemployment benefit provided under a statutory social security scheme', fell within the scope of the Barber Protocol. It followed that Ms Defreyn could not claim the protection of Article 141, since the payments to her were made in respect of an employment relationship which had ended before 1990 and she had not by that date already initiated legal proceedings.

The complexity surrounding this area is increased by the fact that the Court has also ruled that the temporal limitation contained in *Barber* applies only to claims for pension payment, not to claims in relation to the right to join a pension scheme; the right to join a scheme on non-discriminatory terms had been established in

---

[72] Ibid, at 4944–5. Case C-110/91 *Moroni v Collo GmbH* [1993] ECR I-6591, and Case C-200/91 *Coloroll Pension Trustees Ltd v Russell* [1994] ECR I-4389 established that the same temporal limitation applies to non-contracted-out pension schemes; the logic of this holding is dubious in the light of the Court's reasoning in *Barber*, because it has been known since Case 170/84 *Bilka-Kaufhaus Gmbh v Weber Von Hartz* [1986] ECR 1607 (discussed above) that pensions paid under such schemes fall within Art 141; Van Gerven AG got over this difficulty by arguing that in *Bilka* the Court had ruled only on the questions of whether a scheme of the type in point fell within Art 141 and whether the exclusion of part-timers constituted unlawful discrimination, and that it was not until *Barber* that the Court addressed the lawfulness of an age condition which was different for men and women. In Case C-152/91 *Neath v High Steeper Ltd* [1993] ECR I-6935, the Court added: 'As regards transfer benefits and lump-sum options . . . since by virtue of the *Barber* judgment Article 119 cannot be invoked to call in question the financial basis of pension rights accrued before 17 May 1990 on the basis of different retirement ages, it follows . . . that its capital equivalent must necessarily be subject to the consequences of that temporal limitation' (at 6959).   [73] Case C-200/91 *Coloroll*, op cit, n 72.
[74] Case C-166/99 [2000] ECR I-6155.

Bilka-Kaufhaus GmbH v Weber Von Hartz,[75] and in *Fisscher v Voorhuis Hengelo BV*[76] the Court held that this made it impossible to argue that it was thereafter unclear that Article 141 applied to this situation:

[T]he limitation of the effects in time of the *Barber* judgment concerns only those kinds of discrimination which employers and pension schemes could reasonably have considered to be permissible, owing to the transitional derogations for which Community law provided and which were capable of being applied to occupational pensions ... [A]s far as the right to join an occupational pension is concerned, there is no reason to suppose that the professional groups concerned could have been mistaken about the applicability of Article 119. It has indeed been clear since the judgment in the *Bilka* case that a breach of the rule of equal treatment committed through not recognising such a right is caught by Article 119.

Moreover, since the Court's judgment in the *Bilka* case included no limitation of its effect in time, the direct effect of Article 119 can be relied upon in order retroactively to claim equal treatment in relation to the right to join an occupational pension scheme and this may be done as from 8 April 1976, the date of the *Defrenne* judgment in which the Court held for the first time that Article 119 has direct effect.[77] ... [T]he limitation of the effects in time of the *Barber* judgment does not apply to the right to join an occupational pension scheme.[78]

Furthermore, the Court also held in this case and in *Vroege v NCIV Instituut voor Volkshuisvesting BV*[79] that the Barber Protocol did not apply to claims in relation to the right to join a pension scheme; in the latter case, it explained that:

It is clear that Protocol No 2 is linked to the *Barber* judgment, since it refers to the date of that judgment ... While extending it to all benefits payable under occupational social security schemes and incorporating it into the Treaty, Protocol No 2 essentially adopted the same interpretation of the *Barber* judgment as did the *Ten Oever* judgment. It did not, on the other hand, any more than the *Barber* judgment, deal with, or make any provision for, the conditions of membership of such occupational schemes.[80]

This is a perceptive decision on the part of a Court which did not wish to see its earlier decision in *Bilka* effectively restricted by later legislation. *Magorrian and Cunningham v Eastern Health and Social Services Board*[81] then raised the issue of what

[75] Case 170/84, op cit, n 39. See also Case C-256/01 *Allonby*, op cit, n 3, where a requirement of being employed under a contract of employment as a pre-condition for membership of a statutory teachers' pension scheme was held to be potentially indirectly discriminatory against teachers who were technically regarded as self-employed under national law.
[76] Case C-128/93 [1994] ECR I-4583. The pension scheme in this case excluded married women from membership at the material date. See also Case C-57/93 *Vroege v NCIV Instituut voor Volkshuisvesting BV* [1994] ECR I-4541, where part-time workers were excluded; the Court reached the same conclusions as in *Fisscher*, the only significant difference between the two cases being that the discrimination alleged in *Vroege* was indirect whilst that in *Fisscher* was direct. See also Case C-7/93 *Beune*, op cit, n 54.   [77] Op cit, n 11, as to which see discussion below.
[78] [1994] ECR I-4583, at 4595–6. In addition, the ECJ later held in Case C-50/96 *Deutsche Telekom v Schröder* [2000] ECR I-743, Joined Cases C-270 & 271/97 *Deutsche Post v Sievers and Schrage* [2000] ECR I-929, and Joined Cases C-234 & 235/96 *Deutsche Telekom AG v Vick and Conze* [2000] ECR I-799, that EU law does not preclude a Member State from providing an even more extensive retroactive right to membership of a pension scheme.
[79] Case C-57/93, op cit, n 76. See to the same effect Case C-435/93 *Dietz v Stichting Thuiszorg Rotterdam* [1996] ECR I-5223.   [80] [1994] ECR I-4541, at 4579.
[81] Case C-246/96 [1997] ECR I-7153.

precisely is meant by access to a pension scheme; in particular, where workers transfer from full-time working to part-time working, and thereby suffer a diminution in what would otherwise be their pension entitlement, is this an example of discrimination over access or over terms? Advocate General Cosmas submitted that it was an example of discriminatory access. The ECJ agreed and went on to hold that reg 12 of the Northern Ireland Occupational Pension Regulations,[82] which limited the right to join pension schemes to a period no more than two years prior to the initiation of proceedings, was illegal. As seen in chapter 2, national rules on limitation of action may be applied to the enforcement of Community rights, provided that they do not have the effect of frustrating such Community rights and that they are not less favourable than the rules applied to similar domestic law claims. Here the Court found that the national limitation period rendered the enforcement of Community rights 'impossible in practice'.

The same principle was vindicated on a grander scale in *Preston v Wolverhampton Healthcare NHS Trust*.[83] Some 60,000 part-time workers had sought to ascertain their rights in relation to access to pension schemes; they claimed that their exclusion from the relevant schemes, which was grounded on their part-time status, constituted indirect sex discrimination. They went on to argue that the rule contained in reg 12 of the UK Occupational Pension Regulations,[84] barring their rights to claim pensions based on their service more than two years before they instituted proceedings, infringed EU law because it made it virtually impossible to exercise their rights. The ECJ observed that the objective of their claims was not to obtain retroactively arrears of benefits under the pension schemes, but to secure the recognition of their rights to retroactive membership of the schemes for the purpose of calculating benefits to be paid in the future. This it appeared to regard as a crucial distinction, since it has long adhered to the principle that normal limitation periods conduce to legal certainty and are entirely acceptable in EU law. The facts presented to the Court in *Preston* were very similar to those with which it had recently confronted in *Magorrian and Cunningham v Eastern Health and Social Services Board*, and it repeated its earlier remarks:

[U]nlike the rules which, in the interests of legal certainty, merely [limit] the retroactive scope of a claim for certain benefits and [do] not therefore strike at the very essence of the rights conferred by the Community legal order, a procedural rule such as that in issue . . . [is] such as to render any action by individuals relying on Community law impossible in practice . . . Even though the procedural rule at issue does not totally deprive the claimants of access to membership, the fact nevertheless remains that . . . [it] prevents the entire record of service completed by those concerned before the two years preceding the date on which they commenced their proceedings from being taken into account for the purposes of calculating the benefits which would be payable even after the date of the claim.[85]

The House of Lords therefore held that reg 12 of the Occupational Pension Regulations was precluded by EU law and that, subject to the employees concerned paying contributions owing in respect of the periods for which membership was claimed retroactively, they were entitled to pensions calculated by reference to all their service, whether full or part-time, subsequent to 8 April 1976.[86]

The fact that a worker can claim retroactively to join an occupational pension scheme is somewhat undermined in practice (at least as far as contributory schemes are concerned) by the fact that this does not permit the worker to escape paying contributions in relation to the period in question.[87]

The meaning of 'workers or those claiming under them who have [before 17 May 1990] initiated legal proceedings or introduced an equivalent claim under the applicable national law' was in issue in *DEI v Evrenopoulos*.[88] The ECJ held that such proceedings must be brought in accordance with the procedural rules applicable in the relevant Member State. The plaintiff had applied to the Director of the Insurance Fund governing the Greek electricity industry for a pension on the death of his wife, a pensioner of the Fund. His letter remained unanswered, so he brought an action before the Greek Administrative Court of First Instance against the implied rejection of his claim on 12 June 1989. While this action was pending, the Director of the Fund refused his application. By a judgment of November 1990, the Greek Administrative Court rejected his action on the ground that he had not first lodged an objection against the rejection of his claim by the Director with the Staff Insurance Board. However, because the Director had not informed him of the possibility of lodging such an objection, the Court granted him a further three months in which to do so. He then lodged his objection with the Insurance Board in February 1991, and it too was rejected. Against this rejection the plaintiff successfully appealed, and in the course of these appellate proceedings, a ruling was sought from the ECJ. The ECJ held that the judicial proceedings between the plaintiff and the defendant began with the original action, namely the proceedings of 12 June 1989, and were thus commenced before the crucial date of the ruling in the *Barber* case.

Further problems have arisen with respect to transitional arrangements where, pursuant to *Barber*, pension schemes changed their rules so as to stipulate the same pension age for men and women. These problems highlight the mixed blessing which sex equality in pension schemes has proved to be from the point of view of women.[89] In *Smith v Avdel Systems Ltd*,[90] the Court held that, until equalizing measures are adopted by a pension scheme, the only way in which there can be compliance with Article 141 is to grant to persons in the disadvantaged class the advantages of those in the favoured class;[91] thus, where a scheme had pension ages of 60 for women and 65 for men, between 17 May 1990 and the date on

---

[86] [2001] 2 AC 455.   [87] Case C-128/93 *Fisscher*, op cit, n 76.

[88] Case C-147/95, op cit, n 54.

[89] For an interesting analysis of the effect of EU pension equality provisions on the financial position of older people, see Luckhaus and Moffat, *Serving the Market And People's Needs?* (Joseph Rowntree Foundation, York, 1996).   [90] Case C-408/92 [1994] ECR I-4435.

[91] See below for more general discussion of the principle of 'equalization upwards' in relation to Art 141.

which the fund rules were changed, the pension rights of men must be calculated on the basis of a pension age of 60. However, after the fund rules changed, the Court held weakly and with little explanation that Article 141 did not preclude measures producing equality by reducing the advantage of the persons formerly favoured, so that from this date onwards it was permissible to have a common pension age of 65. As to the period before 17 May 1990, the Court held that since Article 141 did not affect the matter, EU law did not justify the retroactive reduction of the advantages which women at that time enjoyed. It added that:

[O]nce discrimination has been found to exist, and an employer takes steps to achieve equality for the future by reducing the advantages of the favoured class, achievement of equality cannot be made progressive on a basis that still maintains discrimination, even if only temporarily ... [T]herefore ... the step of raising the retirement age for women to that for men, which an employer decides to take in order to remove discrimination in relation to occupational pensions as regards benefits payable in respect of future periods of service, cannot be accompanied by measures, even if only transitional, designed to limit the adverse consequences which such a step may have for women.[92]

A second series of difficulties which emerged from *Barber* concerned precisely what amounts to unlawful discrimination within a pension scheme. In *Barber* itself, the discrimination took the seemingly blatant form of setting different pensionable ages for men and women.[93] The Court held:

... Article 119 prohibits any discrimination with regard to pay as between men and women, whatever the system which gives rise to such inequality. Accordingly, it is contrary to Article 119 to impose an age condition which differs according to sex in respect of pensions paid under a contracted-out scheme, even if the difference between the pensionable age for men and that for women is based on the one provided for by the national statutory scheme.[94]

But does the notion of discrimination extend to more subtle differentiation, such as the payment of a survivor's pension to widows but not to widowers? The Court gave an affirmative answer to this in the *Ten Oever* case, saying that

... entitlement to such a benefit is a consideration deriving from the survivor's spouse's membership of the scheme, the pension being vested in the survivor by reason of the employment relationship between the employer and the survivor's spouse and being paid to him or her by reason of the spouse's employment ... [A] survivor's pension ... [therefore] falls within the scope of Article 119.[95]

---

[92] [1994] ECR I-4435, at 4467. See also Case C-28/93 *Van Den Akker v Stichting Shell Pensioenfonds* [1994] ECR I-4527, and Case C-200/91 *Coloroll*, op cit, n 72.

[93] But the setting of different pensionable ages for the two sexes is less obviously discrimination forbidden by Art 141 if a rigid separation is maintained as between the quantum of a pension and the terms of access to it. See further discussion of this distinction in ch 5.

[94] [1990] ECR I-1889, at 1953. For the same principle in relation to supplementary pension schemes, see Case C-110/91 *Moroni*, op cit, n 72. For the application of the principle to survivors' benefits, see Case C-50/99 *Podesta v CRICA* [2000] ECR I-4039.

[95] [1993] ECR I-4879, at 4944. The Editors of the EOR have made the interesting point that this principle might be extended so as to outlaw private medical insurance schemes provided for the spouses of employees (as well as employees themselves) which exclude pregnancy coverage: see (1994) 53 EOR 48.

It added in *Coloroll Pension Trustees Ltd v Russell*[96] that the survivor's rights are directly effective. Furthermore, the Article can be relied upon against the trustees of an occupational pension scheme, even though the trustees are not technically party to the employment relationship, since 'the effectiveness of Article 119 would be considerably diminished and the legal protection required to ensure real equality would be seriously impaired if an employee or an employee's dependants could rely on that provision only as against the employer'.[97] This principle holds good whatever the legal form of the pension scheme; furthermore, it is not undermined by the fact that the pension beneficiary can also proceed against the employer in the case of default by the pension fund, nor by the fact that national legislation guarantees the beneficiary's rights in the event of the employer's insolvency.[98] The temporal limitation in *Barber* also applies to a survivor's pension.[99]

The *Coloroll* case also established that, although Article 141 applies to all benefits payable to an employee by an occupational pension scheme irrespective of whether that scheme is contributory or non-contributory, it does not apply to additional benefits consequent on additional voluntary contributions made by the employee, since these do not arise out of employment.[100]

Neither does the equality principle contained in Article 141 apply to an employer's contributions paid under a defined-benefit scheme, and these may therefore vary as between male and female employees as a result, for example, of the use of gender-specific actuarial tables. This emerged from *Neath v Hugh Steeper Ltd*,[101] which involved a scheme providing employees with a pension corresponding to one-sixtieth of their final salary for each year of service. The scheme was contributory on the part of both employees and the employer. The employees' contributions consisted of a percentage of salary, and in this there was no distinction as between men and women. However, the employer's contributions had to cover the balance of the cost of the pensions promised and so varied over time; they were also higher for female employees than for male employees, because the actuarial tables used reflected the fact that women, on average, live longer than men. Where an employee left employment before reaching the prescribed age, either acquired pension rights could be transferred into another fund or the former employee could receive a capital sum by way of commutation; however,

---

[96] Case C-200/91, op cit, n 72. See also Case C-147/95 *Evrenopoulos*, op cit, n 54.

[97] [1994] ECR I-4389, at 4411. See also Case C-128/93 *Fisscher*, op cit, n 76, and Case C-435/93 *Dietz*, op cit, n 79.

[98] Case C-379/99 *Pensionkasse für die Angestellten der Barmer Ersatzkasse VvaG v Menauer* [2001] ECR I-7275.

[99] [1994] ECR I-4389, at 4419–20. Cf the view of Van Gerven AG, who had proposed a temporal limitation on the survivor's rights from the date of the *Ten Oever* judgment itself (rather than from the date of the *Barber* judgment). In his submissions in *Vroege* and *Fisscher*, the Advocate General said that he had only one explanation for the Court's choice of the date of the *Barber* judgment: 'the Court is disposed to consider that the temporal limitation of the effects of the *Barber* judgment is also applicable in the other situations for which Directive 86/378 allows exceptions to the application of the principle of equal treatment...': [1994] ECR I-4541, at 4560.

[100] [1994] ECR I-4389, at 4427–8.

[101] Case C-152/91 [1993] ECR I-6935. See also Case C-200/91 *Coloroll*, op cit, n 72.

in calculating such transfer value or a capital sum, gender-specific actuarial calculations would again be used, with the result that a man would receive less than a woman. The Court held:

> The assumption . . . is that the employer commits himself, albeit unilaterally, to pay his employees defined benefits or grant them specific advantages and that the employees in turn expect the employer to pay them those benefits or provide them with those advantages. Anything that is not a consequence of that commitment and does not therefore come within the corresponding expectations of the employees falls outside the concept of pay.
>
> In the context of a defined-benefit occupational pension scheme . . . , the employer's commitment to his employees concerns the payment, at a given moment in time, of a periodic pension for which the determining criteria are already known at the time when the commitment is made and which constitutes pay within the meaning of Article 119. However, that commitment does not necessarily have to do with the funding arrangements chosen to secure the periodic payment of the pension, which thus remain outside the scope of application of Article 119.
>
> In contributory schemes, funding is provided through the contributions made by the employees and those made by the employers. The contributions made by the employees are an element of their pay since they are deducted directly from an employee's salary, which by definition is pay (see the judgment in Case 69/80 *Worringham v Lloyds Bank* [1981] ECR 767). The amount of those contributions must therefore be the same for all employees, male and female, which is indeed so in the present case. This is not so in the case of the employer's contributions which ensure the adequacy of the funds necessary to cover the cost of the pensions promised, so securing their payment in the future, that being the substance of the employer's commitment.
>
> It follows that, unlike periodic payment of pensions, inequality of employers' contributions paid under funded defined-benefit schemes, which is due to the use of actuarial factors differing according to sex, is not struck at by Article 119.
>
> That conclusion necessarily extends to the specific aspects referred to in the questions submitted, namely the conversion of part of the periodic pension into a capital sum and the transfer of pension rights, the value of which can be determined only by reference to the funding arrangements chosen.[102]
>
> The answer to be given to the national court must therefore be that the use of actuarial factors differing according to sex in funded defined-benefit occupational pension schemes does not fall within the scope of Article 119 . . .[103]

In *Coloroll Pension Trustees Ltd v Russell*,[104] the Court extrapolated from its reasoning in *Neath* to defined-benefit schemes in the situations involved in the later case, namely:

> . . . where a reversionary pension is payable to a dependant in return for the surrender of part of the annual pension and where a reduced pension is paid when the employee opts for early retirement.

---

[102] It is submitted that this is a particularly obscure passage in the Court's judgment; it is far from clear why it is a 'necessary' extension from the mathematics adopted to calculate the employer's contribution to the scheme that the capital equivalent of a payment which certainly falls within the equality principle contained in Art 141 should cease to be subject to this principle.

[103] [1993] ECR I-6935, at 6962–3. The apparently general nature of the final paragraph quoted in the text must, it is submitted, be read in the context of the preceding paragraphs; thus, it is restricted to the use of sex-specific actuarial calculations in relation to employer contributions only and does not permit their use in relation to employee contributions or benefits. Query the applicability of the *Neath* ruling in the case of defined-contribution schemes, as to which see further discussion below.

[104] Case C-200/91, op cit, n 72.

[In these cases too] the funding arrangements chosen must also be taken into account. Since those arrangements are not covered by Article 119, any inequality in the amounts of those benefits, arising from the use of actuarial factors in the funding of the scheme, is not struck at by that Article.[105]

The acceptability of such gender-specific actuarial calculations to the ECJ is regrettable,[106] especially since it means that, in these cases, it is more expensive to employ women than men, which clearly constitutes an obstacle to the principle of equal treatment. In addition, it may be seen as evidence of the Court's diminishing sensitivity to the demands of an effective anti-discrimination law. It is submitted that there is considerable force in the arguments expressed by the Commission:

[T]he principle of equal pay for men and women must be applied individually and not on a category basis. The fact that women generally live longer than men has no significance at all for the life expectancy of a specific individual and it is not acceptable for an individual to be penalised on account of assumptions which are not certain to be true in his specific case.[107] Moreover, there are a number of risk factors which are not taken into account: risks associated with certain occupations, smoking, state of health and so on. Finally, there is no technical necessity for pension schemes to have a distinction based on life expectancies: some pension schemes, and all state pension schemes, use a system of risk compensation which covers differences in the probable lifespan of men and women... [T]he Supreme Court of the United States has held that similar discrimination in pension schemes is incompatible with the Civil Rights Act 1964.[108]

Van Gerven AG himself likewise rejected the use of such calculations:

The unequal treatment of men and women may... not constitute unlawful discrimination if the difference in treatment is based on objective differences which are relevant, that is to say which bear an actual connection with the subject of the rules entailing unequal treatment. In this regard, I could for instance imagine that factors having a direct impact on the life expectancy of a specific individual, such as risks associated with a particular occupation, smoking, eating and drinking habits and so forth, would be taken into account, if this is technically possible, in order to justify individual differences in contributions and/or benefits. As regards differences in average life expectancy between men and women, the situation is different, however. These differences bear no relation to the life expectancy of a specific individual and are thus irrelevant for the calculation of the contributions and/or benefits which may be ascribed to that individual.[109]

Birds Eye Walls Ltd v Roberts[110] concerned the legality of a so-called 'bridging pension' in the UK. The bridging pension was intended to equalize the financial package received by male and female employees retiring early; but in order to achieve this result, smaller sums were paid to women aged between 60 and 65 than to men of the same age because of the women's earlier entitlement to a State

---

[105] Case C-200/91, op cit, n 72, at 4425–6.
[106] See also Curtin, 'Occupational Pension Schemes and Article 119: Beyond the Fringe?' (1987) 27 CMLRev 215.
[107] It might be added that statistics which held good for a past generation might well not do so for later generations: eg, it would not be surprising if a generation of women who have been subject to the stresses and strains of paid employment (as well as their seemingly inevitable domestic responsibilities) proved to have a shorter average longevity than their male counterparts.
[108] See the submissions of Van Gerven AG in Case C-109/91 *Ten Oever*, op cit, n 45, at 4913.
[109] Ibid, at 4919.   [110] Case C-132/92 [1993] ECR I-5579.

pension (at 60 rather than 65). Mrs Roberts argued that this amounted to a breach of Article 141, but the ECJ disagreed. It held that, albeit that the bridging pension constituted pay, like must be compared with like in order to establish discrimination:

It should be noted that the principle of equal treatment laid down by Article 119 of the Treaty, like the general principle of non-discrimination which it embodies in a specific form, presupposes that the men and women to whom it applies are in identical situations. However, that would not appear to be so where the deferred payment which an employer makes to those of his employees who are compelled to take early retirement on grounds of ill health is regarded as a supplement to the financial resources of the man or woman concerned.

It follows clearly from the mechanism for calculating the bridging pension that the assessment of the amount thereof is not frozen at a particular moment but necessarily varies on account of changes occurring in the financial position of the man or woman concerned with the passage of time.

Accordingly, although until the age of 60 the financial position of a woman taking early retirement on grounds of ill health is comparable to that of a man in the same situation, neither of them as yet entitled to payment of the state pension, that is no longer the case between the ages of 60 and 65 since that is when women, unlike men, start drawing that pension. That difference as regards the objective premise, which necessarily entails that the amount of the bridging pension is not the same for men and women, cannot be considered discriminatory.[111]

Although it has been emphasized above that much of the ECJ's case law on the meaning of 'pay' for the purposes of Article 141 can be extrapolated into the fields covered by the Race Directive and the Framework Directive, there is one very important exception as far as occupational pensions are concerned. This is the consequence of Article 6(2) of the Framework Directive, which permits the Member States to provide that:

The fixing for occupational social security schemes of ages for admission or entitlement to retirement or invalidity benefits, including the fixing under those schemes of different ages for employees or groups or categories of employees, and the use, in the context of such schemes, of age criteria in actuarial calculations, does not constitute discrimination on the grounds of age, provided this does not result in discrimination on the grounds of sex.

(iii)   The Occupational Social Security Directive

Before it became clear just how extensive was the protection extended by Article 141 to the various types of pension schemes, the Council legislated specifically to deal with this matter. The legislation took the form of the so-called Occupational Social Security Directive.[112] The expressed objective of this instrument was to

---

[111] Ibid, at 5604–5. Cf the reasoning of Van Gerven AG. For comment on the post-*Barber* cases, see also Hanlon, 'Some Backward Steps for Equality' (1995) 17 JSWFL 237, and id, 'Some Further Backward Steps for Equality' (1995) 17 JSWFL 399.

[112] Directive 86/378, OJ [1986] L225/40. The Directive was foreshadowed by Art 3(3) of the Social Security Directive (Directive 79/7, OJ [1979] L6/24, as to which see ch 8), which provides: 'With a view to ensuring implementation of the principle of equal treatment in occupational schemes, the

'implement' the principle of equal treatment in occupational social security schemes.[113] Ironically, in the light of the treatment later accorded by the ECJ to Article 141 in relation to pensions, the chief effect of the Directive has actually been a negative one; as seen above, its existence, and in particular the exemptions which it contained in its original form, provided an important part of the reasoning which underlay the Court's temporal restriction of the effect of the Treaty in the *Barber* case.

The Directive was subsequently amended by Directive 96/97,[114] so as to reflect the substance of the Court's rulings in *Barber* and its later jurisprudence on pensions equality; the main changes that this entailed were to make it clear that the substantive right to equality in this field flows from Article 141, not the Directive,[115] and to reduce the number of exceptions permitted. The Member States were required by this later instrument to legislate to comply with its terms by 1 July 1997.[116]

The Occupational Social Security Directive defines 'occupational social security schemes' as

schemes not governed by Directive 79/7/EEC whose purpose is to provide workers, whether employees or self-employed, in an undertaking or group of undertakings, area of economic activity, occupational sector or group of such sectors with benefits intended to supplement the benefits provided by statutory social security schemes or to replace them, whether membership of such schemes is compulsory or optional.[117]

Although both the *Bilka-Kaufhaus*-type supplementary pension scheme and the *Barber*-type substitutive pension scheme are thus within the scope of the Directive, the practical importance of the instrument was largely undermined by the Court's rulings that Article 141 also applies to such schemes. Article 141 has proved to be a far more potent weapon, in part because it is not handicapped by the Directive's lack of horizontal direct effect,[118] and in part because the original version of the Directive provided for a number of exceptions not contained in Article 119.[119]

Council, acting on a proposal from the Commission, will adopt provisions defining its substance, its scope and the arrangements for its application'. In Case C-7/93 *Beune*, op cit, n 54, Jacobs AG commented that 'at first sight the combination of the terms "occupational", apparently in the sense of "non-statutory", and "social security" may seem surprising' (at 4481).

[113] Art 1 of the Directive. According to Jacobs AG in the *Beune* case, op cit, n 112, Art 141 and the Directive were not intended to be mutually exclusive.   [114] OJ [1997] L46/20.

[115] For an application of this principle, see Joined Cases C-4 & 5/02 *Schönheit v Stadt Frankfurt am Main*, judgment of 23 October 2003, nyr. There is a parallel to be drawn with the Equal Pay Directive, Directive 75/117, OJ [1975] L45/19. As discussed below, this merely fleshes out the bare principles contained in Art 141.

[116] Art 3(1) of the amending Directive. France failed to comply within this implementation period: see Case C-354/98 *Commission v France* [1999] ECR I-4927.

[117] Art 2(1) of the Occupational Social Security Directive.

[118] See ch 2 for discussion of the concept of horizontal direct effect.

[119] The Occupational Social Security Directive, however, covers the self-employed, as regards whom the exceptions contained in its original version (namely, for pensionable age, survivors' benefits, and actuarial calculations) are maintained by Art 9; see further below. It must, however, be remembered that some workers who are regarded by national law as self-employed are regarded by EU law as 'workers' for the purposes of Art 141: see Case C-256/01 *Allonby*, op cit, n 3, discussed above.

The Directive does not apply to:

(a) individual contracts for self-employed workers;
(b) schemes for self-employed workers having only one member;
(c) insurance contracts to which the employer is not a party, in the case of salaried workers;
(d) optional provision of occupational schemes offered to participants individually to guarantee them:

 —either additional benefits,[120] or
 —a choice of date on which the normal benefits for self-employed workers will start, or a choice between several benefits;

(e) occupational schemes in so far as benefits are financed by contributions paid by workers on a voluntary basis.[121]

Legislative blessing is given to the ruling in *Birds Eye Walls Ltd v Roberts*[122] by Article 2(3), which states:

This Directive does not preclude an employer granting to persons who have already reached the retirement age for the purposes of granting a pension by virtue of an occupational scheme, but who have not yet reached the retirement age for the purposes of granting a statutory retirement pension, a pension supplement, the aim of which is to make equal or more nearly equal the overall amount of benefit paid to these persons in relation to the amount paid to persons of the other sex in the same situation who have already reached the statutory retirement age, until the persons benefiting from the supplement reach the statutory retirement age.

The Directive governs the treatment of members of the working population, 'including self-employed persons, persons whose activity is interrupted by illness, maternity, accident or involuntary unemployment and persons seeking employment, to retired and disabled workers and to those claiming under them, in accordance with national law and/or practice'.[123]

The hazards against which the scheme must provide protection in order to fall within the ambit of the Directive are defined, apparently exhaustively:

This Directive shall apply to:
(a) occupational schemes which provide protection against the following risks:

 —sickness,
 —invalidity,
 —old age, including early retirement,
 —industrial accidents and occupational diseases,
 —unemployment;

(b) occupational schemes which provide for other social benefits, in cash or in kind, and in particular survivors' benefits and family allowances, if such benefits are accorded to employed persons and thus constitute a consideration paid by the employer to the worker by reason of the latter's employment.[124]

---

[120] As to which, see Case C-200/91 *Coloroll*, op cit, n 72, discussed above.
[121] Art 2(2) of the Directive.   [122] Op cit, n 110, discussed above.
[123] Art 3 of the Directive.   [124] Ibid, Art 4.

The principle of non-discrimination is spelled out in similar but not wholly identical terms to those in the Equal Treatment Directive;[125] there must be no discrimination 'on the basis of sex, either directly or indirectly,[126] by reference in particular to marital or family status'.[127] As in the case of the Equal Treatment Directive, it is unclear from this formulation whether discrimination on the basis of marital or family status on its own is caught by the Directive, or whether it is prohibited only where it also constitutes discrimination on the ground of sex. It is provided that there must be no such discrimination:

especially as regards:
  —the scope of the schemes and the conditions of access to them;
  —the obligation to contribute and the calculation of contributions;
  —the calculation of benefits, including supplementary benefits due in respect of a spouse or dependants, and the conditions governing the duration and retention of entitlement to benefits.[128]

The word 'especially' of course indicates that any other form of discrimination, unless specifically excepted elsewhere in the Directive, is also forbidden. Special protective provisions for women relating to maternity are, however, permitted.[129] The words used here are substantially identical to those used in the Social Security Directive,[130] and they are presumably intended to mean that especially favourable benefits can be extended to women having babies. However, the wording used is somewhat unclear in at least two respects. First, unlike the formula adopted in the Equal Treatment Directive, there is no reference to pregnancy as well as maternity. It may be thought that maternity necessarily implies pregnancy, and the ECJ certainly might interpret the provision in this way; if it did not do so, however, problems could develop, for instance, in relation to counting periods of leave from work prior to the birth of a baby.[131] It is also unclear from the wording of the Directive just how far the maternity exception really goes.[132] The ECJ, of course, usually gives a narrow reading to exceptions to general principles which themselves confer fundamental liberties. But here it might not analyse the exception in this way, and might instead see the fundamental right as the right to maternity and thus be persuaded to give this provision a broad reading, so as to confer the maximum protection on mothers. The extent of the discretion intended to be left to the Member States by the maternity exception is thus far

[125] Discussed in detail in ch 5.
[126] In Joined Cases C-4 & 5/02 Schönheit, op cit, n 115, the ECJ held that the aim of restricting public expenditure would not justify indirect discrimination in an occupational pension scheme; however, a reduced pension entitlement for part-time workers which reflected the proportion of time spent actually working, as compared to full-timers, could be justified.
[127] Occupational Social Security Directive, Art 5.   [128] Ibid, Art 5(1).
[129] Ibid, Art 5(2).   [130] Directive 79/7, OJ [1979] L6/24, discussed in detail in ch 8.
[131] The Pregnancy Directive (Directive 92/85, OJ [1992] L348/1), Art 11(2)(a), guarantees the upkeep of contractual rights to women on the 14-week maternity leave mandated by the Directive; in Case C-411/96 Boyle v EOC [1998] ECR I-6401, the ECJ held that this includes the accrual of pension rights under an occupational pension scheme. See further discussion in ch 5.
[132] Does it, eg, extend to adoption?

from clear.[133] In the view of the present writer the Court ought to countenance the legality of positive measures in favour of pregnant women and those who have recently given birth, since otherwise substantive equality is certainly not accorded to both sexes. The issue is more one of construing the basic right to equality than of implying exceptions into the text of the Article.[134]

Article 6(1) of the Directive, as amended,[135] contains considerable detail as regards the ways in which sex discrimination may arise:

Provisions contrary to the principle of equal treatment shall include those based on sex, either directly or indirectly, in particular by reference to marital or family status, for:

(a) determining the persons who may participate in an occupational scheme;

(b) fixing the compulsory or optional nature of participation in an occupational scheme;

(c) laying down different rules as regards the age of entry into the scheme or the minimum period of employment or membership of the scheme required to obtain the benefits thereof;

(d) laying down different rules, except as provided for in points (h) and (i), for the reimbursement of contributions when a worker leaves a scheme without having fulfilled the conditions guaranteeing a deferred right to long-term benefits;

(e) setting different conditions for the granting of benefits or restricting such benefits to workers of one or other of the sexes;

(f) fixing different retirement ages;

(g) suspending the retention or acquisition of rights during periods of maternity leave or leave for family reasons which are granted by law or agreement and are paid by the employer;

(h) setting different levels of benefit, except in so far as may be necessary to take account of actuarial calculation factors which differ according to sex in the case of defined-contribution schemes. In the case of funded defined-benefit schemes, certain elements (examples[136] of which are annexed) may be unequal where the inequality of the amounts results from the effects of the use of actuarial factors differing according to sex at the time when the scheme's funding is implemented;

(i) setting different levels of worker contributions:

—in the case of defined contribution schemes if the aim is to equalise the amount of the final benefits or to make them more nearly equal for both sexes,

—in the case of funded defined-benefit schemes where the employer's contributions are intended to ensure the adequacy of the funds necessary to cover the cost of the benefits defined;

(j) laying down different standards or standards applicable only to workers of a specified sex, except as provided for in points (h) and (i), as regards the guarantee or retention of entitlement to deferred benefits when a worker leaves a scheme.

---

[133] Whether any such positive measures in favour of pregnancy and maternity are permitted under Art 141 has not yet been decided by the ECJ. For discussion of Art 141(4), added by the Amsterdam Treaty and apparently permitting certain measures of positive action, see ch 6.

[134] Some support for this view is to be derived from the comments of Slynn AG in Case 318/86 *Re Sex Discrimination in the Civil Service, Commission v France* [1988] ECR 3559, esp at 3572, where he said: 'Pregnancy of female staff has to be accommodated by employers as one of the consequences of . . . equal treatment.' Cf Case 177/88 *Dekker v Stichting Vormingscentrum Voor Jonge Volwassen Plus* [1990] ECR I-3941.

[135] In particular, so as to put into statutory form the decisions in Case C-152/91 *Neath*, op cit, n 72 and Case C-200/91 *Coloroll*, op cit, n 72, discussed above.

[136] Note the use of the word 'examples' here; the list is clearly not exhaustive.

The Annex provides:

Examples of elements which may be unequal, in respect of funded defined-benefit schemes, as referred
to in Article 6(h):
    —conversion into a capital sum of part of a periodic pension,
    —transfer of pension rights,
    —a reversionary pension payable to a dependant in return for the surrender of part of a pension,
    —a reduced pension where the worker opts to take early retirement.

Even following its amendment, the Directive therefore continues to permit the use
of gender-specific actuarial calculations in certain circumstances.[137] It was seen above
that the ECJ's decision in *Neath v Hugh Steeper Ltd*[138] outlawed inequality over pension
payments and employee contributions in defined-benefit schemes, but permitted
unequal employer contributions consequent on gender-specific actuarial calculations
in such schemes. The Directive today confirms this position. The Court has not,
however, dealt with these matters in relation to contribution-defined schemes; whilst
accepting that employee contributions must be equal in such schemes, the Directive
permits specified exceptions to the equality principle in relation to employers' contributions and pension payments in contribution-defined schemes. The vulnerability of
these exceptions to successful challenge for breaching Article 141 thus remains to be
tested before the Court. The continued scope for gender-specific actuarial tables
sparked considerable controversy between the Commission and the European Parliament during the legislative process of the amending Directive and was ended only on
the Commission giving its undertaking to give further consideration to this matter. It
2003, it proposed a new Directive to be based on Article 13, 'implementing the
principle of equal treatment between men and women in the access to and supply of
goods and services'.[139] In its Explanatory Memorandum, the Commission explained:

Studies show that sex is not the main determining factor for life expectancy. Other factors have been
shown to be more relevant, such as marital status, socio-economic factors, employment/unemployment,
regional area, smoking and nutrition habits. Lifestyle can be seen as a multidimensional factor which has
a significantly higher impact on individuals' life expectancy than sex. Studies which have tried to remove
lifestyle, social class and environmental factors from the equation have shown that the difference in
average life expectancy between men and women lies between zero and two years with the conclusion
that the growing gap in life expectancy witnessed in the general population in some Member States
cannot be attributed to biological differences. Sex is at the very best a proxy for other indicators of life
expectancy. The inference which can be drawn from such studies is that the practice of insurers to use
sex as a determining factor in the evaluation of risk is based on ease of use rather than real value as a guide
to life expectancy. Commentators have noted that insurers are more likely to pool together the healthy
and the unhealthy than men and women.[140]

The Commission concluded that the separation of men and women into different
pools for actuarial purposes was unjustified and discriminatory. Furthermore, it

---

[137] Cf the Commission's proposal for the original Directive prohibited the determination of benefit
amounts or rates of contribution by reference to such factors: see OJ [1983] C134/7.
[138] Case C-152/91, op cit, n 72.
[139] COM (2003) 657 final. This draft instrument is also discussed in ch 5.   [140] Ibid, at 6.

pointed out that the matter was of escalating practical importance, because Member States are placing increasing reliance on private, rather than State, pension provision. The Commission therefore proposed that the principle of equal treatment should apply to the use of sex-based actuarial factors in the calculation of premiums and benefits in insurance; however, in deference to the commercial difficulties anticipated by insurers, this requirement would be subject to a transitional period of eight years.[141] Political agreement on the draft directive was reached by the Council on 4 October 2004; however, although the agreed text includes insurance and related financial activities within the scope of the new instrument, it significantly dilutes the principle of equal treatment. It provides that Member States may permit proportionate differences in individuals' premiums and benefits where the use of sex is a determining factor in the assessment of risk. However, any different treatment is required to be based on relevant and accurate actuarial and statistical data which has to be made public and regularly updated.

Article 6(2) of the Occupational Social Security Directive states that '[w]here the granting of benefits . . . is left to the discretion of the scheme's management bodies, the latter must take account of the principle of equal treatment'. In response to the argument that it was to be implied from this provision that Article 141 itself was not directly effective as against the trustees of a pension fund, Van Gerven AG commented in *Coloroll Pension Trustees Ltd v Russell*:[142]

I see in that provision merely a confirmation of the Community legislature's intention to give effect to the principle of equal treatment as effectively as possible and certainly not any argument *a contrario* according to which the worker or the person (or persons) claiming under him could not, as regards pay discrimination directly caught by Article 119, rely on Article 119 against trustees as well. In any case, that directive [namely, the Occupational Social Security Directive] cannot detract from the effect of Article 119 . . .[143]

Article 8(1) used to provide that the Member States were to take all necessary steps to ensure that the provisions of occupational schemes contrary to the principle of equal treatment were revised by 1 January 1993. However, the ruling of the ECJ in *Barber* that, albeit subject to the temporal limitation set out in that decision, Article 141 takes direct effect in relation to pension schemes, rendered Article 8(1) nugatory; the Court later explained in *Moroni v Collo GmbH*:[144]

By its second question, the national court wishes to know whether or not Article 8(1) of Directive 86/378 prevents the legal consequences of the incompatibility with Article 119 of the Treaty of the setting of different retirement ages for men and women for the purposes of the payment of company pensions from being drawn before 1 January 1993 . . .

This question is essentially concerned with the relationship between Article 119 and Directive 86/378.

It is sufficient to point out in this regard that it is settled law that Article 119 applies directly to all forms of discrimination which may be identified solely with the aid of the criteria of equal work and equal pay

---

[141] See Art 4 of the proposed Directive.
[142] Case C-200/91, AG's submissions at [1993] ECR I-4879.   [143] Ibid, at 4940–1.
[144] Case C-110/91, op cit, n 72.

referred to by that Article, without national or Community measures being required to define them with greater precision in order to permit their application . . . [145]

Since with the aid of the constitutive elements of the pay in question and of the criteria laid down in Article 119 discrimination may be directly identified as arising from the setting of different retirement ages for men and women in the matter of company pensions, the effects of the Directive do not matter, for its provisions cannot in any way restrict the scope of Article 119.

It follows that, subject to [the temporal limitation contained in the *Barber* case] a worker who is discriminated against by the setting of different retirement ages for men and women may in principle assert his rights to payment of the company pension at the same age as his female counterpart and any reduction in the event of early departure from the service of the undertaking must be calculated on the basis of that age.

The answer to the second question . . . must therefore be that, subject to [the temporal limitation contained in *Barber*], Council Directive 86/378 cannot prevent Article 119 of the Treaty from being relied upon directly and immediately before national courts. [146]

Similarly, although Article 8(2) used to provide that the Directive was not to preclude 'rights and obligations relating to a period of membership of an occupational scheme prior to revision of that scheme from remaining subject to the provisions of the scheme in force during that period', the Court held in the *Beune* case [147] that 'Article 8(2) . . . cannot limit the scope of Article 119 in relation to pension rights in respect of periods of membership prior to revision of the scheme concerned'. [148]

Article 8 is today restricted in its scope so as to provide:

1. Member States shall take the necessary steps to ensure that the provisions of occupational schemes *for self-employed workers* contrary to the principle of equal treatment are revised with effect from 1 January 1993 at the latest.

2. This Directive shall not preclude rights and obligations relating to a period of membership of an occupational scheme *for self-employed workers* prior to revision of that scheme from remaining subject to the provisions of the scheme in force during that period. [149]

Furthermore, Article 2(1) of the amending Directive 96/97 mandates that:

Any measure implementing this Directive, as regards paid workers, must cover all benefits derived from periods of employment subsequent to 17 May 1990 and shall apply retroactively to that date, without prejudice to workers or those claiming under them who have, before that date, initiated legal proceedings or raised an equivalent claim under national law. In that event, the implementation measures must apply retroactively to 8 April 1976 and must cover all the benefits derived from periods of employment after that date . . .

Article 2(2) of the amending instrument goes on to spell out the Court's customary position in relation to the procedural autonomy of the Member States: [150]

The second sentence of paragraph 1 shall not prevent national rules relating to time limits for bringing actions under national law from being relied on against workers or those claiming under them who initiated legal proceedings or raised an equivalent claim under national law before 17 May 1990,

---

[145] For further discussion of the direct effect of Art 141, see below.
[146] [1993] ECR I-6591, at 6616–17.   [147] Case C-7/93 *Beune*, op cit, n 54.
[148] Ibid, at 4523.   [149] Emphases added.   [150] See ch 2.

provided that they are not less favourable for that type of action than for similar actions of a domestic nature and that they do not render the exercise of Community law impossible in practice.

Article 9 of the original Directive contained exceptions, in particular for pensionable age and survivors' benefits, which were later ruled by the ECJ to fall within the scope of Article 141. The amended Article 9 is therefore restricted to the self-employed[151] and provides:

As regards schemes for self-employed workers, Member States may defer compulsory application of the principle of equal treatment with regard to:

(a) determination of pensionable age for the granting of old-age or retirement pensions, and the possible implications for other benefits:

  —either until the date on which such equality is achieved in statutory schemes,
  —or, at the latest, until such equality is prescribed by a directive;

(b) survivors' pensions until Community law establishes the principle of equal treatment in statutory social security schemes in that regard;

(c) the application of the first subparagraph of point (i) of Article 6(1) to take account of the different actuarial calculation factors, at the latest until 1 January 1999.

A new Article 9(a) of the Directive also now provides that, where men and women may claim a flexible pension age under the same conditions, 'this shall not be deemed to be incompatible with this Directive'.

The Directive concludes with provisions guaranteeing the right to legal redress for breaches of its terms[152] and protecting workers against victimization in the form of dismissal where they have complained of a breach of the Directive.[153]

(iv) Other statutorily regulated payments made by employers to their employees

Once the ECJ had conceded in *Bilka-Kaufhaus GmbH v Weber Von Hartz*[154] that an element of statutory regulation of a payment made by employer to employee did not deprive the payment of its status as 'pay' under Article 141,[155] the way was clear for that Article to be extended to a variety of payments made as a result of statutory obligations[156] cast on employers.[157]

Very importantly in practice, the issue arose as to the applicability of Article 141 to redundancy payments. These were involved in *Burton v British Railways*

---

[151] But see n 119 above in relation to the meaning of 'self-employed' in EU law.
[152] Art 10 of the Directive.   [153] Ibid, Art 11.   [154] Op cit, n 39, discussed above.
[155] See also Jacobs AG in Case C-7/93 *Beune*, op cit, n 54, at 4486.
[156] See, eg, Case C-249/97 *Gruber*, op cit, n 15.
[157] The ECJ had, in fact, pointed the way to this conclusion many years earlier in Case 43/75 *Defrenne v Sabena*, op cit, n 11, where it held that 'Article 119 may be relied upon before the national courts and . . . these courts have a duty to ensure the protection of the rights which this provision vests in individuals, in particular as regards those types of discrimination *arising directly from legislative provisions* or collective labour agreements . . .' (at 476, emphasis added).

Board,[158] but since the issue was not discrimination in relation to the amount of the payments receivable, the Court did not there decide whether they fell within the Article 141 notion of 'pay'. However, in *Worringham v Lloyds Bank Ltd*,[159] the Court commented that: 'Sums . . . which are included in the calculation of the gross salary payable to the employee and which directly determine the calculation of other advantages linked to the salary, *such as redundancy payments* . . . form part of the worker's pay . . .'[160] The position was finally clarified as a matter of EU law[161] by *Barber v Guardian Royal Exchange Assurance Group*.[162] The ECJ there held all forms of redundancy payment, whether contractual, statutory, or *ex gratia*, to be within the scope of Article 141:[163]

[T]he concept of pay . . . comprises any other consideration, whether in cash or in kind, whether immediate or future, provided that the worker receives it, albeit indirectly, in respect of his employment from his employer . . . Accordingly, the fact that certain benefits are paid after the termination of the employment relationship does not prevent them from being in the nature of pay, within the meaning of Article 119 of the Treaty.

As regards, in particular, the compensation granted to a worker in connection with his redundancy, it must be stated that such compensation constitutes a form of pay to which the worker is entitled in respect of his employment, which is paid to him on termination of the employment relationship, which makes it possible to facilitate his adjustment to the new circumstances resulting from the loss of his employment and which provides him with a source of income during the period in which he is seeking new employment.

It follows that compensation granted to a worker in connection with his redundancy falls in principle within the concept of pay for the purposes of Article 119 of the Treaty.

At the hearing, the UK argued that the statutory redundancy payment fell outside the scope of Article 119 of the Treaty because it constituted a social security benefit and not a form of pay. In that regard it must be pointed out that a redundancy payment made by the employer . . . cannot cease to constitute a form of pay on the sole ground that, rather than deriving from the contract of employment, it is a statutory or *ex gratia* payment.

In the case of statutory redundancy payments it must be borne in mind that, as the Court held in its judgment of 8 April 1976 in Case 43/75 . . . Article 119 of the Treaty also applies to discrimination arising directly from legislative provisions. This means that benefits provided for by law may come within the concept of pay for the purposes of that provision . . . [B]enefits paid by an employer to a worker in connection with the latter's compulsory redundancy fall within the scope of the second paragraph of Article 119, whether they are paid under a contract of employment, by virtue of legislative provisions or on a voluntary basis.[164]

---

[158] Case 19/81, op cit, n 16. See also Snaith, 'Equal Pay and Sex Discrimination' (1982) 7 ELRev 301.
[159] Case 69/80, op cit, n 23.   [160] Ibid, at 790, emphasis added.
[161] The UK legislature implicitly acknowledged the applicability of Art 141 to redundancy payments when, in s 16 of the Employment Act 1989, it removed the discriminatory age limits applying to eligibility for statutory redundancy pay.   [162] Op cit, n 28.
[163] See also Case C-220/02 *Österreichischer Gewerkschaftsbund v Wirtschaftskammer Österreich*, judgment of 8 June 2004, nyr, where the ECJ held that a 'benefit' consisting of the taking into account of a period of leave for the calculation of a termination payment is 'pay' within the meaning of Art 141. Cf the submissions of Kokott AG.
[164] [1990] ECR I-1889, at 1949–50. This decision was followed shortly afterwards by that of the ECJ in Case 33/89 *Kowalska v Freie und Hansestadt Hamburg* [1990] ECR I-2591.

The Court also made another significant statement of general principle in *Barber*. It held that:

Although it is true that many advantages granted by an employer also reflect considerations of social policy, the fact that a benefit is in the nature of pay cannot be called in question where the worker is entitled to receive the benefit in question from his employer by reason of the existence of the employment relationship.[165]

Once it had become clear that redundancy payments were within Article 141, a large part of the UK's employment protection legislation fell under suspicion. Those covered by the legislation were divided into two classes: employees working for more than 16 hours a week were protected after two years' continuous employment with the same employer; whereas those working between eight and sixteen hours a week were entitled to protection only after five years' of such employment. The argument was that since the first group of workers was predominantly male and the second predominantly female, this constituted unlawful indirect sex discrimination. The Equal Opportunities Commission (EOC) therefore brought judicial review proceedings against the Secretary of State for Employment, alleging that this discrimination in relation to the availability of statutory redundancy pay and compensation for unfair dismissal contravened EU law.[166] The House of Lords[167] granted declarations that the discrimination in relation to redundancy pay contravened Article 141, and that that in relation to compensation for unfair dismissal contravened the Equal Treatment Directive;[168] in the absence of any ruling on the matter by the ECJ, the House left open the question of whether compensation for unfair dismissal constituted 'pay' within the meaning of Article 141, though it was conceded that there is 'much to be said in favour' of this view.[169] However, in *Mediguard Services Ltd v Thame*,[170] the British Employment Appeal Tribunal held that such compensation is within Article 141, so entitling a worker with two years' service of between eight and sixteen hours a week to bring an action for unfair dismissal. Eventually, the issue was referred to the ECJ in *R v Secretary of State for Employment, ex parte Seymour-Smith*,[171] where the House of Lords asked whether compensation for unfair dismissal constitutes pay within the meaning of Article 141 and, if so, whether the right to complain of unfair dismissal also falls under Article 141. The ECJ held that compensation for

---

[165] [1990] ECR I-1889, at 1950.

[166] It emerged in the course of the proceedings that no other Member State, apart from Ireland, had similar thresholds; Ireland, where statute had at one time provided for an 18 hours per week threshold, had recently introduced legislation reducing this to 8 hours.   [167] [1994] 2 WLR 409.

[168] See further in ch 5. The legislation was subsequently amended so as to remove the qualifying thresholds.

[169] See the remarks of Lord Keith of Kinkel in [1994] 2 WLR 409, at 423. In the Court of Appeal, Dillon LJ commented: '... compensation for unfair dismissal, which is compensation payable by the employer for the unfair premature determination of the contract of employment, must, in my judgment, fall within the definition of "pay" ': [1993] 1 WLR 872, at 884.   [170] [1994] IRLR 504.

[171] [1997] 1 WLR 473.

unfair dismissal does indeed fall within the purview of Article 141:[172]

> In this case, the compensation awarded to an employee for unfair dismissal, which comprises a basic award and a compensatory award, is designed in particular to give the employee what he would have earned if the employer had not unlawfully terminated the employment relationship.
>
> The basic award refers directly to the remuneration which the employee would have received had he not been dismissed. The compensatory award covers the loss sustained by him as a result of the dismissal, including any expenses reasonably incurred by him in consequence thereof and, subject to certain conditions, the loss of any benefit which he might reasonably be expected to have gained but for the dismissal.
>
> It follows that compensation for unfair dismissal is paid to the employee by reason of his employment, which would have continued but for the unfair dismissal. That compensation therefore falls within the definition of pay for the purposes of Article 119 of the Treaty.
>
> The fact that the compensation at issue in the main proceedings is a judicial award made on the basis of the applicable legislation cannot, of itself, invalidate that conclusion. As the Court has already stated in this connection, it is irrelevant that the right to compensation, rather than deriving from the contract of employment is, for instance, a statutory right.... [173]

Furthermore, the ECJ added that, since the claim in *Seymour-Smith* was for compensation, the complaint was about access to pay and therefore fell within Article 141.[174]

Another important decision of the ECJ in this context was that in *Rinner-Kühn v FWW Spezial-Gebaudereinigung GmbH*.[175] This concerned sick pay under the German statutory scheme. Under this scheme, an employer was obliged to pay an employee's full salary for the first six weeks of sickness, after which the social security system took over payments at the level of 80% of normal earnings for a statutorily defined period. The employer was not entitled to be reimbursed by the State in respect of the first six weeks, unless there were fewer than twenty employees in the enterprise concerned, in which case the State reimbursed 80% of the payments. In a terse judgment, making very little mention of its other relevant jurisprudence, the ECJ held that the employer's payments under this scheme constituted 'pay' for the purpose of Article 141. It stated simply that: '[T]he continued payment of wages to a worker in the event of illness falls within the definition of "pay" within the meaning of Article 119 of the Treaty.'[176] What was unclear from this judgment was whether the Court regarded the ultimate source of the payment as significant (under the German scheme, of course, all employers had to make at least a contribution to the first six weeks' sick pay). It was seen earlier that the Court laid stress in the *Bilka-Kaufhaus* case on the fact that the benefits concerned there were financed solely by the employer; and in *Barber* it noted specifically that the schemes were financed either wholly by the employer, or by

---

[172] Case C-167/97 [1999] ECR I-623.   [173] Ibid, at 675–6.

[174] It would have been otherwise if the applicants had been seeking reinstatement or re-engagement; in this case the conditions laid down by national law would have concerned *working conditions*, and the claim would therefore have fallen within the ambit of the Equal Treatment Directive.

[175] Case 171/88 [1989] ECR 2743.   [176] Ibid, at 2759.

both the employer and the workers. It adopted a similar approach in *Commission v Belgium*.[177] A scheme, which originated in a collective agreement but was subsequently given statutory force, established special payments for elderly workers on redundancy; however, eligibility for the payments depended upon eligibility for unemployment benefit. Since women were not entitled to unemployment benefit after the age of 60, although men remained so entitled until the age of 65, women were correspondingly excluded from the special redundancy payment after 60. The payments were made by the worker's last employer. The Belgian Government argued that the payments were in the nature of social security since they supplemented the State unemployment benefit, and that the difference between male and female entitlement reflected the difference in State pension age, so that the situation was exempted by the Social Security Directive. The ECJ rejected this contention:

[T]he additional payment at issue, although *sui generis* in certain respects, must be deemed to constitute 'pay' within the meaning of Article 119 of the Treaty. It is clear from Collective Agreement No 17 that that payment is to be received from the redundant worker's last employer . . . and that it is payable by reason of the employment relationship which existed between those two persons, the agreement being applicable only to workers employed in pursuance of a contract of employment and their employers . . . It is also apparent that the additional payment is contractual since it is the result of negotiations between employers and employees. The fact that it was subsequently made compulsory *erga omnes* by legislation cannot therefore detract from its contractual nature . . .

The Belgian government's argument that the additional payment and the unemployment benefit form an indivisible unit, namely the 'contractual early-retirement pension', and that consequently the additional payment should, like unemployment benefit, be regarded as a social security benefit cannot be upheld. It must be observed, first, that whilst it is true that the amount of the payment is dependent both on the reference wage and on the unemployment benefit, the additional payment nevertheless constitutes consideration received by the worker from the employer in respect of the employment relationship which existed between them. Secondly, the fact that the payment supplements a social security benefit such as unemployment benefit is not decisive. Under Collective Agreement No 17, the additional payment, although linked to the unemployment benefit as regards the manner in which it is made, is independent of the general social security scheme as regards both its structure and its financing, *the latter being the responsibility of the employer alone*.[178]

On the other hand, in its ruling in *Barber* in relation to redundancy pay, the Court appeared unconcerned as to the original source of the funds involved, provided only that the payment was actually made by the employer and received by the employee in respect of his or her employment. In addition, it has also been seen that in the *Beune* case,[179] in relation to pension schemes, the Court pointed out that none of the criteria for distinguishing between pay and social security payments is decisive when taken alone, but that the fundamental issue is whether the payment is made to the worker by reason of the employment relationship between the worker and the employer. This view was confirmed by the Court's decision in

---

[177] Case C-173/91 [1993] ECR I-673.   [178] Ibid, at 698–9, emphasis added.
[179] Case C-7/93 *Beune*, op cit, n 54, discussed above.

Gillespie,[180] that maternity pay in the UK[181] is within Article 141; the Court arrived at this conclusion without making any explicit reference to the fact that employers making statutory maternity payments are to all intents and purposes totally reimbursed by the State, and it based its decision wholly on the payment's foundation in the employment relationship. It must therefore now be concluded that a payment can constitute pay within the meaning of Article 141 even if it is not funded to any extent at all by the employer.

(v)   Are all employment benefits 'pay'?

Unlike the British Equal Pay Act of 1970, which in s 1(2) refers to discrimination in respect of any term of a contract of employment, Article 141(1) and (2) refers specifically only to the term 'pay'.[182] However, as has been seen above, 'pay' is not to be confined to the physical contents of the wage packet, but clearly extends to many other forms of consideration granted even indirectly by the employer to the employee in respect of the employment. This being so, is not any benefit extended to the employee via the contract of employment to be regarded as 'pay'? Such benefits as holiday entitlements, periods of sick leave, access to canteen facilities, and so on would also appear to fall within an extended notion of 'pay': the employer does not grant them out of the goodness of his or her heart but as a reward for the job done. Such an argument found favour with the House of Lords in *Hayward v Cammell Laird Shipbuilders (No 2)*.[183] However, it appears to be less attractive to the ECJ.[184] If the Court were to accept the argument, the scope of Article 141 would of course be enormously widened, and in this context the difficulties arising as regards the direct enforcement of the Equal Treatment Directive against persons other than organs of the State would be avoided,[185] although such difficulties would remain for discrimination contrary to the Race Directive and the Framework Directive.

---

[180]   Case C-342/93 *Gillespie*, op cit, n 16, also discussed above.
[181]   The Court was actually asked in this case about both statutory and contractual maternity pay. Since it drew no distinction between the two categories, it seemingly attached no significance to the provenance of the payments.
[182]   However, other aspects of the treatment accorded by an employer to the workforce are also governed by the Equal Treatment Directive, the Race Directive, and the Framework Directive, as discussed in ch 5.
[183]   [1988] 2 WLR 1134. The employers in that case had convinced the Court of Appeal that a distinction could be drawn for the purposes of the British Equal Pay Act 1970 between those terms of a contract of employment relating to the general category of 'pay', and other terms. The House of Lords rejected this argument and Lord Goff said: '[A]lmost any, indeed perhaps any, benefit will fall within "pay" in the very wide sense favoured by [the Court of Appeal]' (at 1145).
[184]   Certain remarks of the ECJ in Case 149/77 *Defrenne v Sabena* [1978] ECR 1365 seem at first sight to reject this argument. However, the issue before the Court there was the enforced retirement of female employees at the age of only 40, and thus concerned working conditions generally, not consideration passing from the employer to the employee. See also *Gerster v Freistaat Bayern* Case C-1/95 [1997] ECR I-5253, and Case C-236/98 *Jämställdhetsombudsmannen v Örebro läns landsting* [2000] ECR I-2189.   [185]   See ch 2 for discussion of the impossibility of enforcing directives horizontally.

However, whatever its ultimate position on the question of how far 'pay' can be taken, the ECJ has taken a perceptive approach to how pay levels are to be compared. In *Barber v Guardian Royal Exchange Assurance Group*,[186] the Court was pressed to apply a global type of assessment to the pay received by each sex, as the House of Lords had been in the *Hayward* case. The national court had asked the ECJ whether, in EU law, equal pay must be ensured at the level of each element of remuneration, or only on the basis of a comprehensive assessment of the consideration paid to the workers concerned. The ECJ, demonstrating considerable sensitivity to the risk of subconscious bias on the part of those carrying out such an assessment, replied that it had already

emphasized the fundamental importance of transparency and, in particular, of the possibility of a review by the national courts in order to prevent and, if necessary, eliminate any discrimination based on sex. With regard to the means of verifying compliance with the principle of equal pay, it must be stated that if the national courts were under an obligation to make an assessment and a comparison of all the various types of consideration granted, according to the circumstances, to men and women, judicial review would be difficult and the effectiveness of Article 119 would be diminished as a result. It follows that genuine transparency, permitting an effective review, is assured only if the principle of equal pay applies to each of the elements of remuneration granted to men or women.[187]

It continued to take this approach in the difficult circumstances presented to it in *Jämställdhetsombudsmannen v Örebro läns landsting*.[188] The case concerned a pay comparison between two (female) midwives and a (male) technician. The basic monthly salaries of the midwives were less than that of the technician, but the midwives were required to work a shift system which resulted in an inconvenient-hours supplement being paid to them. The technician would have been entitled to such a supplement had he worked inconvenient hours, but he did not in fact do so. In addition, the midwives worked a slightly shorter week than the technician, in recognition of their duty to perform shift-work. When the inconvenient-hours supplement and the reduced working hours were taken into account, it was alleged that the midwives did not receive less pay than the technician. The Court ruled that the constituent elements of the pay package must be compared; thus, the basic monthly salaries should be compared. If it was found that they were indeed of unequal value, then a *prima facie* breach of the equal pay principle would be established; this breach could, however, be rebutted by proof that the pay differential was attributable to the difference in the hours worked, provided that this was unrelated to any discrimination on the ground of sex. As the Finnish Government pointed out, these sorts of problems are particularly acute in equal value claims, where the relevant contractual conditions may diverge completely. This argument

---

[186] Op cit, n 28. Cf the remarks of Cosmas AG in *ex parte Seymour-Smith*, op cit, n 172, at 641.
[187] [1990] ECR I-1889, at 1953.
[188] Case C-236/98 [2000] ECR I-2189. Likewise in Case C-381/99 *Brunnhofer v Bank der österreichischen Postsparkasse AG* [2001] ECR I-4961. For the application of the same principle in relation to equal treatment, see *Jørgensen*, op cit, n 42.

led Advocate General Jacobs to make an exception:

> Where ... for historical or other reasons the pay structures are complex, so that individual elements or the bases on which they are granted are difficult or impossible to disentangle, it may be both unrealistic and unprofitable to look at individual components of the pay package in isolation. Moreover, to do so may lead to discrimination against the other sex. In such cases a global assessment may be the only valid—or even feasible—method, pending a re-structuring of the system. ...
>
> That does not mean, however, that one element in the overall package can necessarily be set off against another. Thus in *Barber* itself, in which men who had been made redundant were entitled to an immediate pension if they had attained the age of 55 whereas women who had been made redundant were entitled to an immediate pension if they had attained the age of 50, it is understandable that the Court regarded it as inappropriate to seek to offset discriminatory pension rights by taking into account possible differences in redundancy payments.[189]

The meaning of 'equal work'

(i) Equal pay for 'equal work'

Article 141 expressly mandates equal pay where men and women perform 'equal work'. The same concept must be taken to apply to pay discrimination within the terms of the Race Directive and the Framework Directive since both instruments are predicated on the EU notion of 'non-discrimination' which, as seen in chapter 3, refers to the application of different rules to comparable situations.

The clearest and most obvious case where equal work is performed is, of course, where, as in *Defrenne v Sabena*,[190] two people perform identical jobs for the same employer in a single establishment. Does the Article extend also to the performance of identical jobs for the same employer in different establishments, or to the performance of identical jobs for different employers? It is submitted that, as a matter of logic, the answer should be 'Yes' to both questions. The underlying issue concerns what precisely is being valued when two jobs are classified as constituting equal work. Broadly, there are two approaches: to analyse the value of the jobs in terms of their content and the demands they place on workers; or, alternatively, to measure the value of the jobs to the employer by means of measuring, for example, the benefits they bring to the business, or the cost that the employer would incur by buying in other services to replace the jobs in issue. Both approaches have their drawbacks. The job content approach involves the elusive task of putting a price on particular skills and requirements and, moreover, carries with it the risk that in so assessing job factors subconscious prejudices and discrimination are allowed to creep into the calculation. So, for example, if heavy manual work (performed in the past at least largely by men) has traditionally been rewarded at higher rates than repetitive tasks requiring considerable manual dexterity (largely the domain of women workers), then there is a real danger that a job evaluator may be swayed in

---

[189] [2000] ECR I-2189, at 2199–2200.   [190] Case 43/75, op cit, n 11.

the direction of rating heavy work more highly than dextrous work. On the other hand, if the approach taken is value to the employer then the legislation's potential for radically changing women workers' economic status is wholly undermined: where there is job segregation according to sex, and the women's jobs have come to be paid less than the men's, then the cost of finding another woman to perform the job in issue will be correspondingly depressed. Putting it another way, the 'market value' of women's jobs is the very thing which Article 141 seeks to address and to remedy.

For this reason, the first approach to job evaluation is to be preferred. The ECJ has made it clear that this is its preference too. So, for example, in *Macarthys Ltd v Smith*[191] it held:

> [T]he decisive test lies in establishing whether there is a difference in treatment between a man and a woman performing 'equal work' within the meaning of Article 119. The scope of that concept . . . is entirely qualitative in character in that it is exclusively concerned with the nature of the services in question . . .[192]

It follows that it does not, therefore, matter where or for whom equal work is performed. If the nature of the services is identical then it must be rewarded equally. In its early judgments on the subject, the ECJ did not appear to recognize this argument, and in *Defrenne v Sabena*[193] it said:

> [T]he principle of equal pay contained in Article 119 may be relied upon before the national courts and . . . these courts have a duty to ensure the protection of the rights which this provision vests in individuals, in particular as regards those types of discrimination arising directly from legislative provisions or collective labour agreements, as well as in cases in which men and women receive unequal pay for equal work *which is carried out in the same establishment or service*, whether public or private.[194]

However, as will be discussed later in the present chapter, the ECJ was concerned in this passage to distinguish between those situations in which Article 141 takes direct effect and those in which it does not. Furthermore, the factual situation with which it was presented in *Defrenne v Sabena* involved identical work in the same establishment or service.[195] Later cases suggested that the ECJ might consider that Article 141 extends to comparisons with colleagues in other establishments belonging

---

[191] Case 129/79 [1980] ECR 1275, at 1288–9. See also Crisham, op cit, n 23.

[192] *Macarthys Ltd v Smith*, ibid. As Lord Bridge explained in *Leverton v Clwyd County Council* [1989] 2 WLR 47, this involves examining the nature of what is done, not the hours at which or frequency with which the tasks are performed. He commented: '[I]n job evaluation studies the demands made by different jobs have in practice always been assessed under whatever headings are adopted on a qualitative, not a quantitative, basis. That this is the correct basis, if English law is to conform to Community law, seems to be amply borne out by the judgment of the ECJ in *Macarthys Ltd v Smith* . . . I have no doubt that demand in terms of hours worked is not only beyond the expertise of the job evaluator but is, on the true construction of s 1(2)(c) and (5) [of the Equal Pay Act 1970], a factor which is outside the scope of job evaluation' (at 74–5). [193] Case 43/75, op cit, n 11.

[194] Ibid, at 476, emphasis added. On the other hand, the addition of the word 'service' to 'establishment' provided a seed from which a wider principle might be permitted to emerge.

[195] In Case 96/80 *Jenkins v Kingsgate (Clothing Productions) Ltd* [1981] ECR 911, the ECJ also appeared to confine its remarks to discrimination within a particular 'undertaking', but that again was the situation presented to it on the facts of the case.

to the same employer, and even perhaps with comparators working for different employers.[196] This matter has proved particularly significant in Britain where the scope of comparison permitted under s 1(6) of the Equal Pay Act 1970 is limited to cases where the man and woman are working either in the same establishment, or else at different establishments of the same employer at which common terms and conditions apply.[197] This restriction is self-evidently even narrower than a requirement that the claimant and the comparator must have a common employer. The Employment Appeal Tribunal has held that the scope of s 1(6) is narrower than that permitted under Article 141, and allowed a claimant to enforce the Treaty directly so as to make a pay comparison with a comparator doing a similar job for another employer.[198]

The scope of comparison under Article 141 was raised, but not answered by the ECJ, in *Commission v Denmark*;[199] Advocate General Van Themaat did, however, comment that in his opinion Article 141 extended to comparisons outside the worker's immediate workplace.[200] And the Court's statements in relation to the Equal Pay Directive[201] have contained at least the suggestion that this instrument requires comparisons outside the employer's establishment; for example, in *Commission v UK*,[202] it held that the Directive requires that a worker 'be entitled to claim before an appropriate authority that his work has the same value *as other work*'.[203] When coupled with its frequent statements that the Directive does not extend, but merely gives greater articulation to, Article 141,[204] it would appear to follow that the Court meant that Article 141 itself can require comparisons with the pay of employees outside the claimant's immediate working environment.

The ECJ has now been required to confront this issue head-on. In *Lawrence v Regent Office Care Ltd*,[205] it was asked whether a group of women workers could compare their pay with that of men working for a different employer, in circumstances in which it had already been established that the jobs concerned were

---

[196] In *Hasley v Fair Employment Agency* [1989] IRLR 106, Lord Lowry, in the Northern Ireland Court of Appeal, said: 'It has to be observed that neither the *Defrenne* nor the *Macarthy* judgment treats the remedy given by Article 119 as *confined* to work carried out *in the same establishment or service*' (at 111).

[197] However, this provision has in recent times been given an increasingly broad interpretation by the higher courts; see in particular *Leverton v Clwyd County Council* [1989] 2 WLR 47 and *British Coal Corporation v Smith* [1996] 3 All ER 97.

[198] See *Scullard v Knowles* [1996] IRLR 344; the Tribunal there emphasized that the phrase used in *Defrenne v Sabena* was 'same establishment *or service*', and it proceeded to initiate further inquiries as to whether the claimant could be said to be in the same service as her comparator. See also the decision of the Inner House of the Scottish Court of Session in *South Ayrshire Council v Morton* [2002] ICR 956, a head-teacher was permitted to compare her pay with a comparator employed by another education authority, both because of the existence a national collective agreement covering the pay of all head-teachers in Scotland and because the two head-teachers could be said to be in the same 'service' as each other.   [199] Case 143/83 [1985] ECR 427.

[200] See also the remarks of Capotorti AG in *Macarthys*, op cit, n 191, esp at 1293–4.

[201] Directive 75/117, OJ [1975] L45/19, discussed in detail below.

[202] Case 61/81 [1982] ECR 2601.   [203] Ibid, at 2615–16, emphasis added.

[204] See, eg, Case 96/80 *Jenkins*, op cit, n 195, esp at 927, and see also further discussion below.

[205] Case C-320/00 [2002] ECR I-7325.

of equal value. The Court gave an extremely brief judgment. It acknowledged that there is nothing in the wording of Article 141 to suggest that its applicability is limited to situations in which men and women work for the same employer. However, it went on to say that where pay differences between men and women doing equal work or work of equal value 'cannot be attributed to a single source', there is no body which is responsible for the inequality and which can restore equal treatment, and the situation does not therefore fall within Article 141. It repeated this formulation in *Allonby v Accrington and Rossendale College*,[206] which concerned a woman lecturer who had been dismissed by the college but re-engaged as an independent contractor via an agency called ELS. She sought to compare her pay conditions with those of a male lecturer employed directly by the college. The ECJ held that the fact that the level of pay received by Ms Allonby was influenced by the amount which the college paid ELS was not a sufficient basis for concluding that the college and ELS constituted a 'single source' to which the relevant differences in the employment conditions could be attributed.[207]

The Court in neither case gave any explanation of why the employer paying the lower wage cannot be treated, in the absence of rebutting evidence, as responsible for remedying the breach. Advocate General Geelhoed in *Lawrence* was rather more forthcoming, and it has to be assumed that the Court intended to follow his line of reasoning. He considered that a pay comparison could be made in three cases:

The first covers cases in which statutory rules apply to the working and pay conditions in more than one undertaking, establishment or service . . . Second, there are cases in which several undertakings or establishments are covered by a collective works agreement or regulations governing the terms and conditions of employment. Finally, the third category concerns those cases in which the terms and conditions of employment are laid down centrally for more than one organisation or business within a holding company or conglomerate.

In all of these cases it is possible, going beyond the boundaries of the individual undertaking or service, to compare male with female employees in order to determine whether there is discrimination prohibited by Article 141 EC.

The feature common to these three categories is that regulation of the terms and conditions of employment actually applied is traceable to one source, whether it be the legislature, the parties to a collective works agreement, or the management of a corporate group.[208]

---

[206] Op cit, n 3. See also Fredman, 'Marginalising Equal Pay Laws' (2004) 33 ILJ 281.

[207] It is, however, noteworthy that Geelhoed AG drew attention in *Allonby* to the increasingly prevalent practice by employers of contracting-out jobs, often with the consequence that the equal pay requirement is evaded. He agreed with the Commission that the only solution would be new legislation. The Commission has announced its intention to propose a directive which would protect agency workers and align their treatment to staff in stable employment; however, at the time of writing, progress on this initiative appeared to have stalled.

[208] [2002] ECR I-7325, at 7340–41. It might perhaps be useful to add that the Directive on Part-Time Work (Directive 97/81, OJ [1998] L14/9) and the Directive on Fixed-Term Employees (Directive 1999/70, OJ [1999] L175/43) permit comparisons with the work of full-timers and those on indefinite contracts outside the establishment in which the part-timer or fixed-term worker is employed; see ch 5.

The Advocate General's answer to why this single source was important was the employer's right of defence:

[The employer] is entitled to argue that an established difference in pay is justified on the basis of objective factors unrelated to discrimination on grounds of sex. It is impossible for an employer against whom a claim for equal treatment has been made to examine the reasons why another employer remunerates activities 'of equal value' 'differently' to him. Even if he were able to do so, it is still not certain, given his distinct economic situation, that he would be able to align himself accordingly.[209]

It is respectfully submitted that this is a flawed approach which takes insufficient account of the essentially tortious nature of discrimination.[210] Where it has been established that two jobs are of equal value, the question which has to be answered is whether their unequal remuneration is grounded on discrimination. If it is, the source of that discrimination—the reason why it has come about—is irrelevant. Because it is sometimes difficult to prove discrimination, the way that the law is designed is to assume that discrimination exists where a *prima facie* case can be demonstrated; the employer is then given the opportunity to defend the claim by proving that the unequal pay has its roots in some different cause (for instance, the different qualifications of the persons concerned). This is the stage which had been reached in *Lawrence* and *Allonby*, but the Court, instead of hearing the arguments of the employers, simply gave them the benefit of the doubt. These decisions do not therefore survive analytical scrutiny.

A similar criticism can be levelled against the Court's decision in *Angestellten-betriebsrat der Wiener Gebietskrankenkasse v Wiener Gebietskrahnkenkasse*.[211] Psychotherapy services were provided in the circumstances of this case by both doctors and psychologists; the latter group was predominantly female and complained of receiving lower pay than the doctors. The ECJ was asked whether the different qualifications of the two groups meant that their work could not be considered equal. To this question there are two logical responses: first, that different qualifications may indeed mean that different jobs are required to be done;[212] but, secondly, that where this is not the case and the jobs are in fact the same, different qualifications may provide an objective justification for different pay levels. In other words, in this second instance the reason for the pay difference would be shown to be unrelated to reasons of sex.[213] However, following the advice of Advocate General Cosmas, the ECJ obfuscated this vital distinction and held that different qualifications may mean that what seem to be identical jobs are not in reality the

---

[209] [2002] ECR I-7325, at 7342.   [210] See discussion in ch 3.

[211] Case C-309/97 [1999] ECR I-2865.

[212] Thus, eg, where somebody recruits two people to work in a garden, one a trained landscaper and the other a person untrained in horticulture, on one level it might be said that both were performing the job of 'gardener'; on closer inspection it might, however, be found that the jobs were not equal because the landscaper was employed to re-design the whole garden, whereas the unskilled employee was employed to weed a flowerbed.

[213] On similar lines, note the comment of Jacobs AG in Case C-236/98 *Jämställdhetsombudsmannen*, op cit, n 184, at 2204, that 'working conditions may be relevant both to whether work is of equal value and to whether there is objective justification for any inequality of pay for work of equal value'.

same. The Court concluded that, although the doctors and the psychologists concerned performed 'seemingly identical activities', they drew upon 'knowledge and skills acquired in very different disciplines'.[214] In what appears to the present author to be a vain attempt to validate this conclusion, it added that, 'even though doctors and psychologists both in fact perform work of psychotherapy, the former are qualified also to perform other tasks in a field which is not open to the latter, who may only perform psychotherapy'.[215] The Court was thus led to a ruling which was patently self-contradictory: 'The term "the same work" does not apply . . . where the same activities are performed over a considerable length of time by persons the basis of whose qualification to exercise their profession is different.'

The fact that two employees are classified in the same job category under a collective agreement is of course not enough to prove conclusively that they are doing equal work.[216] In *Brunnhofer*,[217] the ECJ explained that although such a collective agreement provides a general indication, it has to be corroborated by 'precise and concrete factors' based on the activities actually performed by the employees concerned:

It is therefore necessary to ascertain whether, when a number of factors are taken into account, such as the nature of the activities actually entrusted to each of the employees in question in the case, the training requirements for carrying them out and the working conditions in which the activities are actually carried out, those persons are in fact performing the same work or comparable work.[218]

The Court went on to say that equal work is to be understood on the basis of objective criteria, not subjective matters such as an individual's productivity. It followed that:

[As concerns work paid at time rates], circumstances linked to the person of the employee which cannot be determined objectively at the time of that person's appointment but come to light only during the actual performance of the employee's activities, such as personal capacity or the effectiveness or quality of the work actually done by the employee, cannot be relied on by the employer to justify the fixing, right from the start of the employment relationship, of pay different from that paid to a colleague of the other sex performing identical or comparable work . . .

[However], there is nothing to stop individual work capacity from being taken into account and from having an effect on the employee's career development as compared with that of her colleague, and hence on the subsequent posting and pay of the persons concerned, even though they might, at the beginning of the employment relationship, have been regarded as performing the same work or work of equal value.[219]

It has been clear for many years that the concept of 'equal work' is not restricted to jobs held simultaneously. In *Macarthys Ltd v Smith*,[220] the company employed a

[214] [1999] ECR I-2865, at 2917.
[215] Ibid, at 2917. The present writer's view has received the support of Craig and de Búrca, *EU Law: Text, Cases, and Materials*, 3rd edn (Oxford University Press, Oxford, 2003), at 850.
[216] Because it has been clear since Case 43/75 *Defrenne v Sabena* [1976] ECR 455 that discrimination may be contained in a collective agreement.   [217] Case C-381/99 *Brunnhofer*, op cit, n 188.
[218] Ibid, at 4993.   [219] Ibid, at 4999–5000.
[220] Op cit, n 191. See Wyatt, 'Article 119 EEC: Equal Pay for Female Successor to Male Worker' (1980) 5 ELRev 374.

man as manager of their stockroom until 1975 and paid him £60 per week. After he left, his job was unfilled for four months, and then Ms Smith was appointed to it. However, she was paid only £50 per week. The situation was apparently not covered by the British Equal Pay Act of 1970, since that extended only to con-temporaneous comparisons between employees.[221] However, the ECJ held that Article 141 did cover this situation and that its ambit 'could not be restricted by the introduction of a requirement of contemporaneity'.[222] It ruled that:

> The principle of equal pay enshrined in Article 119 applies to the case where it is established that, having regard to the nature of her services, a woman has received less pay than a man who was employed prior to the woman's period of employment and who did equal work for the employer.[223]

It will be observed that this ruling makes no reference to the length of time which has elapsed between the two periods of employment. It would therefore appear that this is not a relevant factor and that, other things being equal, the com-parison can be made even if there has been a very long interval between the two periods of employment. If this is correct then presumably a domestic court applying Article 141 would be entitled to take into account the effect of inflation during the interval, since otherwise there would be little point in seeking parity with a wage paid a number of years before.

Although a comparison may be made under Article 141 with the wage of a predecessor, the ECJ was not prepared in *Macarthys Ltd v Smith* to go further than this and permit hypothetical comparisons.[224] Ms Smith had argued that Article 141 also extends to workers who cannot compare their work with that of persons of the opposite sex because the employer has segregated the jobs into 'women's work' and 'men's work'; she therefore wanted the ECJ to adopt an interpretation of Article 141 which would encompass comparison with a hypothetical, as well as an actual, male worker doing the same job.[225] The Court held that this situation

> is to be classed as indirect and disguised discrimination, the identification of which . . . implies com-parative studies of entire branches of industry and therefore requires, as a prerequisite, the elaboration by the Community and national legislative bodies of criteria of assessment. From that it follows that, in cases of actual discrimination falling within the scope of the direct application of Article 119, comparisons are confined to parallels which may be drawn on the basis of concrete appraisals of the work actually performed by employees of different sex within the same establishment or service.[226]

---

[221] See the judgment of the Court of Appeal at [1979] 3 CMLR 44.

[222] [1980] ECR 1275, at 1289.

[223] Ibid, at 1290. In *Diocese of Hallam Trustee v Connaughton* [1996] IRLR 505, the British Employment Appeal Tribunal permitted an applicant to rely on Art 141 to compare her pay rate with that of a male successor.

[224] Thus Trabucchi AG exaggerated in Case 43/75 *Defrenne v Sabena*, op cit, n 11, when he said: '[A]s regards the abolition, in connection with pay, of *all discrimination* based on sex, Article 119 imposes an obligation which is clear, precise and unconditional' (at 486, emphasis added).

[225] The possibility of making such a comparison became less important as a consequence of the extension of Art 141 to equal value claims. See discussion below.

[226] [1980] ECR 1275, at 1289. See also Case C-200/91 *Coloroll*, op cit, n 72, where the Court held: '. . . a worker cannot rely on Article 119 in order to claim pay to which he could be entitled if

It is to be noted that the Court's remarks on the subject were confined to the context of the direct effect of Article 141.[227] In *Dekker v Stichting Vormingscentrum Voor Jonge Volwassen Plus*,[228] in relation to the Equal Treatment Directive, the ECJ held that the existence of a comparator was essentially an evidential matter, so that where direct discrimination could be proved without such a comparator this should be enough to satisfy a court.[229] Were the ECJ to hold at least that the theoretical scope of Article 141 (but preferably also the area within which it takes direct effect) extends to hypothetical comparisons, its decision in *Lawrence v Regent Office Care Ltd* would be of reduced importance and the utility of the Article would be hugely extended. If the Article forbids discrimination only as between comparable jobs, it fails to cater for the situation where unfair differentials are found between two admittedly different jobs. For example, where a woman is employed to perform a very much more highly skilled job than a male comparator, she could not complain under Article 141 if she were paid more than him, but only slightly more.[230] If hypothetical comparisons were permitted under Article 141, she could argue that, were she a man, she would be paid much more, even though she could not demonstrate this directly by pointing to an actual male comparator. From the point of view of improving the economic lot of women, such an argument possesses enormous potential force. It is reinforced today as a result of the amendment of the Equal Treatment Directive.[231] As seen in chapter 3, this now defines direct discrimination so as to embrace hypothetical comparison. If the Equal Treatment Directive is required to be interpreted in this fashion, it is certainly arguable that the Treaty Article itself must be construed likewise.[232] In addition, the Race Directive and the Framework Directive expressly permit hypothetical comparisons over the whole fields of their respective application including, it would seem, pay.[233] If the intention is to produce a consistent approach both conceptually and in practice to all forms of discrimination, not least in order to assist claims of multiple discrimination, then the conclusion must be that the principle of equal pay

---

he belonged to the other sex in the absence, now or in the past, in the undertaking concerned of workers of the other sex who perform or performed comparable work. In such a case, the essential criterion for ascertaining that equal treatment exists in the matter of pay, namely the performance of the same work and receipt of the same pay, cannot be applied' (at 4430–1).

[227] As to which see below. Note also the qualified way in which the principle was expressed by Geelhoed AG in Case C-256/01 *Allonby*, op cit, n 3: '[I]t is the case that a comparator *or a comparative framework* is necessary in order to determine whether there is discrimination on the ground of sex' (at para 76, emphasis added).   [228] Case 177/88, op cit, n 134.

[229] See also Case C-342/93 *Gillespie*, op cit, n 16, in which the ECJ held that a woman on maternity leave was entitled to receive a pay rise enjoyed by the rest of her colleagues even though her situation was 'not comparable either with that of a man or with that of a woman actually at work' (at 499). See also McGlynn, 'Equality, Maternity and Questions of Pay' (1996) 21 ELRev 327.

[230] See Case 157/86 *Murphy v Bord Telecom Eireann* [1988] ECR 673, also discussed below.

[231] The Equal Treatment Directive was amended by Directive 2002/73, OJ [2002] L269/15.

[232] The importance of extending hypothetical comparison to the Treaty Article as well as to the Equal Treatment Directive of course lies in the fact, discussed in ch 2, that unlike the Directive the Treaty can take horizontal direct effect; it is therefore enforceable against employers who are not organs of the State.   [233] Art 2(2)(a) of both Directives.

for men and women protected by Article 141 also extends today to hypothetical comparisons. This is a tempting conclusion, but, as will be seen in chapter 5, not one to which analysis of the amended Equal Treatment Directive necessarily leads.

(ii)   Work of equal value

It was seen at the beginning of this chapter that the Amsterdam Treaty amended the original version of Article 141 so as expressly to mandate equal pay for work of equal value.[234] However, even before this express insertion of the principle, it seems that the ECJ accepted that the term 'equal work' embraced the situation where two jobs were of equal value,[235] as well as the situation where the two jobs compared were identical.[236] In the early days it did not take this view, and it stated in *Defrenne v Sabena*[237] that Community secondary legislation:

[Implements] Article 119 from the point of view of *extending* the narrow criterion of 'equal work', in accordance in particular with the provisions of Convention 100 on equal pay concluded by the International Labour Organization in 1951, Article 2 of which establishes the principle of equal pay for work 'of equal value'.[238]

However, in its later decision in *Jenkins v Kingsgate (Clothing Productions) Ltd,*[239] it said of the Equal Pay Directive,[240] which expressly requires equal pay for work to which equal value is attributed:

As may be seen from the first recital in the Preamble the primary objective of the above-mentioned Directive is to implement the principle that men and women should receive equal pay which is 'contained in Article 119 of the Treaty.' For that purpose the fourth recital states that 'it is desirable to reinforce the basic laws by standards aimed at facilitating the practical application of the principle of equality.' The provisions of Article 1 of that Directive are confined, in the first paragraph, to restating the principle of equal pay set out in Article 119 of the Treaty and specify, in the second paragraph, the conditions for applying that principle where a job classification system is used for determining pay. It follows, therefore, that Article 1 of Council Directive 75/117 which is principally designed to facilitate

---

[234] See n 1.

[235] This principle has not, however, received full recognition in all the Member States. In its *Memorandum on Equal Pay for Work of Equal Value* (COM (94) 6 final), the Commission noted that there had by 1994 been no litigation on the matter in France, Luxembourg, Greece, or Italy, that in other Member States there had been little litigation in which truly different jobs had been compared, and that the legislation in Luxembourg, Italy, Belgium, Spain, Greece, and Portugal did nothing to clarify the scope of the principle. See also the Report on equal pay for work of equal value produced by the European Parliament's Committee on Women's Rights and Equal Opportunities, 13 July 2001, A5-0275/2001, final; this took a pessimistic view of the wage situation of women in the EU and called on the Commission, the Member States, and the social partners to act more vigorously to outlaw unequal pay for work of equal value. For further discussion of the gender wage gap, see the final section of the present chapter.

[236] The same query exists in this area as in relation to identical jobs, namely, the extent to which Art 141 permits comparison with workers outside the claimant's immediate workplace.

[237] Case 43/75, op cit, n 11.   [238] Ibid, at 472–3, emphasis added.

[239] Case 96/90, op cit, n 195.

[240] Directive 75/117, OJ [1975] L45/19, discussed in detail below.

the practical application of the principle of equal pay outlined in Article 119 of the Treaty in no way alters the content or scope of that principle as defined in the Treaty.[241]

Again, it said in *Worringham v Lloyds Bank Ltd*[242] that 'Article 1 of the Directive explains that the concept of "same work" contained in the first paragraph of Article 119 of the Treaty includes cases of "work to which equal value is attributed".'[243]

A curious twist in this development occurred in *Murphy v Bord Telecom Eireann*.[244] Ms Murphy was employed by the Bord as a factory worker maintaining telephones. She claimed the right to be paid at the same rate as a male colleague employed in the same factory as a stores labourer. The Irish Equality Officer, to whom the claim had been referred under the national Anti-Discrimination (Pay) Act 1974, found that Ms Murphy's work was actually of a higher value than that of her comparator, and so it did not constitute 'like work' within the meaning of the Act. The Equality Officer therefore considered that she could not lawfully recommend that Ms Murphy receive equal pay with the comparator. The Irish High Court, to which the issue came on appeal, asked the ECJ whether

the Community law principle of equal pay for equal work extend[s] to a claim for equal pay on the basis of work of equal value in circumstances where the work of the claimant has been assessed to be of higher value than that of the person with whom the claimant sought comparison.

As Advocate General Lenz pointed out, this was not a claim for pay proportionate to the work performed (as fairness in the circumstances would certainly seem to have justified). It amounted in effect to a claim for 'less than equal pay for equal work'. Nevertheless, the Court held that Article 141 caught the situation:

It is true that Article 119 expressly requires the application of the principle of equal pay for men and women solely in the case of equal work or, according to a consistent line of decisions of the Court, in the case of work of equal value, and not in the case of work of unequal value. Nevertheless, if that principle forbids workers of one sex engaged in work of equal value to that of workers of the opposite sex to be paid a lower wage than the latter on grounds of sex, it *a fortiori* prohibits such a difference in pay where the lower-paid category of workers is engaged in work of higher value. To adopt a contrary interpretation would be tantamount to rendering the principle of equal pay ineffective and nugatory. As the Irish Government rightly emphasized, in that case an employer would easily be able to circumvent the principle by assigning additional or more onerous duties to workers of a particular sex, who could then be paid a lower wage . . . Article 119 must be interpreted as covering the case where a worker who relies on that provision to obtain equal pay within the meaning thereof is engaged in work of higher value than that of the person with whom a comparison is to be made.[245]

---

[241] [1981] ECR 911, at 926–7. The cynic might be tempted to reflect that, by the date of the judgment in *Jenkins*, the ECJ was becoming aware that its reasoning in relation to the direct effect of directives was unlikely to enable it to grant them horizontal effect. (See ch 2.) The Treaty Article thus became a more versatile, and therefore more attractive, basis for its decision.

[242] Case 69/80, op cit, n 23.

[243] Ibid, at 790–1. See also Case 157/86 *Murphy*, op cit, n 230, discussed below.

[244] Case 157/86, op cit, n 230.

[245] Ibid, at 689. This case is sometimes taken as suggesting that the ECJ was not on this occasion prepared to require 'proportionate' pay, and it is contrasted with its later decision in Case C-127/92 *Enderby v Frenchay Health Authority* [1993] ECR I-5535 (discussed below), where it stated (at 5575):

An important practical issue in this area which the ECJ has not yet confronted, is how precise it is necessary to be in assessing equality. The problem is to know whether substantial equality is all that is required by Article 141, or whether there must be absolute mathematical equality. The latter seems unlikely, since the whole business of assessing the value of work is essentially imprecise, but what degree of divergence will be allowed?[246]

Defences to an equal pay claim

Article 141 contains no defences, apart perhaps from the kinds of positive action permitted by para 4.[247] As will be discussed in chapter 5, the Race Directive and the Framework Directive contain a number of express defences, but none seems apposite to the principle of equal pay.

However, it was seen in chapter 3 that, where a claim is made that indirect discrimination has occurred in relation to pay, it is open to the respondent to demonstrate that the adverse impact caused is objectively justified by factors unrelated to discrimination. This is essentially an issue of causation, and was first clearly articulated in relation to sex discrimination over pay in *Bilka-Kaufhaus GmbH v Weber Von Hartz*.[248]

Later cases have filled in important details about the way in which justification can operate in the field of equal pay. For example, *Enderby v Frenchay Health Authority*[249] demonstrated that the justification proved must be proportionate to the particular pay discrepancy in issue:

The state of the employment market, which may lead an employer to increase the pay of a particular job in order to attract candidates, may constitute an objectively justified economic ground . . . How it is to be applied in the circumstances of each case depends on the facts and so falls within the jurisdiction of the national court.

If, as the question referred seems to suggest, the national court has been able to determine precisely what proportion of the increase in pay is attributable to market forces, it must necessarily accept that the pay differential is objectively justified to the extent of that proportion. When national authorities have to apply Community law, they must apply the principle of proportionality.

'If. . . the national court has been able to determine precisely what proportion of the increase in pay is attributable to market forces, it must necessarily accept that the pay differential is objectively justified to the extent of that proportion. When national authorities have to apply Community law, they must apply the principle of proportionality.' In the view of the present writer, this apparent inconsistency is to be explained by the fact that in *Murphy* the true rate of pay due to the plaintiff was not revealed by the evidence, and therefore any upward adjustment would have resulted in the court acting as a wage-fixer; it is otherwise where it is clear what the rate of pay would be were a disproportionate adjustment not being made for market forces. Such a distinction, though regrettable from the point of view of achieving substantive sex equality, is understandable both in terms of the drafting of Art 141 and of the constitutional role of the ECJ.

[246] British employment tribunals, faced with this issue, have reached conflicting conclusions. See, eg, *Wells and Others v Smales Ltd* (1985) 2 EOR 24 and *Brown and Royle v Cearns and Brown Ltd* (1986) 6 EOR 27.   [247] Discussed in ch 6.
[248] Op cit, n 39.   [249.] Case C-127/92, op cit, n 245.

If that is not the case, it is for the national court to assess whether the role of market forces in determining the rate of pay was sufficiently significant to provide objective justification for part or all of the difference.[250]

A further deduction to be made from this ruling is that the Court has accepted the existence in EU law of an economic defence, at least in the field of equal pay,[251] and it has made little attempt to explain where it sees the balance lying as between the commercial profitability of an organization and the elimination of discrimination.[252] The UK courts for a number of years resisted such a defence, on the sensible ground that, if pursued, it would rob the anti-discrimination legislation of all purpose. In the words of Lord Denning MR in *Clay Cross Ltd v Fletcher*:[253]

[A]n employer cannot avoid his obligations under the [Equal Pay Act] by saying: 'I paid him more because he asked for more', or 'I paid her less because she was willing to come for less'. If such excuses were permitted, the Act would be a dead letter. Those are the very reasons why there was unequal pay before the statute. They are the very circumstances in which the statute was intended to operate. Nor can the employer avoid his obligations by giving the reasons why he submitted to the extrinsic forces. As for instance by saying: 'He asked for that sum because it was what he was getting in his previous job', or 'He was the only applicant for the job so I had no option'. In such cases the employer may beat his breast, and say: 'I did not pay him more because he was a man. I paid it because he was the only suitable person who applied for the job. Man or woman made no difference to me'. Those are reasons personal to the employer. If any such reasons were permitted as an excuse, the door would be wide open. Every employer who wished to avoid the statute would walk straight through it.[254]

The danger pointed out by Lord Denning is a real one, and it is therefore vital that the courts scrutinize cases very carefully to make sure that what looks like an objectively justified factor does not in reality have its roots in sex discrimination; for example, where it is alleged in an equal value case that one skill is rarer and more valuable than another, the court must insist on knowing the background to that statement and must ensure that this is not because women have been discriminated against as regards training for that rarer skill.[255] In general, the ECJ in

---

[250] Case C-127/92, op cit, n 245, at 5575.

[251] See also Case 96/80 *Jenkins*, op cit, n 195. However, in Case C-50/96 *Schröder*, op cit, n 78, and Joined Cases C-270 & 271/97 *Sievers and Shrage*, op cit, n 78, it asserted that the economic aim of Art 141 is secondary to its social aim, which constitutes the expression of a fundamental human right; see further discussion in ch 7. See also the comments of Besselink on these cases in (2001) 38 CMLRev 437.

[252] Cf the position in relation to the justification of indirect discrimination in the field of social security, discussed in ch 8.   [253] [1979] ICR 1.

[254] Ibid, at 5. The ECJ's decisions forced the UK courts to retrench somewhat and to accept the possibility of an economic defence. See in particular *Rainey v Greater Glasgow Health Board* [1986] 3 WLR 1017.

[255] In Case C-127/92 *Enderby*, op cit, n 245, Lenz AG observed: 'Since justification of the discriminatory result is called for, it cannot be sufficient to explain the causes leading to the discrimination . . . The historical and social context of a "purely female profession" is most probably sex-related. If an explanatory approach were accepted as sufficient justification, that would lead to the perpetuation of sexual roles in working life. Instead of the equality of treatment which is sought, there would be afforded a legal argument for maintaining the *status quo*' (at 5563). See also Fredman, 'Equal Pay and Justification' (1994) 23 ILJ 37.

guiding the national courts must remain vigilant to ensure that when the 'genuine need' of an enterprise is assessed, it is not merely male-orientated notions of merit and qualifications which are used as the parameters.[256]

In *Handels-OG Kontorfunktionaerernes Forbund i Danmark v Dansk Arbejdsgiverforening (acting for Danfoss)*,[257] the ECJ was presented with some traditional arguments to justify what appeared to be sex discrimination in pay. An employer claimed that incremental payments were made to its employees as a reward for 'mobility', vocational training, and seniority. The Court looked at each separately. 'Mobility' had a rather specific meaning here, and did not merely embrace a willingness to work at different hours; it involved the employer making an overall assessment of the quality of the work carried out by the employees, and would take into account their 'enthusiasm for work', their sense of initiative, and the amount of work done. In scrutinizing such a factor as providing an objective justification for discrimination, the Court was sensitive to the risks it carries. It held:

[A] distinction must be made according to whether the criterion of mobility is employed to reward the quality of the work done by the employee or is used to reward the employee's adaptability to variable work hours and varying places of work.

In the first case, the criterion of mobility is undoubtedly wholly neutral from the point of view of sex. Where it systematically works to the disadvantage of women that can only be because the employer has misapplied it. It is inconceivable that the quality of work done by women should generally be less good. The employer cannot therefore justify applying the criterion of mobility, so understood, where its application proves to work systematically to the disadvantage of women.[258]

In such a case, therefore, the employer would invariably lose the claim. However, the Court went on to say:

The position is different in the second case. If it is understood as covering the employee's adaptability to variable hours and varying places of work, the criterion of mobility may also work to the disadvantage of female employees who, because of household and family duties for which they are frequently responsible, are not as able as men to organize their working time flexibly . . . [The *Bilka-Kaufhaus* principles] apply in the case of a wages practice which specially remunerates the employee's adaptability to variable hours and varying places of work. *The employer may, therefore, justify the remuneration of such adaptability by showing that it is of importance for the performance of specific tasks entrusted to the employee.*[259]

It took the same line in relation to vocational training, saying:

[It cannot] be excluded that [the criterion of vocational training] may work to the disadvantage of women in so far as they have had less opportunity than men for training or have taken less advantage of such opportunity. Nevertheless, in view of the considerations laid down [in *Bilka-Kaufhaus*], the employer may justify remuneration of special training by showing that it is of importance for the performance of specific tasks entrusted to the employee.[260]

---

[256] See discussion in Connolly (ed), *Townshend-Smith on Discrimination Law: Text, Cases and Materials*, 2nd edn (Cavendish Publishing, London, 2004), esp ch 10.
[257] Case 109/88 [1989] ECR 3199.   [258] Ibid, at 3227.
[259] Ibid, at 3227–8, emphasis added.   [260] Ibid, at 3228.

As to seniority, the Court was considerably less perceptive, and was perhaps timorous in its approach because of the admitted practical significance of seniority in pay systems and collective bargaining. It held simply:

[It cannot be ruled out that seniority] may involve less advantageous treatment of women than of men, in so far as women have entered the labour market more recently than men or more frequently suffer an interruption of their career. Nevertheless, since length of service goes hand in hand with experience and since experience generally enables the employee to perform his duties better, *the employer is free to reward it without having to establish the importance it has in the performance of specific tasks entrusted to the employee.*[261]

This last is an illogical deduction, since for many jobs experience does not improve performance, a point subsequently recognized by the Court. In *Nimz v Freie und Hansestadt Hamburg,*[262] a collective agreement provided for reclassification into a higher salary grade after a certain number of years for those employed for at least three-quarters of normal working time. For those, predominantly women, employed between one-half and three-quarters of normal working time, double the number of years was required before reclassification into the higher grade.[263] The employers sought to justify this situation by arguing that full-timers acquired job-related skills more quickly than part-timers. The Court rejected this with some enthusiasm, saying:

Such considerations, in so far as they are no more than generalizations about certain categories of workers, do not make it possible to identify criteria which are both objective and unrelated to any discrimination on grounds of sex ... Although experience goes hand in hand with length of service, and experience enables the worker in principle to improve performance of the tasks allotted to him, the objectivity of such a criterion depends on all the circumstances in a particular case, and in particular on the relationship between the nature of the work performed and the experience gained from the performance of that work upon completion of a certain number of working hours.[264]

Similarly, the ECJ in *Hill and Stapleton v Revenue Commissioners*[265] took a forthright attitude towards indirect discrimination and justification. Under an Irish job-sharing scheme for civil servants, job-sharers were paid on a scale each point of which was 50% of the corresponding point on the scale for full-time staff; in other words, they received the same hourly rate of pay as full-timers. Job-sharers were given a right to convert to full-time work. However, on doing so they discovered

[261] Case 109/88 [1989] ECR 3199, emphasis added.
[262] Case C-184/89 [1991] ECR I-297, commented on by Adinolfi in (1992) 29 CMLRev 637 and by More in 'Seniority Pay for Part-time Workers' (1991) 16 ELRev 320.
[263] It is noteworthy that this case, like Case C-262/88 *Barber,* op cit, n 28 (discussed above), involved access to pay rather than the quantum of pay, but the Court nonetheless held the situation to fall within the scope of Art 141. On the other hand, in Case C-1/95 *Gerster v Freistaat Bayern* [1997] ECR I-5253, where a similar rule to that operating in *Nimz* disadvantaged part-timers as regards promotion, the ECJ held that the matter fell within the scope of the Equal Treatment Directive (discussed in ch 5) because length of service was merely one factor considered by the employer and therefore affected pay only indirectly.
[264] [1991] ECR I-297, at 319. See also Case C-100/95 *Kording v Senator für Finanzen* [1997] ECR I-5289, in which the same principle was applied for the purposes of the Equal Treatment Directive.
[265] Case C-243/95 [1998] ECR I-3739.

that each year spent job-sharing was counted only as six months' full-time service, with the consequence that they regressed on the pay scale. The referring court wished to know whether this constituted indirect discrimination and, if so, whether it was justifiable for the employers to rely on the time actually worked in the job in fixing pay rates. The ECJ had little difficulty in deducing that this arrangement amounted to indirect discrimination: 99.2% of people in the claimants' jobs who job-shared were women, and they suffered a reduction in their hourly rate of pay on conversion from job-sharing to full-time work. Employees working full-time, but who had previously job-shared, were therefore treated less favourably than those who had always worked full-time. The question thus arose as to whether this apparent discrimination was justifiable. The Court rejected the employers' arguments that there was an established practice in the civil service of 'crediting' only actual service and that this maintained staff motivation, commitment, and morale:

The first justification is no more than a general assertion unsupported by objective criteria. With regard to the second, the system of remuneration for employees working on a full-time basis cannot be influenced by the job-sharing scheme.[266]

Furthermore, the employer could not justify discrimination arising from a job-sharing scheme solely on the ground that avoidance of such discrimination would involve increased costs. The Court went on to say:

Community policy in this area is to encourage and, if possible, adapt working conditions to family responsibilities. Protection of women within family life and in the course of their professional activities is, in the same way as for men, a principle which is widely regarded in the legal systems of the Member States as being the natural corollary of the equality between men and women, and which is recognised by Community law. The onus is therefore on the Revenue Commissioners . . . to establish before the Labour Court that the reference to the criterion of service, defined as the length of time actually worked, in the assessment of the incremental credit to be granted to workers who convert from job-sharing to full-time work is justified by objective factors unrelated to any discrimination on grounds of sex.[267]

In *Rinner-Kühn v FWW Spezial-Gebaudereinigung GmbH*,[268] the ECJ held that the *Bilka-Kaufhaus* test for justifying indirect discrimination must be applied to German legislation restricting the payment of sick pay to employees working for longer than ten hours a week or forty-five hours a month. The Court asked the German Government to provide information on the reasons which had motivated the legislation, and the Government answered that the workers affected by the legislation were not integrated in or connected with the undertaking in a comparable way to that of other workers and that therefore the conditions for recognition of a duty of care from the employer towards them, including an

---

[266] Case C-243/95 [1998] ECR I-3739, at 3771.

[267] Ibid, at 3772. For the view that this decision in fact entrenches the traditional role of women, see McGlynn and Farrelly, 'Equal Pay and the "Protection of Women Within Family Life"' (1999) 24 ELRev 202. See also discussion of the non-dynamic nature of the concept of indirect discrimination in ch 3.   [268] Case 171/88 [1989] ECR 2743.

obligation to continue to pay wages, did not exist; in addition, the Government pointed out that the statutory exclusion followed earlier legislation.[269] The ECJ firmly rejected this approach:

It should however be stated that those considerations, in so far as they are only generalizations about certain categories of workers, do not enable criteria which are both objective and unrelated to any discrimination on grounds of sex to be identified. However, if the Member State can show that the means chosen meet a necessary aim of its social policy and that they are suitable and requisite for attaining that aim, the mere fact that the provision affects a much greater number of female workers than male workers cannot be regarded as constituting an infringement of Article 119.[270]

A novel aspect of this ruling was that it applied the *Bilka-Kaufhaus* test not merely to an employer's practices but to the State's legislation, backed up of course by the principle of the supremacy of EU law. The test therefore evolved from the needs of a business to the needs of a State's social policy.[271] It is for the State to justify the legislation, although:

It is for the national court . . . which has sole jurisdiction to assess the facts and interpret the national legislation, to determine whether and to what extent a legislative provision, which, although applying independently of the sex of the worker, actually affects a greater number of women than men, is justified by reasons which are objective and unrelated to any discrimination on grounds of sex.[272]

It will be seen in chapter 8 that this principle has important application in the field of social security, where a Member State may well rely on the alleged aims of its social policy in order to try to justify the adverse impact of a piece of its legislation on one sex. It will also be seen that the ECJ has considerably relaxed its grip over justification in the area of social security, emphasizing the broad margin of discretion enjoyed by the Member States in their choice of measures of social policy and contenting itself with a test of what the national legislature reasonably considers necessary to achieve its legitimate aims;[273] in other words, the dangerous transition has occurred from a test of objective justification to one much closer to subjective

---

[269] These arguments were strikingly similar to those of the British Government in *Building Businesses . . . Not Barriers* (Cmnd 9794), where it was proposed to raise the hours of work qualification for UK statutory rights from 16 to 20.

[270] [1989] ECR 2743, at 2761. Cf the submissions of Darmon AG in this case. In Case C-187/00 *Kutz-Bauer v Freie und Hansestadt Hamburg* [2003] ECR I-2741, the ECJ said in relation to indirect discrimination contrary to the Equal Treatment Directive (as to which see ch 5): '. . . mere generalisations concerning the capacity of a specific measure to encourage recruitment are not enough to show that the aim of the disputed provisions is unrelated to any discrimination based on sex or to provide evidence on the basis of which it could reasonably be considered that the means chosen are or could be suitable for achieving that aim' (at 2790). See also Case C-77/02 *Steinicke v Bundesanstalt für Arbeit* [2003] ECR I-9027, where the ECJ emphasized that, although budgetary considerations may underlie a Member State's choice of social policy and influence the nature or scope of the social protection measures which it wishes to adopt, they do not in themselves constitute an aim pursued by that policy and cannot therefore justify discrimination against one of the sexes.

[271] See also Szyszczak, 'European Court Rulings on Discrimination and Part-Time Work and the Burden of Proof in Equal Pay Claims' (1990) 19 ILJ 114.   [272] [1989] ECR 2743, at 2761.

[273] See in particular Case C-317/93 *Nolte v Landesversicherungsanstalt Hannover* [1995] ECR I-4625, and Case C-444/93 *Megner and Scheffel v Innungskrankenkasse Vorderplatz* [1995] ECR I-4741.

justification. The Court's apparent resolve not to allow this degree of slippage to occur in relation to legislation in the field of equal pay was demonstrated in parts of its judgment in *R v Secretary of State for Employment, ex parte Seymour-Smith*.[274] The UK Government had tried to defend legislation imposing service threshold requirements which had to be proved in order for an employee to claim unfair dismissal; in particular, it had argued that the risk of the exposure of employers to unfair dismissal proceedings brought by employees who had been engaged only fairly recently would deter recruitment. The ECJ agreed that the encouragement of recruitment was a legitimate aim of social policy, and went on to say:

[T]he UK government maintains that a Member State should merely have to show that it was reasonably entitled to consider that the measure would advance a social policy aim. It relies to that end on *Nolte* . . .

It is true that in the judgment in *Nolte* . . . the Court observed that, in choosing the measures capable of achieving the aims of their social and employment policy, the Member States have a broad margin of discretion.

However, although social policy is essentially a matter for the Member States under Community law as it stands, the fact remains that the broad margin of discretion available to the Member States in that connection cannot have the effect of frustrating the implementation of a fundamental principle of Community law such as that of equal pay for men and women.

Mere generalizations concerning the capacity of a specific measure to encourage recruitment are not enough to show that the aim of the disputed rule is unrelated to any discrimination based on sex nor to provide evidence on the basis of which it could reasonably be considered that the means chosen were suitable for achieving that aim.[275]

However, it then held:

Accordingly, . . . if a considerably smaller percentage of women than men is capable of fulfilling the requirement of two years' employment imposed by the disputed rule, it is for the Member State, as the author of the allegedly discriminatory rule, to show that the said rule reflects a legitimate aim of its social policy, that that aim is unrelated to any discrimination based on sex, and that it could reasonably consider that the means chosen were suitable for attaining that aim.[276]

This leaves the test to be applied for the justification of employment legislation extremely unclear. As Barnard and Hepple have commented, it appears that Court could not arrive at a unanimous view and so it produced an unhappy compromise between a rigorous application of the concept of indirect discrimination and a more market-orientated approach.[277] In addition, the result is a hierarchy of tests for the justification of indirect discrimination. The weakest rule applies to the justification of a statutory social security provision.[278] Then follows the justification of a

---

[274] Op cit, n 172.   [275] Ibid, at 686.   [276] Ibid.

[277] Barnard and Hepple, 'Indirect Discrimination: Interpreting *Seymour-Smith*' (1999) 58 CLJ 399.

[278] Hervey has suggested that this development is a consequence of the limits of Community competence: 'The further the application of the EC law principle of equal treatment impinges on elements of national social policy for which the Community has no competence to adopt other harmonisation legislation, the wider a margin of discretion the Court is prepared to give in the justification of indirect sex discrimination'; see 'EC Law on Justifications for Sex Discrimination in Working Life' in Blanpain (ed), *Collective Bargaining, Discrimination, Social Security and European Integration* (Kluwer, Deventer, 2003), at 133.

statutory employment provision. That the strictest rule still applies to the justification of an employer's practices emerged from *Krüger v Kreiskrankenhaus
Ebersberg*.[279] This concerned persons classified by German legislation as being in
'minor employment', defined to mean working fewer than fifteen hours per week.
The ECJ had already held in *Nolte* and *Megner and Scheffel*[280] that, since this group
was predominantly female in composition, its exclusion from social security
benefits constituted *prima facie* indirect discrimination; however, such discrimination was justified because it was intended to meet the social and employment
policy aims of satisfying the demand for part-time employment.[281] Nevertheless,
the Court held in *Krüger* that the same principle did not apply in relation to indirect
discrimination over pay; this resulted from a collective agreement excluding persons in minor employment from eligibility to an annual Christmas bonus, an
exclusion which the Court did not regard as justifiable.[282]

The requirement to justify allegedly indirectly discriminatory legislation, though
wholly welcome in principle, raises considerable practical problems. For example,
in the UK it means that an employer faced with a similar claim to that in *Rinner-
Kühn*[283] must ask the employment tribunal to join the relevant Secretary of State
as a party to the case in order to justify the legislation.[284] There is also the difficulty that, justification being an issue of fact rather than law as far as the British
courts are concerned, different employment tribunals may well reach different conclusions when presented with the same evidence.[285] This, however, is a general
problem as far as the justification of indirect discrimination is concerned. It cannot
be denied that the formula chosen by the ECJ entrusts a considerable discretion to
the deciding judge. Indeed, Sebba has gone so far as to argue that the assessment of
justification is essentially a non-justiciable task: 'The judge can do no more than
express his or her personal political opinion on the matter. The personal perspective of the unelected judge therefore shapes . . . social policy . . .'[286]

In addition to this potential for local inconsistencies in its application, the
Court's own jurisprudence on objective justification has wavered in its underlying
principles, the bullish stance evident in cases such as *Nimz* and *Rinner-Kühn* giving
way on occasion to a weaker form of supervision over the national courts. For
example, in *Kowalska v Freie und Hansestadt Hamburg*,[287] the defendants argued that
discrimination against part-timers in relation to severance pay was justified because
these kinds of workers do not provide for their needs or those of their families
exclusively out of their earned income; one might have expected this argument to

[279] Case C-281/97 [1999] ECR I-5127.
[280] Case C-317/93 *Nolte*, op cit, n 273, and Case C-444/93 *Megner and Scheffel*, op cit, n 273.
[281] See further ch 8.   [282] Cf the view of Léger AG in this case.
[283] The *Seymour-Smith* case took the form of a judicial review action.
[284] See also *R v Secretary of State for Employment, ex parte EOC* [1994] 2 WLR 409.
[285] See the comments of the Editors of the *Equal Opportunities Review* on the *Rinner-Kühn* decision in
'Discriminatory Statutory Rights can be Challenged under EEC Law' (1989) 28 EOR 39.
[286] Sebba, 'The Doctrine of "Direct Effect": A Malignant Disease of Community Law' [1995]
LIEI 35.   [287] Case C-33/89, op cit, n 164.

be dismissed as another mere generalization, but instead the Court simply replied that the assessment of justification was a matter for the national court. This sort of inconsistency of approach is also evident in a series of references from German courts in relation to the employment staff committee system which operates in that country. The first was *Arbeiterwohlfahrt der Stadt Berlin e V v Bötel*.[288] Ms Bötel, a part-time worker, was chair of such a staff committee and exercised her statutory right to paid time off work in order to attend some training courses in connection with this activity which lasted for longer than her normal working hours. Her employers, in accordance with their usual practice, paid her only in respect of her normal working hours. Had she been a full-timer, she would have been reimbursed in respect of all the hours she spent on the courses, and this disparity of treatment she alleged to be indirect discrimination against her. After concluding that the sums paid were within Article 141,[289] the Court held:

[T]he argument that compensation for participation in training courses granted under national legis-lation is calculated solely on the basis of working hours not worked does not alter the fact that staff council members who work on a part-time basis receive less compensation than their full-time col-leagues when in fact both categories of workers receive without distinction the same number of hours of training in order to be able effectively to look after the interests of employees for the sake of good working relations and for the general good of the undertaking . . . [S]uch a situation is likely to deter employees in the part-time category, in which the proportion of women is undeniably preponderant, from serving on staff councils or from acquiring the knowledge needed in order to serve on them, thus making it more difficult for that category of worker to be represented by qualified staff council members. To that extent, the difference in treatment in question cannot be regarded as justified by objective factors unrelated to any discrimination on grounds of sex, unless the Member State concerned proves the contrary before the national court.[290]

Kuratorium fur Dialyse und Nierentransplantation e V v Lewark[291] raised the same 'delicate' issue as *Bötel*[292] and the Federal Labour Court specifically asked the ECJ to reconsider its position. Both the German court and the German Government argued that it was important to the staff council system that those workers serving did so on an unpaid and independent basis; all that should therefore be required should be that they should be reimbursed in respect of the hours that they would have spent at work had they not been serving on a staff committee. The Court reiterated that, irrespective of how these payments were perceived within Germany, they nevertheless fell within the Article 141 notion of 'pay'. Furthermore, it held that there was unequal treatment as between full and part-timers because they received unequal pay in respect of their hours devoted to staff committee service. Since this undoubtedly impacted more severely on women than men, there was therefore a *prima facie* case of indirect discrimination and the issue was whether

---

[288] Case C-360/90, op cit, n 19.
[289] See discussion above as to the meaning of 'pay' in the context of Art 141.
[290] [1992] ECR I-3589, at 3613–14.   [291] Case C-457/93, op cit, n 19.
[292] See Darmon AG in Case C-278/93 *Freers v Deutsche Bundespost*, op cit, n 19, at 1167. The Advocate General also commented that the 'heated debate provoked by the [*Bötel*] judgment in Germany' had prompted the two further references discussed in the text.

that could be justified. On this last point, the Court compromised its former stance, saying:

It is ... apparent from the order for reference in the present case that the Bundesarbeitsgericht considers that the German legislature's wish to place the independence of staff councils above financial induce-ments for performing staff council functions ... is an aim of social policy. Such a social policy aim appears in itself to be unrelated to any discrimination on grounds of sex. It cannot be disputed that the work of staff councils does indeed play a part in German social policy, in that the councils have the task of promoting harmonious labour relations within undertakings and in their interest. The concern to ensure the independence of the members of those councils thus likewise reflects a legitimate aim of social policy.

If a Member State is able to show that the measures chosen reflect a legitimate aim of its social policy, are appropriate to achieve that aim and are necessary in order to do so, the mere fact that the legislative provision affects far more women workers than men cannot be regarded as a breach of Article 119 ...

However, it should be noted that, as the Court held in *Bötel*, ... legislation such as that at issue is likely to deter workers in the part-time category ... from performing staff council functions ...

In the light of all those considerations and taking into account the possibility of achieving the social policy aim in question by other means, the difference in treatment could be justified ... only if it appeared to be suitable and necessary for achieving that aim. It is for the national court to ascertain whether that is so in the present case.[293]

This reasoning is inherently illogical. If the sums in question are 'pay', as the ECJ maintains, then discrimination in relation to them ought not to be able to be justified by an argument which relies on the fact that they are not pay. To argue that inequality over pay is prohibited but not inequality over compensation for loss of pay, is purely semantic.[294] Nevertheless, the Court followed its judgment in *Lewark* in *Freers v Deutsche Bundespost*.[295]

Another important practical issue on which the ECJ has not been wholly consistent is whether the existence of two separate collective agreements, applying essentially to male and female workers respectively, is sufficient to satisfy the *Bilka-Kaufhaus* requirement of objective justification.[296] Such a factor ought not in

---

[293] [1996] ECR I-243, at 269–70.

[294] This factor may have been in the mind of Jacobs AG, who submitted: 'I conclude that, as the Court held in *Bötel*, the compensation paid to a staff council member for attendance at training courses ... is "pay" for the purposes of Article 119 ... However, it must be recognised that on the facts of this case that compensation can be regarded as pay only in the broadest sense of the term. Even if the continuance of salary for undertaking such activities during normal working hours can be regarded as pay, it is less clear that payment for undertaking such activities outside working hours can be so regarded' (at 250).

[295] Case C-278/93, op cit, n 19. Darmon AG, however, submitted that the indirect discrimination was not justified in this case and that *Bötel* should be followed. For comment on *Lewark* and *Freers*, see Shaw, 'Works Councils in German Enterprises and Article 119 EC' (1997) 22 ELRev 256. See also *Manor Bakeries Ltd v Nazir* [1996] IRLR 604, in which the British Employment Appeal Tribunal held that attendance at a trade union conference was not 'work' and did not therefore attract 'pay'. This decision was subsequently disapproved by the same Tribunal in *Davies v Neath Port Talbot Country Borough Council* [1999] IRLR 769, where attendance at a union-organized health and safety training course was held to be 'work'.

[296] It was asked about this matter but declined to answer the question because it found it to be unnecessary in Case C-109/88 *Handels-OG Kontorfunktionaerernes Forbund I Danmark v Dansk Arbejdsgiverforening (acting for Danfoss)*, op cit, n 257.

theory to constitute an 'objectively justified factor unrelated to any discrimination based on sex' since, even if the collective agreements in question did not have their roots in earlier sex discrimination, it is more or less inconceivable that their existence could constitute a 'necessary' response to a 'genuine need' of the employer.[297] The UK Government, which intervened in the *Danfoss* case, argued that the existence of two separate collective agreements does not by itself justify a pay differential.

The issue was put directly to the ECJ in *Enderby v Frenchay Health Authority*,[298] where separate non-discriminatory collective agreements governed the groups of workers whose pay was the subject of comparison. The Court held robustly that this was not sufficient to establish justification:

The fact that the rates of pay at issue are decided by collective bargaining processes conducted separately for each of the two professional groups concerned, without any discriminatory effect within each group, does not preclude a finding of *prima facie* discrimination where the results of those processes show that two groups with the same employer and the same trade union are treated differently. If the employer could rely on the absence of discrimination within each of the collective bargaining processes taken separately as sufficient justification for the difference in pay, he could, as the German government pointed out, easily circumvent the principle of equal pay by using separate bargaining processes.[299]

However, in the Court's later decision in *Specialarbejderforbundet I Danmark v Dansk Industrie, acting for Royal Copenhagen A/S*,[300] it resiled from this clear-cut position, but without substantial reasoning:

[T]he principle of equal pay for men and women...applies where the elements of the pay are determined by collective bargaining or by negotiation at local level but...the national court may take that fact into account in its assessment of whether differences between the average pay of two groups of workers are due to objective factors unrelated to any discrimination on grounds of sex.[301]

The direct effect of the equal pay principle and the remedies for its breach

The concept of direct effect was discussed in general terms in chapter 2. It will be recalled that a provision of EU law is said to be 'directly effective'[302] where it is enforceable by a legal person in the courts of the Member States. The first hint in

---

[297] However, this has not always been the view of UK courts. See, in particular, *Reed Packaging Ltd v Boozer* [1987] IRLR 26 and *Enderby v Frenchay Health Authority and the Secretary of State for Health* [1991] IRLR 44. Cf *British Road Services v Loughran* [1997] IRLR 92.

[298] Case C-127/92, op cit, n 245.

[299] Ibid, at 5574. Lenz AG drew a distinction, apparently taken up by the Court, between collective agreements concluded for whole branches of industry and those where there is a common employer.

[300] Case C-400/93 [1995] ECR I-1275.

[301] Ibid, at 1314. See further Case C-236/98 *Jämställdhetsombudsmannen*, op cit, n 188.

[302] Other terms used to refer to the same concept include 'directly applicable' and 'self-executing'. For reasons explained in ch 2, the term 'direct effect' will be used in this work in this context.

the ECJ that the equal pay principle might be directly effective came in the *First Defrenne* case,[303] where Lamothe AG said:

[Article 119] is thus not limited, as are Articles 117 and 118, to setting out objectives of harmonization of laws and regulations or co-operation between Member States, but it creates an obligation for the Member States. The question could have been asked whether in addition or as a result of the obligation which it created for the states, it gives rise to individual rights in favour of the nationals of Member States and whether it has a 'direct effect'. But this question no longer arises for two reasons:

1. Although the difficulties of application encountered by certain countries were great and although in particular a conference of Member States extended until 31 December 1964 the period initially laid down, it appears to me certain that at least as from this date Article 119 created subjective rights which the workers of the Member States can invoke and respect for which national courts must ensure.

2. It is even more certain in Belgium since, to avoid any difficulty of interpretation by the courts and give additional publicity to this provision of the treaty, the Belgian government by an initiative which was legally superfluous but the intentions of which were highly commendable, has insisted on inserting in Royal Decree No 40 of 27 October 1967 concerning the work of women an Article 14 worded thus:

'In accordance with Article 119 of the Treaty establishing the European Economic Community, adopted by the law of 2 December 1957, any woman worker may institute proceedings in the competent court for the application of the principle of equal pay for men and women workers'.

In these circumstances the reasons may be well understood why the Belgian Conseil d'Etat does not even seem to have considered and in any event has not asked us to consider whether Article 119 had a direct effect or not. This appeared to it, as it does to me, to be obvious.[304]

However, to others the conclusion that the Article takes direct effect was probably less obvious. It was seen in chapter 2 that, in order to take direct effect, a provision must satisfy certain criteria of precision: specifically, the scope of the obligation it creates must be clear; and it must also be unconditional, non-discretionary, and final. Arguably, at least three of these conditions could not be said to be satisfied by the equal pay principle contained in Article 141. The scope of the obligation might be said to be somewhat vague, in particular since the concepts of 'equal work' and 'equal pay' require clarification. Such clarification might confer a discretion on the Member States, and might also mean that the Article could not be regarded as 'final'. Nevertheless, the ECJ, in its dramatic ruling in the *Second Defrenne* case,[305] agreed with Lamothe AG's earlier conclusion. In reaching this result, it clearly showed its frustration with the non-compliance with Article 141 by the Member States and with the weak-willed attitude towards this non-compliance demonstrated by the Commission. It was a proactive ruling given by a Court intent on ascribing useful effect to an important Article of the Treaty. Having explained its belief that Article 141 forms 'part of the foundations of the Community',[306] it went on to say that nothing in the wording of the Article undermined its direct effect:

First of all it is impossible to put forward an argument against its direct effect based on the use in this Article of the word 'principle', since, in the language of the Treaty, this term is specifically used in order

---

[303] Case 80/70 *Defrenne v Belgium*, op cit, n 44.   [304] Ibid, at 456.
[305] Case 43/75 *Defrenne v Sabena*, op cit, n 11.   [306] Ibid, at 472.

to indicate the fundamental nature of certain provisions, as is shown for example by the heading of the first part of the Treaty which is devoted to 'Principles' and by Article 113, according to which the commercial policy of the Community is to be based on 'uniform principles'. If this concept were to be attenuated to the point of reducing it to the level of a vague declaration, the very foundations of the Community and the coherence of its external relations would be directly affected. It is also impossible to put forward arguments based on the fact that Article 119 only refers expressly to 'Member States'. Indeed, as the Court has already found in other contexts, the fact that certain provisions of the Treaty are formally addressed to the Member States does not prevent rights from being conferred at the same time on any individual who has an interest in the performance of the duties thus laid down. The very wording of Article 119 shows that it imposes on states a duty to bring about a specific result to be mandatorily achieved within a fixed period. The effectiveness of this provision cannot be affected by the fact that the duty imposed by the Treaty has not been discharged by certain Member States and that the joint institutions have not reacted sufficiently energetically against this failure to act. To accept the contrary view would be to risk raising the violation of the right to the status of a principle of interpretation, a position the adoption of which would not be consistent with the task assigned to the Court by Article 164[307] of the Treaty. Finally, in its reference to 'Member States', Article 119 is alluding to those states in the exercise of all those of their functions which may usefully contribute to the implementation of the principle of equal pay. Thus, contrary to the statements made in the course of the proceedings, this provision is far from merely referring the matter to the powers of the national legislative authorities. Therefore the reference to 'Member States' in Article 119 cannot be interpreted as excluding the intervention of the courts in direct application of the Treaty.[308]

It is highly probable that the ECJ would come to the same conclusion about the principle of equal pay contained in the Race Directive and the Framework Directive;[309] it is therefore likely to be only a matter of time before someone successfully alleges the direct effect of the pay provisions contained in one or both of these instruments.

Under the original terms of what is today Article 141, the equal pay obligation became unconditional as far as the founding Member States were concerned as from the end of the first stage, in other words from the beginning of January 1962. However, as this date approached, it became clear that some of the Member States had not introduced the necessary legislation in time and so had not put the equality principle into practice within their own jurisdictions. Consequently the Member States adopted the Resolution mentioned by Lamothe AG, by which they agreed to postpone the deadline to the end of 1964.[310] The ECJ held that this Resolution was ineffective to modify the time limit stipulated in the Article, since the Treaty can be amended only by means of the procedure laid down therein.[311]

However, the Court's judgment contained an unfortunate sting in its tail in relation to the operative date of Article 141. Several of the original Member States

---

[307] Today, Art 220.   [308] [1976] ECR 455, at 474–5.

[309] But see ch 5 for discussion of the rather tentative language used in the opening articles of the Race Directive and the Framework Directive, which could be argued to reduce the likelihood of the subsequent substantive provisions taking direct effect.

[310] See Warner, 'European Community Social Policy in Practice: Community Action on Behalf of Women and its Impact in the Member States' (1984) 23 JCMS 141.

[311] [1976] ECR 455, at 478–9. See today Art 48 of the TEU. Cf the apparently different view of Lamothe AG on this point.

did not observe even the later time limit agreed in the Resolution. The Commission therefore held a conference, attended by representatives of the governments and the two sides of industry, and produced several reports on the matter. It also declared its intention to take enforcement proceedings against those States remaining in breach, although it in fact took no further action. The UK and Irish Governments also argued that the economic repercussions of holding Article 141 to be directly effective from its operative date under the Treaty would be disastrous; undertakings might face bankruptcy as a result of large numbers of backdated claims. This argument seems an exaggerated one in the light of the fact that, as seen in chapter 2, national rules of procedure relate to directly effective Community provisions and, in the UK at least, the relevant statute at the date in question provided that no equal pay claim could be backdated further than two years.[312] The ECJ was, however, persuaded by the Member States' arguments and held:

[I]n the light of the conduct of several of the Member States and the views adopted by the Commission and repeatedly brought to the notice of the circles concerned, it is appropriate to take exceptionally into account the fact that, over a prolonged period, the parties concerned have been led to continue with practices which were contrary to Article 119, although not yet prohibited under their national law. The fact that, in spite of the warnings given, the Commission did not initiate proceedings under Article 169[313] against the Member States concerned on grounds of failure to fulfil an obligation was likely to consolidate the incorrect impression as to the effects of Article 119. In these circumstances, it is appropriate to hold that, as the general level at which pay would have been fixed cannot be known, important considerations of legal certainty affecting all the interests involved, both public and private, make it impossible in principle to reopen the question as regards the past. Therefore the direct effect of Article 119 cannot be relied on in order to support claims concerning pay periods prior to the date of this judgment, except as regards those workers who have already brought legal proceedings or made an equivalent claim.[314]

In terms of principle, this is an illogical conclusion. If the Article possesses the qualities required to produce direct effect, then this has been so ever since it ceased to be conditional at the beginning of 1962. To interpose another operative date was a clear example of judicial legislation and highlights the unsatisfactoriness of there being no appeal from decisions of the ECJ.[315] Furthermore, in paying heed to the failure of the Commission to initiate proceedings, the Court was inconsistent in its reasoning, since earlier in its judgment it rejected the notion that the effectiveness of the Treaty Article could be undermined by the dilatoriness of the Commission.[316] The creation of the concept of prospective effect for Article 141

---

[312] Equal Pay Act 1970, s 2(5). See ch 2 for further discussion of the legality of this limitation period.
[313] Today, Art 226.   [314] [1976] ECR 455, at 480–1.
[315] Even today, despite the existence of the Court of First Instance, there would be no possibility of appeal in a case such as *Defrenne*.
[316] See [1976] ECR 455, at 472–3. On this matter, the Court differed from the Advocate General. Burrows, in 'The Promotion of Women's Rights by the European Economic Community' (1980) 17 CMLRev 191, comments that 'the Court did in effect what it said the other institutions of the Community were not entitled to do ie amended the Treaty by a procedure other than that foreseen in [the Treaty itself]'.

also produced an unfortunate precedent in practice.[317] The Court, however, regards prospective direct effect as exceptional,[318] and it held in *Amministrazione delle Finanze dello Stato v Denkavit Italiana Srl*:[319]

[I]t is only exceptionally that the Court may, in application of the general principle of legal certainty inherent in the Community legal order and in taking account of the serious effects which its judgment might have, as regards the past, on legal relationships established in good faith, be moved to restrict for any person concerned the opportunity of relying upon the provisions as thus interpreted with a view to calling into question those legal relationships. *Such a restriction may, however, be allowed only in the actual judgment ruling upon the interpretation sought. The fundamental need for a general and uniform application of Community law implies that it is for the Court of Justice alone to decide upon the temporal restrictions to be placed on an interpretation which it lays down.*[320]

In *Grzelczyk v Centre Public d'Aide Sociale*,[321] the ECJ added that it had granted prospective effect to a provision

only in quite specific circumstances, where there was a risk of serious economic repercussions owing in particular to the large number of legal relationships entered into in good faith on the basis of rules considered to be validly in force and where it appeared that both individuals and national authorities had been led into adopting practices which did not comply with Community law by reason of objective, significant uncertainty regarding the implications of Community provisions, to which the conduct of other Member States or the Commission may even have contributed . . .[322]

The temporal limitation which the Court applies to the enforcement of Article 141 in relation to pensions has been discussed above. It is important to note, however, that the limitation expressed in the *Barber* case[323] does not extend to matters outside the pensions field; as seen above, the Court also dealt with non-discrimination in relation to redundancy payments. It should also be noted that the *Defrenne* time limitation does not prevent Member States from enacting more extensive retroactive rights to equal pay within their own jurisdictions.[324]

The ECJ's ruling in the *Second Defrenne* case[325] also established, very importantly in practice, that the equal pay principle takes horizontal direct effect; in other

---

[317] See Wyatt, 'Prospective Effect of a Holding of Direct Applicability' (1975–6) 1 ELRev 399, and L Neville Brown, 'Agromonetary Byzantinism and Prospective Overruling' (1981) 18 CMLRev 509.

[318] See, eg, its refusal to apply the principle in Case C-366/99 *Griesmar*, op cit, n 57.

[319] Case 61/79 [1980] ECR 1205.

[320] Ibid, at 1223–4, emphasis added. See also Case 33/76 *Rewe-Zentralfinanz eG and Rewe-Zentral AG v Landwirtschaftskammer fur das Saarland* [1976] 2 ECR 1989, esp the remarks of Warner AG at 2005; Cases 66, 127, & 128/79 *Amministrazione delle Finanze dello Stato v Meridionale Industria Salumi Srl* [1980] ECR 1237; Case 69/80 *Worringham*, op cit, n 23; Case 24/86 *Blaizot v University of Liège* [1988] ECR 379; Case C-262/88 *Barber*, op cit, n 28; Case C-163/90 *Administration des Douanes v Legros* [1992] ECR I-4625; Case C-110/91 *Moroni*, op cit, n 72; and Case C-57/93 *Vroege*, op cit, n 76.

[321] Case C-184/99 [2001] ECR I-6193.   [322] Ibid, at 6248.   [323] Op cit, n 28.

[324] See Case C-50/96 *Schröder*, op cit, n 78, and Joined Cases C-270 & 271/97 *Sievers and Shrage*, op cit, n 78.   [325] Case 43/75, op cit, n 11.

words, it may be enforced against employers who are private persons or companies, as well as against organs of the State. The Court held:

[S]ince Article 119 is mandatory in nature, the prohibition on discrimination between men and women applies not only to the action of public authorities, but also extends to all agreements which are intended to regulate paid labour collectively, as well as to contracts between individuals.[326]

In contrast to the width of the class for whom Article 141 creates the obligation to provide equal pay, it seems that the scope of its direct effect may be limited; in other words, there may be some circumstances in which the Article obliges the Member States to provide equal pay for equal work but in which, without further implementing legislation, the Article itself cannot be directly enforced. It was seen in chapter 3 that the Court in the *Second Defrenne* case drew a distinction between what it then described as 'direct and overt' sex discrimination, as regards which Article 141 does take direct effect, and 'indirect and disguised' discrimination, as to which it does not. 'Direct and overt' discrimination can be identified solely with the aid of the criteria based on equal work and equal pay referred to by Article 141, whilst 'indirect and disguised' discrimination can be identified only by reference to more explicit implementing provisions of a Community or national character. The ECJ went on to hold:

Among the forms of direct discrimination which may be identified solely by reference to the criteria laid down by Article 119 must be included in particular those which have their origin in legislative provisions or in collective labour agreements and which may be detected on the basis of a purely legal analysis of the situation. This applies even more in cases where men and women receive unequal pay for equal work carried out in the same establishment or service, whether public or private. As is shown by the very findings of the judgment making the reference, in such a situation the court is in a position to establish all the facts which enable it to decide whether a woman worker is receiving lower pay than a male worker performing the same tasks.[327]

Although the Court in later cases abandoned the use of the phrases 'direct and overt' and 'indirect and disguised', it has stuck to its original reasoning in relation to the direct effect of Article 141. This is unsurprising given that the concept of direct effect calls for the enforcement of the provision in question by the judges of the national courts; its ambit must therefore be clearly defined if there are not to be great discrepancies in application. Warner AG explained the position in *Jenkins v Kingsgate (Clothing Productions) Ltd*,[328] as follows:

A difficulty . . . is . . . caused by certain *dicta* of the Court in Case 43/75 the *Second Defrenne* case and in *Macarthys Ltd v Smith* . . . Those *dicta* could be interpreted as meaning that the test for determining whether there is 'covert' discrimination, in the sense meant in [the nationality cases,] is the same as the test for identifying the kind of discrimination as regards which Article 119 has no direct effect. In my opinion the two tests are not the same and I doubt if the Court can ever have intended to say that they were . . . Article 119 is, in my opinion, more accurately described as not having direct effect where a

---

[326] Case 43/75, op cit, n 11, at 476. See also the remarks of Van Themaat AG in Case 58/81 *Commission v Luxemburg* [1982] ECR 2175.   [327] Case 43/75 [1976] ECR 455, at 473–4.
[328] Case 96/80, op cit, n 195.

court cannot apply its provisions by reference to the simple criteria that those provisions themselves lay down and where, consequently, implementing legislation, either Community or national, is necessary to lay down the relevant criteria.[329]

The Court has held that Article 141 is directly effective where male and female workers perform identical jobs simultaneously in the same establishments,[330] where they perform such jobs at different times,[331] where there is indirect discrimination over pay in relation to men and women performing identical jobs,[332] and where there is gender-plus discrimination in relation to identical jobs.[333]

It remains to be determined in what other situations Article 141 takes direct effect. In particular, in the light of the fact that the Court has now acknowledged that the Article extends to comparisons with workers in other establishments or working for different employers,[334] it is arguable that, so long as the pay discrimination can be ascertained by means of the concepts of pay and work contained in the Article itself, then there is nothing to inhibit direct effect in this situation.

Importantly in practice, there is the question of whether the Article is directly effective where the two jobs compared are not identical but are alleged to be of equal value.[335] It was seen earlier in the present chapter that the ECJ changed its mind in this context and came to consider, even before its amendment by the Amsterdam Treaty, that at least the theoretical scope of the equal pay Article embraced equal value situations. This may well have been because, once it had articulated its position on the horizontal direct effect of directives, it realized that the Equal Pay Directive would be of little help in the equal value situation, so that recourse would have to be made to the Treaty Article. *Dicta* from the early cases about the extent of the Article's direct effect are of course misleading today,[336] although the difficulty referred to in those cases appears a real one: namely, how can the Article apply directly when further explanatory legislation is needed before a court can know how equal value is to be assessed? However, notwithstanding this obstacle, by the time of *Worringham v Lloyds Bank Ltd*[337] the Court seemed prepared to include the equal value situation in its definition of the extent of the direct effect of Article 141:

[The Article applies directly] to all forms of discrimination which may be identified solely with the aid of the criteria of equal work and equal pay referred to by the Article in question, without national or

---

[329] Case 96/80, op cit, at 937–8.

[330] Case 43/74 *Defrenne v Sabena*, op cit, n 11, and Case 69/80 *Worringham*, op cit, n 23.

[331] Case 129/79 *Macarthys*, op cit, n 191.

[332] Case 96/80 *Jenkins*, op cit, n 195, and Case 170/84 *Bilka-Kaufhaus*, op cit, n 39. Cf the remarks of Capotorti AG in Case 149/77 *Defrenne v Sabena*, op cit, n 184, at 1382.

[333] Case 23/83 *Liefting v Directie van het Academisch Ziekenhuis bij de Universiteit van Amsterdam* [1984] ECR 3225.

[334] See Case C-320/00 *Lawrence*, op cit, n 205, and Case C-256/01 *Allonby*, op cit, n 3, nyr, both discussed above.

[335] See Arnull, 'Article 119 and Equal Pay for Work of Equal Value' (1986) 11 ELRev 200.

[336] See, eg, the comments of Trabucchi AG in Case 43/75 *Defrenne v Sabena* [1976] ECR 455, at 485–6.

[337] Case 69/80, op cit, n 23. Cf the opinion of Van Themaat AG in Case 61/81 *Commission v UK* [1982] ECR 2601.

Community measures being required to define them with greater precision in order to permit of their application. Among the forms of discrimination which may thus be judicially identified, the Court mentioned in particular cases where men and women receive unequal pay for equal work carried out in the same establishment or service, public or private. In such a situation the court is in a position to establish all the facts enabling it to decide whether a woman receives less pay than a man engaged in the same work *or work of equal value*.[338]

The issue seems to have been settled by *Murphy v Bord Telecom Eireann*,[339] in which the ECJ held that Article 141 is directly effective where the claimant can demonstrate that she is engaged on work of higher value than that of her male comparator. It would seem to follow from the Court's remarks in this case that the same would have been true were the work established to be of equal value. In *Pickstone v Freemans plc*, the British Court of Appeal also came to the conclusion that Article 141 is directly effect-ive in equal value cases.[340] The House of Lords decided the case on the basis of British law, but the comments of Lord Oliver are significant:

[T]he cases in the European Court to which your Lordships have been referred clearly establish that there is an area within which [Article 141] is not directly applicable.[341] The bounds of that area are far from clear to me, however, but the cases appear to indicate that the Article may not be directly applic-able in an 'equal value' claim, *at any rate where there is no machinery in the domestic law by which the criterion of what is work of equal value can be readily ascertained*.[342]

The last part of Lord Oliver's statement probably explains the ECJ's change of mind in relation to direct effect in equal value cases: where national implementing legislation has been passed explaining how equal value is to be assessed then Article 141 can in principle take direct effect in such cases within that Member State.[343] However, *Pickstone's* case involved a particular difficulty, as Lord Oliver went on to demonstrate. The assessment of equal value in the UK is the job of employment tribunals under s 1(2)(c) of the Equal Pay Act 1970, but their jurisdiction is purely statutory and they possess no inherent powers. The Court of Appeal had held that s 1(2)(c) did not extend, because of its wording, to the precise situation in issue in that case and thus, in his Lordship's opinion, there was no national machinery for the assessment of equal value on the Court of Appeal's analysis. He could not envisage how Article 141 could be enforced either. This would have been

---

[338] [1981] ECR 767, at 792, emphasis added.   [339] Op cit, n 230, also discussed above.

[340] [1987] 3 WLR 811. Cf the view of the Court of Appeal in *O'Brien v Sim-Chem Ltd* [1980] 1 WLR 734.

[341] It is apparent from the context that Lord Oliver is using the expression 'directly applicable' in the same sense as the present writer is using 'directly effective'.

[342] [1988] 2 All ER 803, at 816, emphasis added.

[343] There is a parallel to be drawn here with the reasoning adopted by the ECJ in Case C-271/91 *Marshall v Southampton and South-West Hants Area Health Authority (No 2)* [1993] ECR I-4367, discussed in ch 5. Essentially, the Court held in *Marshall (No 2)* that Art 6 of the Equal Treatment Directive was rendered directly effective so as to provide a remedy for the victim of a discriminatory dismissal where the national legislature had acted to restrict the available remedies in this situation to compensation; the victim was entitled to rely on the direct effect of the otherwise insufficiently specific Art 6 in order to override a national ceiling on damages, the effect of which was to prevent her from recovering in full for the loss which she had sustained.

disastrous for the enforcement of equal value claims in the UK, but there is now a body of case law which takes the view that directly effective EU law automatically amends UK law.[344] Moreover, it does not detract from the general principle that Article 141 appears now to be directly effective in such cases, at least provided that there is national legislation governing the ascertainment of equal value.

Where a litigant relies in a national court on the direct effect of Article 141, it was seen in chapter 2 that the same remedies must be available as would be available in a similar domestic claim, provided that these do not actually frustrate the EU claim. The ECJ has added that the effect of a successful Article 141 claim is to raise the lower pay to the level of that of the comparator, a principle which would appear to apply with equal force to pay discrimination contrary to the Race Directive and the Framework Directive:[345]

[S]ince Article 119 appears in the context of the harmonization of working conditions while the improve-ment is being maintained, the objection that the terms of this Article may be observed in other ways than by raising the lowest salaries may be set aside.[346]

The strength of this principle has been somewhat diluted in the field of occupa-tional pension schemes, where it has been held lawful to re-write the scheme's rules so as to equalize as between men and women, even where such equalization operates downwards.[347]

A rate of pay which violates Article 141 is automatically rendered void and replaced by the higher rate applicable to comparators;[348] this remedy can also be supplemented by national measures imposing penal sanctions on those who dis-obey the equal pay principle.[349] In *Kowalska v Freie und Hansestadt Hamburg*,[350] this principle was applied to discrimination occurring under the terms of a collective agreement.[351] The agreement in question restricted the payment of severance benefits to workers employed for at least thirty-eight hours a week, thereby indirectly discriminating against women since the large majority of those employed for under

---

[344] See, eg, *Biggs v Somerset County Council* [1996] ICR 364.

[345] See in particular Recital 9 of the Preamble to the Race Directive and Recital 11 of the Preamble to the Framework Directive.

[346] Case 43/75 *Defrenne v Sabena*, op cit, n 11, at 472; Case C-200/91 *Coloroll*, op cit, n 72, at 4413. See also Case C-147/95 *Evrenopoulos*, op cit, n 54, where it was alleged that a term in a pension scheme discriminating against widowers was unconstitutional and therefore invalid; the ECJ held that this was not correct as a matter of EU law and that the position of widowers must be levelled-up to match that of widows. Cf the effect of establishing discrimination in a social security scheme contrary to the Social Security Directive, Directive 79/7, OJ [1979] L6/24, where the result may be a general levelling-down of the benefit in question, as discussed in ch 8.

[347] See Case C-408/92 *Smith*, op cit, n 90, discussed above; also Deakin, 'Levelling Down Employee Benefits' [1995] CLJ 35.

[348] See Trabucchi AG in Case 43/75 *Defrenne v Sabena*, op cit, n 11, at 489.

[349] See Case 14/83 *Von Colson and Kamann v Land of North Rhine-Westfalia* [1984] ECR 1891, discussed further in ch 5.

[350] Case 33/89, op cit, n 164, discussed by Reiland in 'Sex Discrimination in Collective Agreements' (1991) 20 ILJ 79, and by More in 'Severance Pay for Part-time Workers' (1991) 16 ELRev 58.

[351] As also Case C-184/89 *Nimz*, op cit, n 262, and Joined Cases C-399, 409, & 425/92, C-34, 50, & 78/93, *Helmig*, op cit, n 13, both discussed above.

thirty-eight hours a week were female. The Court held:

It is apparent from the judgment of 13 December 1989, *Ruzius-Wilbrink* (Case C-102/88 [1989] ECR 4311), that in a case of indirect discrimination the members of the class of persons placed at a disadvantage are entitled to have the same scheme applied to them as that applied to other workers, on a basis proportional to their working time. That ruling applies equally to discriminatory provisions in a collective agreement. It must therefore be stated in reply to the second question that where there is indirect discrimination in a clause in a collective wage agreement, the class of persons placed at a disadvantage by reason of that discrimination must be treated in the same way and made subject to the same scheme, proportionately to the number of hours worked, such scheme remaining for want of correct transposition of Article 119 of the EEC Treaty into national law, the only valid point of reference.[352]

In *Nimz v Freie und Hansestadt Hamburg*,[353] the ECJ added:

It should also be pointed out that the Court has consistently held . . . that a national court which is called upon, within the limits of its jurisdiction, to apply provisions of Community law is under a duty to give full effect to those provisions, if necessary by refusing of its own motion to apply any conflicting provision of national legislation, and it is not necessary for the court to request or await the prior setting aside of such provision by legislative or other constitutional means.

It is equally necessary to apply such considerations to the case where the provision at variance with Community law is derived from a collective labour agreement. It would be incompatible with the very nature of Community law if the court having jurisdiction to apply that law were to be precluded at the time of such application from being able to take all necessary steps to set aside the provisions of a collective agreement which might constitute an obstacle to the full effectiveness of Community rules.

. . . [W]here there is indirect discrimination in a provision of a collective agreement, the national court is required to set aside that provision, without requesting or awaiting its prior removal by collective bargaining or any other procedure, and to apply to members of the group disadvantaged by that discrimination the same arrangements as are applied to other employees, arrangements which, failing the correct application of Article 119 . . . in national law, remain the only valid system of reference.[354]

The Equal Pay Directive[355]

(i) The background to the Equal Pay Directive

The Equal Pay Directive was passed in 1975, in an effort to harmonize the laws of the Member States in relation to the principle of equal pay.[356] It was, accordingly, based on what is today Article 94. That the principle of pay equality had by that date emerged as of fundamental importance to the Community is exemplified by

---

[352] [1990] ECR I-2591, at 2613.   [353] Op cit, n 262.

[354] Ibid, at 321. See also Case C-187/00 *Kutz-Bauer*, op cit, n 270, and Case C-77/02 *Steinicke*, op cit, n 270, in which the ECJ held that the same principle applies to provisions in legislation and collective agreements which produce indirect discrimination contrary to the Equal Treatment Directive (as to which see ch 5).   [355] Directive 75/117, OJ [1975] L45/19.

[356] See the final recital of the Preamble.

the first recital of the Directive's Preamble, which describes the implementation of what is today Article 141 as an 'integral part of the establishment and functioning of the common market'. The Preamble also refers expressly to the Council Resolution of 21 January 1974,[357] which 'recognized that priority should be given to action taken on behalf of women as regards access to employment and vocational training and advancement, and as regards working conditions, including pay'.

The record in relation to equal pay in the various Member States during the early 1970s was, to say the least, patchy.[358] Strong feelings began to be expressed, particularly in the European Parliament, that Article 141 had been legally binding for a period of many years (at least in six of the Member States) and yet it had achieved little practical significance.[359] This was attributed in part to a lack of effective monitoring of what was going on in the Member States, and in part to the lack at that time of wider legislative measures to deal with discrimination against women in employment generally. The Equal Pay Directive was therefore seen as providing a valuable additional means of control by the Commission over the Member States in relation to pay equality.[360] The fifth recital of the Directive's Preamble refers to the differences which in 1975 continued 'to exist in the various Member States despite the efforts made to apply the resolution of the conference of the Member States of 30 December 1961 on equal pay for men and women', and implies that the Directive seeks to impose, at the very least, a uniform minimum standard.

As events turned out, the need for the Directive was greatly reduced very shortly after its enactment, when the ECJ ruled in *Defrenne v Sabena*[361] that Article 141 itself was directly effective.[362] This had the very important consequence in practice that the principle of pay equality, at least on some occasions, could be enforced directly in the courts of the Member States and, even more significantly, that national legislation which conflicted with the Treaty Article was automatically rendered inapplicable. A large part of the Commission's job of chasing up offending Member States was thus performed at a stroke.

---

[357] OJ [1974] C13/1.

[358] See, eg, the Commission's comments in its Sixth General Report on the Activities of the Communities, 1972, para 211. Also the Reports of the Commission to the Council on the Application of the Principle of Equal Pay for Men and Women of 18 July 1973 (SEC (73) 3000 final) and 17 July 1974 (SEC (74) 2721 final), and Sullerot, *The Employment of Women and the Problems it Raises in the Member States of the European Community* (Commission of the European Communities, 1975).

[359] The editors of the *Common Market Law Review* commented in 1974 that a directive on equal pay was long overdue, 'as the failure to give effective enforcement to Article 119 of the EEC Treaty has been the scandal of the stunted development of the social aspect of the Community' ((1974) 11 CMLRev 1–2).

[360] See Bull EC 4–1974, point 2420. Also Burrows, 'The Promotion of Women's Rights by the European Economic Community' (1980) 17 CMLRev 191.   [361] Case 43/75, op cit, n 11.

[362] See above. A similar sequence of events occurred in relation to the Occupational Social Security Directive (Directive 86/379, OJ [1986] L225/40), also discussed above, when the ECJ ruled that Art 141 itself extended to various types of pension scheme.

(ii)   The relationship between the Directive and Article 141

The ECJ experienced a change of heart with respect to the relationship between the Equal Pay Directive and Article 141. This may well have been provoked by its development of the doctrine of the direct effect of directives and its ultimate conclusion that they are incapable of horizontal effect:[363] if the Member States were going to prove recalcitrant in implementing the Directive, then the way to achieve maximum utility for EU law would be via the Treaty Article itself. Its original stance was articulated in *Defrenne v Sabena*,[364] where it commented that Community secondary legislation 'implement[s] Article 119 from the point of view of extending the narrow criterion of "equal work" ', thus suggesting that the Directive went further in its provisions than the Treaty Article. However, by the early 1980s, it had decided that this was not so and that the Directive does no more than flesh out the bare bones of Article 141; it is for this reason that analysis of the Directive has been deferred until the final section of the present chapter. The Court's amended view has the logical support of the wording of the Directive itself, both in Article 1(1) and in the fourth recital of its Preamble, which states that 'it is desirable to reinforce the basic laws by standards aimed at facilitating the practical application of the principle of equality in such a way that all employees in the Community can be protected in these matters'. This enabled the ECJ to hold in *Jenkins v Kingsgate (Clothing Productions) Ltd*[365] that: 'Article 1 of Council Directive 75/117 which is principally designed to facilitate the practical application of the principle of equal pay outlined in Article 119 of the Treaty in no way alters the content or scope of that principle as defined in the Treaty.'[366] The fact that the Directive does not extend the scope of Article 141 does not, of course, mean that it can diminish it either, because, as noted above, a measure of secondary legislation cannot restrict the scope of primary legislation.[367] The ECJ applied this general principle to the present context in *Defrenne v Sabena*,[368] saying:

[T]he principle contained in Article 119 has been fully effective in the new Member States since the entry into force of the Accession Treaty . . . It was not possible for this legal situation to be modified by Directive 75/117, which was adopted on the basis of Article 100[369] dealing with the approximation of laws and was intended to encourage the proper implementation of Article 119 by means of a series of measures to be taken on the national level, in order, in particular, to eliminate indirect forms of discrimination, *but was unable to reduce the effectiveness of that Article or modify its temporal effect.*[370]

---

[363] Discussed in ch 2.   [364] Case 43/75, op cit, n 11, at 473.

[365] Case 96/80, op cit, n 195.

[366] Ibid, at 927. See also Case 69/80 *Worringham*, op cit, n 23; Case 192/85 *Newstead*, op cit, n 27; Case 262/88 *Barber*, op cit, n 28; and Joined Cases C-399, 409, & 425/92 and C-34, 50, & 78/93, *Helmig*, op cit, n 13. And see Arnull, 'Article 119 and Equal Pay for Work of Equal Value' (1986) 11 ELRev 200.

[367] See the discussion of the relationship between the Occupational Social Security Directive (Directive 86/378, OJ [1986] L225/40) and Art 141, and the remarks of the ECJ in Case C-110/91 *Moroni*, op cit, n 72.   [368] Case 43/75, op cit, n 11.

[369] Today, Art 94.   [370] [1976] ECR 455, at 478–9, emphasis added.

If the Directive therefore merely spells out the detail of Article 141, without in any way undermining its scope, it follows that its chief practical effect today is to shed light on the more obscure aspects of Article 141. Whether it will be held to perform the same service for the equal pay provisions contained in the Race Directive and Framework Directive remains to be seen, but it seems logical to suppose that it will. The major object of the discussion of the Directive which follows is therefore to explore the ways in which it might be said to elucidate Article 141 and, by implication, also the pay provisions of the Race Directive and the Framework Directive.

It should be remembered that the scope of Article 141 is important in two different ways. First, it places obligations on the Member States to ensure that its terms are complied with; and, secondly, it is capable of conferring directly enforceable rights on individuals. The Directive may play a part in each of these processes, both explaining more clearly what duties are cast on the Member States (and therefore conditioning the interpretation and effect given by national courts to any national implementing legislation) and also facilitating the direct effect of the Article.

Given this analysis, and bearing in mind that it may not in any event be enforced horizontally, the possible direct effect of the Directive itself assumes only limited significance. The question whether the Directive takes direct effect has in fact been referred to the ECJ on several occasions[371] but has not been resolved, largely because the more potent effects of Article 141 have proved more useful to litigants.[372]

(iii)   Content of the Equal Pay Directive

Article 1(1) of the Directive provides:

The principle of equal pay for men and women outlined in Article 119 of the Treaty, hereinafter called 'principle of equal pay', means, for the same work or for work to which equal value is attributed, the elimination of all discrimination on grounds of sex with regard to all aspects and conditions of remuneration.

There are essentially two aspects of substance to this provision: first is the nature of the work to be compared, and second is the scope of the prohibition on discrimination. As regards the nature of the work to be compared, the Article refers to the 'same work' or 'work to which equal value is attributed'. These phrases suggest, unfortunately, a necessity for an actual comparator of the opposite sex. Whilst they do not expressly rule out the possibility of hypothetical comparison, they are more appropriate to deal with the situation where a man and a woman are actually engaged on the same work, or on work of equal value to one another. It was seen

---

[371] See in particular Case 129/79 *Macarthys*, op cit, n 191; Case 69/80 *Worringham*, op cit, n 23; Case 96/80 *Jenkins*, op cit, n 195; Case 12/81 *Garland*, op cit, n 12; Case 192/85 *Newstead*, op cit, n 27; Case 19/81 *Burton*, op cit, n 32; and Case 157/86 *Murphy*, op cit, n 230.

[372] In *Preston v Wolverhampton Healthcare NHS Trust* [1997] IRLR 233, Schiemann LJ commented that it is clear that the Equal Pay Directive is not directly effective (at 239).

above that the ECJ has held that the direct effect of Article 141 does not extend to the situation of hypothetical comparison.[373] However, it was also seen that it is nevertheless strongly arguable that the Article today creates binding obligations for the Member States in this respect.[374] Since the Equal Pay Directive may not in any way diminish the scope of Article 141, but is merely intended to facilitate its application, this argument remains open.

The expression 'same work' is presumably designed primarily to cover the case where two people are employed to perform identical jobs. Even this matter is not, however, entirely free from doubt. It follows from *Jenkins v Kingsgate (Clothing Productions) Ltd*[375] that what is relevant for this purpose is the nature of the tasks performed, rather than the overall job description. Thus, a full-timer and a part-timer engaged on the same process would seem to be performing the same work, even though their job descriptions would vary because of the different hours worked.[376]

Even more elusive is the meaning of 'work to which equal value is attributed'. What is the meaning of 'equal value' for this purpose? By whom, and when, must it be attributed? It has been seen that, for the purposes of Article 141, the ECJ has focused on job content (rather than the market value of the work performed from the point of view of the employer) in assessing the value of work.[377] Logic clearly demands that the Court adopt the same analysis for the purposes of the Equal Pay Directive, and this conclusion is reinforced by Article 1(2) of the Directive,[378] which gives its blessing to the use of non-discriminatory job classification schemes for determining pay. The issues of who must attribute equal value, and when the attribution must take place, for the purposes of the Directive were considered by the ECJ in *Commission v UK*.[379] This was a prosecution of the UK by the Commission under what is today Article 226 of the Treaty for failure to implement the Equal Pay Directive fully. UK legislation at the time of the action provided for equal pay as between the sexes only where the man and woman concerned were engaged on 'like work' (meaning broadly similar work), or where their work had been 'rated as equivalent' in a job evaluation study. It made no provision for a claimant to demand equal pay with a colleague of the opposite sex where he or she merely alleged that their work was of equal value, but where no job evaluation study had been conducted. Since a job evaluation study could be conducted only with the consent of the employer, this left a considerable lacuna in the legislation: the lacuna was of enormous practical significance because large numbers of women were known to be working in sex-segregated occupations, so that they could not rely on the 'like work' provision, but neither could they insist on having a job evaluation study conducted in their organization generally if the employer did not agree. The UK

---

[373] Case 129/79 *Macarthys*, op cit, n 191; Case C-200/91 *Coloroll*, op cit, n 72.

[374] See discussion above, especially in relation to the effect of the Race Directive and Framework Directive.   [375] Case 96/80 [1981] ECR 911.

[376] See Warner AG in *Jenkins*, ibid, at 933.

[377] See in particular its remarks in Case 129/79 *Macarthys*, op cit, n 191.   [378] Discussed below.

[379] Case 61/81 [1982] ECR 2601. See Atkins, 'Equal Pay for Work of Equal Value' (1983) 8 ELRev 48.

Government defended its position by arguing that the requirements of the Directive take effect only *after* the jobs concerned have been found to be of equal value; neither the Directive nor Article 141, it said, gave an individual employee the right to take steps to determine the value of the jobs to be compared. It stressed the precise wording of the Directive in this context, and pointed out that the words 'is attributed' are used; this wording suggests that it is not until equal value *has been* attributed that the claim to equal pay arises. According to the UK Government, if the drafters of the Directive had intended otherwise, they would have simply used the words 'work of equal value'. In addition, it was pointed out that Article 1(2) of the Directive suggests that equal value has, as a matter of EU law, to be determined on the basis of a job classification system, and that that indeed was the only practicable way of comparing the value of two different jobs. Lastly, the UK argued that, at the time the Directive was agreed by the Council, the situation under UK legislation was recorded in the minutes of the Council meeting; since neither the Council nor the Commission raised any objections then, it was said that they were subsequently estopped from doing so. Both the Court itself and the Advocate General rejected all the UK's arguments. The Court held that perusal of the Directive showed that job classification is merely one of several methods for determining whether work is of equal value; Article 1(2) begins with the words '*In particular,* where a job classification system is used for determining pay . . . '.[380] Van Themaat AG observed that all sorts of different methods were in use for evaluating jobs in the Member States of the Community in practice, and job classification constituted merely one method. The Court went on to hold:

British legislation does not permit the introduction of a job classification system without the employer's consent. Workers in the UK are therefore unable to have their work rated as being of equal value with comparable work if their employer refuses to introduce a classification system. The UK attempts to justify that state of affairs by pointing out that Article 1 of the Directive says nothing about the right of an employee to insist on having pay determined by a job classification system. On that basis it concludes that the worker may not insist on a comparative evaluation of different work by the job classification method, the introduction of which is at the employer's discretion. The UK's interpretation amounts to a denial of the very existence of a right to equal pay for work of equal value where no classification has been made. Such a position is not consonant with the general scheme and provisions of the Equal Pay Directive 75/117. The recitals in the Preamble to that Directive indicate that this essential purpose is to implement the principle that men and women should receive equal pay contained in Article 119 of the Treaty and that it is primarily the responsibility of the Member States to ensure the application of this principle by means of appropriate laws, regulations and administrative provisions in such a way that all employees in the Community can be protected in these matters.[381]

To the UK's arguments about the practicality of giving effect to equal value claims, the Court replied:

[W]here there is disagreement as to the application of . . . [the equal value] concept a worker must be entitled to claim before an appropriate authority that his work has the same value as other work and, if

---

[380] Emphasis added.   [381] [1982] ECR 2601, at 2615.

that is found to be the case, to have his rights under the Treaty and the Directive acknowledged by a binding decision. Any method which excludes that option prevents the aims of the Directive from being achieved . . . The implementation of the Directive implies that the assessment of the 'equal value' to be 'attributed' to particular work may be effected notwithstanding the employer's wishes if necessary in the context of adversary proceedings. The Member States must endow an authority with the requisite jurisdiction to decide whether work has the same value as other work, after obtaining such information as may be required.[382]

Thus, the Court made it clear that national legislation must not deny a claimant the right to allege that his or her work is of equal value to that of a comparator irrespective of the employer's wishes; and this allegation must be investigated by an 'authority' endowed by the State concerned with the 'requisite jurisdiction'. The right to claim equal pay for work of equal value is therefore certainly not restricted to the period of time subsequent to a finding of equal value through job classification.

Van Themaat AG also rejected the UK's argument about its statement in the Council minutes, saying:

As for the statement itself, I share the Commission's view that it simply explains that in order to determine the equal value of different jobs in the UK a job classification system must be used. As I have already stated, no objection can be taken to that. However, the statement does not indicate in practical terms how far such a system is dependent on the consent of the employer. It is this, in particular, which in my opinion is of crucial importance in this case. The argument that the Commission forfeited its right to take action under Article [226] by not raising any objection against the UK's statement cannot be accepted in my judgment. In my view such conduct on the part of the Commission cannot diminish its responsibility under Article [211] of the Treaty. Nor is it possible in my view to accept the argument that the UK can rely on the statement when construing the provision in question. As the Court has held on several occasions (for instance in Case 39/72 *Commission v Italy* [1973] CMLR 439 at paragraph (22)) such a statement made by a Member State for recording in the minutes of the Council when a decision is adopted cannot modify the objective scope of Community rules enacted by the Community decision.[383]

The Court's final ruling was that:

By failing to introduce into its national legal system in implementation of the provisions of Council Directive 75/117/EEC of 10 February 1975 such measures as are necessary to enable all employees who consider themselves wronged by failure to apply the principle of equal pay for men and women for work to which equal value is attributed and for which no system of job classification exists to obtain recognition of such equivalence, the UK has failed to fulfill its obligations under the Treaty.[384]

This ruling clearly required a change to the national legislation to cover the case of the employee alleging non-equal pay for work of equal value to that of another worker, where the employer was unwilling to commission a job evaluation study. The new legislation took the form of the Equal Pay (Amendment) Regulations 1983.[385]

---

[382] Ibid, at 2616–17.   [383] Ibid, at 2625.   [384] Ibid, at 2617–18.
[385] SI 1983 No 1794, as to which, see in particular Rubenstein, *Equal Pay For Work of Equal Value* (Macmillan, London and Basingstoke, 1984). The Equal Pay Regulations proved inordinately

Denmark has also been prosecuted by the Commission for inadequate implementation of the Directive.[386] The relevant Danish legislation provided:

Every person who employs men and women to work at the same place of work must pay them the same
salary for the *same work* under this Act if he is not already required to do so pursuant to a collective
agreement.[387]

The Commission argued that this was defective, first, because it made no reference
to work to which equal value is attributed and, secondly, because it did not
provide for any means of redress enabling workers alleging unequal pay for work
of equal value to pursue their claims. Van Themaat AG took the somewhat
eccentric view that, since Article 1 of the Directive merely spells out the detail of
Article 141, and since Article 141 can itself be enforced in the national courts, it
is unnecessary to implement the precise wording of the Directive as a matter of
national law. This approach is inconsistent with that hitherto taken by the ECJ,
namely, that the fact that a directive takes direct effect does not remove the
requirement that it be transformed into national law. [388] The Court itself took a
different view. The Danish Government had argued that its legislation constituted
only a subsidiary guarantee of the principle of equal pay in cases where the
principle was not already ensured under collective agreements. Collective agreements governed most contracts of employment in Denmark and they upheld
the principle of equal pay for work of equal value. The Court, however, ruled
that this was not sufficient and that the Danish legislation should refer specifically
to the equal value situation:

It is true that Member States may leave the implementation of the principle of equal pay in the first
instance to representatives of management and labour. That possibility does not, however, discharge
them from the obligation of ensuring, by appropriate legislation and administrative provisions, that all
workers in the Community are afforded the full protection provided for in the Directive. The state
guarantee must cover all cases where effective protection is not ensured by other means, for whatever
reason, and in particular cases where the workers in question are not union members, where the sector
in question is not covered by a collective agreement, or where such an agreement does not fully
guarantee the principle of equal pay.[389]

The situation was not saved by Denmark's argument (akin to that of the UK in
the earlier case) that it had entered a declaration in the Council minutes when

cumbersome in practice; in 1993 and 1994, the TUC and the EOCs for both Britain and Northern
Ireland made formal complaints to the EC Commission to the effect that the inadequacies of the
legislation meant that the UK remained in breach of the Equal Treatment Directive. The Commission,
however, declined to begin further infringement proceedings. See Ellis, 'Equal Pay for Work of Equal
Value: the United Kingdom's Legislation Viewed in the Light of Community Law' in Hervey and
O'Keefe (eds), *Sex Equality Law in the European Union* (Wiley, Chichester, 1996). The Regulations have
subsequently been amended in a number of detailed respects.

[386] Case 143/83 *Commission v Denmark*, op cit, n 199.   [387] Emphasis added.
[388] See discussion in ch 2.
[389] [1985] ECR 427, at 434–5. The Danish legislation was subsequently amended to reflect the ECJ's
decision: see Nielsen, *Equality in Law between Men and Women in the European Community: Denmark*
(Martinus Nijhoff, The Hague/Boston/London, 1995).

the Equal Pay Directive was passed, saying: 'Denmark is of the view that the expression "same work" can continue to be used in the context of Danish labour law.' The ECJ pointed out that it had

consistently held that such unilateral declarations cannot be relied upon for the interpretation of Community measures, since the objective scope of rules laid down by the common institutions cannot be modified by reservations or objections which Member States may have made at the time the rules were being formulated.[390]

Another aspect of the nature of the work to be compared under Article 1(1) of the Directive which remains unclear is the geographical or spatial scope of the comparison which the worker may demand. It was seen above that Article 141 may sometimes extend to comparisons with workers in other establishments of the same employer, and even to comparisons with workers employed by different employers. Van Themaat AG was prepared in *Commission v Denmark*[391] to submit that the Equal Pay Directive also mandates such comparisons. As already noted, the Danish legislation challenged in that case specifically restricted claims for equal pay to men and women working 'at the same place of work'. The Danish Government argued that this phrase had been put in in order to permit geographical differences in pay within Denmark, but the Advocate General found this unconvincing because such differences in pay, if genuine and if applied equally to men and women, are not grounded on sex and are therefore not prohibited anyway. He went on to say:

As appears from the second sentence of Article 1 of the Directive . . . a comparison of duties within the same fixed establishment of an undertaking or even within a single undertaking will not always be sufficient. In certain circumstances comparison with work of equal value in other undertakings covered by the collective agreement in question will be necessary. As is correctly observed in the annual report for 1980 of the Danish Council for Equal Treatment of Men and Women ('Ligestillingsradet'), submitted by the Commission in evidence, in sectors with a traditionally female workforce comparison with other sectors may even be necessary. In certain circumstances the additional criterion of 'the same place of work' for work of equal value may therefore place a restriction on the principle of equal pay laid down in Article 119 of the EEC Treaty and amplified in the Directive in question. The mere fact that such a supplementary condition for equal pay which has no foundation in Article 119 or in the Directive has been added must in any event be regarded as an infringement of the Treaty.[392]

The Court itself did not deal with this issue, apparently because the Commission did not formally raise it in its pleadings.[393] As seen above, its remarks on this subject in *Commission v UK*[394] were equivocal. It said merely:

[W]here there is disagreement as to the application of [the concept of non-discrimination] a worker must be entitled to claim before an appropriate authority that his work has the same value as other work and, if that is found to be the case, to have his rights under the Treaty and the Directive acknowledged

[390] Ibid, at 436.　[391] Op cit, n 386.　[392] Ibid, at 430.
[393] Ibid, at 436.　[394] Op cit, n 379.

by a binding decision. Any method which excludes that option prevents the aims of the Directive from being achieved.[395]

The Directive thus, as so far construed by the ECJ, does not cast any further light on the question of when Article 141 requires comparisons outside the worker's immediate workplace.

The second limb of Article 1(1) of the Directive is concerned with the scope of the prohibition of discrimination. It refers first of all to 'the elimination of all discrimination'. This strongly suggests that indirect, as well as direct, discrimination is outlawed by the combined forces of Article 141 and the Directive, and this conclusion was first confirmed by the ECJ's decision in *Jenkins v Kingsgate (Clothing Productions) Ltd*.[396] However, the discrimination in question must of course be 'on grounds of sex', which means that it must be proved to the satisfaction of the court or tribunal that sex is the cause of the differential treatment of the man and woman. This element will not be established where it can be shown that there is some wholly independent cause for the differentiation.[397]

Thus far, this part of the Directive appears to say little which could not be deduced from Article 141 itself. However, it goes on to add that sex discrimination is forbidden 'with regard to all aspects and conditions of remuneration'.[398] Although Article 141 explains that 'pay' may be expected to embody a wide variety of forms and to arise in various circumstances, it does not explicitly focus on its 'aspects' and 'conditions'. Two specific consequences might be said to follow from these words. First, the word 'aspects' provides reinforcement for the argument suggested in relation to Article 141 to the effect that any benefit extended to an employee by an employer via the contract of employment could be regarded as 'pay' and therefore could be argued to fall within Article 141. For example, a generous contractual holiday entitlement might be said to be an 'aspect' of 'pay', since it enters into the calculation of the size of the worker's pay packet. The word 'conditions' suggests that the Directive enables a worker to challenge the *way* in which, or the *terms* on which, pay is made available. In other words, this part of the wording of the Directive reinforces the view taken in *Barber v Guardian Royal*

---

[395] Op cit, n 379, at 2616.

[396] Op cit, n 195. See also Case 170/84 *Bilka-Kaufhaus*, op cit, n 39, and Joined Cases C-399, 409, & 425/92 and C-34, 50, & 78/93 *Helmig*, op cit, n 13, both discussed above. For an ingenious, though ill-fated, attempt to establish indirect discrimination over pay in relation to the qualifications required in order to receive an expatriation allowance where the Commission was the employer, see Case 246/83 *De Angelis v Commission* [1985] ECR 1253.

[397] See, eg, Van Themaat AG's argument mentioned above in Case 143/83 *Commission v Denmark*, op cit, n 199, in relation to geographically determined pay differences. And see also the discussion of this matter in ch 3 and in relation to Art 141.

[398] In Case 69/80 *Worringham*, op cit, n 23, at 807, Warner AG commented: 'Nothing turns on the change from the use of the word "pay" in Article 119 to the use of the word "remuneration" in the Directive. That is a feature of the English texts only. In all the other texts the same word is used in Article 119 and in the Directive: "remuneration" in French, "Entgelt" in German, and so forth'.

Exchange Assurance Group[399] and the later pensions equality cases that Article 141 forbids discriminatory access to pay, as well as discrimination in relation to the quantum of pay received. The same conclusion should arguably therefore be drawn in relation to the Race Directive and the Framework Directive.

Article 1(2) provides:

In particular, where a job classification system is used for determining pay, it must be based on the same criteria for both men and women and so drawn up as to exclude any discrimination on grounds of sex.

The opening phrase 'In particular' underlines a point made clear by the ECJ in *Commission v UK*,[400] namely, that job classification systems merely constitute one of the permissible ways in which equal value can be established. The meaning and effect of this provision were tested in *Rummler v Dato-Druck GmbH*.[401] Ms Rummler brought proceedings against her employer, a printing firm, with the object of having herself placed in a higher category in the pay scale relating to the printing industry. This pay scale, which was nationally agreed, provided for seven wage groups varying according to the work carried out and determined on the basis of degree of knowledge required, concentration, muscular demand or effort, and responsibility. The activities in Wage Group II were those which could be executed with slight previous knowledge and after brief instruction or training, required little accuracy, placed a slight to moderate demand on the muscles, and involved slight or occasionally moderate responsibility. Group III comprised activities which could be executed with moderate previous knowledge and instruction or training related to the particular job, required moderate accuracy, required moderate or occasionally great muscular effort, and involved slight or occasionally moderate responsibility. Group IV covered activities requiring previous knowledge on the basis of instruction or training related to the particular job, occasionally a fair degree of occupational experience requiring moderate accuracy, moderate and occasionally great effort of different kinds, particularly as a result of work dependent on machines, and involved moderate responsibility. It was specified that the evaluation criteria must not be regarded as cumulative in all cases. Ms Rummler was classified in Group III, but argued that she ought to be placed in Group IV, in particular since she was required to pack parcels weighing more than 20 kg, which for her represented heavy physical work. Her employer disagreed, contending that because her job in fact made only slight muscular demands she ought to be classified in Group II. The national court dealing with the case sought a preliminary ruling from the ECJ, asking whether the Equal Pay Directive permits a job classification system to include muscular effort as a criterion of evaluation and, if so, whether account must be taken of the amount of such effort required of women in particular. The practical point at issue was,

---

[399] Op cit, n 28.   [400] Op cit, n 379.
[401] Case 237/85 [1986] ECR 2101. See Arnull, 'Equal Treatment and Job Classification Schemes (1987) 12 ELRev 62.

of course, that certain types of physical work require more effort from women on average than men; it might be said to follow from this that women should be more highly remunerated for such tasks than men, but this might in turn produce the unfortunate consequence that women would become more expensive to employ than men and so might in practice find themselves excluded from the type of work in question.

The ECJ avoided this trap. The employers argued, in accordance with generally accepted theories of the role of job evaluation, that pay criteria must be established to reflect the duties actually performed and not by reference to the personal attributes of the worker who carries them out. They therefore took the view that the criteria of muscle demand and the heaviness of work were not discriminatory in so far as they corresponded to the characteristics of the work actually performed and were used in a system which also referred to the criteria of ability, mental effort, and responsibility. The UK Government, which submitted observations, added its view that the principle of non-discrimination does not preclude the use of a criterion in relation to which one sex has greater natural ability than the other, so long as that criterion is representative of the range of activities involved in the job in question. The Commission pointed out that what has to be judged is whether the classification system as a whole is or is not discriminatory; in other words whether, because of the factors it takes into account, it is in reality loaded in favour of one sex. With these submissions the Court overall agreed, saying:

Where a job classification system is used in determining remuneration, that system must be based on criteria which do not differ according to whether the work is carried out by a man or by a woman and must not be organized, as a whole, in such a manner that it has the practical effect of discriminating generally against workers of one sex. Consequently, criteria corresponding to the duties performed meet the requirements of Article 1 of the Directive where those duties by their nature require particular physical effort or are physically heavy. In differentiating rates of pay, it is consistent with the principle of non-discrimination to use a criterion based on the objectively measurable expenditure of effort necessary in carrying out the work or the degree to which, reviewed objectively, the work is physically heavy. Even where a particular criterion, such as that of demand on the muscles, may in fact tend to favour male workers, since it may be assumed that in general they are physically stronger than women workers, it must, in order to determine whether or not it is discriminatory, be considered in the context of the whole job classification system, having regard to other criteria influencing rates of pay. A system is not necessarily discriminatory simply because one of its criteria makes reference to attributes more characteristic of men. In order for a job classification system as a whole to be non-discriminatory and thus to comply with the principles of the Directive, it must, however, be established in such a manner that it includes, if the nature of the tasks in question so permits, jobs to which equal value is attributed and for which regard is had to other criteria in relation to which women workers may have a particular aptitude. It is for the national courts to determine on a case-by-case basis whether a job classification system as a whole allows proper account to be taken of the criteria necessary for adjusting pay rates according to the conditions required for the performance of the various duties throughout the undertaking.[402]

[402] [1986] ECR 2101, at 2115.

The only difficulty with this view is that the concept of the 'objective' measurement of the amount of physical effort demanded by a particular job is an obscure one. It postulates the existence of an inter-sex person whose characteristics and abilities are neither all-male nor all-female. This is a problem encountered in connection with all analytical systems of job evaluation and carries within it the inherent risk that the assessment will be biased in favour of traditional values, rather than being truly neutral and 'objective'.[403]

The difficulty becomes even more marked in relation to the second part of the national court's questioning, namely, how precisely physical demand is to be measured and what value is to be placed on it. In particular, the national court wanted to know whether values reflecting the average performance of workers of each sex ought to be used. The Court held that they should not:

The answer to Questions 2 and 3 . . . follows from what has already been said in answer to Question 1, that is to say that nothing in the Directive prevents the use in determining wage rates of a criterion based on the degree of muscular effort objectively required by a specific job or the objective degree of heaviness of the job. The Directive lays down the principle of equal pay for equal work. It follows that the work actually carried out must be remunerated in accordance with its nature. Any criterion based on values appropriate only to workers of one sex carries with it a risk of discrimination and may jeopardize the main objective of the Directive, equal treatment for the same work. That is true even of a criterion based on values corresponding to the average performance of workers of the sex considered to have less natural ability for the purpose of that criterion, for the result would be another form of pay discrimination: work objectively requiring greater strength would be paid at the same rate as work requiring less strength.

The failure to take into consideration values corresponding to the average performance of female workers in establishing a progressive pay scale based on the degree of muscle demand and muscular effort may indeed have the effect of placing women workers, who cannot take jobs which are beyond their physical strength, at a disadvantage. That difference in treatment may, however, be objectively justified by the nature of the job when such a difference is necessary in order to ensure a level of pay appropriate to the effort required by the work and thus corresponds to a real need on the part of the undertaking (see the judgment in Case-170/84 *Bilka-Kaufhaus v Von Hartz*).[404]

The answer to the second and third questions must therefore be that it follows from Directive 75/117 that:

(a) criteria governing pay-rate classification must ensure that work which is objectively the same attracts the same rate of pay whether it is performed by a man or a woman;

(b) the use of values reflecting the average performance of workers of one sex as a basis for determining the extent to which work makes demands or requires effort or whether it is heavy constitutes a form of discrimination on grounds of sex, contrary to the Directive;

---

[403] See the remarks of Van Themaat AG in Case 61/81 *Commission v UK*, op cit, n 379, at 2624–5. See also the Report on equal pay for work of equal value by the European Parliament's Committee on Women's Rights and Equal Opportunities, 13 July 2001, A5-0275/2001 final; in its accompanying Resolution, the Committee urged the Commission to propose updating the Equal Pay Directive, in particular in relation to job classification and to the ways in which gender discrimination could be avoided in job classification.   [404] Op cit, n 39.

(c) in order for a job classification system not to be discriminatory as a whole, it must, in so far as the nature of the tasks carried out in the undertaking permits, take into account criteria for which workers of each sex may show particular aptitude.[405]

The practical effect of this judgment is potentially useful. Although it is still far from clear exactly when a job classification system will be discriminatory taken as a whole, not least because there will always be room for argument about what demands a particular job actually makes on the workers carrying it out, there is acknowledged at least the possibility of alleging that a particular classification system falls short of the requirements of EU law. In such a situation, it would be helpful to be able to rely on the direct effect of Article 1(2) of the Directive; whilst this would be impossible, at least as against an employer who was not an organ of the State, if the Directive stood alone,[406] it remains to be seen whether the ECJ would be prepared to enforce Article 141 itself in this situation.[407] It is arguable that if all the Directive achieves legally is a practical elucidation of the general principle articulated in Article 141, then Article 141 itself extends to forbidding discrimination in job classification systems. A litigant facing an allegedly sex dis-criminatory job classification system could then rely simply on the direct effect of Article 141 to have it declared inapplicable. A second way in which this provision could prove of practical use is through the doctrine of supremacy of EU law; if a national law precludes challenge, or makes excessively difficult challenge to a job classification system on the ground of its being sex discriminatory, then that national law itself could be rendered inapplicable because of the conflict with the Directive and Article 141. Such an argument might, for example, be used in the UK, where the Equal Pay (Amendment) Regulations 1983 make it difficult for a litigant to attack a job evaluation study as discriminatory.[408]

Article 2 provides:

Member States shall introduce into their national legal systems such measures as are necessary to enable all employees who consider themselves wronged by failure to apply the principle of equal pay to pursue their claims by judicial process after possible recourse to other competent authorities.

Although physically distanced from it, this provision must be read in conjunction with Article 6, which states:

Member States shall, in accordance with their national circumstances and legal systems, take the measures necessary to ensure that the principle of equal pay is applied. They shall see that effective means are available to take care that this principle is observed.

Together, these provisions require a proper judicial hearing for a claim of denial of the equal pay principle and an effective remedy if the claim proves successful at

---

[405] [1986] ECR 2101, at 2116–17.

[406] Because of the lack of possible horizontal direct effect for directives, discussed in ch 2.

[407] A fortiori does this remain an open question were the situation to arise under either the Race Directive or the Framework Directive.

[408] See the Equal Pay Act 1970, s 2A(2). The EOC might, in such circumstances, bring an action for judicial review of the UK legislation.

the end of the day. One issue of importance in the present context is the relationship between these provisions and Article 141. It has already been seen that, in so far as Article 141 is directly effective, it may be relied on in the national courts to provide a remedy within the same procedural limitations as parallel national proceedings; and it has also been seen that the direct effect of Article 141 may be relied on to demand an equal pay rate with that of the comparator. Neither Article 141 nor the Directive prescribes remedies or procedures which are more precise than this. Under both measures there exists the possibility, however, of alleging that the relevant national remedies and procedures are *defective*; here, the wording of Article 6 of the Directive might be relied upon to lend weight to the direct effect of Article 141, since it provides expressly for 'effective means' of redress. So, for example, if national equal pay legislation allowed only a small claim for compensation in cases where unequal pay was established, rather than a full claim for the difference between what was received and what ought to have been received, the Directive and Article 141 together might be relied upon to enforce the more effective remedy.[409] The remedies provided in the UK before the passage of the Equal Pay (Amendment) Regulations 1983 were certainly inadequate. The Directive requires that 'all employees who consider themselves wronged by failure to apply the principle of equal pay' shall have a right to judicial redress. As seen above, the Commission's successful prosecution of the UK[410] was provoked by the absence of a remedy in the UK at that date for a complainant alleging work of equal value but where the employer was unwilling to commission a job evaluation study. Whether or not the cumbersome procedures available today in UK equal pay claims still fall short of the requirements of the Directive and Article 141 remains to be tested in future litigation.[411]

In cases of sex discrimination over pay which fall outside the scope of the direct effect of Article 141, there is nothing in Articles 2 or 6 of the Directive which creates greater precision and which might therefore supply the missing ingredients for direct effect. A person seeking a remedy in such a claim would therefore be unable to enforce the EU equal pay legislation directly, but might be able to rely on the *Francovich* principle[412] in order to claim damages from the State itself for its breach of EU obligations.

Article 2 of the Directive also refers to the pursuit of claims by 'judicial process'. This wording implies that the issue must be decided by an independent judge, after the hearing of arguments and representations from both parties and in an established court or tribunal. This provision was influential during the drafting of the

---

[409] This is essentially the same argument as that used successfully in Case C-271/91 *Marshall v Southampton and South-West Hants Area Health Authority* [1993] ECR I-4367, discussed in ch 5, to challenge the UK's statutory ceiling on damages for sex discriminatory treatment contrary to the Equal Treatment Directive.   [410] Case 61/81 *Commission v UK*, op cit, n 379.

[411] However, improved procedures for equal value claims were introduced in the UK in 2004; see the Equal Pay Act 1970 (Amendment) Regulations 2004 (SI 2004 No 2352) and the Employment Tribunal (Constitution and Rules of Procedure) Regulations 2004 (SI 2004 No 1861).

[412] Discussed in ch 2.

UK's Equal Pay (Amendment) Regulations 1983, in particular in relation to the way in which equal value was to be assessed. The Regulations provide for the appointment of an 'independent expert' to assess value, but it was regarded as essential that the expert's report be open to challenge before the tribunal hearing the claim, otherwise the process would not be a 'judicial' one.[413] Similarly, where a job evaluation study has already been conducted and has resulted in a finding that the complainant's work is not of equal value to that of the comparator, this must also be open to challenge on the grounds of the scheme being discriminatory in design or operation, otherwise the assessment of value would not be 'judicial'. The words 'judicial process' clearly elucidate Article 141 in a significant respect, and could prove useful to an individual complainant. Quite how they would be useful would again depend on the type of claim being brought: if it was a claim within the area of direct effect of Article 141, it would appear that the allegation of a denial of proper 'judicial process' could also be made directly; if the matter fell outside the direct effect of Article 141 but the defendant was an organ of the State, then it might be argued that this part of the Directive is vertically directly effective; if the Directive were held not to take direct effect, or if the defendant were not an organ of the State, the claimant would need to rely on the *Francovich* principle.

Article 3 requires the repeal of all legislation which conflicts with the equal pay principle:

Member States shall abolish all discrimination between men and women arising from laws, regulations or administrative provisions which is contrary to the principle of equal pay.

Once again, to the extent to which Article 141 is directly effective, it can of course be relied upon to take precedence over any conflicting national law; this is the practical operation of the doctrine of supremacy of EU law.[414] To the extent that it is not so effective, this provision merely casts a duty on the Member States. This duty is unqualified[415] and so extends even to legislation which pre-dated the Directive. There can therefore be no saving legislative provisions preserving pay inequalities, for example, for historical reasons. If the cause of the pay differential between men and women is their difference of sex, then any legislation approving such a situation, whether directly or indirectly, must be repealed.

Article 4 provides:

Member States shall take the necessary measures to ensure that provisions appearing in collective agreements, wage scales, wage agreements or individual contracts of employment which are contrary to the principle of equal pay shall be, or may be declared, null and void or may be amended.

[413] The appointment of an independent expert was subsequently made optional and tribunals empowered to determine equal value by themselves: see the Sex Discrimination and Equal Pay (Miscellaneous Amendments) Regulations 1996 (SI 1996 No 438).   [414] See ch 2.
[415] Apart from in the exceptional circumstances in which Art 307 applies.

This wording indicates that all types of pay discrimination on the ground of sex are barred from collective agreements and the rest; the bar is not restricted merely to direct discrimination, or to that which is overt.[416] By analogy with a decision of the ECJ under a parallel provision of the Equal Treatment Directive,[417] it would appear irrelevant that the collective agreement or wage scale itself produced no binding legal effects; pay discrimination on the ground of sex in its terms is still prohibited, since its existence misleads all who are affected by it. This part of the Directive was given effective teeth by the decision of the ECJ in *Kowalska v Freie and Hansestadt Hamburg*.[418]

Article 5 is concerned with the victimization of those who allege a breach of the equal pay principle:

Member States shall take the necessary measures to protect employees against dismissal by the employer as a reaction to a complaint within the undertaking or to any legal proceedings aimed at enforcing compliance with the principle of equal pay.

This provision is broad, in that it mentions those who have merely made 'a complaint within the undertaking', as well as those who have actually launched legal proceedings. However, it is undesirably narrow in its reference merely to protection against dismissal;[419] the Article appears to provide no protection for those who are ill-treated in some way which falls short of dismissal, such as through a wrongful refusal to promote, or the denial of some benefit extended to other employees.[420] The possible direct effect of this provision is also a matter of some doubt. This is the type of provision which an individual person might well wish to enforce. The ECJ, in its statements about the Equal Pay Directive and its role merely as the elucidator of Article 141, probably did not have this Article specifically in mind, and thus this might perhaps be a way in which the Directive does in fact extend beyond the scope of Article 141. If this were so, Article 5 could of course be enforced (if at all) only vertically, as against an employer who was an organ of the State.[421] If, on the other hand, the Court were prepared to hold that

---

[416] Unlike the position in the UK under the Equal Pay Act 1970, s 3, before the latter's repeal by the Sex Discrimination Act 1986. See also *R v CAC, ex parte Hy-Mac Ltd* [1979] IRLR 461.

[417] Case 165/82 *Commission v UK* [1983] ECR 3431, discussed in ch 5.

[418] Case C-33/89, op cit, n 164. See also Case C-184/89 *Nimz*, op cit, n 262; Case C-127/92 *Enderby*, op cit, n 245; and Joined Cases C-399, 409, & 425/92 and C-34, 50, & 78/93 *Helmig*, op cit, n 13, all discussed above. This case law was of particular significance in the UK before the enactment the Trade Union Reform and Employment Rights Act 1993, s 32, which enabled an individual to bring employment tribunal proceedings to challenge an allegedly discriminatory term of a collective agreement; this amendment to the legislation was introduced in order to settle infringement proceedings which had been threatened by the EC Commission. See also discussion in ch 5.

[419] Contrast the broader protection against victimization contained in the Race Directive, the Framework Directive, and the amended Equal Treatment Directive, discussed in ch 5.

[420] Note, however, that the ECJ gave the equivalent provision in the original version of the Equal Treatment Directive a wide interpretation in Case C-185/97 *Coote v Granada Hospitality Ltd* [1998] ECR I-5199; see ch 5.   [421] Failing this, the *Francovich* principle might provide a remedy.

Article 5 of the Directive simply spells out a principle already contained in Article 141, then, so long as it was regarded as precise enough in its ambit to be capable of direct effect, it could be enforced both vertically and horizontally, in other words, against any type of employer.

Article 7 provides:

Member States shall take care that the provisions adopted pursuant to this Directive, together with the relevant provisions already in force, are brought to the attention of employees by all appropriate means, for example at their place of work.

The Member States were given the unusually short period of one year within which to put into force the legislation necessary to ensure compliance with the Directive:[422] this period was presumably chosen because Article 141 itself had by that time already supposedly been in operation for a number of years. However, there is an essential logical flaw in imposing a time limit in this Directive at all; if, as the Court has maintained, the Directive does no more than spell out the details already required by Article 141, then any action which has to be taken by national legislatures is a response to the Article and not to the Directive.[423] This point was taken by Van Themaat AG in *Commission v Luxembourg*,[424] although not by the Court itself. The Commission had brought an Article 226 enforcement action in respect of legislation which remained in force in Luxembourg after the period for implementing the Equal Pay Directive had expired. The legislation in question granted to central government and local authority officials a 'head of household allowance', but did so on discriminatory terms, because it was only in exceptional cases (for example, where her husband was incapacitated) that a female official would qualify for the payment. The Luxembourg Government admitted that discrimination was occurring and tried unsuccessfully to defend itself by arguing that it was engaged in procuring the necessary legislative amendments. Van Themaat AG considered that the Commission had made out a successful case of breach of Article 141, rather than of Article 8 of the Equal Pay Directive; he pointed out that, as the Court itself had held in the *Second Defrenne* case,[425] Article 141 became binding as far as the original Member States were concerned as from 1 January 1962.[426] He went on to say:

[T]he terms 'shall ensure . . . and . . . maintain' used in Article 119 do not, in my opinion, stand in the way of the interpretation that the Member States were required to adopt within the said period all the measures needed to ensure the application of that principle, despite the fact that the Article does not expressly refer to 'abolition' or 'the adoption of measures'. That idea is in my view also to be found in the same *Defrenne* judgment in which it is stated, in paragraph 56 of the decision, that as from 1 January 1962 the application of the principle 'was to be fully secured and irreversible . . .'[427]

---

[422] Art 8(1) of the Directive.
[423] See above for discussion of the similar situation in relation to Art 119 and the Occupational Social Security Directive (Directive 86/378, OJ [1986] L225/40).   [424] Case 58/81, op cit, n 14.
[425] Case 43/75, op cit, n 11.   [426] See above.   [427] [1982] ECR 2175, at 2185.

And he concluded:

[T]he Court ruled in the *Defrenne* judgment and reaffirmed in its recent decisions, for example Case 96/80 *Jenkins*,[428] that the purpose of the Directive was to ensure the proper implementation of Article 119, but was unable to reduce the effectiveness of that Article or modify its temporal effect. According to paragraph 54 of the decision in the *Defrenne* case, the Directive clarifies certain aspects of the material scope of Article 119 and contains various provisions 'whose essential purpose is to improve the legal protection of workers...' In my opinion, however, the present case is not concerned with such measures but with what is laid down by Article 3 of the Directive, namely that 'Member States shall abolish all discrimination between men and women arising from laws, regulations or administrative provisions which is contrary to the principle of equal pay'. However, that provision no longer serves any purpose in relation to Article 119 in the light of the Court's interpretation of the latter. Accordingly, I consider that it was incorrect to seek a declaration from the Court that the Grand Duchy of Luxembourg had failed to fulfil its obligations under Article 119 and the provisions of the Directive. In my view, the Court should confine itself to finding that the Grand Duchy of Luxembourg has infringed Article 119.[429]

The Court itself, in an unusually terse judgment, made no reference to this point at all and merely ruled that Luxemburg was in breach of Article 8(1) of the Directive because of its failure to adopt the necessary legislation within the period prescribed.

The Directive also obliged the Member States to send to the Commission the texts of all the legislation adopted by them by way of implementation of the Directive.[430] Within three years of the Directive's notification they were to forward all necessary information to the Commission to enable it to draw up a report on the application of the Equal Pay Directive for submission to the Council.[431] This report was produced by the Commission on 16 January 1979.[432] It demonstrated clearly that all the Member States had failed in practice to give full implementation to the principle of equal pay, and Article 226 enforcement proceedings were begun in March 1979 against no fewer than seven Member States. Ultimately, the report resulted in the Commission's prosecutions of the UK and Luxembourg before the ECJ, discussed above. A judicial action was also begun against Belgium,[433] but was discontinued after the Belgian Government adopted the measures necessary to fulfil its obligations under the Directive.

Even in recent times, however, the principle of equal pay has remained unfulfilled in practice. In 1994, the Commission issued a Memorandum on Equal Pay for Work of Equal Value,[434] which demonstrated that the pay gap between men and women remained wide and was, in some cases, still widening. Although it observed that there was an absence of adequate data on this matter, it was able to find some statistical evidence to support its claims: it found that in no Member State did women earn more than 84.5% of men's earnings; in the UK, women on average earned 68.2% of the male rate in manual jobs and only 54.2% in

---

[428] Op cit, n 195.   [429] [1982] ECR 2175, at 2186.   [430] Art 8(2) of the Directive.
[431] Ibid, Art 9.   [432] COM (78) 711 final.   [433] Case 57/81.   [434] COM (94) 6 final.

non-manual jobs; only two Member States scored worse: 69.1% for manual rates in Ireland and 65.1% for manual rates in Luxembourg.[435] The impoverished position of women in the pay leagues was attributed by the Commission to their vertical and horizontal segregation in the workforce, to a general lack of objectivity in pay evaluation systems, and to inequality in collective agreements. It submitted that a strategy to improve matters should focus on better systems for data collection to enable wage comparisons between men and women across broad sectors of activity, and on the improved dissemination of information about the law; it also promised to continue to have recourse to its power of prosecution of Member States under Article 226 'where this is considered appropriate'.[436] In addition, it floated the idea of issuing a Code of Practice on the implementation of the equal pay principle, a step it ultimately took in 1996. Sadly, in 2004 it concluded that the picture had hardly changed, the gender pay gap still averaging 16% throughout the EU. It commented that this pay gap is significantly higher in the private sector than the public sector, and attributed it in large part to differences in labour market participation, sex segregation, career and wage structures, and the relative under-valuing of female-dominated areas of employment. However, the 2004 Report conceded that the gender pay gap has taken on a higher profile in recent years within the Member States and that some countries have taken significant steps to implement policies to address the link between it and labour-market segregation. It nevertheless ended by inviting the European Council to urge the Member States to pay special attention to taking specific measures, in cooperation with the social partners, to reduce the gender pay gap.[437]

The Code of Practice on the Implementation of Equal Pay for Work of Equal Value for Women and Men[438] 'aims to provide *concrete advice* for employers and collective bargaining partners at business, sectoral or intersectoral level to ensure that the principle of equality between women and men performing work of equal value is applied to all aspects of pay. In particular it aims to eliminate sexual discrimination whenever pay structures are based on job classification and evaluation systems'.[439] It proposes that:

[N]egotiators at all levels, whether on the side of the employers or the unions, who are involved in the determination of pay systems, should carry out an *analysis of the remuneration system* and evaluate the data required to detect sexual discrimination in the pay structures so that remedies can be found,

---

[435] See also Clarke, 'Earnings of men and women in the EU: the gap narrowing but only slowly' (Eurostat, 2001). Clarke found that the difference in average earnings between men and women in the 10 countries which acceded to the EU in 2004 was similar to that in the pre-existing Member States: in most, women's earnings as a percentage of men's averaged between 75% and 80%, although it was lower in Cyprus (70%) and higher in Slovenia (almost 90%). [436] COM (94) 6 final, at 40.

[437] 'Report on equality between women and men, 2004', Commission of the European Communities, COM (2004) 115 final. See also the Report on equal pay for work of equal value by the European Parliament's Committee on Women's Rights and Equal Opportunities, 13 July 2001, A5-0275/2001 final. [438] COM (96) 336 final.

[439] Ibid, at 4.

[And] that a *plan for follow-up* should be drawn up and implemented to eliminate any sexual discrimination evident in the pay structures.[440]

The Code goes on to provide details of the kind of information to be collected, how it should be assessed, and appropriate courses of follow-up action.[441]

---

[440] COM (96) 336 final.

[441] Unfortunately, in making suggestions for the evaluation of follow-up action, the Code appears to sanction transitional introduction of the equality principle, a course of action which is plainly contrary to Art 141: see the Code, at 14.

5

The scope and enforcement of the anti-discrimination provisions

It has been seen in earlier chapters that EU law directly prohibits discrimination on the grounds of sex, part-time and temporary working, race or ethnic origin, religion or belief, disability, age, sexual orientation, and nationality. The law prohibiting discrimination on the ground of nationality is not specifically analysed in the present work. Sex discrimination is prohibited by the Treaty, and the aspects of Article 141 devoted to the principle of equal pay were discussed in chapter 4; other types of workplace discrimination based on sex are also forbidden under EU law, primarily as a consequence of the Equal Treatment Directive,[1] but also as a result of further supporting instruments of secondary EU law, which are discussed below. Discrimination on the ground of racial or ethnic origin in a number of different contexts is addressed by the Race Directive,[2] and discrimination in the workplace[3] on the grounds of religion or belief, disability, age, and sexual orientation by the Framework Directive.[4] The Race Directive and the Framework Directive share a number of common features with the Equal Treatment Directive and are likely to be interpreted by the ECJ congruently, not least because of the

[1] Directive 76/207, OJ [1976] L39/40.
[2] Directive 2000/43, OJ [2000] L180/22. The Race Directive was required to be implemented by 19 July 2003. At the time of writing, the Commission had announced its intention of bringing enforcement proceedings against five Member States (Austria, Germany, Finland, Greece, and Luxembourg) for failure to implement the Race Directive by the due date.
[3] The limitation of the scope of the Framework Directive to the workplace is especially significant for those complaining of discrimination on the ground of age; in practice, discrimination is frequently alleged by the elderly in relation to such matters as health care and education, and these matters are not covered by the Directive.
[4] Directive 2000/78, OJ [2000] L303/16. The Framework Directive was required to be implemented by 2 December 2003, except in relation to age and disability; in these last two cases, Member States were permitted to delay implementation until 2 December 2006, provided that they informed the Commission and reported annually to it on the steps they were taking to tackle discrimination in these areas. This stay of execution in relation to age and disability was the result of last-minute political negotiation in the Council, discussed below. It was felt to be especially necessary in relation to age discrimination because of the extreme complexity of regulating this matter in detail. The UK, Sweden, Germany, The Netherlands, and Belgium notified the Commission that they would rely on the three-year extension of the deadline for implementation in relation to age; Denmark notified that it would use one extra year for age. As regards disability, France and Sweden notified the Commission that they would use the extra three years, and the UK and Denmark that they would use one extra year. See further Baker, 'Age Discrimination: implementing the Directive in Europe' (2004) 125 EOR 14.

need for consistency of approach in situations where discrimination on several grounds is alleged to have occurred simultaneously.[5]

Scope of the Equal Treatment Directive, Race Directive, and Framework Directive

The earliest of these three instruments was the Equal Treatment Directive. In common with the Equal Pay Directive,[6] it was prompted by the Council's Resolution of 21 January 1974[7] concerning a social action programme, which included amongst its priorities 'action for the purpose of achieving equality between men and women as regards access to employment and vocational training and promotion and as regards working conditions, including pay'.[8] The Equal Pay Directive was regarded as carrying forward the programme in the field of pay. The Equal Treatment Directive aimed to regulate the other areas mentioned, with the exception of the 'definition and progressive implementation of the principle of equal treatment in matters of social security', which was to be dealt with by means of later instruments.[9] The Preamble to the Directive explains its specific aims as follows:

Whereas Community action to achieve the principle of equal treatment for men and women in respect of access to employment and vocational training and promotion and in respect of other working conditions also appears to be necessary; whereas equal treatment for male and female workers constitutes one of the objectives of the Community, in so far as the harmonization of living and working conditions while maintaining their improvement are *inter alia* to be furthered.[10]

In view of these far-reaching objectives, Article 94, the 'harmonization' Article, was thought to constitute an insufficient legal authority for the Equal Treatment Directive. It is therefore based instead on Article 308, available where action by the EU proves 'necessary to attain, in the course of the operation of the common market, one of the objectives of the Community, and [the] Treaty has not provided the necessary powers'. As discussed in chapter 2, such a legal basis in no way inhibits the potential direct effect of a legal provision, and indeed, as will be seen later in the present chapter, important parts of the Equal Treatment Directive have been held by the ECJ to confer rights directly on individuals. It is unfortunate, however, that a directive was chosen as the type of instrument to be used here, rather than a regulation; the latter could theoretically have been passed, since Article 308 authorizes the taking of 'appropriate measures', and it would have obviated the problem of lack of horizontal direct effect[11] which continues to present a serious practical obstacle to the utility of social policy directives.

---

[5] See Recital 14 of the Preamble to the Race Directive and Recital 3 of the Preamble to the Framework Directive.   [6] Discussed in ch 4.

[7] OJ [1974] C13/1.   [8] See Recital 1 of the Preamble to the Directive.

[9] See Recital 4 of the Preamble to the Directive, and also chs 4 and 8 on the legislation subsequently enacted.   [10] Recital 3.

[11] See discussion in ch 2.

The Equal Treatment Directive was amended in 2002,[12] primarily in order to achieve consistency between itself and the Race and Framework instruments (in so far as they cover common ground).[13] In the discussion of the Equal Treatment Directive which follows, reference will be made to the Directive as amended.

The background to the enactment of the Race and Framework Directives was discussed in chapter 1, where it was noted that there was, at the time of adoption of these instruments, a general and growing concern about racism within the EU, and a desire on the part of the Commission to exploit the political momentum to ensure that the ensuing legislation covered all the grounds set out in the mandating Article 13. It was also regarded as of prime importance that the new anti-discrimination provisions should form part of the *acquis communautaire* before the EU admitted any new Member States. All these considerations led to a somewhat unseemly rush to get the new legislation onto the statute book; whilst there was little real controversy surrounding the content of the Race Directive,[14] the same was not true in relation to the Framework Directive. A formal English text of the final draft of the Framework Directive, which was substantially different from earlier drafts, reached the British Government only one day before the Council meeting at which the instrument was adopted. This meant that the Select Committees on the EU within the UK Parliament were unable to scrutinize it before adoption.[15] In addition, since it too did not see the final draft, the European

---

[12] By Directive 2002/73, OJ [2002] L269/15. The amended instrument must be implemented by the Member States by 5 October 2005.

[13] See in particular Recital 6 of the Preamble to Directive 2002/73.

[14] The Portuguese Presidency of the Council decided to make adoption of the Race Directive its urgent priority in view of the crisis in the relations between the EU and Austria at the time. The UK Government overrode the House of Lords scrutiny reserve on the instrument in its haste to give its assent by the end of June 2000. (The scrutiny reserve applies to all legislative proposals which have been reported on and are awaiting debate; once that debate has taken place the proposal is cleared from scrutiny.) The House of Commons European Scrutiny Committee was able to clear the Directive from scrutiny before the Government assented to it; however, it is noteworthy that the whipping system applies to the Commons Committee, making it much easier for the Government in office to impose its view on it.

[15] Contrary to the Protocol on the role of national parliaments, annexed to the TEC by the Treaty of Amsterdam, which states that the Member States wish 'to encourage greater involvement of national parliaments in the activities of the European Union and to enhance their ability to express their views on matters which may be of particular interest to them'. The Protocol goes on to provide:

'1. All Commission consultation documents (green and white papers and communications) shall be promptly forwarded to national parliaments of the Member States.

2. Commission proposals for legislation as defined by the Council in accordance with Article 151(3) of the Treaty establishing the European Community, shall be made available in good time so that the government of each Member State may ensure that its own national parliament receives them as appropriate.

3. A six-week period shall elapse between a legislative proposal or a proposal for a measure to be adopted under Title VI of the Treaty on European Union being made available in all languages to the European Parliament and the Council by the Commission and the date when it is placed on a Council agenda for decision either for the adoption of an act or for adoption of a common position pursuant to Article 189b or 189c of the Treaty establishing the European Community, subject to exceptions on grounds of urgency, the reasons for which shall be stated in the act or common position'.

Parliament's right to be consulted pursuant to Article 13 was effectively side-stepped;[16] this procedural defect unfortunately raises the spectre of the ECJ ultimately one day declaring the whole instrument *ultra vires*.[17]

A number of significant exceptions were introduced into the Framework Directive at the eleventh hour, and these will be discussed in chapter 6. However, the general point should be made here that this kind of hasty legislation, not to mention the evasion of the process of democratic scrutiny, is extremely undesirable. In the words of the House of Lords Select Committee on the EU:

Nine months of detailed examination . . . failed to produce a text to which all fifteen Member States were prepared to agree. There were then six hours of intense negotiation by the Council, in which several highly significant amendments were made. This extraordinary acceleration was dictated by a Presidency determined to secure political agreement on a given day—prepared, it seems, to make almost any concession in order to secure that agreement. Hurried last-minute bargaining is not the way to prepare good legislation . . . We endorse the comments made in a letter . . . to the Foreign Secretary by Jimmy Hood MP, Chairman of our sister Committee in the House of Commons, that where Ministers negotiate at such a pace, 'the net result may well be poorly drafted and inadequate legislation that leads to severe problems in interpretation and implementation'.[18]

Article 1 of the Equal Treatment Directive enacts the aims of that instrument:

1. The purpose of this Directive is to put into effect in the Member States the principle of equal treatment for men and women as regards access to employment, including promotion, and to vocational training and as regards working conditions and, on the conditions referred to in paragraph 2, social security. This principle is hereinafter referred to as 'the principle of equal treatment.'

2. With a view to ensuring the progressive implementation of the principle of equal treatment in matters of social security, the Council, acting on a proposal from the Commission, will adopt provisions defining its substance, its scope and the arrangements for its application.[19]

The corresponding provision of the Race Directive, Article 1, states simply:

The purpose of this Directive is to lay down a framework for combating discrimination on the grounds of racial or ethnic origin, with a view to putting into effect in the Member States the principle of equal treatment.

The dissatisfaction of the House of Lords Select Committee on the EU with the procedure adopted in relation to the Framework Directive was expressed forcefully in 'The EU Framework Directive on Discrimination', Session 2000-01, 4th Report, HL Paper 13.

[16] The European Parliament had formally asked to be consulted again if the Council were minded to depart from the text which the Parliament had approved; this re-consultation never took place.

[17] Although the time limit for bringing a direct challenge to the Directive has passed, an allegation that the instrument was *ultra vires* might be made in an action invoking domestic legislation based on the Directive; a national court faced with such an allegation might well refer to the ECJ for a preliminary ruling on the matter. The less than edifying role played by the Commission in the procedure surrounding the adoption of the Framework Directive is recounted in the House of Lords Select Committee Report, op cit, n 15.

[18] Ibid, para 17.

[19] The first draft of the Equal Treatment Directive itself included social security as part of the 'working conditions' to which the principle of equal treatment must apply. It was removed from later versions of the instrument because of the complexities involved, but the Commission insisted that a commitment to cover social security in a future piece of legislation be written into the Equal Treatment Directive nevertheless.

Similarly, Article 1 of the Framework Directive provides:

The purpose of this Directive is to lay down a general framework for combating discrimination on the grounds of religion or belief, disability, age or sexual orientation as regards employment and occupation, with a view to putting into effect in the Member States the principle of equal treatment.

It is to be observed at the outset that these formulations are subtly different from one another. The Equal Treatment Directive does not refer to discrimination, but instead simply seeks to put into effect the wider principle of equal treatment. The other two instruments refer both to non-discrimination and to the principle of equal treatment. On the other hand, they express their aims in more tentative terms, speaking of putting a mere 'framework' or 'general framework' into place 'with a view to' the achievement of equality. It is to be hoped that this less determined phraseology will not be interpreted by the Court as undermining the capacity of these instruments to take direct effect.[20]

The exclusion of social security schemes from the ambit of the Equal Treatment Directive in consequence of Article 1(2) is not complete.[21] The ECJ held in *Marshall v Southampton and South West Hants Area Health Authority*[22] that since the Equal Treatment Directive expresses a principle of fundamental importance, the derogation from it contained in Article 1(2) must be strictly construed.[23] Indeed, as Lenz AG has pointed out,[24] 'If matters of social security were to be excluded entirely from the scope of the Directive, the express reference to social security in Article 1(1) would make no sense'.[25] This is important in view of the limitations on the scope of the Social Security Directive,[26] discussed in chapter 8. In *Meyers v Adjudication Officer*,[27] the Court held that a social security scheme falls within the Equal Treatment Directive, 'if its subject-matter is access to employment, including vocational training and promotion, or working conditions'.[28] Thus, the payment of family credit in the UK was governed by the Equal Treatment Directive because, albeit within the formal scheme of social security, family credit was linked to the employment relationship; it was payable only where, at the time of making the claim, the claimant, or his or her spouse or partner, was employed,[29] and the purpose of the benefit was to encourage low-paid workers to remain in employment.[30] Its status was not undermined, according to the Court, by the fact that the benefit was always payable to the female partner, even where it was the male partner who was

---

[20] There is an obvious parallel with the robust attitude which the ECJ took to the direct effect of the equal pay principle in Case 43/75 *Defrenne v Sabena* [1976] ECR 455, as to which see ch 4.

[21] Cf Case 192/85 *Newstead v Department of Transport* [1987] ECR 4753.

[22] Case 152/84 [1986] ECR 723, discussed further below.   [23] Ibid, at 746.

[24] In *Meyers v Adjudication Officer* Case C-116/94 [1995] ECR I-2131, at 2136.

[25] See also Van Gerven AG in Joined Cases C-63 & 64/91 *Jackson and Cresswell v Chief Adjudication Officer* [1992] ECR I-4737, at 4767.   [26] Directive 79/7, OJ [1979] L6/24.

[27] Op cit, n 24.

[28] Ibid, at 2149. But cf the comments of Jacobs AG in Joined Cases C-245 & 312/94 *Hoever v Land Nordrhein-Westfalen* [1996] ECR I-4895.

[29] In addition, the claimant's income must not exceed a stated level and there must be a child or other dependent person in the household.

[30] See also Case C-78/91 *Hughes v Chief Adjudication Officer* [1992] ECR I-4839.

employed, nor by the fact that entitlement to the benefit lasted for twenty-six weeks irrespective of the earnings of the family during that period. Conversely, the Court held in *Jackson and Cresswell v Chief Adjudication Officer*[31] that income support in the UK was not within the scope of the Equal Treatment Directive because the 'subject matter' of the scheme was not access to employment; rather, its purpose was exclusively the support of people in receipt of low incomes.[32] As regards the Race Directive, the borderline between social security and access to employment does not pose a problem since, as will be seen below, the directive applies expressly to social protection, including social security, as well as to access to employment. However, the Framework Directive in Article 3(3) states that it is not to apply to 'payments of any kind made by state schemes or similar, including state social security or social protection schemes'. Recital 13 of the Preamble to the Directive also provides that the instrument does not apply 'to any kind of payment made by the state aimed at providing access to employment or maintaining employment'. Situations of the type presented in *Meyers* would therefore not fall within its field of application.

It should be noted that the Equal Treatment Directive and the Framework Directive are confined in their application to the workplace, whilst the Race Directive is not so confined.[33] In addition, as discussed in chapter 6, the Framework Directive contains some very wide-ranging exceptions, especially in relation to age. This has led to the frequent comment that there is now a hierarchy of provisions in the sphere of non-discrimination law, with racial discrimination at the top and age discrimination at the bottom.[34]

It would seem to be the intention of all three of these articles that equal treatment should be the rule throughout the territory covered by the Community. However, they do not make plain the precise geographical scope of the obligations they place on the Member States. At the heart of the difficulty is the fact that they do not define such crucial terms as 'treatment' and 'employment'. This leads to potential, but as yet unresolved, difficulties in cases with a multi-national element. For example, do the Directives govern the case where a job offer is made in a Member State but the job is to be performed outside that Member State? If so, does it make any difference whether the job is to be performed inside or outside the territory of the EU? Does it make any difference where a job offer is actually made if the prospective employer is based in a Member State? In the light of the fundamental importance which the ECJ attaches to the principle of equality, it is arguable that the Directives should be engaged whenever there is a factual link between the employment and a Member State; thus, where a job offer (or other potentially discriminatory act) takes place on the territory of a Member State, or where the employer is based in that Member State, or where the job is to be

---

[31] Op cit, n 25.

[32] See also discussion of these cases by Stix-Hackl AG in Case C-186/01 *Dory v Germany* [2003] ECR I-2479.   [33] This is discussed further below.

[34] See, eg, Schiek, 'A New Framework on Equal Treatment of Persons in EC Law?' (2002) 8 ELJ 290.

performed in that Member State, then the requirements of the Directives should have to be complied with by the State concerned.[35]

It is evident from the subject matter of all three Directives that they are intended to protect human beings, and the instruments frequently use expressions such as 'men', 'women', 'individual', and 'persons'. However, the Race Directive is also apparently intended to protect legal entities such as companies or other associations; this appears from Recital 16 of its Preamble (of which there is no counterpart in the Equal Treatment Directive or the Framework Directive), which states:

It is important to protect all natural persons against discrimination on grounds of racial or ethnic origin. Member States should also provide, where appropriate, and in accordance with their national traditions and practice, protection for legal persons where they suffer discrimination on grounds of the racial or ethnic origin of their members.

A subtle distinction between the wording of the three Directives is encountered in their respective Articles 2(1). The Equal Treatment Directive provides:

For the purposes of the following provisions, the principle of equal treatment shall mean that there shall be no discrimination whatsoever on grounds of sex . . .

Likewise, the Framework Directive states:

For the purposes of this Directive, the 'principle of equal treatment' shall mean that there shall be no direct or indirect discrimination whatsoever . . .

However, the Race Directive omits the word 'whatsoever':

For the purposes of this Directive, the principle of equal treatment shall mean that there shall be no direct or indirect discrimination . . .

It is to be hoped that this discrepancy will be taken to be of no theoretical or practical importance by the ECJ.[36]

Article 2(1) of each of the three Directives would appear, taken alone, to be incapable of taking direct effect, since the provision does not elaborate on the circumstances in which it is to operate. When combined with the later provisions of the Directives, however, outlawing discrimination in relation to specifically defined matters, there seems little doubt that this paragraph can be relied upon by individual litigants to ensure that both direct and indirect discrimination are forbidden.[37]

[35] As regards nationality, the ECJ has held that the principle of non-discrimination applies in judging all legal relationships in so far as those relationships, by reason either of the place where they are entered into or of the place where they take effect, can be located within the territory of the Community: Case 36/74 *Walrave and Koch v Union Cycliste Internationale* [1974] ECR 1405, and Case C-237/83 *Prodest v Caisse Primaire d'Assurance Maladie de Paris* [1984] ECR 3153.

[36] However, in Case C-13/94 *P v S and Cornwall County Council* [1996] ECR I-2143, the ECJ quoted the wording of Article 2(1) to support its conclusion that the Equal Treatment Directive is the expression, within its field, of the principle of equality which it holds to be one of the fundamental principles of Community law; see discussion in chs 1 and 7.

[37] See the Court's comments to this effect in relation to sex discrimination in *Marshall*, op cit, n 22, and in Case 222/84 *Johnston v Chief Constable of the RUC* [1986] ECR 1651. It is highly likely that the same principle will apply in relation to the Race Directive and the Framework Directive.

Workplace provisions of the Equal Treatment Directive, Race Directive, and Framework Directive

Article 3 of each of these Directives sets out the circumstances in which discrimination within the workplace is prohibited. Thus, Article 3 of the Equal Treatment Directive provides:

1. Application of the principle of equal treatment means that there shall be no direct or indirect discrimination on the grounds of sex in the public or private sectors, including public bodies, in relation to:

   (a) conditions for access to employment, to self-employment or[38] to occupation, including selection criteria and recruitment conditions, whatever the branch of activity and at all levels of the professional hierarchy, including promotion;
   (b) access to all types and to all levels of vocational guidance, vocational training, advanced vocational training and retraining, including practical work experience;
   (c) employment and working conditions, including dismissals, as well as pay as provided for in Directive 75/117/EEC;
   (d) membership of, and involvement in, an organisation of workers or employers, or any organisation whose members carry on a particular profession, including the benefits provided for by such organisations.

The equivalent provisions in the Race Directive and the Framework Directive are in substantially identical terms.[39]

Article 3 of the Equal Treatment Directive was amended by Directive 2002/73.[40] One technical consequence of this is that the provisions formerly contained in Articles 3, 4, and 5 are now all absorbed into Article 3. A much more important consequence of the amendment, however, is that pay appears to have been brought within the purview of the Equal Treatment Directive. If it were the case that pay had by this process been subjected to exactly the same rules as any other aspect of employment, this would make it possible to engage in hypothetical comparisons between the pay of the two sexes; in other words, there would be the potential to challenge sexually discriminatory differentials as between male and female work which is not alleged to be identical or of equal value. As seen in chapter 4, the ECJ does not appear to permit this pursuant to Article 141, whereas the definition of

[38] For reasons unknown to the present author, the word 'and' takes the place of 'or' here in the Race Directive.
[39] Note, however, that the opening words are different. Art 3(1) of the Race Directive begins: 'Within the limits of the powers conferred upon the Community, this Directive shall apply to all persons, as regards both the public and private sectors, including public bodies...' Art 3(1) of the Framework Directive provides: 'Within the limits of the areas of competence conferred on the Community, this Directive shall apply to all persons, as regards both the public and private sectors, including public bodies...' This formulation was, no doubt, adopted in order to make it clear that discrimination could not be proscribed using Art 13 as a base outside the limits of competence of the European Community itself. The relevance of this is more obvious in relation to the Race Directive than the Framework Directive, since the former, but not the latter, steps outside the area of work which it is clearly within the Community's sphere of competence to regulate.   [40] OJ [2002] L269/15.

direct discrimination now contained in Article 2(2) of the Equal Treatment Directive does permit such comparisons.[41]

There are strong arguments both in support of and in opposition to the contention that pay is now subject to the regime of the amended Equal Treatment Directive. The most obvious argument in favour of the contention is that this is what the new paragraph actually says; this is the natural meaning of the language used. To this the reply may be made that the paragraph goes on to qualify the statement by adding 'pay as provided for in Directive 75/117'. One way in which this phrase might be interpreted is as meaning that the principles relating to equal pay are to be applied as in the same fashion as they have hitherto been applied pursuant to the Equal Pay Directive; in other words, the way in which the equality principle is to be applied in the field of pay is not intended to change. If this is what was meant, it may be asked why the paragraph does not refer expressly to the way in which the equal pay principle applies pursuant to the far more important Article 141 of the Treaty. Perhaps the answer is that the drafter of the amending Directive was being careful not to appear to be suggesting that secondary EU law could encroach upon a Treaty provision. However, this is an unconvincing response if the whole purpose of the qualifying phrase is intended to suggest that the old law on equal pay as applied in the past remains untouched. It would be wholly different if it was intending to reform that old law.

A second argument in favour of the proposition that pay is indeed today within the regime created by the amended Equal Treatment Directive flows from the explicit intention underlying the amending instrument, namely, the alignment of the law on sex discrimination with that pursuant to the Race Directive and the Framework Directive. The whole idea was to achieve consistency across the board, in the interests of fairness and ease of understanding. If equal pay is not included within the scope of the amended Equal Treatment Directive, this purpose will not be achieved. There will remain one body of law on pay and another on the other aspects of sex equality. Indeed, there will be two bodies of law applicable to Article 141 of the Treaty, since its expansion by the Amsterdam Treaty to cover equal treatment in addition to equal pay. Worse, since there is nothing to suggest that the old law on equal pay will apply to discrimination in relation to pay contrary to either the Race Directive or the Framework Directive, there may possibly develop different bodies of law on pay equality depending on whether the ground of discrimination is sex on the one hand, or one of the other prohibited categories on the other hand.

Nevertheless, there are powerful arguments to support the notion that the amending instrument did not intend to re-write the ECJ's case law on equal pay. The wording 'pay as provided for in Directive 75/117' was inserted into the text of the amending instrument after the intervention of the European Parliament, and it appears that it was inserted specifically in order to indicate that there was no intention to upset the *acquis communautaire*. Pay, it might be said, has always been treated differently from other aspects of sex discrimination, and there would be a general expectation that this tradition would continue. This proposition is lent support by

[41] See ch 3.

Recital 16 of the Preamble to the instrument amending the Equal Treatment Directive, which describes the principle of equal pay as established by the ECJ as an 'essential and indispensable part of the *acquis*'. In addition, a change of this magnitude might be expected to be presaged by some of the earlier *travaux* and working documents which preceded the amending Directive, but there is no evidence to this effect. Again, this argument is open to criticism; the definition of indirect discrimination which was contained in the Burden of Proof Directive was re-cast by the amending Directive, without so much as a mention of its former authority. If such a change can be made without further explanation, then it is hard to see why the same should not be said of the inclusion of pay within the amended Equal Treatment Directive.

However, the Commission appears to be proceeding on the assumption that the law on equal pay for men and women has not been changed by the amended Equal Treatment Directive; this is evidenced by a proposal which it published in April 2004 for a consolidation of all the existing law on sex discrimination.[42] The proposed Directive would simply enact the existing case law of the ECJ on the need for, and scope of, comparison in equal pay claims.[43]

On balance, it therefore seems likely that the old law on pay equality will continue to apply, as least as far as sex discrimination is concerned. This then raises the further problem of the relationship between Article 141 and the Equal Treatment Directive.[44] Can the Directive be taken to influence the concept of discrimination in any way at all for the purposes of the Treaty Article? If not (and of course secondary legislation is not normally permitted to re-write primary legislation), what are the lines of demarcation between the two instruments? It can perhaps be postulated that the meaning of 'pay' for the purposes of Article 141[45] will be thrown into sharp focus. On the one hand, the ability of Article 141 to take horizontal direct effect and to trump exceptions linked to pensionable age[46] encourages litigants to argue for a broad interpretation of 'pay' as therein defined; on the other hand, the ability of the Equal Treatment Directive to accommodate claims for hypothetical comparison may drive litigants to argue that aspects of a contract of employment, though they could in a broad sense be regarded as consideration provided for the employee by the employer, are not 'pay' within the meaning of Article 141, or can anyway also be regarded as also falling within the scope of the Directive. The vexed relationship between Article 141 and the Directive is discussed in greater detail below in relation to discrimination over dismissal and working conditions.

[42] COM (2004) 279 final.

[43] As to which, see ch 4. The Commission's proposal is not entirely internally consistent, however, since it also refers to the need to apply the same definitions in all the areas covered by the new directive.

[44] The Court has, at least in the past, taken the view that Art 141 and the Equal Treatment Directive are mutually exclusive; see Case C-342/93 *Gillespie v Northern Health and Social Services Board* [1996] ECR I-475, at 501. This was said to be clear from the second recital to the Directive's Preamble, which provides: 'Whereas, with regard to pay, the Council adopted [the Equal Pay Directive] . . .' See also Case C-411/96 *Boyle v EOC* [1998] ECR I-6401, and Case C-166/99 *Defreyn v Sabena SA* [2000] ECR I-6155. Cf the view expressed by Van Gerven AG in C-262/88 *Barber v Guardian Royal Exchange Assurance Group* Case [1990] ECR I-1889, at 1925.   [45] Discussed in ch 4.

[46] See ch 4.

A particular difficulty in relation to the scope of the Framework Directive arises in the context of sexual orientation discrimination. It was seen in chapter 4 that 'pay' has generally been given a broad interpretation for the purposes of equal pay for men and women, and that it includes employment benefits in the form of survivors' pensions in occupational pension schemes.[47] It would therefore appear strongly arguable, at least at first glance, that a surviving partner to a gay partnership would be entitled to rely on the Directive to forbid discrimination in relation to such a pension. However, Recital 22 of the Preamble to the Framework Directive provides that the instrument is 'without prejudice to national laws on marital status and the benefits dependent thereon'. A curious feature of the drafting of the Directive is that this provision is not replicated in the body of the instrument. The issue therefore is whether it can actively constrain the meaning to be placed on Article 3, given the usual principle that a provision in a preamble is no more than an aid to interpretation. The question had not at the time of writing come before the ECJ, but it was put to Richards J in *R (on the application of Amicus—MSF section) v Secretary of State for Trade and Industry*.[48] When the claim was brought, it was not possible under UK law for gay couples to marry or to contract any form of civil partnership akin to marriage, and the allegation therefore was that implementing legislation which restricted access to benefits to married people was discriminatory on the ground of sexual orientation.[49] Richards J proceeded on the assumption that issues of discrimination by reference to marital status fall within the Community's competence. He concluded that, despite the difficulty of giving legal force to a mere provision of a preamble, Recital 22 does limit the substantive scope of the Framework Directive since '[t]o hold otherwise would be to frustrate the legislative intention'.[50] He distinguished the decision in *KB v National Health Service Pensions Agency*,[51] in which the ECJ had held that UK legislation making it impossible for transsexuals to marry breached Article 141 by excluding a transsexual partner from the right to a survivor's pension; he held that the same principle could not be extended to homosexuals since the ECJ's reasoning had been specifically restricted to transsexuals and had relied heavily on a decision of the European Court on Human Rights that the relevant UK legislation breached the ECHR.[52] Even if it were wrong to conclude that Recital 22 limits the scope of the Framework Directive, Richards J nevertheless concluded that a restriction on occupational benefits by reference to marital status was neither directly nor indirectly discriminatory against homosexuals. It was not directly discriminatory because it was based on marriage, not sexual orientation. The judge rejected the argument that a requirement of being married was a requirement with which (at the

---

[47] See, in particular, Cases 75 & 117/82 *Razzouk and Beydoun v Commission* [1984] ECR 1509; Joined Cases C-109, 110, 152, & 200/91 *Ten Oever v Stichting Bedrijfspensioenfonds voor het Gazenwassers- en Schoonmaakbedrijf* [1993] ECR I-4879; and the Occupational Social Security Directive, Art 4(b).
[48] [2004] IRLR 430.
[49] The UK Government's view that such legislation was permitted by the Framework Directive was made clear in *Equality and Diversity: the Way Ahead* (DTI, 2002).   [50] [2004] IRLR 430, at 451.
[51] Case C-117/01 [2004] 1 CMLR 28, discussed in ch 1.
[52] *Goodwin v UK* (2002) 35 EHRR 447, discussed in ch 7.

time of the litigation) only opposite-sex partners could comply and that it was therefore necessarily discriminatory; he did so on the basis that the consistent approach of the ECJ in this area has been to hold that marriage cannot be compared with other relationships. Similarly, the situation was not indirectly discriminatory, since married and unmarried couples are not in a materially similar situation. Finally, he ruled that, even if the UK implementing legislation could be held to be indirectly discriminatory, it was justifiable because its aims fell within the broad margin of discretion permitted to the Member States over social policy.

Decisions of the ECJ in sex discrimination claims have established some important principles about the substance and effect of what is now Article 3. It is to be anticipated that much of this case law will also be applicable to the Race Directive and the Framework Directive. In particular, what are today paras (a) and (b), in conjunction with Article 2(1) of the Directive, were held by the ECJ in *Johnston v Chief Constable of the RUC*[53] to take direct effect. What is today contained in para (c) relating to working conditions was also held to be directly effective in *Marshall v Southampton and South-West Hants Area Health Authority*.[54]

'Access' to employment has been given a wide meaning.[55] In *Meyers v Chief Adjudication Officer*,[56] the Court held that it is 'not only the conditions obtaining before an employment relationship comes into being' which are covered by the concept of 'access' to employment; it also extends to factors which influence a person's decision as to whether or not to accept a job offer. Thus, 'the prospect of receiving family credit if he accepts low-paid work encourages an unemployed worker to accept such work, with the result that the benefit is related to considerations governing access to employment'.[57] On the other hand, in *Jackson and Cresswell v Chief Adjudication Officer*,[58] the Court held that where a social security benefit scheme is merely intended to provide income support for those with insufficient means:

[T]he assertion that the method of calculating claimants' actual earnings, which are used as the basis for determining the amount of the benefits, might affect sole mothers' ability to take up access to vocational training or part-time employment, is not sufficient to bring such schemes within the scope of Directive 76/207.[59]

'Working conditions' are not confined to those set out in the contract of employment or applied by the employer in respect of a worker's employment. Having established this principle, the Court was able to go to hold in *Meyers v Chief Adjudication Officer*[60] that family credit in the UK, although a social security benefit, also constituted part of a person's 'working conditions'.

---

[53] Case 222/84, op cit, n 37. See also Morris, 'Sex Discrimination, Public Order and the European Court' (1987) PL 334, and Arnull, 'The Beat Goes On' (1987) 12 ELRev 56.   [54] Op cit, n 22.

[55] For example, in Case C-79/99 *Schnorbus v Land Hessen* [2000] ECR I-10997, the ECJ held that national provisions governing the date of admission to practical legal training (which was a prerequisite for the relevant judicial or higher civil service) fell within the scope of the Equal Treatment Directive.

[56] Op cit, n 24.

[57] Ibid, at 2151. But note the non-applicability of the Framework Directive to social security schemes, discussed above.   [58] Op cit, n 25.

[59] Ibid, at 4782. See also Case C-77/95 *Züchner v Handelskrankenkasse Bremen* [1996] ECR I-5689.

[60] Op cit, n 24

What is today para (c) is breached where a Member State maintains in force a law prohibiting night work in industry by women (but not men).[61] The direct effect of the paragraph can be relied upon in such circumstances.[62] In accordance with the Court's usual reasoning in this regard, the direct effect of the Article does not excuse a Member State from legislating to give effect to the Directive.[63]

Discrimination in relation to dismissal has proved an important area in practice; this is unsurprising, since recent decades have witnessed several periods of economic difficulty. In addition, an employee who has been dismissed may well be less reluctant to sue a former employer than one who is still hoping to be employed or promoted. Although the ECJ has generally shown considerable sympathy for the dismissed employee, there are limits to its compassion, as demonstrated by *Kachelmann v Bankhaus Herman Lampe KG*.[64] German legislation provided that employers seeking to make their employees redundant must choose those for whom redundancy would be the least damaging. However, it had been established that full- and part-timers could not be compared for this purpose. The ECJ held that this constituted *prima facie* indirect sex discrimination, since part-timers would find it more difficult to find new jobs than full-timers because of the significantly larger number of full-time jobs on the market. However, the Court went on to hold that the purpose of the national legislation was to protect workers facing redundancy whilst at the same time taking into account the employer's needs. It was clear that:

[J]ob comparability [was] determined according to the actual content of the respective employment contracts, by assessing whether the worker whose job is being abolished . . . would be capable, having regard to his professional qualifications and the activities he has hitherto been carrying out . . . , of carrying out the different but equivalent work done by other workers.

Application of those criteria may well create an indirect disadvantage for part-time workers because their jobs cannot be compared with those of full-time workers. However . . . if job comparability between full-time and part-time workers were to be introduced . . . that would have the effect of placing part-time workers at an advantage, while putting full-time workers at a disadvantage. In the event of their jobs being abolished, part-time workers would have to be offered a full-time job, even if their employment contract did not entitle them to one.

The question whether part-time workers should enjoy such an advantage is a matter for the national legislature, which alone must find a fair balance in employment law between the various interests concerned.[65]

---

[61] Case C-197/96 *Commission v France* [1997] ECR I-1489.

[62] Case C-345/89 *Stoeckel* [1991] ECR I-4047. Cf Case C-158/91 *Levy* [1993] ECR I-4287, and Case C-13/93 *Office National de l'Emploi v Minne* [1994] ECR I-371, where, as discussed in ch 2, France was permitted to rely on Art 307 to preserve national legislation which conflicted with the Directive but which was necessary in order to comply with a pre-existing international obligation pursuant to ILO Convention No 89 which France had not at the relevant date yet renounced. See also Wuiame, 'Night Work for Women—*Stoeckel* Revisited' (1994) 23 ILJ 95, and Kilpatrick, 'Production and Circulation of EC Night Work Jurisprudence' (1996) 25 ILJ 169.

[63] Case C-197/96 *Commission v France* [1997] ECR I-1489.

[64] Case C-322/98 [2000] ECR I-7505.

[65] Ibid, at 7530–31. It would not presumably be open to the national legislature to introduce a rule which positively favoured part-timers over full-timers, since this could constitute *prima facie* indirect discrimination against men.

Difficult problems have emerged as regards the relationship between what is today para (c) (formerly Article 5 of the Equal Treatment Directive) and certain other provisions of EU law. First of all, how is the principle of equality as regards 'dismissal' to be reconciled with continuing permissible differential State pensionable ages for men and women and their knock-on effects as regards other benefits? The ECJ's case law in this area is really comprehensible only on the basis that it has shifted its ground to a more radical approach over recent years. The issue was first raised before the ECJ in *Burton v British Railways Board*.[66] British Rail had decided to pay voluntary redundancy benefits to certain of its employees, provided that they were aged 55 or over in the case of women and 60 or over in the case of men. Mr Burton was 58 years of age. He wished to take advantage of the scheme and argued that he was being discriminated against unlawfully. Since this issue was at the time of the action excluded from the ambit of the British Sex Discrimination Act 1975 by s 6(4) of that Act, the effect of the Equal Treatment Directive became crucial. The case was sent to the ECJ for a preliminary ruling, and it held that 'dismissal' must be 'widely construed so as to include termination of the employment relationship between a worker and his employer, even as part of a voluntary redundancy scheme'.[67] Access to such a scheme was therefore held to be potentially within the scope of what is now para (c) of the Directive; however, on the facts, this situation did not fall foul of the Directive, it was held, because the qualifying ages for access to the scheme were linked to the differential State retirement pension ages for men and women; both men and women became eligible for entrance to the scheme five years before each reached the State retirement pension age. Since the Social Security Directive[68] permits differential State retirement pension ages to continue for the present, the Court said that it followed that EU law had not been breached. It seems unlikely that the ECJ would today decide this case in the same way in the light of its decision in *Barber v Guardian Royal Exchange Assurance Group*.[69]

Marshall v Southampton and South-West Hants Area Health Authority[70] then made it clear that compulsory retirement also falls within the ambit of the Directive. Ms Marshall, who had been employed as a dietician by the Health Authority, was dismissed by the Authority when she was 62 years of age. The Authority had a policy, which had become an implied term of Ms Marshall's contract of employment, that employees were to retire at the age at which they became entitled to draw the State retirement pension (that is to say, at 65 for men and 60 for women). Ms Marshall did not want to retire at 60, and the Authority waived its normal policy in her case for two years. She complained that her dismissal caused her financial loss

[66] Case 19/81 [1982] ECR 555.   [67] Ibid, at 575.

[68] As to which see ch 8. Note that Recital 14 of the Preamble to the Framework Directive also states that that instrument is 'without prejudice to national provisions laying down retirement ages'.

[69] Case-262/88 [1990] ECR I-1889. See the comments to this effect of the British Court of Appeal in *Thomas v Adjudication Officer and Secretary of State for Social Security* [1990] IRLR 436.

[70] Op cit, n 22.

because of the difference between her earnings as a dietician and her pension, and she also complained of the premature loss of job satisfaction. Her allegation that the situation contravened the national anti-discrimination legislation was met with the answer that it was saved by the then very broadly drafted s 6(4) of the Sex Discrimination Act 1975. The issue became, as in *Burton*, whether or not the case fell foul of EU law, particularly the 'dismissal' provision of the Equal Treatment Directive. The Health Authority argued that, as in *Burton*, account must be taken of the link between the retirement ages it stipulated contractually and the State retirement pension ages. The laying down of different ages for the compulsory termination of a contract of employment, it argued (with considerable logic on its side), merely reflected the minimum ages fixed by the State scheme: a male employee was allowed to continue in employment until the age of 65 precisely because he was not protected by the provision of a State pension until that age, whereas a female employee could draw a State pension at the age of 60. The ECJ, however, rejected this argument, in doing so drawing a somewhat artificial distinction between retirement age and pensionable age.[71] With the benefit of hindsight, this case can be identified as the beginning of a trend in which the ECJ began to erode the Social Security Directive's exception for State pensionable age and its knock-on effects. It held:

Article 5(1) of Council Directive 76/207/EEC provides that application of the principle of equal treatment with regard to working conditions, including the conditions governing dismissal, means that men and women are to be guaranteed the same conditions without discrimination on grounds of sex. In its judgment in the *Burton* case . . . the Court had already stated that the term 'dismissal' contained in that provision must be given a wide meaning. Consequently, an age limit for the compulsory dismissal of workers pursuant to an employer's general policy concerning retirement falls within the term 'dismissal' construed in that manner, even if the dismissal involves the grant of a retirement pension.

As the Court emphasised in its judgment in the *Burton* case, Article 7 of Council Directive 79/7/EEC [the Social Security Directive] expressly provides that the Directive does not prejudice the right of Member States to exclude from its scope the determination of pensionable age for the purposes of granting old age and retirement pensions and the possible consequences thereof for other benefits falling within the statutory social security schemes. The Court thus acknowledged that benefits tied to a national scheme which lays down a different minimum pensionable age for men and women may lie outside the ambit of the aforementioned obligation.

However, in view of the fundamental importance of the principle of equality of treatment, which the Court has reaffirmed on numerous occasions, Article 1(2) of Council Directive 76/207/EEC, which excludes social security matters from the scope of that Directive, must be interpreted strictly. Consequently, the exception to the prohibition of discrimination on grounds of sex provided for in Article 7(1)(a) of Council Directive 79/7/EEC applies only to the determination of pensionable age for the purposes of granting old age and retirement pensions and the possible consequences thereof for other benefits.

In that respect it must be emphasised that, whereas the exception contained in Article 7 of Council Directive 79/7/EEC concerns the consequences which pensionable age has for social security benefits, this case is concerned with dismissal within the meaning of Article 5 of Council Directive 76/207/EEC.

---

[71] In *Duke v Reliance Systems Ltd* [1988] 2 WLR 359, at 373, Lord Templeman protested that the respondent in that case 'could not reasonably be expected to appreciate the logic of Community legislators in permitting differential retirement pension ages but prohibiting differential retirement ages'.

Consequently, the answer to the first question referred to the Court by the Court of Appeal must be that Article 5(1) of Council Directive 76/207/EEC must be interpreted as meaning that a general policy concerning dismissal involving the dismissal of a woman solely because she has attained the qualifying age for a state pension, which age is different under national legislation for men and for women, constitutes discrimination on grounds of sex, contrary to that Directive.[72]

The Court went on to conclude that what is now Article 3(1)(c) of the Equal Treatment Directive was also directly effective, so as to confer on Ms Marshall rights which she could enforce 'vertically' against an organ of the State.[73]

It therefore appeared after *Marshall* that the ECJ regarded as vital the question of whether the age prescribed governed access to retirement benefits (apparently excluded from the scope of the Directive), or merely dismissal (covered by the Directive). This distinction, however, became blurred, in part as a result of the Court's decision in *Roberts v Tate & Lyle Ltd*.[74] This case clearly demonstrates the impossibility of simultaneously respecting the notion of equality in the context of retirement and preserving differential State retirement pension ages. Ms Roberts was made redundant by Tate & Lyle when she was aged 53, as part of a mass redundancy which followed the closure of the depot at which she worked. She was a member of the Tate & Lyle occupational pension scheme, which was contracted out of the State scheme and thus in a sense constituted a substitute for a State social security benefit.[75] It provided for compulsory retirement with a pension at the age of 65 for men and 60 for women. On the closure of the depot, the employers had agreed severance terms with Ms Roberts's trade union, by virtue of which all employees made redundant were to be offered either a cash payment, or an early pension up to five years before the date of their entitlement under the scheme; thus, the pension would have been payable to women over 55 and to men over 60. The male employees, however, protested that this constituted discrimination against them, so eventually the employers agreed to pay an immediate pension to both men and women over 55. Ms Roberts in turn protested against this solution, arguing that the situation contravened EU law because a male employee was now entitled to receive a pension ten years before his normal retirement age, whereas a female employee received the pension only five years before her normal retirement age. The Court, however, chose to treat this as essentially a dismissal case, saying:

[T]he question of interpretation which has been referred . . . does not concern the conditions for the grant of the normal old-age or retirement pension but the termination of employment in connection with a mass redundancy caused by the closure of part of an undertaking's plant. The question therefore concerns the conditions governing dismissal and falls to be considered under Council Directive 76/207.

Article 5(1) of Council Directive 76/207 provides that application of the principle of equal treatment with regard to working conditions, including the conditions governing dismissal, means that men and women are to be guaranteed the same conditions without discrimination on grounds of sex.

---

[72] [1986] ECR 723, at 745–6.
[73] See ch 2 for discussion of direct effect in relation to directives.
[74] Case 151/84 [1986] ECR 703, noted by Arnull in 'Some More Equal than Others?' (1986) 11 ELRev 229.   [75] See ch 4.

In its judgment in the *Burton* case the Court has already stated that the term 'dismissal' contained in that provision must be given a wide meaning. Consequently, an age limit for the compulsory redundancy of workers as part of a mass redundancy falls within the term 'dismissal' construed in that manner, *even if the redundancy involves the grant of an early retirement pension.*[76]

The Court went on to hold:

Even though the retirement scheme at issue does not *prima facie* discriminate between men and women with regard to the conditions for dismissal, it is still necessary to consider whether the fixing of the same age for the grant of an early pension nevertheless constitutes discrimination on grounds of sex in view of the fact that under the UK statutory social security scheme the pensionable age for men and women is different . . . As the Court emphasised in its judgment in the *Burton* case, Article 7 of Council Directive 79/7 expressly provides that the Directive does not prejudice the right of Member States to exclude from its scope the determination of pensionable age for the purposes of granting old-age and retirement pensions and the possible consequences thereof for other benefits falling within the statutory social security schemes. The Court thus acknowledged that benefits linked to a national scheme which lays down a different minimum pensionable age for men and women may lie outside the ambit of the aforementioned obligation.

However, in view of the fundamental importance of the principle of equality of treatment, which the Court has reaffirmed on numerous occasions, Article 1(2) of Council Directive 76/207, which excludes social security matters from the scope of that Directive, must be interpreted strictly. Consequently, the exception to the prohibition of discrimination on grounds of sex provided for in Article 7(1)(a) of Council Directive 79/7 applies only to the determination of pensionable age for the purposes of granting old-age and retirement pensions and to the consequences thereof for other social security benefits.

In that respect it must be emphasised that, whereas the exception contained in Article 7 of Council Directive 79/7 concerns the consequences which pensionable age has for social security benefits, this case is concerned with dismissal within the meaning of Article 5 of Council Directive 76/207. In those circumstances the grant of a pension to persons of the same age who are made redundant amounts merely to a collective measure adopted irrespective of the sex of those persons in order to guarantee them all the same rights.[77]

Again with the benefit of hindsight, it is probably implicit in this judgment that the ECJ was not concerned about the early retirement pensions granted here, since they were granted to both sexes at the same age. This development was explicitly articulated in *Barber v Guardian Royal Exchange Assurance Group*,[78] in which the ECJ ruled that it is contrary to Article 141 for an occupational pension scheme to adopt different retirement ages for men and women, and for redundancy payments to be related to different ages for the two sexes. The effect of this ruling was clearly to take much of the force and significance out of the ECJ's former distinction between retirement age and pensionable age.

A second line of demarcation which has proved difficult to draw in this area is that between what is now para (c) of the Equal Treatment Directive in its reference to 'working conditions' (formerly Article 5) and Article 141 of the Treaty. Some of the steam may have gone out of this area with the inclusion of 'pay' within the scope of the Equal Treatment Directive, although the Directive's lack of horizontal effect will

---

[76] [1986] ECR 703, at 720, emphasis added.   [77] Ibid, at 720–1.
[78] Case C-262/88 [1990] ECR I-1889, also discussed in ch 4.

as usual render the Treaty a more attractive alternative where the respondent is not an organ of the State.[79] One group of cases before the ECJ seemed to support a distinction between the quantum of the benefit involved (an Article 141 issue) and the conditions under which access to the benefit was granted (an Equal Treatment Directive issue). For example, in the *Burton, Marshall*, and *Roberts* decisions, the Court ruled that, where an age-limit was applied in relation to selection for compulsory retirement, that fell within the Equal Treatment Directive, even though there were financial implications for the litigants involved. However, in *Bilka-Kaufhaus GmbH v Weber Von Hartz*,[80] the Court held that the conditions of access to a supplementary pension scheme were challengeable via Article 141[81] and in *Rinner-Kühn v FWW Spezial-Gebaudereinigung GmbH*,[82] it ruled that an hours-based exclusion from the right to sick pay fell within Article 141.[83] *Barber v Guardian Royal Exchange Assurance Group*[84] also takes this approach. Mr Barber was a member of a pension fund established by Guardian which operated a non-contributory, contracted-out[85] occupational pension scheme. Normal pensionable age under the scheme was 62 for men and 57 for women, but employees' contracts of service also provided that, in the event of redundancy, members of the pension fund were entitled to an immediate pension provided only that they had reached the age of 55 in the case of men and 50 in the case of women. Staff who did not fulfil these conditions received cash benefits calculated on the basis of the number of years of their service and a deferred pension payable at normal pensionable age. Mr Barber was made redundant when he was 52. Guardian paid him the cash benefits just referred to, a statutory redundancy payment, and an *ex gratia* payment. He complained of unlawful sex discrimination on the basis that a woman of his age and in his position would have received an immediate retirement pension, as well as the statutory redundancy payment, and that the total value of these benefits would have been greater than the amount Mr Barber in fact received. One of the questions referred by the Court of Appeal to the ECJ asked whether this was contrary to Article 141, in particular in the light of the fact that the age conditions imposed by Guardian reflected the differential contained in the State pension scheme. The ECJ did not explain how it distinguished this situation from its earlier decisions in *Burton, Marshall*, and *Roberts*, which of course suggested that this was an Equal Treatment Directive issue rather than an Article 141 issue; it simply held:

Article 119 prohibits any discrimination with regard to pay as between men and women, whatever the system which gives rise to such inequality. Accordingly, it is contrary to Article 119 to impose an age

---

[79] See ch 2.   [80] Case 170/84 [1986] ECR 1607.

[81] In Case C-57/93 *Vroege v NCIV Instituut voor Volkshuisvesting BV* [1994] ECR I-4541 and Case C-128/93 *Fisscher v Voorhuis Hengelo BV* [1994] ECR I-4583, the ECJ repeated that it followed from *Bilka* 'that Article 119 covers not only entitlement to benefits paid by an occupational pension scheme but also the right to be a member of such a scheme' (at 4573 and 4593 respectively).

[82] Case 171/88 [1989] ECR 2743.

[83] See also Case C-184/89 *Nimz v Freie und Hansestadt Hamburg* [1991] ECR I-297, and Case C-1/95 *Gerster v Freistaat Bayern* [1997] ECR I-5253.   [84] Op cit, n 78.

[85] See ch 4 for further discussion of 'contracted-out' pension schemes.

condition which differs according to sex in respect of pensions paid under a contracted-out scheme, even if the difference between the pensionable age for men and that for women is based on the one provided for by the national statutory scheme.[86]

Van Gerven AG was considerably more analytical in his treatment of this matter, although it is not clear whether the Court accepted his analysis since it made no reference to it. He submitted:

The judgments in *Defrenne III, Burton, Marshall, Beets-Proper*, and apparently in *Roberts* as well, are all connected with an (age) condition or (age) limit regarding the termination of an employment relationship. That condition or limit was intended to select employees with whom the employment relationship was to be terminated on certain financial conditions. Viewed in those terms, the age condition or age-limit is clearly revealed as a working condition, more particularly as a condition governing dismissal or, in a wider context, termination, that is to say a condition for the selection of employees whose employment relationship is to be terminated ... If, on the other hand, the age condition or limit does not play such a role but relates, as in this case, to the grant of a terminal payment or a pension to employees the termination of whose employment relationship has already been decided upon on the basis of other (supposedly non-discriminatory) factors, then it constitutes a condition governing pay which comes within Article 119. The *Bilka-Kaufhaus* case, in which no age condition was involved, was also concerned with the grant of entitlement to a pension (as was the recent judgment in *Rinner-Kühn* where a condition for the payment of remuneration in the event of illness was brought within Article 119).

Essentially, the distinction does amount to bringing within Article 119 working conditions (including conditions governing dismissal or other forms of redundancy) which directly govern access to, that is to say the grant of, remuneration (including a payment or pension benefit in connection with redundancy), but not the conditions precedent thereto which govern the inception, continuation or termination of the employment relationship, even though those conditions are attended by financial consequences or accompanied by financial provisions (such as terminal payments or pension benefits).[87]

The decision in *R v Secretary of State for Employment, ex parte Seymour-Smith*[88] supports the Advocate General's distinction between a condition governing the grant of a payment and a condition governing the continuation of the employment relationship, although without referring explicitly to his reasoning. The ECJ held there that conditions determining an employee's entitlement to compensation on unfair dismissal fall within Article 141 since they concern access to a form of pay; on the other hand, conditions determining the right to re-engagement or reinstatement fall within the Directive since they involve working conditions.[89]

The fact that the fixing of certain working conditions may have financial consequences is not sufficient to bring such conditions within the scope of Article 141; thus, in *Lommers v Minister van Landbouw*,[90] the ECJ held that the making available to employees of nursery places was a working condition, even though the cost of the nursery places was partly borne by the employer. Similarly, in

[86] [1990] ECR I-1889, at 1953.   [87] Ibid, at 1926–7.
[88] Case C-167/97 [1999] ECR I-623.
[89] See also Case C-236/98 *Jämställdhetsombudsmannen v Örebro läns landsting* [2000] ECR I-2189.
[90] Case C-476/99 [2002] ECR I-2891.

Kutz-Bauer v Freie und Hansestadt Hamburg[91] and *Steinicke v Bundesanstalt für Arbeit*,[92] the Court ruled that schemes offering the possibility of part-time working to older employees affected the exercise of the occupation of the workers concerned and therefore fell within the Equal Treatment Directive, notwithstanding that they had financial consequences.

The application of the principle of equality for men and women has brought to the fore two special cases which merit further consideration. They are where the discrimination encountered is based on pregnancy and where the discrimination takes the form of harassment.

(i) Pregnancy discrimination

In *Dekker v Stichting Vormingscentrum Voor Jonge Volwassen Plus*,[93] the ECJ held that the Directive (today para 3(1)(a)) forbade an employer to refuse to employ a pregnant woman, who was otherwise suitable for the job. The fact of her pregnancy was the most important reason for her non-employment and, since this is a condition which can only apply to members of the female sex, this meant that the employer's action necessarily constituted direct discrimination on the ground of sex.[94] The same principle was applied in *Mahlburg v Land Mecklenburg-Vorpommern*[95] to preclude the non-appointment of a woman to a permanent job in circumstances where it was unlawful under national legislation to employ a pregnant woman;[96] this was notwithstanding the fact that the unequal treatment was 'not based directly on the woman's pregnancy but on a statutory prohibition on employment attaching to that condition'.[97] In both cases, the Court was unimpressed by arguments about the economic plight in which this placed the employer. Neither is the size of the employing undertaking of any relevance.[98] In *Handels-OG Kontorfunktionaerernes*

---

[91] Case C-187/00 [2003] ECR I-2741.   [92] Case C-77/02 [2003] ECR I-9027.

[93] Case 177/88 [1990] ECR I-3941, noted by Asscher-Vonk in (1991) 20 ILJ 152.

[94] For discussion of the meaning of direct discrimination, see ch 3. In Case C-79/99 *Schnorbus v Land Hessen* [2000] ECR I-10997, it was argued that a provision which favoured those who had completed compulsory military service was directly discriminatory against women, since under the relevant national legislation only men could be conscripted. However, Jacobs AG rejected this argument, saying: '[T]here is a distinction to be drawn between a criterion based on an obligation imposed by law on one sex alone and a criterion based on a physical characteristic inherent in one sex alone. No amount of legislation can render men capable of bearing children, whereas legislation might readily remove any discrimination between men and women in relation to compulsory national service' (at 11009). But see also Wintemute, 'When is Pregnancy Discrimination Indirect Discrimination?' (1998) 27 ILJ 23, and Honeyball, 'Pregnancy and Sex Discrimination' (2000) 29 ILJ 43; the latter has argued that *Dekker* does not represent an example of a strict 'but for' test.   [95] Case C-207/98 [2000] ECR I-549.

[96] Query whether the Court would have been prepared to stretch this principle to the non-appointment of a pregnant woman to a fixed-term contract.

[97] [2000] ECR I-549, at 572-3. Non-renewal of a fixed-term contract, if grounded on pregnancy, also breaches the Equal Treatment Directive: see Case C-438/99 *Melgar v Ayuntamiento de Los Barrios* [2001] ECR I-6915.

[98] Case C-109/00 *Tele Danmark A/S v Handels- og Kontorfunktionaerernes Forbund I Danmark (HK)* [2001] ECR I-6993.

Forbund i Danmark v Dansk Arbejdsgiverforening (acting for Aldi Marked K/S),[99] the Court added that the *Dekker* principle holds good throughout the relevant period of maternity leave.[100]

The ECJ has also applied the same principle for the purpose of what is today Article 3(1)(c) of the Equal Treatment Directive; so, for example, it held in *Habermann-Beltermann v Arbeiterwohlfahrt*[101] that the termination of an employment contract on account of the employee's pregnancy, whether by annulment or avoidance, concerns women alone and therefore constitutes direct discrimination on the ground of sex. As will be seen below, dismissal of a pregnant woman is also today rendered unlawful by the Pregnancy Directive.[102]

As discussed in chapter 3, some of the earlier case law of the Court on this subject contained hints that direct discrimination on the ground of pregnancy might sometimes be justifiable,[103] although the Court never actually applied this idea in any of the cases referred to it. Thus, in *Habermann-Beltermann*, it held that where a woman's contract of employment is for an indefinite period, termination on account of her pregnancy is not 'justified' by a statutory provision prohibiting pregnant women from engaging in nightwork.[104] Rather more worryingly, in *Webb v EMO (Air Cargo) Ltd*,[105] where a woman employee was dismissed on account of pregnancy because she would be absent from work during the leave of another employee whom she had been engaged to replace, it held:

[D]ismissal of a pregnant woman recruited for an indefinite period cannot be justified on grounds relating to her inability to fulfil a fundamental condition of her employment contract. The availability of an employee is necessarily, for the employer, a precondition for the proper performance of the employment contract. However, the protection afforded by Community law to a woman during pregnancy and after childbirth cannot be dependent on whether her presence at work during maternity is essential to the proper functioning of the undertaking in which she is employed. Any contrary interpretation would render ineffective the provisions of the Directive.

In circumstances such as those of Mrs Webb, termination of a contract for an indefinite period on grounds of the woman's pregnancy cannot be justified by the fact that she is prevented, on a purely temporary basis, from performing the work for which she has been engaged...[106]

---

[99] Case 179/88 [1990] ECR I-3979; both *Dekker* and *Aldi* are noted by Nielsen in (1992) 29 CMLRev 160. See also More, 'Reflections on Pregnancy Discrimination under EC Law' [1992] JSWFL 48.

[100] See also discussion below of the Pregnancy Directive, Directive 92/85, OJ [1992] L348/1.

[101] Case C-421/92 [1994] ECR I-1657.   [102] Op cit, n 100.

[103] Cf the submissions of Ruiz-Jarabo Colomer AG in *CNAVTS v Thibault* [1998] ECR I-2011, at 2023.

[104] It is, however, clear from the context that the Court was referring here to the possibility of defending the employer's actions through reliance on the defence contained in the Directive for the protection of pregnant women (discussed below); the word 'justified' is sometimes used loosely to connote 'excused', and it seems likely that this was the sense in which the Court intended it here. In other words, it was contemplating a cognate defence, rather than some broad general notion of justification.

[105] Case C-32/93 [1994] ECR I-3567, commented on by More in 'Sex, Pregnancy and Dismissal' (1994) 19 ELRev 653, by Boch in (1996) 33 CMLRev 547, and by Fredman in 'Parenthood and the Right to Work' (1995) 111 LQR 220.   [106] [1994] ECR I-3567, at 3587–8.

The corollary of this holding seemed of course to be that, had Mrs Webb been engaged on a temporary contract, her dismissal might have been 'justified' and thus lawful.[107] That this was not, however, the Court's intention was revealed by its later decision in *Tele Danmark A/S v Handels-og Kontorfunktionaereernes Forbund I Danmark (HK)*.[108] Here it held:

Since the dismissal of a worker on account of pregnancy constitutes direct discrimination on grounds of sex, whatever the nature and extent of the economic loss incurred by the employer as a result of her absence because of pregnancy, whether the contract of employment was concluded for a fixed or an indefinite period has no bearing on the discriminatory character of the dismissal. In either case the employee's inability to perform her contract of employment is due to pregnancy.

Moreover, the duration of an employment relationship is a particularly uncertain element of the relationship in that, even if the worker is recruited under a fixed-term contract, such a relationship may be for a longer or shorter period, and is moreover liable to be renewed or extended.

Finally, Directives 76/207 and 92/85 [the Equal Treatment Directive and the Pregnancy Directive] do not make any distinction, as regards the scope of the principle of equal treatment for men and women, according to the duration of the employment relationship in question.[109]

This case demonstrated what a particularly strict view the ECJ takes of discrimination on account of pregnancy; it ruled there that the Directive precluded the dismissal of a woman on the ground of her pregnancy, notwithstanding that she had been recruited for a fixed term[110] during a substantial part of which she would have been unable to work and despite the fact that she had failed to inform her employer that she was pregnant, even though she was aware of this when the contract of employment was concluded.

The width of the right granted to pregnant employees by the Equal Treatment Directive, and the corresponding difficulties which an employer faces,[111] were well illustrated in *Busch v Klinikum Neustadt GmbH*.[112] A nurse took parental leave after the birth of her first child; although this leave could have lasted for three years, she requested permission to terminate it early and to return to full-time work. At the time of making this request, which her employer granted, she was pregnant again. She did not inform her employer of this second pregnancy, and it had the effect of disbarring her, under the provisions of national legislation, from certain parts of her job as a nurse. Her return to work in these circumstances was motivated by her desire to obtain maternity allowance, which was higher than the allowance paid during parental leave, and also certain supplements to maternity allowance. Her employer considered this conduct to be a breach of the good faith which is implicit

---

[107] See also discussion below in relation to Art 10 of the Pregnancy Directive, op cit, n 100, prohibiting dismissal of a worker on the ground of her pregnancy. On the relationship between the Equal Treatment Directive and the Pregnancy Directive, see Jacqmain, 'Pregnancy As Grounds for Dismissal' (1994) 23 ILJ 355. Article 1(7) of Directive 2002/73 (OJ [2002] L269/15), amending the Equal Treatment Directive, states that the Equal Treatment Directive is 'without prejudice to' the Pregnancy Directive.   [108] Case C-109/00 [2001] ECR I-6993.

[109] Ibid, at 7025.   [110] The ECJ confirmed this statement in Case C-438/99 *Melgar*, op cit, n 97.

[111] As to which see Stott, 'What Price Certainty?' (2002) 27 ELRev 351.

[112] Case C-320/01 [2003] ECR I-2041.

in a contract of employment. It therefore rescinded its consent to her return to work. The ECJ, on being asked about the compatibility of this series of events with the Equal Treatment Directive, reiterated that the Directive prohibits all sex discrimination over working conditions. Such conditions include those applicable to employees who return to work following parental leave. When an employer takes an employee's pregnancy into consideration in refusing to allow her to return to work after parental leave, it is therefore guilty of direct sex discrimination. Furthermore, since the employer may not take the employee's pregnancy into consideration, she is under no obligation to inform the employer that she is pregnant. In addition, the Court pointed out that it was already established that the situation was not excused by a legislative provision which temporarily prevented the employee from carrying out all her employment duties. Neither was Ms Busch's financial motivation of any relevance. Lastly, the Court held that, since the employer could not take the pregnancy into consideration, it could not plead that its consent to the employee's reinstatement was vitiated because it was unaware of her pregnancy; any national law which might serve as a basis for such a claim had therefore to be set aside.

Despite its early case law, some doubt persists in this area as regards the role which might be played by a male, or indeed another female, comparator. The Court began by stating clearly in *Dekker*, and in its subsequent decision in *Webb v EMO (Air Cargo) Ltd*,[113] that there is no need to resort to comparison with the treatment afforded, or which would be afforded, to a member of the opposite sex where the detrimental treatment complained of can be shown to be referable to pregnancy; thus, it is incorrect to draw comparisons between the treatment received by a pregnant woman and that which would be received by a male comparator suffering from some temporary medical ailment.[114] In *Gillespie v Northern Health and Social Services Board*,[115] it also held that women on maternity leave are in a special position which requires them to be given special protection but which is not comparable to that of either a man or of a woman who is actually at work.[116]

However, the spectre of the comparator has nevertheless crept back in in certain circumstances. For example, once the protected period of maternity leave has expired, the treatment received by a woman may be compared with that receivable by a colleague of the opposite sex, even where pregnancy continues to play a causative role in the matter. Thus, in *Aldi*,[117] a woman dismissed for prolonged

---

[113] Case C-32/93, op cit, n 105.

[114] That this principle can also work to the detriment of a woman was revealed by Case C-411/96 *Boyle v EOC* [1998] ECR I-6401, where the ECJ held that it meant that a woman on maternity leave could, unlike a fellow worker on sick leave, be required to repay additional maternity pay above the level of the statutory sick pay minimum in the event of her not returning to work after giving birth.

[115] Case C-342/93, op cit, n 44.

[116] See also Case C-411/96 *Boyle v EOC* [1998] ECR I-6401; Case C-218/98 *Abdoulaye v Renault SA* [1999] ECR I-5723; and Case C-147/02 *Alabaster v Woolwich plc and Secretary of State for Social Security*, judgment of 30 March 2004, nyr, but note the compelling criticism of the ECJ's logic in the submissions of Léger AG.   [117] Case 179/88, op cit, n 99.

absence from work some time after her maternity leave had expired but because of an illness which had its roots in her earlier pregnancy, did not experience unlawful discrimination, since a man who was away from work for comparable periods on account of illness would also have been dismissed. In *Larsson*,[118] this principle was extended to cover a case where the woman's illness began during her pregnancy and was a consequence of that pregnancy but continued after her statutory period of maternity leave had expired. The Court repeated its remarks in *Aldi*, saying:

[I]n the case of an illness manifesting itself after the maternity leave, there is no reason to distinguish an illness attributable to pregnancy or confinement from any other illness, and . . . such a pathological condition is therefore covered by the general rules applicable in the event of illness.[119]

It went on to add that it did not mean by that to draw a distinction

on the basis of the moment of onset or first appearance of the illness. It merely held that, in the factual situation submitted to it on that occasion, there was no reason to distinguish, from the point of view of the principle of equal treatment enshrined in the Directive, between an illness attributable to pregnancy or confinement and any other illness . . .

. . . [M]ale and female workers are equally exposed to illness. Although certain disorders are, it is true, specific to one or other sex, the only question is whether a woman is dismissed on account of absence due to illness in the same circumstances as a man; if that is the case, then there is no direct discrimination on grounds of sex . . .

The Directive therefore does not preclude dismissal on the ground of periods of absence due to an illness attributable to pregnancy or confinement, even where such illness first appeared during pregnancy and continued during and after the period of maternity leave.[120]

Ms Larsson argued that it was discriminatory to take into account her absence from work due to sickness in the interval between the beginning of her pregnancy and the beginning of her maternity leave. If those absences were discounted, together with her annual leave which she had tacked onto the end of her maternity leave, she would have been absent on account of her illness for less than four weeks prior to her dismissal. The Court accepted that during whatever period was permitted to her as maternity leave under national law, she was protected from dismissal on account of absence from work. However:

Outside the periods of maternity leave laid down by the Member States to allow female workers to be absent during the period in which the problems inherent in pregnancy and confinement occur, . . . and in the absence of national or, as the case may be, Community provisions affording women specific protection, a woman is not protected under the Directive against dismissal on grounds of periods of absence due to an illness originating in pregnancy . . . [A]s male and female workers are equally exposed to illness, the Directive does not concern illnesses attributable to pregnancy or confinement.

The principle of equal treatment enshrined in the Directive does not, therefore, preclude account being taken of a woman's absence from work between the beginning of her pregnancy and the beginning of her maternity leave when calculating the period providing grounds for her dismissal under national law.[121]

---

[118] Case C-400/95 *Handels- og Kontorfunktionaerernes Forbund i Danmark, acting on behalf of Helle Elisabeth Larsson v Dansk Handel & Service, acting on behalf of Fotex Supermarked A/S* [1997] ECR I-2757.
[119] Ibid, at 2780.   [120] Ibid, at 2780–1.   [121] Ibid, at 2781–2.

The only mitigation offered by the Court was that today the situation would be dealt with by the Pregnancy Directive:[122]

[T]he Community legislature subsequently provided . . . for special protection to be given to women, by prohibiting dismissal during the period from the beginning of their pregnancy to the end of their maternity leave, save in exceptional cases unconnected with their condition . . . It is clear from the objective of that provision that absence during the protected period, other than for reasons unconnected with the employee's condition, can no longer be taken into account as grounds for subsequent dismissal. However, Directive 92/85 had not yet been adopted when Ms Larsson was dismissed.[123]

However, shortly after this decision, the full ECJ changed its mind.[124] *Brown v Rentokil Ltd*[125] concerned a woman dismissed from her job during pregnancy as a result of absence due to pregnancy-related illness. Her employers argued that a man who had been absent from work for a similar time would also have been dismissed, pursuant to a term contained in the contracts of all Rentokil employees providing that absence for twenty-six weeks would result in dismissal. Advocate General Ruiz-Jarabo Colomer observed that the Court's existing case law in this area was so opaque that it had enabled all the parties, and those who had submitted written observations to the Court, to rely on the same paragraphs of the relevant judgments in support of their disparate views. The Advocate General also pointed out that the decision in *Brown*, though dealing with a time before the entry into operation of the Pregnancy Directive, would continue to have relevance; this was because it would answer the question of whether absence due to pregnancy-related illness during pregnancy could be taken into account to excuse dismissal after the mother's return to work. He submitted that a pregnant woman finds herself in a unique position and cannot be compared with a man; it therefore followed that no absence from work during pregnancy which was attributable to pregnancy-related illness could be taken into account to excuse dismissal. The ECJ agreed, saying:

Articles 2(1) and 5(1) of Directive 76/207 preclude dismissal of a female worker at any time during her pregnancy for absences due to incapacity for work caused by an illness resulting from that pregnancy.

However, where pathological conditions caused by pregnancy or childbirth arise after the end of maternity leave, they are covered by the general rules applicable in the event of illness . . . In such circumstances, the sole question is whether a female worker's absences, following maternity leave, caused by her incapacity for work brought on by such disorders, are treated in the same way as a male worker's absences, of the same duration, caused by incapacity for work; if they are, there is no discrimination on grounds of sex.

It is also clear . . . that, contrary to the Court's ruling in Case C-400/95 *Larsson* . . . , where a woman is absent owing to illness resulting from pregnancy or childbirth, and that illness arose during pregnancy and persisted during and after maternity leave, her absence not only during maternity leave but also during the period extending from the start of her pregnancy to the start of her maternity leave cannot be

---

[122] Op cit, n 100, discussed below.
[123] [1997] ECR I-2757, at 2782. It remains significant nevertheless, for the purposes of UK law, whether the claim is for sex discrimination or for unfair dismissal on account of pregnancy: in the latter, but not in the former, cases there is a cap on the level of compensation receivable.
[124] *Larsson* was decided by the Sixth Chamber of the Court.
[125] Case C-394/96 [1998] ECR I-4185.

taken into account for computation of the period justifying her dismissal under national law. As to her absence after maternity leave, this may be taken into account under the same conditions as a man's absence, of the same duration, through incapacity for work.[126]

It is submitted that this was a well-intentioned decision, from a Court intent on protecting the interests of pregnant women. It does not, however, stand up to logical scrutiny for two reasons.[127] First, it distorts the existing principle that discrimination on the ground of pregnancy is direct discrimination on the ground of sex; this is because it extends it into the postulate that discrimination on the ground of an illness which may occur in pregnancy is discrimination on the ground of that pregnancy. This is to fall into the error of equating pregnancy with illness, contrary to the Court's own earlier assertions. Secondly, the Court's abandonment of its usual yardstick for measuring the kind of treatment which constitutes discrimination is unfortunate; its usual path is to compare the treatment received, or receivable, by the two sexes. Its departure from this path has the consequence that a relatively tangible test is replaced by a subjective judgement. In the absence of the tangible test, problems are to be anticipated where pregnant women allege forms of discrimination other than dismissal (which is automatically caught by the Pregnancy Directive). What, for example, of the pregnant woman, sick or healthy, who is not promoted during her pregnancy? Is such treatment to be presumed to be discriminatory and, if not, how is it to be assessed?

Perhaps for reasons such as that mentioned in the preceding paragraph, the Court has continued to waiver over its test for what amounts to detrimental treatment in the case of pregnant women. It has on several occasions strayed close to comparing the situation of a pregnant woman with that of a male colleague. For example, in *CNAVTS v Thibault*,[128] it was confronted by a woman who had been excluded from an assessment of performance with a view to 'career advancement' to which a collective agreement entitled her colleagues. She was denied this opportunity because the collective agreement extended the right only to those who had been at work for six months of the year; Ms Thibault had been away from work through sickness and as a result of taking maternity leave for longer than six months. The ECJ nevertheless held, in an extremely short judgment, that she must be offered an assessment of performance:

The principle of non-discrimination requires that a woman who continues to be bound to her employer by her contract of employment during maternity leave should not be deprived of the benefit of working conditions which apply to both men and women and are the result of that employment relationship. In circumstances such as those of this case, to deny a female employee the right to have her performance assessed annually would discriminate against her merely in her capacity as a worker because, if she had not been pregnant and had not taken the maternity leave to which she was entitled, she would have been assessed for the year in question and could therefore have qualified for promotion.[129]

---

[126] Case C-394/96 [1998] ECR I-4185, at 4233–4.

[127] For a fuller account of the present writer's criticisms of the ECJ's decision in *Brown*, see the case-note in (1999) 36 CMLRev 625.   [128] Op cit, n 103.

[129] Ibid, at 2035–6.

This analysis appears strikingly similar to a comparison between the woman on maternity leave and her colleagues who remain at work. The Court made no mention of this, but neither did it make its usual statement that a pregnant woman, or a woman on maternity leave, is not to be compared with a male colleague.

Again, in *Handels- og Kontorfunktionaerernes Forbund I Danmark v Faellesforeningen for Danmarks Brugsforeninger*,[130] the Court held that it was contrary to Article 141 for national law to provide that sick workers were entitled to full pay from their employers but to exclude from this principle pregnant employees whose sickness was pregnancy-related. The Court itself was once again brief in its analysis of the situation, saying merely that this was treatment based essentially on pregnancy and was thus discriminatory. However, Advocate General Ruiz-Jarabo Colomer submitted that the issue was 'whether a pregnant woman whose unfitness for work is caused by pregnancy is entitled to the same treatment, as regards pay, as a man who is unfit for work by reason of illness'.[131] He concluded that their situations were indeed comparable and that this was therefore unlawful discrimination. Similarly, in *Boyle v EOC*,[132] the Court held that the Equal Treatment Directive did not preclude an employment contract from stipulating that entitlement to annual leave did not accrue during contractual maternity leave; this was because the accrual of annual leave was stopped for all EOC employees taking unpaid leave, male as well as female.

At the core of many of the difficulties faced by the Court in these cases are two main issues. The first is how to reconcile, on the one hand, the need to recognize that women suffer material disadvantages in the workplace on account of childbirth with, on the other hand, the imperative of not reinforcing traditional, stereotypical role-playing within family life; to grant apparent substantive equality to women now, in recognition that they do indeed do far more child-caring than men, does not encourage the development of child-caring by men, nor stimulate the dismantling of structural disadvantages faced by employees with domestic responsibilities.[133] The second issue is the tension between the essentially even-handed or symmetrical concept of discrimination, formal equality, and the wholly one-sided situation of pregnancy. The Court's decisions show that to use the concept of formal equality as the law's chief method of reconciling pregnancy with employment risks corrupting the underlying principles of discrimination law. Yet, in most employment situations, it is vital to protect the fundamental right to equality which is enshrined in the formal principle. It is therefore very much preferable, for the welfare of pregnant women, for the promotion of real substantive equality and for the coherence of discrimination law, that a separate regime be maintained conferring positive rights in relation to pregnancy, as the Pregnancy

[130] Case C-66/96 [1998] ECR I-7327.   [131] Ibid, at 7348.
[132] Case C-411/96, op cit, n 44.
[133] See McGlynn, 'Pregnancy, Parenthood and the Court of Justice in *Abdoulaye*' (2000) 25 ELRev 654.

Directive has begun to do.[134] Furthermore, it is essential that this regime does not confuse child-bearing with child-rearing.

It is heartening to see that the Commission is sensitive to the obstacles which children and other domestic responsibilities present to making a reality of equality of opportunity. In its Report on equality between men and women in 2004,[135] it stressed that this is not a 'women's issue' and that policies must be put in place to encourage men to take up family responsibilities. It urged the Member States to promote parental leave, saying that 'negative effects that extended parental leave schemes can have on the employment of women, through disincentives inherent in the combination of poor wage prospects and benefit systems and the risk of outdated skills and potential job loss after long periods of absence from the labour market, should be avoided'.[136] It stressed the need for better, cheaper, and more flexible child-care services, and also flagged up the need to prioritize care facilities for elderly people.

(ii)   Harassment and sexual harassment

The gist of the concepts of 'harassment' and 'sexual harassment' is unwanted behaviour in the workplace, which causes some kind of damage or detriment to its victim. The existence of workplace harassment has been recognized for many years but, because of the lack until recently of legal definitions of these terms, it has been difficult to assess the extent of the problem posed in practice.

The first empirical evidence as to the incidence of sexual harassment came from the USA, where the problem was originally articulated and given a name; the US Merit Systems Protection Board questioned 23,000 Federal civil servants (both male and female) and found that 42% of the female employees reported having experienced sexual harassment during the two-year period from May 1978 to May 1980; 15% of male employees also reported having been sexually harassed during the same period.[137] This picture is roughly reflected by the findings of more recent European surveys. The most extensive study of the situation within the EU was conducted by Rubenstein for the EC Commission,[138] who concluded:

Whatever its precise incidence, all the available data now indicates that sexual harassment at work is not an isolated phenomenon perpetuated by the odd socially-deviant man. On the contrary, it is clear that for millions of women in the EEC today, sexual harassment is an unpleasant and unavoidable part of their working lives.[139]

[131] See further Fredman, 'A Difference With Distinction: Pregnancy and Parenthood Reassessed' (1994) 110 LQR 106; Wintemute, op cit, n 94; Honeyball, op cit, n 94; and Di Torella and Masselot, 'Pregnancy, Maternity and the Organisation of Family Life: an Attempt to Classify the Case Law of the Court of Justice' (2001) 26 ELRev 239.   [135] COM (2004) 115 final.
   [136] Ibid, at 9.
   [137] 'Sexual Harassment in the Federal Workplace', US Merit Systems Protection Board Study, 1981.
   [138] Rubenstein, *The Dignity of Women at Work* (Commission of the European Communities, 1988). See this study for details of empirical data on the incidence of sexual harassment within the Member States of the EC. The galvanizing effect of the report on the governments of the Member States is recounted by Rubenstein in (1992) 42 EOR 27.   [139] *The Dignity of Women at Work*, at 16.

Empirical studies suggest a clear link between status and the likelihood of being sexually harassed. The US Merit Systems Protection Board Study found that the most sexual harassment was experienced by young women, and especially those who were well-educated and trying to break out of traditional occupational confines. In most instances, the harasser was the woman's supervisor, which obviously compounds the difficulty she faces in making a complaint within the organization concerned. Similarly, the European evidence collected by Rubenstein suggests that 'sexual harassment is disproportionately perpetrated by male supervisors or managers upon female subordinates'.[140] The cost of sexual harassment to society in general, and to businesses in particular, is likely to be colossal. Again, the empirical studies show that it frequently damages the victim's health, causing anxiety and depression which leads to her taking time off work, and sometimes to her leaving her employment altogether. These sorts of consequences of sexual harassment led the US Merit Systems Protection Board to conclude that sexual harassment had cost the US Federal Government $189 million over the two years surveyed.

There has never seemed to be much doubt that most forms of sexual harassment in the workplace are forbidden by Article 3(c) of the Equal Treatment Directive, and indeed today that harassment on any of the other protected grounds would (without further definition or articulation) constitute a breach of the equivalent provisions of the Race Directive and the Framework Directive: to subject an employee to harassment is not to grant equal working conditions to those enjoyed by colleagues.[141] Rubenstein found, however, that at the date of his study, even though the majority of Member States had passed national legislation ostensibly carrying out their obligations under the Equal Treatment Directive, the principle that sexual harassment constitutes unlawful discrimination had yet to receive recognition by the courts.[142] In addition, as will be seen later in the present chapter, the remedies mandated for breach of the Equal Treatment Directive are not specific, and thus do not guarantee an appropriate remedy in cases of sexual harassment. Rubenstein therefore concluded that there was a need for a separate directive dealing with sexual harassment, which would declare that sexual harassment at work is contrary to the Equal Treatment Directive, but would contain certain further provisions as well. As will be seen below, some

---

[140] Ibid, at 15. The Commission's Code of Practice on sexual harassment, discussed below, comments: 'Some specific groups are particularly vulnerable to sexual harassment. Research in several Member States, which documents the link between sexual harassment and the recipient's perceived vulnerability, suggests that divorced and separated women, young women and new entrants to the labour market and those with irregular or precarious employment contracts, women in non-traditional jobs, women with disabilities, lesbians and women from racial minorities are disproportionately at risk. Gay men and young men are also vulnerable to harassment.'

[141] But see Dine and Watt, 'Sexual Harassment: Moving Away From Discrimination' (1995) 58 MLR 343, for the argument that discrimination law provides an inadequate theoretical basis for the remedying of sexual harassment.

[142] He found, in fact, that it was only in the UK and Ireland that there was relatively unequivocal judicial acceptance that sexual harassment constitutes unlawful sex discrimination.

(but not all) of his conclusions have now found fulfilment in the amended Equal Treatment Directive. Rubenstein's proposed directive focused on preventing sexual harassment from occurring in the first place, or from recurring. It would have defined sexual harassment as 'verbal or physical conduct of a sexual nature which the perpetrator knew or should have known was offensive to the victim'. Under the proposal, it would be the duty of every employer to take reasonably practicable steps to maintain a workplace free of the risk to employees of sexual harassment, and employers would be liable for any unlawful sexual harassment committed by their employees at the workplace unless they could show that reasonably practicable steps had been taken to prevent harassment. In addition, the Commission would be deputed to publish a Code of Practice giving guidance on reasonably practicable steps to prevent and deal with sexual harassment at work. As to sanctions for unlawful sexual harassment, the proposed directive would have required Member States to ensure that the relevant courts or tribunals were empowered to provide 'assistance' where appropriate to those found liable for unlawful sexual harassment by requiring them to present to the court or tribunal for its approval a suitable plan outlining the corrective and preventive action to be taken to ensure that similar acts did not occur in the future. In the view of the present writer, an effective measure should also require that courts and tribunals dealing with harassment claims be given specifically enforceable powers to enjoin harassment, breach of any such an order being a serious offence (such as contempt of court); whilst a preventive and educative role for a directive on harassment is clearly a laudable aim, there is also an overriding need to protect victims who actually suffer such harassment.

A formal response to the Rubenstein Report came on 29 May 1990, when the Council of Ministers passed not a directive, but a resolution on the dignity of women and men at work.[143] It was of course both legally and politically significant that a binding legal instrument was not used here, but the importance of 'soft law' as an aid to the construction of domestic legislation should be borne in mind.[144] The resolution endorsed many of Rubenstein's proposals. The Commission was also charged with the production of a Code of Conduct on the matter by 1 July 1991, the specific aim of the Code being to 'provide guidance based on examples and best practice in the Member States on initiating and pursuing positive measures designed to create a climate at work in which women and men respect one another's human integrity'. It adopted a recommendation on the protection of the dignity of women and men at work on 27 November 1991, and annexed a 'Code of Practice'[145] to this.[146]

---

[143] OJ [1990] C157/3.   [144] See discussion in ch 2.   [145] *Sic.*

[146] Commission Recommendation 92/131, OJ [1992] L49/1. Michael Rubenstein and the Dutch social affairs journalist, Ineke de Vries, acted as consultants to the Commission in the drafting of the Code. Rubenstein has pointed out, in 'Sexual Harassment: European Commission Recommendation and Code of Practice' (1992) 21 ILJ 70, that the Code was annexed to a recommendation in order to enhance its status. The Code was referred to by the Employment Appeal Tribunal in *Wadman v Carpenter Farrer Partnership* [1993] IRLR 374 as a means of elucidating the law on sexual harassment to be

The Member States were required by the recommendation to inform the Commission within three years of the measures taken by them in pursuance of it, to enable the Commission to draw up a report on the overall position within the Community.[147] That subsequent report showed 'a clear lack of progress' on the matter.[148] Few Member States were found to have taken coherent action and, in particular, only Belgium, France, and The Netherlands had enacted specific legislation requiring employers to be proactive in combating sexual harassment. In other Member States the existing legislation was found to be inadequate, and the Commission also questioned whether national collective agreements had been implemented at local level. In view of these disappointing findings, the Commission suggested a new 'global approach', involving comparison of different national policies to try to identify a strategy for improving the efficacy of existing measures; significantly, it also reverted to the original view of Rubenstein that a binding instrument might be required. The Commission began a new round of negotiations with the two sides of industry in 1997 in an attempt to draw up a collective EU-wide agreement to combat sexual harassment in the workplace, but in the end this proved unsuccessful.

However, as seen in chapter 3, all three Directives now contain provisions prohibiting harassment and deeming it to be unlawful discrimination. Only time will tell whether the ECJ and the national courts find these new provisions a useful tool in the fight against harassment. Although deemed to be types of discrimination, the new torts of harassment and sexual harassment do not reflect the accepted concept of discrimination, not least in containing no element of actual or hypothetical comparison. Indeed, in some respects it is arguable that their requirements are actually more stringent than simply demonstrating unlawful discrimination in the usual way. It was seen in chapter 3 that there are essentially two elements of a successful claim of unlawful discrimination: harm and causation (basis on a prohibited ground). However, in order to satisfy the definition of harassment contained in Article 2(2) of the Equal Treatment Directive and Article 2(3) of the Race and Framework Directives, it is necessary to prove additional elements, specifically: the conduct of which complaint is made must be 'unwanted' (presumably a subjective criterion); it must have the purpose or effect of 'violating the dignity' of the complainant (a phrase which will no doubt eventually have to be explained by the ECJ and may come to contain an objective element); and it must have the purpose or effect of creating an 'intimidating, hostile, degrading, humiliating or offensive environment' (again perhaps at least partially an objective matter). This third element is in fact a narrower criterion than simply proving harm or adverse impact more generally.

---

applied by an industrial tribunal. See also Lester, 'Some Reflections on the EC's Code of Conduct on Sexual Harassment' [1994] JSWFL 354, and Dine and Watt, 'Sexual Harassment: Hardening the Soft Law' (1994) 19 ELRev 104.

[147] Art 4 of the recommendation.

[148] 'Consultation of management and labour on the prevention of sexual harassment at work' COM (96) 373 final.

The conduct need not, according to the Directives, be directed specifically against the victim, although of course it is also prohibited where it is so directed; it is enough, for example, if a generally homophobic atmosphere, or an atmosphere antipathetic to a particular religion, prevails in a workplace.

The concept of harassment is permitted by the Directives to be 'defined in accordance with the national laws and practice of the Member States'.[149] Although at first sight this might appear to give the Member States *carte blanche* over the definition of harassment, it would be illogical to interpret the Directives in this way; the opening sentence of the harassment provision contains a definition for the purposes of EU law and, in accordance with the usual principle, this must be understood as setting a minimum threshold for domestic law. If the Member States wish to go further, then it is within their discretion to do so.

Confusion is also created by the addition of a separate category of sexual harassment,[150] whose definition appears to reduce the proof of an intimidating, etc environment to an aspect of the violation of personal dignity. In addition, the definition of sexual harassment restricts the unwanted conduct of which complaint can be made to that which is either 'verbal, non-verbal or physical'. Whilst it is difficult to envisage relevant conduct which does not fit within one of these descriptions, it is not obvious why this further refinement was felt necessary.

It is also unclear why the concept of *quid pro quo* harassment and sexual harassment is expressly mentioned in the Equal Treatment Directive but not in the Race or Framework Directives. Article 2(3) of the Equal Treatment Directive now provides that a person's rejection of, or submission to, harassment or sexual harassment may not be used as a basis for a decision affecting that person. There is, however, no equivalent provision in the other instruments. It is to be hoped that this is merely a drafting error and that it is not intended to mean that such *quid pro quo* harassment is not contrary to the Race and Framework Directives.

It is also evident that the new approach to harassment does little or nothing to meet the arguments put forward so cogently by Rubenstein, namely, that the law should deter harassment from occurring in the first place, and also that it should contain effective sanctions to compensate the victim and to prevent recurrence when harassment has actually been proved. Article 2(5) of the Equal Treatment Directive merely provides:

Member States shall encourage, in accordance with national law, collective agreements or practice, employers and those responsible for access to vocational training to take measures to prevent all forms of discrimination on grounds of sex, in particular harassment and sexual harassment at the workplace.

[149] Race Directive, Art 2(3); Framework Directive, Art 2(3). There is no equivalent phrase in the Equal Treatment Directive.

[150] Inserted into the amended Equal Treatment Directive at the instigation of the European Parliament. It is noteworthy that the amended Equal Treatment Directive was adopted under the authority of Art 141(3), which gives a power of co-decision to the European Parliament, whilst the Race Directive and the Framework Directive were adopted pursuant to Art 13, which requires only consultation of the European Parliament; the potential for drafting infelicity contained in these different legislative bases may be said to have been realized in the cases of the harassment provisions.

This is notably weak wording and there are no equivalent provisions in the Race or Framework Directives.

The directives supplementing the principle of non-discrimination on the ground of sex

(i)   The Pregnancy Directive[151]

The Long Title and Article 1 of this Directive[152] explain that its purpose is to introduce measures to encourage improvements in the safety and health at work of pregnant workers and workers who have recently given birth or are breastfeeding.[153] In so far as this instrument attempts to create a special legal regime to deal with the rights of pregnant workers, it is to be welcomed;[154] in the view of the present writer, and as discussed above, since pregnancy and childbirth are situations which are unique to women, it is inappropriate to use the anti-discrimination legislation as the chief legal vehicle to cater for them. It is certainly vital to the concept of substantive equality for special rules to exist to cater for maternity rights for workers, but such rules need to be additional to the normal non-discrimination principle. However, as will be seen below, the Directive in large measure equates the position of pregnant women and those who have recently given birth with sick workers, which is not only inaccurate and patronizing but also risks making women workers appear generally weaker than men, thereby seeming to legitimize exclusionary policies.[155]

The Preamble to the instrument explains at length that the Community legislature considers pregnant workers to constitute a specially vulnerable group. In *Webb v EMO (Air Cargo) Ltd*,[156] the ECJ described the legislative intention underlying the part of the Directive prohibiting the dismissal of pregnant workers[157] thus:

In view of the harmful effects which the risk of dismissal may have on the physical and mental state of women who are pregnant, have recently given birth or are breastfeeding, including the particularly

---

[151] Directive 92/85, OJ [1992] L348/1, discussed by Hargreaves in 'Pregnancy and Employment: a Change of Direction in EC Law' (1995) 17 JSWFL 491.

[152] The Directive is based on the pre-Amsterdam Art 118a. This permitted the Council to adopt directives setting minimum requirements for the harmonization of conditions relating to the health and safety of workers. The legitimacy of using this Article as the basis for measures protecting pregnant workers appeared to be assured by Case C-84/94 *UK v Council* [1996] ECR I-5755, where the ECJ held that the Article was to be interpreted broadly, so as to authorize measures of social policy the principal aim of which was the protection of the health and safety of workers.

[153] In reality, the purposes underlying the Directive would seem to include the protection of the health and safety of the foetus too, but this would have been outwith the scope of the former Art 118a.

[154] However, the robustness of the measure was considerably weakened during the political negotiations surrounding its adoption; see Ellis, 'The Pregnancy Directive' (1993) 22 ILJ 63.

[155] See Beveridge and Nott, 'Women, Wealth and the Single Market' in *Making Ourselves Heard* (Feminist Legal Research Unit, Faculty of Law, University of Liverpool, 1995), (WP No 3).

[156] Case C-32/93, op cit, n 105.   [157] Art 10 of the Directive, discussed below.

serious risk that pregnant women may be prompted voluntarily to terminate their pregnancy, the Community legislature subsequently provided, pursuant to Article 10 of [the Pregnancy Directive] . . . for special protection to be given to women, by prohibiting dismissal during the period from the beginning of their pregnancy to the end of their maternity leave.[158]

The Directive forbids any reduction in the standards of protection already existing in the Member States.[159] The Commission is required to draw up guidelines on the assessment of the chemical, physical, and biological agents and industrial processes considered hazardous to pregnant workers,[160] and employers are required to take action to avoid such hazards either by adjusting the woman's working conditions or hours, or by moving her to another job, or by granting her leave.[161] In addition, Member States must ensure that women are not obliged to perform night work during pregnancy, nor for a period following childbirth to be determined by the appropriate national authority.[162]

A continuous period of maternity leave of at least fourteen weeks, of which at least two weeks must be compulsory, is required to be allocated before and/or after confinement in accordance with national rules.[163] It is for the Member States to choose when maternity leave begins. Thus, an employment contract may require an employee who has expressed her intention to start maternity leave during the six weeks preceding the expected birth, and who is on sick leave with a pregnancy-related illness immediately before that date and gives birth during the sick leave, to bring forward the date on which her paid maternity leave begins either to the beginning of the sixth week before the expected week of birth, or to the beginning of the period of sick leave, whichever is the later; this is so notwithstanding that the sick pay scheme is more favourable to the employee than the maternity pay scheme.[164]

Women on the fourteen-week leave are guaranteed their contractual employment rights, apart from those relating to pay.[165] In *Boyle v EOC*,[166] the ECJ held that the accrual of annual leave is a contractual employment right for this purpose. However, the Directive requires the preservation of contractual rights only during the fourteen-week compulsory maternity leave period, and therefore does not preclude a contractual clause according to which annual leave ceases to accrue during any period of supplementary maternity leave. In the same case, the Court also held that the accrual of pension rights under an occupational scheme wholly financed by the employer is a contractual right within Article 11(2)(a); an employment contract cannot therefore limit the accrual of such pension rights to a period during which the woman is receiving income either from that contract, or from the statutory maternity pay scheme. *Merino Gómez v Continental Industrias del*

---

[158] [1994] ECR I-3567, at 3586.   [159] Art 1(3) of the Directive.   [160] Ibid, Art 3(1).

[161] Ibid, Art 5. See Case C-66/96 *Brugsforeninger*, op cit, n 130. See also Art 6.

[162] Ibid, Art 7.   [163] Ibid, Art 8.   [164] Case C-411/96, op cit, n 44.

[165] Art 11(2)(a) of the Directive. But note that in Case C-147/02 *Alabaster*, op cit, n 116, Léger AG submitted that a pay *rise* granted during maternity leave constituted such a contractual right.

[166] Op cit, n 44.

Caucho SA[167] confirmed that the right to annual leave is a protected contractual right. Ms Merino Gomez was on maternity leave during the entire period of the annual shutdown prescribed by collective agreement for her place of work. The issue was whether she could claim her annual leave, contrary to the collective agreement, at a different time of the year. The Working Time Directive[168] requires a minimum of four weeks' paid leave, but the employers in this case in fact provided thirty days' annual leave. The ECJ held that the purposes of annual leave and maternity leave are different, the first being to protect health and safety by permitting the worker to rest, and the second being to protect the woman's biological condition and the special relationship with her child. The principle of equality enshrined in the Equal Treatment Directive, when combined with the statutory rights to annual leave and maternity leave, therefore meant that the worker must be able to claim her annual leave at a different time from her maternity leave. Furthermore, since the annual leave was a contractual entitlement, she was entitled to thirty days and not merely the minimum period prescribed by the Working Time Directive.

Whilst on the fourteen-week leave, women are also entitled to a payment or allowance which is at least equivalent to statutory sick pay in the Member State concerned, but this can be made conditional on the worker concerned fulfilling the national conditions for sick pay eligibility, which must not provide for a qualifying period of employment of longer than 12 months immediately prior to the birth.[169] In *Boyle v EOC*,[170] it was argued that these provisions required the payment to a worker on maternity leave of an amount at least equivalent to that which a woman would receive under her employment contract if she were on sick leave; where, as in *Boyle* itself, the employer has undertaken to pay workers on sick leave their full salary, women on maternity leave should therefore receive an equivalent income. The ECJ rejected this view, saying that the concept of 'allowance' adopted by the Pregnancy Directive is different from 'pay' for the purposes of Article 141 and includes all income received by the worker during her maternity leave which is not paid to her by her employer pursuant to the employment relationship. The Directive merely requires it to be equivalent to the sickness allowance provided for by national social security legislation, payable either in the form of an allowance, pay, or a combination of the two; it does not require the employer to guarantee to the woman any higher income to which she would be contractually entitled if she were on sick leave. It was therefore not a breach of the Directive for the employer to require women employees to repay any payments received which exceeded the statutory sick pay minimum in the event of their not returning to work after giving birth. In *Lewen v Denda*[171] the Court repeated its remarks in *Boyle* and added that a Christmas bonus, not being intended to ensure a level of income at least equal to statutory sick pay, was not a 'payment' for the purposes of the Pregnancy Directive.

---

[167] Case C-342/01 judgment of 29 April 2004, nyr.
[168] Directive 93/104, OJ [1993] L307/18.
[169] Pregnancy Directive, Arts 11(2)(b), 11(3) and 11(4).   [170] Case C-411/96, op cit, n 44.
[171] Case C-333/97 [1999] ECR I-7243.

The original draft of the Directive would have provided for full pay to be maintained during the fourteen weeks' leave. The UK, however, resisted such a provision on the ground of expense. The resulting compromise in practice undermines the utility of the Directive; in the UK, for example, many part-time workers do not earn more than the national insurance threshold and therefore do not satisfy the conditions for eligibility for UK statutory sick pay; they are consequently not entitled to any payment or allowance during maternity leave, and this may well pressurize them into a return to work well before their theoretical entitlement to fourteen weeks' leave has elapsed. It is relevant to note in this context that the ECJ held in *Gillespie v Northern Health and Social Services Board*[172] that, although Article 141 and the Equal Pay Directive do not lay down criteria for determining the quantum of maternity pay, they guarantee a minumum level:

The amount payable could not... be so low as to undermine the purpose of maternity leave, namely the protection of women before and after giving birth. In order to assess the adequacy of the amount payable from that point of view, the national court must take account, not only of the length of maternity leave, but also of the other forms of social protection afforded by national law in the case of justified absence from work.[173]

Pregnant workers must also be entitled to time off without loss of pay in order to attend ante-natal examinations, where such examinations have to take place during working hours.[174]

Article 10 requires that:

1. Member States shall take the necessary measures to prohibit the dismissal of workers... during the period from the beginning of their pregnancy to the end of the maternity leave referred to in Article 8(1), save in exceptional cases not connected with their condition which are permitted under national legislation and/or practice and, where applicable, provided that the competent authority has given its consent;

2. If a worker... is dismissed during the period referred to in point 1, the employer must cite duly substantiated grounds for her dismissal in writing;

3. Member States shall take the necessary measures to protect workers... from consequences of dismissal which is unlawful by virtue of point 1.

This constitutes a blanket ban on pregnancy-related dismissal[175] and it contains no exceptions.[176] Thus, the Court held in *Tele Danmark A/S v Handels- og*

---

[172] Case C-342/93, op cit, n 44.

[173] Ibid, at 500. In *Gillespie v Northern Health and Social Services Board (No 2)* [1997] IRLR 410, the Northern Ireland Court of Appeal held that, since the Directive expressly deems statutory maternity pay to be adequate if it guarantees income at least equivalent to statutory sickness benefit, it cannot be said that contractual maternity pay is inadequate if it is higher than such sickness benefit.

[174] Art 9 of the Directive.

[175] But it should be noted that, in Case T-45/00 *Speybrouck v Parliament* [1992] ECR II-33, the CFI denied that there was any fundamental principle of EU law prohibiting absolutely the dismissal of pregnant women.

[176] However, it applies only to dismissal and not, eg, to failure to renew a fixed-term contract: Case C-438/99 *Melgar*, op cit, n 97. Such failure may, however, on the usual principles constitute a breach of the Equal Treatment Directive: see discussion above.

Kontorfunktionaererernes Forbund I Danmark (HK),[177] that Article 10 renders dismissal illegal even where the pregnant woman is employed on a temporary contract, where she failed to inform her employer that she was pregnant despite her being aware of this when the contract of employment was concluded, and notwithstanding that she is unable to work during a substantial part of the term of that contract. Dismissal of a pregnant woman is possible under the terms of the Directive only in exceptional cases which have nothing to do with the pregnancy; Advocate General Ruiz-Jarabo Colomer explained that examples of such exceptional situations might be 'a *force majeure* situation which permanently prevented a person from working, or a collective dismissal for financial, technical, organisational or production reasons'.[178] In *Melgar v Ayuntamiento de Los Barrios*,[179] the ECJ explained that Article 10 does not impose on the Member States any obligation to draw up a specific list of such exceptional reasons for dismissal; on the other hand, neither does it prevent the Member States from providing for higher protection for pregnant workers by laying down specific grounds on which dismissal can take place. In relation to the final phrase contained in Article 10(1), which refers to the consent of a competent authority, the Court held that all this does is to take account of the existence in some Member States of prior consent procedures; if such a procedure does not exist in a particular Member State, Article 10(1) does not require it to introduce one. The Court also held in *Melgar* that Article 10 is sufficiently precise to take direct effect.[180]

The Directive requires the Member States to introduce national measures to enable all workers who consider themselves wronged by a breach of its terms 'to pursue their claims by judicial process (and/or, in accordance with national laws and/or practices) by recourse to other competent authorities'.[181]

The Member States were given two years (in other words, until October 1994) to bring into force the provisions needed to comply with the Directive.[182] These provisions had to be communicated to the Commission,[183] which is obliged to report periodically to the Parliament, Council, and Economic and Social Committee on the implementation of the instrument.[184]

Although the Court has to date ruled on the direct effect only of Article 10 of the Pregnancy Directive, it would seem strongly arguable that a number of its other

---

[177] Op cit, n 98. It is particularly difficult in this situation to balance the rights of women to substantive equality with those of an employer trying to run a commercial enterprise; see further McGlynn, 'Pregnancy Dismissals and the *Webb* Litigation' (1996) Vol IV, No 2, Feminist Legal Studies 229.   [178] [2001] ECR I-6993, at 7009.
[179] Case C-438/99, op cit, n 97.   [180] For discussion of the concept of direct effect, see ch 2.
[181] Art 12 of the Pregnancy Directive. In the UK, protection against dismissal on account of pregnancy takes the form of a right to claim unfair dismissal pursuant to s 99 of the Employment Rights Act 1996; since the damages in such a claim are subject to a statutory ceiling, it would seem to be open to a claimant to assert the vertical direct effect of Art 10 and argue, on the authority of *Marshall v South-West Hants Area Health Authority (No 2)* Case C-271/91 [1993] ECR I-4367, that the ceiling must be set aside where it inhibits the award of damages which are adequate in the circumstances (see discussion of *Marshall (No 2)* below).   [182] Art 14(1) of the Directive.
[183] Art 14(3).   [184] Art 14(5).

articles take direct effect,[185] in particular those prohibiting the reduction of existing protection, nightwork, and those conferring entitlement to maternity leave, ante-natal care, minimum allowances, and contractual rights.

(ii)   The Directive on Parental Leave[186]

This Directive enacts a framework agreement concluded on 14 December 1995 pursuant to the Protocol and Agreement on Social Policy.[187] The Preamble stresses the importance of the instrument as a means of reconciling work and family life, and for the promotion of equal opportunities between men and women. Part I goes on to proclaim:

5. Whereas the Council Resolution of 6 December 1994 recognizes that an effective policy of equal opportunities presupposes an integrated overall strategy allowing for better organization of working hours and greater flexibility, and for an easier return to working life, and notes the important role of the two sides of industry in this area and in offering both men and women an opportunity to reconcile their work responsibilities with family obligations;

6. Whereas measures to reconcile work and family life should encourage the introduction of new flexible ways of organizing work and time which are better suited to the changing needs of society and which should take the needs of both undertakings and workers into account . . .

8. Whereas men should be encouraged to assume an equal share of family responsibilities, for example they should be encouraged to take parental leave by means such as awareness programmes . . .

A right to parental leave for at least three months is granted to all workers on the birth or adoption of a child.[188] Advocate General Ruiz-Jarabo Colomer pointed out in *Busch v Klinikum Neustadt GmbH*[189] that the right is not confined to workers employed on permanent contracts of employment. It persists until the child reaches an age defined for each Member State up to eight years, and it is non-transferable.[190] It is left to the Member States to decide whether to grant parental leave on a full or part-time basis, in a piecemeal way, or in the form of a time-credit system; they can subject the right to a service qualification not exceeding one year and can require the worker to give notice to the employer.[191] Employers may postpone the granting of parental leave 'for justifiable reasons related to the operation of the undertaking (eg, where work is of a seasonal nature, where a replacement cannot be found within the notice period, where a significant pro-portion of the workforce applies for parental leave at the same time, where a specific function is of strategic importance)',[192] and special arrangements are allowed 'to meet the operational and organizational requirements of small undertakings'.[193]

---

[185] Subject, of course, to the inability of directives to take horizontal effect, as to which see ch 2.
[186] Directive 96/34, OJ [1996] L145/4. Directive 96/34 was amended and extended to the UK (which had opted out of the Agreement on Social Policy) by Directive 97/75, OJ [1998] L10/24.
[187] As to which, see ch 1.   [188] Part II, clause 2(1) of the Agreement.
[189] Case C-320/01 [2003] ECR I-2041.   [190] Part II, clause 2(1) and (2) of the Agreement.
[191] Ibid, clause 2(3)(a), (b), and (d).   [192] Ibid, clause 2(3)(e).   [193] Ibid, clause 2(3)(e).

Member States are required to protect workers against dismissal (though not other forms of retributive treatment) on the ground of seeking or taking parental leave.[194] When parental leave ends, the worker has the right to return to the same job, or, if that is not possible, to 'an equivalent or similar job consistent with their employment contract';[195] and rights acquired, or being acquired, at the start of the leave must be maintained until the end of the leave.[196] This last provision was in issue in *Lewen v Denda*,[197] in which a woman on parental leave challenged her employer's refusal to pay her a Christmas bonus. It was unclear from the facts as referred to the ECJ whether the bonus was intended to represent a reward for work actually done in the preceding year, or an incentive for future work. The Court approached the matter on both bases and held that, on either, the bonus represented 'pay' within the meaning of Article 141.[198] The question then arose as to whether that Article was breached in the situation under review. There was clearly no direct discrimination, since the bonus was not paid to either mothers or fathers on parental leave. However, the Court held that it might constitute indirect discrimination, since it accepted that women take parental leave far more often than men and that was also the case in the employer's undertaking.[199] It repeated its familiar formula that discrimination involves the application of different rules to comparable situations, or the application of the same rule to different situations. If the bonus in this case were paid by way of incentive, the Court concluded that there would be no discrimination, because a worker on parental leave is in a special situation which cannot be compared with that of a man or woman at work since the contract of employment is suspended.[200] On the other hand, if the bonus constituted retroactive pay:

[A]n employer's refusal to award a bonus, even one reduced proportionally, to workers on parenting leave who worked during the year in which the bonus was granted, on the sole ground that their contract of employment is in suspense when the bonus is granted, places them at a disadvantage as compared with those whose contract is not in suspense at the time of the award and who in fact receive the bonus by way of pay for work performed in the course of that year. Such a refusal therefore constitutes discrimination . . . [201]

The logic relied upon in this case by the ECJ is somewhat obscure, in particular because it is unclear why workers on parental leave are permitted to compare their

---

[194] Ibid, clause 2(4).
[195] Ibid, clause 2(5). This right is a 'working condition' within the meaning of the Equal Treatment Directive, and must therefore be provided on non-discriminatory terms: see Case C-320/01 *Busch*, op cit, n 189.   [196] Ibid, clause 2(6).
[197] Op cit, n 171.   [198] See ch 4.
[199] For the view that this decision reinforces the existing division of labour within families, see Di Torella, 'Childcare, Employment and Equality in the European Community: First (False) Steps of the Court' (2000) 25 ELRev 310.
[200] See also the submissions of Kokott AG in Case C-220/02 *Österreichischer Gewerkschaftsbund v Wirtschaftskammer Österreich*, judgment of 8 June 2004, nyr.
[201] [1999] ECR I-7243, at 7282. The Court also added that, for this purpose, any period during which the mother was prohibited by protective legislation from working must be assimilated to the period actually worked.

situations with those still at work in one scenario but not in the other. However, the outcome appears sensible, since where the bonus constitutes retroactive pay it has actually been earned by Christmas and cannot therefore lawfully be confiscated by the employer.

In addition to parental leave, the Directive entitles workers to time off work 'on grounds of *force majeure* for urgent family reasons in cases of sickness or accident making the immediate presence of the worker indispensable', although this may be limited to a certain amount of time per year.[202]

It seems likely that the chief effect of this instrument will be a symbolic one, emphasizing as it clearly does the importance of both parents to the welfare of families and to making a reality of equal opportunities legislation for women.[203] The obvious shortcomings of the measure are the short period of leave permitted, the exclusions with which the right is surrounded, and the fact that no provision is made for payment of the worker during leave; the instrument even concedes that all relevant matters relating to social security remain to be determined by the Member States individually.[204]

The Member States were given until 3 June 1998 to comply with the terms of the Directive.[205]

(iii)   The Directive on Part-time Work[206]

This instrument implements the Framework Agreement on Part-time Work concluded pursuant to the Protocol and Agreement on Social Policy. The purposes of the Agreement are expressed to be:

(a) to provide for the removal of discrimination against part-time workers and to improve the quality of part-time work;

(b) to facilitate the development of part-time work on a voluntary basis and to contribute to the flexible organisation of working time in a manner which takes into account the needs of employers and workers.[207]

Part-time workers are defined as employees whose normal hours of work are 'less than the normal hours of work of a comparable full-time worker'; interestingly,[208] where there is no comparable full-time worker in the same establishment, the comparison is to be made by reference to the applicable collective agreement, or, in the absence of such an agreement, in accordance with national

---

[202] Part II, clause 3 of the Agreement.

[203] In similar vein, see also the Recommendation on Childcare, Recommendation 92/241, OJ [1992] L123/16, which encourages the Member States to take initiatives to enable both sexes to reconcile their occupational, family, and upbringing responsibilities arising from the care of children.   [204] Part II, clause 2(8) of the Agreement.

[205] Art 2 of the Directive. The Article goes on to give them an additional year, if this is necessary 'to take account of special difficulties or implementation by a collective agreement'.

[206] Directive 97/81, OJ [1998] L14/9.   [207] Clause 1 of the Agreement.

[208] See discussion in ch 4 of the scope of comparison permitted by Art 141.

law, collective agreements, or practice.[209] Part-timers working on a casual basis may be excluded from the coverage of the instrument 'for objective reasons'.[210]

The core of the Agreement appears to add little to the existing case law of the Court on indirect sex discrimination, with the important exception that it protects male as well as female part-time workers.[211] Indeed, as can be seen from the wording of clause 4 set out below, it actually detracts from the existing sex discrimination law in that it permits the justification of direct discrimination;[212] thus, women part-time workers will continue to prefer to rely on Article 141 of the Treaty and the Equal Treatment Directive. Clause 4 states:

1. In respect of employment conditions, part-time workers shall not be treated in a less favourable manner than comparable full-time workers solely because they work part-time unless different treatment is justified on objective grounds.

2. Where appropriate, the principle of *pro rata temporis* shall apply...

However, the instrument is at pains to stress the importance of providing opportunities for part-time work at all levels within enterprises, providing in particular in clause 5(1) that:

(a) Member States, following consultation with the social partners in accordance with national law or practice, should identify and review obstacles of a legal or administrative nature which may limit the opportunities for part-time work and, where appropriate, eliminate them;

(b) the social partners, acting within their sphere of competence and through the procedures set out in collective agreements, should identify and review obstacles which may limit opportunities for part-time work and, where appropriate, eliminate them.

Clause 5(2) adds that a worker's refusal to transfer from full-time to part-time work, or vice versa, should not in itself constitute a valid reason for dismissal.

The Directive was required to be implemented by 20 January 2000.[213]

(iv) The Directive on Fixed-term Employees[214]

This is another Directive which implements a Framework Agreement concluded pursuant to the Protocol and Agreement on Social Policy. The Agreement explicitly recognizes that more than half of the fixed-term workers in the EU are women, and that it therefore contributes to improving equality of opportunity between the two sexes.[215] It expresses its purposes as to:

---

[209] Clause 3 of the Agreement.   [210] Ibid, clause 2.

[211] See also Barnard and Hepple, 'Substantive Equality' (2000) 59 CLJ 562.

[212] See ch 3 for discussion of the undesirability of the concept of justification being applied to direct discrimination.

[213] Art 2 of the Directive. For criticism of many aspects of the Directive, see Jeffery, 'Not Really Going To Work? Of the Directive on Part-time Work, "Atypical Work" and Attempts to Regulate it' (1998) 27 ILJ 193.   [214] Directive 1999/70, OJ [1999] L175/43.

[215] See para 9 of the General Considerations of the Agreement.

(a) improve the quality of fixed-term work by ensuring the application of the principle of non-discrimination;[216]

(b) establish a framework to prevent abuse arising from the use of successive fixed-term employment contracts or relationships.[217]

A fixed-term worker is defined as:

A person having an employment contract or relationship entered into directly between an employer and a worker where the end of the employment contract or relationship is determined by objective conditions such as reaching a specific date, completing a specific task, or the occurrence of a specific event.[218]

A 'comparable permanent worker' is someone with an employment contract or relationship of indefinite duration, 'in the same establishment, engaged in the same or similar work/occupation, due regard being given to qualifications or skills'.[219]

Clause 4 of the Agreement articulates the non-discrimination principle:

1. In respect of employment conditions, fixed-term workers shall not be treated in a less favourable manner than comparable permanent workers solely because they have a fixed-term contract or relation unless different treatment is justified on objective grounds.[220]

2. Where appropriate the principle of *pro rata temporis* shall apply . . .

Clause 5 contains measures intended to prevent abuse through the use of successive fixed-term contracts, including a requirement for objective reasons to justify the renewal of contracts and a maximum total duration of successive fixed-term contracts. Employers are required to inform fixed-term workers when vacancies for permanent jobs occur within their undertakings and must facilitate their access to training.[221]

The Directive on Fixed-term Employees had to be complied with by 10 July 1999.[222]

---

[216] Murray has pointed out that temporary workers require not so much the protection of the principle of non-discrimination as a guarantee of the portability of their work-related entitlements; the problems faced by temporary workers are quite distinct from those faced by part-time workers: see 'Normalising Temporary Work' (1999) 28 ILJ 269.   [217] Clause 1 of the Agreement.

[218] Ibid, clause 3(1). Certain workers, including apprentices, are permitted to be excluded by clause 2.

[219] Ibid, clause 3(2), which goes on to make the same provision as the Directive on Part-time Work in the event of there being no such comparator; comparison is then to be made 'by reference to the applicable collective agreement, or where there is no applicable collective agreement, in accordance with national law, collective agreements or practice'.

[220] As with the Directive on Part-time Work, this has the unfortunate consequence that direct as well as indirect discrimination can be justified for the purposes of the Directive on Fixed-term Employees. See discussion in ch 3. However, in Case C-109/00 *Tele Danmark*, op cit, n 98, Ruiz-Jarabo Colomer AG submitted (at 7004–5) that 'there can be no doubt that the circumstances in which a dismissal takes place form part of the working conditions and that pregnancy is not an objective ground capable of justifying a difference in treatment between permanent and fixed-term workers'.

[221] Clause 6 of the Agreement.

[222] Art 2 of the Directive, which also granted the Member States one further year for compliance in the event of special difficulties.

(v) The Directive on Equal Treatment of the Self-employed[223]

The long title of this instrument is 'Council Directive on the Application of the Principle of Equal Treatment between Men and Women Engaged in an Activity, including Agriculture, in a Self-employed Capacity, on the Protection of Self-employed Women during Pregnancy and Motherhood'. The mischief at which it was specifically directed was the problem that self-employed women, especially those engaged in agriculture, of whom many are farmers' wives who in fact play an active role in the running of their farms, complained that they did not enjoy a clearly defined occupational status. They did not receive an identifiable sum by way of pay, and this had the consequence that their social security entitlements, including pensions, were often unclear. They were also rarely to be found on the bodies representing the agriculture industry and other self-employed sectors. Perhaps even more importantly, they faced grave difficulties in the event of pregnancy, being normally ineligible for maternity allowances related to employment. The Commission, in making its proposal on which the Directive was based, considered that a system of compensatory allowances should be devised for self-employed women taking maternity leave in general, but that for women engaged in agriculture what was also needed was access to a replacement service to cover for them during their absence.[224] Given the seriousness of these underlying problems, the solutions adopted by the Directive appear extremely weak and read more like those in a recommendation than a binding legal instrument.

The Directive is based on both Articles 94 and 308 of the TEC. In its Preamble it makes special note of the fact that specific provision is required to protect persons engaged in a self-employed capacity in an activity in which their spouses are also engaged. It explains in Article 1 that its purpose is:

[T]o ensure . . . application in the Member States of the principle of equal treatment as between men and women in an activity in a self-employed capacity, or contributing to the pursuit of such an activity, as regards those aspects not covered by Directives 76/207/EEC and 79/7/EEC.[225]

As a result of Article 2, it covers:

(a) self-employed workers ie all persons pursuing a gainful activity for their own account, under the conditions laid down by national law, including farmers and members of the liberal professions;
(b) their spouses, not being employees or partners, where they habitually, under the conditions laid down by national law, participate in the activities of the self-employed worker and perform the same tasks or ancillary tasks.

---

[223] Directive 86/613, OJ [1986] L359/56.   [224] COM (84) 57 final/2.
[225] The Equal Treatment and Social Security Directives respectively.

Article 3 applies to these persons the principle of equal treatment, using language similar, but puzzlingly not identical, to that of the Equal Treatment Directive:

For the purposes of this Directive the principle of equal treatment implies the absence of all discrimination on grounds of sex, either directly or indirectly, by reference in particular to marital or family status.[226]

From this point onwards, the provisions of the Directive are markedly unhelpful. There is no provision guaranteeing equal pay to those covered by the Directive irrespective of sex, nor to any kind of defined occupational status. Instead, Article 4 merely obliges the Member States to take the measures necessary to ensure

the elimination of all provisions which are contrary to the principle of equal treatment as defined in Directive 76/207/EEC, especially in respect of the establishment, equipment or extension of any other form of self-employed activity including financial facilities.[227]

This does not address the real problem, since it is not the existence of provisions contrary to the principle of equal treatment which have hitherto prevented the formalization of these women's positions; it is rather the absence of any national legislation requiring the recognition of their status. The Directive should therefore have been cast in positive terms, requiring the Member States to take action to achieve such recognition. All that the instrument provides in this respect is contained in the completely open-ended Article 7:

Member States shall undertake to examine under what conditions recognition of the work of the spouses referred to in Article 2(b) [ie, working spouses of self-employed persons] may be encouraged and, in the light of such examination, consider any appropriate steps for encouraging such recognition.[228]

Article 5 requires the Member States to take the measures necessary to ensure that the conditions for the formation of a company between spouses are not more restrictive than the conditions for the formation of a company between unmarried persons. This is obviously of no help where the circumstances of the spouses are not such that they wish to form a company.

Again, as regards coverage by the national social security systems, the Directive permits the Member States an enormous amount of freedom. There is no requirement to ensure that those within the scope of the Directive are in fact covered by adequate social security schemes. Instead, Article 6 merely provides:

Where a contributory social security system for self-employed workers exists in a Member State, that Member State shall take the necessary measures to enable the spouses referred to in Article 2(b) who are not protected under the self-employed workers' social security scheme to join a contributory social security scheme voluntarily.

---

[226] Note in particular the absence of the word 'whatsoever' from this definition. Cf Art 2(1) of the Equal Treatment Directive, as to which see the discussion above.

[227] The close linkage between this Directive and the Equal Treatment Directive was stressed by the ECJ in Case C-226/98 *Jørgensen v Foreningen af Speciallaeger* [2000] ECR I-2447.

[228] See also Arnull, 'Equal Treatment and the Self-Employed' (1988) 13 ELRev 58.

One obvious problem resulting from this solution is that only better-off women can benefit from it because only they are likely to join voluntarily.[229]

Most disappointing of all are the Directive's provisions in the field of pregnancy and maternity. These make no guarantee whatsoever that women within the scope of the Directive will receive maternity allowances as they would if they were employed; still less do they confer any entitlement to replacement services, contrary to the advice of the Commission. Article 8 states:

Member States shall undertake to examine whether, and under what conditions female self-employed workers and the wives of self-employed workers may, during interruptions in their occupational activity owing to pregnancy or motherhood,

    —have access to services supplying temporary replacements or existing national social services, or
    —be entitled to cash benefits under a social security scheme or under any other public social
      protection system.

The Directive contains the usual general and final provisions, requiring the Member States to provide proper judicial redress for breach of its provisions[230] and to bring the relevant national implementing measures to the notice of those covered by the instrument.[231] The Member States were given until 30 June 1989 to comply with the Directive, except where, in order to comply with Article 5 on the formation of companies, amendment was needed to the national legislation dealing with matrimonial rights and obligations, in which case the deadline for compliance with Article 5 was extended to 30 June 1991.[232]

The non-workplace provisions of the Race Directive

The coverage of the Race Directive, unlike that of the Equal Treatment and Framework Directives, extends beyond the workplace. Its ultimate reach is, of course, determined by the competence of the European Community, from which it derives its authority. The Community itself enjoys only those powers which have been conferred upon it,[233] although those powers will be formally set out in the

---

[229] See the interview with Cecile Boeraeve, President of the Women's Committee of COPA, which represents European Community farming organizations, reported in CREW Reports (1989), vol 9, no 4, 10.   [230] Art 9 of the Directive.
[231] Ibid, Art 10.
[232] Ibid, Art 12. The Commission reported on the implementation of the Directive on Equal Treatment of the Self-employed in 1994; it concluded that, although in strictly legal terms it appeared that the instrument had been implemented in the Member States, the practical result was 'not entirely satisfactory' when measured against the prime objectives of the Directive. In addition, it observed that the terms of the Directive were quite vague and this 'lack of direction' might be 'responsible in part for the minimal response in the Member States'. Overall, it commented that even the more straightforward requirements of the Directive did not appear to have been implemented 'with anything like the necessary vigour' (see COM (94) 163 final, esp Part III).
[233] Opinion 2/94 *On Accession by the Community to the ECHR* [1996] ECR I-1759.

Constitution if and when it is adopted. Thus, no matter what its ostensible coverage, the Race Directive cannot extend to areas which it is outside the competence of the Community to regulate.[234]

Nevertheless, as its Preamble makes clear, the instrument is based on the premise that the achievement of real equality irrespective of racial or ethnic origin depends on action in a number of areas of which the world of work is only one.[235] Laudable though this acknowledgement undoubtedly is, the EU and its institutions made no attempt at the time of the enactment of the Race Directive and the Framework Directive to explain why the realization of the aim of equality in the field of race requires provision outside the workplace, whilst its realization in the other areas of sex, religion, disability, age, and sexual orientation does not. Subsequently, the Commission proposed a new Directive to implement the principle of equal treatment between both sexes in the access to and supply of goods and services.[236] Political agreement on the text of this instrument was reached by the Council at a meeting on 4 October 2004.

Article 3(1) of the Race Directive provides:

Within the limits of the powers conferred upon the Community, this Directive shall apply to all persons, as regards both the public and private sectors, including public bodies, in relation to:

...

(e) social protection, including social security and healthcare;[237]

(f) social advantages;

(g) education;

(h) access to and supply of goods and services which are available to the public, including housing.

The sparse wording of this provision is noteworthy; the Article contains no definitions and no examples. A great deal of controversy and resulting litigation can therefore be expected to flow from it. Each of the four categories listed raises obvious and immediate difficulties. 'Social protection' is a very broad expression, which is clearly intended to extend beyond the field of social security systems—but

---

[234] See the opening words of the authorizing Art 13(1) TEC: 'Without prejudice to the other provisions of this Treaty and within the limits of the powers conferred by it upon the Community...' A draft of the Directive included 'cultural activities' within its remit, but this was later excluded because it was realized that the competence of the Community to intervene in this area was limited to the field of application of Art 151 TEC, ie, to promoting cooperation between the Member States and with third countries.

[235] See, in particular, Recital 12 of the Preamble to the Race Directive. See also the Commission's Explanatory Memorandum on the draft Directive, COM (1999) 566 final, esp at 5.

[236] COM (2003) 657 final. The Commission justified this proposal on the basis that discrimination over access to goods and services acts as a barrier to social and economic integration, especially but not exclusively in the area of finance. It rejected the idea of extending its proposal to education, taxation, and media portrayal of the sexes on the ground that the most effective ways of tackling discrimination in these areas was still being debated. However, it did not directly address the issue of why discrimination on the ground of race was unacceptable in some areas outside the workplace and the supply of goods and services, yet the same did not apply to discrimination on the ground of sex.

[237] The provision of healthcare would appear to be an excellent example of the kind of situation in which age discrimination might be highly relevant, yet, as pointed out above, the Framework Directive does not extend to this sphere.

how far?[238] In as much as the Directive covers social security systems, is it to be taken to embrace all the detailed rules painstakingly set out, and thereafter interpreted by the ECJ, in the Social Security Directive?[239] How far does the Community's competence extend into the field of healthcare, especially given the proviso contained in Article 152(5) TEC that 'Community action in the field of public health shall fully respect the responsibilities of the Member States for the organisation and delivery of health services and medical care'? Support for Community competence in relation to healthcare might, however, be derived from the cases establishing that the freedom to provide services, guaranteed by Articles 49 to 55, extends to freedom to receive healthcare.[240]

The expression 'social advantages' has been transplanted from the law on the free movement of persons,[241] and the Community's competence in this area is therefore undisputed. The Commission, in its Explanatory Memorandum on the draft Directive,[242] explained that the meaning of 'social advantages' was intended to follow that arrived at in relation to free movement. In other words, it was to cover benefits of an economic or a cultural nature granted either by public authorities or by private organizations, including such things as concessionary travel on public transport, reduced prices for cultural or other events, and subsidized school meals. However, it may well be that, given the fundamental importance attached by the ECJ to the principle of equality and the basis of the Race Directive in human rights protection, the Court will give a more generous interpretation to 'social advantages' in the field of race than it has for free movement.[243]

Article 3(1)(g) on education is potentially problematic. The Community's competence in this area derives from Articles 149 and 150 of the TEC. Paragraph 1 of each Article contains similar wording:

Article 149

1. The Community shall contribute to the development of quality education by encouraging cooperation between Member States and, if necessary, by supporting and supplementing their action, while fully respecting the responsibility of the Member States for the content of teaching and the organisation of educational systems and their cultural and linguistic diversity.

Article 150

1. The Community shall implement a vocational training policy which shall support and supplement the action of the Member States, while fully respecting the responsibility of the Member States for the content and organisation of vocational training.

---

[238] Art 137(1)(c) gives the Community competence in relation to the social protection of workers, and Art 136(1)(k) refers in general to the modernization of social protection systems.

[239] Directive 79/7, OJ [1979] L6/24, discussed in ch 8.

[240] See Case C-158/96 *Kohll v Union des Caisses de Maladie* [1998] ECR I-1931; Case C-157/99 *Peerbooms v Stichting CZ Groep Zorgverzekeringen* [2001] ECR I-5473; and Case C-385/99 *Müller Fauré v Onderlinge Waarborgmaatschappij* [2003] ECR I-4509.

[241] Specifically, Art 7(2) of Regulation 1612/68, OJ Sp Ed [1968] L257/2.

[242] COM (1999) 566 final, at 7.

[243] See further Ellis, 'Social Advantages: A New Lease of Life?' (2003) 40 CMLRev 639.

The difficulty lies in the apparent exclusion of the Community from competence over matters of educational curriculum and organization. Yet these are very important areas in which racial discrimination may occur, for example through the inclusion in the curriculum of material with a racial bias (say, biological theory about differential racial ability), or through the non-admission of children of a particular origin (say the Roma) to a school. It is therefore greatly to be hoped that the ECJ, when called upon to decide the reach of the Directive in the field of education, will adopt a robust approach. Cause for optimism on this score might be derived from its decisions in the analogous cases dealing with freedom of movement; in particular, at a time when the relevant Treaty Article dealing with vocational training provided only that the Council was 'to lay down general principles for implementing a common vocational training policy', the Court held that what is today Article 12 prohibited discrimination on the ground of nationality in relation to access to vocational training.[244] In addition, it has been argued that the expansion by the ECJ of the notion of services 'provided for remuneration', covered by Articles 49 to 55, might allow for the inclusion of general education as a service.[245] The Court's commitment to the protection of human rights might also justify a broad approach in this area.

As regards access to and the supply of goods and services, the Community enjoys competence in this area as a result of its powers in relation to freedom to provide services and consumer protection. However, the phrase 'which are available to the public' confines the scope of Article 3(1)(h). Brown has pointed that it is important that the goods and services provision be interpreted by the ECJ as catching bodies such as the police if 'institutional racism' of the type discussed in chapter 1 is to be proscribed by EU law.[246] Housing falls within the scope of the Article as an aspect of the supply of goods and services, and the Directive would therefore appear to forbid racial discrimination in relation to the allocation of, for example, council housing, or even in relation to a sale of real property by a private seller.

If and when the Constitution comes into operation, the problems of competence in relation to the non-workplace provisions of the Race Directive will largely be resolved, assuming that the provisions of the Directive are ambulatory. Article I-11 of the Constitution states that the Union is to enjoy only those competences conferred on it by the Member States in that instrument.

---

[244] Case 152/82 Forcheri v Belgium [1983] ECR 2323; Case 293/83 Gravier v City of Liège [1985] ECR 593; Case 24/86 Blaizot v University of Liège [1988] ECR 379; and Case C-357/89 Raulin [1992] ECR I-1027. See discussion in Arnull, The European Union and its Court of Justice (Oxford University Press, Oxford, 1999), at 376–81.

[245] See the (critical) comments of Spaventa in 'Public Services and European Law: Looking for Boundaries' (2002–3) 5 CYELS 271. Cf Case 263/86 Belgium v Humbel [1988] ECR 5365, and Case C-102/92 Wirth v Landeshaupstadt Hannover [1993] ECR I-6447.

[246] Brown, 'The Race Directive: Towards Equality for All the Peoples of Europe?' (2002) 21 YEL 195. The concept of 'institutional racism' was highlighted by Sir William MacPherson's Stephen Lawrence Inquiry, Cm 4262-I (HMSO, London, 1999).

However, in Article I-14 it is expressly given shared competence with the Member States in a number of areas, including the internal market, social policy (for the aspects defined in the substantive areas dealt with in Part III), consumer protection, and common safety concerns in public health matters (again, for the aspects defined in Part III). In addition, Article I-17 gives the Union competence to carry out supporting, coordinating, or complementary action in areas which include the protection and improvement of human health and education.

Remedies and enforcement

It has already been noted that the non-discrimination principle has been held to be directly effective in sex discrimination cases in many of the circumstances which are today also set out in the Race Directive and the Framework Directive. The concept of direct effect provides what the Court calls a 'safety net'[247] for claimants where Member States do not comply with their EU obligations; an aggrieved individual may therefore enforce the relevant EU law directly in his or her national courts, even in the face of conflicting national law, subject only to the principle that a directive may not of itself take horizontal effect. It was also seen in chapter 2 that, despite their non-horizontal direct effect, directives appear to limit the power of the Member States to enact contradictory legislation; national legislation which contradicts a provision of one of the anti-discrimination directives may therefore prove inapplicable. Furthermore, as also discussed in chapter 2, the *Francovich* principle enables an individual injured in certain circumstances by a Member State's breach of EU law to claim damages; in the present context this means that, were a Member State not to implement a provision of one of the Directives and to cause resulting loss to an individual, that individual might well have a claim to damages.

However, the Directives also provide a number of specific remedies. For example, Article 3(2) of the Equal Treatment Directive provides:

Member States shall take the necessary measures to ensure that:
(a) any laws, regulations and administrative provisions contrary to the principle of equal treatment are abolished;
(b) any provisions contrary to the principle of equal treatment which are included in contracts or collective agreements, internal rules of undertakings or rules governing the independent occupations and professions and workers' employers' organisations shall be, or may be declared, null and void or are amended.[248]

The Race and Framework Directives contain substantially identical provisions.[249]

[247] See Case 102/79 *Commission v Belgium* [1980] ECR 1473, discussed in ch 2.
[248] A para (c) dealing with protective provisions was repealed by Directive 2002/73, OJ [2002] L269/15.   [249] Art 14 of the Race Directive; Art 16 of the Framework Directive.

Paragraph (b) of Article 3(2) provided the basis for a successful infringement action brought by the Commission against the UK under Article 226.[250] The Commission alleged that, at the date of the action (1982), no legislative instrument in force in the UK provided that discriminatory provisions contained in collective agreements, rules of undertakings, or rules governing independent occupations and professions were, or could be declared, void, or could be amended. The UK Government replied that s 18 of the Trade Union and Labour Relations Act 1974 provided that collective agreements were presumed not to have been intended by the parties to be legally enforceable unless they were in writing and contained a provision in which the parties expressed their intention that the agreements were to be legally enforceable. Collective agreements, it said, were not usually legally binding in the UK in practice for this reason. Accordingly, to require them to be annulled would be like 'beating the air'. In any event, it pointed out that, even if collective agreements containing sex discriminatory terms did exist, those terms would be rendered void by s 77(1) of the Sex Discrimination Act 1975, which provides:

A term of a contract is void where:
(a) its inclusion renders the making of the contract unlawful by virtue of this Act, or
(b) it is included in furtherance of an act rendered unlawful by this Act, or
(c) it provides for the doing of an act which would be rendered unlawful by this Act.

Similarly, said the Government, any discriminatory provisions contained in the internal rules of an undertaking, or of an occupational body, would be void if they were incorporated into an individual's contract of employment; and if any discrimination in employment were to result from the existence of such a discriminatory provision in the internal rules of an undertaking, or of an occupational or professional body, that discrimination would be caught by s 6 of the Sex Discrimination Act 1975, which outlaws discrimination by employers against their employees as regards all aspects of the employment relationship. The Government also pointed to s 13(1) of the Sex Discrimination Act, which makes it unlawful for a body which can confer an authorization or qualification to discriminate on the ground of sex. However, both the Advocate General and the Court rejected these contentions. Rozès AG submitted:

[W]orkers have easier access to collective agreements, the internal rules of undertakings and the rules governing the independent occupations and professions than to Directive 76/207 or to the UK laws depriving those documents, in general, of legal binding force. Thus, workers may believe that because their contracts of employment reproduce possibly discriminatory provisions from the types of document referred to they are legal and may not be challenged at law and the workers may therefore be deprived of the advantages of a Directive which was in fact adopted for their benefit. In order to avoid such risks of confusion, the best course is to make it possible for such discriminatory provisions to be removed from those documents, as required by the Directive.[251]

---

[250] Case 165/82 *Commission v UK* [1983] ECR 3431.   [251] Ibid, at 3454.

The Court held:

> The Directive . . . covers all collective agreements without distinction as to the nature of the legal effects which they do or do not produce. The reason for that generality lies in the fact that, even if they are not legally binding as between the parties who sign them or with regard to the employment relationships which they govern, collective agreements nevertheless have important *de facto* consequences for the employment relationships to which they refer, particularly in so far as they determine the rights of the workers and, in the interests of industrial harmony, give undertakings some indication of the conditions which employment relationships must satisfy or need not satisfy. The need to ensure that the Directive is completely effective therefore requires that any clauses in such agreements which are incompatible with the obligations imposed by the Directive upon the Member States may be rendered inoperative, eliminated or amended by appropriate means.[252]

The UK responded to this ruling by enacting s 6 of the Sex Discrimination Act 1986, providing for the automatic invalidity of discriminatory provisions contained in collective agreements, employers' rules, and the rules of trades unions, employers' associations, professional organizations, and qualifying bodies. In its original form, this was merely a declaratory provision, and it was not until its amendment by s 32 of the Trade Union Reform and Employment Rights Act 1993 (following the threat of further infringement proceedings against the UK by the Commission) that a statutory remedy was prescribed by means of which an affected individual could ascertain the nullity of a discriminatory collective provision.

The nullity provision contained in the Directives does not, however, of itself require a discriminatory term to be replaced by a non-discriminatory one; the ECJ's decision in *Kowalska v Freie and Hansestadt Hamburg*[253] is consequently of particular importance. The Court held, in apparently general terms, that:

> [W]here there is indirect discrimination in a clause in a collective wage agreement, the class of persons placed at a disadvantage by reason of that discrimination must be treated in the same way and made subject to the same scheme, proportionately to the number of hours worked, as other workers . . .[254]

Although the Court ultimately based its ruling in this case on Article 141, it appears that precisely the same principle applies to terms of the agreement other than pay, at least where the respondent to the claim is an organ of the State so that the Directive is being enforced vertically. In *Kutz-Bauer v Freie und Hansestadt Hamburg*,[255] a collective agreement appeared to be indirectly discriminatory against women as regards working conditions. The Court observed that what is today Article 3(1)(c) of the Equal Treatment Directive takes direct effect,[256] and that it would therefore be enforceable by Ms Kutz-Bauer as against a public authority

---

[252] Ibid, at 3447.

[253] Case 33/89 [1990] ECR I-2591. See also Case C-184/89 *Helga Nimz v Freie und Hansestadt Hamburg* [1991] ECR I-297, and Joined Cases C-399, 409, & 425/92 and C-34, 50, & 78/93 *Stadt Lengerich v Helmig* [1994] ECR I-5727.　　　　　　　　　　[254] [1990] ECR I-2591, at 2613.

[255] Op cit, n 91.　　　[256] See discussion above.

such as the City of Hamburg. It went on to hold:

It would be incompatible with the very nature of Community law if the court having jurisdiction to apply that law were to be precluded at the time of such application from being able to take all necessary steps to set aside the provisions of a collective agreement which might constitute an obstacle to the full effectiveness of Community rules . . .

. . . [I]n the case of a breach of Directive 76/207 by legislative provisions or by provisions of collective agreements introducing discrimination contrary to that directive, the national courts are required to set aside that discrimination, using all the means at their disposal, and in particular by applying those provisions for the benefit of the class placed at a disadvantage, and are not required to request or await the setting aside of the provisions by the legislature, by collective negotiation or otherwise.[257]

In relation to individual claims, all three Directives provide that:

Member States shall ensure that judicial and/or administrative[258] procedures, including where they deem it appropriate conciliation procedures, for the enforcement of obligations under this Directive are available to all persons who consider themselves wronged by failure to apply the principle of equal treatment to them, even after the relationship in which the discrimination is alleged to have occurred has ended.[259]

This formulation consolidates the ECJ's ruling in *Coote v Granada Hospitality Ltd*,[260] in which it held that the Directive required the Member States to ensure judicial protection for workers whose employers, after the employment relationship has ended, refuse to provide references as a reaction to legal proceedings brought complaining of earlier sex discrimination.[261] The more weakly worded predecessor to this provision in the unamended Equal Treatment Directive (Article 6) proved to have significant teeth.[262] Its importance was first revealed in *Von Colson and Kamann v*

---

[257] [2003] ECR I-2741, at 2795. See also Case C-77/02 *Steinicke*, op cit, n 92, where the ECJ repeated its formulation in *Kutz-Bauer*, apparently in circumstances involving the vertical enforcement of the Equal Treatment Directive.

[258] It is doubtful whether a mere administrative procedure would satisfy the standard set out in Art 6 of the ECHR; in Case C-185/97 *Coote v Granada Hospitality Ltd* [1998] ECR I-5199, the ECJ held that the principle of the judicial protection of fundamental rights underlies the constitutional traditions common to the Member States and enshrined in Art 6 of the ECHR; it went on to say that the Equal Treatment Directive, interpreted in the light of this general principle of judicial protection, meant that 'all persons have the right to obtain an effective remedy in a competent court against measures which they consider to interfere with the equal treatment for men and women laid down in the Directive' (at 5220).

[259] Art 6(1) of the Equal Treatment Directive; Art 7(1) of the Race Directive; Art 9(1) of the Framework Directive. The usual rule applies, namely, that national time limits govern such actions; see Art 6(4) of the Equal Treatment Directive; Art 7(3) of the Race Directive; Art 9(3) of the Framework Directive. It is to be presumed that the principles that remedies and procedures must be the same as those applied to similar domestic actions, and that they must not frustrate the enforcement of the EU right (discussed in ch 2), apply as usual in this context.   [260] Case C-185/97, op cit, n 258.

[261] Mischo AG (with whose submissions the Court did not concur) pointed out that, with regard to equal pay, the prohibition of discrimination by an employer on the ground of sex does not cease to have effect on termination of the contract of employment. See discussion in ch 4.

[262] The old provision stated: 'Member States shall introduce into their national legal systems such measures as are necessary to enable all persons who consider themselves wronged by failure to apply to them the principle of equal treatment . . . to pursue their claims by judicial process after possible recourse to other competent authorities.'

Land Nordrhein-Westfalen.[263] Women social workers had applied for vacant posts in a German prison for male offenders. Although they were placed at the top of the list of candidates by the social workers' committee, they were moved down by the recruiting authority, which eventually selected two male candidates. The local labour court found that it was quite clear from the attitude of the authority that the female candidates had been discriminated against on the ground of their sex. Their problems were compounded by the fact that, under German law, they were not entitled to demand that the jobs be offered to them and, indeed, even their right to compensation appeared to be severely limited: they were entitled only to be reimbursed their expenses incurred in making the unsuccessful job applications (for example, postage and travel expenses, and the cost of compiling a *curriculum vitae*). The German court sought a preliminary ruling from the ECJ, asking essentially what remedies are mandated by the Equal Treatment Directive in such a situation. The ECJ pointed out that, although Article 249 leaves Member States freedom to choose the ways and means of ensuring that a directive is implemented, they nevertheless remain under an obligation to ensure that the substance of the directive is complied with; they must see that 'the directive is fully effective, in accordance with the objective which it pursues'.[264] It went on to hold that the Equal Treatment Directive did not prescribe any specific remedies for sex discrimination, so that it did not, for example, entitle a victim of discrimination to demand a contract of employment where the non-selection was on grounds of sex. However, since the Directive required there to be proper judicial remedies, what remedies there were must be sufficient to fulfil the objectives of the legislation. Thus:

Although . . . full implementation of the directive does not require any specific form of sanction for unlawful discrimination, it does entail that that sanction be such as to guarantee real and effective judicial protection. Moreover it must also have a real deterrent effect on the employer. It follows that where a Member State chooses to penalize the breach of the prohibition of discrimination by the award of compensation, that compensation must in any event be adequate in relation to the damage sustained. In consequence it appears that national provisions limiting the right to compensation of persons who have been discriminated against as regards access to employment to a purely nominal amount, such as, for example, the reimbursement of expenses incurred by them in submitting their application, would not satisfy the requirements of an effective transposition of the directive.[265]

It followed from this that the Directive could be used by litigants in national courts to challenge undue restrictions placed on national remedies, the only proviso to this being the usual one in the case of directives, namely, that the directive itself can be enforced directly only against organs of the State.[266] Thus, in

---

[263] Case 14/83 [1984] ECR 1891, noted by Arnull in 'Sanctioning Discrimination' (1984) 9 ELRev 267. See also Curtin, 'Effective Sanctions and the Equal Treatment Directive: The *Von Colson* and *Hartz* Cases' (1985) 22 CMLRev 505.   [264] [1984] ECR 1891, at 1905–6.

[265] Ibid, at 1908. When the case returned to the local court, compensation amounting to six months' pay was awarded.

[266] But note the technique relied on in *Von Colson* itself, whereby a national court interprets what national legislation there is so as to accord with the terms of a directive; this may be done whether or not the defendant is an organ of the State. See discussion in ch 2.

Dekker v Stichting Vormingscentrum Voor Jonge Volwassen Plus,[267] the ECJ held that

> when the sanction chosen by a Member State is contained within the rules governing an employer's civil liability, any breach of the prohibition of discrimination must, in itself, be sufficient to make the employer liable, without there being any possibility of invoking the grounds of exemption provided by national law.[268]

The presence or absence of fault, which was normally relevant in Netherlands law, was therefore irrelevant here.[269] Similarly, the ECJ held in *Draehmpaehl v Urania Immobilienservice oh G*[270] that 'the Directive precludes provisions of domestic law which . . . make reparation of damage suffered as a result of discrimination on grounds of sex in the making of an appointment subject to the requirement of fault'.[271] It went on to add:

> That conclusion cannot be affected by the German government's argument that proof of such fault is easy to adduce since, in German law, fault entails liability for deliberate or negligent acts. It must be pointed out in this regard that . . . the Directive does not provide for any ground of exemption from liability on which the person guilty of discrimination could rely and does not make reparation of such damage conditional on the existence of fault, no matter how easy it would be to adduce proof of fault.[272]

In *Marshall v Southampton and South-West Hants Area Health Authority (No 2),*[273] an industrial tribunal assessing the compensation due to Ms Marshall following her enforced discriminatory retirement found that the then UK statutory maximum for such compensation,[274] which was £6,250 at the time of Ms Marshall's dismissal and £8,500 at the date of the hearing, was 'inadequate' within the meaning intended by the ECJ in *Von Colson.* The case was appealed up to the House of Lords, which sought a preliminary ruling from the ECJ on the matter. The ECJ held:

> [The Directive] does not prescribe a specific measure to be taken in the event of a breach of the prohibition of discrimination, but leaves Member States free to choose between the different solutions suitable for achieving the objective of the Directive, depending on the different situations which may arise.
>
> However, the objective is to arrive at real equality of opportunity and cannot therefore be attained in the absence of measures appropriate to restore such equality when it has not been observed . . . [T]hose measures must be such as to guarantee real and effective judicial protection and have a real deterrent effect on the employer.
>
> Such requirements necessarily entail that the particular circumstances of each breach of the principle of equal treatment should be taken into account. In the event of discriminatory dismissal . . . , a situation of equality could not be restored without either reinstating the victim of discrimination or, in the alternative, granting financial compensation for the loss and damage sustained.

---

[267] Op cit, n 93.   [268] Ibid, at 3976.

[269] In the UK, s 66(3) of the Sex Discrimination Act 1975 originally provided that no damages were available in respect of unintentional indirect discrimination; in view of the argument that this breached the principles of adequate compensation and full liability, this limitation was removed by the Sex Discrimination and Equal Pay (Miscellaneous Amendments) Regulations 1996, SI 1996 No 438.

[270] Case C–180/95 [1997] ECR I–2195.   [271] Ibid, at 2220.   [272] Ibid.

[273] [1988] IRLR 325.

[274] Under s 65(2) of the Sex Discrimination Act 1975. The statutory maximum was removed after the decision in the *Marshall (No 2)* by the Sex Discrimination and Equal Pay (Remedies) Regulations 1993, SI 1993 No 2798. The statutory maximum for race claims was removed by the Race Relations (Remedies) Act 1994.

Where financial compensation is the measure adopted in order to achieve the objective indicated above, it must be adequate, in that it must enable the loss and damage actually sustained as a result of the discriminatory dismissal to be made good in full in accordance with the applicable national rules.[275]

Later, it added:

[T]he fixing of an upper limit of the kind at issue in the main proceedings cannot, by definition, constitute proper implementation of ... the Directive, since it limits the amount of compensation *a priori* to a level which is not necessarily consistent with the requirement of ensuring real equality of opportunity through adequate reparation for the loss and damage sustained as a result of discriminatory dismissal.

... [F]ull compensation for the loss and damage sustained ... cannot leave out of account factors, such as the effluxion of time, which may in fact reduce its value. The award of interest, in accordance with the applicable national rules, must therefore be regarded as an essential component for the purposes of restoring real equality of treatment.[276]

However, in its later decision in *Draehmpaehl v Urania Immobilienservice ohG*,[277] the Court resiled somewhat from its tough stance that an upper limit on damages contravened the Directive. The German legislation involved limited to three months' salary the compensation payable for discrimination over appointment to a job; it also limited to six months' salary the total compensation payable in such a situation where claims were made by several people. The Court held that these limitations were in most cases precluded by the Directive, in particular since there were no similar limitations to be found in analogous provisions of German law. Nevertheless, despite repeating its earlier comments that compensation must guarantee real and effective judicial protection, have a real deterrent effect on the employer, and be adequate in relation to the damage sustained, it conceded that the ceiling on compensation was permissible where the applicant would not have got the job even had there been no discrimination:

... reparation may take account of the fact that, even if there had been no discrimination in the selection process, some applicants would not have obtained the position to be filled since the applicant appointed had superior qualifications. It is indisputable that such applicants, not having suffered any damage through exclusion from the recruitment process, cannot claim that the extent of the damage they have suffered is the same as that sustained by applicants who would have obtained the position if there had been no discrimination in the selection process.

Consequently, the only damage suffered by [such] an applicant ... is that resulting from the failure, as a result of discrimination on grounds of sex, to take his application into consideration ...

---

[275] Case C-271/91 [1993] ECR I-4367, at 4407–8. Cf the view of Van Gerven AG that 'compensation must be adequate in relation to the damage sustained but does not have to be equal thereto' (at 4390). The ECJ's judgment is analysed by Curtin in (1994) 31 CMLRev 63, by Grief in 'Compensation for Sex Discrimination' (1993) 22 ILJ 314, and by Fitzpatrick and Szyszczak in 'Remedies and Effective Judicial Protection in Community Law' (1994) 57 MLR 434.

[276] [1993] ECR I-4367, at 4409. As More points out in 'Compensation for Discrimination?' (1993) 18 ELRev 533, the judgment does not provide an answer to the question of whether national courts can restrict the period over which interest is payable, by excluding the time between the unlawful conduct and the date when the claim is brought, if this delay can be attributed to the conduct of the applicant. See also the Editorial Comment on this decision in (1993) 18 ELRev 365. [277] Op cit, n 270.

> ... [I]t does not seem unreasonable for a Member State to lay down a statutory presumption that the damage suffered by [such] an applicant ... may not exceed a ceiling of three months' salary.
>
> In this regard, it must be made clear it is for the employer, who has in his possession all the applications submitted, to adduce proof that the applicant would not have obtained the vacant position even if there had been no discrimination.[278]

This unprincipled and unimaginative conclusion did not respect the Court's own rule that compensation must be an adequate reflection of the loss sustained in the particular circumstances; where, for example, an employer discriminates in such a way as to cause extreme distress and injury to feelings, there is no logical reason to suppose that the amount of damages which would properly compensate for that head of loss would necessarily be limited in such an arbitrary fashion.

In *Marshall (No 2)*,[279] the Court held the enforcement Article to be directly effective so as to enable a victim of discrimination to rely on it as against an authority of the State. To the argument that this frustrated the discretion entrusted to the Member States by the Directive in relation to remedies, the Court replied:

> The fact that Member States may choose among different solutions in order to achieve the objective pursued by the Directive depending on the situations which may arise, cannot result in an individual's being prevented from relying on Article 6 in a situation such as that in the main proceedings where the national authorities have no degree of discretion in applying the chosen solution.
>
> It should be pointed out in that connection that, as appears from the judgment in Joined Cases C-6 & 9/90 *Francovich v Italy* [1991] ECR I-5357, at paragraph 17, the right of a state to choose among several possible means of achieving the objectives of a directive does not exclude the possibility for individuals of enforcing before national courts rights whose content can be determined sufficiently precisely on the basis of the provisions of the directive alone.[280]

Putting this in a slightly different way, the Member State had constrained its own discretion in this situation by choosing the remedy of damages; having done so, the then Article 6 was directly effective so as to ensure the efficacy of this remedy.[281]

The emphasis placed by the ECJ in *Von Colson*, *Marshall (No 2)*, and *Draehmpaehl* on the element of deterrence is interesting; deterrence is not normally regarded as one of the objectives of the civil law, which traditionally concentrates its attention on restitution and compensation rather than on seeking to change future behaviour patterns. The express mention of deterrence in the context of remedies for sex discrimination seems to underline what a serious view the ECJ takes of the issue of sex equality. It is to be hoped that it will take a similar view when it encounters

---

[278] Op cit, n 270, at 2223–4.   [279] Case C-271/91, op cit, n 181.   [280] Ibid, at 4410.

[281] It is therefore strongly arguable that, where a Member State chooses to make some sort of specific enforcement available in sex discrimination cases, as the UK does in providing for a recommendation that the employer take certain action under the Sex Discrimination Act 1975, s 65(1)(c), that specific enforcement must be effective. A recommendation is, however, not effective, because there are very limited sanctions for its non-observance under the Sex Discrimination Act 1975, s 65(3). It follows that more effective specific remedies, such as reinstatement, engagement, and injunctions to restrain continuing acts of discrimination, must be granted by UK courts and tribunals as a result of Art 6 of the Directive. Injunctions are today available in the UK in the limited sphere of application of the Protection From Harassment Act 1997.

discrimination on the grounds of race, religion, disability, age, and sexual orientation. It remains to be seen from the future case law of the Court whether it also indicates that exemplary, as well as purely compensatory, damages should be available in appropriate cases of unlawful discrimination.[282]

Johnston v Chief Constable of the RUC[283] also cast important light on the meaning of the old Article 6. Ms Johnston, who was a member of the Royal Ulster Constabulary's full-time Reserve, complained that the Chief Constable's refusal to renew her contract of employment was unlawfully discriminatory. Her action before the Belfast industrial tribunal was obstructed by the Secretary of State issuing a certificate under Article 53 of the Sex Discrimination (Northern Ireland) Order 1976, stating that Ms Johnston's contract was not renewed in order to safeguard national security and to protect public safety and public order. The effect of such a certificate under Northern Ireland law was to withdraw the matter from the consideration of courts and tribunals. Ms Johnston argued that this contravened Article 6 of the Directive. The ECJ agreed with her, saying:

The requirement of judicial control stipulated by [Article 6 of the Equal Treatment Directive] reflects a general principle of law which underlies the constitutional traditions common to the Member States. That principle is also laid down in Articles 6 and 13 of the European Convention for the Protection of Human Rights and Fundamental Freedoms of 4 November 1950 (1953) (Cmd 8969.) As the European Parliament, Council and Commission recognized in their joint declaration of 5 April 1977 (OJ 1977 No C 103, p 1) and as the Court has recognized in its decisions, the principles on which that Convention is based must be taken into consideration in Community law.

By virtue of Article 6 of Council Directive 76/207/EEC, interpreted in the light of the general principle stated above, all persons have the right to obtain an effective remedy in a competent court against measures which they consider to be contrary to the principle of equal treatment for men and women laid down in the Directive. It is for the Member States to ensure effective judicial control as regards compliance with the applicable provisions of Community law and of national legislation intended to give effect to the rights for which the Directive provides.

A provision which, like Article 53(2) of the Sex Discrimination (Northern Ireland) Order 1976, requires a certificate such as the one in question in the present case to be treated as conclusive evidence that the conditions for derogating from the principle of equal treatment are fulfilled allows the competent authority to deprive an individual of the possibility of asserting by judicial process the rights conferred by the Directive. Such a provision is therefore contrary to the principle of effective judicial control laid down in Article 6 of the Directive.[284]

---

[282] The availability of exemplary damages in discrimination cases in the UK is now a matter of doubt; it had been held, on the basis of *AB v South West Water Services* [1993] 1 All ER 609, that such damages could not be obtained in either sex discrimination or race discrimination claims: see *Deane v London Borough of Ealing* [1993] IRLR 209; *Ministry of Defence v Cannock* [1994] IRLR 509; and *Ministry of Defence v Meredith* [1995] IRLR 539, as to which see further Arnull, 'EC Law and the Dismissal of Pregnant Servicewomen' (1995) 24 ILJ 215. (Cf *Bradford City Metropolitan Council v Arora* [1991] 2 QB 507 and *London Borough of Lambeth v D'Souza* [1999] IRLR 240.) The same reasoning could be applied to the other heads of discrimination. However, the House of Lords in *Kuddus v Chief Constable of Leicestershire* [2002] 2 AC 122 disapproved *AB v South West Water Services*. If exemplary damages are required to be made available in appropriate cases by EU law, and if UK law does not respect this principle, it will of course be in breach of EU law.   [283] Case 222/84, op cit, n 37.

[284] Ibid, at 1682–3.

Exactly as in *Von Colson* and *Marshall (No 2)*, although the complainant here could not enforce her rights under the Directive within the sphere of freedom of action allowed to the Member States, she could enforce the instrument directly (against an organ of the State) when the State outstepped the limits of the discretion conferred on it. It was, in other words, directly effective where the State attempted to withdraw from her all possible routes to judicial redress.

This body of ECJ case law in relation to the unamended Article 6 of the Equal Treatment Directive is today consolidated in Article 6(2) of the amended instrument:

Member States shall introduce into their national legal systems such measures as are necessary to ensure real and effective compensation or reparation as the Member States so determine for the loss and damage sustained by a person injured as a result of discrimination contrary to Article 3, in a way which is dissuasive and proportionate to the damage suffered; such compensation or reparation may not be restricted by the fixing of a prior upper limit, except in cases where the employer can prove that the only damage suffered by an applicant as a result of discrimination within the meaning of this Directive is the refusal to take his/her job application into consideration.

There is no provision equivalent to this in the Race or Framework Directives. This is highly regrettable, and it is to be hoped that it is merely a consequence of a slip of the drafter's pen, rather than an intimation that the sanctions for these latter instruments are not intended to be as powerful as those applying to the Equal Treatment Directive. All three instruments nevertheless contain a provision in the following terms:

Member States shall lay down the rules on sanctions applicable to infringements of the national provisions adopted pursuant to this Directive, and shall take all measures necessary to ensure that they are applied. The sanctions, which may comprise the payment of compensation to the victim, must be effective, proportionate and dissuasive.[285]

Whatever provisions the Member States adopt for enforcement of the Directives must not be regressive—in other words, must not reduce the level of protection afforded against discrimination in the State concerned. Member States nevertheless remain free to introduce legislation which is more favourable to protection of the principle of equal treatment than the Directives demand.[286]

The Equal Treatment Directive and the Race Directive (but not the Framework Directive) require the Member States to set up a body to promote the equal treatment principle in their respective fields.[287] Article 8(a) of the Equal Treatment Directive provides:

1. Member States shall designate and make the necessary arrangements for a body or bodies for the promotion, analysis, monitoring and support of equal treatment for all persons without discrimination

---

[285] Art 8(d) of the Equal Treatment Directive (query its necessity in the light of Art 6(2) discussed above); Art 15 of the Race Directive; Art 17 of the Framework Directive.

[286] Art 8(e) of the Equal Treatment Directive; Art 6 of the Race Directive; Art 8 of the Framework Directive.

[287] Presumably the Framework Directive does not include such a provision because such a body supporting all the aims of that instrument would have a very wide-ranging portfolio.

on the grounds of sex. These bodies may form part of agencies charged at national level with the defence of human rights or the safeguard of individuals' rights.

2. Member States shall ensure that the competences of these bodies include:

(a) without prejudice to the rights of victims and of associations, organisations or other legal entitles referred to in Article 6(3),[288] providing independent assistance to victims of discrimination in pursuing their complaints about discrimination;
(b) conducting independent surveys concerning discrimination;
(c) publishing independent reports and making recommendations on any issue relating to such discrimination.

The powers of this body in the race field are slightly narrower and do not include monitoring, a practice which is regarded by some Member States as improper when applied to such matters as racial origin.[289]

In addition, all three Directives provide for enforcement by organizations acting on behalf of individuals. This is of considerable importance to the practical efficacy of the principle of equality; in a system which relies heavily on individuals' complaints, it is necessary to support such complaints both financially and morally, since individual litigants will inevitably lack the money and the psychological strength to pursue all their lawful rights. In addition, a claim on behalf of a number of complainants is more likely to produce results since it operates as a greater threat to the respondent. A body with representative enforcement powers is also able to take a more strategic view of the overall direction and development of the law than an individual can do. All three instruments provide:

Member States shall ensure that associations, organisations or other legal entities which have, in accordance with the criteria laid down by their national law, a legitimate interest in ensuring that the provisions of this Directive are complied with, may engage, either on behalf of or in support of the complainant,[290] with his or her approval, in any judicial and/or administrative procedure provided for the enforcement of obligations under this Directive.[291]

The victimization of those complaining of discrimination, either internally within their organization or as a matter of law, is prohibited. The Race Directive sets out

[288] Discussed below.
[289] Art 13 of the Race Directive provides: '1. Member States shall designate a body or bodies for the promotion of equal treatment of all persons without discrimination on the grounds of racial or ethnic origin. These bodies may form part of agencies charged at national level with the defence of human rights or the safeguard of individuals' rights. 2. Member States shall ensure that the competences of these bodies include:—without prejudice to the rights of victims and of associations, organisations or other legal entities referred to in Article 7(2), providing independent assistance to victims in pursuing their complaints about discrimination,—conducting independent surveys concerning discrimination,—publishing independent reports and making recommendations on any issue relating to such discrimination.' [290] 'Complainants' in the Equal Treatment Directive.
[291] Art 6(3) of the Equal Treatment Directive; Art 7(2) of the Race Directive; Art 9(2) of the Framework Directive. The UK Government takes the view that this provision gives the Member States a discretion to decide whether such organizations can undertake representative actions in their own name: see the evidence submitted by the DfEE to the House of Lords Select Committee on the EU, reported in 'The EU Framework Directive on Discrimination', Session 2000–01, 4th Report, HL Paper 13, at 14.

a particularly broad rule in this respect:

> Member States shall introduce into their national legal systems such measures as are necessary to protect individuals from any adverse treatment or adverse consequence as a reaction to a complaint or to proceedings aimed at enforcing compliance with the principle of equal treatment.[292]

It is noteworthy that this formulation shields complainants from any possible adverse consequences of making a complaint, and it does not appear on its face to be restricted to actions taken by or on behalf of the respondent. The Equal Treatment Directive is more guarded:

> Member States shall introduce into their national legal systems such measures as are necessary to protect employees, *including those who are employees' representatives provided for by national laws and/or practices*, against dismissal or other adverse treatment by the employer as a reaction to a complaint within the undertaking or to any legal proceedings aimed at enforcing compliance with the principle of equal treatment.[293]

This provision is, however, broader than its predecessor under the unamended Equal Treatment Directive, which expressly protected only against dismissal.[294] The victimization provisions contained today in all three Directives would appear to be sufficiently specific to take direct effect and thus be enforceable against an employer who is an organ of the State.[295]

The parts of the Directives directed towards specific enforcement of the principle of equality are supported by softer provisions promoting information and dialogue. Thus, the Member States are required to ensure that their national laws giving effect to the Directives are brought to the attention of those likely to be affected, for example at their place of work.[296] They are also required to promote social dialogue between the social partners with a view to fostering equal treatment and to concluding collective agreements,[297] and to encourage dialogue with non-governmental organizations which have a legitimate interest in the promotion of equality.[298] In the case of the Equal Treatment Directive, employers too are brought

---

[292] Art 9 of the Race Directive.

[293] Art 7 of the Equal Treatment Directive. Art 11 of the Framework Directive is framed identically but excludes the words italicized in the text.

[294] Nevertheless, the ECJ was not prepared to interpret this provision restrictively. In Case C-185/97 *Coote*, op cit, n 258, it declined to follow the advice of Mischo AG and held: '[H]aving regard to the objective of the Directive, which is to arrive at real equality of opportunity for men and women . . . and to the fundamental nature of the right to effective judicial protection, it is not, in the absence of a clear indication to the contrary, to be inferred from Article 7 of the Directive that the legislature's intention was to limit the protection of workers against retaliatory measures decided on by the employer solely to cases of dismissal, which, although an exceptionally serious measure, is not the only measure which may effectively deter a worker from making use of the right to judicial protection' (at 5222).

[295] See discussion of the parallel point in relation to the Equal Pay Directive in ch 4.

[296] Art 8 of the Equal Treatment Directive; Art 10 of the Race Directive; Art 12 of the Framework Directive.

[297] Art 8(b)(i) and (ii) of the Equal Treatment Directive; Art 11 of the Race Directive; Art 13 of the Framework Directive.

[298] Art 8(c) of the Equal Treatment Directive; Art 12 of the Race Directive; Art 14 of the Framework Directive.

into this process; thus, Article 8(b) states:

3. Member States shall, in accordance with national law, collective agreements or practice, encourage employers to promote equal treatment for men and women in the workplace in a planned and systematic way.

4. To this end, employers should be encouraged to provide at appropriate regular intervals employees and/or their representatives with appropriate information on equal treatment for men and women in the undertaking.

Such information may include statistics on proportions of men and women at different levels of the organisation and possible measures to improve the situation in cooperation with employees' representatives.

6

Exceptions to the non-discrimination principle

Introduction

The Equal Treatment Directive, the Race Directive, and the Framework Directive all contain exceptions to the principle that discrimination contrary to their terms is unlawful. As will be seen, the Framework Directive contains a number of exceptions additional to those contained in the other instruments, several of which were included as a consequence of last-minute political settlement. Each exception will be examined separately,[1] but two general points need to be made before doing so.

The first is that the list of permissible exceptions is likely to be limited to those expressly mentioned in the three Directives. This can be deduced from the ECJ's decision in *Johnston v Chief Constable of the RUC*,[2] where it revealed itself unwilling to imply extra defences into the Equal Treatment Directive.[3] The UK Government in that case had argued that public safety exonerated the Chief Constable's discriminatory treatment of Ms Johnston. The ECJ, however, held:

[T]he only Articles in which the EEC Treaty provides for derogations applicable in situations which may involve public safety are Articles 36, 48, 56, 223 and 224,[4] which deal with exceptional and clearly defined cases. Because of their limited character those Articles do not lend themselves to a wide interpretation and it is not possible to infer from them that there is inherent in the EEC Treaty a general proviso covering all measures taken for reasons of public safety.[5] If every provision of Community law were held to be subject to a general proviso, regardless of the specific requirements laid down by the provisions of the EEC Treaty, this might impair the binding nature of Community law and its uniform application.

It follows that the application of the principle of equal treatment for men and women is not subject to any general reservation as regards measures taken on grounds of the protection of public safety, apart from the possible application of Article 224 of the EEC Treaty which concerns a wholly exceptional

---

[1] Positive action is the subject of a separate section below; as will be discussed, argument remains about the extent to which positive action can excuse unlawful discrimination.

[2] Case 222/84 [1986] ECR 1651.

[3] See further Arnull, 'EC Law and the Dismissal of Pregnant Servicewomen' (1995) 24 ILJ 215.

[4] Now Arts 30, 39, 46, 296, and 297.

[5] But note that, as discussed below, the Framework Directive contains a general defence for measures necessary for public security, public order, protection of health, and the protection of the rights and freedoms of other; it also contains a specific exception in relation to the armed forces as regards discrimination on the grounds of disability and age.

situation . . . [and which the Court later found to be inapplicable on the facts of this case.][6] The facts which induced the competent authority to invoke the need to protect public safety must therefore if necessary be taken into consideration, in the first place, in the context of the application of the specific provisions of the Directive.

The answer to the first question must therefore be that acts of sex discrimination done for reasons related to the protection of public safety must be examined in the light of the exceptions to the principle of equal treatment for men and women laid down in Council Directive 76/207/EEC.[7]

Secondly, the Court will usually accord a strict construction to any exception to a general principle, where that general principle exists for the protection of individuals.[8] A strict view can therefore be predicted for all the exceptions listed in the three Directives.

The exceptions

(i)   Genuine and determining occupational requirement

Such a requirement constitutes a defence for the purpose of all three Directives. Thus, for example, the Race Directive provides:

Notwithstanding Article 2(1) and (2), Member States may provide that a difference of treatment which is based on a characteristic related to racial or ethnic origin shall not constitute discrimination[9] where, by reason of the nature of the particular occupational activities concerned or the context in which they are carried out, such a characteristic constitutes a genuine and determining occupational requirement, provided that the objective is legitimate and the requirement is proportionate.[10]

The Preambles to both the Race Directive and the Framework Directive explain that this defence is intended to operate only in 'very limited circumstances'.[11] It is indeed difficult to imagine many situations in which it would come into play as regards discrimination on the ground of sexual orientation. However,

---

[6] Art 224 is now Art 297; for further discussion of its potential, see Koutrakos, 'Is Article 297 EC a "reserve of sovereignty"?' (2000) 37 CMLRev 1339.

[7] Op cit, n 2, at 1684. See also Case C-273/97 *Sirdar v Army Board and Secretary of State for Defence* [1999] ECR I-7403, Case C-285/98 *Kreil v Germany* [2000] ECR I-69, and Case C-186/01 *Dory v Germany* [2003] ECR I-2479, in all of which the Court replaced the word 'safety' with 'security'. The view that the exceptions to the Directives are expressed exhaustively in the instruments concerned has also been expressed by Mme Odile Quintin on behalf of the Commission in evidence to the House of Lords Select Committee on the EU: see 'EU Proposals to Combat Discrimination', Session 1999–2000, 9th Report, HL Paper 68, at 29.

[8] See, eg, Case 41/74 *Van Duyn v Home Office* [1974] ECR 1337; Case 222/84 *Johnston*, op cit, n 2; and Case C-328/91 *Secretary of State for Social Security v Thomas* [1993] ECR I-1267.

[9] This is an undesirable formulation: the situation envisaged by the Article does in reality constitute discrimination, but it is of a sort which is excusable.

[10] Art 4 of the Race Directive. Art 4 of the Framework Directive is in substantially identical terms as regards discrimination on any of the grounds it covers.

[11] Recital 18 of the Preamble to the Race Directive; Recital 23 of the Preamble to the Framework Directive.

it is arguable that the defence would operate to protect the choice of a homosexual where a job involves the provision of gay and lesbian counselling services; it might also apply to protect an employer's insistence on appointing a heterosexual where an employee is contractually required to work abroad in a country which criminalizes homosexuality. Oliver has also pointed out that, whilst individuals are protected from discrimination based on perceptions of their sexual orientation, the genuine occupational requirement exception appears to permit employers to use these very perceptions in deciding whether or not a person falls within the exception.[12]

It should also be noted that this exception excuses essentially positive, rather than negative, discrimination;[13] in other words, it provides an excuse for providing more (not less) favourable treatment for members of a protected class than for other people on the ground of their membership of that class; the classic examples are the choice of a black actor to play the part of Othello and of a woman to model women's clothes. For this reason, the exception is not of importance in relation to discrimination on the ground of disability; since, as discussed in chapter 3, it is only unlawful to discriminate on the ground of disability, it is not in principle unlawful to discriminate in favour of the disabled.

Article 2(6) of the Equal Treatment Directive (but not the other two instruments) confines the ambit of the defence to 'access to employment including the training leading thereto'. It therefore only applies to discrimination contrary to Article 3(1)(a) and (b) of the instrument. Thus, for example, it might be arguable that, where women had been traditionally under-represented within a trade union, it would be lawful to offer them free membership, even though men were charged a subscription.

The original text of the Equal Treatment Directive referred to the exclusion by Member States of occupational activities generally; the amended wording, like that used in the Race and Framework Directives, refers to 'particular' occupational activities. This makes it clear that the exclusion does not apply today to whole classes of jobs but that instead each case must be examined individually.[14] That Member States were formerly unabashed in attempting to exclude whole sectors of the employment market from the provisions of the Equal Treatment Directive appeared from the early cases on the exception, in particular *Commission v UK*.[15]

---

[12] Oliver, 'Sexual Orientation Discrimination: Perceptions, Definitions and Genuine Occupational Requirements' (2004) 33 ILJ 1. This view was accepted by Richards J in *R (on the application of Amicus—MSF section) v Secretary of State for Trade and Industry* [2004] IRLR 430.

[13] Although, of course, positive discrimination in favour of one person usually amounts to negative discrimination against someone else.

[14] Recital 11 of the Preamble to the amending Directive 2002/73 (OJ [2002] L269/15) states: 'The occupational activities that Member States may exclude from the scope of Directive 76/207/EEC should be restricted to those which necessitate the employment of a person of one sex by reason of the nature of the particular occupational activities concerned, provided that the objective sought is legitimate, and subject to the principle of proportionality as laid down by the case-law of the Court of Justice.'   [15] Case 165/82 [1983] ECR 3431.

The Commission alleged there that three of the exceptions contained in the British Sex Discrimination Act 1975 conflicted with Article 2(2) of the Directive. The first two were the exceptions then conferred by s 6(3) of the statute, excusing all employment for the purposes of a private household and also employment where the number of persons employed did not exceed five. The Commission reported that there were no equivalent exceptions provided for by the legislation of any of the other Member States, but the UK Government argued that these exceptions were permitted since they involved 'close personal relationships between employee and employer, so that it would not be legally possible to prevent the latter from employing persons of a particular sex'. In the case of employment in private households, it contended that the employee often lives in the household, as in the case of resident companions and personal maids, and it also contended (contrary to the Commission's view) that the concept of a 'private household' was perfectly clear: 'Thus, if a chauffeur is not actually employed in his employer's household but for the purposes of his business, the exception will not apply. On the contrary, a family cook or gardener will normally come within that exception.'[16] As to the small business exception, the UK Government took as an example female owners and managers of small shops, particularly the elderly, who wish to employ assistants of their own sex. These arguments all had an extraordinarily old-fashioned ring to them and suggested a lack of touch with the modern world of employment. They found no favour with either the Advocate General or with the Court, except that the Advocate General considered that the term 'private household' was susceptible of satisfactory definition through case law. Nevertheless, her general view was that:

[T]he UK has not furnished proof that in all the cases covered by the exception at issue the conditions in which the work in question is performed make it necessary to allow employers to practise discrimination. It is not true that all occupational and professional activities capable of being covered by the exception contained in that provision involve the close personal relationships which constitute the justification for it. As the Commission rightly points out, the defendant itself admits this in the words it uses: employment for the purposes of a private household frequently (and therefore not always) involves very close personal relationships; close personal relationships often (here too, not always) exist in small undertakings.

I also consider that the terms of section 6, subsection 3, do not satisfy the condition laid down in Article 2(2) by virtue of which the exclusion must relate to 'occupational activities'. There is no doubt that it is not necessary, as the UK rightly points out, for the exclusion of occupational activities pursuant to Article 2(2) to be effected by listing them activity by activity; it seems to me to be perfectly permissible for a Member State to implement the Directive by enacting laws which prohibit discrimination, reiterating the actual wording of that Article and, for the rest, leaving the national courts to determine case by case, subject to review by this Court under Article [234] of the Treaty, what occupational activities are excluded from the general prohibition. But it cannot be considered, without stretching the meaning of the words, that the concepts of employment for the purposes of a private household (and not for example the concept of resident domestic staff) and employment in undertakings with five or fewer employees correspond to occupational activities.[17]

---

[16] These are the words of Rozès AG, ibid, at 3456.   [17] Ibid, at 3456–7.

The Court itself held:

It must be recognized that the provision of the 1975 Act in question is intended, in so far as it refers to employment in a private household, to reconcile the principle of equality of treatment with the principle of respect for private life, which is also fundamental. Reconciliation of that kind is one of the factors which must be taken into consideration in determining the scope of the exception provided for in Article 2(2) of the Directive. Whilst it is undeniable that, for certain kinds of employment in private households, that consideration may be decisive, that is not the case for all the kinds of employment in question.

As regards small undertakings with not more than five employees, the UK has not put forward any argument to show that in any undertaking of that size the sex of the worker would be a determining factor by reason of the nature of his activities or the context in which they are carried out.

Consequently, by reason of its generality, the exclusion provided for in the contested provision of the 1975 Act goes beyond the objective which may be lawfully pursued within the framework of Article 2(2) of the Directive.[18]

Unfortunately, the subsequent decision in *Kirsammer-Hack v Sidal*[19] suggested that the Court later modified the rigour of its approach in relation to small businesses. The impugned German law on unfair dismissal did not apply to small businesses, that is to say, those employing five or fewer persons. Part-timers had the right to claim unfair dismissal but, in calculating the total number of employees in an enterprise, those working fewer than ten hours per week were excluded. Ms Kirsammer-Hack, who worked part-time but for more than ten hours per week, alleged unfair dismissal but was met by the small business exception. The Labour Court referred to the ECJ the question of whether the domestic legislation constituted indirect discrimination in breach of the Equal Treatment Directive. The ECJ held that the national law did not impact specifically on part-timers, but rather on everybody employed by small businesses; since there was no evidence to suggest that small businesses employ a considerably larger number of women than men, there was therefore no indirect discrimination. Significantly, however, the Court went on to hold that, even if the legislation were *prima facie* indirectly discriminatory, it would be justifiable as intended to relieve the constraints weighing on small businesses:

[The legislation in question] forms part of a series of measures intended to alleviate the constraints burdening small businesses which play an essential role in economic development and the creation of employment in the Community.

In that respect, it should be noted that, by providing that directives adopted in the fields of health and safety of workers are to avoid imposing administrative, financial and legal constraints in a way which would hold back the creation and development of small and medium-sized undertakings, Article 118a[20] of the EEC Treaty . . . indicates that such undertakings may be the subject of special economic measures.[21]

---

[18] Case 165/82 [1983] ECR 3431, at 3448. The Sex Discrimination Act 1986 subsequently narrowed down the private household exception and removed the small business exception altogether.

[19] Case C-189/91 [1993] ECR I-6185, noted by Horspool in (1994) 31 CMLRev 1115, and by Hervey in 'Small Business Exclusion in German Dismissal Law' (1994) 23 ILJ 267.

[20] Now Art 138.   [21] [1993] ECR I-6185, at 6223.

The decision in *Kirsammer-Hack* was not directly comparable with that in *Commission v UK*. The latter involved an exclusion from the scope of UK anti-discrimination legislation, which was automatically a breach of the Equal Treatment Directive unless excused by one of the exceptions contained in that Directive. *Kirsammer-Hack* involved an allegation that the German legislation on unfair dismissal operated in an indirectly discriminatory fashion and thus it had to be determined whether or not it was justifiable; only had it been found not to be justifiable would the issue of the applicability of the defence have arisen. Nevertheless, the ECJ's readiness to accept that the commercial viability of small businesses outweighed the right to equal treatment contrasted sharply with the attitude of the House of Lords in *R v Secretary of State for Employment, ex parte EOC*.[22] There, the House refused to accept the UK Government's assertion that the hours of work thresholds contained in UK employment protection legislation, which deprived many part-timers of the right to rely on this legislation, were justified on the ground that they encouraged part-time employment; although increasing the availability of part-time work was thought by the House to be a proper aim of social policy, the threshold provisions had not been shown to be either suitable or requisite to achieve that aim.

The third exception challenged by the Commission in *Commission v UK* was the exclusion of midwives (at that date) from the general operation of the Sex Discrimination Act 1975. Section 20 of the Act provided that midwives were excluded from the employment and training provisions of the Act. However, men were permitted to train as midwives at two centres in the UK, and to work as midwives in four designated hospitals. At the time of the action, these provisions, which had been intended to be transitional only, were about to be amended so as to remove the restrictions on men working as midwives and so to extend the protection of the Sex Discrimination Act to them.[23] Advocate General Rozès considered that nevertheless this had no bearing on the issue before the Court, which concerned only the state of the legislation at the time the proceedings were begun. However, Article 9(2) of the Directive requires Member States to assess periodically 'the occupational activities referred to in Article 2(2) in order to decide, in the light of social developments, whether there is justification for maintaining the exclusions concerned. They shall notify the Commission of the results of this assessment'.[24] The UK Government gave evidence that the exception for midwives had been kept under review as a result of this provision, and indeed that it was as a consequence of this review that the restrictions on male midwives were

---

[22] [1994] 2 WLR 409. See also Deakin, 'Part Time Employment, Qualifying Thresholds and Economic Justification' (1994) 23 ILJ 151, and Villiers and White, 'Agitating for Part-Time Workers' Rights' (1995) 58 MLR 560.

[23] See now the Sex Discrimination Act (Amendment of section 20) Order 1983, SI 1983 No 1202, Art 2. Patients can still, however, choose to be cared for by a female midwife if they prefer, and if a male midwife is provided, he must be subject to appropriate supervision.

[24] It is anomalous that this provision was not repealed when the Equal Treatment Directive was amended so as to cover only 'particular occupational activities' rather than occupational activities generally.

about to be lifted. It argued that midwives are often alone with their patients, especially after the mother has returned home after giving birth, and that in particular members of certain ethnic minorities living in the UK might object to the presence of a male midwife, to the ultimate endangerment of both mother and baby. All this was insufficient to persuade Advocate General Rozès of the legality of the exception, and she said:

I do not consider that the alleged specific nature of the conditions in which the occupation of midwife is practised in the UK is such as to justify, under Article 2(2) of the Directive, the discriminatory rules against men. I think that the guarantee of a free choice for patients, which is maintained in the proposed British rules, is a condition which is necessary and sufficient to allay the fears expressed by the UK Government.[25]

However, the Court itself held:

It is undeniable that in the area in question, as the UK acknowledges, the Member States are under an obligation to implement the principle of equality of treatment. It must however be recognized that at the present time personal sensitivities may play an important role in relations between midwife and patient. In those circumstances, it may be stated that by failing fully to apply the principle laid down in the Directive, the UK has not exceeded the limits of the power granted to the Member States by Articles 9(2) and 2(2) of the Directive. The Commission's complaint in that regard cannot therefore be upheld.[26]

It is likely that the principles governing the applicability of the 'genuine and determining occupational requirement' exception established by the ECJ in relation to the Equal Treatment Directive will in the future shape its application for the purposes of all three Directives. This may be surmised from the fact that the new wording consolidates the existing case law on sex discrimination, in particular in relation to the requirement of proportionality which the Court set out in *Johnston v RUC*.[27] The ECJ held there that the Chief Constable could not justify his refusal to provide women police reservists with firearms training (which had subsequently led to the non-renewal of their contracts of employment) by relying on the part of the Directive which referred to the exclusion of those occupational activities whose 'nature' required male workers, because the Sex Discrimination (Northern Ireland) Order 1976 expressly applied to employment in the police. However, that still left the part of the Article referring to the 'context' in which a job was performed. The Chief Constable argued that if women police officers were armed they might become a more frequent target for assassination and their firearms might fall into the hands of their assailants, that the public would not welcome the carrying of firearms by women, and that armed policewomen would be less effective in police work of a social nature. The Court held:

[T]he reasons which the Chief Constable thus gave for his policy were related to the special conditions in which the police must work in the situation existing in Northern Ireland, having regard to the

---

[25] [1983] ECR 3431, at 3460. [26] Ibid, at 3449.
[27] Op cit, n 2. See Recital 11 of the Preamble to the Directive amending the Equal Treatment Directive, op cit, n 14.

requirements of the protection of public safety in a context of serious internal disturbances. As regards the question whether such reasons may be covered by Article 2(2) of the Directive, it should first be observed that that provision, being a derogation from an individual right laid down in the Directive, must be interpreted strictly. However, it must be recognized that the context in which the occupational activity of members of an armed police force are carried out is determined by the environment in which that activity is carried out. In this regard, the possibility cannot be excluded that in a situation characterized by serious internal disturbances the carrying of firearms by policewomen might create additional risks of their being assassinated and might therefore be contrary to the requirements of public safety. In such circumstances, the context of certain policing activities may be such that the sex of police officers constitutes a determining factor for carrying them out.[28]

This was unsatisfactory because the Court made no attempt to explain why policewomen in this situation were more liable to be assassinated than policemen. When it referred to 'additional risks' to policewomen, it appeared confused: instead of comparing the risk to a police*woman* carrying out general police duties with the risk to a police*man* performing those same duties, it seemed to compare the risk to a policewoman between general police duties and those special few on which women were currently being employed.[29] The Court did, however, somewhat redeem itself by also pointing out that proportionality had a part to play in relation to this defence, and indeed with respect to all derogations from the equal treatment principle:

[I]n determining the scope of any derogation from an individual right such as the equal treatment of men and women provided for by the Directive, the principle of proportionality, one of the general principles of law underlying the Community legal order, must be observed. That principle requires that derogations remain within the limits of what is appropriate and necessary for achieving the aim in view and requires the principle of equal treatment to be reconciled as far as possible with the requirements of public safety which constitute the decisive factor as regards the context of the activity in question.

By reason of the division of jurisdiction provided for in Article [234] of the EEC Treaty, it is for the national court to say whether the reasons on which the Chief Constable based his decision are in fact well founded and justify the specific measure taken in Mrs Johnston's case. It is also for the national court to ensure that the principle of proportionality is observed and to determine whether the refusal to renew Mrs Johnston's contract could not be avoided by allocating to women duties which, without jeopardizing the aims pursued, can be performed without firearms.[30]

A later case on somewhat similar facts to *Johnston* was *Re Sex Discrimination in the Civil Service, Commission v France*,[31] in which the Commission prosecuted France for, *inter alia*, maintaining a quota based on sex for recruitment into various ranks of the police service. The French Government argued that sex was a determining factor because members of the national police force must at any time be able to use force in order to deter potential troublemakers, and that this prevented the

[28] Op cit, n 2, at 1686–7.
[29] See Ellis, 'Can Public Safety Provide an Excuse for Sex Discrimination?' (1986) 102 LQR 496.
[30] [1986] ECR 1651, at 1687. See also the ECJ's remarks to similar effect in Case 318/86 *Re Sex Discrimination in the Civil Service, Commission v France* [1988] ECR 3559, esp at 3582.
[31] Op cit, n 30.

inclusion of a large proportion of women in the police generally. Advocate General Slynn seemed more than willing to accept such an explanation,[32] but the Court did not have to address the issue directly since the parties had agreed that certain of the police duties involved had to be performed by men only, others by women only, and the remainder by either sex.[33] In these circumstances, the question became how the exception would apply, and the Court made an important statement about the practical enforcement of the anti-discrimination legislation. It held:

[T]he Directive leaves the Member States the power to exclude certain 'occupational activities' from its field of application[34] and . . . Article 9(2) of the Directive requires them periodically to assess the activities in question in order to decide, in the light of social developments, whether there is justification for maintaining the exclusions concerned. Article 9(2) further provides that the Member States are to notify the Commission of the results of that assessment.

It follows from those provisions that the exceptions . . . may relate only to specific activities, that they must be sufficiently transparent so as to permit effective supervision by the Commission and that in principle they must be capable of being adapted to social developments. The last requirement gives rise to no difficulties in this case; however, French law is not in accordance with the other two requirements.

As regards the requirement of transparency, it must be concluded that it is not fulfilled. Under the system of separate recruitment, the percentage of posts to be allotted to men and women respectively are fixed in the decision ordering the holding of a competition; the fixing of those percentages is not governed by any objective criterion defined in a legislative provision.

This lack of transparency also has consequences for compliance with the second requirement laid down by the Directive, which relates to the activities involved. *The contested system of recruitment makes it impossible to exercise any form of supervision, not only by the Commission and the courts but also by persons adversely affected by the discriminatory measures, in order to verify whether the percentages fixed for the recruitment of each sex actually correspond to specific activities for which the sex of the persons to be employed constitutes a determining factor within the meaning of . . . the Directive.*[35]

It was seen in chapter 3 that the ECJ has emphasized the significance of the principle of transparency in relation to the computation of pay, and the effect of its

[32] He commented: 'The argument is . . . that police officers have to be interchangeable and that all may be liable to perform police duties which involve the display of force. The latter, it is said, are unsuitable to be carried out by women. There is force in this argument, but it seems to me that it seeks to extend [the defence] too far. It may well be that for some police activities (where the use of force or a display of the capacity to use force are required) sex could be a determining factor not simply because on average men are bigger and stronger than women (which in itself would not necessarily be sufficient) but because potential delinquents regard men as more ready to use force, and perhaps because men are more willing to use force. These however, are matters which it seems to me are not necessary or, on the evidence available, not possible to decide, especially if regard is had to the role which women now appear to play in warfare and in police forces in some parts of the world. There may be a difference between handling violent crowds and situations where one or two individuals are threatening violence. As to the former, the Commission appears to accept that the exception . . . would apply to . . . bodies . . . whose activities regularly involve the use of force where substantial numbers of people may be involved. As to the latter, there may be an argument that in some situations with which the police have to deal the presence of women could be a deterrent to violence' (ibid, at 3571).
[33] It is unsatisfactory that the Commission conceded this important point, and it is to be hoped that the Court will have a future opportunity to examine the logic of the argument relied on.
[34] Cf under the amended Equal Treatment Directive.
[35] [1988] ECR 3559, at 3581–2, emphasis added.

remarks in both that field and the equal treatment field is to create a far-reaching principle: namely, that individuals involved are entitled to know the basis upon which employment decisions affecting them are reached, at least where the facts demonstrate a *prima facie* case of discrimination.

The applicability of the determining factor defence has arisen in a number of important sex discrimination cases concerning the military;[36] in these cases, the ECJ has shown marked deference to political sensibilities surrounding the armed forces and their deployment by the Member States. Its first decision was *Sirdar v Army Board and Secretary of State for Defence*,[37] in which a woman was denied access to the British Royal Marines on the ground that the unit needed to be all-male in order to ensure its combat effectiveness; reliance was placed by the Ministry of Defence on s 85(4) of the Sex Discrimination Act 1975, excluding acts done for the purpose of ensuring the combat effectiveness of the armed forces. The Royal Marines constitute a small proportion of the British army, designed in the words of Advocate General La Pergola to act as the 'point of the arrow head' and to intervene first in combat situations. The Ministry's argument was that the Marines depended on the principle of 'inter-operability', in other words, the ability of all its members to act both in specific capacities and also as fighting members of the infantry; the principle of inter-operability precluded the presence of women, it was alleged, because male soldiers might be tempted to try to protect their female colleagues and because women might prove physically unsuited for offensive hand-to-hand combat. The ECJ rejected the UK Government's argument that decisions concerning the organization of the armed forces, especially those taken in relation to combat effectiveness, remain within the sovereign competence of the Member States and therefore fall outside the scope of the Treaty. The question therefore became whether or not the exclusion of women from the Royal Marines could be excused by Article 2(2) of the Directive. Again, the UK Government argued for especially benevolent treatment of the armed services, claiming that judicial review in this area was limited to whether the national authorities could reasonably have formed the view that the policy was necessary and appropriate. The Court appeared to be swayed by this argument:

In determining the scope of any derogation from an individual right such as the equal treatment of men and women, the principle of proportionality, one of the general principles of Community law, must...be observed...That principle requires that derogations remain within the limits of what is appropriate and necessary in order to achieve the aim in view and requires the principle of equal treatment to be reconciled as far as possible with the requirements of public security which determine the context in which the activities in question are to be performed.

However, depending on the circumstances, national authorities have a certain degree of discretion when adopting measures which they consider to be necessary in order to guarantee public security in a Member State...[38]

---

[36] See also discussion below about the special exemption for the armed services in relation to disability and age.   [37] Case C-273/97, op cit, n 7.

[38] Ibid, at 7442, emphasis added.

The Court went on to hold that the British authorities were entitled, in the exercise of this discretion, to conclude that the specific conditions for deployment of the Royal Marines, in particular the principle of inter-operability, fell within the scope of the defence both as regards the nature of the activities concerned and the context in which they are carried out. What is surprising about this conclusion is the degree of gender-stereotyping adopted by the Court: it simply accepted the arguments of the British Government without questioning whether they were properly grounded on evidence, or merely on prejudice.[39]

Kreil v Germany[40] next raised the legality of a much more extensive German law (itself a reflection of a national constitutional provision) confining women volunteers to the medical and musical services of the military, and excluding them completely from any kind of armed service. The Court repeated its statements of principle made in *Sirdar*, but held that the present exclusion fell outside the legitimate sphere of action open to the Member States; this was because, since the exclusion applied to almost all posts in the German army, it could not be explained either by the specific nature of the jobs concerned, or by their particular context.[41]

If the confinement of women volunteers to particular posts within the armed forces constitutes discrimination against them, does it follow that Germany's policy of requiring compulsory military service only from men amounts to unlawful discrimination against men? This was the question asked in *Dory v Germany*.[42] Since this practice indubitably involves the unequal treatment of men and women, the only real issue was whether such conscription fell within the scope of EU law, in particular within the scope of the Equal Treatment Directive. One obvious answer might have been to hold that compulsory military service does not constitute employment.[43] However, Mr Dory constructed his argument cleverly, alleging that compulsory military service had the effect of prohibiting the exercise by him of an occupation during the period of that service, and also of delaying

---

[39] Cf the considerable attention paid by La Pergola AG to this matter. See also Ellis, 'The Recent Jurisprudence of the Court of Justice in the Field of Sex Equality' (2000) 37 CMLRev 1403. Hervey has suggested that a preferable analysis of *Sirdar* is that the context of the work of the Royal Marines, in particular its being a small force operating in difficult and unsanitary conditions, justified the exception from the point of view not of public safety but of personal privacy: see 'EC Law on Justifications for Sex Discrimination in Working Life' in Blanpain (ed), *Collective Bargaining, Discrimination, Social Security and European Integration* (Kluwer, Deventer, 2003).

[40] Case C-285/98, op cit, n 7. For discussion of both this case and *Sirdar*, see Koutrakos, 'Community Law and Equal Treatment in the Armed Forces' (2000) 25 ELRev 433.

[41] For discussion of the reaction within Germany to this decision, see Langer's note on *Sirdar* and *Kreil* in (2000) 37 CMLRev 1433.

[42] Case C-186/01, op cit, n 7. The German legislation confining compulsory military service to men formed part of the context in Case C-79/99 *Schnorbus v Land Hessen* [2000] ECR I-10997, but the Court was not asked there to rule on its compatibility with the Equal Treatment Directive. For comment critical of the decision in *Dory*, see Trybus in (2003) 40 CMLRev 1269.

[43] Stix-Hackl AG inclined to this view, saying (at 2497): 'Since compulsory military service is a unilateral civic duty imposed by authority with no entitlement to pay, [it] . . . could indeed be doubtful' whether it constituted 'employment' for the purposes of the Equal Treatment Directive.

his access to employment; it thus interfered with his right to equality under the terms of the Equal Treatment Directive. The ECJ nevertheless rejected this argument, but without distinguishing *Kreil* and on a basis the logic of which is elusive:

Certainly, decisions of the Member States concerning the organisation of their armed forces cannot be completely excluded from the application of Community law, particularly where observance of the principle of equal treatment of men and women in connection with employment, including access to military posts, is concerned. But it does not follow that Community law governs the Member States' choices of military organisation for the defence of their territory or of their essential interests.

It is for the Member States, which have to adopt appropriate measures to ensure their internal and external security, to take decisions on the organisation of their armed forces . . . [44]

The German Government had submitted that compulsory military service was very important to it, making a contribution to the 'democratic transparency of the military, national integration, the link between the armed forces and the population, and the mobilisation of the manpower needed by the armed forces in the event of a conflict'.[45] The Court concluded:

Such a choice, enshrined in the Grundgesetz, consists in imposing an obligation to serve the interests of territorial security, albeit in many cases to the detriment of access of young people to the labour market. It thus takes precedence over the objectives of policies aimed at the work prospects of young people.

The decision of the Federal Republic of Germany to ensure its defence in part by compulsory military service is the expression of such a choice of military organisation to which Community law is consequently not applicable.[46]

There is, in truth, a very fine line dividing these decisions, and one cannot help but wonder whether the Court was not unconsciously influenced by traditional gender-stereotyping; could it have reached the same decision in *Dory* if, for example, conscription had been confined to black or to Christian members of the population? However, Koutrakos has observed that, although the Court in *Dory* failed to articulate a criterion to define the outer reach of EU law in relation to the armed forces, the relevant measure in *Dory* was qualitatively different from that in *Sirdar* and *Kreil*:

[T]he German measure in *Dory* entailed a primary choice as to how national defence should be organised, whereas the British measure in *Sirdar* and the German one in *Kreil* entailed a secondary choice as to the regulation of access to the protection of national defence once its fundamental character had been decided.[47]

---

[44] [2003] ECR I-2479, at 2522–3. Stix-Hackl AG adopted a different analysis and submitted: 'Since . . . national compulsory military service for men only has a *subject-matter other than access to employment*, . . . —namely the guaranteeing of the external security of Germany by means of a specific form of organisation of the armed forces—this national measure is in principle outside the material scope of Directive 76/207' (at 2506, emphasis added).   [45] Ibid, at 2523.

[46] Ibid.

[47] Koutrakos, 'How Far is Far Enough? EC Law and the Organisation of the Armed Forces after *Dory*' (2003) 66 MLR 759, at 765.

(ii) The special occupational exception for religious bodies

During the gestation of the Framework Directive, the provision which caused the most public controversy was that protecting the right of religious bodies to maintain their beliefs where those beliefs would otherwise run counter to the instrument. There is a genuine clash here between freedom of religion and freedom from discrimination, in particular discrimination grounded on sexual orientation, because a number of religious sects condemn homosexuality. The Article which emerged, Article 4(2), is possibly one of the most opaque to be found on any statute book:

Member States may maintain national legislation in force at the date of adoption of this Directive or provide for future legislation incorporating national practices existing at the date of adoption of this Directive pursuant to which, in the case of occupational activities within churches and other public or private organisations the ethos of which is based on religion or belief, a difference of treatment based on a person's religion or belief shall not constitute discrimination where, by reason of the nature of these activities or of the context in which they are carried out, a person's religion or belief constitute a genuine, legitimate and justified occupational requirement, having regard to the organisation's ethos. This difference of treatment shall be implemented taking account of Member States' constitutional provisions and principles, as well as the general principles of Community law, and should not justify discrimination on another ground.

Provided that its provisions are otherwise complied with, this Directive shall thus not prejudice the right of churches and other public or private organisations, the ethos of which is based on religion or belief, acting in conformity with national constitutions and laws, to require individuals working for them to act in good faith and with loyalty to the organisation's ethos.[48]

At least at first sight, it is far from clear that this wording (which was considerably altered during the final Council negotiations at the instigation of the Irish Government)[49] adds anything of significance to that contained in Article 4(1), the exception for genuine and determining occupational requirements. Its basic intention is clearly to preserve the right of religious organizations, such as churches, schools, and hospices, to appoint staff of their own religious persuasion to key positions. However, this right has already been catered for by Article 4(1).

The meaning of 'public or private organisations the ethos of which is based on religion or belief' will also have to be worked out by the ECJ in future litigation. The use of the word 'ethos' clearly extends beyond personal belief and suggests some outward demonstration of adherence to a particular religion. Undoubtedly,

---

[48] See also Recital 24 of the Preamble to the Framework Directive. There is no equivalent provision in either the Equal Treatment Directive, or the Race Directive. It is especially significant that it was thought sufficient for the purposes of the Equal Treatment Directive to rely simply on the existence of the exception for genuine and determining occupational requirements, notwithstanding the fact that many religions hold strong views on the role to be played by men and women respectively.

[49] The Article as originally drafted appeared to limit the ability of religious organizations to rely on the genuine and determining occupational requirement defence.

many practical questions will arise, such as, for example, whether and to what extent Catholic practices of doctors, Jewish care homes, Muslim schools, or evangelical Christian partnerships of solicitors will be able to avail themselves of the exception.

Tessa Jowell, on behalf of the UK Government, set out to the House of Lords Select Committee on the EU the intended relationship between the two paragraphs of Article 4(2). She explained that the first paragraph permits religious organizations to treat employees or applicants differently on the ground of their religion where membership of the relevant religion is a genuine occupational requirement. However, the closing words of the paragraph indicate that, in so doing, they may not discriminate on any other ground, such as homosexuality (a matter categorized by the Minister as one of 'identity'). The second paragraph, however, then goes on to deal with the person's 'conduct' and would permit an employee's dismissal where his or her conduct undermined the organization's ethos. The House of Lords Select Committee remained unconvinced that this distinction was workable:

> It is not easy to draw clear lines between identity and conduct or to determine the constraints that may be imposed on the enjoyment of private life. One could imagine a situation in which the headmaster of a religious school was homosexual, but kept this part of his life wholly private and separate from his work in the school. He might then be exposed by a newspaper. In such circumstances it is not clear what rights either he or his employer would be able to claim under Article 4(2) of the Directive.[50]

The relationship between Article 4(1) and Article 4(2) is also worthy of scrutiny. Article 4(1) demands a more stringent test for the connection between the work and the characteristic; the characteristic must be a genuine and determining occupational requirement, the objective legitimate, and the requirement proportionate. For Article 4(2), it is sufficient that the relevant religion or belief constitutes a genuine, legitimate, and justified requirement; the word 'determining' is omitted. On the other hand, Article 4(1) does not conclude with a prohibition of discrimination on other grounds. Thus it would appear, for example, that a fundamentalist sect which disapproved of homosexuality could rely upon Article 4(1), but not Article 4(2), to excuse the non-appointment of a gay person, where the job to be performed is that of a minister or someone else close to the core of the organization's values. Where the job is not so vitally connected to the organization concerned, Article 4(2) might excuse the rejection of an applicant on the ground that that person did not share the same religion, but it would not excuse further discrimination on another ground, such as sex or sexual orientation, unless the person concerned then went on to act in a way which conflicted with the ethos of the organization.

The drafting of Article 4(2) contains a number of mysterious features, notably in the opening words of its second paragraph. It is unclear what is meant by 'Provided

---

[50] House of Lords Select Committee on the EU, 'The EU Framework Directive on Discrimination', Session 2000–01, 4th Report, HL Paper 13, para 48.

that its provisions are otherwise complied with', although presumably the intention is to permit the employer to discipline or dismiss an employee who acts in contravention of the organization's ethos but not to permit discrimination against that person on any other ground. The word 'thus' in the second paragraph is also difficult to explain, since the second paragraph does not follow as a matter of logic from the first.[51]

(iii) Provisions protecting women

The amended Equal Treatment Directive contains a detailed provision dealing with the protection of women. It repeats the old Article 2(3) of the instrument, consolidates the existing case law of the ECJ[52] on the subject, and refers also to the other statutory material in this area. Article 2(7) states:

This Directive shall be without prejudice to provisions concerning the protection of women, particularly as regards pregnancy and maternity.[53]

A woman on maternity leave shall be entitled, after the end of her period of maternity leave, to return to her job or to an equivalent post on terms and conditions which are no less favourable to her and to benefit from any improvement in working conditions to which she would be entitled during her absence.[54]

Less favourable treatment of a woman related to pregnancy or maternity leave within the meaning of Directive 92/85/EEC[55] shall constitute discrimination within the meaning of this Directive.[56]

This Directive shall also be without prejudice to the provisions of Council Directive 96/34/EC of 3 June 1996 on the framework agreement on parental leave concluded by UNICE, CEEP and the ETUC[57] and of Council Directive 92/85/EEC of 19 October 1992 on the introduction of measures to encourage improvements in the safety and health at work of pregnant workers and workers who have recently given birth or are breastfeeding . . . It is also without prejudice to the right of Member States to recognise distinct rights to paternity and/or adoption leave. Those Member States which recognise such rights shall take the necessary measures to protect working men and women against dismissal due to exercising those rights and ensure that, at the end of such leave, they shall be entitled to return to their jobs or to equivalent posts on terms and conditions which are no less favourable to them, and to benefit from any improvement in working conditions to which they would have been entitled during their absence.

---

[51] In the context of special dispensations for religious practices, note also Art III-121 of the proposed Constitution; this requires the Union and the Member States in formulating and implementing Union policies to pay full regard to the requirements of animal welfare, whilst at the same time respecting particular religious rites.

[52] See Recital 12 of the Preamble to Directive 2002/73 (OJ [2002] L269/15).

[53] This provision only excuses treatment favourable to the woman employee; thus, in Case C-66/96 *Handels- og Kontorfunktionaerernes Forbund I Danmark v Faellesforeningen for Danmarks Brugsforeninger* [1998] ECR I-7327, the Court held that it did not excuse a national rule permitting an employer to send home a healthy pregnant employee when he could not find work for her: such a rule was 'aimed not so much at protecting the pregnant woman's biological condition as at preserving the interests of her employer' (at 7375). See also Case C-136/95 *CNAVTS v Thibault* [1998] ECR I-2011, and Case C-207/98 *Mahlburg v Land Mecklenburg-Vorpommern* [2000] ECR I-549.

[54] See Case C-342/93 *Gillespie v Northern Health and Social Services Board* [1996] ECR I-475.

[55] Discussed in ch 5.

[56] Case C-177/88 *Dekker v Stichting Vormingscentrum voor Jonge Volwassen Plus* [1990] ECR I-3941.

[57] Discussed in ch 5.

The old Article 2(3) was in issue before the ECJ on a number of occasions. *Commission v Italy*[58] concerned, *inter alia*, Italian legislation which extended certain maternity rights to women, but not to men, when they adopted children under six years of age. It allowed them to claim three months' leave from employment, together with a financial allowance. Advocate General Rozès considered that this constituted a breach of the equal treatment principle as regards working conditions, and that it could not be justified by reference to the exception for maternity:

I believe that leave after giving birth to a child in order to allow the mother to rest may rightly be regarded as a provision to protect women in relation to maternity. On the other hand, I consider that leave after adoption benefits the child above all in so far as it is intended to foster the emotional ties necessary to settle the child in the family adopting it . . . I therefore consider that the leave referred to . . . is part of the working conditions within the meaning of . . . of the Directive. That is why I consider that adoptive fathers must be entitled to it on the same basis as their working wives.[59]

The full Court, however, unfortunately did not adopt such an analytical approach and held simply:

[The distinction in relation to maternity leave] is justified . . . by the legitimate concern to assimilate as far as possible the conditions of entry of the child into the adoptive family to those of the arrival of a newborn child in the family during the very delicate initial period. As regards leave from work after the initial period of three months the adoptive father has the same rights as the adoptive mother.[60]

This ruling suggested that the Court was prepared to give an extensive interpretation to the word 'maternity'. This view was confirmed by *Hofmann v Barmer Ersatzkasse*,[61] in which a father alleged that it was unlawfully discriminatory for Federal German law to grant mothers, but not fathers, an optional period of paid leave from employment between the ending of the statutory period of maternity leave eight weeks after childbirth and the child reaching the age of six months. The father argued that, since this additional period of leave was essentially provided for the benefit of the baby, it should be open to fathers too. The Advocate General and the Court both rejected this argument, the latter explaining:

[B]y reserving to Member States the right to retain or introduce provisions which are intended to protect women in connection with 'pregnancy and maternity', the Directive recognizes the legitimacy, in terms of the principle of equal treatment, of protecting a woman's needs in two respects. First, it is legitimate to ensure the protection of a woman's biological condition during pregnancy and thereafter until such time as her physiological and mental functions have returned to normal after childbirth; and secondly, it is legitimate to protect the special relationship between a woman and her child over the period which follows pregnancy and childbirth, by preventing that relationship from being disturbed by the multiple burdens which would result from the simultaneous pursuit of employment.

In principle, therefore, a measure such as maternity leave granted to a woman on expiry of the statutory protective period falls within the scope of Article 2(3) of Directive 76/207, inasmuch as it seeks to protect a woman in connection with the effects of pregnancy and motherhood. That being so, such

[58] Case 163/82 [1983] ECR 3273.   [59] Ibid, at 3297–8.   [60] Ibid, at 3288.
[61] Case 184/83 [1984] ECR 3047.

leave may legitimately be reserved to the mother to the exclusion of any other person, in view of the fact that it is only the mother who may find herself subject to undesirable pressures to return to work prematurely.[62]

It is significant that the language used by the ECJ evolved here from 'maternity' (the word used in the Directive) to 'motherhood'. The Court was apparently saying that different provision is permissible in connection with 'motherhood', which, in ordinary language, is a state of very much longer duration than 'maternity'. The unfortunate innuendo here, of course, was that it signalled that the exception might be interpreted in future by the ECJ to legitimize other forms of preferential treatment for mothers which were based on outdated notions of parental role-playing within families. On the other hand, the *Hofmann* case was only in fact concerned with leave periods up to six months from the child's birth, and it did not necessarily follow that the Court would have accepted the same argument had it been faced with a returner scheme allowing a mother only a period of, say, one or two years of leave after the birth. It would appear logically that, if the exception is to be construed strictly, in accordance with the usual principle, such a scheme could not be excused as attributable to 'maternity'.

Some of the more recent cases suggest that the Court may be moving in this direction.[63] *Commission v France*[64] was a prosecution of France for enacting legislation providing that, although contractual employment equality was to be the norm as between men and women, there could remain in operation terms of contracts and collective agreements in force on the date at which the legislation was enacted 'granting particular rights to women'. The French Government argued that this was justifiable by means of the then Article 2(3) of the Directive. The particular rights in question related to extended maternity leave, reduction in working hours for women aged 59, the bringing forward of retirement age, time off for sick children, extra days' holiday each year per child, a day off on the first day of the school term, some hours off on Mothers' Day, daily breaks for women working on computer equipment, or as typists or switchboard operators, pension bonuses after the birth of a second child, and allowances for nurseries and childminders. The Commission agreed that some of these matters might fall within Article 2(3), but argued that in general effect the French legislation enabled inequalities in treatment between men and women contrary to the Directive to continue indefinitely. The Court agreed with the Commission, pointing out that some of the examples given of the particular rights for women which were being protected 'relate to the protection of women in their capacity as older workers or parents—categories to which both men and women may equally belong'.[65] In other words, the Court would not countenance any extension of Article 2(3)

---

[62] Case 184/83 [1984] ECR 3047, at 3075.

[63] Cf Case C-218/98 *Abdoulaye v Renault SA* [1999] ECR I-5723, as to which see the comments of McGlynn in 'Pregnancy, Parenthood and the Court of Justice in *Abdoulaye*' (2000) 25 ELRev 654.

[64] Case 312/86 [1988] ECR 6315.

[65] Ibid, at 6336. See also Case C-366/99 *Griesmar* [2001] ECR I-9383.

beyond cases connected in some fairly close but unspecified way with the process of childbearing. Unfortunately, the Court said nothing about how it saw the limits to the exception and, in particular, at what point maternity matures into parenthood. Advocate General Slynn was somewhat more forthcoming in this respect, saying that the *Hofmann* case had established that the exception was confined to 'the period which follows pregnancy and childbirth, and not any later period'.[66]

Part of the doubt which surrounds the extent of this exception is due to its drafting. The inclusion of the word 'particularly' ('particularly as regards pregnancy and maternity') is unfortunate: it suggests, although it does not articulate, that there are other grounds on which women may lawfully be protected. This reasoning could of course be used to justify differential treatment of women on the basis of some spurious supposed vulnerability or weakness. In its decision in *Johnston v Chief Constable of the RUC*,[67] the Court left tantalizingly open the question of whether there were any other grounds, besides pregnancy and maternity, on which women could lawfully be protected. After asserting that the Article must, like the exception for genuine and determining occupational requirements, be construed strictly, it said:

[I]t is clear from the express reference to pregnancy and maternity that the Directive is intended to protect a woman's biological condition[68] and the special relationship that exists between a woman and her child. That provision of the Directive does not therefore allow women to be excluded from a certain type of employment on the ground that public opinion demands that women be given greater protection than men against risks that affect women and men in the same way *and which are distinct from women's special needs of protection, such as those expressly mentioned.* It does not appear that the risks and dangers to which women are exposed when performing their duties in the police force in a situation such as exists in Northern Ireland are different from those to which any man is also exposed when performing the same duties.[69]

In the later decision in *Commission v France*[70] Advocate General Slynn commented, with almost equal opacity: 'Although the word "particularly" in Article 2(3) indicates that situations other than pregnancy and maternity may fall within its scope, those words colour the scope of the exemptions'.[71] At present, therefore, all

---

[66] [1988] ECR 6315, at 6328.   [67] Op cit, n 2, also discussed above.
[68] Recital 12 of the Preamble to Directive 2002/73 (OJ [2002] L269/15) consolidates this view by referring specifically to the need to protect 'a woman's biological condition during and after pregnancy'.
[69] [1986] ECR 1651, at 1688–9, emphasis added. See also Case C-285/98 *Kreil*, op cit, n 7. In Case C-345/89 *Stoeckel* [1991] ECR I-4047, the ECJ held that a ban on night work by women was not permitted; it stated that '[a]s far as the aims of protecting female workers are concerned, they are valid only if... there is a justified need for a difference of treatment as between men and women. However, whatever the disadvantages of night work may be, it does not seem that, except in the case of pregnancy or maternity, the risks to which women are exposed when working at night are, in general, inherently different from those to which men are exposed' (at 4066). See also Case C-13/93 *Office National de l'Emploi v Minne* [1994] ECR I-371.   [70] Op cit, n 64.
[71] Ibid, at 6328.

that can be concluded about the scope of Article 2(7) is that it can certainly be used to justify special treatment for women in employment in relation to pregnancy[72] and up to at least six months from the date of their giving birth; beyond this, it can seemingly be used to justify the 'protection' of women against biological risks which are specific to their sex, but quite what these risks are, and how 'biological' is to be defined, has yet to be worked out in the case law of the ECJ.

(iv)   Differences of treatment based on nationality

Article 3(2) of the Race Directive provides:

This Directive does not cover difference of treatment based on nationality and is without prejudice to provisions and conditions relating to the entry into and residence of third-country nationals and stateless persons on the territory of Member States, and to any treatment which arises from the legal status of the third-country nationals and stateless persons concerned.

The apparent rationale for this exception is to prevent third-country nationals from circumventing the limitation of Article 12 of the TEC; this restricts unlawful discrimination on the ground of nationality to cases where the nationality involved is that of one of the Member States. Article 3(2) of the Directive appears to deny the possibility of alleging race discrimination in a situation where the real underlying cause of the discrimination experienced by a third-country national is nationality. However, the provision may well open the door to what are actually examples of racial discrimination being excused on the basis of nationality. Lord Lester has commented that this exception is incompatible with the effective protection of human rights,[73] and Brown has perceptively observed that 'by maintaining a distinction in the field of racial discrimination between EU nationals and third-country nationals, the Directive risks feeding xenophobia rather than diminishing it'.[74]

Nevertheless, one positive message which can be drawn from this provision is that, in situations other than those specified, the Race Directive (and its partner

---

[72]   Where special treatment is actually extended to pregnant women, it appears to be assumed that that treatment is logically related to their pregnancy; thus, eg, in Case C-421/92 *Habermann-Beltermann v Arbeiterwohlfahrt* [1994] ECR I-1657, Tesauro AG submitted: '...with respect to Article 2(3) of the Directive, the legality of...German legislation prohibiting night-time work for pregnant women is beyond dispute. That legislation accords special protection to female workers in such circumstances and is clearly covered by the derogations provided for in the Directive' (at 1663). The Court agreed that 'the prohibition on night-time work by pregnant women [was]...unquestionably compatible with Art 2(3) ...' (at 1675). However, there was no inquiry here into why night-time (as distinct from day-time) work was perceived as especially hazardous to pregnant women.

[73]   Lester, 'New European equality measures' [2000] PL 562.

[74]   Brown, 'The Race Directive: Towards Equality for *All* the Peoples of Europe?' (2002) 21 YEL 195, at 212. See also Brennan, 'The Race Directive: Recycling Racial Inequality' (2002–3) 5 CYELS 311.

Framework Directive) is intended to apply to all persons within the EU, irrespective of their nationality.[75]

The provision was inserted into the Directive in order to make it clear that the ever-sensitive matter of immigration was not within its terms.[76] In addition, the UK Government wished to make it clear that such matters as social protection and social security for third-country nationals and stateless persons was excluded from the scope of the Race Directive. However, the breadth of the wording used is significant and regrettable;[77] in particular, the final phrase of the provision permits 'any' adverse treatment of third-country nationals and stateless persons which is based on their status.[78] Thus, for example, it would appear to legalize discrimination by anybody in relation to housing or the provision of education, provided that the action could be said to be grounded on the victim's third-country nationality or statelessness, even though it also constituted discrimination on racial grounds.

Puzzlingly, though perhaps it was simply the consequence of a misplaced striving for consistency, the Framework Directive was amended during its gestation so that it contains a provision in virtually identical terms to Article 3(2) of the Race Directive.[79] It is difficult to imagine how the Framework Directive would impinge on immigration.[80] Tessa Jowell, on behalf of the UK Government, offered the view that 'it is unlikely that a situation would in fact arise where this would impact in practice and we do not consider that this Directive . . . touches on immigration at all'; nevertheless, it was helpful to make it 'crystal clear' that entry conditions relating to access to particular types of employment, and setting different standards for different ages, were not caught by the Directive.[81]

---

[75] This intention is confirmed by Recital 13 of the Preamble to the Directive and by Recital 12 of the Preamble to the Framework Directive.

[76] The UK Government, having secured an opt-out from measures taken under Title IV of the TEC and the Schengen Agreement, was instrumental in the exclusion of immigration from the Race Directive. It cited the example of the exceptional leave to remain in the UK granted to the Kosovan Albanians; such leave was not granted to the Kosovan Serbs and, without the exception now contained in Art 3(2), similar action in the future would amount to unlawful discrimination on the ground of ethnic origin. In a letter to Lord Lester (quoted in Lester, op cit, n 73), Baroness Blackstone, the responsible Government Minister, stated that the exception was necessary for the effective operation of the UK's immigration and asylum policies, and to safeguard the provisions of domestic law which 'allow the government to impose restrictions on, for example, the access to employment enjoyed by third-country nationals resident in the UK in a temporary capacity, including those awaiting the outcome of their asylum applications and appeals' (at 565).

[77] For further criticism of this exception and its potential impact on third-country nationals, see Hepple, 'Race and Law in Fortress Europe' (2004) 67 MLR 1.

[78] Cf Recital 13 of the Preamble to the Race Directive, which merely says: 'This prohibition of discrimination . . . is without prejudice to . . . access to employment and to occupation'.

[79] Art 3(2) of the Framework Directive. The Equal Treatment Directive (mercifully) contains no equivalent provision.

[80] Note, however, that, as originally proposed, the Framework Directive would also have covered racial discrimination. This nevertheless does not explain why the immigration exception was inserted into the Framework instrument after the provisions on racial discrimination had been removed from it and enacted in a separate Directive.

[81] House of Lords Select Committee on the EU, 'The EU Framework Directive on Discrimination', Session 2000–01, 4th Report, HL Paper 13.

(v) Measures necessary for public security, public order, the prevention of criminal offences, the protection of health, and the protection of the rights and freedoms of others

Article 2(5) of the Framework Directive[82] provides:

This Directive shall be without prejudice to measures laid down by national law which, in a democratic society, are necessary for public security, for the maintenance of public order and the prevention of criminal offences, for the protection of health and for the protection of the rights and freedoms of others.

This wording is based loosely on that contained in the ECHR, in particular Article 8 on the right to respect for private and family life, Article 9 on freedom of thought, conscience, and religion, Article 10 on freedom of expression, and Article 11 on freedom of assembly and association; the ECJ may therefore well look to the interpretation of these Articles by the European Court of Human Rights for guidance as to how to construe Article 2(5).

The provision is one which was inserted into the Directive during the final hours of negotiation on it[83] and no version of it was contained in the original draft of the instrument. It was thought necessary to prevent members of harmful cults, paedophiles,[84] and people with dangerous physical and mental illnesses from gaining protection from the Directive. It is, however, an extremely broadly drafted provision, especially given that the Framework Directive covers only workplace discrimination. The ECJ will have to patrol its boundaries carefully.

(vi) Payments made by State schemes

Article 3(3) excepts from the scope of the Framework Directive 'payments of any kind made by state schemes or similar, including state social security or social protection schemes'.[85] Recital 13 of the Preamble to this Directive explains that it is intended to align the meaning of 'pay' for the purposes of the Framework Directive with that adopted in relation to Article 141, and it adds that the Directive does not apply to 'any kind of payment by the State aimed at providing access to employment or maintaining employment'. This exception is somewhat less controversial than the others which (like it) were introduced during the final

---

[82] There is no equivalent provision in either the Equal Treatment Directive, or the Race Directive.

[83] Apparently at the insistence of the UK Government: see the House of Lords Select Committee on the EU, 'The EU Framework Directive on Discrimination', Session 2000–01, 4th Report, HL Paper 13, para 37.

[84] It is of course highly questionable whether paedophilia could be considered to be a sexual orientation.

[85] There is no equivalent exception in the Race Directive. The principle of sex equality in relation to social security is discussed in ch 8.

negotiations on the Directive, since it merely articulates a conclusion which the ECJ would probably have reached in any event.

(vii)   The armed forces

The same can certainly not be said of Article 3(4) of the Framework Directive. Also introduced at the end of the negotiations on the instrument,[86] this provides that the Directive, 'in so far as it relates to discrimination on the grounds of disability and age, shall not apply to the armed forces'.[87] This provision must be viewed against the background of the Preamble to the instrument, which states:

(17) This Directive does not require the recruitment, promotion, maintenance in employment or training of an individual who is not competent, capable and available to perform the essential functions of the post concerned or to undergo the relevant training, without prejudice to the obligation to provide reasonable accommodation for people with disabilities.

(18) This Directive does not require, in particular, the armed forces and the police, prison or emergency services to recruit or maintain in employment persons who do not have the required capacity to carry out the range of functions that they may be called upon to perform with regard to the legitimate objective of preserving the operational capacity of those services.

(19) Moreover, in order that the Member States may continue to safeguard the combat effectiveness of their armed forces, they may choose not to apply the provisions of this Directive concerning disability and age to all or part of their armed forces. The Member States which make that choice must define the scope of that derogation.

This is a serious erosion of the protection offered by the Directive, especially as far as disabled people are concerned. It is unnecessary to exclude all jobs (even, for example, clerical jobs) within the armed forces, rather than simply those relevant to combat effectiveness. However, the UK Government justified its support for this provision with the argument that decisions on combat effectiveness should not be challengeable before the courts.

(viii)   Reasonable accommodation for the disabled

Article 5 of the Framework Directive articulates the very important principle of reasonable accommodation for disabled people:

In order to guarantee compliance with the principle of equal treatment in relation to persons with disabilities, reasonable accommodation shall be provided. This means that employers shall take appropriate measures, where needed in a particular case, to enable a person with a disability to have access

---

[86] When it became apparent that the genuine and determining occupational requirement exception would not deal with the situation.

[87] There is no equivalent express exception in the Equal Treatment Directive or the Race Directive. See discussion above about the cases in which the determining factor exception from the Equal Treatment Directive has been invoked in relation to the armed forces.

to, participate in, or advance in employment, or to undergo training, unless such measures would impose a disproportionate burden on the employer. This burden shall not be disproportionate when it is sufficiently remedied by measures existing within the framework of the disability policy of the Member State concerned.[88]

Thus, a concept of equilibrium underlies the law on non-discrimination on the ground of disability. Unlike most of the other prohibited grounds of discrimination, disability describes a spectrum of conditions. This makes it difficult to lay down absolutes and, for the law to operate properly in practical terms, it must focus on individual cases as well as generalities. The solution opted for in the Framework Directive is to require employers to take 'appropriate measures' to accommodate disabled employees, in the 'particular' case as well as more generally, but to limit this principle to measures which are 'proportionate'. There will clearly be an important role for the ECJ in explaining what is meant by 'appropriate measures' and according to what parameters proportion is to be judged. Some guidance is provided by the Preamble to the Framework Directive, which indicates that the appropriateness of the employer's measures is to be measured by their effectiveness; Recital 20 states that 'appropriate measures' are 'effective and practical measures to adapt the workplace to the disability, for example by adapting premises and equipment, patterns of working time, the distribution of tasks or the provision of training or integration resources'. In determining whether the burden is disproportionate, the Preamble states that 'account should be taken in particular of the financial and other costs entailed, the scale and financial resources of the organisation or undertaking and the possibility of obtaining public funding or other assistance'.[89]

It has been argued that there is a risk that the defence provided by Article 2(5)[90] may undermine the principle of reasonable accommodation and thus the extent to which the Framework Directive really protects disabled people. In particular, the protection of public health and the protection of the rights and freedoms of others 'may prove a fertile area for defending claims of failure to make reasonable accommodation', and it is therefore vital that the ECJ interprets the Article 2(5) derogations particularly strictly in the context of disability.[91]

---

[88] Note that this principle applies only to discrimination on the ground of disability and not, eg, to religious discrimination. Note also, the obligation to provide reasonable accommodation originated in relation to religious discrimination in North America, and it applies in Canada to all the grounds covered by the Charter of Fundamental Freedoms and the Federal Human Rights Act. It would have greatly aided the effectiveness of the proscription of discrimination on the ground of religion or belief if the requirement of reasonable accommodation had applied to it; despite growing cultural diversity throughout Europe, the world of work reflects a predominantly Christian model; see, eg, the tenor of the remarks of the Court of Appeal in *Ahmad v ILEA* [1978] QB 36. However, it would have presented huge practical difficulties for employers, in view of the probable breadth of meaning of 'religion or belief', to have required them to provide reasonable accommodation for the religious needs of their workforces.   [89] Recital 21.

[90] Discussed above.

[91] See Wells, 'The Impact of the Framework Employment Directive on UK Disability Discrimination Law' (2003) 32 ILJ 253, at 265–6.

The notion of reasonable accommodation is especially relevant in the context of indirect discrimination, although, since Article 5 creates an independent and free-standing obligation, this must not be taken to imply that the requirement to provide reasonable accommodation does not apply with equal force in cases where direct discrimination is alleged. Indirect discrimination against disabled people may be justified in the usual way.[92] However, in addition, Article 2(2)(b)(ii) of the Framework Directive provides that what is *prima facie* indirect discrimination can also be negatived provided:

As regards persons with a particular disability, the employer or any person or organisation to whom this Directive applies, is obliged, under national legislation, to take appropriate measures in line with the principles contained in Article 5 in order to eliminate disadvantages entailed by such provision, criterion or practice.

This arrangement is comprehensible, if at all, only in the light of its history. The UK's existing disability legislation does not distinguish between direct and indirect discrimination, but applies a concept akin to reasonable accommodation to both.[93] When the draft Framework Directive appeared, and proposed applying the concept of indirect discrimination in the field of disability, there was much discussion in the UK of the relationship between it and reasonable accommodation.[94] A practical illustration illustrates the problem: suppose that an employer requires an office-worker to deliver packages to a number of different offices within a building. Somebody confined to a wheel-chair would find this task difficult and time-consuming; the requirement therefore constitutes *prima facie* indirect discrimination on the ground of disability. If the concept of justification were held to legalize this situation, the employer would have to prove that there was a genuine need for the packages to be delivered, that this was an appropriate way for delivery to be achieved, and that there was no alternative way. If, on the other hand, the concept of reasonable accommodation were to apply, the employer would have to examine whether there were measures which could be taken which, short of imposing a disproportionate burden, would make it possible for the wheel-chair user to deliver the packages (for example, the installation of ramps or appropriate doors). The two tests are simply different. Furthermore, although reasonable accommodation is helpful from the victim's viewpoint, because it enables him or her to engage in the occupation concerned, it does not require the employer to remove the obstacle for other potential disabled candidates; it does not, in other words, yield a group benefit. If a practice has to be justified, on the other hand, an employer who fails to justify it will have to discontinue the practice, with consequential benefits to other disabled applicants.

---

[92] See the general discussion of justification in ch 3.

[93] See the Disability Discrimination Act 1995, esp s 6.

[94] See the House of Lords Select Committee on the EU, 'EU Proposals to Combat Discrimination', Session 1999–2000, 9th Report, HL Paper 68, paras 94–95.

The House of Lords Select Committee on the EU considered one intellectually attractive solution in its investigation of the draft Directive. Professor Bob Hepple suggested that the two concepts could be combined in a single provision, thus:

A provision, criterion or practice shall not be regarded as appropriate and necessary in the case of indirect discrimination which disadvantages disabled persons . . . unless the needs of that group cannot be reasonably accommodated without causing undue hardship on the person responsible for accommodating those needs, having regard to factors such as cost and health and safety requirements.[95]

As has been seen, this is not the solution adopted in the Directive. Instead, the Directive appears to allow the Member States to choose whether ('under national legislation') they apply justification or reasonable accommodation in cases of alleged indirect discrimination on the ground of disability.[96] However, this still leaves a conundrum; since Article 5 creates a free-standing obligation, it requires employers to provide reasonable accommodation even in Member States which opt to apply the concept of justification to alleged indirect discrimination. What appears to be an option is therefore not in reality an option.

(ix)   Justification on grounds of age

Article 6 of the Framework Directive creates an exception applicable only to discrimination on the ground of age.[97] Its heading itself is sinister: 'Justification of differences of treatment on grounds of age.' As discussed in chapter 3, justification is a concept which serves to negative causation in the context of indirect discrimination. It is not logically applicable to direct discrimination, and an attempt to apply it to direct discrimination also risks seriously eroding the utility of that concept. It is therefore disturbing that Article 6 of the Framework Directive does not limit the application of justification to indirect discrimination but instead creates a general defence:

1. Notwithstanding Article 2(2), Member States may provide that differences of treatment on grounds of age shall not constitute discrimination,[98] if, within the context of national law, they are objectively and reasonably justified by a legitimate aim, including legitimate employment policy, labour market and vocational training objectives, and if the means of achieving that aim are appropriate and necessary.

Such differences may include, among others:

(a) the setting of special conditions on access to employment and vocational training, employment and occupation, including dismissal and remuneration conditions, for young people, older

---

[95] See the House of Lords Select Committee on the EU, 'EU Proposals to Combat Discrimination', Session 1999–2000, 9th Report, HL Paper 68, at para 94. This approach is based on the Ontario Human Rights Code.

[96] This is certainly the view that the UK Government takes of the Directive; see the House of Lords Select Committee on the EU, 'The EU Framework Directive on Discrimination', Session 2000–01, 4th Report, HL Paper 13, para 39.

[97] No equivalent exception is contained in the Equal Treatment Directive, or in the Race Directive.

[98] The same point applies here as in relation to the wording of the genuine and determining occupational qualification defence, namely, that this is in fact discrimination but that it is rendered lawful by a specific defence.

workers and persons with caring responsibilities in order to promote their vocational integration or ensure their protection;

(b) the fixing of minimum conditions of age, professional experience or seniority in service for access to employment or to certain advantages linked to employment;

(c) the fixing of a maximum age for recruitment which is based on the training requirements of the post in question or the need for a reasonable period of employment before retirement.[99]

The breadth of this provision is to be noted. It explicitly sacrifices the principle of non-discrimination to commercial interests. An important discretion will therefore lie with the ECJ when it is called on to determine the meaning of 'reasonably justified by a legitimate aim'. If the Court does not take a firm line on this, age discrimination will have been effectively legalized by this provision, a serious matter in the present demographic climate.[100]

As discussed in chapter 4, this Article also removes occupational pensions from the reach of the Directive's provisions on age discrimination.

It is noteworthy that, although para (2) of Article 6[101] prohibits practices which result in sex discrimination, para (1) makes no such reference. The imposition of age limits, for example in relation to access to the employment market, frequently constitutes indirect discrimination on the ground of sex, since women spend more time out of the labour market than men as a result of bearing children. It is therefore to be hoped that the Court will imply this limitation into the whole Article; the spirit of the Article implies such a limitation since it envisages especially favourable treatment for certain groups, including those with 'caring responsibilities'.

(x) The exceptions for Northern Ireland

Two exceptions applicable only to Northern Ireland appeared mysteriously during the final negotiations on the Framework Directive, apparently in deference to the unique circumstances of that Province. Article 15 of that instrument provides:

1. In order to tackle the under-representation of one of the major religious communities in the police service of Northern Ireland, differences in treatment regarding recruitment into that service, including its support staff, shall not constitute discrimination insofar as those differences in treatment are expressly authorised by national legislation.

2. In order to maintain a balance of opportunity in employment for teachers in Northern Ireland while furthering the reconciliation of historical divisions between the major religious communities there, the provisions on religion or belief in this Directive shall not apply to the recruitment of teachers in schools in Northern Ireland insofar as this is expressly authorised by national legislation.

---

[99] Recital 14 of the Preamble to the Directive states that the instrument is without prejudice to national provisions laying down retirement ages.

[100] It is estimated that, in the EU, the number of elderly people will have doubled between 2000 and 2050: see *Finance and Development*, June 2004.   [101] As to which see ch 4.

The intention of this Article appears to be to except from the Framework Directive two particularly sensitive issues in Northern Ireland,[102] namely, the Patten reforms to the police service,[103] which demand an equal number of Catholic and Protestant recruits to the service, and the long-standing religious segregation of the teaching profession.[104] Ironically, perhaps as a consequence of the haste with which Article 15 was constructed, it might not prove sufficient to preserve the legality of the present arrangements. There is no equivalent provision in either the Equal Treatment Directive, or the Race Directive; it may very well be that discrimination of the types envisaged in Article 15 of the Framework Directive constitutes discrimination prohibited by the Race Directive, since membership of either the Catholic or the Protestant community in Northern Ireland might be held to be a matter of 'ethnic origin'.

Positive action

The term 'positive action' has not as yet been comprehensively defined by the ECJ. It appeared expressly for the first time in EU legislation in the Race Directive and the Framework Directive.[105] In colloquial use, it describes a range of measures intended to promote substantive equality, from the mere encouragement of under-represented groups to reverse discrimination and quotas in favour of those under-represented groups.[106] It was seen in chapter 1 that schemes for positive action are all essentially in tension with the liberal, individual notion of equality. Divergent views are consequently held within the Member States as to what the permissible scope of positive action should properly be: some strongly advocate the legalization of what would otherwise constitute discrimination, provided that it is carried out in the cause of equality; others, with equal vehemence, assert that this undermines the very principle of equality itself.

The first EU provision to address the matter, albeit not expressly under the label of positive action, was Article 2(4) of the Equal Treatment Directive. This has now been amended,[107] but since it received some judicial attention in its original form, it is necessary to examine its original wording. This stated:

This Directive shall be without prejudice to measures to promote equal opportunities for men and women, in particular by removing existing inequalities which affect women's opportunities in the areas referred to in Article 1(1).

---

[102] Recital 34 of the Preamble to the Framework Directive explains that the rationale for Art 15 is the 'need to promote peace and reconciliation between the major communities in Northern Ireland'.

[103] Contained in the Police (Northern Ireland) Act 2000; see also ch 1.

[104] Schoolteachers in Northern Ireland are exempted from the fair employment legislation.

[105] See further below. [106] See Fredman, 'Reversing Discrimination' (1997) 113 LQR 575.

[107] By Directive 2002/73, OJ [2002] L269/15.

In *Hofmann v Barmer Ersatzkasse*,[108] although the Court itself said nothing of substance about the scope of Article 2(4), Advocate General Darmon commented:

The exception set out in Article 2(4) is in a category of its own. The provision opens the way for national measures 'to promote equal opportunity for men and women, in particular by removing existing inequalities'. It merely appears to make an exception to the principle: in aiming to compensate for existing discrimination it seeks to re-establish equality and not to prejudice it. In other words, since it presupposes that there is an inequality which must be removed, the exception must be broadly construed.[109]

He went on to say that the grant of an additional period of paid leave from employment after childbirth to mothers but not fathers:

[A]ffords a means of mitigating the *de facto* inequalities suffered by women as a result of the deterioration of their health following childbirth and thus preserves their opportunities on the resumption of work. In that sense, the leave is included amongst the measures referred to by Article 2(4) of the Directive. Thus, the question necessarily arises as to whether the exception in Article 2(3)[110] is not an illustration, selected by the Community legislature, of the general derogation contained in Article 2(4). I incline towards that view and see it as confirming the rejection of the restrictive interpretation placed on the exception in Article 2(3).[111]

This led the French Government to put forward the radical argument in *Commission v France*[112] that, since women experience *de facto* inequality as regards employment because they continue to shoulder more domestic responsibilities than men, therefore the exception in Article 2(4) justified special compensatory treatment in favour of women. The Court seemed to have been prepared to accept this argument, had France been able to prove it. It held:

The exception provided for in Article 2(4) is specifically and exclusively designed to allow measures which, although discriminatory in appearance, are in fact intended[113] to eliminate or reduce actual instances of inequalities which may exist in the reality of social life. Nothing in the papers of this case, however, makes it possible to conclude that a generalised preservation of special rights for women in collective agreements may correspond to the situation envisaged by that provision.[114]

It seemed to follow from what the Court said that special measures—perhaps even positively discriminatory ones—benefiting women would be excused by Article 2(4) to the extent that they compensated for specific instances of pre-existing inequality. However, the Court was clearly not prepared to construe the provision so as to justify positive discrimination in favour of women in employment generally, on the basis that women have, as a sex, suffered negative discrimination

---

[108] Case 184/83 [1984] ECR 3047.   [109] Ibid, at 3082.

[110] Now Art 2(7) of the amended Equal Treatment Directive, discussed above.

[111] [1984] ECR 3047, at 3086.   [112] Op cit, n 64.

[113] It is noteworthy that the test articulated by the Court here is a subjective, not an objective, one; query whether the Court would insist that the national measures concerned must be reasonably apt to achieve their purpose.

[114] [1988] ECR 6315, at 6336–7. In Case C-450/93 *Kalanke v Freie Hansestadt Bremen* [1995] ECR I-3051, discussed below, Tesauro AG characterized the Court's decision in *Commission v France* as one of 'excessive severity' (at 3063).

in the past which has resulted in their current inequitable distribution throughout the world of work.

No doubt encouraged by this ruling, the Commission subsequently instructed Professor Eliane Vogel-Polsky of the Brussels National Centre for the Sociology of Labour Law to conduct a study of positive action schemes within the Community. Professor Vogel-Polsky reported[115] that a directive would be the best way of ensuring that all Member States took action in this field and would operate in a non-discriminatory way as between the Member States. Such a directive would have made positive action programmes obligatory in the Community's own institutions and in national public bodies, and it would have worked in a similar fashion to the federal contract compliance scheme in the USA. However, only a few months after this report was presented, the EC's own Advisory Committee on Equal Opportunities for Women and Men rejected the idea of a directive, preferring a mere non-binding recommendation, which it believed was far more likely to command the support of the Member States. The Commission therefore opted for a recommendation only on positive action, despite the contrary views of the European trade unions and the European Parliament.

A Recommendation on the Promotion of Positive Action for Women was adopted by the Council in December 1984.[116] Certain of the Commission's more radical proposals had been removed by the Council, in particular the fixing of recruitment targets to ensure greater female representation in industry. Being only a recommendation, the instrument also of course contains no sanctions for non-compliance. However, it does adopt quite sensitively forthright language, for example in Article 1, urging the Members States

to adopt a positive action policy designed to eliminate existing inequalities affecting women in working life and to promote a better balance between the sexes in employment, comprising appropriate general and specific measures, within the framework of national policies and practices, while fully respecting the spheres of competence of the two sides of industry, in order:

  (a) to eliminate or counteract the prejudicial effects on women in employment or seeking employment which arise from existing attitudes, behaviour and structures based on the idea of a traditional division of roles in society between men and women;

  (b) to encourage the participation of women in various occupations in those sectors of working life where they are at present under-represented, particularly in the sectors of the future, and at higher levels of responsibility in order to achieve better use of all human resources.[117]

In Article 8, it stresses the need to make particular efforts to promote equal opportunities in the public sector, especially in those fields where new information technologies were being used or developed, because they could serve as models for the private sector to emulate. The Commission was obliged by the instrument to

---

[115] See CREW Reports (1983), vol 3, no 3, p 4.

[116] Recommendation 84/635, OJ [1984] L331/34.

[117] This provision has been referred to by the ECJ in its interpretation of the hard law on positive action: see in particular Case C-409/95 *Marschall v Land Nordrhein-Westfalen* [1977] ECR I-6363; Case C-158/97 *Badeck v Landesanwalt Beim Staatsgerichtshof des Landes Hessen* [1999] ECR I-1875; and Case C-476/99 *Lommers v Minister van Landbouw* [2002] ECR I-2891.

report to the Council within three years on the progress achieved in the implementation of the recommendation: its consequent report in 1988 concluded that in general the Member States had begun to introduce positive action programmes although their methodology varied widely.[118]

The Commission also pledged itself[119] to present to the Council, the Member States, the two sides of industry, and potential promoters of positive action plans, a Code of Practice to assist and inform them on the implementation of such schemes. This promise it fulfilled in 1988 in *Positive Action—Equal Opportunities for Women in Employment—A Guide*.[120] In answer to the elusive question 'What exactly is positive action?', the *Guide* replies:

Positive action aims to complement legislation on equal treatment and *includes any measure contributing to the elimination of inequalities in practice*.

The setting up of a positive action programme allows an organisation to identify and eliminate any discrimination in its employment policies and practices, and to put right the effects of past discrimination.

Thus a positive action programme is a type of management approach which an employer can adopt with a view to achieving a more balanced representation of men and women throughout the organisation's workforce and thus a better use of available skills and talents.[121]

The *Guide* explains that a full positive action programme is likely to include:

—a commitment stage, where the organisation announces its commitment to positive action;
—an analysis stage, in which relevant data on the organisation's workforce and employment practices are collected and analysed so as to:

   —get an insight into the relative position of women to men and of married to single people within the organisation; and to
   —identify any barrier to women's or married persons' progress within the organisation;

—an action stage, in which measures are worked out in detail for implementation;
—a monitoring and evaluation stage, in which the way the programme progresses is assessed and—if required—measures for adapting aspects of the programme are devised.[122]

This was the background against which the Court was asked in *Kalanke v Freie und Hansestadt remen*:[123]

Is national legislation under which women are given priority in recruitment and/or in obtaining promotion provided that they have the same qualifications as the male applicants and that women

---

[118] COM (88) 370 final.
[119] In its 'Medium Term Community Programme 1986–90', Bull Supp EC 3/86.
[120] Office for Official Publications of the European Communities, Luxembourg.
[121] Emphasis added.
[122] The Community's Third Medium-Term Action Programme on Equal Opportunities (1991–5), OJ [1991] C142/1, also underlined the need for positive action and, in the Fourth Action Programme (1996–2000), OJ [1995] L335/37, sex desegregation of the labour market was expressed as one of the objectives which was to be pursued *inter alia* by positive action. However, the language had subtly shifted to a more general desire to promote gender equality by the date of the 2001–2005 Programme relating to the Community framework strategy on gender equality, OJ [2001] L17/22.
[123] Case C-450/93, op cit, n 114. See Szyszczak, 'Positive Action After *Kalanke*' (1996) 59 MLR 876; Moore, 'Nothing Positive From the Court of Justice' (1996) 21 ELRev 156; Schiek, 'Positive

are under-represented—in so far as they do not constitute one half of the personnel—in the individual remuneration brackets in the relevant personnel group, compatible with the principle of equal treatment for men and women laid down by the relevant Community legislation? In other words, does a system of quotas in favour of women, even if it is dependent on the conditions . . . just described, embody sex discrimination contrary to Community law or does it constitute permitted positive action inasmuch as it is designed to promote effective equal opportunities in the world of work?[124]

The *Kalanke* case arose in Bremen, where a law of 1990 expressly gave women priority in relation to appointment or promotion to official posts, provided that they had 'qualifications equal to those of their male co-applicants'[125] and that women were under-represented in the relevant sector in the sense that they constituted less than half its personnel.[126] The City of Bremen had advertised the post of section manager in its Parks Department. Mr Kalanke was the section manager's deputy. Ms Glissman had the same formal qualifications in horticulture and landscape gardening as Mr Kalanke. Women were under-represented in the sector involved, and a dispute resulted as to the applicability of the 1990 law. This dispute was submitted to a Conciliation Board, which ruled that the 1990 law did indeed apply so as to give preference to Ms Glissman. Mr Kalanke complained of this ruling to the local labour court, which dismissed his claim. On appeal to the Bundesarbeitsgericht, that court agreed that the case fell within the scope of the 1990 law but referred to the ECJ the compatibility of that 1990 law with EU law, in particular, with the Equal Treatment Directive.

The conceptual springboard for Advocate General Tesauro was the distinction between individual and group rights. He explained that the concept of formal equality essentially focuses on the right to equal treatment as between individuals belonging to different groups, whereas substantive equality tries to achieve equal treatment as between groups.[127] Since positive action is generally understood to refer to the elimination of the obstacles faced by groups, it marks what the Advocate General described as 'a transition from the individual vision to the collective vision of equality'.[128]

Action in Community Law' (1996) 25 ILJ 239; and Fenwick, 'Perpetuating Inequality in the Name of Equal Treatment' (1996) 18 JSWFL 263.

[124] In the words of Tesauro AG [1995] ECR I-3051, at 3053.

[125] Although easy to formulate in theory, such a condition is only easy to operate in practice in a system (such as it is understood is often to be found in Germany) where a precise mathematical formula is used to determine a person's qualifications for a job. It is very much more difficult to apply where suitability for a job is determined according to more subjective criteria, including, eg, such matters as personality. Indeed, this is an aspect of a wider difficulty, namely, the application in practice of the so-called 'merit' principle: everything depends on how 'merit' is defined and what qualities are considered to be relevant.

[126] The national court had indicated in its order for reference that the Bremen law had to be interpreted in accordance with the Grundgesetz, which meant that, even if priority was in principle to be given to women, exceptions could be made in individual cases; although the Court noted this point, it seemingly proceeded on the basis that the priority for women was absolute; see also Moore, op cit, n 123. For general discussion of the use of quotas in Germany, see Shaw, 'Positive Action for Women in Germany: The Use of Legally Binding Quota Systems' in Hepple and Szyszczak (eds), *Discrimination: the Limits of Law* (Mansell, London, 1992).   [127] See also the discussion in ch 1.

[128] [1995] ECR I-3051, at 3058.

He also pointed out that, as has already been mentioned above, the expression 'positive action' embraces a variety of different types of provision. The first measures of positive action described by the Advocate General are those designed to remove the disadvantages and reduced opportunities encountered by women in employment; they consist of measures, for example, to attract and train women employees. Such provisions are often described in the UK as 'out-reach' measures.[129] A second type of positive action seeks to redistribute family and career opportunities as between the two sexes, and it therefore deals with such matters as working hours, child-care arrangements, and social security or tax policies which take account of family duties. The third and strongest model identified by the Advocate General seeks to remedy 'the persistent effects of historical discrimination of legal significance' and has a 'compensatory nature, with the result that preferential treatment in favour of disadvantaged categories is legitimised, in particular through systems of quotas and goals'.[130]

It is unfortunate that the Advocate General chose this formulation for his third model. To begin with, it is by no means clear that this type of positive action is to be differentiated from all other types in its attempt to remedy historical discrimination; this is surely also the motive for some actions falling into the first two categories, for example, the provision of training for jobs for which women were formerly not trained. Secondly, it seems to be the Advocate General's intention to indicate that the third model involves reverse discrimination and, by implication, that the other two models do not; this is of such critical legal importance that it is regrettable that it was not articulated more clearly. Moreover, the underlying logic is complex and requires some unravelling: any action taken to favour one group inevitably has a negative effect on the rest of society, since resources (and therefore opportunities) are finite. A distinction can, however, be drawn between those forms of positive action which favour one group but do not breach the anti-discrimination laws (such as the advertising of a vacancy in a women's magazine in addition to other more traditional places), and those which do breach the anti-discrimination laws (such as the choice of a woman on the ground of her sex). Furthermore, it is unfortunate that the Advocate General did not attempt to make a legal distinction between quotas and goals; they are of course essentially different from one another, in that the former are mandatory whereas the latter confer a discretion; both have frequently been examined by the courts in the USA, which have generally frowned on quotas but accepted goals provided that they are used for a transitional period only in order to remedy the effects of past discrimination, or they are used to achieve diversity.[131] The articulation of goals and timetables in

---

[129] See McCrudden, 'Rethinking Positive Action' (1986) 15 ILJ 219.

[130] [1995] ECR I-3051, at 3058.

[131] See n 10 in the submissions of Tesauro AG, and also Douglas-Scott, 'Ruling out Affirmative Action' (1995) 145 NLJ 1586. See further *Adarand Constructors v Pena* 515 US 200; *Regents of the University of California v Bakke* 98 S Ct 2733; *Grutter v Bollinger* 123 S Ct 2325; and *Gratz v Bollinger* 123 S Ct 2411.

an effort to secure fair participation in the workforce irrespective of religion or political belief is also a feature of the Fair Employment and Treatment (Northern Ireland) Order 1998;[132] its chief purpose in that context is to raise awareness levels and to cause employers to question their own previous practices.

Quotas are clearly most at odds with the notion of equality of opportunity as between individuals, and they overtly sacrifice the principle of individual merit to that of the greater good. It is arguable that they constitute an effective tool for putting into place and accustoming the public to non-traditional role models and for ensuring that representatives of a disadvantaged group achieve strategically important positions.[133] Conversely however, quotas are objectionable on a number of grounds, most importantly that they constitute too crude a form of compensation to be just, since it is by no means necessarily the victims of discrimination who derive any direct benefit from them; in addition, they can be viewed as patronizing and they tend to result in the undervaluing of the qualities of those who do benefit directly, since observers conclude that they have achieved their position on the basis of belonging to the group in question rather than on the basis of their individual qualities. Furthermore, the attempt sometimes made to distinguish quotas in jurisprudential terms from other types of discrimination by focusing on the intention underlying them,[134] involves a misunderstanding of the nature of anti-discrimination law: discrimination is a statutory tort for which intention or motive are not essential ingredients.[135]

Kalanke itself involved a quota system, albeit one of a kind which is often described as 'soft'. In other words, the German law did not demand that a precise percentage of official posts be allocated invariably to women, irrespective of the individual qualifications possessed by those women. Instead, it sprang into operation only where the contenders for a particular post were equally qualified, a system often described as a 'tie-break'. It was argued that no male careers were thwarted by such a system, since a better qualified male would be appointed in preference to a female candidate. The question was whether such a scheme, whilst clearly discriminatory against men in its immediate impact, was permitted by Article 2(4) of the Directive in the light of its more far-reaching social and equitable goals. Since the discrimination involved was of a weak type, the case provided an ideal basis

---

[132] SI 1998 No 3162 (NI 21). See in particular Art 55. Art 4 of the Order defines 'affirmative action' as 'action designed to secure fair participation in employment by members of the Protestant, or members of the Roman Catholic, community in Northern Ireland by means including—(a) the adoption of practices encouraging such participation, and (b) the modification or abandonment of practices that have or may have the effect of restricting or discouraging such participation'.

[133] For a powerful articulation of the arguments in favour of such types of positive action, see Bhikhu Parekh, 'A Case for Positive Discrimination' in Hepple and Szyszczak (eds), op cit, n 126.

[134] See, eg, the dissenting judgment of Justice Stevens in the US Supreme Court in *Adarand Constructors Inc v Federico Pena, Secretary of Transportation et al* (1995) 132 L Ed 2d 158, where he asserted that to confuse positive and negative discrimination was like disregarding 'the difference between a "No Trespassing" sign and a welcome mat'.

[135] See Case 177/88 *Dekker*, op cit, n 56, discussed in this respect in ch 3, and *James v Eastleigh Borough Council* [1990] 2 AC 751.

on which to test the issue of whether the original Article 2(4) permitted reverse discrimination in any circumstances, or whether alternatively it was limited to forms of action which benefit women but do not discriminate against men; unfortunately, as will be seen, the Court failed to grasp this nettle.

In the view of Advocate General Tesauro, since the expressed aim of Article 2(4) was the promotion of equality of opportunity, it was essential to define that term and to keep it uppermost in mind when determining the limits of Article 2(4). In particular, did it refer to equality 'with respect to starting points or with respect to points of arrival'? The Advocate General preferred the former view:

[G]iving equal opportunities can only mean putting people in a position to attain equal results and hence restore conditions of equality as between members of the two sexes as regards starting points . . .

It seems to me to be all too obvious that the national legislation at issue in this case is not designed to guarantee equality as regards starting points. The very fact that two candidates of different sex have equivalent qualifications implies in fact by definition that the two candidates have had and continue to have equal opportunities: they are therefore on an equal footing at the starting block. By giving priority to women, the national legislation at issue therefore aims to achieve equality as regards the result or, better, fair job distribution simply in numerical terms between men and women. That does not seem to me to fall within either the scope or the rationale of Article 2(4) . . . [136]

However, the Advocate General went on to reason that the ultimate objective of equal opportunities legislation is to attain substantive equality; since equality as regards starting points alone will not guarantee equal results because of the generally disadvantaged position of women in society, it still remained to consider whether Article 2(4) also permitted actions entailing the 'predetermination of "results"'.[137] The principle of substantive equality, the Advocate General submitted (non-controversially), requires the elimination or neutralization of existing inequalities which hold back a particular group; to that extent, it is not gender-neutral because it involves facing up to the fact that the group is indeed disfavoured. However, any action taken must be limited to that necessary to eradicate the existing disadvantage 'so as to raise the starting threshold of the disadvantaged category'.[138] Thus, the Advocate General concluded:

Article 2(4) . . . only enables existing inequalities affecting women to be eliminated, but certainly not through pure and simple reverse discrimination, that is to say, through measures not in fact designed to remove the obstacles preventing women from pursuing the same results on equal terms, but to confer the results on them directly or, in any event, to grant them priority in attaining those results *simply because they are women*.

In the final analysis, measures based on sex and not intended to eliminate an obstacle—to remove a situation of disadvantage—are, in their discriminatory aspect, as unlawful today for the purposes of promotion as they were in the past.[139]

The Advocate General thus opted for an interpretation of the original Article 2(4) which preserved the legality of most examples of his first two categories of

---

[136] [1995] ECR I-3051, at 3060.   [137] Ibid, at 3061.   [138] Ibid, at 3063.
[139] Ibid, at 3065.

positive action, that is to say, out-reach measures and those designed to reorganize family and career patterns, but which outlawed reverse discrimination by way of quotas. Unfortunately, his argument concealed his view of what many would consider to be one of the most productive and the least morally objectionable forms of positive action, namely, goals or targets.

The Court, in an extremely brief judgment, apparently endorsed the views of its Advocate General. It began by reiterating two points concerning Article 2(4) which it had made in earlier judgments, namely, that it permitted measures 'intended to eliminate or reduce actual instances of inequality which may exist in the reality of social life'[140] and that, as a derogation from an individual right, it must be construed strictly.[141] In concluding that a system such as that in operation in Bremen contravened the Directive, it held:

National rules which guarantee women absolute and unconditional priority for appointment or promotion go beyond promoting equal opportunities and overstep the limits of the exception in Article 2(4) . . .

Furthermore, in so far as it seeks to achieve equal representation of men and women in all grades and levels within a department, such a system substitutes for equality of opportunity as envisaged in Article 2(4) the result which is only to be arrived at by providing such equality of opportunity.[142]

Although formally answering the question posed it by the referring court, this judgment did little to shed light on the detail of the law in this difficult and sensitive area. In particular, it left open an important issue in relation to the scope of Article 2(4). Although quotas of the type at issue in *Kalanke* were clearly out-with Article 2(4), it was not so clear from the *Kalanke* judgment whether a less per-emptory system would also have been forbidden. The Court merely disapproved measures guaranteeing women 'absolute and unconditional' job priority; this formulation might simply have been intended to limit the decision to the facts of the case as it perceived them, or, alternatively, it might have been meant to imply that some conditional sort of priority is permissible. That the latter inter-pretation was what the Court had in mind[143] was revealed by its subsequent decisions in *Marschall v Land Nordrhein-Westfalen*[144] and *Badeck v Landesanwalt Beim Staatsgerichtshof des Landes Hessen*.[145] In the former case, a male German school teacher had been denied promotion because of a law providing for preference to

---

[140] See Case 312/86 *Commission v France*, op cit, n 64, also discussed above.

[141] See Case 222/84 *Johnston*, op cit, n 2, discussed above.

[142] [1995] ECR I-3051, at 3078. See also *Jepson and Dyas-Elliott v Labour Party* [1996] IRLR 116, where an industrial tribunal held that Article 2(4) did not excuse all-women shortlists for the selection of Parliamentary candidates which had been part of an effort to boost female representation in Parliament; the tribunal considered its conclusion to be 'fully endorsed by the decision of the European Court in the *Kalanke* case' (at 119). Sadly for Mr Kalanke, he won no damages when the action returned to the German courts because his case was regarded as insufficiently serious: see Prechal's case note in (1996) 33 CMLRev 1245.

[143] Alternatively perhaps the critical outcry provoked by *Kalanke* caused the Court to change its mind: see More's comment in (1999) 36 CMLRev 443.   [144] Case C-409/95, op cit, n 117.

[145] Case C-158/97, op cit, n 117.

be given to an equally qualified female candidate where there were fewer women than men in the grade in question; the relevant legislation, however, contained a saving clause and laid down the rule preferring women only where 'reasons specific to another candidate' did not predominate.[146] Advocate General Jacobs submitted with compelling logic that this national law, like that in *Kalanke*, involved discrimination prohibited by the Directive and that it was not saved by Article 2(4):

It is axiomatic that there is no equal opportunity for men and women in an individual case if, where all else is equal, one is appointed or promoted in preference to the other solely by virtue of his or her sex...

In my view the proviso to the national rule at issue in the present case does not affect the conclusion that that rule is unlawful for the following reasons.

First, ... if the proviso operates it merely displaces the rule giving priority to women in a particular case: it does not alter the discriminatory nature of the rule in general.

Furthermore, ... the scope of the proviso at issue in the present case is (and was apparently intended to be) unclear. It is settled law that the principles of legal certainty and the protection of individuals require, in areas covered by Community law, that the Member States' legal rules should be worded unequivocally so as to give the persons concerned a clear and precise understanding of their rights and obligations and enable national courts to ensure that those rights and obligations are observed.[147]

However, the Full Court disagreed and distinguished *Kalanke* on the basis that there had been no saving clause there. It went on to state:

[I]t appears that even where male and female candidates are equally qualified, male candidates tend to be promoted in preference to female candidates particularly because of prejudices and stereotypes concerning the role and capacities of women in working life and the fear, for example, that women will interrupt their careers more frequently, that owing to household and family duties they will be less flexible in their working hours, or that they will be absent from work more frequently because of pregnancy, childbirth and breastfeeding.

For these reasons, the mere fact that a male candidate and a female candidate are equally qualified does not mean that they have the same chances.

It follows that a national rule in terms of which, subject to the application of the saving clause, female candidates for promotion who are equally as qualified as the male candidates are to be treated preferentially in sectors where they are under-represented may fall within the scope of Article 2(4) if such a rule may counteract the prejudicial effects on female candidates of the attitudes and behaviour described above and thus reduce actual instances of inequality which may exist in the real world.[148]

It concluded that:

A national rule which, in a case where there are fewer women than men at the level of the relevant post in a sector of the public service and both female and male candidates for the post are equally qualified in terms of their suitability, competence and professional performance, requires that priority be given to the

---

[146] The Spanish, Austrian, Finnish, Swedish, and Norwegian Governments, in addition to the Land of Nordrhein-Westfalen and the Commission, all argued that the legislation fell within the protection conferred by Art 2(4).   [147] [1997] ECR I-6363, at 6374–5.
[148] Ibid, at 6392.

promotion of female candidates unless reasons specific to an individual male candidate tilt the balance in his favour is not precluded by Article 2(1) and (4) . . . , provided that:

—in each individual case the rule provides for male candidates who are equally as qualified as the female candidates a guarantee that the candidatures will be the subject of an objective assessment which will take account of all criteria specific to the candidates and will override the priority accorded to female candidates where one or more of the criteria tilts the balance in favour of the male candidate, and

—such criteria are not such as to discriminate against the female candidates.[149]

In *Badeck*,[150] the ECJ took the same view in relation to a number of provisions contained in the positive action law of Hessen. These required the adoption of 'advancement plans' for women in the public service, with the ultimate aim of securing equality of access for both sexes. Although some of the specific schemes envisaged appeared to operate a strict quota scheme, guaranteeing a fixed number of places to women, the ECJ nevertheless found all to be flexible in reality and therefore legitimate. In terms of general principle, it re-stated the position it had adopted in *Marschall*:

[A] measure which is intended to give priority in promotion to women in sectors of the public service where they are under-represented must be regarded as compatible with Community law if it does not automatically and unconditionally give priority to women where women and men are equally qualified, and the candidatures are the subject of an objective assessment which takes account of the specific personal situations of all candidates.[151]

It therefore appeared after *Marschall* and *Badeck* that the old Article 2(4) excused discrimination in favour of women in tie-break cases, conduct which would otherwise amount to unlawful discrimination.[152] Putting this another way, it had become clear by this time that—however the Court might attempt to dress this up verbally— some decisions grounded upon sex were permitted by Article 2(4). This position was confirmed in *Lommers v Minister van Landbouw*.[153] The Dutch Minister of Agriculture made a number of nursery places open to the children of his female employees; such places were provided for the children of male employees only in emergencies. The stated purpose of the arrangement was to address the under-representation of women within the Ministry, especially at higher levels. The ECJ held that the provision of nursery places was a 'working condition' within the meaning of the Equal Treatment Directive and, furthermore, that there was discrimination on the ground of sex in respect of it. The only question was whether that discrimination was permitted by Article 2(4), and the Court held that in principle it was. It stated:

[A] measure such as that at issue in the main proceedings, which forms part of the restricted concept of equality of opportunity in so far as it is not places of employment which are reserved for women but

---

[149] [1997] ECR I-6363, at 6393.   [150] Case C-158/97, op cit, n 117.   [151] Ibid, at 1919.
[152] In Case C-79/99 *Schnorbus*, op cit, n 42, Jacobs AG expressly stated that Art 2(4) provided a defence to be examined once the existence of discrimination has been established (at 11008).
[153] Case C-476/99, op cit, n 117.

enjoyment of certain working conditions designed to facilitate their pursuit of, and progression in, their career, falls in principle into the category of measures designed to eliminate the causes of women's reduced opportunities for access to employment and careers and are intended to improve their ability to compete on the labour market and to pursue a career on an equal footing with men.[154]

Nevertheless, the ECJ held that the Article must be applied with due respect for the principle of proportionality. Particularly relevant to this principle was the contention that the arrangement might actually help to perpetuate inequality by reinforcing the traditional division of roles between men and women; if its aim could still be achieved if male employees were also included, then it was arguably disproportionate. The Court addressed this concern by pointing out that the number of nursery places available under the scheme was limited, and indeed that there was a waiting list for them even amongst women employees. In addition, the scheme did not wholly exclude male employees; but if it did so in the case of male employees who took care of their children by themselves, it would indeed breach the limits Article 2(4).

Support for the conclusion that Article 2(4) provided a defence to what would otherwise be unlawful discrimination could also be derived from its wording and position in the old version of the Directive.[155] Article 2(1) explained[156] that pursuit of the principle of equality of opportunity entails the elimination of sex discrimination; the following two paragraphs of the Article then went on to articulate circumstances in which discrimination on the ground of sex was, exceptionally, apparently permitted. It made sense, at least in terms of symmetry, if Article 2(4) was interpreted as dealing with another set of circumstances in which, in order to further the goal of equality of opportunity, certain acts of discrimination were permitted.[157] The Court's own judgments confirmed this view, since in *Kalanke, Marschall,* and *Lommers* it referred to Article 2(4) as a 'derogation' from an individual right.[158] Furthermore, there would appear to be little point in using the words 'without prejudice to' if the measures involved would not anyway be prohibited.

Nevertheless, in the view of the present writer, the approach taken by EU law in this area is to be regretted; it would be far better if the EU concentrated its energies on achieving deep-seated structural changes through mainstreaming,[159] contract and grant compliance, requirements for Member States to articulate and

---

[154] Ibid, at 2936.

[155] For further discussion of whether positive action should be seen as an exception to the normal principle of formal equality, see Fenwick, 'From Formal to Substantive Equality: the Place of Affirmative Action in European Union Sex Equality Law' (1998) 4 EPL 507.

[156] As indeed it still does after amendment.

[157] See further Barnard, 'The Principle of Equality in the Community Context: P, Grant, Kalanke and *Marschall*: Four Uneasy Bedfellows?' (1998) 57 CLJ 352.

[158] It is also noteworthy that Tesauro AG, in his remarks quoted above, confined his outlawing of reverse discrimination to that which was 'pure and simple'. From the context, it would seem that he intended by this to prohibit only that type of reverse discrimination which does not seek to remove an existing obstacle to women's employment.   [159] As to which, see ch 3.

aim for equality targets in all their social policies, legislation demanding that employers monitor their workforces and thereby raise their consciousness levels in respect of inequalities, and other measures designed to attack social and economic disadvantage at grass-roots level.[160] There is something deeply unattractive about trying to remedy the shortcomings in the non-discrimination principle by further acts of discrimination: two wrongs simply do not make a right, notwithstanding seductive statements about the achievement of substantive equality; and, as discussed above, this defect manifests itself in a particularly acute form when one group is advantaged and another disadvantaged through the use of quotas.[161] There is also a real risk of patronizing judgements being arrived at on the basis of stereotyping and over-broad generalizations. In addition, it remains difficult to predict the limits to the kinds of positive action which the ECJ will permit, to the ultimate detriment of legal certainty and the financial cost of individual litigants.

Whilst argument about the ambit of the original Article 2(4) of the Directive was rumbling on, the Member States decided to create primary legislation on the subject of positive action.[162] The amended formulation had first appeared in the Agreement on Social Policy (from which the UK was excluded) annexed at Maastricht to the TEC;[163] it was, however, modified and generalized by the Amsterdam Treaty. It breaks important new ground in extending the notion of positive action to the field of equal pay, in addition to that of equal treatment.[164] In addition, at least on their face, the words chosen to express the principle appear to

[160] See also Barrett, 'Re-examining the Concept and Principle of Equality in EC Law' (2003) 22 YEL 117.

[161] Cf the view of Saggio AG in Case C-158/97 *Badeck*, op cit, n 117, at 1888: 'Moreover, while . . . it is true that the legality of such measures [of positive action] depends on whether the positive action can be reconciled with the general principle of non-discrimination, it is equally true . . . that the principle of non-discrimination, designed . . . to ensure equal treatment for employees, and the principle of equal opportunity—on which positive action is based—designed to ensure equality in the actual conditions of employees, or in other words the principles of formal and substantive equality, are not completely at odds: if substantive equality can be achieved by measures that are, by their very nature, discriminatory, then such measures are in fact pursuing the same objective as the first principle, but with the additional twist that the legislature finds itself obliged to remedy a situation where some sections of the population face a real difficulty which cannot be addressed by applying the general principle of non-discrimination. If we follow this line of reasoning, we may come to doubt whether substantive equality is the exception to the rule of formal equality or, in other words, whether the provisions on which positive action is based . . . are in the nature of exceptions and must therefore be interpreted strictly.'

[162] Jacobs AG commented in Case C-409/95 *Marschall*, op cit, n 117, that the Directive was drafted two decades ago and that 'social developments since then may mean that a provision whose intention and scope were apposite when adopted is now in need of review' (at 6379).

[163] In 'Whither the Social Security Directives? Developments in Community Law relating to sex equality' in McCrudden (ed), *Equality of Treatment between Women and Men in Social Security* (Butterworths, London, 1994), Banks makes the amusing suggestion that this provision might have enabled the maintenance of different pensionable ages for men and women in occupational schemes and that, if this were so, it would only have been the UK which would have been excluded from this possibility.

[164] In Case C-366/99 *Griesmar*, op cit, n 65, the ECJ refused to countenance its application to a pension scheme in which an extra year of service was credited to the record of female (but not male) employees for each of their children. This was because the scheme did nothing to offset the disadvantages to which the careers of women were exposed and did not help them in their professional lives.

be calculated to go further than the old Article 2(4) of the Directive.[165] Article
141(4) provides:

With a view to ensuring full equality in practice between men and women in working life, the principle
of equal treatment shall not prevent any Member State from maintaining or adopting measures providing for specific advantages in order to make it easier for the under-represented sex to pursue a
vocational activity or to prevent or compensate for disadvantages in professional careers.[166]

The amended Equal Treatment Directive today adopts this same formulation.[167]

It is clear, however, that even the expanded new wording contains limits which
must not be exceeded. Although the expression 'specific advantages' used in
Article 141(4) at first sight connotes quite distinctly preferential treatment, it is to
be observed that the Court used very similar language in *Kalanke, Marschall*, and
Lommers to describe the ambit of the old Article 2(4) of the Equal Treatment
Directive:

It . . . permits national measures relating to access to employment, including promotion, which give a
specific advantage to women with a view to improving their ability to compete on the labour market and
to pursue a career on an equal footing with men.[168]

As already noted, the Court nevertheless concluded that the Article did not permit
the giving of 'absolute and unconditional priority'. In *Abrahamsson*,[169] the ECJ was
asked about the legality of a scheme pursuant to which some posts in Swedish
universities were reserved for women, provided that the women concerned had
sufficient qualifications for the post and that the difference in qualifications
between the candidates chosen and the candidates who would otherwise have been
successful was not so great as to be 'contrary to the requirement of objectivity in
the making of appointments'. The ECJ expressly treated this as an example of
'positive discrimination'[170] and pointed out that the national legislation in issue
here was different from that concerned in *Kalanke, Marschall*, and *Badeck* in
enabling preference to be given to a candidate who had inferior qualifications to

---

[165] That the new wording is broader than the old Art 2(4) of the Directive was expressly accepted
by the ECJ in Case C-158/97 *Badeck*, op cit, n 117, and in Case C-407/98 *Abrahamsson* [2000] ECR
I-5539.
[166] This provision will become Art III-214(4) of the Constitution, if and when that instrument is
adopted (the only modification being the reversal of the phrase 'men and women'). Declaration No 28
on Art 141(4), annexed to the Treaty of Amsterdam, states: 'When adopting measures referred to in
Article 141(4) . . . Member States should, in the first instance, aim at improving the situation of women
in working life'. Cf. in Case C-79/99 *Schnorbus*, op cit, n 42, Jacobs AG pointed out that the old Art 2(4)
of the Equal Treatment Directive was not to be confined as a matter of law to measures favouring
women. Hepple and Barnard have commented that the new Art 141(4) cannot be described as a
'derogation' from the principle of equal treatment in a formal sense; it expressly aims to achieve 'full
equality in practice', that is substantive equality: see 'Substantive Equality' (2000) 59 CLJ 562, at 576–7.
[167] Art 2(8) provides: 'Member States may maintain or adopt measures within the meaning of
Article 141(4) of the Treaty with a view to ensuring full equality in practice between men and women.'
[168] [1995] ECR I-3051, at 3077, emphasis added. See also the Court's judgments in Case C-409/95
Marschall, op cit, n 117, at 6391, and Case C-476/99 *Lommers*, op cit, n 117, at 2934.
[169] Case C-407/98, op cit, n 165.   [170] Ibid, at 5579.

her comparator. The Court referred to its judgment in *Badeck* and went on to explain:

[I]t is legitimate . . . for certain positive and negative criteria to be taken into account which, although formulated in terms which are neutral as regards sex and thus capable of benefiting men too, in general favour women. Thus, it may be decided that seniority, age and the date of last promotion are to be taken into account only in so far as they are of importance for the suitability, qualifications and professional capability of candidates. Similarly, it may be prescribed that the family status or income of the partner is immaterial and that part-time work, leave and delays in completing training as a result of looking after children and dependants in need of care must not have a negative effect.

The clear aim of such criteria is to achieve substantive, rather than formal, equality by reducing *de facto* inequalities which may arise in society and thus, in accordance with Article 141(4), to prevent or compensate for disadvantages in the professional career of persons belonging to the under-represented sex.[171]

Advocate General Saggio usefully summarized the position:

Community law does not preclude an administrative practice whereby a candidate belonging to the under-represented sex may be given priority over a candidate of the opposite sex as long as they are equal or nearly equal in terms of qualifications, provided that the national legislation requires the authorities, in assessing candidates who are not the subject of positive action, to give due consideration to particular personal circumstances which may indicate social situations that are just as significant as those normally faced by women.[172]

The application of these criteria must also be transparent and reviewable in order to prevent arbitrary selection. Applying these principles to the Swedish legislation at issue in *Abrahamsson*, it did not appear to the ECJ that the assessment of candidates was based on clear and unambiguous criteria intended to prevent or compensate for the career disadvantages of women; on the contrary, the legislation automatically granted preference to women provided that its criteria were fulfilled. The process was therefore not permitted by Article 2(4) of the Equal Treatment Directive. The ECJ then went on to ask whether it was permitted by the more extensive provisions of Article 141(4); unfortunately, it was very brief in its analysis of the difference in scope between the two provisions and merely said that it could not be inferred that Article 141(4) 'allows a selection method of the kind at issue in the main proceedings which appears, on any view, to be disproportionate to the aim pursued'.[173]

It therefore appears that Article 141(4) does not permit what the ECJ calls 'positive discrimination', in other words, an automatic preference based on sex. However, where two candidates of different sex possess equivalent qualifications, it remains permissible to prefer the female candidate, provided that there is an objective assessment which takes account of the specific personal situations of all the candidates.[174]

---

[171] Case C-407/98, op cit, n 165, at 5581–2.   [172] Ibid, at 5558.   [173] Ibid, at 5583.
[174] In the view of the present writer, this is also a form of positive or reverse discrimination, since the decisions concerned are in reality still made on the ground of sex.

The language of the two newer instruments in the field of non-discrimination, the Race Directive and the Framework Directive, appears to be more permissive than that of the old Article 2(4) of the Equal Treatment Directive but, on the other hand, to be weaker than that of Article 141(4). Thus, Article 5 of the Race Directive provides:

> With a view to ensuring full equality in practice, the principle of equal treatment shall not prevent any Member State from maintaining or adopting specific measures to prevent or compensate for disadvantages linked to racial or ethnic origin.[175]

Article 7(1) of the Framework Directive is in substantially identical terms.[176] According to the UK Government, the reason for the difference in wording between the new Directives and Article 141(4) is not significant: the provision in the Framework Directive was simply read across from the Race Directive. The latter could not replicate exactly the language of Article 141(4) because it is not restricted to the workplace.[177] It can perhaps be deduced that the ECJ will take a similar view of these provisions to that which it takes of Article 141(4), namely, that they permit measures of positive action (as that expression is understood by the Court) but fall short of permitting positive discrimination.

Article 7(2) of the Framework Directive provides:

> With regard to disabled persons, the principle of equal treatment shall be without prejudice to the right of Member States to maintain or adopt provisions on the protection of health and safety at work or to measures aimed at creating or maintaining provisions or facilities for safeguarding or promoting their integration into the working environment.[178]

This paragraph is oddly phrased, given that its express purpose[179] is to promote positive action; the tenor of its first half could be taken to suggest that health and safety concerns could actually preclude the employment of disabled people.[180] However, one way in which it appears to extend the scope of positive action in

---

[175] Note, in particular, that the Article does not refer to specific *advantages*. Recital 17 of the Preamble to the Race Directive adds that 'such measures may permit organisations of persons of a particular racial or ethnic origin where their main object is the promotion of the special needs of those persons'. Recital 26 of the Preamble to the Framework Directive is in similar terms.

[176] The UK Government did not consider this Article to be wide enough to permit the exceptions for teachers or the police in Northern Ireland, discussed above. It therefore pressed for separate provisions to be inserted into the Directive to deal with these matters. It has also expressed the view that the new provisions are unlikely to be interpreted differently from the ECJ's existing case law 'in which it has attempted to draw a line between positive action (which is permitted) and positive discrimination (which is not permitted)': see the DfEE's evidence to the House of Lords Select Committee on the EU, 'The EU Framework Directive on Discrimination', Session 2000–01, 4th Report, HL Paper 13, at 13.

[177] See the DfEE's evidence to the House of Lords Select Committee on the EU, 'The EU Framework Directive on Discrimination', Session 2000–01, 4th Report, HL Paper 13, at 13. This does not really explain the change of wording from *specific advantages*, which could presumably have been used in the Race Directive.   [178] See also Recital 27 of the Preamble to the Framework Directive.

[179] Art 7 is headed 'Positive action'.

[180] See also Whittle, 'The Framework Directive for Equal Treatment in Employment and Occupation: An Analysis from a Disability Rights Perspective' (2002) 27 ELRev 303.

relation to the disabled is that such measures are not restricted to those designed to compensate for previous disadvantages.

Positive action in the sphere of disability is also different from the other areas of anti-discrimination law as a result of the asymmetrical approach to disability adopted by the Framework Directive. As seen in chapter 3, it is only unlawful to discriminate on the ground of disability; it is not unlawful to treat an able-bodied person less favourably than a disabled person on the ground of being able-bodied. Thus, to treat a disabled person more favourably than a comparable able-bodied person is not (without more) prohibited by the Directive.

7

General principles and equal treatment

General principles as part of EU law

General principles of law are an important part of the 'common law' of the EU. That is to say, they constitute an unwritten source of law which is, where relevant, applied by the ECJ. Unlike the International Court of Justice, which is expressly enjoined by Article 38 of its Statute to apply 'the general principles of law recognized by civilized nations', the ECJ is under no such general, formal obligation.[1] However, as the Court pointed out in its Opinion[2] on the Accession by the Community to the European Convention for the Protection of Human Rights and Fundamental Freedoms,[3] it has relied on the general principles of Community law in particular in its protection of fundamental rights:

[F]undamental rights form an integral part of the general principles of law whose observance the Court ensures. For that purpose the Court draws inspiration from the constitutional traditions common to the Member States and from the guidelines supplied by international treaties for the protection of human rights on which the Member States have collaborated or of which they are signatories. In that regard, the Court has stated that the [European] Convention [on the Protection of Human Rights] has special significance (see, in particular, the judgment in Case C-260/89 *ERT* [1991] ECR I-2925, paragraph 41).[4]

The other EU institutions have likewise endorsed the Court's recognition that EU law is based upon the recognition of fundamental human rights. In particular,

---

[1] However, Art 288(2) of the TEC provides in the case of non-contractual liability that 'the Community shall, in accordance with the general principles common to the laws of the Member States, make good any damage caused by its institutions or by its servants in the performance of their duties'. Art 220 also provides in extremely broad terms that it is the job of the ECJ to 'ensure that in the interpretation and application of this Treaty *the law* is observed' (emphasis added). On the part played by general principles of law in the jurisprudence of the ECJ, see Arnull, *The European Union and its Court of Justice* (OUP, Oxford, 1999), ch 6, and Tridimas, *General Principles of Community Law* (OUP, Oxford, 1999). [2] Opinion 2/94 [1996] ECR I-1759.

[3] ETS No 5, 1950.

[4] [1996] ECR I-1759, at 1789. See also Case 4/73 *Nold KG v Commission* [1974] ECR 491; Case 36/75 *Rutili v Minister of the Interior* [1975] ECR 1219; and Case 44/79 *Hauer v Land Rheinland-Pfalz* [1979] ECR 3727. However, in Case C-249/96 *Grant v South-West Trains Ltd* [1998] ECR I-621, although the Court recognized the International Covenant on Civil and Political Rights (UNTS Vol 999, p 171) as an instrument informing its views on fundamental rights, it held that the Covenant could not have the effect of extending the scope of the TEC beyond the competences of the Community; thus, it could not be used to support the argument that EU law prohibited discrimination on the ground of sexual orientation before the TEC was amended to include Art 13.

in a Joint Declaration by the European Parliament, the Council, and the Commission of 5 April 1977, it was stressed that these institutions attach 'prime importance ... to the protection of fundamental rights, as derived in particular from the constitutions of the Member States and the European Convention for the Protection of Human Rights', and they promised 'in the exercise of their powers and in pursuance of the aims of the European Communities' to respect these rights.[5]

In legislative terms, the third recital to the Preamble of the Single European Act 1986 pledged the Member States to work together to promote democracy on the basis of the fundamental rights recognized in the constitutions and laws of the Member States, in the European Convention on Human Rights (ECHR), and in the European Social Charter,[6] notably freedom, equality, and social justice.[7] The TEU, especially after its amendment by the Amsterdam Treaty, gives further support to this process. Thus, the third and fourth recitals to its Preamble state:

Confirming their attachment to the principles of liberty, democracy and respect for human rights and fundamental freedoms and of the rule of law,

Confirming their attachment to fundamental social rights as defined in the European Social Charter signed at Turin on 18 October 1961 and in the 1989 Community Charter of the Fundamental Social Rights of Workers ...

In addition, as seen in chapter 1, Article 6(1) of the TEU states that the principles of 'liberty, democracy, respect for human rights and fundamental freedoms, and the rule of law, principles which are common to the Member States', provide the foundation for the EU; and Article 6(2) pledges the Union to respect fundamental human rights as guaranteed by the ECHR and the constitutional traditions of the Member States as 'general principles of Community law'.[8]

The exact relationship between EU law and the law pursuant to the ECHR is a subtle one. The Court has held that the Community in its present form has no power to accede to the ECHR;[9] however, Advocate General Jacobs commented in *Bosphorus v Hava Yollari*[10] that:

Although the [Human Rights] Convention may not be formally binding upon the Community, nevertheless for practical purposes the Convention can be regarded as part of Community law and can be invoked as such both in this Court and in national courts where Community law is in issue.[11]

That there are, however, limits to this influence was demonstrated in *Kremzow v Austria*.[12] Mr Kremzow was convicted of murder and sentenced in circumstances

---

[5] OJ [1977] C103/1. See also the other acts of the institutions listed by the ECJ in its Opinion 2/94 op cit, n 2, at 1768.   [6] ETS No 35. Revised version ETS No 163.

[7] See also Art 136 of the TEC.

[8] Art 46 of the TEU, as amended by the Amsterdam Treaty, confers jurisdiction (in curiously circular language) on the ECJ in relation to Art 6(2) 'with regard to action of the institutions, in so far as the Court has jurisdiction under the Treaties establishing the European Communities and under this Treaty'.   [9] Opinion 2/94, op cit, n 2.

[10] Case C-84/95 [1996] ECR I-3953.   [11] Ibid, at 3972.

[12] Case C-299/95 [1997] ECR I-2629.

which were found by the European Court of Human Rights to breach his right under Article 6 of the ECHR to a fair trial. He subsequently sought compensation, pursuant to Article 5(5) of the ECHR.[13] The Austrian court sought a preliminary ruling from the ECJ, asking whether Articles 5 and 6 of the ECHR form part of Community law. Mr Kremzow argued that, as a citizen of the EU, he enjoyed freedom of movement around the Union, and that a State which impeded that right by executing an unlawful penalty of imprisonment must be held liable in damages. The ECJ reiterated that fundamental rights form an integral part of the general principles of Community law and that the ECHR has a 'special significance' in this regard.[14] However, it went on to point out that Mr Kremzow was an Austrian national whose situation was not connected in any way with any of the situations contemplated by the Treaty provisions on the free movement of persons; furthermore, a purely hypothetical prospect of exercising the right of free movement was not sufficient to establish a connection with Community law. The national legislation applicable in these proceedings therefore related to a situation which did not fall within the field of application of Community law and the ECJ could not, in consequence, give a ruling on whether that national legislation was in conformity with the ECHR.

When it draws on national constitutional provisions as a source of general principles, the Court does not (for obvious reasons of practicality) require completely identical formulation of the principle in question in all the Member States; rather, it regards individual national rules as a source of ideas and as a guide to the solution of particular problems. So, in particular, the German principles of 'proportionality' (in other words, the notion that a penalty or sanction must not be out of scale with the wrong committed), and the protection of legitimate business and other interests, have played a very important part in the ECJ's developing jurisprudence.[15] Britain is also a source of such principles. It can be argued, for instance, that the mechanism allowing for the direct effect of directives, discussed in chapter 2 and formulated by the ECJ in *Pubblico Ministero v Ratti*,[16] owes much to the maxims that equity regards that as done which ought to be done, and that a claimant should come to court with 'clean hands'. Similarly, the natural justice principle known as *audi alteram partem* was applied by the Court in *Transocean Marine Paint Association v Commission*.[17]

The EU Charter of Fundamental Rights, agreed in 2000, also informs the general principles of EU law despite its present status as a non-binding

---

[13] Art 5(5) of the ECHR provides: 'Everyone who has been the victim of arrest or detention in contravention of the provisions of this Article shall have an enforceable right to compensation.'

[14] See also Case C-7/98 *Krombach v Bamberski* [2000] ECR I-1935.

[15] See, eg, Case 11/70 *Internationale Handelsgesellschaft GmbH v Einfuhr-und Vorratsstelle fur Getreide und Futtermittel* [170] ECR 1125; Case 44/79 *Hauer v Land Rheinland-Pfalz* [1979] ECR 3727; and Case 81/72 *Commission v Council* [1973] ECR 575. Note also the vitally important place of proportionality in establishing the defence of justification in relation to indirect discrimination, discussed in ch 3.

[16] Case 148/78 [1979] ECR 1629. See Usher, 'The Direct Effect of Directives' (1979) 4 ELRev 268.

[17] Case 17/74 [1974] ECR 1063.

instrument.[18] In particular, in *max.mobil Telekommunikation Service GmbH v Commission*,[19] the CFI held that the right to sound administration is one of the general principles, common to the constitutional traditions of the Member States, that are observed in a State governed by the rule of law, and it went on to observe that Article 41(1)[20] of the Charter of Fundamental Rights confirms that every person has the right to have his or her affairs handled impartially, fairly and within a reasonable time by the institutions and bodies of the Union. It also referred expressly to Article 47[21] of the Charter in support of the right to an effective remedy for every person who alleges a violation of EU rights. Again, in *Jégo-Quéré v Commission*,[22] the CFI invoked Article 47 of the Charter in order to justify a test for the *locus standi* of individuals in annulment proceedings which was broader than that hitherto accepted.[23]

The proposed Constitution of the EU places fundamental rights at the heart of the Union's workings and Article I-9 provides:

1. The Union shall recognise the rights, freedoms and principles set out in the Charter of Fundamental Rights which constitutes Part II.

2. The Union shall accede to the European Convention for the Protection of Human Rights and Fundamental Freedoms.[24] Such accession shall not affect the Union's competences as defined in the Constitution.

3. Fundamental rights, as guaranteed by the European Convention for the Protection of Human Rights and Fundamental Freedoms and as they result from the constitutional traditions common to the Member States, shall constitute general principles of the Union's law.[25]

It is evident from what has been said above that, apart from the national constitutions of the Member States, the instruments which constitute the most prominent sources of general principles are the ECHR, the European Social Charter of 1961, the Community Charter on the Fundamental Social Rights of Workers of 1989,[26] and the EU Charter of Fundamental Rights agreed in 2000.[27] Although space precludes extensive discussion of these instruments, their most relevant aspects in the present context are summarized below. In particular, focus is

---

[18] OJ [2000] C364/01. See discussion in the Sixth Report of the HL Select Committee on the EU, 'The Future Status of the EU Charter of Fundamental Rights', 3 February 2003, HL 48, Part 2, paras 30–35.   [19] Case T-54/99 [2002] ECR II-313.

[20] Now Art II-101 of the proposed Constitution.

[21] Now Art II-107 of the proposed Constitution.   [22] Case T-177/01 [2002] ECR II-2365.

[23] See further discussion below. In 'From Charter to Constitution and Beyond: Fundamental Rights in the New European Union' [2003] PL 774, Arnull points out that, by the Autumn of 2003, the Charter had been cited by all the Advocates General of the ECJ as well as by the CFI.

[24] This would formally ensure that the Convention operated as a direct source of EU law and that it was able to be invoked as such before the ECJ.

[25] The Charter adds, in Art II-112(4), that in so far as it recognizes fundamental rights as they result from the constitutional traditions common to the Member States, 'those rights shall be interpreted in harmony with those traditions'.

[26] The so-called 'Social Charter', Commission of the European Communities, Luxembourg, 1990.

[27] See also Recital 5 of the Preamble to the Charter of Fundamental Rights.

placed on the extent to which they may broaden the scope of the substantive principles of EU law discussed in the rest of the present work.

(i)   The European Convention on Human Rights[28]

The ECHR arose out of the Hague Congress of the International Committee of Movements for European Unity of May 1948, which resulted in the creation of the Council of Europe in May 1949. The Member States of the Council of Europe drafted the Human Rights Convention, guaranteeing essential civil and political rights, and it became open for signature from November 1950.[29] The scope of the protection provided by the ECHR for the principle of non-discrimination is in a number of respects wider than that otherwise to be found in EU law.[30] Such protection may be derived in two different ways.

First, several substantive provisions of the Convention themselves support the rights to equality and non-discrimination. The most notable examples are Article 8 guaranteeing respect for private and family life, home, and correspondence, Article 9 protecting freedom of thought, conscience, and religion, and Article 12 on the right to marry and to found a family. Thus, for example, in *Goodwin v UK*,[31] the European Court of Human Rights held that the UK's non-recognition of a transsexual person's new gender for purposes such as social security, national insurance, and marriage contravened Article 8 on respect for family life and Article 12 on the right to marry. Most of the gains achieved in the fight for equality pursuant to the ECHR have indeed derived from substantive provisions of the Convention.

The second way in which the ECHR protects against discrimination is through Article 14, which provides:

The enjoyment of the rights and freedoms set forth in this Convention shall be secured without discrimination on any ground such as sex, race, colour, language, religion, political or other opinion, national or social origin, association with a national minority, property, birth or other status.[32]

---

[28]   There is an extensive body of literature on the ECHR, including Feldman, *Civil Liberties and Human Rights in England and Wales*, 2nd edn (Clarendon Press, Oxford, 2002); Harris, Boyle, and Warbrick (eds), *The Law of the European Convention on Human Rights* (Butterworths, London, 1995); Janis, Kay, and Bradley, *European Human Rights Law*, 2nd edn (Oxford University Press, Oxford, 2000); Ovey, *Jacobs and White: The European Convention on Human Rights*, 3rd edn (Oxford University Press, Oxford, 2002); van Dijk and van Hoof, *Theory and Practice of the European Convention on Human Rights*, 3rd edn (Kluwer, The Hague, 1998); and Starmer, *European Human Rights Law* (LAG, London, 1999).

[29]   At the time of writing, the ECHR had been ratified by 45 States, including all the Member States of the EU.

[30]   However, as noted in ch 3 and discussed further below, the concept of discrimination which has been adopted by the European Court of Human Rights is much weaker than that adopted by the ECJ.

[31]   (2002) 35 EHRR 447.

[32]   The 'Convention' in this context includes the First and Fourth Protocols (on property, education, political rights, personal liberty, and freedom of movement) since these Protocols themselves stipulate that all provisions of the Convention are to apply to them. For a detailed analysis of the jurisprudence of the European Court of Human Rights on Art 14, see Arnardóttir, *Equality and Non-Discrimination under the European Convention on Human Rights* (Martinus Nijhoff, The Hague, 2003).

It is clear from the wording of this Article that, taken on its own, it confers no substantive rights; it does so only in conjunction with another Article in the Convention or its Protocols.[33] However, the Convention of course guarantees a broad range of fundamental civil and political rights.[34] The result is thus that, where the Convention stipulates the enjoyment of a particular right, or expressly permits a specific limitation on a right, the Member States may not confer the right, or phrase the limitation, in a way which discriminates, *inter alia*, on any of the stipulated grounds.[35] Moreover, it is not necessary to show that another Convention right has actually been breached in order to rely on Article 14; it is sufficient to show that the matter as regards which discrimination is alleged falls within the ambit of a Convention right.[36] It is nevertheless generally accepted that the reliance of Article 14 on other substantive rights protected by the ECHR seriously limits its effectiveness; where such another right is infringed, the European Court of Human Rights is usually reluctant to go on to examine the additional possible breach of Article 14. In addition, where there is a defence to an ostensible breach of one of the substantive rights, that often results in a defence to an Article 14 claim too.[37] The net result is that Article 14 has not often provided a remedy.

It is also noteworthy that Article 14 contains what to modern eyes looks an outmoded list of prohibited grounds; in particular, unlike the Framework Directive, it makes no express mention of disability, sexual orientation, or age. However, its wording is not exhaustive; the admission of new grounds reflecting changing social *mores* is made possible through the concluding words 'or other status', a term which must be interpreted *eiusdem generis* with the grounds mentioned expressly. Thus, for example, in *Salgueiro da Silva Mouta v Portugal*,[38] the European Court of Human Rights treated as included within Article 14 discrimination on the ground of sexual orientation.[39]

It is evident from its text that Article 14 itself makes no attempt to spell out the meaning of 'discrimination', perhaps unsurprisingly in view of the Convention's

---

[33] *National Union of Belgian Police v Belgium* [1979–80] 1 EHRR 578; *Inze v Austria*, Judgment of 28 October 1987, Series A No 126, p 17. See also *R (Pretty) v DPP* [2002] 1 AC 800 and *Pretty v UK* (2002) 35 EHRR 1.

[34] For an important addition to the procedural weaponry available for the vindication of such rights, see *Schuler-Zgraggen v Switzerland* [1996] 21 EHRR 404.

[35] Thus, eg, in *AP v Austria* (1995) 20 EHRR CD 63, the European Commission of Human Rights considered that an Austrian rule limiting parental leave payments to mothers was in breach of Arts 8 and 14 of the Convention on respect for family life without discrimination on the ground of sex.

[36] *Belgian Linguistic Case (Merits)* [1979–80] 1 EHRR 252; *Van Raalte v Netherlands* (1997) 24 EHRR 503.

[37] Eg, *Pretty v UK* (2002) 35 EHRR 1, and *Sheffield and Horsham v UK* (1999) 27 EHRR 163.

[38] (1999) 31 EHRR 1055.

[39] See also the decision of the House of Lords in *Ghaidan v Godin-Mendoza* [2004] 3 WLR 113. Query whether, given that the ECJ is bound by the principles contained in the ECHR, that court too might some day feel able to extend the general principle of non-discrimination to grounds not expressly specified in EU law. Such a development would be facilitated if the proposed Constitution's pledge to accede to the ECHR were fulfilled.

relative antiquity and the breadth of Article 14. The French version of the Convention contains an even broader formulation than the English: 'sans distinction aucune'. The European Court of Human Rights, faced with an allegation of unlawful discrimination, begins by inquiring whether there is a difference of treatment between two persons placed in analogous situations.[40] If it finds such a difference and that the ground for that difference is one forbidden by Article 14, it proceeds to examine the issue of justification. Thus, it has explained that:

It is important . . . to look for the criteria which enable a determination to be made as to whether or not a given difference in treatment, concerning of course the exercise of one of the rights and freedoms set forth, contravenes Article 14. On this question the Court, following the principles which may be extracted from the legal practice of a large number of democratic States, holds that the principle of equality of treatment is violated if the distinction has no objective and reasonable justification. The existence of such a justification must be assessed in relation to the aims and effects of the measure under consideration, regard being had to the principles which normally prevail in democratic societies. A difference of treatment in the exercise of a right laid down in the Convention must not only pursue a legitimate aim: Article 14 is likewise violated when it is clearly established that there is no reasonable relationship of proportionality between the means employed and the aim sought to be realized.[41]

It thus appears that the concept of discrimination is very different for the purposes of the ECHR from that understood in EU law. In particular, even direct discrimination can in general be excused or 'justified' under the Convention in any case where it pursues an acceptable aim and is not disproportionate to that aim.[42] The European Court of Human Rights has, however, in recent times demanded a more rigorous standard for justification than in its earlier jurisprudence.[43] It applies a high level of scrutiny to allegations of sex discrimination,[44] and may apply a similar level in relation to discrimination on the grounds of religion[45] and nationality.[46] However, the fact remains that this is a considerably wider formulation of

[40] For an example of situations not regarded as analogous, see *Fredin v Sweden* (1991) 13 EHRR 784.
[41] *Belgian Linguistic Case (Merits)* [1979–80] 1 EHRR 252, at 284. It repeated these principles in *Abdulaziz, Cabales and Balkandali v UK* (1985) 7 EHRR 471. The approach of British courts to an Art 14 claim was set out by the Court of Appeal in *Wandsworth London Borough Council v Michalak* [2003] 1 WLR 617; it involves a fourfold test: (i) do the facts fall within the ambit of a substantive Convention provision? (ii) if so, was there different treatment as respects that right between the complainant and the comparators? (iii) were the comparators in an analogous situation to the complainant? and (iv) if so, did the difference have an objective and reasonable justification?
[42] Cf the confinement of justification to indirect discrimination as a general rule in EU law; see Case 170/84 *Bilka-Kaufhaus GmbH v Weber Von Hartz* [1986] ECR 1607 and discussion in ch 3.
[43] See *Hoffmann v Austria* (1994) 17 EHRR 293; *Burghartz v Switzerland* (1994) 18 EHRR 101; and *Karlheinz Schmidt v Germany* Ser A No 291-B 18 EHRR 503.
[44] In *Abdulaziz, Cabales and Balkandali v UK* (1985) 7 EHRR 471, the European Court of Human Rights commented, at 501: '[I]t can be said that the advancement of the equality of the sexes is today a major goal in the Member States of the Council of Europe. This means that very weighty reasons would have to be advanced before a difference of treatment on the ground of sex could be regarded as compatible with the Convention.'   [45] *Hoffmann v Austria* (1993) 17 EHRR 293.
[46] In *Gaygusuz v Austria* (1997) 23 EHRR 364, the European Court of Human Rights held that 'very weighty reasons' would have to be put forward before it would regard a difference of treatment based exclusively on nationality as compatible with the ECHR.

the law than one which (like the EU's equal treatment provisions) contains discrete defences to be applied in particular situations, although this is probably inevitable given the ambit of Article 14. It follows that the Convention (at least potentially) erects into a general principle of EU law the right not to be discriminated against on a number of grounds in fields not otherwise governed by EU law, but that this gain is partially offset by the standard for determining whether or not discrimination has occurred.[47]

On the other hand, in some respects the ECHR concept of discrimination is a broad one. This breadth was demonstrated in *Thlimmenos v Greece*,[48] where the applicant was a Jehovah's Witness who had refused, on the ground of his religious beliefs, to serve in the Greek Army. For this offence of 'insubordination' he was convicted and served a sentence of imprisonment. Some years later he qualified as a chartered accountant, but could not take up this profession because Greek law prohibited the appointment to the civil service, including the accountancy profession, of those convicted of serious criminal offences. He complained that this amounted to a breach of his rights under Article 9 of the ECHR (protecting his right to freedom of thought, conscience, and religion) combined with Article 14. His argument was that his Convention rights were breached because the law excluding him from the civil service made no distinction between those convicted of serious crimes in consequence of their religious beliefs and those convicted of other crimes. The European Court of Human Rights, in upholding this complaint, made an important statement of principle:

The Court has so far considered that the right under Article 14 not to be discriminated against in the enjoyment of the rights guaranteed under the Convention is violated when States treat differently persons in analogous situations without providing an objective and reasonable justification... However, the Court considers that this is not the only facet of the prohibition of discrimination in Article 14. *The right not to be discriminated against in the enjoyment of the rights guaranteed under the Convention is also violated when States without an objective and reasonable justification fail to treat differently persons whose situations are significantly different.*[49]

The Court went on to rule that the State's exclusion of the applicant was not objectively and reasonably justified because, although States have a legitimate interest in excluding some people from becoming accountants, the applicant's crime did not imply any dishonesty or immorality such as might have undermined his professional ability; furthermore, he had already served a term of imprisonment so that further punishment was disproportionate.

A new Protocol to the Convention, Protocol 12, was agreed and opened for signature by Member States of the Council of Europe in November 2000. It requires

---

[47] It should also be borne in mind that, as will be discussed below, the part played by general principles of EU law in the jurisprudence of the ECJ restricts the importance of the Convention, no matter how broad its potential scope.   [48] (2001) 31 EHRR 411.

[49] Ibid, at 424, emphasis added. For the articulation of a similar view of the meaning of discrimination by the ECJ, see discussion below.

ratification by ten States before it can enter into force. By October 2004, it had received only eight ratifications.[50] If and when it becomes effective, it will establish a free-standing right to equality. It provides:

1. The enjoyment of any right set forth by law shall be secured without discrimination[51] on any ground such as sex, race, colour, language, religion, political or other opinion, national or social origin, association with a national minority, property, birth or other status.

2. No one shall be discriminated against by any public authority on any ground such as those mentioned in paragraph 1.

Despite its more recent origin, Protocol 12 thus replicates the grounds set out in Article 14. The Explanatory Report on the Protocol states that it was considered unnecessary to update the wording to include such matters as disability, sexual orientation, and age because of the non-exhaustive nature of the list of prohibited grounds, and also because any inclusion of a particular additional ground might be taken to imply that other grounds not added were not intended to be included. 'Any right set forth by law' must be taken to refer at the very least to the national laws of the States party to the ECHR; it is of course this aspect of the Protocol which gives it a scope additional to that of Article 14.[52] It is unclear whether it also refers to rights set out in international agreements, although the Explanatory Report states that such international rights 'may' be covered.[53]

(ii)   The European Social Charter

Economic and social rights proved harder to reach agreement on in the aftermath of the Second World War than civil and political rights. In part this was because they were not imbued with the same sense of post-war urgency, and in part also

---

[50] The ratifying States are Bosnia–Herzegovena, Croatia, Cyprus, Georgia, The Netherlands, San Marino, Serbia-Montenegro, and the former Yugoslav Republic of Macedonia. The UK had not even signed Protocol 12 by October 2004; the UK Government, although in principle in favour of a free-standing right not to be discriminated against, considers the text of Protocol 12 'too general and open-ended': see HL Deb, Vol 617, Col WA 37, 11 October 2000.

[51] The French wording of Art 1 of Protocol 12 is 'sans discrimination aucune' but, according to the Explanatory Report on that Protocol, no difference of meaning from Art 14 of the ECHR is intended: 'on the contrary, this is a terminological adaptation intended to reflect better the concept of discrimination within the meaning of Article 14 by bringing the French text into line with the English'.

[52] However, as Feldman has observed, even Protocol 12 does not go as far as Art 26 of the International Covenant on Civil and Political Rights 1966, which provides: 'All persons are equal before the law and are entitled without any discrimination to the equal protection of the law'; see Feldman, op cit, n 28, at 142–3.

[53] This is one of the problems which inhibits UK acceptance of Protocol 12; the Government is particularly concerned about international instruments which have not been implemented in UK law because they are essentially aspirational. However, Fredman has pointed out that the Protocol only applies to rights 'set forth by law'; unimplemented international rights are not, under the UK's dualist constitution, 'set forth by law': see 'Why the UK government should sign and ratify Protocol 12' (2002) 105 EOR 21.

because they require constructive action, rather than a mere undertaking by States not to interfere, in order to give them content.[54] The European Social Charter was, however, eventually agreed. It was subsequently revised to take account of recent 'fundamental social changes' and so as to include a number of additional rights. Its new version was opened for signature in May 1996.[55]

By its very nature it is a somewhat different type of instrument from the ECHR. In particular, it is not drafted in terms of legal rights which can be invoked before judicial authorities by individuals, although in a number of instances it recapitulates rights also conferred by EU law. It is instead supposed to set standards to be achieved by its Contracting States, with a fluid, time-consuming, and non-binding supervision procedure. Perhaps for this reason, its content is not generally as well known as that of the ECHR. Although it adds little of direct legal substance to the anti-discrimination provisions today contained in EU law, it does provide a more detailed and sympathetic back-drop against which those provisions should be viewed and enforced.

Part I of the Charter today lists thirty-one rights and principles in the field of employment and social welfare which are aimed at by the Contracting States; Part II then spells out these matters in greater detail. Of particular importance in the present context are the following:

Article 8: The right of employed women to protection of maternity

With a view to ensuring the effective exercise of the right of employed women to the protection of maternity, the Parties undertake:

1. to provide either by paid leave, by adequate social security benefits or by benefits from public funds for employed women to take leave before and after childbirth up to a total of at least fourteen weeks;
2. to consider it as unlawful for an employer to give a woman notice of dismissal during the period from the time she notifies her employer that she is pregnant until the end of her maternity leave, or to give her notice of dismissal at such a time that the notice would expire during such a period;[56]
3. to provide that mothers who are nursing their infants shall be entitled to sufficient time off for this purpose;

---

[54] See further Jaspers and Betten, *Twenty-Five Years, European Social Charter* (Kluwer, The Hague, 1988).

[55] At the time of writing, the Revised Charter had been ratified by the following Member States of the EU: Belgium, Cyprus, Estonia, Finland, France, Ireland, Italy, Lithuania, Portugal, Slovenia, and Sweden. It had been signed by: Austria, The Czech Republic, Denmark, Greece, Luxembourg, The Netherlands, Slovakia, Spain, and the UK. It became operative after the first three Member States acceded to it on 1 July 1999.

[56] The appendix to the Charter nevertheless adds that this provision is not to be interpreted as laying down an absolute prohibition; it states that '[e]xceptions could be made, for instance, ... (a) if an employed woman has been guilty of misconduct which justifies breaking off the employment relationship; (b) if the undertaking concerned ceases to operate; (c) if the period prescribed in the employment contract has expired'.

4. to regulate the employment in night work of pregnant women, women who have recently given birth and women nursing their infants;
5. to prohibit the employment of pregnant women, women who have recently given birth or who are nursing their infants in underground mining and all other work which is unsuitable by reason of its dangerousness, unhealthy or arduous nature and to take appropriate measures to protect the employment rights of these women.

Article 15: The right of persons with disabilities to independence, social integration and participation in the life of the community

With a view to ensuring persons with disabilities, irrespective of age and the nature and origin of their disabilities, the effective exercise of the right to independence, social integration and participation in the life of the community, the Parties undertake, in particular:

1. to take the necessary measures to provide persons with disabilities with guidance, education and vocational training in the framework of general schemes wherever possible or, where this is not possible, through specialised bodies, public or private;
2. to promote their access to employment through all measures tending to encourage employers to hire and keep in employment persons with disabilities in the ordinary working environment and to adjust the working conditions to the needs of the disabled or, where this is not possible by reason of the disability, by arranging for or creating sheltered employment according to the level of disability. In certain cases, such measures may require recourse to specialised placement and support services;
3. to promote their full social integration and participation in the life of the community in particular through measures, including technical aids, aiming to overcome barriers to communication and mobility and enabling access to transport, housing, cultural activities and leisure.

Article 20: The right to equal opportunities and equal treatment in matters of employment and occupation without discrimination on the grounds of sex

With a view to ensuring the effective exercise of the right to equal opportunities and equal treatment in matters of employment and occupation without discrimination on the grounds of sex, the Parties undertake to recognize that right and to take appropriate measures to ensure or promote its application in the following fields:

(a) access to employment, protection against dismissal and occupational reintegration;
(b) vocational guidance, training, retraining and rehabilitation;
(c) terms of employment and working conditions, including remuneration;
(d) career development, including promotion.

The Appendix states, however, in relation to Article 20:

1. It is understood that social security matters, as well as other provisions relating to unemployment benefit, old age benefit and survivor's benefit, may be excluded from the scope of this article.

2. Provisions concerning the protection of women, particularly as regards pregnancy, confinement and the post-natal period, shall not be deemed to be discrimination as referred to in this article.

3. This article shall not prevent the adoption of specific measures aimed at removing *de facto* inequalities.

4. Occupational activities which, by reason of their nature or the context in which they are carried out, can be entrusted only to persons of a particular sex may be excluded from the scope of this article or some of its provisions. This provision is not to be interpreted as requiring the Parties to embody in laws or regulations a list of occupations which, by reason of their nature or the context in which they are carried out, may be reserved to persons of a particular sex.

Article 23: The right of elderly persons to social protection

With a view to ensuring the effective exercise of the right of elderly persons to social protection, the Parties undertake to adopt or encourage, either directly or in co-operation with public or private organisations, appropriate measures designed in particular:

- to enable elderly persons to remain full members of society for as long as possible,[57] by means of:

  (a) adequate resources enabling them to lead a decent life and play an active part in public, social and cultural life;

  (b) provision of information about services and facilities available for elderly persons and their opportunities to make use of them;

- to enable elderly persons to choose their life-style freely and to lead independent lives in their familiar surroundings for as long as they wish and are able by means of:

  (a) provision of housing suited to their needs and their state of health or of adequate support for adapting their housing;

  (b) the healthcare and the services necessitated by their state;

- to guarantee elderly persons living in institutions appropriate support, while respecting their privacy, and participation in decisions concerning living conditions in the institution.

Article 26: The right to dignity at work

With a view to ensuring the effective exercise of the right of all workers to protection of their dignity at work, the Parties undertake, in consultation with employers' and workers' organizations:

1. to promote awareness, information and prevention of sexual harassment in the workplace or in relation to work and to take all appropriate measures to protect workers from such conduct;
2. to promote awareness, information and prevention of recurrent reprehensible or distinctly negative and offensive actions directed against individual workers in the workplace or in relation to work and to take all appropriate measures to protect workers from such conduct.[58]

Article 27: The right of workers with family responsibilities
to equal opportunities and equal treatment

With a view to ensuring the exercise of the right to equality of opportunity and treatment for men and women workers with family responsibilities and between such workers and other workers, the Parties undertake:

---

[57] The Appendix states that the term 'for as long as possible' here refers to the elderly person's physical, psychological, and intellectual capacities.

[58] The Appendix further provides that this article does not require the enactment of legislation and that para 2 does not cover sexual harassment.

1. to take appropriate measures:

   (a) to enable workers with family responsibilities to enter and remain in employment, as well as to re-enter employment after an absence due to those responsibilities, including measures in the field of vocational guidance and training;

   (b) to take account of their needs in terms and conditions of employment and social security;

   (c) to develop or promote services, public or private, in particular child day-care services and other childcare arrangements;

2. to provide a possibility for either parent to obtain, during a period after maternity leave, parental leave to take care of a child, the duration and conditions of which should be determined by national legislation, collective agreements or practice;

3. to ensure that family responsibilities shall not, as such, constitute a valid reason for termination of employment.[59]

Article E provides that:

The enjoyment of the rights set forth in this Charter shall be secured without discrimination on any ground such as race, colour, sex, language, religion, political or other opinion, national extraction or social origin, health, association with a national minority, birth or other status.

This wording is very similar to that used in Article 14 of the ECHR[60] and the Appendix adds, in line with the jurisprudence of the European Court of Human Rights discussed above, that 'differential treatment based on an objective and reasonable justification shall not be deemed discriminatory'.

(iii) The Community Social Charter

The European Community Charter on the Fundamental Social Rights of Workers was signed in December 1989 by all of the then twelve Member States except the UK.[61] It is a formal, hortatory declaration.[62] Although without binding legal force it was supported by an action programme containing numerous proposals for legislation, many of which were subsequently acted upon. It addresses a number of 'Fundamental Social Rights of Workers'. The eighth recital of its Preamble refers

---

[59] The Appendix states: 'It is understood that this article applies to men and women workers with family responsibilities in relation to their dependent children as well as in relation to other members of their immediate family who clearly need their care or support where such responsibilities restrict their possibilities of preparing for, entering, participating in or advancing in economic activity. The terms "dependent children" and "other members of their immediate family who clearly need their care and support" mean persons defined as such by the national legislation of the Party concerned.'

[60] But note the addition of health and the subtraction of property.

[61] The Charter on the Fundamental Social Rights of Workers provided the basis for the Maastricht Social Chapter. As discussed in ch 1, when Labour came into office in the UK in 1997, it reversed Britain's opt-out from the Social Chapter and the Charter was given general legal recognition by the Treaty of Amsterdam.

[62] See ch 2 for discussion of the requirement to interpret domestic legislation in the light of even non-binding EU instruments, so-called 'soft law'.

to the importance of combating every form of discrimination, 'including discrimination on grounds of sex, colour,[63] race, opinions and beliefs'. It contains three Articles specifically targeted at the types of discrimination examined in the present work:

Article 16: Equal treatment for men and women

Equal treatment for men and women must be assured. Equal opportunities for men and women must be developed.

To this end, action must be intensified to ensure the implementation of the principle of equality between men and women as regards in particular access to employment, remuneration, working conditions, social protection, education, vocational training and career development.

Measures should also be developed enabling men and women to reconcile their occupational and family obligations.

Articles 24 and 25: Elderly persons[64]

24. Every worker of the European Community must, at the time of retirement, be able to enjoy resources affording him or her a decent standard of living.

25. Every person who has reached retirement age but who is not entitled to a pension or who does not have other means of subsistence, must be entitled to sufficient resources and to medical and social assistance specifically suited to his needs.

Article 26: Disabled persons

All disabled persons, whatever the origin and nature of their disablement, must be entitled to additional concrete measures aimed at improving their social and professional integration.

These measures must concern, in particular, according to the capacities of the beneficiaries, vocational training, ergonomics, accessibility, mobility, means of transport and housing.

(iv)   The Charter of Fundamental Rights

Although until such time as the Constitution is adopted by all the Member States of the Union the Charter of Fundamental Rights has no formal legal status, it was drafted in precise legal terms on the supposition that it would one day become binding[65] and, even before adoption of the Constitution, it is therefore apt to influence the interpretation placed on instruments of EU and national law.[66]

---

[63] Note the use of the word 'colour' here; it is omitted from the grounds stipulated by the Race Directive although, as noted in ch 1, colour is frequently at the root of racial discrimination.

[64] Arts 20–23 also contain provisions protecting children and adolescents in the workplace.

[65] See the remarks of Dr Roman Herzog, chairman of the Convention drafting the Charter, quoted by Arnull in 'From Charter to Constitution and Beyond: Fundamental Rights in the New European Union' [2003] PL 774.

[66] The wording of the original Charter contains slight differences from its wording as Part II of the Constitution; the formulation and numbering system adopted here is that used in the Constitution.

If and when the Constitution comes into operation, the Charter will constitute a direct source of EU law, since the final recital of its Preamble provides that the 'Union recognises the rights, freedoms and principles' which it sets out; to what extent the ECJ will differentiate between the legal qualities of 'rights, freedoms and principles' is a matter for it to resolve. As a source of law the Charter is, however, somewhat limited. In the first place, as will be examined further below, it is addressed to the Union's own rule-makers and to the Member States only when they are implementing EU law;[67] in addition, the provisions of the Charter containing 'principles' are to be 'judicially cognisable' only in interpreting and ruling on the validity of implementing acts of the Union and the Member States.[68] They do not, therefore, it would appear, create free-standing rights, even potentially capable of taking direct effect. Neither does the Charter extend the field of application of EU law, establish any new power or task for the Union, or modify powers and tasks defined elsewhere in the Constitution.[69] Moreover, rights recognized by the Charter for which provision is also made in other parts of the Constitution must be exercised under the conditions and within the limits defined by those other parts.[70]

A number of the Charter's provisions replicate those set out in the ECHR, although not always in identical terms; a further problem to be confronted by the ECJ will therefore be the extent to which a substantive divergence from the ECHR is intended, although in many instances it is clear that the change merely reflects modern circumstances. Article II-112(3) provides that, in so far as the Charter contains rights which 'correspond'[71] to those in the ECHR, their meaning and scope shall be identical. It adds that this is not to 'prevent Union law providing more extensive protection'; this provision appears deceptively simple but is in reality complex, because one person's more extensive right is often bought at the expense of another's freedom.

The Charter sits oddly in the middle of the proposed Constitution and, most incongruously in that context, opens with a Preamble; this refers expressly to equality[72] and to respect for 'the diversity of the cultures and traditions of the peoples of Europe'.[73] It contains a number of provisions directly relevant to the principles of equality and non-discrimination.[74] Article II-70 guarantees freedom of thought, conscience, and religion:

1. Everyone has the right to freedom of thought, conscience and religion. This right includes freedom to change religion or belief and freedom, either alone or in community with others and in public or in private, to manifest religion or belief, in worship, teaching, practice and observance.

---

[67] Art I-111(1) of the Constitution.   [68] Art II-112(5) of the Constitution.
[69] Art II-111(2) of the Constitution.   [70] Art II-112(2) of the Constitution.
[71] Presumably the word 'correspond' is used by the Article to indicate that up-dated wording is not intended to disturb the substantive meaning of a provision.   [72] In Recital 2.
[73] In Recital 3.
[74] For the view that most of the social rights and freedoms guaranteed in the Charter have either already been recognized by the ECJ or are mentioned in existing EU legal documents, see Lenaerts and Foubert, 'Social Rights in the Case-Law of the European Court of Justice' (2001–2) 28 LIEI 267.

2. The right to conscientious objection is recognised, in accordance with the national laws governing the exercise of this right.[75]

Title III of the Charter is devoted to 'Equality':

Article II-80: Equality before the law

Everyone is equal before the law.

Article II-81: Non-discrimination

1. Any discrimination based on any ground such as sex, race, colour,[76] ethnic or social origin, genetic features, language, religion or belief, political or other opinion, membership of a national minority, property, birth, disability, age or sexual orientation shall be prohibited.[77]

2. Within the scope of application of the Constitution, and without prejudice to any of its specific provisions, any discrimination on grounds of nationality shall be prohibited.[78]

Article II-82: Cultural, religious and linguistic diversity

The Union shall respect cultural, religious and linguistic diversity.

Article II-83: Equality between women and men

Equality between women and men must be ensured in all areas, including employment, work and pay.[79]

The principle of equality shall not prevent the maintenance or adoption of measures providing for specific advantages in favour of the under-represented sex.[80]

Article II-84: The rights of the child

1. Children shall have the right to such protection and care as is necessary for their well-being. They may express their views freely. Such views shall be taken into consideration on matters which concern them in accordance with their age and maturity.

2. In all actions relating to children, whether taken by public authorities or private institutions, the child's best interests must be a primary consideration.

---

[75] Cf Art 9 ECHR, which does not deal expressly with conscientious objection but does contain a paragraph permitting limitations prescribed by law and necessary in a democratic society in the interests of public safety, for the protection of public order, health or morals, or for the protection of the rights and freedoms of others. However, Art II-112(2) of the Constitution accepts limitations on the exercise of the rights and freedoms recognized by the Charter so long as they are provided by law and are proportionate.

[76] Once again, the inclusion of 'colour' in this provision is noteworthy; see also n 63.

[77] The ambit of this prohibition is noteworthy because, unlike the anti-discrimination directives, it apparently extends to discrimination over any matter within the scope of EU law, and it also includes a number of grounds not expressly covered by those instruments

[70] This formulation appears to preserve the distinction between the rights of EU citizens and those of third-country nationals and, unfortunately, to sanction covert racial discrimination in the guise of nationality discrimination, as discussed in relation to the Race Directive in ch 6. See also McInerney, 'The Charter of Fundamental Rights of the European Union and the Case of Race Discrimination' (2002) 27 ELRev 483.

[79] Once again, it is to be noted that this provision mandates sex equality 'in all areas', not merely in those areas dealt with by the existing directives.

[80] This provision appears to permit positive action undertaken by the EU institutions, as well as by Member States. Cf the provisions discussed in ch 6 which deal only with action by the Member States.

3. Every child shall have the right to maintain on a regular basis a personal relationship and direct contact with both his or her parents, unless that is contrary to his or her interests.

Article II-85: The rights of the elderly

The Union recognises and respects the rights of the elderly to lead a life of dignity and independence and to participate in social and cultural life.

Article II-86: Integration of persons with disabilities

The Union recognises and respects the right of persons with disabilities to benefit from measures designed to ensure their independence, social and occupational integration and participation in the life of the community.

In addition, Article II-93 is concerned with family and professional life:

1. The family shall enjoy legal, economic and social protection.

2. To reconcile family and professional life, everyone shall have the right to protection from dismissal for a reason connected with maternity[81] and the right to paid maternity leave and to parental leave following the birth or adoption of a child.[82]

The role played by general principles of EU law

General principles play a part in EU law in two subtly different situations. In the words of Capotorti AG in *Defrenne v Sabena*:[83]

First, the respect for fundamental rights is a limitation on all Community acts: any measure whereby the powers of the Community institutions are exercised is subject to that limitation and in that sense the entire structure of the Community is under an obligation to observe that limitation. Secondly where directly applicable Community measures exist (by the effect of the Treaties or secondary legislation) they must be interpreted in a manner which accords with the principle that human rights must be respected.[84]

The ECJ has summarized the first of these situations thus: 'Respect for fundamental rights is . . . a condition of the lawfulness of Community acts.'[85]

Judicial review of Community action takes a number of forms. A direct action may lie under Article 230 or under Article 241 where a regulation is declared inapplicable. A similar jurisdiction is exercised by the ECJ under Article 234 when it rules on the validity of Community acts, and under Article 288(2) when it adjudicates tort claims against the Community based on acts of the institutions.[86]

---

[81] This is noticeably broad in its reference to 'maternity' rather than 'pregnancy'; it is doubtful whether it can be reconciled with a genuine right to equal treatment of the sexes, as proclaimed by Art II-80.

[82] Art II-94 also recognizes entitlement to social security benefits and social services in relation, *inter alia*, to maternity and old age.   [83] Case 149/77 [1978] ECR 1365.

[84] Ibid, at 1385.

[85] Opinion 2/94, op cit, n 2, at 1789. See also Jacobs AG in Case C-84/95 *Bosphorus*, op cit, n 10, at 3972.

[86] See also TEU, Art 46(d), and the comments thereon by Lenaerts in 'Fundamental Rights in the European Union' (2000) 25 ELRev 575.

Article 230 permits judicial review of administrative action on four broadly defined grounds, of which the most important in the present context is 'infringement of this Treaty *or of any rule of law relating to its application*'.[87] In practice, the Court has fairly frequently exercised its powers of review where the administrative decision in question contravened a general principle of law. Thus, for example, an EU act might be annulled by the ECJ because it infringed the general principle of freedom of religion, as derived from the ECHR.[88] However, there are serious limitations on the scope of this jurisdiction in the present context. Where the person seeking judicial review is an individual (whether human or corporate), it is clear that it is the intention of Article 230 to restrict the circumstances in which the action is admissible, but the Court's jurisprudence as to the extent of any such restriction is disturbingly confused and self-contradictory.[89] First, it is unclear whether it interprets Article 230(4) as conferring on individuals the right only to seek annulment of an instrument that is in substance a 'decision' within the definition contained in Article 249, or whether the individual is entitled also to challenge a true 'regulation'.[90] There has even been the suggestion in some recent cases that an individual may, at least in special circumstances, challenge a directive.[91] Secondly, despite the fact that the individual can establish that the act impugned is one which he or she may challenge, the Court has made inconsistent statements as to the degree of interest required on the part of the applicant in order for there to be *locus standi*.[92] Article 230(4) provides that it must be shown either that the decision is addressed to the applicant, or else that it is of 'direct and individual concern' to that applicant. This requirement, in particular the element of individual concern, has at times been extremely narrowly construed by the

[87] Emphasis added.
[88] For a case in which an act was challenged (unsuccessfully on the facts) on the ground that it infringed freedom of religion, see Case 130/75 *Prais v Council* [1976] ECR 1589.
[89] See in particular Case 789/79 *Calpak SpA v Commission* [1980] ECR 1949; Cases 239/82 and 275/82 *Allied Corporation v Commission* [1984] ECR 1005; Case C-358/89 *Extramet Industrie v Council* [1991] ECR I-2501; and Case 309/89 *Codorníu v Council* [1994] ECR I-1853. The confusion has been exacerbated by the failure of the CFI (which inherited this jurisdiction from the ECJ by Council Decision 93/350, OJ [1993] L144/21) to follow the lead provided by the ECJ in *Codorníu*: see, eg, its decisions in Case T-489/93 *Unifruit Hellas v Commission* [1994] ECR II-1201; Case T-472/93 *Campo Ebro v Council* [1995] ECR II-421; and Case T-585/93 *Stichting Greenpeace Council v Commission* [1995] ECR II-2205. For further discussion, see Greaves, 'Locus Standi under Article 173 EEC when Seeking Annulment' (1986) 11 ELRev 119, and Arnull, 'Private Applicants and the Action for Annulment under Article 173 of the EC Treaty' (1995) 32 CMLRev 7.
[90] Contrast, eg, the Court's decision in *Calpak SpA v Commission*, op cit, n 89, with that in *Codorníu v Council*, also op cit, n 89. See also Case C-49/88 *Al-Jubail Fertilizer v Council* [1991] ECR I-3187, and Case T-99/94 *Asocarne v Council* [1994] ECR II-871.
[91] See Case C-298/89 *Gibraltar v Council* [1993] ECR I-3605; Case C-10/95P *Asocarne v Council* [1995] ECR I-4149; Case T-135/96 *UEAPME v Council* [1998] ECR II-2335; and Joined Cases T-172 & 175-177/98 *Salamander AG v Parliament and Council* [2000] ECR II-2487.
[92] It is, however, clear that an applicant must have some interest in challenging the impugned act, in the sense that annulment would have a tangible effect on the applicant's rights; see Case T-26/97 *Antillean Rice Mills v Commission* [1997] ECR II-1347, and Case T-134/95 *Proderec v Commission* [1997] ECR II-823.

ECJ;[93] in these narrow decisions, far from simply requiring the applicant to demonstrate some sort of interest in the subject matter of the action over and above that of other members of the public (as a British administrative lawyer might perhaps anticipate), the ECJ has ruled that an applicant will be individually concerned only where he or she belongs to a closed and ascertainable class of people whose interests are particularly affected by the decision in question. On the other hand, in some of its decisions, the Court has inclined to the wider view that a close factual connection with the instrument impugned will be sufficient for an applicant to establish *locus standi*.[94]

These procedural uncertainties and limitations have meant in practice that actions brought by members of the Community's own work force have assumed a particular significance in this field, since Community employees are especially prone to receiving 'decisions' addressed to themselves.

Article 241 is likewise of fairly restricted scope. Known in its parent French as the *exception d'illegalité*, it provides a means of challenge to a decision affecting an individual (or a Member State), where the decision is itself based on an illegal regulation in respect of which the very strict time limit of two months for a direct challenge under Article 230 may well have run out. A successful action under Article 241 results not in the annulment of the regulation, but merely in its being declared 'inapplicable'. Once again, given the dearth of occasions in ordinary life on which an individual is liable to receive a decision addressed to him or her, this Article has also proved of particular use to Community staff.[95]

The inability of the EU itself to legislate in defiance of general principles extends in certain circumstances also to the actions of the Member States.[96] In particular, the ECJ has made it clear that the Member States are constrained by the general principles when they implement Community measures.[97] This is in essence because the States are in these circumstances operating as agents of the Community itself in furthering its legislation. It is an important principle in practice because of the

[93] See Cases 106 and 107/63 *Toepfer v Commission* [1965] ECR 405; Case 62/70 *Bock v Commission* [1971] ECR 897; Case C-209/94P *Buralux v Council* [1996] ECR I-615; and Case C-321/95P *Stichting Greenpeace Council v Commission* [1998] ECR I-1651.

[94] See in particular *Extramet Industrie v Council* and *Codorniu v Council*, op cit, n 89, and the submissions of Jacobs AG in Case C-50/00 P *UPA v Council* [2002] ECR I-6677. If and when the Constitution enters into force, the right of natural and legal persons to bring annulment actions will be slightly extended as regards the acts which they may challenge, and the requirement of proving individual concern will be dispensed with where the act impugned is merely a regulatory one; Art III-365(4) of the Constitution permits such persons to bring proceedings 'against an act addressed to that person or which is of direct and individual concern to him or her, and against a regulatory act which is of direct concern to him or her and does not entail implementing measures'.

[95] For general discussion of the scope of judicial review in EU law, see Arnull, Dashwood, Ross, and Wyatt, *Wyatt and Dashwood's European Union Law*, 4th edn (Sweet & Maxwell, London, 2000), ch 10.

[96] See Wyatt, 'Article 119 and the Fundamental Principle of Non-discrimination on Grounds of Sex' (1978) 3 ELRev 483.

[97] See Case 5/88 *Wachauf v Germany* [1989] ECR 2609; Case C-351/92 *Graff v Hauptzollamt Köln-Rheinau* [1994] ECR I-3361; Case C-84/95 *Bosphorus;* op cit, n 10; and Case C-292/97 *Karlsson* [2000] ECR I-2737.

huge number of instances in which the Member States are required to implement EU law. However, there is a second situation in which general principles also constrain the actions of Member States; in *Elliniki Radiophonia Tileorassi AE v Dimotiki Etairia Pliroforissis*,[98] the ECJ explained that it had

> no power to examine the compatibility with the European Convention on Human Rights of national rules which do not fall within the scope of Community law.[99] On the other hand, where such rules do fall within the scope of Community law, and reference is made to the Court for a preliminary ruling, it must provide all the criteria of interpretation needed by the national court to determine whether those rules are compatible with the fundamental rights the observance of which the Court ensures and which derive in particular from the European Convention on Human Rights.
>
> In particular, where a Member State relies on the combined provisions of Articles [46 and 55 of the EC Treaty] in order to justify rules which are likely to obstruct the exercise of the freedom to provide services, such justification, provided for by Community law, must be interpreted in the light of the general principles of law and in particular of fundamental rights. Thus the national rules in question can fall under the exceptions provided for by the combined provisions of Articles [46 and 55] only if they are compatible with the fundamental rights the observance of which is ensured by the Court.
>
> It follows that in such a case it is for the national court and, if necessary the Court of Justice, to appraise the application of those provisions having regard to all the rules of Community law, including freedom of expression, as embodied in Article 10 of the European Convention on Human Rights, as a general principle of law the observance of which is ensured by the Court.
>
> ... [T]he limitations imposed on the power of the Member States to apply the provisions referred to in Articles [46 and 55] of the Treaty on grounds of public policy, public security and public health, must be appraised in the light of the general principle of freedom of expression embodied in Article 10 of the European Convention on Human Rights.[100]

It is thus clear that the Member States must also observe the general principles of EU law, including those derived from the ECHR, when they rely upon a derogation from a Community rule.

If and when the Constitution is adopted, the relationship between the principles set out in the Charter of Fundamental Rights and the legality of other measures will be dealt with expressly. Article II-111(1) provides that the Charter is addressed to 'the institutions, bodies, offices and agencies of the Union ... and to the Member States only when they are implementing Union law'.[101] This formulation appears to give a more limited effect to the Charter than hitherto to general principles of EU law since, as seen above, general principles constrain the Member States not only when they are implementing EU law, but also when they are making use of a derogation permitted by EU law.[102]

---

[98] Case C-260/89 [1991] ECR I-2925. See also Case C-260/89 *ERT* [1991] ECR I-2925, and Case C-368/95 *Familiapress v Bauer Verlag* [1997] ECR I-3689. [99] See also discussion above.
[100] [1991] ECR I-2925, at 2964. [101] See also Art II-112(5) of the Constitution.
[102] Jacobs AG has suggested, extra-judicially, that the formulation contained in Art II-111(1) is not the result of an oversight but is deliberate and to be welcomed. He is critical of the logic underlying the ECJ's involvement in cases involving derogations: '[D]ifficulty arises I think from the apparent suggestion that, even after the Court of Justice has held that the derogation is in principle applicable, there is a further question: is the exercise compatible with human rights—and that this further question

The second situation in which general principles of law assume importance is when it comes to construing the TEC or secondary EU law.[103] Although general principles of law will not be permitted by the Court to override specific provisions of the Treaty,[104] they are from time to time utilized by the ECJ to justify a liberal interpretation of what might otherwise seem to be a narrow rule.[105] Thus, for example, a principle already worked out pursuant to the ECHR might inform the interpretation by the ECJ of one of the many undefined terms used in the Race Directive and the Framework Directive. There is, in addition, considerable potential here for improving the lot of the individual, since the provision concerned may of course prove directly effective. The procedure provided by Article 234 of the Treaty for seeking preliminary rulings on interpretation has facilitated this process.[106]

Having established the ways in which general principles of law play their part in the workings of the EU legal system, it is important now to focus on the general principle of non-discrimination in the sphere of sex equality. Whether this general principle of non-discrimination will also develop specialized offshoots in areas other than sex, especially those areas identified today in Article 13 TEC, can only be a matter for speculation at present, but it seems highly likely that it will.

The general principle of non-discrimination on the ground of sex

EU law has long subscribed to a general principle of non-discrimination, or consistency; it is essentially a rule of fairness and good administration. It may be expressed in broad terms as requiring like situations to be treated alike, and different situations to be treated differently, unless there is a good reason for not doing so.[107] The general principle of non-discrimination has most often found application in

is also a question of Community law. As it seems to me, the position is as follows: if a Member State seeks to justify a restriction in the interest of human rights—eg to preserve plurality of the press—then that is to be examined as part of the public policy derogation under the Treaty. Once that question has been answered, there is no further question of Community law. If the restriction proves to be permissible under Community law, then it must still be applied with respect for human rights. But that is no longer, at that stage, a question of Community law': 'Human Rights in the European Union: the Role of the Court of Justice' (2001) 26 ELRev 331, at 336–7.

[103] See, eg, Case T-93/94 *Becker v Court of Auditors* [1996] ECR II-141.

[104] Case 40/64 *Sgarlata v Commission* [1965] ECR 215.

[105] See, eg, Case C-260/89 *Elliniki Radiophonia Tileorassi AE v Dimotiki Etairia Pliroforissis* [1991] ECR I-2925.

[106] A general principle may also play an important part in the outcome of a case pending before a national court where the implementation of Community law by a Member State is in issue: see Case C-84/95 *Bosphorus v Hava Yollari* [1996] 3 CMLR 257, in which Jacobs AG submitted: 'Community law cannot release Member States from their obligations under [the European Convention on Human Rights]' (at 286). See also discussion above.

[107] See further Tridimas, op cit, n 1, ch 2, and Arnull, op cit, n 1, ch 6.

relation to goods and their producers, and has its roots in Article 34(2) TEC, which prohibits discrimination between producers or consumers within the Community in relation to the common organization of agricultural markets.[108] In this context, it is outwith the scope of the present work.

However, the principle has also found precise expression in the field of sex discrimination.[109] Thus, in *Defrenne v Sabena*,[110] the ECJ held:

> The Court has repeatedly stated that respect for fundamental personal human rights is one of the general principles of Community law, the observance of which it has a duty to ensure. There can be no doubt that the elimination of discrimination based on sex forms part of those fundamental rights.[111]

In *Deutsche Telekom v Schröder*,[112] it added that:

> [T]he economic aim pursued by Article 119 of the Treaty, namely the elimination of distortions of competition between undertakings established in different Member States, is secondary to the social aim pursued by the same provision, which constitutes the expression of a fundamental human right.[113]

This approach was moreover lent greater strength by the Amsterdam Treaty which, as seen elsewhere in the present work, considerably emphasized the importance of the principle of sex equality in a number of its provisions.

The ECJ has relied on the principle on non-discrimination on the ground of sex both to quash discriminatory administrative decisions and to justify a broad interpretation for various pieces of EC legislation. In the words of Trabucchi AG in *Defrenne v Sabena*:[114]

> [I]n interpreting Article 119, the Court cannot overlook the fact that the principle of equal treatment is enshrined in the legal system of Member States, the majority of which have erected it into a principle

---

[108] In Case C-292/97 *Karlsson* [2000] ECR I-2737, the Court described Art 34(2) as 'merely a specific expression of the general principle of equal treatment, which requires that comparable situations not be treated differently and different situations not be treated alike unless such treatment is objectively justified' (at 2775).

[109] See Docksey, 'The Principle of Equality Between Women and Men as a Fundamental Right Under Community Law' (1991) 20 ILJ 258.

[110] Case 149/77, op cit, n 83 the so-called *Third Defrenne* case.

[111] Ibid, at 1378. See also Case C-13/94 *P v S and Cornwall* [1996] ECR I-2143. The CFI confirmed this position in Case T-45/90 *Speybrouck v Parliament* [1992] ECR II-33. In Case C-381/99 *Brunnhofer v Bank der österreichischen Postsparkasse AG* [2001] ECR I-4961 (at 4988), it described the principle of equal pay as a particular expression of the general principle of equality and as 'part of the foundations of the Community'.   [112] Case C 50/96 [2000] ECR I-743.

[113] Ibid, at 794. See also Joined Cases C-270 & 2/1/97 *Deutsche Post v Sievers and Shrage* [2000] ECR I-929, commented on by the present writer in 'The supremacy of Community pensions equality law: a two-edged sword?' (2000) 25 ELRev 564. Cosmas AG, in his submissions in all these cases, said that, regardless of whether the economic objective truly reflected the intentions of the historical Community legislature, 'it no longer corresponds to present-day thinking. In a community governed by the rule of law, which respects and safeguards human rights, the requirement of equal pay for men and women is founded mainly on the principles of human dignity and equality between men and women and on the precept of improving working conditions...' ([2003] ECR I-743, at 769).

[114] Case 43/75 [1976] ECR 455.

formally underwritten by the constitution itself. In its judgment of 17 December 1970 in Case 11/70, *Internationale Handelsgesellschaft*, the Court stated that respect for fundamental human rights forms an integral part of the general principles of law and that the protection of such rights within the Community can and must be inspired by the constitutional traditions common to the Member States. In view of this it seems to me that the prohibition of all discrimination based on sex (particularly on the subject of pay) protects a right which must be regarded as fundamental in the Community legal order as it is elsewhere.[115]

He went on to add:

Undoubtedly, action by the Member States and by the Community institutions in the form of legislation, regulations or administrative measures is essential for the reason that, if the principle of equal treatment were to apply only to pay in the strict sense of the word or to absolutely identical work, the practical effect of Article 119 would be rather small. This gives the Member States and the Community institutions enormous scope in taking action to put into effect the principle of non-discrimination laid down in Article 119 without having to rely on its direct applicability.[116]

A good example of the use of the principle of non-discrimination on the ground of sex to justify judicial review of administrative action came in *Razzouk and Beydoun v Commission*.[117] The widower of a deceased Commission employee was refused a survivor's pension by the Commission in circumstances in which, under the Staff Regulations, a surviving widow would have received such a pension. He argued that this treatment amounted either to the breach of a principle analogous to Article 141 which applied to Community employees, or else to the breach of a general rule of EU law that employees should be treated equally in like or comparable situations. His claim was, in essence therefore, for the annulment of the Commission's decision which had denied him the pension. Advocate General Slynn commented that there was clearly discrimination between Community employees, and consequently between their spouses, on the ground of sex, since both male and female officials made the same pension contributions during their employment but stood to receive different benefits in the event of their predeceasing their spouses. This discrimination, he went on to say, could not be shown to be justified on any objective ground,[118] and he would have annulled it both on the ground that it offended against the general principle of non-discrimination and the narrower principle akin to Article 141. The Court agreed that the decision should be annulled, but based its decision wholly on the general principle of non-discrimination, saying that the Staff Regulations were 'contrary to a fundamental right and . . . therefore inapplicable in so far as they treat the surviving spouses of officials unequally according to the sex of the person concerned'.[119]

---

[115] Ibid, at 490.   [116] Ibid, at 491.

[117] Cases 75 and 117/82 [1984] ECR 1509, also discussed in ch 4.

[118] By this, Slynn AG presumably meant that no other 'cause' for the differential treatment of male and female employees had been found. See discussion in ch 3 of the concept of discrimination.

[119] [1984] ECR 1509, at 1530.

Usher has raised the fascinating question of whether this same principle could be used to challenge the Social Security Directive,[120] which permits differential State pensionable ages for men and women; he points out that the Court has made no comment on this matter, though it has often interpreted the relevant provisions of the Directive.[121]

The *Razzouk and Beydoun* case involved direct discrimination on the ground of sex. However, it has been clear since *Sabbatini v European Parliament*[122] that the general principle of non-discrimination can also be useful when indirect discrimination is concerned. Ms Sabbatini was a Community employee who, before her marriage, had received an expatriation allowance to compensate for her having to live in a foreign country in order to work for the Communities. Once married, she ceased to be paid the allowance because of the Civil Service Regulations, which at the time provided: 'An official loses entitlement to the allowance, if, marrying a person who, at the time of the marriage, does not fulfil the conditions required for the grant of that allowance, he (or she) does not become the head of the family'. Under the Regulations, the 'head of the family' was normally the husband, except in the event of his disability. Ms Sabbatini contested the decision stopping her allowance on the basis of Article 241, arguing that the decision was based on the Regulations, which were invalid because they breached the 'higher' rule prohibiting discrimination on the ground of sex. The discrimination alleged here was of course indirect, since both sexes were subjected to facially neutral treatment, but in reality that treatment disadvantaged women rather than men. Roemer AG submitted that the claim should be dismissed, in doing so denying that any general principle of non-discrimination on the ground of sex existed in EU law.[123] The Court, however, upheld the claim, saying:

[I]t is . . . clear that the provision the validity of which is contested does in fact create a difference of treatment as between male and female officials, in as much as it renders the retention of the expatriation allowance conditional upon the acquisition of the status of head of household within the meaning of the Staff Regulations. It is therefore necessary to examine whether this difference of treatment is such as to affect the validity of the contested provision of the Regulations. The purpose of the expatriation allowance is to compensate for the special expenses and disadvantages resulting from entry into the service of the Communities for those officials who—in the conditions more fully set out in detail in Article 4(1) of Annex VII [to the Regulations]—are thereby obliged to change their place of residence.

Article 4, taken as a whole, indicates that the expatriation allowance is paid to married officials, not only in consideration of the personal situation of the recipient, but also of the family situation created by

---

[120] Directive 79/7, OJ [1979] L6/24, discussed in ch 8. Likewise also the Occupational Social Security Directive 86/378, OJ [1986] L225/40, discussed in ch 4, which contains a similar exemption in respect of the self-employed.

[121] Usher, 'European Community Equality Law: Legal Instruments and Judicial Remedies', in McCrudden (ed), *Women, Employment and European Equality Law* (Eclipse Publications, London, 1987). See also the submissions of Van Gerven AG in Case C-9/91 *R v Secretary of State for Social Security, ex parte EOC* [1992] ECR I-4297, at 4324.

[122] Case 32/71 [1972] ECR 345, also discussed in ch 4.

[123] See in particular his remarks in ibid, at 355.

the marriage. Thus Article 4(3) takes into account the new family situation entered upon by the official when he or she marries a person who does not satisfy the conditions for the grant of the expatriation allowance. The withdrawal of the allowance following the marriage of the recipient might be justified in cases in which this change in the family situation is such as to bring to an end the state of 'expatriation' which is the justification for the benefit in question.

In this respect, the Regulations cannot, however, treat officials differently according to whether they are male or female, since termination of the status of expatriate must be dependent for both male and female officials on uniform criteria, irrespective of sex.

Consequently, by rendering the retention of the allowance subject to the acquisition of the status of 'head of household' . . . the Staff Regulations have created an arbitrary difference of treatment between officials. Consequently the decisions taken with regard to the applicant are devoid of any legal basis and must be annulled . . . [124]

A similar result was arrived at in *Airola v Commission*,[125] where a woman Community employee ceased to be paid an expatriation allowance on her marriage to a national of the country in which she was employed; the local law concerned automatically and irrevocably granted her the husband's nationality, which nationality, according to the Staff Regulations, disentitled her to the allowance. The Court upheld her claim to continued payment of the allowance, pointing out that the Regulations operated in a discriminatory fashion since under no national legislation in existence at the time in any of the Member States did a husband automatically acquire his wife's nationality on marriage. It held:

Though 'expatriation' is a subjective state conditioned by the official's assimilation into new surroundings, the Staff Regulations of officials cannot treat officials differently in this respect according to whether they are of the male or female sex since, in either case, payment of the expatriation allowance must be determined by considerations which are uniform and disregard the difference in sex. The concept of 'nationals' contained in Article 4(a) must therefore be interpreted in such a way as to avoid any unwarranted difference of treatment as between male and female officials who are, in fact, placed in comparable situations. Such unwarranted difference of treatment between female officials and officials of the male sex would result from an interpretation of the concept of 'nationals' . . . as also embracing the nationality which was imposed by law on an official of the female sex by virtue of her marriage, and which she was unable to renounce. It is therefore necessary to define the concept of an official's present or previous nationality under Article 4(a) of Annex VII as excluding nationality imposed by law on a female official upon her marriage with a national of another state, when she has no possibility of renouncing it.[126]

However, the efficacy of the notion of indirect discrimination in the field of sex discrimination is, as has already been noted, heavily dependent on the sensitivity of the deciding court as to what is truly adverse to a greater number of women than

---

[124] Ibid, at 350–1.   [125] Case 21/74 [1975] ECR 221.

[126] Ibid, at 228–9. Cf Case 37/74 *Van Den Broeck v Commission* [1975] ECR 235, in which the Court rejected such a claim because the applicant in that case had the choice, under the local law concerned, of renouncing the nationality conferred on her by marriage. The Staff Regulations were subsequently retrospectively amended so as to reflect these rulings: Art 21(2) of Council Regulation 912/78 of 2 May 1978, OJ [1978] L119/1. See also Case 257/78 *Devred v Commission* [1979] ECR 3767, where the situation, though more complicated, was similar to that in *Van Den Broeck*.

men. The tenor of the ECJ's remarks, although not its overall conclusion on the
facts, in *De Angelis v Commission*[127] suggested that it needed, at least in 1985, to be
made more aware of the practical issues in this field. Ms De Angelis became an
employee of the Commission in Brussels in December 1982. Although an Italian
national, she had been living in Brussels since 1970, when she had gone there in
order to accompany her husband, who at that earlier date had also become a
Commission employee. She contested the Commission's decision not to pay her an
expatriation allowance. Her position was governed by Article 4(1)(a) of Annex VII
to the Staff Regulations, providing:

An expatriation allowance shall be paid . . . (a) to officials:

　—who are not and never have been nationals of the state in whose territory the place where they
　　are employed is situated, and
　—who during the five years ending six months before they entered the service did not habitually
　　reside or carry on their main occupation within the European territory of that state. For the
　　purposes of this provision, circumstances arising from work done for another state or for an
　　international organization shall not be taken into account.

Until February 1982, the Commission had interpreted this provision benevolently,
especially for the benefit of the spouses and children of Community officials who
were themselves recruited by a Community institution. In practice, what this meant
was that a period spent by a wife accompanying her husband to another Member
State was not taken into account in relation to the expatriation allowance. However, this construction was abandoned after criticism by the Court of Auditors
that it amounted to a rewriting of the Staff Regulations. Ms De Angelis argued that
the denial of an expatriation allowance to her amounted to a breach of the principle
of equal pay; the Commission's new, restrictive interpretation of the Staff Regulations, she claimed, led to discrimination between male workers, who are free to
carry on their occupation without delay, and female workers, who are 'subject to
social and cultural pressure to raise their children until they have reached school-
age and must therefore delay their careers by several years'.[128] In so constructing
her argument, Ms De Angelis would seem to have been misguided: there certainly may be indirect discrimination where an employer stipulates an age or time qualification for applicants for employment;[129] however, there was no attempt made
here to prove that age or time had stood in Ms De Angelis's way. What she really
appears to have been trying to argue is that, since wives accompany their husbands
to the latter's place of work more frequently than occurs vice versa, any
employment stipulation which ignores that fact is potentially indirectly discriminatory. The case failed because the Court found, understandably in the circumstances, that discrimination had not been proved. However, both its remarks and
those of the Advocate General had a disturbingly unperceptive quality. Advocate

---

[127] Case 246/83 [1985] ECR 1253.　　　[128] In the words of Darmon AG, ibid, at 1257.
[129] See, eg, the British cases *Price v Civil Service Commission* [1977] IRLR 291, and *Huppert v UGC*
(1986) 8 EOR 38.

General Darmon, for example, commented:

No one has any intention of challenging the sociological and cultural factors relied upon by the applicant. However, neither the provision at issue nor the new application thereof can be criticized on the ground that they do not contribute towards mitigating the effects of those factors. Neither that provision nor the application thereof discriminate, either directly or indirectly, against employed women in the manner complained of by the applicant.

   The Staff Regulations must not contain any provisions which give rise to unequal treatment ... However, the provisions of the Staff Regulations cannot necessarily be expected to correct any pre-existing inequalities.[130]

This slavish commitment to the principle of formal equality of course disregarded the requirements of substantive equality which the concept of indirect discrimination is intended to facilitate. The Court's remarks were hardly more encouraging:

[N]either the wording of the provision in question nor the application thereof by the Commission provides the slightest indication of direct or indirect discrimination based on the sex of officials ... [T]he principle of equal treatment implies that both men and women must be afforded identical working conditions without discrimination but it cannot require the institution to interpret the provisions of the Staff Regulations in a different manner in order to offset any domestic or social expenses or obligations.[131]

It is vital to the efficacy of all the EU's anti-discrimination laws that the Court should be made properly conscious of how and when indirect discrimination may occur; this is of special importance in relation to the new prohibited grounds of discrimination where the consequences of social and cultural practices may not yet be widely appreciated. As the concept of discrimination becomes more familiar to the population generally, it seems likely that the incidence of direct discrimination can be expected to decline. What people are less likely to be aware of are the ways in which indirect discrimination can take place, and it is on this level that the Court's intervention is probably most needed. However, more recent cases display considerably more sensitivity on the part of the ECJ to the potential for indirect discrimination.[132] An important instance was provided in *Rinke v Ätztekammer Hamburg*.[133] Two directives intended to harmonize the training of doctors required a period of full-time training to be completed before a doctor could qualify as a general medical practitioner. Ms Rinke alleged that, on the usual principle that many more women than men have to work part-time, these instruments were unlawfully discriminatory. The ECJ accepted that there was *prima facie* indirect discrimination because of 'the unequal division of domestic tasks between men and women'. However, it held that in pursuing the objectives of the free movement of doctors and a high general level of health protection, the Community legislation enjoyed a 'wide margin of discretion'; on the facts it concluded that that discretion had not

[130] [1985] ECR 1253, at 1257.   [131] Ibid, at 1264.
[132] See, eg, the remarks of the ECJ in Case C-243/95 *Hill and Stapleton v Revenue Commissioners* [1998] ECR I-3739, discussed in ch 4.   [133] Case C-25/02 [2003] ECR I-8349.

been exceeded. The adverse impact of the measures on part-time doctors was justified by the necessity for them to obtain professional relevant experience, in particular by following patients' pathological conditions as they evolve over time. On a broader canvass, the case provided an important endorsement that sex equality is nevertheless a fundamental principle of EU law. After reiterating that the elimination of sex discrimination is a fundamental right respect for which is a condition for the legality of Community acts, it held:

It follows that a provision of a directive adopted by the Council in disregard of the principle of equal treatment for men and women is vitiated by illegality.

. . . compliance with the prohibition of indirect discrimination on grounds of sex is a condition governing the legality of all measures adopted by the Community institutions.[134]

Efforts to persuade the ECJ to regard the principle of non-discrimination on the ground of sex as a positive and enforceable right have, on the whole, not proved so successful as efforts to persuade it to exercise its powers of judicial review on this ground. Of course, by its nature, this is a matter which is not susceptible to precise measurement and, furthermore, there can be little doubt that the Court's frequent liberal interpretations of Article 141 and of the Equal Treatment Directive are attributable in part to a desire to further the general principle of the equality of the sexes. However, this is an area where advances could still be made. It is important that the Court's case law be developed so as to articulate the general principle of non-discrimination clearly and to raise the consciousness of both judges and advocates to its presence in the background when any relevant legislation is being construed. One thing which would help this process would be a much clearer indication from the ECJ as to the precise scope of the principle. In the staff cases, of which the most numerous are those dealing with expatriation allowances, and in *Defrenne v Sabena*,[135] although the principle is expressed in broad terms, in reality it boils down to little more in practice than the application of the principle of equal pay for equal work[136] and, since this is guaranteed anyway by Article 141, the Court is only in effect holding that the Staff Regulations infringe the Treaty itself. Nevertheless, as seen above, the Court on several occasions has referred to the principle of equal treatment,[137] and implied that it sees pay equality merely as an example of this grander principle.[138] In addition, it is clear from the cases so far decided that the Court will not be satisfied by facially equal treatment but will also concern itself with the notion of indirect discrimination. What is not so clear is how far the principle of equal treatment extends: is it restricted, for example, to employment, or does it go further? If it extends, for example, to vocational training, might it not also govern education in other areas, as does the ECHR?

---

[134] Case C-25/02 [2003] ECR I-8349, at 8382.   [135] Case 43/75, op cit, n 114.

[136] In particular in the light of Roemer AG's words in Case 32/71 *Sabbatini* op cit, n 122, discussed in ch 4 to the effect that the expatriation allowance constitutes pay.

[137] Most recently and most clearly in Case C-25/02 *Rinke*, op cit, n 133.

[138] Legislative support for this approach can now be drawn from Art 141, since it now deals with the whole field of equal treatment in employment.

Does it, for example, apply to the supply of services, or to taxation? Does a general principle of sex equality in fact influence all law that the Community is empowered to make, as might be implied from the complementary provisions of the ECHR and the European Social Charter? A clear positive response to these questions would be a tremendously important step towards improving the protection afforded by EU sex equality law.

One limitation on the utility of the general principle of equality to shed light on the meaning of EU law is, however, undoubted: there must be some definite EU law for the principle to bite on. This was illustrated by *Defrenne v Sabena*,[139] and is reflective of the civil law principle that the judge's role is restricted to the enforcement of enacted law. The redoubtable Ms Defrenne had brought an action before the Belgian courts claiming, *inter alia*, an increase in the allowance she received on the termination of her service with Sabena as her contract required when she reached the age of 40 (the airline was prepared to pay her a sum equal to twelve months' pay), and compensation for the damage she suffered as regards her old-age pension in consequence of her enforced premature retirement. The Cour de Cassation sought a preliminary ruling from the ECJ, asking:

Must Article 119 of the Treaty of Rome which lays down the principle that 'men and women should receive equal pay for equal work' be interpreted by reason of the dual economic and social aim of the Treaty as prescribing not only equal pay but also equal working conditions for men and women and, in particular, does the insertion into the contract of employment of an air hostess of a clause bringing the said contract to an end when she reaches the age of 40 years, it being established that no such limit is attached to the contract of male cabin attendants who are assumed to do the same work, constitute discrimination prohibited by the said Article 119 of the Treaty of Rome or by a principle of Community law if that clause may have pecuniary consequences, in particular, as regards the allowance on termination of service and pension?[140]

The ECJ held, first of all, that the old version of Article 141 (dealing expressly only with the principle of equal pay for equal work) did not extend to this situation. In so doing, it demonstrated that, despite the fact that it is prepared to interpret EU legislation broadly and teleologically, there are limits beyond which it will refuse to go. Ms Defrenne had argued that Article 141 must be given a wide interpretation because it was only a specific statement of the more general principle of non-discrimination. In particular, she claimed that her enforced retirement at the age of 40 fell within the scope of Article 141, first, because 'a woman worker can receive pay equal to that received by men only if the requirement regarding equal conditions of employment is first satisfied' and, secondly, because 'the age limit imposed on air hostesses by the contract of employment has pecuniary consequences which are prejudicial as regards the allowance on termination of service and pension'. The Court rejected these arguments on the basis that the Treaty's Social Provisions were divisible into those provisions requiring a harmonization of the laws of the Member States in relation to working conditions (today

---

[139] Case 149/77, op cit, n 83.   [140] Ibid, at 1367.

Articles 136 and 137) and the more specific and prescriptive, of which Article 141 is an example.[141] It implied that these two categories are mutually exclusive, and then went on to add, in somewhat sinister vein:

[T]he fact that the fixing of certain conditions of employment—such as a special age-limit—may have pecuniary consequences is not sufficient to bring such conditions within the field of application of Article 119, which is based on the close connection which exists between the nature of the services provided and the amount of the remuneration. That is all the more so since the touchstone which forms the basis of Article 119—that is, the comparable nature of the services provided by workers of either sex—is a factor as regards which all workers are *ex hypothesi* on an equal footing, whereas in many respects an assessment of the other conditions of employment and working conditions involves factors connected with the sex of the workers, taking into account considerations affecting the special position of women in the work process.[142]

As to the allegation that a general principle of EC law was breached in this situation, and that that general principle was specifically enforceable, the Court had this to say:

[A]s regards the relationships of employer and employee which are subject to national law, the Community had not, at the time of the events now before the Belgian court, assumed any responsibility for supervising and guaranteeing the observance of the principle of equality between men and women in working conditions other than remuneration.[143]

In other words, there was at the time of this action no enforceable EU law on working conditions to which the general principle of non-discrimination could be attached. This situation was of course reversed with the coming into force of the Equal Treatment Directive.

The potency of the principle of sex equality would, of course, be vastly increased if the Treaty were to be amended so as to contain a provision which articulated it in directly effective terms. The same is true for all the other grounds on which discrimination is today forbidden by EU law. The opportunity for such a reform was not made use of when the Amsterdam Treaty was agreed, nor when the Constitution was drafted. Were such directly effective provisions to be included in some future version of the Treaty, the doctrine of supremacy would enable individual litigants to use it not only to assert a positive right to equality throughout the entire field of application of the Treaty, but also to impugn any national law which sought to deny equality. This would amount to truly fundamental constitutional protection for this basic human right.

---

[141] See ch 1 for discussion of the origins of this distinction.

[142] [1978] ECR 1365, at 1377. In later decisions, particularly Case C-262/88 *Barber v Guardian Royal Exchange Assurance Group* [1990] ECR I-1889, discussed in chs 4 and 5, the Court has considerably eroded this distinction.   [143] [1978] ECR 1365, at 1378.

8

Equality in social security

The scope of the non-discrimination principle in the field of social security

The provision of just and adequate social security is vital to the achievement of the goals of non-discrimination and equality. Not only is it the flip-side to employment, aiming to protect the income and living standards of those—often the poorest members of the community—involuntarily out of the workforce, but it sets a very public standard by which people's roles within society are defined and measured. It was seen in chapter 5 that the relevance of social security to the achievement of sex equality was accepted in 1976 when the Equal Treatment Directive was enacted, but that the matter was regarded as meriting separate legislative treatment; the major instrument subsequently passed to address sex discrimination in social security is the Council Directive of 19 December 1978 on the progressive implementation of the principle of equal treatment for men and women in matters of social security, the so-called Social Security Directive;[1] it forms the subject matter of the present chapter. It will be recalled that the Occupational Social Security Directive[2] was discussed, in the context of equal pay, in chapter 4.

It was also seen in chapter 5 that the Race Directive expressly states that it is to apply to 'social protection, including social security';[3] however, no attempt is made by that instrument to define the consequent detailed rules. The possibility is therefore a live one that the rules developed by the ECJ in relation to sex discrimination in social security will come to be applied *mutatis mutandis* in relation to discrimination by social security schemes on the ground of racial or ethnic origin; the rest of the present chapter should be read with this possibility in mind. Whilst it is (it is hoped) unlikely that direct discrimination on the ground of racial or ethnic origin will be encountered within the social security systems of the Member States, it is certainly possible that claims of indirect discrimination will arise.

The Framework Directive, however, excludes all payments made by State schemes.[4] It is obvious that considerable, and perhaps intractable, difficulties were to be anticipated in relation to age, and therefore it is reasonably understandable

---

[1] Directive 79/7, OJ [1979] L6/24.   [2] Directive 86/378, OJ [1986] L225/40.
[3] Art 3(1)(e).
[4] See Art 3(3); cf Recital 13 of the Preamble to the instrument, which is expressed in more limited terms.

that the Directive excludes discrimination on the ground of age from its scope. However, it is equally clear that there is considerable potential mileage in claims that social security legislation discriminates against the other protected categories, in particular against the disabled and against homosexuals (for example, in relation to survivors' benefits). There is therefore a serious lacuna in the Framework Directive in this regard.

The objectives of the Social Security Directive

Mayras AG, in *Worsdorfer v Raad van Arbeid*,[5] described the Social Security Directive as extending to the sphere of social security 'the principle of equal treatment for men and women set out in Article 119 of the EEC Treaty as regards equal pay for equal work'. The instrument itself, even in its Preamble, is somewhat more guarded, explaining that:

[T]he principle of equal treatment in matters of social security should be implemented in the first place in the statutory schemes which provide protection against the risks of sickness, invalidity, old age, accidents at work, occupational diseases and unemployment, and in social assistance in so far as it is intended to supplement or replace the above-mentioned schemes.[6]

It adds that:

[T]he implementation of the principle of equal treatment in matters of social security does not prejudice the provisions relating to the protection of women on the ground of maternity; whereas in this respect, Member States may adopt specific provisions for women to remove existing instances of unequal treatment.[7]

The potential scope of the Directive may not have been quite clear to all those involved in its drafting and negotiation.[8] At the very least, its rationale could be assumed to be to extend the principle of equal treatment of the sexes from the employment situation to those situations in which the State makes payments to compensate persons who are unable to continue in paid work, for example, because of physical disability: it is a logical counterpart to the equal pay principle in such cases. The Directive outlaws both direct and indirect sex discrimination in social security, and this has had wide-ranging and important implications. Many of the national social security systems of the Member States of the EU were based upon the model of the family unit consisting of one breadwinner (traditionally, of course, male), together with one adult dependant (traditionally female) and dependent children. Such a model is highly prone to discrimination against the female sex, of a direct kind where the legislation is expressed in gender-specific terms, and of an indirect kind where the 'non-breadwinning' partner receives lesser social security

---

[5] Case 9/79 [1979] ECR 2717, at 2728.   [6] Recital 2.
[7] Recital 3. See also the discussion below.
[8] See Hoskyns and Luckhaus, 'The European Community Directive on Equal Treatment in Social Security' (1989) Policy and Politics, Vol 17, No 4, 321.

benefits than the 'breadwinner' and it can be shown that this former group is composed primarily of women. It may also discriminate against some groups on the ground of race and ethnicity, where it can be shown that the cultural traditions of the group concerned do not favour this type of domestic organization. Whether or not the inclusion of indirect discrimination within its terms enables the Social Security Directive to require radical recasting of the social security systems of the Member States—not apparently an intended consequence at the time of its enactment—is examined later in the present chapter.

It is important to observe, however, that the Directive does not go so far as to mandate the individualization of benefits, in other words, the treatment of each adult person as a separate unit; couples can therefore still be aggregated for the purpose of determining benefits, so long as the system operates in a gender-neutral fashion.[9] This remains one of the most serious shortcomings of the legislation in the view of its more radical critics (because of its basis in an outmoded stereotype). Moreover, neither does the Directive require the harmonization of all the systems in operation in the Member States. There was clearly no political consensus to go this far when the instrument was drafted, and indeed even today such an aspiration appears distant. The Commission, commenting on the Social Charter agreed in principle by the Heads of Government at the Summit Meeting of December 1989,[10] ruled out harmonization of social security systems, but said that divergence between the Member States in this matter might place 'a brake on free movement and exacerbate regional imbalances, particularly north–south'.[11] In the Action Programme published by the Commission as an accompaniment to the Social Charter,[12] it commented:

The social security systems vary greatly in nature from one Member State of the Community to another. They reflect the history, traditions and social and cultural practices proper to each Member State, which cannot be called into question. There can therefore be no question of harmonizing the systems existing in these fields.

As a result, it merely proposed in the Action Programme two Recommendations in the field of social security, one on the convergence of objectives in national schemes[13] and the other on resourcing.[14]

---

[9] Cf the comment of Laurent, Principal Administrator in the European Commission, in 'European Community Law and Equal Treatment for Men and Women in Social Security' (1982) 121 International Labour Review 373, at 385: '[T]he whole orientation of European Community law in matters of equal treatment for men and women . . . aims at setting in motion an irreversible evolutionary process in which each of the spouses will be granted independent social rights, as in matters of civil and political rights, where such equality is already broadly achieved.'   [10] See ch 7.

[11] See CREW Reports (Nov/Dec 1989), Vol 9, Nos 11/12, 15.   [12] COM (89) 568.

[13] Subsequently Council Recommendation on the convergence of social protection policies and objectives, 92/442, OJ [1992] L245/49. This provides that social benefits should be granted, inter alia, in accordance with the principle of 'equal treatment in such a way as to avoid any discrimination based on nationality, race, sex, religion, customs or political opinion' (at IA2(a)) and so as to 'help remove obstacles to occupational activity by parents through measures to reconcile family and professional responsibilities' (at IA6(c)).

[14] Subsequently Council Recommendation on common criteria concerning sufficient resources and social assistance in social protection systems, 92/441, OJ [1992] L245/46.

Nevertheless, the Commission's 1994 White Paper on Social Policy pledged it to give consideration to a 'Recommendation on the adaptation of social protection systems to changing family structures, notably through the individualization of rights and contributions on the basis of a comparison of actual gender inequalities in social security'.[15] In the Fourth Action Programme[16] the Commission also promised to undertake further studies on the individualization of rights in social security, tax, and related areas, drawing on experience gained in the Member States. In the light of these findings, it said that it would publish a Communication on social protection in 1997, and would thereafter decide on proposals for progressive change in this area.

However, the problem of high levels of unemployment forced the Member States to concentrate on employment policy, rather than on individualization or harmonization of social protection systems, in the closing years of the twentieth century. The Dublin Summit meeting of December 1996, for example, stressed the need to make social security more employment-friendly by developing systems capable of adapting to new patterns of work and of providing appropriate protection to people engaged in such work; and, at the Luxembourg Jobs Summit in late 1997, the Council called for a more active approach to increase the employability of those out of work. The growing costs of social protection, attributable to ageing populations across Europe together with more and longer unemployment and changed work patterns for women, also led to a change of focus by the Commission. In its Report on Social Protection in Europe (1997),[17] it commented that the response of governments in Europe to the economic, social, and demographic changes taking place was to try to limit expenditure on social protection and to reduce the number of people dependent on it; it also noted an increasing debate on where State responsibility should end and individual responsibility take over. It observed a trend to reduce the number of people receiving disability benefits, by making the tests for assessing incapacity more stringent and by helping the disabled to find jobs, in particular through the introduction of legislation prohibiting discrimination in this area. It also identified a recent reversal of policy in relation to older workers, encouraging them to stay on at work rather than retire early, a development supported by schemes permitting a transfer from full-time to part-time working. Although it noted the demand in some quarters for individualization, the Commission's conclusions were ultimately directed towards economic reality:

The twin concern of present social policy on social protection across the Union, to contain costs and reduce dependency, is being achieved in part by increasing the effectiveness of expenditure through the adoption of a more active approach and targeting resources on those most in need.... While the

---

[15] *European Social Policy—A Way Forward for the Union*, COM (94) 333 final, at 36.
[16] Fourth Community Action Programme on Equal Opportunities for Women and Men (1996–2000), COM (95) 381 final; OJ [1995] L335/37.
[17] COM (1998) 243 final. See also *Modernising and Improving Social Protection in the European Union*, COM (97) 102.

consensus on maintaining the universal nature of social protection accessible to all holds firm, this does not rule out some shift in responsibility from the state to the individual or the private sector in certain areas.[18]

Sjerps has pointed out[19] that the principle of equality as regards social security benefits finds readier and more general acceptance in relation to wage-related benefits (usually granted for a limited period in cases of unemployment, disability, and sickness) than in relation to means-tested benefits (guaranteeing a minimum income in cases where the recipient has no other income). She has noted that people find it increasingly logical that, when a man and woman do the same job and pay the same contributions, they should also receive the same wage-related benefits. On the other hand, many also still seem to incline to the view that when it comes to means-tested or 'safety-net' benefits, people should turn first for subsistence not to the State but to members of their families and others closest to them. Such a view of course also militates against the individualization of the latter type of benefits.

The complexity and diversity of the social security systems to be found in the Member States led the Council to adopt a phased approach to the EU legislation. It was originally envisaged that social security would be included as part of the working conditions to which the principle of equality of treatment was applied by the Equal Treatment Directive. However, as the ramifications of this plan became appreciated, it was abandoned in favour of specific legislation dealing with social security, the undertaking to introduce such legislation being expressly written into Article 1(2) of the earlier Directive. Somewhat similarly, the original plans for the Social Security Directive covered occupational social security schemes, but these were eventually omitted from the 1979 instrument on the understanding, articulated in Article 3(3) of the Directive, that they would be covered by subsequent legislation. That legislation took the form of the Occupational Social Security Directive,[20] discussed in chapter 4 because of its close connection in practice with Article 141 of the Treaty. A third social security directive was proposed by the Commission in 1987.[21] This aimed to take the process of equalizing treatment in social security systems yet further, in particular by removing the existing exceptions for pensionable age and survivors' and family benefits.[22] It was to some extent overtaken by events, notably the ECJ's decision in *Barber v Guardian Royal Exchange Assurance Group*,[23] and was subsequently withdrawn.

The Social Security Directive is based upon Article 308[24] of the EC Treaty, as is the Equal Treatment Directive, no doubt because, like the latter instrument, its

[18] Ibid, at 19–20.
[19] Sjerps, 'Indirect Discrimination in Social Security in the Netherlands: Demands of the Dutch Women's Movement', in Buckley and Anderson (eds), *Women, Equality and Europe* (Macmillan, London, 1988).   [20] Directive 86/378, OJ [1986] L225/40.
[21] COM (87) 494 final; OJ [1987] C309/10.   [22] As to which, see below.
[23] Case C-262/88 [1990] ECR I-1889, discussed in ch 4.
[24] Usher has questioned the *vires* of the Social Security Directive, on the ground that, in permitting differential State pensionable ages for men and women (discussed later in the present chapter), it

aims are not the harmonization or 'approximation' envisaged by Article 94. The possible direct effect of its provisions, not of course precluded by its legal basis in Article 308,[25] is less problematic than in the case of the Equal Pay and Equal Treatment Directives; the inability of directives to produce horizontal direct effects leads to anomalies where the provision in question is relevant to the legal position vis-à-vis two individuals (in this context, employer and employee). The Social Security Directive, however, seeks to regulate relations between the State and individuals, and therefore its applicability is of the 'vertical' kind.[26]

Substantive rights conferred by the Social Security Directive

Article 1 articulates the aim of the instrument:

The purpose of this Directive is the progressive implementation, in the field of social security and other elements of social protection provided for in Article 3, of the principle of equal treatment for men and women in matters of social security, hereinafter referred to as 'the principle of equal treatment'.

The essentially limited nature of this purpose was pointed out by Darmon AG in *De Weerd, née Roks*,[27] where he observed that the Directive 'is in no way intended to regulate the operation of Member States' social security schemes, nor to determine a lower or upper limit on the amount of the benefits given to victims of one of the risks listed in the Directive'.[28]

Article 2, in defining the persons to whom the Directive applies, points to a logical link with financially remunerated work. It provides:

This Directive shall apply to the working population—including self-employed persons, workers and self-employed persons whose activity is interrupted by illness, accident or involuntary unemployment and persons seeking employment—and to retired or invalided workers and self-employed persons.

The instrument thus appears to extend to those not currently in work because of their inability to work, unemployment, or old age,[29] but also seems from its wording to omit certain important categories.[30] In particular, the use of the word 'interrupted'

---

infringes the fundamental principle of the equality of the sexes under EU law (discussed in ch 7); see Usher, 'European Community Equality Law: Legal Instruments and Judicial Remedies' in McCrudden (ed), *Women, Employment and European Equality Law* (Eclipse Publications, London, 1987).

[25] See ch 2.   [26] See generally the discussion in ch 2.
[27] Case C-343/92 [1994] ECR I-571.   [28] Ibid, at 580.
[29] The ECJ in Case C-280/94 *Posthuma-Van Damme v Bestuur van de Bedrijfsvereniging voor Detailhandel, Ambachten en Huisvrouwen* [1996] ECR I-179, therefore rejected the contrary argument of the Commission and held that a person who, in the year preceding commencement of an incapacity to work, did not receive a certain income from or in connection with work, did not necessarily fall outside the scope *ratione personae* of the Directive.
[30] Eg, on its face, it would appear not to cover persons seeking to set themselves up as self-employed, as distinct from those seeking employment.

suggests that those who have never been in work (for example, because of dis-ability) are excluded; similarly, its reference to those seeking 'employment' unfortunately seems to rule out those persons (mainly women) who are engaged in non-paid domestic work caring for children, spouses, and infirm relatives, unless they can demonstrate that they belong within some other category of persons covered by the Directive. The non-application of the Directive to many home-makers constitutes one of the major shortcomings of the instrument and demon-strates how a heavily male-orientated work model dominated the thinking of even the drafters of the equality legislation.

This essentially textual analysis of the provision has been supported by the case law, which shows that, though the ECJ is prepared in some instances to give a broad reading to the Article, there are limits beyond which it will not pass and which have the effect of excluding significant sections of the population, a large proportion of whom are probably women.[31]

The ECJ's first decision on the scope of Article 2 came in *Drake v Chief Adjudication Officer.*[32] Ms Drake gave up her paid employment in 1984 in order to look after her severely disabled mother. The mother received an attendance allowance under the relevant UK social security legislation, but, as a result of s 37 of the Social Security Act 1975, Ms Drake was refused an invalid care allowance because she was a married woman living with her husband. She claimed that this refusal contravened the Social Security Directive and the case was referred to the ECJ for a preliminary ruling. One of the issues which arose before the ECJ was whether Ms Drake was a person covered by Article 2 of the Directive (despite the fact that the adjudication officer had conceded this point). The difficulty was that she was not *herself* currently seeking employment, and though her previous employ-ment had been interrupted by disability, it was not her own disability but her mother's. The ECJ nevertheless took a generous view of the scope of the Directive *ratione personae* and held:

[Article 2 of the Directive] is based on the idea that a person whose work has been interrupted by one of the risks referred to in Article 3 belongs to the working population. That is the case of Mrs Drake, who has given up work solely because of one of the risks listed in Article 3, namely the invalidity of her mother. She must therefore be regarded as a member of the working population for the purposes of the Directive.[33]

Such reasoning, of course, would not apply to women giving up work to look after their healthy spouses or children, since the fact of having a family is not one of the 'risks' specified by Article 3. This was confirmed by the Court's later ruling in *Acterberg-te Riele v Sociale Verzekeringsbank.*[34] Under The Netherlands' old-age pensions system, which was in operation until legislative amendment in 1985,

[31] See Cousins, 'Equal Treatment and Social Security' (1994) 19 ELRev 123, and Sohrab, 'Women and Social Security: the Limits of EEC Equality Law' [1994] JSWFL 5.

[32] Case 150/85 [1986] ECR 1995.

[33] Ibid, at 2009. The risks referred to in Art 3 are examined below.

[34] Cases 48/88, 106/88, & 107/88 [1989] ECR 1963.

a married woman resident in The Netherlands did not qualify for a pension if her husband, though also a resident of The Netherlands, had worked and was insured abroad. The system was discriminatory because the reverse was not also the case, so that a husband retained his right to a Netherlands pension even if his wife was insured abroad. The Social Insurance Bank refused to grant a full old-age pension on this basis to three women whose husbands had worked abroad; two of the women had themselves had jobs until they voluntarily ceased work, and the third had never had a job. The ECJ held that it could be inferred from Article 2 of the Directive, when read together with Article 3, that it only covered persons who were working at the time when they were entitled to claim an old-age pension, and persons whose economic activity had previously been interrupted by one of the other risks set out in Article 3(1)(a).[35] This meant that the Directive was not applicable to persons who had never been available on the labour market, or who had ceased to be so where the reason for their giving up work was not the materialization of one of the risks referred to in the Directive. Furthermore, the Court added, in a disappointingly narrow spirit, that this interpretation was consistent with the purpose of EU law and with the wording of the other provisions forming the background to the Social Security Directive. The purpose of Article 141 of the Treaty and the Equal Pay and Equal Treatment Directives was to bring about equal treatment for men and women not in a general way, but solely in their capacity as workers.

This approach was confirmed by the Court's decision in *Züchner v Handelskrankenkasse Bremen*.[36] This involved a claim to a welfare benefit in respect of the caring services provided by a wife who looked after her severely disabled husband. It was argued that, although Ms Züchner had not given up an occupation in order to care for her husband, neither could she thereafter have taken up an occupation because of the extent and intensity of the care she provided; no distinction, it was maintained, could sensibly be drawn between giving up work to look after a disabled person (the *Drake* situation) and being prevented from taking up work for that reason. Moreover, she had had to undergo training in order to be able to care for her husband; and were she not to provide it, care would have had to be provided by someone else who would require payment. Advocate General Ruiz-Jarabo Colomer submitted:

It is well known that the Court has always construed 'working population' widely in that it considers that the Directive applies also to persons whose work or search for work has been interrupted because one of the specified risks has materialised in relation to another person. Nevertheless I would point out that, when deciding whether the person concerned belongs to the working population, the Court has on no occasion overlooked the requirement that he must be employed or self-employed or seeking work, that is to say a person who is available for employment or is seriously trying to find employment.[37]

[35] See also the remarks of Darmon AG in Case C-31/90 *Johnson v Chief Adjudication Officer* [1991] ECR I-3723, at 3739–40.   [36] Case C-77/95 [1996] ECR I-5689.
[37] Ibid, at 5707–8.

The Court's reluctance to recognize the true financial value of work undertaken in the home was more or less explicit in its judgment:

[T]he term 'activity' referred to in relation to the expression 'working population' in Article 2 of the Directive can be construed only as referring at the very least to an economic activity, that is to say an activity undertaken in return for remuneration in the broad sense . . . [A]n interpretation purporting to include within the concept of working population a member of a family who, without payment, undertakes an activity for the benefit of another member of the family on the ground that such activity calls for a degree of competence, is of a particular nature or scope or would have to be provided by an outsider in return for remuneration if the member of the family in question did not provide it would have the effect of infinitely extending the scope of the Directive, whereas the purpose of Article 2 of the Directive is precisely to delimit that scope . . .

Article 2 of the Directive must be interpreted as not covering a person who undertakes, as an unremunerated activity, the care of his or her handicapped spouse, regardless of the extent of that activity and the competence required to carry it out, where the person in question did not, in order to do so, abandon an occupational activity or interrupt efforts to find employment.[38]

This conclusion can be criticized as unduly harsh on two counts. First, it failed to recognize the very real economic value of Ms Züchner's services, without which the State would have had to pay for equivalent skilled care; the nature of the care which she provided went far beyond the expectations of normal married life, and the Court could without much difficulty therefore have held that Ms Züchner in fact constituted a member of the working population. Secondly, through its concentration on the policy objective of limiting the scope of Article 2, the Court was led into the error of ignoring what is surely the more important policy objective underlying the Directive, that of outlawing discrimination; it is highly probable that the majority of persons who are excluded from the traditional paid labour market on account of having to care for severely disabled relatives are women, and thus to interpret the Directive so as to exclude them from its protection is to sacrifice the true aim of the instrument to a patriarchal, out-dated, and unjust view of family life.

The Court has, however, made one limited concession in this area. In *Johnson v Chief Adjudication Officer*,[39] it held that Article 2 extends to a person who has interrupted paid employment in order to bring up children and who thereafter seeks to return to the labour market, where that return to work is prevented by the materialization of one of the risks listed in Article 3:

In order to be a member of the working population within the meaning of Article 2 of the Directive, it is sufficient for the person concerned to be a person seeking employment; no distinction according to the reason for which the person concerned left previous employment or even according to whether or not that person previously carried on an occupational activity is necessary.

However, the person concerned must prove that he or she was a person seeking employment when one of the risks specified in Article 3(1)(a) of the Directive materialised. In this regard, it is for the national court to determine whether the person concerned was actually seeking employment at the time when he or she was affected by one of the risks specified in the Directive by looking to see in particular whether that person was registered with an employment organisation responsible for dealing with offers

---

[38] Ibid, at 5726–7.   [39] Op cit, n 35, noted by Laske in (1992) 29 CMLRev 1011.

of employment or assisting persons seeking employment, whether the person had sent job applications to employers and whether certificates were available from firms stating that the person concerned had attended interviews.

It follows that the protection guaranteed by Directive 79/7 to persons who have given up their occupational activity in order to attend to the upbringing of their children is afforded only to those persons in that category who suffered incapacity for work during a period in which they were seeking employment.[40]

In response to the argument that its interpretation of the scope of Article 2 has the effect of disproportionately disadvantaging women, the Court stated:

[A]ccording to the first recital of the preamble to Directive 79/7 and Article 1 thereof, the Directive has in view only the progressive implementation of the principle of equal treatment for men and women in matters of social security. As far as the social protection of mothers remaining at home is concerned, it follows from Article 7(1)(b)[41] . . . that the acquisition of entitlement to benefits following periods of interruption of employment due to the upbringing of children is still a matter for the Member States to regulate.

. . . [I]t is for the Community legislature to take such measures as it considers appropriate to remove the discrimination which still exists in this regard in some bodies of national legislation.[42]

Despite the refusal of the ECJ to regard persons working within the home as within the scope of the Directive (or perhaps in consequence of its unease at thus excluding so many women from the reach of the Directive), it has been willing to extend the coverage of the instrument to those engaged in a very small way in paid employment. *Nolte v Landesversicherungsanstalt Hannover*[43] raised the issue of whether the Directive extended to persons engaged in what German legislation defined as 'minor' employment, which meant working for fewer than fifteen hours a week for a wage of not more than one-seventh of the average of that earned by persons insured under the statutory old-age insurance scheme. *Megner and Scheffel v Innungskrankenkasse Vorderplatz*[44] concerned (additionally) those in 'short-term' employment, defined by the relevant national legislation as being for no more than eighteen hours a week. In both cases, the Court held that the definition of the working population intended by Article 2 is 'very broad', and that it covered persons in 'minor' and 'short-term' employment:

The fact that a worker's earnings do not cover all his needs cannot prevent him from being a member of the working population. It appears from the Court's case-law that the fact that his employment yields an income lower than the minimum required for subsistence (see Case 53/81 *Levin v Staatssecretaris van Justitie* [1982] ECR 1035, paragraphs 15 and 16) or normally does not exceed 18 hours a week (see Case C 102/88 *Ruzius-Wilbrink* [1989] ECR 4311, paragraphs 7 and 17) or 12 hours a week (see Case 139/85 *Kempf v Staatssecretaris van Justitie* [1986] ECR 1741, paragraphs 2 and 16) or even 10 hours a week (see Case 171/88 *Rinner-Kühn* [1989] ECR 2743, paragraph 16) does not prevent the person in such employment from being regarded as a worker within the meaning of Article 48[45] (the *Levin* and

---

[40] [1991] ECR I-3723, at 3752.   [41] As to which see below.   [42] [1991] ECR I-3723.
[43] Case C-317/93 [1995] ECR I-4625.   [44] Case C-444/93 [1995] ECR I-4741.
[45] Today Art 39.

Kempf cases) or Article 119 of the EEC Treaty (the *Rinner-Kühn* case) or for the purposes of Directive 79/7 (the *Ruzius-Wilbrink* case).

The German Government . . . argues that a different view ought to be taken in this case, since what is at issue is not the concept of a worker within the meaning of Article 48 of the Treaty . . . but the concept of a worker within the meaning of social security law. The definition of the concept of a worker in the latter sphere falls within the competence of the Member States.

It should be observed in that connection that as long ago as the judgment in Case 75/63 *Hoekstra (née Unger)* [1964] ECR 177 (paragraph 1 of the operative part) the Court ruled that the concept of 'wage-earner or assimilated worker' referred to in Regulation No 3 of the Council of 25 September 1958 concerning social security for migrant workers . . . had, like the term 'worker' in Articles 48 to 51, a Community meaning. Consequently, the fact that the *Levin, Kempf* and *Rinner-Kühn* cases do not relate to social security law and are not concerned with the interpretation of Article 2 of Directive 79/7 cannot call in question the finding made [above], since those judgments define the concept of a worker in the light of the principle of equal treatment.[46]

It is thus clear that, in order to be able to invoke the protection of the Directive, a claimant must personally fall within the technical scope of Article 2.[47] One limited exception to this principle emerged from *Verholen v Sociale Verzekeringsbank*,[48] which involved the same Dutch old-age pension legislation which was in issue in *Acterberg-te Riele v Sociale Verzekeringsbank*.[49] Mr Heiderijk, one of the plaintiffs in this joined action, had reached the age of 65 and was drawing an old-age pension. This pension contained an extra element which recognized that he had a dependent spouse who had not yet reached the age of 65. Under the legislation, married women became entitled to a personal pension only at 65, and that pension was normally payable to the husband. In this instance, the extra component was reduced, to reflect periods during which Mr Heiderijk was not insured under the Dutch system because he had been working in Germany. One of the questions referred to the Court was whether an individual may rely before a national court on Directive 79/7 when he bears the effects of a discriminatory national provision regarding his spouse, who is not a party to the proceedings. The Court held:

It should be pointed out straight away that the right to rely on the provisions of Directive 79/7 is not confined to individuals coming within the scope *ratione personae* of the Directive, in so far as the possibility cannot be ruled out that other persons may have a direct interest in ensuring that the principle of non-discrimination is respected as regards persons who are protected.

While it is, in principle, for national law to determine an individual's standing and legal interest in bringing proceedings, Community law nevertheless requires that the national legislation does not undermine the right to effective judicial protection (see the judgments in Case 222/84 *Johnston v Chief Constable of the RUC* [1986] ECR 1651 and in Case 222/86 *Unectef v Heylens* [1987] ECR 4097) and the

---

[46] [1995] ECR I-4625, at 4656–7, and [1995] ECR I-4741, at 4752–3. See also Case C-280/94 *Posthuma-Van Damme*, op cit, n 29, where the ECJ held that Art 2 does not necessarily exclude a person who, in the year preceding his or her incapacity for work, did not receive an income from employment.

[47] See also Case C-343/92 *De Weerd, née Roks*, op cit, n 27.

[48] Joined Cases C-87, 88, & 89/90 [1991] ECR I-3757.

[49] Joined Cases C-48, 106, & 107/88, op cit, n 34, discussed above. For comment on *Verholen* and *Acterberg*, together with Case C-31/90 *Johnson v Chief Adjudication Officer*, op cit, n 35, see Cousins, 'The Personal and Temporal Scope of Directive 79/7/EEC' (1992) 17 ELRev 55.

application of national legislation cannot render virtually impossible the exercise of the rights conferred by Community law (judgment in Case 199/82 *Amministrazione delle Finanze dello Stato v San Giorgio* [1983] ECR 3595).

In so far as this case is concerned, however, it should be stated that an individual who bears the effects of a discriminatory national provision may be allowed to rely on Directive 79/7 only if his wife, who is the victim of the discrimination, herself comes within the scope of that Directive.[50]

Article 3(1) of the Directive provides:

This Directive shall apply to:

    (a) statutory schemes which provide protection against the following risks:

      sickness,

      invalidity,

      old age,

      accidents at work and occupational diseases,

      unemployment;[51]

    (b) social assistance, in so far as it is intended to supplement or replace the schemes referred to in (a).[52]

The ECJ in the *Drake* case[53] ruled that this provision must be given a purposive interpretation, a decision of considerable potential significance given the diversity of social security provision available in the various Member States. One of the questions referred in that case had asked whether a benefit (in this instance, invalid care allowance) which was payable to a person in the claimant's position, not herself directly suffering from any invalidity but in respect of someone else's invalidity, constituted a statutory scheme providing protection against invalidity within the meaning of Article 3(1)(a) of the Directive. Could the 'risk' be a risk to someone other than the claimant? The Court gave a positive answer to this question, holding:

[I]t is possible for the Member States to provide protection against the consequences of the risk of invalidity in various ways. For example, a Member State may, as the UK has done, provide for two

---

[50] [1991] ECR I-3757, at 3790–1. See Waddington, 'The Court of Justice Fails to Show its Caring Face' (1997) 22 ELRev 587, in which the author argues that the *Züchner* case (discussed above) should have been decided on the same basis as *Verholen*: Ms Züchner suffered the effects of the discriminatory treatment directed against her husband, in that care allowances were not paid to her, and her husband, who had worked before becoming disabled, fell within Art 2.

[51] In Case C-187/00 *Kutz-Bauer v Freie und Hansestadt Hamburg* [2003] ECR I-2741, the ECJ concluded that a legislative scheme providing an opportunity for part-time work for older employees, intended to make easier their subsequent transition to retirement and intended also to provide recruitment opportunities for young workers, was not within the scope of the Social Security Directive. The scheme affected the exercise of the occupation of the workers concerned by adjusting their working time, and therefore related to working conditions, thereby bringing it within the scope of the Equal Treatment Directive (as to which see ch 5).

[52] Joined Cases C-245 and 312/94 *Hoever v Land Nordrhein-Westfalen* [1996] ECR I-4895 concerned alleged indirect discrimination over access to a child-raising allowance available to employed people. In deciding that this allowance was not covered by the Directive, the Court pointed out that Art 3(2) (discussed further below) excludes from the scope of the instrument 'provisions concerning . . . family benefits, except in the case of family benefits granted by way of increases of benefits due in respect of the risks referred to in paragraph (1)(a)'. It held that a family benefit, such as a child-raising allowance, does not provide direct and effective protection against one of the Art 3(1)(a) risks but is intended rather to secure the maintenance of the family whilst the children are young.   [53] Case 150/85, op cit, n 32.

separate allowances, one payable to the disabled person himself and the other payable to a person who provides care, while another Member State may arrive at the same result by paying an allowance to the disabled person at a rate equivalent to the sum of those two benefits. In order, therefore, to ensure that the progressive implementation of the principle of equal treatment referred to in Article 1 of Council Directive 79/7/EEC and defined in Article 4 is carried out in a harmonious manner throughout the Community, Article 3(1) must be interpreted as including any benefit which in a broad sense forms part of one of the statutory schemes referred to or a social assistance provision intended to supplement or replace such a scheme.

Moreover, the payment of the benefit to a person who provides care still depends on the existence of a situation of invalidity inasmuch as such a situation is a condition *sine qua non* for its payment . . . It must also be emphasized that there is a clear link between the benefit and the disabled person, since the disabled person derives an advantage from the fact that an allowance is paid to the person caring for him.[54]

In reaching this conclusion, the Court effectively ignored the arguments put forward on behalf of the UK Government by the adjudication officer. He had maintained that invalid care allowance was not a work-related benefit, since it was paid to persons who sacrificed work opportunities and relieved the social services of the burden of caring for the invalid. Furthermore, it was payable to persons not working, and who might never have worked. Luckhaus has argued[55] that the Court was chiefly motivated by its desire to condemn such an unabashed example of direct discrimination against women in the social security system of a Member State, and in its enthusiasm for achieving this result it engaged in 'some well-meaning subterfuge', in particular appearing to restrict the EU law to employment-related areas whilst in reality extending its reach 'into the realm of domestic, traditionally unpaid work and private family relationships'.

In any event, any tendency on the part of the ECJ to stray from the work-related sphere and into a wider social context in its interpretation of Article 3 has since been curbed. *R v Secretary of State for Social Security, ex parte Smithson*[56] concerned differential entitlement as between men and women to a 'higher pensioner premium'. Housing benefit is payable, under UK law, to people whose income falls below a notional sum known as the 'applicable amount'. One of the elements to be taken into account in determining the 'applicable amount' is the 'higher pensioner premium' which is payable to those aged between 60 and 80, who live alone, and who are in receipt of one or more other social security benefits, which used to include an invalidity pension. Invalidity pension[57] was payable up to pensionable age (60 for women and 65 for men), but also for a further five years thereafter for persons who remained in work. Anyone (otherwise qualified) who had retired but not yet reached the age of 65 (for women) or 70 (for men) might elect to withdraw

---

[54] Ibid, at 2009–10. In the face of a well-orchestrated political campaign in favour of Ms Drake's claim, the UK Government announced its intention (subsequently carried out) to extend invalid care allowance to all men and women on equal terms.

[55] Luckhaus, 'Payment for Caring: A European Solution?' [1986] PL 526.

[56] Case C-243/90 [1992] ECR I-467.

[57] Invalidity pensions were subsequently replaced by incapacity benefit, as to which see Wikeley, 'The Social Security (Incapacity for Work) Act 1994' (1995) 58 MLR 523.

from the pension scheme and opt instead for an invalidity pension. Ms Smithson, who was 67, was unable to claim the 'higher pensioner premium' because she did not receive an invalidity pension and, as a woman of this age, was now unable to opt to claim one. The first question asked by the High Court was whether this patent sex discrimination over access to 'higher pensioner premium' contravened the Directive. Advocate General Tesauro considered that it did:

It is essential to interpret Article 3 broadly . . . Any other approach would enable Member States to escape their obligations under the Directive with ease: they would only need in that case to include in a scheme of general scope, or at least one not specifically intended to provide protection against one of the risks set out in Article 3 of the Directive, a benefit which was, on the contrary, taken in isolation, designed precisely to provide protection against those risks.

. . . I cannot endorse the United Kingdom's view that the premium may be regarded in isolation from the benefit of which it forms part because it is merely one of the elements which go to make up the applicable amount for the purposes of calculating housing benefit and not an amount paid out in its own right.

I consider it quite irrelevant, in fact, that the premium is not technically a financial benefit paid as such to the beneficiary. On the contrary, what is relevant in my view is the fact that the premium constitutes, *de facto* and in every case, an economic advantage for those who benefit from it, who become entitled when such a component is applied to higher housing benefit.

In view of the fact that according to the contested United Kingdom legislation the purpose of that increase is to provide additional support for pensioners who have a recognised form of invalidity . . . I do not think there can be any doubt that the premium is covered by Directive 79/7.

It is in essence a 'benefit' which, although encompassed in the more general housing benefit scheme, may be separated from it in as much as it has a well-defined purpose and scope: to aid pensioners who are suffering particular hardship. Consequently, in view of the categories of persons for whom it is intended and its effects, the premium rightly belongs to the scope *ratione materiae* of Directive 79/7. More especially, in as much as it is intended to provide additional support for disabled pensioners to enable them to meet the cost of housing, it should be regarded as a form of social assistance intended to supplement the statutory schemes providing protection against the risks of old age and invalidity.[58]

The Court, however, subtly but significantly re-worded the High Court's question so as to ask about the applicability of Article 3 to housing benefit in general, as distinct from its applicability specifically to the 'higher pensioner premium'. This led it to disagree with its Advocate General:

[A]lthough the mode of payment is not decisive as regards the identification of a benefit as one which falls within the scope of Directive 79/7, in order to be so identified the benefit must be directly and effectively linked to the protection provided against one of the risks specified in Article 3(1) of the Directive.

However, Article 3(1)(a) of Directive 79/7 does not refer to statutory schemes which are intended to guarantee any person whose real income is lower than a notional income calculated on the basis of certain criteria a special allowance enabling that person to meet housing costs.

The age and invalidity of the beneficiary are only two of the criteria applied in order to determine the extent of the beneficiary's financial need for such an allowance. The fact that those criteria are decisive as

[58] [1992] ECR I-467, at 479–80.

regards eligibility for the higher pensioner premium is not sufficient to bring that benefit within the scope of Directive 79/7.

The premium is in fact an inseparable part of the whole benefit which is intended to compensate for the fact that the beneficiary's income is insufficient to meet housing costs, and cannot be characterised as an autonomous scheme intended to provide protection against one of the risks listed in Article 3(1) . . . [59]

A determination on the part of the Court to separate general schemes for supplementing low incomes from schemes covered by the Directive was also evident in *Jackson and Cresswell v Chief Adjudication Officer*,[60] where discrimination was alleged in respect of the award of income support and its predecessor, supplementary benefit, under UK law. The Court of Appeal asked the ECJ whether Article 3 of the Directive applies to a benefit which may be granted in a variety of situations to persons whose means are insufficient to meet their needs as defined by statute, and whether the answer to that question depends on whether the claimant is suffering from one of the Article 3 risks.

Significantly, the Advocate General (Van Gerven on this occasion) again inclined to the view that such schemes could fall within the scope of Article 3 of the Directive. The net result of the *Drake* and *Smithson* cases, he concluded, was that, to fall within Article 3, a benefit must be granted pursuant to an autonomous statutory scheme or a form of social assistance which is directly and effectively linked to one of the Article 3 risks. He distinguished the *Smithson* decision from the circumstances under consideration on the basis that the relationship in that case between the Article 3 risk and housing benefit was only indirect: invalidity was only a criterion for receipt of an invalidity pension, the grant of which was a precondition for the higher pensioner premium, which itself was only one of the factors contributing to the calculation of notional income for the purpose of housing benefit. He examined the issue of whether the Directive applies only to those schemes *intended* by the legislature to afford protection against the Article 3 risks (the UK Government's view), or whether it extends simply to those which *in fact* afford such protection. Stressing that it was important to take a teleological view so as to ensure the effectiveness of the Directive, he opted for the second alternative; in doing so, he pointed out that the English version of the Directive is the only one to use the word 'intended' in Article 3(1)(b), the others all referring to schemes which 'supplement' or 'replace' Article 3(1)(a) schemes. It was, therefore, in his view, a matter for the national court to decide whether income support in the UK in reality provided protection against one or more of the risks specified in Article 3. However, in deciding this matter, he drew the national court's attention to the fact that, since in many cases unemployment benefit ceased and gave way to income support after a stated time under UK law, income support was in fact

---

[59] Ibid, at 489–90. See Hervey's criticisms of this conclusion in [1992] JSWFL 461.

[60] Joined Cases C-63 & 64/91 [1992] ECR I-4737, also discussed in ch 5, and noted by Durston in '*Jackson and Cresswell v Chief Adjudication Officer*: No Help for Women in the Poverty Trap' (1994) 57 MLR 641.

an important part of the protection provided in the event of unemployment; furthermore, unemployed persons claiming income support had at the relevant date generally to be available for work,[61] thus underlining the role of the scheme in providing protection against unemployment. His conclusion of this part of his argument was that the link between income support and protection against unemployment was a much closer link than that in *Smithson*.

Once again, however, the Court rejected this approach in favour of a stricter construction of Article 3. Building on its pre-existing case law, it held:

Article 3(1)(a) . . . does not refer to a statutory scheme which, on certain conditions, provides persons with a means below a legally defined limit with a special benefit designed to enable them to meet their needs. That finding is not affected by the circumstance that the recipient of the benefit is in fact in one of the situations covered by Article 3(1) . . .

Indeed, in the judgment in *Smithson* . . . the Court held with regard to a housing benefit that the fact that some of the risks listed in Article 3(1) . . . were taken into account in order to grant a higher benefit was not sufficient to bring that benefit as such within the scope of the Directive.

Consequently, exclusion from the scope of Directive 79/7 is justified *a fortiori* where, as in the cases at issue in the main proceedings, the law sets the amount of the theoretical needs of the persons concerned, used to determine the benefit in question, independently of any consideration relating to the existence of any of the risks listed in Article 3(1) . . .

Moreover, in certain situations, in particular those of the appellants in the main proceedings, the national schemes at issue exempt claimants from the obligation to be available for work. That shows that the benefits in question cannot be regarded as being directly and effectively linked to protection against the risk of unemployment.[62]

The Court has also been asked whether the Directive governs schemes for the benefit of elderly persons, where eligibility is tied to pensionable age. In particular, a number of statutory schemes in the UK have in the past exempted persons of pensionable age from paying charges for certain services, and the issue has been raised as to the legality of such schemes in the light of the current different pensionable ages of men and women. *R v Secretary of State for Health, ex parte Richardson*[63] concerned the applicability of Directive 79/7 to UK legislation exempting women

---

[61] This rule changed with the introduction in October 1996 of jobseekers' allowance pursuant to the Jobseekers Act 1995.

[62] [1992] ECR I-4737, at 4779–80. Cousins (op cit, n 31) comments that the effect of the ECJ's decisions in *Smithson* and *Jackson and Cresswell* is to exclude many claimants from recourse to the Directive; furthermore, a high proportion of excluded claimants are likely to be women, who have to rely on means-tested payments because they do not satisfy the work-related contribution conditions for insurance payments. See also Van Gerven et al, 'Current Issues of Community Law concerning Equality of Treatment Between Women and Men in Social Security' in McCrudden (ed), *Equality of Treatment Between Women and Men in Social Security* (Butterworths, London, 1994); the authors argue that *Smithson* and *Jackson and Cresswell* lead to uneven application of the Directive across the Member States. Thus, in countries such as the UK, where classic social security benefits have been supplanted by means-tested schemes, there is a risk that many benefits now fall outwith the Directive: 'This is exactly what the Court wanted to avoid in *Drake*, namely that a Member State, by making formal changes to existing benefits covered by the Directive, could remove them from its scope' (at 11–12).

[63] Case C-137/94 [1995] ECR I-3407.

from medical prescription charges from the age of 60, but exempting men only from the age of 65. The ECJ held that the exemption scheme fell within Article 3:

First, being provided for by statute and implemented by regulation it forms part of a statutory scheme.

Secondly, it affords direct and effective protection against the risk of sickness referred to in Article 3(1) ... in so far as grant of the benefit to any of the categories of people referred to is always conditional on materialisation of the risk in question.

Lastly, in view of the fundamental importance of the principle of equal treatment and the aim of Directive 79/7, which is the progressive implementation of that principle in matters of social security, a system of benefits cannot be excluded from the scope of the Directive simply because it does not strictly form part of national social security rules. The fact, relied on by the United Kingdom, that the exemption from prescription charges is provided for in the National Health Service Act 1977 does not therefore affect the foregoing conclusion.[64]

R v Secretary of State for Social Security, ex parte Taylor[65] concerned eligibility to a £20 payment by the State towards winter fuel, and the Court reached a similar conclusion. UK legislation entitled two groups of people to winter fuel payments. One was men over 65 and women over 60 who were also entitled to certain other benefits, some means-tested and others not, and including old-age pensions. Mr Taylor was 62 and alleged that the non-payment of a winter fuel allowance to him contravened the Directive. The ECJ concluded that the benefit was payable to elderly persons, whether or not they had financial or material difficulties. Contrary to the allegation of the UK Government, it was therefore not aimed at lack of financial means. On the other hand, the age limits prescribed indicated clearly that the benefit was intended to protect people against the risk of old age, within the meaning of Article 3(1) of the Directive. Thus, the payment 'must be deemed to protect directly and effectively against that risk'.[66]

On the other hand, in *Atkins v Wrekin District Council*,[67] the Court[68] held that a UK statutory scheme operated by a local authority which granted concessionary fares on public transport to those of pensionable age did not fall within Article 3. The relevant statute gave discretion to local authorities to grant concessions to various groups of persons, including those of pensionable age, and thus the scheme could not be said to 'afford direct and effective protection against one of the risks listed in Article 3(1) ... Old age and invalidity, which are among the risks listed in Article 3(1) ..., are only two of the criteria which may be applied to define the classes of beneficiaries of such a scheme'.[69] Furthermore, the fact that the local

---

[64] Ibid, at 3428–9. Cousins points out in 'Free Movement of Workers and Social Security: Two Steps Forward, One Step Back' (1996) 21 ELRev 233, that the ironic result of this case is that the ECJ has held that a measure which would not be seen as social security at all in the UK is within the scope of the Directive, whilst core elements of the UK social security system (in particular, income support) are outside the Directive's scope.   [65] Case C-382/98 [1999] ECR I-8955.

[66] Ibid, at 8981.   [67] Case C-228/94 [1996] ECR I-3633.

[68] Rejecting the submissions of Elmer AG.

[69] *Atkins*, op cit, n 67, at 3664. Cf the benefit involved in Case C-139/95 *Balestra v INPS* [1997] ECR I-549 (discussed further below), which was payable to employees within a specified age group taking early retirement from an undertaking facing 'critical difficulties'. As Elmer AG explained, the

authority involved here had actually chosen to single out those of pensionable age for eligibility for the concession was irrelevant:

> The fact that the recipient of a benefit is, as a matter of fact, in one of the situations envisaged by Article 3(1) . . . does not suffice to bring that benefit as such within the scope of the Directive (see Joined Cases C-63 & 64/91 *Jackson and Cresswell* [1992] ECR I-4737, paragraphs 18 and 19).
>
> The fact that . . . the local scheme set up by Wrekin District Council . . . benefits only classes of persons who are in fact in such situations, cannot affect that conclusion. Were importance attached to that, some local schemes would come within the scope of Directive 79/7 and others would not—despite all having been set up under the same statutory authorisation—depending on whether or not the persons eligible under such schemes consisted exclusively of classes of persons in one of the situations listed in Article 3(1) . . . [70]

The Court also rejected the Commission's argument that the scope of Directive 79/7 was wider than the scope of social security and social assistance, and that it extended to 'social protection as a whole', which had led it to contend that the Directive applied to measures of 'social protection' such as concessionary fares on public transport granted to persons affected by an Article 3 risk.

One interesting potential extension of the scope of the Directive emerged in *Integrity v Rouvroy*.[71] The case concerned a straightforward incident of discrimination, in that Belgian legislation exempted married women, widows, and students, but not married men or widowers, from the obligation to make social security contributions in certain circumstances. Some of the benefits obtainable as a consequence of paying the contributions in question were not within the ambit of Article 3. Advocate General Jacobs, whose remarks in this respect were specifically endorsed by the Court, pointed out that:

> The question therefore arises . . . whether the Directive applies only in so far as the contributions are related to benefits covered by the Directive . . . I would take the view that the Directive applied globally to the contributions payable . . . if they could not be linked to any particular benefit. If the Directive were not to apply in such circumstances, then its application would be frustrated, as regards the obligation to contribute, whenever Member States included within the ambit of discriminatory national provisions benefits which were not covered by the Directive alongside benefits which were so covered.[72]

He went on to say, however, that it appeared to have been the Belgian Government's intention that, although single contributions would be made, the amounts paid would be apportioned among the risks covered. The Advocate General submitted that if the contributions could be so apportioned, the equality principle would apply only to those contributions attributable to the risks listed in the Directive. He concluded that the 'fact that Belgium chose to incorporate in the same legislation provisions concerning benefits which fall within the scope of the Directive together with provisions concerning benefits which fall outside its scope cannot . . . render the Directive applicable to the latter provisions'.[73]

---

fundamental condition for the payment was age; thus, the benefit was directly and effectively linked to the risk of old age, and therefore fell within the scope of Directive 79/7.

[70] *Atkins*, op cit, n 67, at 3664–5.   [71] Case C-373/89 [1990] ECR I-4243.
[72] Ibid, at 4255.   [73] Ibid.

Article 4 is the kernel of the instrument because it defines the principle to be applied to all situations falling within the ambit of the Directive:

1. The principle of equal treatment means that there shall be no discrimination whatsoever on ground of sex either directly, or indirectly[74] by reference in particular to marital or family status, in particular as concerns:

—the scope of the schemes and the conditions of access thereto, the obligation to contribute and the calculation of contributions,

—the calculations of benefits including increases due in respect of a spouse and for dependants and the conditions governing the duration and retention of entitlement to benefits.

This phraseology is familiar from the Equal Treatment Directive, and it is significant that the all-embracing word 'whatsoever' is found in the context of the Social Security Directive too.[75] The mention of discrimination by reference to marital or family status is especially important in relation to social security since—as, for example, the *Drake* case demonstrates—social security systems are apt to include distinctions on these bases.[76] However, despite the strength with which the principle of equal treatment is articulated in Article 4, it must be remembered that all that the Directive mandates is formal equality. It merely requires that male and female be treated equally (not even identically), not that the less favourably treated be brought up to the standard of the more favourably treated, so-called 'levelling-up' of provision.[77]

The first prerequisite for Article 4, if it is to have real teeth, is that it must be directly effective in the hands of individual litigants.[78] This was demonstrated at an early stage of its existence. It was implicit in the Court's ruling in *Drake v Chief Adjudication Officer*,[79] but was not discussed explicitly there because it was not contested by the adjudication officer. It was first directly ruled on by the ECJ in *Netherlands v Federatie Nederlandse Vakbeweging*.[80] Under Dutch law, which remained in force after the Social Security Directive came into operation, married women (other than those permanently separated from their husbands) were ineligible for unemployment benefit unless they were 'head of the household' within

---

[74] Note that the Burden of Proof Directive (Directive 97/80, OJ [1998] L14/6), defining indirect discrimination and discussed in ch 3, does not extend to discrimination contrary to the Social Security Directive. The amended definition of indirect discrimination pursuant to the Equal Treatment Directive, also discussed in ch 3, applies only for the purposes of that instrument. Query therefore the definition of indirect discrimination which should apply for the purposes of the Social Security Directive. [75] See discussion in ch 5.

[76] In Case C-187/98 *Commission v Greece* [1999] ECR I-7713, the ECJ held, eg, that Greece had breached Art 4 by its failure to abolish retroactively from 1984 (the date on which the Social Security Directive came into operation) regulations which discriminated against female employees in relation to the payment of family and marriage allowances; such allowances were taken into account in calculating a person's income for the purpose of determining pension rights. [77] See discussion in ch 4.

[78] Although it should be appreciated that the device of vindicating individual rights through litigation is somewhat inappropriate in the area of social security where, *ex hypothesi*, the claimant is likely to be in straitened financial circumstances and in practice is unlikely to be able to sustain an action without the help of some other funding body, eg, a pressure group. [79] Case 150/85, op cit, n 32.

[80] Case 71/85 [1986] ECR 3855, noted by Arnull in (1987) 12 ELRev 276.

the meaning of the relevant ministerial regulations. The Federatie (the Netherlands Trades Union Federation) summoned the State before the President of the District Court in The Hague, in proceedings in which it requested that the State be ordered to repeal the requirement about the status of head of the household, or at least refrain from applying it, on the ground that it contravened Article 4 of the Social Security Directive. The President ordered the State to amend its legislation and, in the subsequent appeal, a preliminary ruling was sought from the ECJ, asking whether Article 4 of the Directive is directly effective. Both Advocate General Mancini and the Court held, in the clearest terms, that it is. The Advocate General submitted:

[I]t must be established whether, intrinsically, Article 4(1) satisfies the requirements of being uncon-ditional and sufficiently precise ... If, as the Commission observes, this prohibition is read in the light of the obligation, laid down by Articles 1 and 8(1) of [the] Directive, as to the result to be obtained it is impossible not to consider it *clear, complete* and *precise*. If then, the Federatie Nederlandse Vakbeweging points out in addition, it is read in conjunction with Article 5, under which the Member States have a duty to 'abolish' provisions contrary to the principle of equal treatment, it becomes equally clear that the provision is *unconditional* and hence that there is no discretion on the part of the Member States as regards bringing about the result sought by the Directive.[81]

The Court held:

It must be pointed out that, standing by itself, in the light of the objective and contents of Directive 79/7, Article 4(1) precludes, generally and unequivocally, all discrimination on ground of sex. The provision is therefore sufficiently precise to be relied upon in legal proceedings by an individual and applied by the courts. However, it remains to be considered whether the prohibition of discrimination which it contains may be regarded as unconditional having regard to the exceptions provided for in Article 7 and to the fact that according to the wording of Article 5 Member States are to take certain measures in order to ensure that the principle of equal treatment is applied in national legislation.

As regards, in the first place, Article 7, it must be observed that that provision merely reserves to Member States the right to exclude from the scope of the Directive certain clearly defined areas but lays down no condition with regard to the application of the principle of equal treatment as regards Article 4 of the Directive. It follows that Article 7 is not relevant in this case.

As for Article 5, which obliges Member States to take 'the measures necessary to ensure that any laws, regulations and administrative provisions contrary to the principle of equal treatment are abolished', it cannot be inferred from the wording of that Article that it lays down conditions to which the pro-hibition of discrimination is subject. Whilst Article 5 leaves the Member States a discretion with regard to methods, it prescribes the result which those methods must achieve, that is to say, the abolition of any provisions contrary to the principle of equal treatment.

Consequently, Article 4(1) of the Directive does not confer on Member States the power to make conditional or to limit the application of the principle of equal treatment within its field of application and it is sufficiently precise and unconditional to allow individuals, in the absence of implementing measures adopted within the prescribed period, to rely upon it before the national courts as from 23 December 1984 in order to preclude the application of any national provision inconsistent with that Article.[82]

---

[81] [1986] ECR 3855, at 3867.   [82] Ibid, at 3875–6.

The Dutch Government had attempted to preclude direct effect by arguing that the Article was insufficiently precise as to how exactly equality as between the sexes is to be achieved, and it contended that the provision contested in this case could be amended in at least four different ways, all of which would result in equality. Advocate General Mancini explained that this

confuses the issue of direct effect with that of the discretion available to Member States in transposing the Directive into national law ... [T]he clear and unconditional provisions set out in the Directive are capable of being superimposed on conflicting national laws and precluding their applicability or limiting it. That does not mean, however, that that solution is obligatory. A state which considers such a solution to be too onerous may alter its own law by prescribing other procedures, provided that they are compatible with the result sought by the Community legislation. By legislating in that manner the state will inevitably implement in good time the obligation imposed on it.[83]

Despite the point made earlier in the present chapter that the Social Security Directive does not generally require a levelling-up of social security provisions, that was its effect in the circumstances of this case, where the only standard for the treatment that women could expect was that already provided for men. In the words of the Court:

It follows that until such time as the national government adopts the necessary implementing measures women are entitled to be treated in the same manner, and to have the same rules applied to them, as men who are in the same situation since, where the Directive has not been implemented, those rules remain the only valid point of reference.[84]

It should be noted that, as in relation to Article 141 of the TEC, the ECJ implicitly accepted in this case that gender-plus discrimination constitutes direct discrimination[85] forbidden by the Social Security Directive; the discrimination here was not against women in general, but only against those who were married and not heads of household.[86]

McDermott and Cotter v Minister for Social Welfare and the Attorney General[87] involved similar facts occurring within the Irish social security system. The claimants were both married women who complained of breach of Article 4 of the Directive, in that the relevant national legislation provided for a lesser amount of unemployment benefit, over a shorter period of time, for them than for men or for single women. Both the Advocate General and the Court reiterated their earlier remarks and rejected the Irish Government's argument that the Article was discretionary because there were a number of ways in which the State could comply

---

[83] Ibid, at 3867–8.

[84] Ibid, at 3876. This principle applies irrespective of which group is disadvantaged on the ground of sex; it was therefore able to be relied on so as to improve the treatment afforded to men in Case C-154/92 *Van Cant v Rijksdienst voor Pensioenen* [1993] ECR I-3811.   [85] See discussion in ch 3.

[86] See also Case C-337/91 *Van Gemert-Derks v Bestuur van de Nieuwe Industriele Bedrijfsvereniging* [1993] ECR I-5435.

[87] Case 286/85 [1987] ECR 1453. For the background to this case and its successor, Case C-377/89 *Cotter and McDermott v Minister for Social Welfare (No 2)* [1991] ECR I-1155, see Whyte and O'Dell, (1991) 20 ILJ 304.

with it. Once again, the direct effect of the equality principle contained in the Directive required the levelling-up of the provision made for married women so that it matched that available to men (and to single women.)

The principle involved in *Clark v Chief Adjudication Officer*[88] was the same as in the preceding cases, but the factual situation to which it applied was somewhat different, and the potency of the principle was again demonstrated. Ms Clark suffered from a medical condition from 1983 onwards which rendered her incapable of work. She applied under the then applicable UK legislation for a non-contributory invalidity pension (NCIP), but was refused the pension because she was unable to satisfy the statutory test, demanded only in the case of married women such as herself, of incapacity to perform 'normal household duties'. The NCIP was abolished in late 1984, in anticipation of the coming into operation in December of that year of the Social Security Directive, and it was replaced by a new benefit, known as severe disablement allowance. The conditions for entitlement to severe disablement allowance were, in general, stricter than those for NCIP had been, and Ms Clark, again, did not meet them.[89] However, transitional arrangements were also made, because it was feared that some people who had been entitled to the old NCIP would cease to be eligible for severe disablement allowance and it was felt to be politically unacceptable for benefit in effect then to be withdrawn from them. The transitional legislation therefore provided that everybody entitled to the old benefit on certain dates in 1984 was automatically to acquire entitlement to the new benefit. Ms Clark, of course, was unable to take advantage of this rule, and argued that it perpetuated discrimination against married women contrary to the Social Security Directive and after that instrument had become operative (a subtle form of direct discrimination). With this contention both the Advocate General and the Court agreed. The direct effect of Article 4 could be relied on to prohibit the perpetuation of discrimination which had been lawful before the Directive came into force. Advocate General Da Cruz Vilaca commented that the Directive makes no exception 'for the continuing discriminatory effects of national provisions previously in force, since to maintain those effects is as much contrary to the provisions of the Directive as it would be to maintain those national provisions themselves'.[90]

The Court itself was quite unmoved by the UK Government's protestations about the legitimate expectations of those receiving NCIP before the Social Security Directive came into effect, and once again its solution was to require the levelling-up of the provision made. It held:

[I]t must be emphasized that the Directive does not provide for any derogation from the principle of equal treatment laid down in Article 4(1) in order to authorize the extension of the discriminatory effects

---

[88] Case 384/85 [1987] ECR 2865. Similarly Case 80/87 *Dik v College van Burgemeester en Wethouders, Arnhem* [1988] ECR 1601. See also Luckhaus, 'Equal Treatment for Men and Women in Social Security?' (1987) 137 NLJ 1006.

[89] Hoskyns and Luckhaus argued that the provisions relating to severe disablement allowance also discriminated (this time indirectly) against women: see op cit, n 8.   [90] [1987] ECR 2865, at 2875.

of earlier provisions of national law. It follows that a Member State may not maintain beyond 22 December 1984 any inequalities of treatment which have their origin in the fact that the conditions for entitlement to benefit are those which applied before that date. That is so notwithstanding the fact that those inequalities are the result of transitional provisions adopted at the time of the introduction of a new benefit.

Consequently, Article 4(1) of the Directive in no way confers on Member States the power to make conditional or to limit the application of the principle of equal treatment within its field of application and it is sufficiently precise and unconditional to allow individuals, in the absence of appropriate implementing measures, to rely upon it before the national courts as from 22 December 1984 in order to preclude the application of any provision of national law inconsistent with that Article.

As is also apparent from the judgments in *FNV* and *McDermott and Cotter*, it follows from Article 4(1) of the Directive that, as from 22 December 1984, women are entitled to be treated in the same manner, and to have the same rules applied to them, as men who are in the same situation since, where the Directive has not been implemented correctly, those rules remain the only valid point of reference. In this case that means that if, as from 22 December 1984, a man in the same position as a woman was automatically entitled to the new severe disablement allowance under the aforesaid transitional provisions without having to re-establish his rights, a woman was also entitled to that allowance without having to satisfy an additional condition applicable before that date exclusively to married women.[91]

The Court's reluctance to allow transitional provisions to perpetuate former sex discrimination was also evident in *Van Cant v Rijksdienst voor Pensioenen*,[92] where Advocate General Darmon explained that:

[A]lthough the principle of the progressive nature of the implementation of equal treatment appears in the actual title of the Directive, the Court [has] clearly ruled against the maintenance of any transitional provision contrary to Article 4 . . . [The Court is determined] not to allow earlier or transitional schemes which delay genuine equality of treatment to linger on . . . The uniform application of Community law in each Member State requires that the interpretation of the Directive be detached from the national context and, consequently, from the merits of a scheme compared with those of the previous scheme. Justification by progressiveness has its limits.[93]

The vital question of the meaning of indirect discrimination in the context of social security was first raised before the ECJ in *Teuling v Bedrijfsvereniging voor de Chemische Industrie*.[94] Ms Teuling had been incapable of work since 1972. From 1975 onwards, she received invalidity benefit under the Netherlands social security legislation equal to the statutory minimum wage. However, from the beginning of 1984 her benefit was reduced in accordance with new legislation to 70% of the statutory minimum wage. Supplements were payable to certain persons, but she was not one because the relevant legislation took into account the income of a spouse and/or the presence of dependent children. Ms Teuling, at the material time, was married and her husband's income was over the maximum prescribed limit. She argued that the system for the payment of supplements discriminated

[91] Ibid, at 2880–81. The direct effect of Art 4 was reiterated in Case C-31/90 *Johnson v Chief Adjudication Officer*, op cit, n 35 and by Van Gerven AG in Joined Cases C-63 & 64/91 *Jackson and Cresswell v Chief Adjudication Officer*, op cit, n 60, at 4770, both also discussed above.
[92] Case C-154/92 [1993] ECR I-3811, discussed further below.   [93] Ibid, at 3827.
[94] Case 30/85 [1987] ECR 2497.

indirectly against women and therefore should be disapplied, because it breached the directly effective Article 4 of the Social Security Directive. Both Advocate General Mancini and the Court agreed that the rules disproportionately disadvantaged women. The Dutch Government had provided statistics which showed that a significantly greater number of married men than married women received a supplement on the basis of having a dependent family; that was because in The Netherlands at the relevant date there were considerably more married men than married women who carried on occupational activities, and therefore considerably fewer women with a dependent spouse. The Court held that it was clear:

[F]rom the very words of Article 4(1) that increases are prohibited if they are directly or indirectly based on the sex of the beneficiary. In that regard, it should be pointed out that a system of benefits in which, as in this case, supplements are provided for which are not directly based on the sex of the beneficiaries but take account of their marital status or family situation and in respect of which it emerges that a considerably smaller proportion of women than of men are entitled to such supplements is contrary to Article 4(1) of the Directive if that system of benefits cannot be justified by reasons which exclude discrimination on grounds of sex.[95]

What the Court did not say explicitly here, although it seemed implicit in its words, was that Article 4(1) of the Directive is directly effective in the context of indirect discrimination as well as in the more obvious cases of direct discrimination.[96] However, it has remedied this omission in later cases, holding, for example, in *De Weerd, née Roks*[97] that 'Article 4(1) of Directive 79/7 precludes the application of a national measure which, although formulated in neutral terms, works to the disadvantage of far more women than men, unless that measure is based on objectively justified factors unrelated to any discrimination on grounds of sex'.[98]

An important rider to add in cases where the discrimination is indirect is that the Court's usual technique for producing equality may prove inappropriate, as was demonstrated in *Jackson and Cresswell v Chief Adjudication Officer*.[99] Advocate General Van Gerven proceeded on the assumption (actually rejected by the Court, as seen above) that income support fell within the scope of Directive 79/9; the question then arose as to how to apply the equal treatment principle in the particular circumstances of the case. childminding expenses were not permitted to be deducted from income when determining eligibility to the benefit, which was alleged to produce indirect discrimination against women. The Advocate General observed that the Court's usual approach is to require the application of the same

---

[95] Case 30/85 [1987] ECR 2497, at 2520–1. To the same effect, see Case C-317/93 *Nolte*, op cit, n 43, at 4659; Case C-444/93 *Megner and Scheffel*, op cit, n 44, at 4754; and Case C-280/94 *Postuma-Van Damme*, op cit, n 29, at 203. See also the submissions of Ruiz-Jarabo Colomer AG in Case C-77/95 *Züchner*, op cit, n 36, at 5713.

[96] It will be recalled from the discussion in chs 3 and 4 that this issue caused problems in relation to Art 141 of the Treaty, but that the Court eventually accepted the direct effect of this Article even in cases of indirect discrimination.   [97] Case C-343/92, op cit, n 27.

[98] Ibid, at 600. See also Case C-229/89 *Commission v Belgium* [1991] ECR I-2205.

[99] Joined Cases 63 & 64/91, op cit, n 60.

rules to the disadvantaged group as are applied to the advantaged group. However, he pointed out that:

That approach affords no comfort to the appellants in the main proceedings: even in the case of lone fathers, childminding expenses are not deductible from income . . .

Consequently, as Community law stands at present, the most realistic solution seems to me for the national court to decide, where appropriate, at the request of the appellants in the main proceedings that, having regard to the criteria developed in this connection, the British authorities have not complied with their obligations under Directive . . . 79/7, and to declare them liable to pay compensation to Ms Jackson and Ms Cresswell on the basis of the rules specified in the Court's case-law, in particular . . . in *Francovich and Bonifaci* (Joined Cases C-6 & 9/90 [1991] ECR I-5357).[100]

Since indirect discrimination is not unlawful where it can be justified,[101] the strength of the non-discrimination principle in cases of indirect discrimination is directly proportional to the robustness with which the ECJ is prepared to treat the concept of justification.[102] The first indication of the Court's attitude to justification in the field of social security came in the *Teuling* case,[103] where both the Court and the Advocate General agreed that the *de facto* indirect discrimination which had been demonstrated could be excused. Examining the purpose intended to be served by the supplementary payments for which Ms Teuling did not qualify, they found that the Netherlands legislation did not aim to link invalidity benefit to previous salary earned but just to provide a minimum subsistence income for persons with no earnings. The Court held:

[S]uch a guarantee granted by Member States to persons who would otherwise be destitute is an integral part of the social policy of the Member States.

Consequently, if supplements to a minimum social security benefit are intended, where beneficiaries have no income from work, to prevent the benefit from falling below the minimum subsistence level for persons who, by virtue of the fact that they have a dependent spouse or children, bear heavier burdens than single persons, such supplements may be justified under the Directive.

If a national court, which has sole jurisdiction to assess the facts and interpret the national legislation, finds that supplements such as those in this case correspond to the greater burdens which beneficiaries having a dependent spouse or children must bear in comparison with persons living alone, serve to ensure an adequate minimum subsistence income for those beneficiaries and are necessary for that purpose, the fact that the supplements are paid to a significantly higher number of married men than married women is not sufficient to support the conclusion that the grant of such supplements is contrary to the Directive.[104]

This ruling offered some, albeit limited, scope for argument to litigants; if it could be demonstrated that the payment of higher benefit levels to claimants with dependants was not an effective means of making provision for those dependants, because the payments were not passed on to them, then the *de facto* discrimination against women would not, seemingly, be justified. It is to be noted that, apart from the fact that it did not use the expression 'objectively justified factors', the Court's

[100] Ibid, at 4771. See ch 2 for discussion of *Francovich and Bonifaci v Italy*.
[101] See discussion in particular in ch 3.   [102] See Cousins, op cit, n 31.
[103] Case 30/85, op cit, n 94.   [104] Ibid, at 2521–2.

formulation here was substantially identical to that relied on by it in relation to Article 141 in *Bilka-Kaufhaus GmbH v Weber Von Hartz*.[105]

The Court's decision in *Ruzius-Wilbrink v Bestuur van de Bedrijfsvereniging voor Overheidsdiensten*[106] underscored the fact that the burden falls on the State to prove objective justification and that, if it does not discharge that burden, it will be guilty of indirect discrimination. Dutch invalidity payments which differentiated between full-time and part-time workers were there found to be discriminatory by the ECJ. The Court held that the scheme discriminated indirectly against women who made up the majority of those working part-time in The Netherlands. Ms Ruzius-Wilbrink had been refused the full benefit because she had only worked an average of 18 hours a week in the year preceding her incapacity. Under the scheme, everyone with an incapacity had a right to a minimum subsistence income benefit irrespective of previous salary, the only exception being for part-timers, for whom the scheme linked the level of benefit to the person's previous salary. The Government explained the rule by arguing that it was designed to prevent part-timers from receiving a benefit which was more than their previous income. The Court held that this could not amount to an objective justification of the difference in treatment because the level of the benefit granted in many other cases also was greater than the income previously received. It went on to rule that, just as in cases of direct discrimination, the members of the group disadvantaged in these circumstances were entitled to have applied to them the same scheme as that applied to other recipients of the benefit, in other words, to receive the full benefit.

This decision provided grounds for optimism that the Court would scrutinize critically the arguments put forward by the Member States as alleged justification for indirect discrimination. However, subsequent cases have not fulfilled this promise and they have, in general, illustrated the enormous difficulties faced by those who seek to challenge measures of social security policy. A good example is provided by *Commission v Belgium*,[107] where the national law on unemployment and sickness benefits assigned claimants to three groups: (1) workers cohabiting with one or more persons, the latter having no income; (2) workers living alone; and (3) workers cohabiting with a person receiving an income. For both unemployment benefit and sickness benefit, entitlement under the system was calculated on the basis of previous earned income, but tiered to allow a different rate for each group, the highest being enjoyed by group (1), the next highest by group (2), and the lowest by group (3). In addition, an adaptation supplement of 20% of previous income was payable to all claimants, but stopped after the first year of unemployment for groups (2) and (3). The alleged indirect discrimination arose from the fact that a clear majority of group (1) were men, whereas the majority of group (3) were women. The Belgian Government argued first that the difference in the ratio of

<hr>

[105] Case 170/84 [1986] ECR 1607, discussed in chs 3 and 4. See also Case 171/88 *Rinner-Kühn v FWW Spezial-Gebaudereinigung GmbH* [1989] ECR 2743, discussed in ch 4.
[106] Case C-102/88 [1989] ECR 4311.
[107] Case C-229/89 [1991] ECR I-2205, noted by Banks in (1991) 20 ILJ 220.

men to women between the three groups was the product of a social phenomenon arising from the fact that fewer women than men were employed. The Court held that this could not be regarded as forming the basis of objective criteria unrelated to any discrimination on the ground of sex. However, the Belgian Government went on to contend that its legislation sought to assure a minimum replacement income to each individual claimant, in the light of the family situation of that person, and this the Court accepted as objective justification. It stated:

> The aim of the Belgian legislation is to take into consideration the existence of different needs. On the one hand, it recognises the greater burdens resulting from unemployment for households with only one income and, on the other hand, it takes into account the financial aid which the spouse's income represents for the unemployed person. Moreover, it seeks to encourage the persons concerned to adapt themselves to their new financial situation by avoiding too sudden a drop in their income during the first year, whilst enabling the unemployed person with dependants to bear the expenses of a household beyond a period of 18 months. Those principles and objectives form part of a social policy which in the current state of Community law is a matter for the Member States which enjoy *a reasonable margin of discretion* as regards both the nature of the protective measures and the detailed arrangements for their implementation . . .
>
> With regard to a guaranteed minimum subsistence level, the Court has already held that Community law does not preclude a Member State, in controlling its social expenditure, from taking into account the relatively greater needs of beneficiaries who have a dependent spouse or a dependent child or receive only a very small income, in relation to the needs of single persons . . .
>
> [T]he Belgian Government has shown that its system of unemployment and invalidity benefits corresponds to a legitimate objective of social policy, involving increases suitable and requisite for attaining that aim; it is therefore justified by reasons unrelated to discrimination on grounds of sex.[108]

The real degree of latitude thus entrusted to the Member States emerged from *Molenbroek v Bestuur van de Sociale Verzekeringsbank*.[109] The Court was asked whether Article 4 of the Directive precluded national legislation on old-age pensions from making the grant and amount of a supplement payable to a pensioner whose spouse had not yet reached retirement age depend on that spouse's earned income, excluding any other income of the pensioner, given that far more men than women qualified for the supplement and that the supplement was payable even where it was not essential to guarantee the couple a minimum income. In holding that this *de facto* discrimination was justified, the Court stated:

> [T]he allowance granted . . . is in the nature of a basic allowance, in that it is intended to guarantee those concerned an income equal to the social minimum, irrespective of any income which they receive from other sources.

---

[108] Ibid, at 2229–30, emphasis added. It is noteworthy that the effect of this reasoning was that a Commission prosecution under Art 226 was rejected. This is an, extremely rare occurrence: according to Weatherill and Beaumont *EU Law*, 3rd edn (Penguin, 1999), of the cases of this type which have got as far as the ECJ, only about one-tenth have been decided in favour of the Member State. With the benefit of hindsight, the case discussed in the main text may be seen as evidence of the beginning of the Court's resolve to allow the Member States a wide measure of discretion in relation to the organization of their social security systems.   [109] Case C-226/91 [1992] ECR I-5943.

Furthermore, the Court has already held that the allocation of an income equal to the social minimum formed an integral part of the social policy of the Member States . . .

Finally, in leaving out of account any other income received by an old-age pensioner when determining the supplement payable to him in respect of a younger dependent spouse, the national legislation . . . ultimately allocates to the couple an aggregate income equal to that to which both spouses will be entitled when they are both in receipt of a pension and the supplement has consequently been discontinued.

The supplements scheme is therefore essential in order to preserve the nature of the allowance . . . as a basic allowance and in order to guarantee the couple, where one of the spouses has not yet reached pensionable age, an income equal to the social minimum which they will receive when they are both pensioners.

In those circumstances, the fact that at times the supplement is granted to persons who, having regard to the income which they receive from other sources, do not need it in order to guarantee a minimum level of subsistence cannot affect the fact that the means chosen are necessary having regard to the aim pursued.[110]

In this somewhat obscure passage, the Court failed to investigate whether the legitimate aim pursued, namely the guaranteeing of a minimum income, could have been achieved by a means which did not involve overpayment in some cases. In the absence of such scrutiny, it is hard to feel convinced that the means chosen in these circumstances were 'necessary' for the achievement of the legitimate aim.

A glimmer of hope was offered to claimants by the ruling in *De Weerd, née Roks*,[111] where the Court held that 'although budgetary considerations may influence a state's choice of social policy and affect the nature or scope of the social protection measures it wishes to adopt, they cannot themselves constitute the aim pursued by that policy and cannot, therefore, justify discrimination against one of the sexes'.[112] This was in part because 'to concede that budgetary considerations may justify . . . indirect discrimination . . . would be to accept that the application and scope of as fundamental a rule of Community law as that of equal treatment between men and women might vary in time and place according to the state of the public finances of the member States'.[113] However, in the *Nolte* and *Megner and Scheffel* cases,[114] which concerned indirect discrimination against women resulting from the exclusion of those in 'minor' or 'short-term' employment from compulsory old-age insurance, the Court reverted to an approach which was much more indulgent to the Member States. It reiterated its earlier principles but added a significant tailpiece:

[S]ocial policy is a matter for the Member States . . . Consequently, it is for the Member States to choose the measures capable of achieving the aim of their social and employment policy. *In exercising that competence, the Member States have a broad margin of discretion.*[115]

[110] Case C-226/91 [1992] ECR I-5943, at 5968–9, emphasis added.
[111] Case C-343/92, op cit, n 27.
[112] Ibid, at 600. See also Case C-104/98 *Buchner v Sozialversicherungsanstalt der Bauern* [2000] ECR I-3625.   [113] Ibid. Cf the submissions of Darmon AG.
[114] Case C-317/93 *Nolte*, op cit, n 43, and Case C-444/93 *Megner and Scheffel*, op cit, n 44.
[115] Ibid, at 4660 and 4755 respectively, emphasis added. See also Case C-8/94 *Laperre v Bestuurscommissie* [1996] ECR I-273. The effect of these decisions is to make it very unlikely that an

The German Government argued that the exclusion of the affected groups from compulsory insurance was basic to the structure of the national social security scheme, in which equivalence had to be maintained between the contributions paid in and the benefits paid out. It also maintained that the system favoured the creation of minor and short-term employment, for which there was a social demand,[116] and that in the absence of the existing system this demand would be satisfied by unlawful employment practices. The Court decided that:

[T]he social and employment policy aim relied on by the German Government is objectively unrelated to any discrimination on grounds of sex and . . . , in exercising its competence, the national legislature was reasonably entitled to consider that the legislation in question was necessary in order to achieve that aim.[117]

This ruling led the Editors of the *Equal Opportunities Review* to comment that it reduced 'significantly the standard of proof required of a Member State in order to justify indirectly discriminatory legislation'. They went on to point out that, 'instead of having to show empirical evidence that the measure actually was necessary to achieve the objective pursued, it now appears sufficient under EC law if the Member State government could reasonably be entitled to take that view'.[118]

Furthermore, in *Posthuma-van Damme v Bestuur van de Bedrijfsvereniging voor Detailhandel, Ambachten en Huisvrouwen*,[119] the Court made it clear that, although it had held in *De Weerd, née Roks* that budgetary considerations could not justify indirect discrimination resulting from a change in the Dutch social security rules which required claimants for incapacity benefit to have received 'some income' in the

---

allegation of indirect discrimination would be successful in relation to the exclusion of those in the UK who earn less than the lower earnings limit from liability to pay national insurance contributions. Many of those so excluded are women: according to the Green Paper, *A New Contract for Welfare: Partnership in Pensions* (Cm 4170, 1998, at para 2.14), the percentages of men and women who qualify for State basic pensions through a full record of national insurance contributions is respectively 86% and 49%. Nevertheless, the Court would seem to be prepared to condone the resulting discrimination against women on the basis of the Member State's choice of social policy.

[116] Léger AG pointed out that the Court had 'lent a sympathetic ear to this type of argument in the judgment in Case C-189/91 *Kirsammer-Hack* [1993] ECR I-6185 [discussed in ch 6], where it held that there was objective justification for " . . . legislation which . . . forms part of a series of measures intended to alleviate the constraints burdening small businesses which play an essential role in economic development and the creation of employment in the Community" ' ([1995] ECR I-4625, at 4645). But contrast the view of the House of Lords in *R v Secretary of State for Employment, ex parte EOC* [1994] 2 WLR 409, also discussed in ch 6.

[117] [1995] ECR I-4625 and [1995] ECR I-4741, at 4660 and 4755 respectively. See also Case C-226/98 *Jørgensen v Foreningen af Speciallaeger* [2000] ECR I-2447, where the ECJ said that 'social policy is a matter for the Member States, which enjoy a reasonable margin of discretion as regards the nature of social protection measures . . . [B]udgetary considerations cannot in themselves justify discrimination on grounds of sex. However, measures intended to ensure sound management of public expenditure on specialised medical care and to guarantee people's access to such care may be justified if they meet a legitimate objective of social policy, are appropriate to attain that objective and are necessary to that end' (at 2482).

[118] (1996) 67 EOR 43, at 44. See also Hepple, 'The Principle of Equal Treatment in Article 119 EC and the Possibilities for Reform' in Dashwood and O'Leary (eds), *The Principle of Equal Treatment in EC Law* (Sweet & Maxwell, London, 1997).   [119] Case C-280/94, op cit, n 29.

year preceding the onset of their incapacity, nevertheless other considerations of social policy might provide such justification. The decision of the Dutch legislature amounted in effect to a decision to switch from a system of pure national insurance to one which protected against loss of income, and the Court concluded that:

[G]uaranteeing the benefit of a minimum income to persons who were in receipt of income from or in connection with work which they had to abandon owing to incapacity for work satisfies a legitimate aim of social policy and . . . to make the benefit of that minimum income subject to the requirement that the person concerned must have been in receipt of such an income in the year prior to the commencement of incapacity for work constitutes a measure appropriate to achieve that aim which the national legislature, in the exercise of its competence, was reasonably entitled to consider necessary in order to do so.

The fact that that scheme replaced a scheme of pure national insurance and that the number of persons eligible to benefit from it was further reduced to those who had actually lost income from or in connection with work at the time when the risk materialised cannot affect that finding.[120]

Laperre v Bestuurscommissie[121] involved two Dutch unemployment schemes, the RWW, which granted subsistence benefits but was means-tested, and the IOAW, which was not means-tested but was subject to specific conditions relating to the employment record, age, and incapacity of the claimant. Indirect discrimination was said to arise from the fact that more men than women qualified under the second, more generous scheme. The Dutch Government argued that the purpose underlying the two schemes was different. That underlying the RWW was to encourage claimants to provide for their own needs and to go back into employment. The IOAW, on the other hand, was intended for unemployed workers who had worked for a relatively long period, had received earnings-related unemployment benefits for the maximum permitted period, and thereafter had little chance of finding new employment before they reached retirement age. The IOAW scheme was not means-tested because the legislature wished to protect its beneficiaries from having to break into their lifetime savings from earnings, especially in view of the very small likelihood of their being able to rebuild those savings from earned income. The Court accepted that this reasoning constituted justification; it represented a legitimate aim of social policy and was objectively unrelated to any discrimination on the ground of sex; in exercising its competence, the Dutch legislature was reasonably entitled to consider that its scheme was necessary in order to achieve its aim.

It is submitted that the cases discussed above, which deal with indirect discrimination and its justification, demonstrate clearly some of the limitations inherent in the concept of indirect discrimination as a tool for the radical alteration of social security systems, in other words, as a means to achieve true substantive equality between the sexes in this field. As already pointed out, in particular in chapter 3, the concept is essentially a non-dynamic one, which takes the workforce as it finds it, and does not attempt social engineering in any dramatic sense. In addition, even

[120] Case C-280/94, op cit, n 29, at 204–5.   [121] Case C-8/94, op cit, n 115.

where a measure has been shown to be potentially indirectly discriminatory because it has an adverse impact for one sex, it is still permissible provided that it serves a legitimate policy which is not itself discriminatory. Thus, a court which is called upon to assess whether a measure is justified is required to engage in a balancing process, weighing the social utility of the measure against its discriminatory effect. This would not necessarily be detrimental to the effectiveness of the concept of indirect discrimination were the ECJ to demand a very strict standard for justification.[122] However, the cases decided to date in general display an extreme reluctance on the part of the ECJ to interfere with the subjective legislative decisions of the Member States in the area of social policy. It therefore remains hard to resist the conclusion arrived at by Luckhaus as long ago as 1988 that any sex-neutral social security provision operating to women's disadvantage will be lawful if the purpose of the provision is to ensure a minimum subsistence income to protect people from poverty: 'women's needs must always be subordinated to those of the "poor" '.[123]

Article 5 of the Directive provides that the Member States must take the measures necessary to ensure that any laws, regulations, and administrative provisions contrary to the principle of equal treatment are abolished. However, provided that equality as between the sexes is maintained, the effect of legislative reform pursuant to the Directive can lawfully be to withdraw benefits. The Court made this clear in *De Weerd, née Roks*,[124] where it stressed that Directive 79/7 leaves intact the powers of the Member States to legislate on social policy and that the control of public expenditure may provide the rationale for such an even-handed withdrawal.

Article 6 mirrors the old, unamended Article 6 of the Equal Treatment Directive, providing:

Member States shall introduce into their national legal systems such measures as are necessary to enable all persons who consider themselves wronged by failure to apply the principle of equal treatment to pursue their claims by judicial process, possibly after recourse to other competent authorities.

It was seen in chapter 2 that the ECJ originally took the view[125] that, where a Member State had not properly implemented a directive, it might not rely on a domestic limitation period in order to defeat an individual's claim based on the direct effect of the instrument; that principle was subsequently reversed in *Fantask A/S v Industrimininsteriet*.[126] Nevertheless, even whilst the original view held good,

[122] See the generally stricter approach that it takes in regard to equal pay, discussed in ch 4, and its remarks in Case C-50/96 *Deutsche Telekom v Schröder* [2000] ECR I-743, and Joined Cases C-270 & 271/97 *Deutsche Post v Sievers and Shrage* [2000] ECR I-929.
[123] Luckhaus, 'Sex Discrimination in State Social Security Schemes' (1988) 13 ELRev 52. See also Sjerps, op cit, n 19.
[124] Case C-343/92, op cit, n 27. See also Case C-226/91 *Molenbroek v Bestuur van de Sociale Verzekeringsbank* [1992] ECR I-5943; Case C-137/94 *ex parte Richardson*, op cit, n 63; and Case C-280/94 *Posthuma-Van Damme*, op cit, n 29.
[125] In Case C-208/90 *Emmott v Minister for Social Welfare* [1991] ECR I-4269.
[126] Case C-188/95 [1997] ECR I-6783, discussed in ch 2.

the Court ruled in *Steenhorst-Neerings*[127] that it did not preclude the State concerned from limiting back-payment of a social security benefit entitlement to which arose by virtue of the direct effect of Directive 79/7.[128] Dutch law used to grant incapacity benefits only to men and unmarried women; on introduction of the principle of sex equality, entitlement was extended to married women, with the exception of those whose incapacity had arisen before 1975. This last condition was ruled invalid on the ground of discrimination by the Dutch Higher Social Security Court in 1988, which enabled the plaintiff, whose incapacity had originated in 1963, to claim the benefit. However, she was then met with a national procedural rule which limited back payments of such benefits to not more than one year. The Court distinguished this situation from the imposition of a limitation period, saying:

[A] time-bar resulting from the expiry of the time-limit for bringing proceedings serves to ensure that the legality of administrative decisions cannot be challenged indefinitely. The judgment in *Emmott* indicates that that requirement cannot prevail over the need to protect the rights conferred on individuals by the direct effect of provisions in a directive so long as the defaulting Member State responsible for those decisions has not properly transposed the provisions into national law.

On the other hand, the aim of the rule restricting the retroactive effect of claims for benefits for incapacity for work is quite different from that of a rule imposing mandatory time-limits for bringing proceedings . . . [T]he first type of rule . . . serves to ensure sound administration, most importantly so that it may be ascertained whether the claimant satisfied the conditions for eligibility and so that the degree of incapacity, which may well vary over time, may be fixed. It also reflects the need to preserve financial balance in a scheme in which claims submitted by insured persons in the course of a year must in principle be covered by the contributions collected during that same year.[129]

This decision was followed in *Johnson v Chief Adjudication Officer*,[130] which concerned a claim to severe disablement allowance in the UK, which was also subject to a one-year limitation on back payments. This was notwithstanding the claimant's argument that her situation was distinguishable from that in *Steenhorst-Neerings* on the basis that there was no problem in determining whether she satisfied the conditions for the grant of the benefit and that the benefit involved was non-contributory.

In *R v Secretary of State for Social Security, ex parte Sutton*,[131] the UK High Court asked the ECJ whether an individual was entitled to interest on arrears of a social security benefit, where the delay in payment of the benefit concerned resulted from discrimination prohibited by Directive 79/7. The claimant's case for the payment of interest rested on the similarity between Article 6 of Directive 79/7 and the unamended Article 6 of the Equal Treatment Directive; as seen in chapter 5, the ECJ had held in *Marshall v Southampton and South-West Hants Area Health*

---

[127] Case C-338/91 *Steenhorst-Neerings v Bestuur van de Bedrijfsvereniging voor Detailhandel, Ambachten en Huisvrouwen* [1993] ECR I-5475, noted by Sohrab in (1994) 31 CMLRev 875.
[128] Cf the submission of Darmon AG.   [129] [1993] ECR I-5475, at 5503–4.
[130] Case C-410/92 [1994] ECR I-5483.   [131] Case C-66/95 [1997] ECR I-2163.

Authority (No 2)[132] that the latter Article required the payment of interest on compensation for unlawful discrimination. The Court rejected this comparison:

[Social security] benefits are paid to the person concerned by the competent bodies, which must, in particular, examine whether the conditions laid down in the relevant legislation are fulfilled. Consequently, the amounts paid in no way constitute reparation for loss or damage sustained and the reasoning of the Court in its judgment in *Marshall II* cannot be applied to a situation of that kind.[133]

Furthermore, the Court rejected the Commission's argument, which was based on *Jackson and Cresswell v Chief Adjudication Officer*[134] and *Meyers v Chief Adjudication Officer*, [135] to the effect that a social security benefit relating to employment may fall within the scope of the Equal Treatment Directive:

According to the Commission, when such benefits are awarded belatedly on account of discrimination prohibited by Directive 76/207, interest is payable on the arrears of benefit in conformity with the principle laid down in *Marshall II*. There is nothing to suggest that in the case of a social security benefit falling under Directive 79/7, the principle of equal treatment is narrower in scope than that laid down by Directive 76/207, so that the conclusion drawn in the case of both Directives should be the same.

  That reasoning is based on a false premise. Although it follows from the judgments in *Jackson and Cresswell* and in *Meyers* that certain social security benefits do fall within the scope of Directive 76/207, that does not mean that Article 6 of that Directive, as interpreted in the judgment in *Marshall II*, requires interest to be paid on arrears of benefit when the delay in payment is due to discrimination on grounds of sex prohibited by the Directive. Whichever directive applies, amounts paid by way of social security benefit are not compensatory in nature, with the result that payment of interest cannot be required on the basis either of Article 6 of Directive 76/207 or of Article 6 of Directive 79/7.[136]

Article 8(1) of the instrument gave the Member States six years from its notification, that is to say, until 23 December 1984, within which to bring into force the legislation necessary to implement it. This unusually long implementation period,[137] the result of a compromise at the drafting stage, was adopted in recognition of the complexity of the subject matter and the legislation involved.[138] It meant that the practical effects of the legislation took a long time to make themselves evident. In *Dik v College van Burgemeester en Wethouders, Arnhem*,[139] the ECJ held that where a Member State had wrongfully delayed implementation of the Social Security Directive, it could nevertheless belatedly pass such legislation and make it retroactive to the date when implementation was required.

Article 8(2) of the Directive required the Member States to communicate to the Commission the text of laws, regulations, and administrative provisions adopted by them in the field covered by the Directive. This procedure played a significant

---

[132] Case C-271/91 [1993] ECR I-4367.   [133] [1997] ECR I-2163, at 2188.

[134] Joined Cases C-63 & 64/91, op cit, n 60, discussed as to this aspect in ch 5.

[135] Case C-116/94 [1995] ECR I-2131, also discussed as to this aspect in ch 5.

[136] [1997] ECR I-2163, at 2189. For criticism of the paucity of this reasoning, see van Casteren's comment on *Sutton* in (1998) 35 CMLRev 493.

[137] The same as the maximum period permitted by Art 18 of the Framework Directive for its implementation in the fields of age and disability.

[138] The Commission had originally proposed an implementation period of only two years.

[139] Case 80/87 [1988] ECR 1601.

part in the Court's refusal in *R v Secretary of State for Health, ex parte Richardson*[140] to impose a temporal limitation on the effect of its ruling [141] that the national system of exemption from prescription charges fell within the scope of the Directive:

First, . . . the United Kingdom was not unaware that an exemption from prescription charges fell within the scope of Directive 79/7 as defined in Article 3(1). In a letter of 11 June 1985 it had in fact informed the Commission, pursuant to Article 8(2) . . . , that it was relying on Article 7(1)(a)[142] in order to maintain the difference in treatment between men and women in relation to prescription charges, the implication being that the exemption fell within the scope of the Directive.

Secondly, the mere fact that the Commission did not respond to that information could not reasonably have caused the United Kingdom to believe that that difference of treatment was excluded from the scope of Directive 79/7 pursuant to Article 7(1)(a). The Directive contains no specific provision obliging the Commission to approve or disapprove measures communicated to it pursuant to Article 8(2). Moreover, in performing its general task of acting as the guardian of the Treaties, the Commission has a discretion in assessing the expediency of initiating the procedure [for prosecuting Member States] laid down in Article 169[143] of the Treaty.[144]

By Article 9, within seven years of notification, Member States were required to forward all information necessary to the Commission to enable it to draw up a report on the application of the Directive for submission to the Council and to propose such further measures as might be required for the implementation of the principle of equal treatment.[145]

Exceptions to the Social Security Directive

The Social Security Directive contains a number of important exceptions. As discussed earlier in the present chapter, Article 3(3) appears to except occupational schemes and foreshadows later legislation in this area, which has now taken the form of the Occupational Social Security Directive.[146]

Article 3(2) excepts survivors' benefits:

This Directive shall not apply to the provisions concerning survivors' benefits nor to those concerning family benefits, except in the case of family benefits granted by way of increases of benefits due in respect of the risks referred to in [Article 3(1)(a)].[147]

---

[140] Case C-137/94, op cit, n 63.   [141] For discussion of prospective direct effect, see ch 4.
[142] Discussed below.   [143] Today Art 226,
[144] [1995] ECR I-3407, at 3434–5. See also Elmer AG in Case C-228/94 *Atkins*, op cit, n 67; he submitted that 'there may well be more scope for restricting the temporal effects of a judgment than there has hitherto appeared in the case law of the Court in cases where the judgment would otherwise involve considerable administrative consequences or an enormous strain on the national court system' (at 3655).
[145] In its subsequent report, the Commission in particular invited the Member States to ensure that their national legislation did not result in the exclusion of part-time workers from the right to social security (COM (88) 769 final).   [146] Directive 86/378, OJ [1986] L225/40, discussed in ch 4.
[147] The exclusion of these matters from the scope of the Directive means that they remain subject to regulation by national and, where relevant, international law; thus, in Case C-337/91 *Van Gemert-Derks v Bestuur van de Nieuwe Bedrijfsvereniging* [1993] ECR I-5435, the ECJ held that EU law did not prevent

As seen in chapter 4, the Occupational Social Security Directive used to contain a similar exception, which fell foul of Article 141; there is little chance of such an allegation being proved in relation to the Social Security Directive because of the ECJ's continued insistence on the distinction between pay for the purposes of Article 141 of the Treaty and social security schemes.[148] The very existence of the exception at all is yet more evidence of the essentially conservative nature of the Directive and the political compromises which underlay it.

In *Steenhorst-Neerings*,[149] one of the questions referred to the ECJ concerned the legality of a national rule which provided that women forfeited incapacity benefit on being awarded a widow's pension, but did not make an equivalent provision in relation to men. The Court held that incapacity benefit fell within the scope of Directive 79/7 and that it was 'irrelevant that the withdrawal [of incapacity benefit occurred] as the result of the award of a benefit, in this case survivors' benefits, falling outside the scope' of the Directive.[150]

Article 4(2) of the Directive provides: 'The principle of equal treatment shall be without prejudice to the provisions relating to the protection of women on the grounds of maternity.' As commented in chapter 4 in relation to the parallel provision in the Occupational Social Security Directive, it is generally assumed that this permits only specially *favourable* treatment for women having babies, but the period of pregnancy is not specifically included and it is not clear just how far the exception extends.

Article 7 is exclusively devoted to exceptions to the Social Security Directive.[151] The first and most significant exception that it lists is that in para (1)(a): 'the determination of pensionable age for the purposes of granting old age and retirement pensions and the possible consequences thereof for other benefits.' This exception, another result of political compromise,[152] was included in the Directive in deference to the differential State pension ages then to be found in the Member States.

---

a Dutch court from interpreting Art 26 of the International Covenant on Civil and Political Rights of 19 December 1966 (*Treaty Series*, Vol 999, p 171) as requiring equal treatment for men and women as regards survivors' benefits.

[148] See Case C-7/93 *Bestuur van Het Algemeen Burgerlijk Pensioenfonds v Beune* [1994] ECR I-4471.

[149] Case C-338/91 *Steenhorst-Neerings*, op cit, n 127.

[150] Ibid, at 5505. See also Case C-337/91 *Van Gemert-Derks*, op cit, n 147.

[151] In Joined Cases C-245 & 312/94 *Hoever v Land Nordrhein-Westfalen* [1996] ECR I-4895, Jacobs AG asserted that Case 151/84 *Roberts v Tate & Lyle Ltd* [1986] ECR 703, Case 152/84 *Marshall v Southampton and South-West Hants Area Health Authority* [1986] ECR 723, and Case 262/84 *Beets-Proper v Van Lanschot Bankiers* [1986] ECR 773 provided authority that 'Article 7 of Directive 79/7, being *a* derogation from a fundamental principle of Community law . . . , calls for a strict construction' (at 4915). See also the submissions of Van Gerven AG in Case C-9/91 *R v Secretary of State for Social Security, ex parte EOC* [1992] ECR I-4297 (but contrast the actual outcome in that case, discussed below); Van Gerven AG additionally commented that he was assuming the legality of Art 7 'even though it permits the Member States to maintain provisions which are contrary to the principle of equal treatment for men and women, which has been recognised by the Court as fundamental'. He added that '[n]either the national court nor the parties nor the Commission have raised the question of the validity of that provision. Moreover, the Court has already repeatedly ruled on it without questioning its validity' (at 4324).   [152] Its second limb was proposed by the UK.

Its original rationale is, however, diminished today, since all but four[153] of the Member States either now have the same pension age for the two sexes, or else have begun the process leading to such equalization. The UK introduced differential pension ages in 1940. Before that date, the age for both sexes had been 65. One of the reasons given in 1940 for making the change was so as to enable a married couple to retire at the same time (it being assumed that husbands were normally slightly older than their wives); husbands also at that time were not able to claim an increased pension for their dependent wives. In 1993 the UK Government announced that it intended to equalize the State pension age at 65, the change being phased in between the years 2010 and 2020; more specifically, the pension age for women will increase by one month every two months between 2010 and 2020, only women born after 5 April 1950 being affected.[154] These proposals were subsequently enacted in the Pensions Act 1995.

The first element of the exception for pensionable age—the determination of pensionable age for the purposes of granting old-age and retirement pensions— was in issue in *Haackert v Pensionsversicherungsanstalt der Angestellten*.[155] The ECJ was confronted there with a scheme granting an early old-age pension which was dependent on the claimant having been unemployed for a prescribed period. It held that such a benefit could not constitute an old-age pension within the meaning of Article 7(1)(a), since that Article is a derogation from the fundamental principle of equality and must therefore be interpreted strictly.

The same provision was in issue in *Marshall v Southampton and South-West Hants Area Health Authority*.[156] As discussed in more detail in chapter 5, the ECJ apparently experienced a change of heart in *Marshall* from its opinion in *Burton v British Railways Board*,[157] and it held that the exception was confined to the age at which entitlement to pensions begins and must not be extended to other matters (notably dismissal) which are regulated by the Equal Treatment Directive. *Roberts v Tate & Lyle Ltd*,[158] however, showed that this distinction was virtually impossible to operate in practice, and in *Barber v Guardian Royal Exchange Assurance Group*[159] the ECJ apparently abandoned it, holding that there must be no discrimination in relation to age in occupational pension schemes. In truth, the potential for intractable problems in this area will remain until such time as EU law and the national legal systems simply prohibit outright differential State pension ages.

The question has also arisen as to whether the exception extends to the arrangements surrounding the granting of old-age pensions. Under the old UK system currently being phased out, in order to qualify for a full State old age pension men must have paid national insurance contributions for at least forty-four years of

---

[153] The four exceptions are Italy, Poland, the Czech Republic, and Slovenia.
[154] *Equality in State Pension Age*, HMSO, 1993, Cmnd 2420.
[155] Case C-303/02, judgment of 4 March 2004, nyr.   [156] Case 152/84, op cit, n 151.
[157] Case 19/81 [1982] ECR 555.   [158] Case 151/84, op cit, n 151.
[159] Case C-262/88, op cit, n 23.

their working life, whereas for women the requirement was only thirty-nine years. In addition, after the age of 60, a woman could not make any further national insurance contributions, whereas a man working between the ages of 60 and 64 was required to pay national insurance contributions even if he had already made forty-four years of contributions. The Equal Opportunities Commission (EOC), believing these arrangements to discriminate contrary to the Social Security Directive, and not to be saved by Article 7(1)(a), brought judicial review proceedings against the Government. Both Advocate General Van Gerven and the Court analysed the problem as being whether the exception merely allows men and women to be treated unequally with respect to the moment at which they become entitled to a pension, or whether it also covers other consequences flowing from differential pensionable ages. Upholding the latter interpretation, the Court confirmed the legality of the UK system:

The [Directive] does not ... refer expressly to discrimination in respect of the extent of the obligation to contribute for the purposes of the pension or the amount thereof. Such forms of discrimination therefore fall within the scope of the derogation only if they are found to be necessary in order to achieve the objectives which the Directive is intended to pursue by allowing Member States to retain a different pensionable age for men and women ...

Although the preamble to the Directive does not state the reasons for the derogations which it lays down, it can be deduced from the nature of the exceptions contained in Article 7(1) ... that the Community legislature intended to allow Member States to maintain temporarily the advantages accorded to women with respect to retirement in order to enable them progressively to adapt their pension systems in this respect without disrupting the complex financial equilibrium of those systems, the importance of which could not be ignored. Those advantages include the possibility for female workers of qualifying for a pension earlier than male workers, as envisaged by Article 7(1)(a) ...

In a system such as the one concerned in the main proceedings, whose financial equilibrium is based on men contributing for a longer period than women, a different pensionable age for men and women cannot be maintained without altering the existing financial equilibrium, unless such inequality with respect to the length of contribution periods is maintained.

Consequently, any interpretation of Article 7(1) ... whose effect would be to restrict the scope of the derogations provided for in subparagraph (a) to that of allowing Member States to provide that men and women do not become entitled to a pension at the same time and to exclude discrimination with respect to contribution periods would lead to the financial disequilibrium of the pension schemes.[160]

On the other hand, *Van Cant v Rijksdienst voor Pensioenen*[161] demonstrated that, once pensionable ages have been equalized, there is no longer scope for differences between the sexes over the calculation of the amount of pension benefits. Belgian law had seemingly equalized pension age, but had retained the former system of calculating the amount of pension receivable which took as its annual basis

---

[160] Case C-9/91 *ex parte EOC*, op cit, n 151, at 4337–8. Hervey has argued that this judgment represents an unjustifiably broad construction of the derogation permitted by Art 7(1)(a): see (1993) 30 CMLRev 653.

[161] Case C-154/92 [1993] ECR I-3811, noted by De Vos in 'Pensionable Age and Equal Treatment from Charybdis to Scylla' (1994) 23 ILJ 175.

one forty-fifth of salary for men but one fortieth for women. The ECJ condemned this situation, holding that:

Articles 4(1) and 7(1) of Directive 79/7 preclude national legislation which authorises male and female workers to take retirement as from an identical age from retaining in the method of calculating the pension a difference according to sex which is itself linked to the difference in pensionable age which previously existed.[162]

The second limb of the exception—the possible consequences of differential pensionable age for other benefits—is also fraught with difficulties. How far does this limb extend? It has been seen in chapters 4 and 5 that the ECJ in *Barber v Guardian Royal Exchange Assurance Group*[163] held that occupational pensions may not discriminate between the sexes on the basis of age (despite the attempt to create such an exception in the Occupational Social Security Directive). The remarks of the ECJ in *Marshall v Southampton and South-West Hants Area Health Authority*[164] and *Roberts v Tate & Lyle Ltd*[165] also showed that the Court now regards the exception for pensionable age contained in the Social Security Directive as confined exclusively to the field of social security benefits and as no longer being able to excuse any type of private discriminatory financial provision.[166] For example, in *Marshall*, it commented: 'It must be emphasized that ... the exception contained in Article 7 of Council Directive 79/7/EEC concerns the consequences which pensionable age has *for social security benefits* ...'[167] However, even on this limited basis, the question remains of how 'consequences' should be defined and what sort of benefits the exception might still embrace. Does the exception, for example, permit the abatement of other social security benefits as pensionable age approaches, or is it confined to the age at which other benefits are actually payable?

Several questions of this type were helpfully discussed by the UK Social Security Commissioner, Mr Monroe, in *Re Severe Disablement Allowance*.[168] He had been referred to a decision of a Tribunal of Commissioners in which a male claimant had tried to establish that a statutory provision then in operation, under which a person who had attained the age of 60 was liable to have unemployment benefit restricted if he or she received an occupational pension, discriminated against men. There was no similar rule in relation to women over the age of 55, so that there was no issue as to direct discrimination. However, it was argued that the rule was indirectly discriminatory, because in fact it applied to many more men than women because

---

[162] [1993] ECR I 3811, at 3834. For an account of the background to this case, see Clotuche's 'Comment' in McCrudden (ed), *Equality of Treatment Between Women and Men in Social Security* (Butterworths, London, 1994). The practical difficulties inherent in attempted transition to a uniform pensionable age for both sexes were also manifested in Case C-377/96 *De Vriendt v Rijksdienst voor Pensioenen* [1998] ECR I-2105 and in Case C-154/96 *Wolfs v Office Nation des Pensions* [1998] ECR I-6173; in both cases, the ECJ held that, if pensionable ages had not yet been equalized, discrimination in the method of calculating pensions was permitted.   [163] Case C-262/88, op cit, n 23.
[164] Case 152/84, op cit, n 151.   [165] Case 151/84, op cit, n 151.
[166] Cf Case 19/81 *Burton v British Railways Board*, op cit, n 157.
[167] [1986] ECR 723, at 746, emphasis added.   [168] [1989] 3 CMLR 379.

of women's pensionable age being 60. It was held that the situation was excepted from the Directive because it was clearly a consequence of the difference in pensionable age, and with this conclusion Mr Monroe agreed, saying that the same conclusion was bound to be reached even on the narrowest interpretation of Article 7(1)(a). Similarly, he took the case of a woman who had attained pensionable age and was actually receiving her retirement pension, who was precluded by the Overlapping Benefit Regulations from also receiving a severe disablement allowance. A man below pensionable age would not be so precluded, but there was nevertheless, according to Mr Monroe, a sufficient link in these circumstances between the benefit rules and the differential pensionable ages for the exception to apply. But he went on to point out that:

A more difficult question arises when there is a provision that the right to a benefit comes to an end at pensionable age as happened with mobility allowance when it was first introduced by section 22 of the Social Security Pensions Act 1975 . . . subsection (4)(a) being material on the present point. Again the rate of some benefits may change at pensionable age (as happens under section 14 subsection 2 of the 1975 Act in relation to sickness, invalidity and unemployment benefits) and can disappear altogether five years later. I should be disposed to think that these provisions fell to be associated with the fact that the beneficiary having reached pensionable age fell to be treated as sufficiently provided for by whatever provision he had made for pension and could not expect to look beyond that; and that accordingly these too were possible consequences for other benefits of the differential . . . pensionable ages.[169]

On the facts of *Re Severe Disablement Allowance* itself, the claimant had reached pensionable age (60) in 1983. She had continued to work after this date, but had ceased work on becoming disabled. She applied for a severe disablement allowance in 1986, but was refused it because she had already attained pensionable age and had not been entitled to the allowance immediately before she reached that age (as stipulated by s 36(4)(d) of the Social Security Act 1975). If she had been a man, she would not already have reached pensionable age and so could have claimed the allowance.[170] Mr Monroe held that the intention behind the statutory provision was to permit those whose incapacity set in before 'the infirmities of age' begin to assume significance to continue to receive the allowance, whereas those whose incapacity does not set in until an age when the infirmities of age assume significance shall never be entitled to it. For this purpose, pensionable age was selected by the legislature as the critical time, but for a purpose unconnected with title to the pension itself. He therefore held that the differentiation between the sexes in relation to severe disablement allowance was not a consequence of the difference in pensionable age: '[i]t is rather the consequence of a differential view being taken of the setting in of infirmity in the two sexes'. The claimant was therefore entitled to be treated in the same way as if she were a man, in other words, to be able to claim the allowance provided only that her disablement set in

---

[169] Ibid, at 386. There appears to be an error in the last paragraph of this quotation, as printed in the Common Market Law Reports, which the present writer has attempted to correct.
[170] See now SI 1993 No 3194.

before she reached the age of 65. As a matter of general principle, Mr Monroe commented:

[I]t is not sufficient to escape the Directive simply to gear a different benefit to the differential pension ages if the resulting differentiation between sexes in that benefit cannot be shown to have some objective link with pensionable age. If it were it would make it all too easy to evade the provisions of the Directive.[171]

On appeal, the case was consolidated with several others on similar facts, and in particular with three involving invalid care allowances (awarded to those caring for a severely disabled person), which were also excluded by UK legislation where the carer had reached pensionable age, unless he or she was entitled to the allowance immediately before reaching pensionable age.[172] The House of Lords referred a number of questions to the ECJ on the ambit of Article 7(1)(a).[173] The Court took a strict view of the scope of the defence, saying:

[F]orms of discrimination provided for in benefit schemes other than old-age and retirement pension schemes can be justified, as being the consequence of determining a different retirement age according to sex, *only if such discrimination is objectively necessary in order to avoid disrupting the complex financial equilibrium of the social security system or to ensure consistency between retirement pension schemes and other benefit schemes.*[174]

It justified an excursion into the facts of the case on the basis of its role being to furnish the national court with worthwhile answers, and added:

As regards the requirement of preserving financial equilibrium as between the old-age pension scheme and the other benefit schemes, it should be noted that the grant of benefits under non-contributory schemes, such as severe disablement allowance and invalid care allowance, to persons in respect of whom certain risks have materialised, regardless of the entitlement of such persons to an old-age pension by virtue of contribution periods completed by them, has no direct influence on the financial equilibrium of contributory pension schemes.[175]

Furthermore . . . discrimination between men and women under non-contributory schemes, such as that of the severe disablement allowance and the invalid care allowance, is unnecessary to preserve the financial equilibrium of the entire social security system, particularly since the national rules contain provisions to prevent overlapping between benefits such as severe disablement allowance or invalid care allowance and the old-age pension and, in fact, the grant of those benefits takes the place of benefits paid under other non-contributory schemes, such as benefits paid to people who have insufficient resources to support themselves.[176]

The ECJ also made short shrift of the UK Government's reliance on statistics relating to male and female working and retirement patterns in its attempt to justify differential treatment of the two sexes. The Court referred to its holding in

---

[171] [1989] 3 CMLR 379, at 384.
[172] *Sub nom Thomas v Adjudication Officer and the Secretary of State for Social Security.*
[173] Case C-328/91 *Secretary of State for Social Security v Thomas* [1993] ECR I-1247.
[174] Ibid, at 1273, emphasis added.
[175] See also Case C-382/98 *R v Secretary of State for Social Security, ex parte Taylor* [1999] ECR I-8955.
[176] [1993] ECR I-1247, at 1273.

Marshall v Southampton and South-West Hants Area Health Authority,[177] that women are entitled to go on working beyond the qualifying age for an old-age pension, and held:

As to the United Kingdom's argument that the vast majority of women receive an old-age pension once they have attained the age of 60, suffice it to say that the grant of benefits such as severe disablement allowance or invalid care allowance constitutes, for women who are not yet in receipt of old-age pension despite their having attained the normal retirement age, an individual right which cannot be denied them on the ground that, statistically, their situation is exceptional by comparison with that of most women.[178]

It is clear from *Thomas* that the Court regards as extremely important the coherence between a Member State's retirement benefits scheme and its other social security benefits. This was further evidenced in *Secretary of State for Social Security v Graham*,[179] which concerned discrimination in relation to entitlement to invalidity pensions in the UK. The invalidity pension was a benefit designed to be replaced by the old-age pension. To be more specific, women receiving invalidity pension after the female State pensionable age of 60 had the rate of their pension reduced to what they would have been entitled to by way of retirement pension, whereas for men this did not occur until they reached the male pensionable age of 65. The ECJ reiterated its holding in *Thomas* that Article 7(1)(a) justifies only discrimination which is necessarily and objectively linked to the difference in pensionable age between men and women. However, notwithstanding that invalidity benefits were contributory (unlike the benefits involved in *Thomas*), it went on to find that Article 7(1)(a) excused the discrimination on these facts:

As regards the forms of discrimination at issue in the main proceedings, the Court finds that they are objectively linked to the setting of different pensionable ages for women and men, inasmuch as they arise directly from the fact that that age is fixed at 60 for women and 65 for men.

As to the question whether the forms of discrimination are also necessarily linked to the difference in pensionable age for men and women, it should be noted, first, that since invalidity benefit is designed to replace income from occupational activity, there is nothing to prevent a Member State from providing for its cessation and replacement by a retirement pension at the time when the recipients would in any case stop working because they have reached pensionable age.[180]

Further, to prohibit a Member State which has set different pensionable ages from limiting, in the case of persons becoming incapacitated for work before reaching pensionable age, the rate of invalidity benefit payable to them from that age to the actual rate of the retirement pension to which they are entitled under the retirement pension scheme would mean restricting to that extent the very right which a Member State has under Article 7(1)(a) of Directive 79/7 to set different pensionable ages.[181]

---

[177] Case 152/84, op cit, n 151.   [178] [1993] ECR 1247, at 1274.
[179] Case C-92/94 [1995] ECR I-2521.
[180] Cf the Court's insistence in Case 152/84 *Marshall*, op cit, n 151, that retirement age and pensionable age are not necessarily to be equated with one another.
[181] [1995] ECR I-2521, at 2553–4. As Cousins comments in 'Free Movement of Workers and Social Security: Two Steps Forward, One Step Back' (1996) 21 ELRev 233, 'this statement simply begs the question as to whether or not such a restriction is allowed under Community law'.

The Court went on to explain that:

Such a prohibition would also undermine the coherence between the retirement pension scheme and the invalidity benefit scheme in at least two respects.

First, the Member State in question would be prevented from granting to men who become incapacitated for work before reaching pensionable age invalidity benefits greater than the retirement pensions which would actually have been payable to them if they had continued to work until reaching pensionable age unless it granted to women over pensionable age retirement pensions greater than those actually payable to them.

Second, if women did not have their invalidity pension reduced to the level of their retirement pension until they reached the age of 65, as in the case of men, women aged between 60 and 65, thus over pensionable age, would receive an invalidity pension at the rate of a full retirement pension if their incapacity for work commenced before they reached pensionable age and a retirement pension corresponding to the rate actually payable if it did not.[182]

Later cases have adhered to the principles that discrimination will be excused by Article 7(1)(a) only where it is objectively and necessarily linked to the difference in pensionable age, and that this link will be present only where the discrimination is necessary to preserve the financial equilibrium of the social security system or to preserve its coherence. For example, in *Haackert v Pensionsversicherungsanstalt der Angestellten*,[183] an early old-age pension was provided under Austrian legislation three and a half years before normal pensionable age to both men and women on proof of a prescribed period of unemployment. The ECJ held that this differentiation between the sexes was not necessary to preserve the financial equilibrium of the social security system because the scheme in question accounted for only 1.2 % of old-age and early old-age pensions paid in Austria. However, it could be excused on the ground of coherence of the system:

[T]he retirement age fixed for the benefit in issue . . . and the normal retirement age are objectively linked, not only because the old-age pension is substituted for the early old-age pension on account of unemployment where the persons concerned attain the normal retirement age, but also because the age at which that benefit may be claimed is the same for men as for women . . .[184]

In addition, . . . the system of early old-age pension on account of unemployment . . . is designed to establish an early entitlement to old-age pension where, for reasons connected with age, illness or reduced working capacity, or for other reasons, it is no longer possible, save at the cost of certain difficulties, for the insured person to find a job during a certain period. That benefit is therefore designed to assure an income to a person who is no longer capable of being reintegrated into the employment market before attaining the age entitling him or her to an old-age pension.[185]

By contrast, in *R v Secretary of State for Health, ex parte Richardson*,[186] the UK's dispensation from the requirement to pay prescription charges, which applied from the two different pensionable ages, was not permissible. Just as in *Thomas*, removal

---

[182] [1995] ECR I-2521, at 2554–5.   [183] Case C-303/02, judgment of 4 March 2004, nyr.

[184] Cf Case C-104/98 *Buchner v Sozialversicherungsanstalt der Bauern* [2000] ECR I-3625, which the Court distinguished on the basis that the benefit involved there was provided to women five years before normal retirement age and to men eight years before normal retirement age.

[185] Case C-303/02, op cit, n 183, at paras 34–36.   [186] Case C-137/94, op cit, n 63.

of the discrimination would not affect the financial equilibrium of either the pension scheme or of the social security system as a whole. Neither was it necessary to discriminate in order to ensure coherence of the system. The Court concluded that:

> Although the fact that the elderly will generally incur more prescription charges than younger people at a time when they will normally have less disposable income may provide some justification for exempting them from prescription charges above a certain age, that consideration does not require this benefit to be granted at statutory pensionable age and therefore at different ages for men and women.[187]

Similarly, in *Atkins v Wrekin District Council*,[188] Advocate General Elmer considered that Article 7(1)(a) did not excuse the provision of concessionary fares on public transport at different pensionable ages. He pointed out that:

> An interpretation according to which a benefit such as that operated by Wrekin District Council was regarded as covered by Article 7(1)(a) would, in my view, lead to every benefit protecting against old age being covered by that derogating provision. The Member State would merely have to make the benefit conditional on the recipient's having reached pensionable age. Such a legal position would, however, be hard to reconcile with the fact that the risk of old age is expressly covered by the Directive and must accordingly be intended to have a real content. It should, therefore, be an exception and not the rule that benefits for the elderly which are not in the nature of an old-age pension should be regarded as covered by Article 7(1)(a).[189]

However, the discrimination encountered in *Balestra v INPS*[190] was held to fall within the derogation contained in Article 7(1)(a). It stemmed from Italian legislation which credited pension contributions to persons employed by undertakings facing 'critical difficulties' where those persons took early retirement five years or less from State pensionable age. State pensionable age in Italy at the relevant date was 60 for men and 55 for women, but women were permitted to continue working if they so chose until the age of 60. The plaintiff in this action was aged 54 years 7 months when her employer was declared to be in critical difficulty; she was accordingly credited with five months' contributions, but claimed that she should have been credited with a full five years' contributions. The discrimination alleged arose in that a woman retiring at 55 was not credited with any contributions, whereas a man of the same age and who had the same contribution record would be credited with a further five years' worth of contributions; thus, a woman aged 55 would actually have to work for five years longer than her male colleague in order to achieve the same ultimate pension as he received. The ECJ found that

---

[187] Ibid, at 3432. Likewise, in Case C-382/98 *ex parte Taylor*, op cit, n 175, the ECJ ruled that if, as it had held, a State winter fuel payment was designed to protect against the risk of old age, it did not follow that the age triggering payment should necessarily coincide with the State pension age and therefore be different for men and women in the UK.

[188] Case C-228/94, op cit, n 67, also discussed above.

[189] Ibid, at 3653. The Court itself had no need to deal with this issue since (as discussed above) it held that the benefit in question was not within the scope *ratione materiae* of the Directive.

[190] Case C-139/95, op cit, n 69.

this discrimination was indeed objectively linked to the difference in pensionable ages between the two sexes because it ensued directly from it. As to whether or not it was necessary, the Court held:

If women taking early retirement at an age between 50 and 55 were credited with five years' contributions, without account being taken of the ordinary retirement age, the closer their entry into early retirement was to the ordinary pensionable age, the clearer it would become that those women were receiving a definitive pension higher than that of women who had paid contributions until they reached the age of 55 and then retired, without being able to claim a credit of contributions.

Second, such a scheme is also liable to give rise to discrimination against men. Whereas a man taking early retirement at an age between 55 and 60 is only entitled to a credit of contributions covering the period from the date on which he takes early retirement until he reaches the ordinary pensionable age, a woman who also takes early retirement during the five years prior to the date on which she qualifies for a retirement pension would, as a matter of course, be entitled to a credit of five years' contributions.

Consequently, even though women are entitled to work until they reach the age of 60, denying them a credit of contributions in respect of the period after the date on which they reach the age of 55, the age at which they are entitled to a retirement pension, is necessary in order to preserve the coherence between the retirement-pensions scheme and the early-retirement scheme in question.[191]

Hepple v Adjudication Officer[192] made the at first sight surprising point that the Article 7(1)(a) defence can in some circumstances be relied upon even where a Member State has introduced new discriminatory measures after the expiry of the period for implementation of the Directive. The case concerned the payment of a reduced earnings allowance (REA) in the UK, a benefit payable to people suffering a reduction in earnings following an accident at work or occupational disease, and intended to compensate for consequential reduced earning capacity. From 1986 (two years after the Social Security Directive should have been implemented), a number of legislative amendments were made to REA, in particular limiting its payment to those of normal working age. In addition, a new retirement allowance (RA) was introduced to replace REA for those who had reached pensionable age and had ceased regular employment. Five recipients of benefit claimed that the amount of allowance they received after reaching retirement age, whether REA or RA, was lower than that receivable by a member of the opposite sex in comparable circumstances. The ECJ held that the temporary maintenance of different retirement ages for men and women (as in the UK):

[M]ay necessitate the subsequent adoption, after expiry of the period prescribed for transposition of the Directive, of measures indissociable from that derogation and also amendments to such measures.

To prohibit a Member State which has set different retirement ages for men and women from adopting or subsequently amending, after expiry of the period prescribed for transposition of the Directive, measures linked to that age difference would be tantamount to depriving the derogation for which Article 7(1)(a) of the Directive provides of its practical effect.[193]

---

[191] Case C-139/95, op cit, n 69, at 581–2.   [192] Case C-196/98 [2000] ECR I-3701.
[193] Ibid, at 3737. But note the more stringent test for the compatibility of the Member State's measures with the principle of equality which was proposed by Saggio AG.

The ECJ concluded:

As regards . . . coherence between the retirement pension scheme and other benefit schemes, it must be considered whether it is objectively necessary for different age conditions based on sex to apply to the benefit at issue in this case.

In that respect, the principal aim of the successive legislative amendments . . . was to discontinue payment of REA . . . to persons no longer of working age by imposing conditions based on the statutory retirement age.

Thus, as a result of those legislative amendments, there is coherence between REA, which is designed to compensate for a decrease in earnings, and the old-age pension scheme. It follows that maintenance of the rules at issue . . . is objectively necessary to preserve such coherence.[194]

The remainder of Article 7(1) permits Member States to exclude a number of other matters, in relation in particular to wives, from the scope of the Directive. It itemizes:

(b) advantages in respect of old-age pension schemes granted to persons who have brought up children; the acquisition of benefit entitlements following periods of interruption of employment due to the bringing up of children;

(c) the granting of old age or invalidity benefit entitlements by virtue of the derived entitlements of a wife;[195]

(d) the granting of increases of long-term invalidity, old age, accidents at work and occupational disease benefits for a dependent wife;

(e) the consequences of the exercise, before the adoption of this Directive, of a right of option not to acquire rights or incur obligations under a statutory scheme.

Bramhill v Chief Adjudication Officer[196] demonstrated the considerable potential of, in particular, Article 7(1)(d) to preserve discrimination. UK legislation used formerly to provide for increases in long-term old-age benefits in respect of a dependent spouse to be granted only to men. However, legislation enacted in 1984 extended this right to women, but only on condition that immediately before payment of the retirement pension the claimant was entitled to an increase in unemployment benefit, sickness benefit, or invalidity pension in respect of an adult dependant. From 1984 onwards, therefore, the increases applied to all men with dependent spouses but only to certain women with dependent spouses. The claimant relied on the wording of two provisions contained in the Directive: first, Article 4(1), which, as seen above, lays down the general principle that all discrimination on grounds of sex is prohibited as regards the calculation of benefits, including increases due in respect of a 'spouse' and for dependants; and, secondly, she observed that Article 7(1)(d) excludes discrimination only as regards benefits for a dependent 'wife'. The ECJ

---

[194] Ibid, at 3739. Cf Case C-104/98 *Buchner v Sozialversicherungsanstalt der Bauern* [2000] ECR I-3625, in which the ECJ rejected as incompatible with Art 7(1)(a) a difference in eligibility to an incapacity benefit which was based on sex, notwithstanding different pensionable ages for men and women in the Member State concerned; the difference, which had been newly introduced after the period for transposition of the Directive had expired, was not the consequence of the different pensionable ages for men and women, but rather of a desire to save costs.

[195] For an application of this exception, see Case C-165/91 *Van Munster v Rijksdienst voor Pensioenen* [1994] ECR I-4661.   [196] Case C-420/92 [1994] ECR I-3191.

nevertheless held that the discrimination involved here was excusable. After noting that the Directive states its purpose to be the progressive implementation of the principle of equal treatment in social security, it held:

> To interpret the Directive in the way contended for by Mrs Bramhill, which would mean that in the case of benefits which a Member State has excluded from the scope of the Directive pursuant to Article 7(1)(d) it could no longer rely on the derogation provided for by that provision if it adopted a measure which, like that in question in the main proceedings, has the effect of *reducing the effect of unequal treatment based on sex*, would therefore be incompatible with the purpose of the Directive and would be likely to jeopardise the implementation of the aforesaid principle of equal treatment.[197]

The desire of the Court not to penalize a Member State which has gone some way towards providing equal treatment for men and women was particularly evident here.[198] The relevant UK legislation patently contravened the general principle of sex equality and was not itself saved by Article 7(1)(d), because that permits discrimination only as regards long-term benefits for dependent *wives*; the 1984 legislation was outwith the terms of the exception because it discriminated as regards long-term benefits for some *husbands*.

The Member States are required periodically to examine the matters excluded under Article 7(1) in order to ascertain, in the light of relevant social developments, whether there is justification for continuing to maintain the exclusions concerned.[199] They must also communicate to the Commission the text of any measures they adopt pursuant to this obligation, and must inform the Commission of their reasons for maintaining exclusions under Article 7(1) and of the possibilities for reviewing them at a later date.[200]

---

[197] Case C-420/92 [1994] ECR I-3191, at 3211, emphasis added.

[198] The Court might alternatively have held that the enactment of the Directive deprived the Member States henceforth of the power to enact further social security legislation which was sexually discriminatory and thus in breach of its terms, an argument considered by Saggio AG in Case C-196/98 *Hepple*, op cit, n 192. See also the submissions of Mancini AG in Case 30/85 *Teuling v Bedrijfsvereniging voor de Chemische Industrie* [1987] ECR 2497 and Case C-129/96 *Inter-Environnement Wallonie ASBL v Region Wallonne* [1997] ECR I-7411, both discussed in ch 2.   [199] Art 7(2) of the Directive.

[200] Ibid, Art 8(2).

Index